THE CASE OF

CARDINAL ALOYSIUS STEPINAC

THE CASE OF
Cardinal
Aloysius Stepinac

By RICHARD PATTEE

THE BRUCE PUBLISHING COMPANY
MILWAUKEE

FOREWORD

THE trial and conviction of the Metropolitan of Croatia initiated the series of public demonstrations of injustice that have distinguished the so-called popular democracies since 1946. The indictment of Archbishop, now Cardinal, Stepinac was aimed at arousing public indignation against him; at fostering antagonism to the Holy See, and at securing a mass support for the regime of Marshal Josip Broz Tito. The formal charges against the Archbishop were the fruit of the passions and bitterness of the war years, and especially of the critical events that took place in Croatia between 1940 and the end of the conflict. Despite the repeated refutation of the indictment against the prelate, there linger on in the West certain doubts and reservations concerning his entire innocence. In many circles it is felt that perhaps after all *some* of the charges may be true; that the Archbishop could not have been entirely innocent in the face of the aggressively hostile attitude of the Belgrade government. Up to the present, only the documents for the prosecution have been made public. Here, for the first time, the documents for the defense are made available.

The case of Archbishop Stepinac typifies the regimes of terror that have been set up in eastern Europe. There is danger that his case may be forgotten or that many of its details never be sufficiently known. It is important now, seven years after his conviction and while he remains under strict surveillance in Krašić, to bring together a considerable number of documents and source materials to the end that the truth regarding the charges and trial may be known fully. There is danger of forgetting that the martyrdom of Cardinal Stepinac and of his people continues; that he is the

victim of untold indignities at the hand of the Tito government;
that he is not allowed to exercise his Archiepiscopal functions or to
communicate as he would wish with the faithful. In his foreword
to the study entitled *Tito and the Church* by Michael Derrick, Cardinal Griffin, Archbishop of Westminster, notes that Marshal Tito
told his followers recently that, "We need not fear any campaign.
They will shout to their hearts content and then the storm will abate
and they will weary of it." The initial outburst of indignation that
greeted the travesty of justice that was the trial of the Archbishop
of Zagreb did abate. Here and there the light of protest has been
kept alive. It is important that it continue to be kept alive because
Cardinal Stepinac is the symbol of unyielding resistance to the dema-
goguery and chicanery that constitute the essence of Marxist practice.
His integrity and rare moral courage are a permanent indictment
of the cynicism and shoddiness of the Tito regime. The policy
of rapprochement between Tito and the West, as evidenced in his
visit in March, 1953, to England, may easily lead us to forget the
flagrant injustice toward one of the very great ecclesiastics of this
century, injustice that extends to hundreds of other ecclesiastics and
to organized religion as a whole.

The source material has been selected in order to present every
aspect of the Archbishop's public life, especially during the critical
years of the so-called autonomous government of Ante Pavelić. For
the first time, so far as is known, the full text of the indictment and the
addresses of the principal counsel for the defense is made available in
a Western language. Sermons, circular letters, pastoral communications, and messages of various kinds are here brought together to tell
the connected story of Archbishop Stepinac's relations with the
Ustasha government, with the occupying powers, and later with the
communist regime.

I am indebted for many suggestions in the preparation of these texts
to a number of persons, clerical and lay, now living outside of
Yugoslavia, whose knowledge and experience have been of inestimable assistance. Various members of the Croatian College of St.
Jerome in Rome deserve the greatest praise for the devoted and
selfless enthusiasm with which they have contributed to this effort
to present the case of their Metropolitan in its true light.

I am profoundly grateful to His Eminence, Samuel Cardinal Stritch, Archbishop of Chicago, for his constant encouragement and keen interest in this project; to His Excellency Archbishop Joseph P. Hurley, Bishop of St. Augustine, and for several years Regent of the Nunciature of the Holy See in Belgrade, whose personal knowledge of the events described here is unsurpassed and with whom it has been my privilege more than once to discuss aspects of the trial, its antecedents and aftermath; and finally to Right Reverend Monsignor Howard J. Carroll, General Secretary of the National Catholic Welfare Conference, Washington, D. C., without whose support and innumerable facilities the work could not have been accomplished.

RICHARD PATTEE

CONTENTS

Part II :: DOCUMENTS

Contents

Contents

III. THE "FORCED CONVERSIONS"

IV. THE MILITARY VICARIATE

V. CONSPIRACY AGAINST THE NEW AUTHORITY AND RELATIONS WITH IT

Part I :: ANALYSIS

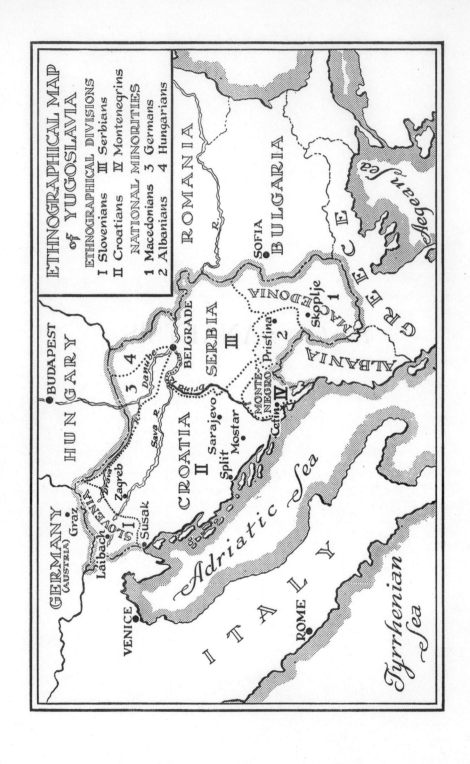

ETHNOGRAPHICAL MAP
of YUGOSLAVIA

ETHNOGRAPHICAL DIVISIONS
I Slovenians   III Serbians
II Croatians   IV Montenegrins

NATIONAL MINORITIES
1 Macedonians   3 Germans
2 Albanians   4 Hungarians

Chapter I

THE HISTORICAL BACKGROUND

THE dramatic trial and condemnation of Cardinal Aloysius Stepinac in 1946, with its many confusing aspects, has been too frequently treated as an isolated event, out of context with the complicated and tumultuous history of Croatia which forms its natural historical background. No real understanding of the attitudes, reactions, sentiments, and emotions of this trial and the accompanying persecution of the Catholic Church in contemporary Yugoslavia, is conceivable without an outline of the historical forces that culminated in the short-lived independent Croatian state and the recreation of the Yugoslav state under Partisan direction.

Yugoslavia is more an ideal than a reality. It was a vision, along with Pan-Slavism, that stirred the hearts and imaginations of many South Slavs in the past century. It is often misleading in that it creates the impression of singleness and unity when the opposite characterizes the experience of the large area embraced in this name. The new Constitution of the Federal People's Republic of Yugoslavia given at Belgrade, January 31, 1946, makes clear just how mosaic-like this new political structure really was:

Article 2

The Federal People's Republic of Yugoslavia is composed on the People's Republic of Serbia, the People's Republic of Croatia, the People's Republic of Slovenia, the People's Republic of Bosnia and Hercegovina, the People's Republic of Macedonia and the People's Republic of Montenegro.

The People's Republic of Serbia includes the autonomous province of the Vojvodina and the autonomous Kosovo-Metohijan region.

These various regions, designated by the Tito inspired constitution, as *People's Republics,* represent much more than convenient adminis-

3

trative units or departments. The Yugoslav state was created after World War I and was an attempt to bring under single political rule the most varied and clashing ethnic and cultural elements.

These diverse streams of culture, religion, and social organization date from the earliest times and their origins are often lost in legend and mist. For the purposes of this review of the case of the Archbishop of Zagreb, the specific place of Croatia in the Yugoslav scheme of things is of paramount interest. In this historical sketch, aimed at suggesting the high lights of Croatian development, one central theme recurs over and over again down through the centuries: that Serb and Croat are not the same people, and have operated within a spiritual and emotional framework considerably different one from the other. The cleavage between the two nationalities is clear-cut. From the earliest record of the presence of the South Slavs in their present domicile, numerous factors tend to separate Serb from Croat. The story of how this came about is the backdrop for the events that transpired in 1945. Without this necessary historical résumé, Croat nationalism becomes a petulant anachronism; a seditious reaction to the centrifugal pull toward Yugoslav unity.

These South Slavs entered the Balkan Peninsula in all probability sometime in the sixth or seventh century. One view holds that the South Slavs arrived as a unit and split during the course of permanent settlement.

Whether the ancestors of the modern Serbs and Croatians came together from some spot east of the Carpathians, or separately at different periods, the fact remains that geography soon separated them. The Croats were forced by natural and historical circumstances to look westward, out to the Adriatic and toward the Italian peninsula. The Serbs, constrained to an inland outlook, moved southward through the Vardar valley and it was the Aegean that attracted them.[1] Two focal points emerged from the character of Balkan geography to pull the two peoples away from each other. Croat writers emphasize the extreme antiquity of their nationality and very particularly the early evidences of a conscious political life.

The Croats displayed a precocious aptitude for political organiza-

---

[1] Cf. Robert J. Kerner, "The Yugoslav Movement," in *Yugoslavia*, edited by Robert J. Kerner in the *United Nations Series* (Berkeley: U. of California Press, 1949).

tion when we recall that in the seventh century, soon after their arrival, they entered into an agreement with the Holy See under Pope Agatho. The collaboration of the Croats with the Roman world and the contact with Christianity led quickly to conversion. In a treaty of peace and friendship signed by the Croatian leaders and the Holy See, the former swore to refrain from aggressive warfare beyond their borders and in this earliest international agreement entered into by the Croats, it is not without significance that the other contracting party was the Holy See. This is perhaps symptomatic of the role Croatia was destined to play during the next twelve centuries. The country was menaced then as later by growing pressure from both East and West; the advance of the Germanic Franks on one side and the expansion of Byzantium on the other placed Croatia in a critical position between these two forces. The struggle for independence absorbed the national energies during these early centuries, from the time of the first known Croatian prince, Višeslav (*circa* 800) to Tomislav, first Croatian king (925). The Hungarians represented another growing danger as they pushed farther and farther through the Danubian valley while the territorial ambitions of Simeon of Bulgaria in the east added to the travail of primitive Croatia. Two wars consolidated Croatia's independence under Tomislav who assumed the crown with the blessing of Pope John X cementing more firmly than ever the ties between Croatia and the Holy See. Pope John X wrote of the Croatians in most flattering terms, calling them "specialissimi filii Sanctae Romanae Ecclesiae." Under Zvonimir, in the eleventh century, the Pope was formally declared the protector of Croatia.

The development of this organic link between Rome and Croatia continued, conferring on Croatia what one writer has called "its peculiar spiritual character."[2] The "latinization" of the country and its close bonds with the Roman West met with inevitable opposition among certain sectors of the recently converted Croatians. The earliest conflict within the nation — curiously indicative of the later struggle — was between what may be called the Latin party and the patriarchal. One element was favorable to the growing authority of the monarch, greater ecclesiastical influence, close ties with Rome and the West, and a strongly centralized state, while the so-called patriarchal

---

[2] Ivo Guberina, *La formazione cattolica della Croazia*, Rome, 1943, p. 11.

party, made up of those who lived further inland, clinging tenaciously to tribal customs and outlook, was eager to return to the vernacular language in the liturgy and maintain a loosely ordered decentralized state.

This early history of Croatia reveals clearly the existence of a national consciousness. Events from the eleventh century on demonstrate with equal clarity that despite attack and mutilation, incorporation and disappearance, the Croat national sense persisted, even when the Croat state as such was scarcely discernible as a political entity. In 1102 came the personal union of the crowns of Croatia and Hungary. It was carefully provided that this union did not mean the absorption of Croatia as part of Hungary nor was it to signify the loss of the separate, particular national character of the Croat people. This union with Hungary continued for centuries constituting the leading factor in the long and heroic story of Croatia. Bosnia became separated from Croatia to the extent of creating what was for all purposes a schismatic church. The fourteenth century was a turbulent one with the rise of Stephan Dušan, ardent defender of the Greater Serbian idea, while in the next century Venice became the dominant power in the Adriatic with the purchase of Dalmatia in 1409. In 1463 the victorious Turks annexed Bosnia to their expanding dominions and Croatia became very much diminished. This did not mean however that the Croat spirit was dead, for the Crusade of 1464, proclaimed by Pope Pius II, merited very considerable Croatian help. Four years later, the Turks penetrated Croatia proper and all of western Hungary, Styria, and Carniola were under the shadow of this threat. This was the opening of the heroic chapter of resistance of the Croats against Turkish domination. The Croatian leaders, under the title of Ban, waged unceasing warfare against the intruders until temporarily paralyzed by the decisive Battle of Mohacs in 1526 which terminated the Croat-Hungarian dynasty and destroyed Hungary itself as a state.

The tenacity of the Croats in resisting the Turks won acclaim from the popes. Julius II informed the legate of Ban Berislavić in December, 1519, that "the Head of the Catholic Church will not allow Croatia to fall, for it is the shield and bulwark of Christianity." No higher compliment could be paid the valiant Croats than their designation as the "Antemurale Christianitatis." Heroism became the rule of life for the embattled Croats. Nikola Zrinjski, Ban of Croatia, defended Siget with exemplary valor against Suleiman the Magnificent, whose army was moving on Vienna and in 1593, Ban Thomas Bakač defeated the Turks at Sisak. Defeats and victories alternated. The Croats through their persistent refusal to capitulate hampered and harassed the Turks and in a literal sense contributed to the final victory that ended the Turkish peril to Europe forever.

Croatia itself was made a desert. The tiny republic of Ragusa became a haven of peace and safety in these troubled times and from it emerged a legion of Croatians to contribute mightily to the Renaissance and the learning and culture of Western Europe. The personal unity with Hungary continued even in the days when both people were scarcely more than serfs to the Turks. The sixteenth century produced the phenomenon of the new religious heresy, which penetrated Hungary. Lutheranism won adherents in the Danubian basin and threatened the religious unity of the entire area. Its penetration of Hungary alarmed the Croatians. The reaction in defense of orthodoxy was immediate. In 1567 the Croatian diet deprived any citizen abandoning the Catholic faith of his civil and property rights. The Croats gave their unstinting support to Rudolph of Hapsburg in his struggle against the inroads of Protestantism under the leadership of Bočkaj. At the joint Croat-Hungarian diet of 1606 at Bratislava, the Croat Ban, Drašković declared that he preferred the secession of Croatia from the dual arrangement to any concession to the Protestant reform. Croatia demanded in 1607 that freedom of worship for Protestants be denied within its territory. Despite the deep penetration of the Reform in neighboring Hungary, Croatia suffered none of the effects of the religious division precipitated by the schism. The Croatian diet was so convinced of the soundness of its stand that it hailed the nation as the *Regnum Catholicissimum.*

Under Hapsburg rule, Croatia felt the full impact of the West, although in many ways, and particularly the political, the nation was less independent than before. What was lost in the political field was gained in others for under Maria Teresa and Joseph II, education, agriculture, bridge and road building, were immensely stimulated.

Administration was reformed and a general improvement came about in the lot of the ordinary Croatian. During this period Croatia was cut off totally from Turkish Serbia. The juxtaposition of the two territories, linked by a very similar language, did not mean an identical evolution in other respects. Austrian Croatia was Roman Catholic, western, oriented toward German speaking Vienna and entirely attuned to the movements and the currents of occidental culture and thought. Most of Serbia was under Ottoman occupation — a Turkish province, with the handicaps and drawbacks implied in that servitude.

The year 1848 was crucial for Croatia. The revolutionary movements of that year in the Austrian empire were an integral part of the wave of revolt that swept Europe from West to East. In the midst of the tension following the events in Vienna, the Croatian diet, composed not only of the nobility, but of intellectuals and peasants, met for solemn deliberation. Its task in 1848 was to reaffirm the historical, national personality of Croatia. It was a vibrant, vehement reaction to the Hungarian nationalism *à outrance* of Louis Kossuth. In the conflict that developed between Vienna and the Hungarians, Croatia took its stand resolutely on the side of the Hapsburgs. The reason was simple. The shifts and fluctuations had produced a wide autonomy in Croatia and federalism was winning its way as the solution of the vexing problem of unity within variety: the great historical problem of the Hapsburg empire. Under the distinguished Ban, Jelačić, Croatia became the defender of federalism and it is no exaggeration to say that Croatian influence saved the empire at this critical moment in its history.

Nevertheless, the practical consequences were not favorable. Instead of relaxing the centralizing influence of Vienna, the Constitution of 1849 accentuated a new absolutism. Although the position of the Croatian Ban was recognized, it could hardly be said that the Croatian claims to autonomy or equal status within the empire were recognized. The Hungarians, defeated in the hostilities of 1848, were prone to claim that the Croatians received as compensation the identical treatment Hungary received as punishment.

The Austrian defeat at the hands of Prussia in 1866 ended for all time any pretense on the part of Vienna to playing the role of the preponderant element among the German states. The war meant quite definitely that Austria was no longer to exert leadership in guiding the emerging German nation. The Hapsburg monarchy was thrown back upon its own territories — one small, pivotal German state in uneasy association with a variety of peoples and cultures. The dual monarchy was born out of this distress. The new Austro-Hungarian agreement placed the Croatians under Magyar domination once more; a return in a sense to the arrangement that had characterized Croatian history for centuries. Between 1861 and 1868 there had been considerable restlessness in Croatia and a growing demand for broader autonomy, granted in 1868 by agreement with Austria. The currents of thought during those seven years of struggle became the basis of the political groupings in the new Croatia.

On the one hand, there were the conservatives, made up largely of the aristocracy and convinced partisans of close union with the Hapsburgs for the defense of autonomy, under leadership at this time of Levin Rauch. In the second group were to be found the bourgeoisie, lawyers, professional men, and intellectuals, with the lesser nobility. Western liberalism played a very large role in the thought of this group and philological nationalism found its expression here. Among other leaders was Bishop Joseph Strossmayer of Djakovo, who sought a meeting ground for the members of the eastern and western churches. Some of the followers of this tendency were favorable to the Yugoslav idea. In the third category were the Croat nationalists, the most outstanding leader of whom was Ante Starčević. To him and to his followers, Illyrianism, Yugoslavism, Pan-Slavism, and the like were simply so many *isms* without any real basis in experience or aspiration. The only reality for this group was Croatian nationalism and the ultimate independence of the Croatian people.

The military crisis of 1875, followed by the political events of 1878, was a turning point in the history of Croatia. The Bosnian question loomed large as the major difficulty in the way of tranquillity. Prior to 1875, Hercegovina had been the seat of numerous uprisings against the Turks, particularly in 1852 and 1857. In 1861, inflamed by the example of Garibaldi in Italy, the province seethed with unrest, and in 1875 the drama reached major proportions with the widespread outbreak of rebellion in both Hercegovina and Bosnia. The Russo-Turkish war of that year overshadowed the immediate controversy in the two provinces and projected the dispute into the wider area of Balkan politics. The smashing victory of the Russian armies and the rigorous Treaty of San Stefano led to the Congress of Berlin at which the limitations placed on Russian encroachment were favorable to the Austro-Hungarian empire. Andrassy managed, in Article 25 of the convention, to obtain recognition of Austrian administration of Bosnia and Hercegovina. From then on, despite the theoretical sovereignty of the Sultan every step led in the direction of permanent incorporation in 1908 of the provinces in the dominions of the Hapsburgs.

The negligence and psychological ineptitude of the dominant nationalities also accelerated the rapproachment of Croatians and Serbs. The establishment in Belgrade of the dynasty of Karadjordjević in 1903 paved the way for the improvement of relations between the two nations, despite the centuries of separate development. The Croatians were becoming increasingly convinced that the hope of Trialism, as against Dualism, within the Austro-Hungarian monarchy, was impossible and that their place was doomed to be secondary in the concert of peoples making up the empire. The natural and inevitable reaction was to look for reorientation beyond the borders of the Dual Monarchy. The success of Serbian arms in the two Balkan Wars of 1912 and 1913 was a powerful factor in this direction. Despite every effort by the Hungarians to discourage it, Yugoslavism became a more and more popular concept and the idea became fixed in the minds of some Croatians that the solution of their problem depended on Serbia.

Since the history of Croatia is so closely bound up with that of Serbia during the present century, a word may be added regarding the latter kingdom, destined to become the nucleus of the new Yugoslavia that emerged after 1918. During the nineteenth century Serbia was dominated economically and to a considerable extent politically by the Austro-Hungarian Empire. Under the Karadjordjevićs a real effort to achieve national independence was made. The rise of the Karadjordjević dynasty implied a reaction in favor of Serbian independence and release from this irksome control. After

1903, Serbia sought to throw off the shackles of the economic treaty of 1893 and obtain certain of her imports elsewhere, notably arms in France, livestock in Turkey, and ammunition in Germany. The annexation of Bosnia and Hercegovina in 1908 produced profound repercussions in Serbia where resentment against the Dual Monarchy on the economic front was now intensified on the political. The bitter rancor against the predominance of Magyar and German administrators in the annexed territories fed this rising anti-Hapsburg sentiment. The Croatians at the same time could obtain no position of real leadership within the monarchy. As brothers in misery and spurred by very similar motives, the two peoples tended to move toward each other. The treason trial at Zagreb in 1909 evidenced the fear and anxiety of the Austro-Hungarian authorities at this trend.

The complex story of the events surrounding the annexation and the conspiracies that led to the outbreak of war in 1914 must be told in extremely summary form, to set the proper stage for the new phenomenon known as Yugoslavia. The tranquillity of Europe was violently disturbed in 1908 by the outbreak of the revolt led by the Young Turks. These audacious reformers sought to transform the decrepit empire of Abdul-Hamid and threatened by their program the whole structure of the ancient and corrupt Ottoman Empire. The rebels convoked a parliament, to which delegates from Bosnia and Hercegovina were invited, as still nominally under Ottoman sovereignty. Thus the issue was placed before the Austrian government. In the midst of negotiations and consultations, Count Alois Aehrenthal, Austrian foreign minister, obtained the conditional consent of Russia to the annexation by the promise of supporting the opening of the Straits to Russian vessels. European reaction was varied to the annexation as proclaimed on October 6, 1908. In London, Paris, and Rome there was considerable agitation with accusations of violation of the Treaty of Berlin and recriminations between Russia and Austria regarding details of the alleged agreement between the two powers. If Izvolsky, Russian foreign minister, was more or less willing to go along, Serbia was definitely not. The reaction in Belgrade and in Montenegro was violent. The Foreign Minister Milovanović expressed the total deception of his people at this blow. Since the accession of Peter to the Serbian throne, the sentiment had grown in favor of the ejection of Austria from the two provinces. Milovanović made a series of visits to various European capitals to seek support for Serbia's position, with the proposal that Bosnia and Hercegovina become autonomous territories under the guarantee of the powers and as compensation Serbia receive an outlet to the Adriatic Sea. London was reserved and St. Petersburg assured the Serbian minister that the situation could be solved only through war. Russia refused to recognize the validity of the annexation and Izvolsky argued that Russia had been tricked as to the date and before suitable conversations could be held regarding the freedom of movement through the Straits. Austria managed to satisfy Turkey with monetary compensation. The situation was tense and the *malaise* produced by the annexation endured through the winter of 1908–1909. Izvolsky proposed in his speech to the Duma on December 24, an international conference regarding the disputed issues but Austria was adamant without prior approval of the annexation. The rise of intense anti-Austrian sentiment in Serbia led certain of the imperial leaders to think of a quick war as the best solution of this vexing problem.

Into this confusion was injected the problem of the Serbians and Croatians living within the boundaries of Austria-Hungary. On March 25, 1909, the historian Friedjung published in the *Neue Freie Presse* a virulent article accusing the Croatian leaders of illicit relations with Belgrade. It has since been demonstrated that many of the documents presented were false. Austria proposed the formal cancellation of Article 25 of the Treaty of Berlin with reference to the occupation of Bosnia and Hercegovina and Russia accepted, largely because of the danger of an Austro-Serbian war. This was followed by similar action on the part of the major powers. On March 31, Serbia informed Vienna that the annexation of the provinces was recognized as a *fait accompli*. The diplomatic triumph of Aehrenthal was complete. The threat of war against Serbia had produced the desired result. Russia was unable to envisage war at that time against the Triple Alliance and was obliged to sacrifice the interests of Serbia.

The Serbian government undertook, moreover, "to renounce henceforth the attitude of protest and opposition which it has adopted since last summer with regard to the annexation." In addition, Serbia would make every effort to live on good neighborly terms with the Austro-Hungarian monarchy. Behind the whole façade of apparent cordiality and resignation to reality was the cold fact that Russia did not recognize the annexation and gave Serbia to understand that in due time the injustice would be rectified and the only form of rectification, obviously, was by arms. The years between 1909 and 1914 were packed with intrigue and feverish maneuvering for position with the South Slavs directly involved, at all times, in this development.

Russian influence on Bulgaria was decisive in bringing about in 1912 the long desired alliance of Serbia and that kingdom and, despite their rivalries and frequently unfriendly relations, the two joined in a pact which was patently directed against the Ottoman Empire. The atmosphere of 1912 was disquieting. The death of Aehrenthal removed an able, audacious diplomat who, albeit devoted to the cause of Austrian expansionism, had stood for peace against the bellicose Conrad von Hötzendorff. In April, the French Ambassador reported that the Emperor Francis Joseph was convinced that the cause of peace had been seriously weakened in the course of the past eight months. The story of the Serbo-Bulgarian accord is typical of the tortuous, sinuous negotiations that preceded World War I. The frustration of both small countries with reference to Turkey and Austria brought them together. In March of 1909 the treaty was signed, the principal article stipulating mutual aid if either of the two undertook to annex or occupy territory then held by Turkey. Conditions were laid down for other eventualities, including Austrian participation in any armed conflict that might arise. Greece joined the combination in 1912, thanks to the new policy of Venizelos.

War broke out between Turkey and the Balkan League in 1912. The rapid advance of the three Balkan armies and the collapse of Turkish resistance stupefied all Europe. Austria massed a hundred thousand troops on the Serbian frontier and everything pointed to a spread of the conflict. The peaceful intentions of Germany at that moment probably contributed as much as anything to restraining Austria, although the danger for the Hapsburg monarch was evident.

If Serbia managed to gain a foothold on the Adriatic, the last vestige of Austrian control over that nation would vanish. Since in the Austro-Hungarian dominions enthusiasm among the Slav minorities had been very great and volunteers streamed into Serbia to join the forces, it would have been dangerous and impolitic to provoke open hostilities with Serbia in the moment of her triumph. Berchtold, Austrian foreign minister, proposed that Serbia obtain an outlet by way of Salonika, a solution which would have produced almost instant tension between Serbia and Bulgaria, which was, perhaps, the purpose of the Austrian chancery in suggesting it. Prime Minister Pašić undertook to satisfy the Austrians regarding Serb claims westward and to propose various economic concessions as compensation for the retention of territory on the Adriatic. Serbia was deeply humiliated, after the conquest of Albania, by the international pressure brought to bear, to deprive her of the fruits of victory.

The Serbian government, faced by the hostility of Austria and the certainty of future conflict, sought support in Russia. Early in 1914 Pašić visited Russia to secure arms and materials of war for the exhausted Serbian forces and engaged in an exchange of amenities that indicated the increasing cordiality between the two peoples and the fact that by this time Serbia had virtually passed completely out of the orbit of Austria-Hungary and was now firmly tied to the Russian chariot. Rising Serbian prestige exerted a magnetic attraction on the peoples of the Dual Monarchy. The vacillating policy of Vienna did not reduce this sentiment or restore Austro-Hungarian authority among the component elements of the Empire. The Austrian foreign office sought to re-establish some sort of equilibrium through renewal of negotiations with Romania, temporarily alienated by the pro-Bulgarian policy of Vienna. The substance of the efforts of Count Tisza was the formation of a new Balkan alliance with Serbia excluded. None of these proposals bore fruit, thanks to the startling events of June, 1914.

There was recognition within the Austrian government circles of the need for an imaginative solution of the problem and the conviction that repression would only exacerbate the already violent sentiments. The Archduke Francis Ferdinand was one of the few who saw that the elimination or containment of Serbia was obviously not enough since satisfaction must be given the peoples of the empire itself influenced by the Yugoslav and Great Serbian propaganda. Trialism, of which mention has already been made, seemed the answer to the difficulty, although the practical complications of such a solution were evident. The Austrian and Hungarian governments were reluctant to give in to what seemed pressure through terror and the partisans of Yugoslav federalism in the provinces themselves were unwilling to participate in any scheme which perpetuated Austro-Hungarian rule.

It is not surprising that the visit of the Archduke to Sarajevo on June 28, 1914, should have been chosen as the moment for action. The atmosphere was charged; the emotions of the underground movements aroused beyond control and the murder of the heir to the Austrian throne the fatal result. Abundant documentation and sources have been published to establish the nature of this crime and the complicated links that existed between the act of Gavrilo Princip, his associates, and the government in Belgrade.

This is not the place to describe the four years of heartless struggle and martyrdom of the Serbian people at the hands of the combined onslaught of Germans, Austrians, and Bulgarians. From the point of view of the evolution of political ideas, it may be noted that Croatia received most belatedly the promise of separation from Hungary when, at the coronation of Charles as Emperor on December 28, 1916, the complete autonomy of Croatia was recognized. The new coat of arms symbolized the empire as composed of three units: Austria, Hungary, and Croatia, a recognition *in articulo mortis,* for the Hapsburg monarchy was already doomed.

Efforts were being made during the war years to create the basis of the Yugoslav state. The Serbian parliament had declared in December, 1914, that its principal war aim was the liberation of all "our subjugated brothers: Serbs, Croats and Slovenes." A Yugoslav Committee in London carried on the work of propaganda and organization among South Slavs everywhere looking toward the creation of the new homeland. King Alexander, who had succeeded the aged Peter as regent, issued a statement on April 7, 1916, that the allies of Serbia were willing to extend aid "in order that we may make Serbia great and that she may include all Serbs (in Serbia) and Yugoslavs (in

Austria-Hungary) — in a word, that we may make her into a strong and mighty Yugoslavia." Within the Austrian parliament, the South Slav members agitated for full recognition of their autonomy, insisting on achieving it within the framework of the empire.

On July 20, 1917, the Pact of Corfu was signed by Dr. Pašić of Serbia and Dr. Ante Trumbić, Croatian nationalist and leader of the Yugoslav Committee. This document proposed that all South Slavs, Slovenes, Croats, Serbians, and Montenegrins form a single kingdom under the Karadjordjević dynasty.[3] There had been considerable confusion and hesitation among the Croats of the empire regarding the future structure of the new state. The issue was primarily between those who believed in the firm historical continuity of Croatia and that the moment would come for its reassertion as an independent state, and those who were won over to the Yugoslav idea and the powerful influence it exerted during the period of the war. In August, 1917, the leader of the Croatian Peasant Party, Stjepan Radić, expressed disapproval of the proposed union with the Serbs, emphasizing his preference for a republic.

The collapse of Austria-Hungary and of Bulgaria in the great offensive of 1918 left a very considerable vacuum in the southeast of Europe, the breakup of the empire providing an excellent testing ground for the principle of self-determination so much emphasized by President Woodrow Wilson. In the case of the South Slavs the problem was singularly difficult because the secret agreement of 1915 between the Allies and Italy had promised the latter considerable stretches of territory along the Adriatic coast inhabited exclusively by Croats. This agreement was a powerful factor in turning opinion in Croatia and the other South Slav areas against the allied position as there was little inclination to substitute for Austro-Hungarian domination that of a resurgent and vitalized Italy. As the war came to an end, the Croatian diet, as it had done so many times in the nation's history, gathered to take the necessary decisions for the future of its people. The intellectual atmosphere was that of the Fourteen Points and the high sounding promises

---

[3] See the excellent survey of this period by John Clinton Adams, entitled: "Serbia in the First World War," in *Yugoslavia, United Nations Series, op. cit.,* p. 88 *seq.*

of self-determination. The diet promptly broke all ties with the Austro-Hungarian empire and proclaimed the independence of "Dalmatia, Croatia, and Slavonia with Fiume"; a state that lasted exactly one month, overwhelmed by the wave toward the creation of united Yugoslavia.

The Allies in general and Italy in particular made certain specific commitments to the Yugoslavs toward the end of the war such as the Rome agreement of 1918, and the later declarations of responsible Italian statesmen in which the creation of a separate, independent Yugoslavia was hailed as a necessary consequence of the defeat of the Dual Monarchy. On September 3, 1918, the United States acknowledged the justice of the Yugoslav aspirations; on November 24, Yugoslav unity was proclaimed at Zagreb and on December 1 accepted by Alexander in the name of the dynasty. On December 5, less than a week after the proclamation of the new state, Zagreb was the scene of violent disorders and protests against the proclamation and Serbian troops appeared in Croatia to assist in putting down the disturbances.

The birth of the new state was infinitely complicated by the fact that Italy would not recognize it at all, despite the numerous pacts and agreements to which the Italian government had been a party. The problem of satisfying Italian claims loomed by far as one of the most serious problems at the Paris conference. There was a tendency to prefer to make concessions in Europe rather than in Asia or Africa and frequently to the detriment of the Yugoslavs. The Yugoslav position — or the Serbian if we wish to use the accurate expression — was that territorial allocation should follow recognizable linguistic and national lines. Obviously this offers endless possibility of conflict in the area where Italy and Yugoslavia meet and the dominant characteristic is precisely the confusion of speech and race, with Italian groups in cities and ports surrounded by a Croatian speaking hinterland.

The settlement of 1919 was, aside from the Italo-Yugoslav aspect, extremely favorable to the emerging nationality. Hungary surrendered the rich Vojvodina area and a compromise was reached with Romania in the Banat. The problem of Albania was more complex and until 1921 Yugoslav troops occupied the northern portion of the country when the Great Powers forced a settlement. Despite President Wilson's very considerable efforts to satisfy the Italian demands, and despite his statement to the Italian people in late April, 1919, the Italo-Yugoslav frontier was not settled in detail at the peace conference.

What was this thing called Yugoslavia as set up after 1919? The understanding of its complexities and conflicts is part of the whole story of its tumultuous development, crisis, and collapse into communism. First, a word regarding the traditional regions making up this multiform and mosaic-like kingdom. Serbia provided the dynasty, and the political and military leadership of the new state. Serbia in 1913 was a small land locked kingdom with a three million peasant population under Peter I, the grandson of a pig-dealer, Karadjordje. This somewhat primitive, close to the earth peasant people was enured to war and to discomfort. Since the first successful uprising against Ottoman rule in 1830, down through the numerous conflicts of the nineteenth century, the Serbians had won a reputation as tough and valiant warriors. Serbia acquired Macedonia from Turkey and with it came the problem of assimilating a turbulent, difficult to classify people, most of whom were not Serbs at all. It took its place at the peace conference as a stalwart, heroic little people, aspiring to serve as the nucleus around which all those speaking forms of Serbian and Croatian might rally.

Second, there was Montenegro, a tiny state of 250,000 people in 1912, and which had long been the refuge of Serbs unwilling to accept Ottoman rule. These highland tribes maintained their independence under their Bishops, and after 1853 the hereditary Prince of Montenegro. After the Austro-Hungarian occupation of 1916, and the exile of Montenegro's king, Nicholas, the country vanished until the arrival of Serbian forces in 1918. These, without much concern for the wishes of either dynasty or people, organized their supporters and voted the incorporation of Montenegro into Yugoslavia. There were revolts afterward and despite the close affinity of Montenegro and Serbia, the tradition of separatism and autonomy did not die.

The other South Slav peoples had lived under Austria and Hungary prior to 1918; the Slovenes in Carniola, southern Styria, and the region around Trieste; the Croats in Istria and Dalmatia. The

Slovenes numbered about a million and a quarter, whose initiative and talent made it possible for this peasant people to create considerable national culture, make Ljubljana a Slovene center, and develop an efficient and up-to-date administration. The Croats of Istria were separated from the Italians and in general enjoyed a less privileged status than the northern Slovenes. Of the 635,000 inhabitants of Dalmatia, 500,000 were Croats and about 100,000 Serbs with a small minority of perhaps 20,000 Italians. In general Dalmatia was poor, but its accessibility to Vienna, the sea, and Italy gave it contact with the Western world.

The Slavs of Hungary were divided, prior to the formation of Yugoslavia, into two important groups. Croatia-Slavonia constituted an area extending from the Slovene Mountains to the Adriatic Sea and eastward toward the Drava and Sava to near Belgrade with a population of some 2,548,000 Croats and 743,000 Serbs. In the former imperial Hungary there were some 650,000 South Slavs, divided between some 70,000 Slovenes, 95,000 Croats, and over 400,000 Serbs in the Vojvodina. Finally, there was Bosnia and Hercegovina where Hungarian and Serbian influence found expression and Turkish Islam had left a deep and lasting imprint. Serbs had poured in from the east, so that contemporary Bosnia included some 1,000,000 inhabitants of traditionally Serbian stock. The Croats were 640,000 strong and were Catholic; 700,000 of the total population professed the faith of Islam. Added to this Yugoslav portion of the population, the various racial and linguistic elements such as the Magyars, Albanians, Romanians, Germans, and Jews. Broadly speaking, Yugoslavia represents some six and a half million Serbs, 5,500,000 Croats, and 1,100,000 Slovenes. The distribution of population may be indicated in the following manner.

	Per cent
Serbs, Croats, Slovenes	84.33
Germans	4.22
Hungarians	3.90
Albanians	3.67
Romanians	1.93
Turks	1.26
Italians	0.11
Others	0.58

If the racial or linguistic divisions are complex, the religious diversity is even more so. This is, fundamentally, the source of the strife and tension between the various elements of the population, particularly between the Serbs and the Croats. The Eastern Orthodox religion is the mark of the Serb and of the small non-Serb minorities settled in the country, such as the Romanians and the Vlachs. It is impossible to exaggerate the place of the Orthodox faith in the development and maintenance of Serb nationalism, for it is linked with innumerably family customs, festivities, and folkways and the Serbian way of life is profoundly impregnated with this influence. The Orthodox clergy has exerted a very real influence on Serbian affairs, both religious and political, and frequently they have participated actively in politics and sat in parliament. It is difficult to exaggerate the mission and relation of the Orthodox church to the survival of Serb nationalism during the trying period of Turkish control.

The Catholics in communion with Rome include almost all the Slovenes and Croats, plus the greater portion of the half million Magyars and the still larger German communities. Protestants number in all less than two per cent of the Yugoslav population. The Slovenes have a reputation for piety and one of the striking features of their society was the large place of the clergy in the defense of the national tradition, and in the creation, through the co-operative movement, of a more balanced economy. Up to the outbreak of World War II the Slovenes were represented politically almost entirely by the Catholic People's Party. The Croats are also in very large proportion Catholics, with a traditional attachment to the See of Rome, described elsewhere in these brief pages. In politics there appeared to be less emphasis on the purely clerical nature of the parties, as in Slovenia, and the Croat Peasant's Party was less directly influenced by the clergy than its counterpart in the Slovene area.

The actual administration of the Roman Catholic portions of Yugoslavia was more complicated than the Orthodox. For one thing, the various units of the nation, with a Catholic population, continued to be administered according to traditional attachments: Croatia and Slavonia in conformity with the Austro-Hungarian Concordat of 1855; Slovenia and Dalmatia by an arrangement dating from 1874; Montenegro by the Concordat of 1886; and Serbia by

the Concordat of 1914. It was plain after the formation of Yugoslavia
that some arrangement was necessary to make uniform the various
agreements and concordats under which Catholicism operated within
the national boundaries. The centralizing tendency of Belgrade and
the preponderance of the Serbs made the independent and separate
activity of the Roman Catholic Church something of an obstacle
to the closer relations of the Yugoslav peoples. This is summarized
by Prof. Matthew Spinka:

> Political unity between the Serbian and the Croatian-Slovene groups depended
> in large degree on satisfactory settlement of the ecclesiastical problem. Whereas
> the nationalism or separatism of the Serbs found religious expression in Orthodoxy,
> that of the Croatian-Slovene group was traditionally under the leadership of the
> Catholic priesthood. . . . The government was under pressure to take action
> in the matter.[4]

After 1918 the Church in Yugoslavia was impoverished and dis-
rupted. The clergy lost much of their income from forest and agricultural lands for the nationalization of the forests in part and the
agrarian reform left the Church shorn of its traditional source of
revenue. The Yugoslav state delayed for years an arrangement to
subsidize the Church as it did in the case of the Orthodox. In 1921,
Pope Benedict XV declared that the six agreements or concordats in
effect were all invalid in view of the creation of the new state. It was
not until 1935 that a Concordat was finally reached between
Yugoslavia and the Holy See that was to be submitted to
the Skupština and the Senate of Yugoslavia. The government of
Premier Milan Stojadinović hesitated to present it for fear of the
violent Orthodox reaction. In fact when it was submitted to the
chambers, in November, 1936, the opposition was extremely articulate,
with Patriarch Barnabas and the Orthodox clergy leading in the
hostility to the new agreement. The Holy Synod of the Orthodox
Church denounced the document as giving the Catholic clergy
privileges which the Orthodox did not enjoy. The specific complaints
were against the readmission of the Society of Jesus; the right to
establish as many schools and seminaries as it wished at state
expense, and the obligatory teaching of Catholic doctrine in Catholic
schools. Approval of the proposal risked alienating large sectors

---

[4] Spinka, "The Church," in *Yugoslavia, op. cit.,* p. 256.

of the Orthodox; its rejection would encourage the Croat-Slovene separatists. After six months of debate and discussion the Concordat was approved, with the stipulation that the Council of Ministers be empowered to grant similar rights to the Orthodox. The Orthodox Synod threatened with excommunication the members of parliament and the ministers voting for the Concordat and after its passage, there were strong currents of resentment and rancor on the part of the Orthodox circles. Catholic groups under the leadership of Archbishop Ante Bauer of Zagreb protested against the Orthodox attacks and insisted that the rights of the six million Catholics be recognized. Premier Stojadinović did not submit the Concordat to the Senate and in 1938 announced its withdrawal, leaving the status of the Catholic Church undefined and ambiguous.

The Moslems are the third largest religious group in Yugoslavia. Islam was transmitted to Yugoslavia by the Turks and by the Albanians, many of whom pushed out beyond their own borders into Yugoslav territory. These two forces confused the ethnic and linguistic situation very considerably as South Slavs in many cases became Albanized as they went over to the new religion while others, although accepting Islam, retained their own Croatian customs and speech through the centuries. Remnants of the Turkish population from the days of Ottoman hegemony form islands of population here and there as do a number of entirely Albanian communities. Most of the Moslems are Bosnian, who are genuinely Croat in speech and racial composition. The census of 1931 gave a total of 1,561,166 Moslem for all Yugoslavia and in 1939 it was estimated that 858,140 of this total lived in Bosnia and Hercegovina, constituting 31.2 per cent of the entire population of the two provinces. Despite the religious attachment with Turkey and the fact that not a few Croat Moslems attained high position in the Turkish administration, there has always been a strong sense of belonging to the Croatian community. The Moslem position has never been uniform or consistent. Many supported Turkey in the heyday of the empire while Austro-Hungarian policy tended to maintain a lively sense of Islam as against excessive identification with the Croatians or Serbs. Some Moslems were strongly pro-Serb and applauded the leadership of Serbia in the struggle against Austria-Hungary while the majority were drawn more closely to Croatia and partook of Croatian nationalism. The pro-Croat Moslems were the object of very considerable attention on the part of the nationalists, their plight was depicted as stemming from the neglect and abandonment of Belgrade. One of the numerous elements in the ancient rivalry of Serbs and Croats was the future of Bosnia and the fate of its Moslem people.

Protestantism is confined to minorities among the Germans, Magyars, and Slovaks, and Jews belong to two groups: those of East European origin and German or Hungarian speech and the Sephardic Jews, descendants of those expelled from the Iberian peninsula in the late fifteenth century. The following table may be useful in indicating the religious distribution of the Yugoslav population.[5]

	Per cent		Per cent
Greek Orthodox	48.70	Protestant (Calvinist)	0.40
Roman Catholic	37.45	Other Christians	0.12
Greek Catholic	0.32	Moslem	11.20
Old Catholic	0.05	Jewish	0.49
Protestant (Lutheran)	1.26		

If the ethnic and religious composition of the country is complex and varied with obvious difficulties of effective unification, the importance of the cultural problem cannot be overemphasized. The three major languages of Yugoslavia are Croat, Serb, and Slovenian. It is well known that the Cyrillic alphabet is employed in the Serbian form of the language, while in the Croatian the Latin is used. This difference is far more than mere usage; it reflects an orientation, a different center of attraction and participation in a different cultural stream. Moreover, not only have the religious and spiritual differences contributed to a distinction between the languages, but the various efforts during the past to bring them to a high cultural level and make them the common form of intellectual expression sprang from diverse sources and with different characteristics.

"The crux of Yugoslav politics, from the very formation of the new state to this day, has been the alternative of centralization and federalism — the Serbs fostering the notion of the 'Greater Serbia' and the Croats advocating regionalism," writes Professor Roucek in

---

[5] Joseph S. Roucek, *Balkan Politics: International Relations in No-Man's Land* (Stanford University Press, 1948), p. 84.

his lucid account of this complex period of Balkan history.[6] The experience of Yugoslavia from 1918 to the outbreak of the war in 1941 illustrates this statement. The Croat-Serb issue more than any other was constantly in the forefront of Yugoslav politics and was the dominating question threatening Yugoslavia again and again. This historical experience teaches one very plain thing: that the sentiment of Croat nationality was extremely strong, and that there was no enduring basis for the perpetual union of the two peoples — Serbs and Croats — in a single, harmonious society.

The Yugoslav state was harassed from the beginning by the passion for diversity and the indestructible urge toward separatism. The peoples of the new state, despite their common origin, had lived too long under other sovereignties and there was little consciousness of oneness to offset the perplexing economic and international problems that plagued the unified administration. The Croats in favor of the union were quite certain that they did not wish to become merely a prolongation of Serbia, and the trend toward a large and cumbersome bureaucracy, staffed in many cases by Serbs, caused complaint and resistance. The rivalry of Zagreb and Belgrade became more and more accentuated with the Croat and the Slovene, with a far lesser proportion of illiteracy, looking on the Serb as something of a *parvenu* and an oriental. The Serb, on the other hand, deemed Zagreb and its "Western" atmosphere distinctly decadent and smacking strongly of the Hapsburg tradition. Economic factors contributed in this misunderstanding for there was no comparison between semi-industrialized Croatia and Slovenia, achieved under the administration of Vienna and Budapest, and the purely agrarian economies of the rest of Yugoslavia. There was the inevitable resentment of the industrial society, or at least one that had savored some of the advantages of that type of society, against the less developed regimes of Macedonia, Montenegro, and Old Serbia.

The political future of the new state was relatively unpromising, in the light of the widely varying political experience and habits of the South Slav peoples. The Montenegrins saw in party politics simply a carry-over of the brigand tactics to which they had been accustomed

---

[6] Roucek, *op. cit.*, p. 87.

for centuries, while the Macedonians and others brought to the new scene the habits of the underground.

The emergence of political parties accentuated this regionalism and furnished the leitmotiv of Yugoslav politics. The elections of 1920, hailed as relatively free from pressure, witnessed the participation of fifteen political parties, the largest of which was the Radical, under the leadership of Pašić, the traditional Serbian party, conservative in doctrine despite its name. The Democrats occupied second place, becoming after 1924 the Independent Democratic Party and conforming broadly to the continental Liberals. The Communist Party was relatively strong, even in 1920, with 58 deputies in Parliament. The Croat Peasant's Party, led by two most distinguished spokesmen, Stjepan Radić and Vladimir Maček, laid strong emphasis on Croatian nationalism. There was the Slovene Catholic People's Party, led by Father Korošec; the Moslem party with its strength in Bosnia; the Serbian Peasant's Party; and a number of minor groups.

The Radical Party, founded in 1881, had become the political expression of the ruling classes in Serbia and especially of the more privileged economic groups. Under the leadership of Nicholas Pašić, the party had dominated during the Balkan wars and through the world war to see Serbia enlarged and expanded in the new Yugoslavia. Pašić was largely responsible for the centralistic constitution of 1921 and for the firm stand against the federalist demands of the Croatians. During the discussions of the constitution, the Croatians had urged a decentralized arrangement of provinces with a high degree of local autonomy. Nevertheless, the so-called Vidovdan constitution, adopted on June 28, 1921, symbolized the triumph of unitary Serbianism, to such an extent that there is little in the first Yugoslav constitution that differs from the purely Serbian document of 1889. Pašić and his Radical Party managed to extend to all of the new units of the Yugoslav state the precepts that for years had served as the constitutional basis of Serbia. The conservatism of Pašić was strictly Great Serbian and Yugoslavism as a federalist conception meant little to him in his political activities which ended with his death in 1926.

Toward the end of the past century a group of Young Radicals rebelled against the Pašić leadership and in 1918, with elements from

Bosnia and Slovenia formed the Democratic Party, under the leadership of Ljuba Davidović and Svetozar Pribičević. The Croat Peasant's Party was led, as has been indicated, by the remarkable Radić who had long been a critic of Austro-Hungarian rule, and who organized his group in 1904, rejected the Yugoslav idea in 1918, and was the bitter opponent of the Vidovdan constitution of 1921. His role in Yugoslav politics was a contradictory one, since he abstained for years from any participation in parliament giving Pašić and his partisans full opportunity to play the Great Serbian game. During the years immediately after the war, Radić was strongly republican, and during the periods when he was not in prison, he appealed in the name of Croat nationalism to the tribunals of the world against what he considered the tyranny of Belgrade. His political success was unquestionable and the official figures of the elections show that in 1920, he secured 230,000 votes; in 1923 some 475,000; and in 1925, when he was imprisoned and his movement declared illegal, over 532,000. Once his strength was demonstrated, Radić decided to collaborate with the existing Yugoslav government. On June 20, 1928, he was shot in the Skupština together with several of his closest collaborators — an assassination that was denounced by the Croatians as a carefully planned plot by King Alexander to eliminate one of the most able and energetic of the leaders of the anti-Serb cause. The event was certainly far more than an act of personal vengeance; it was a confession of the failure of parliamentary government and of the inability of the Yugoslav state to provide a forum where the issues of regionalism and federalism would be debated. King Alexander acted almost without delay, setting aside the Vidovdan constitution and initiating the period of dictatorship. The murder of Radić and the implantation of the dictatorship brought to the surface all the forces of Croatian nationalism. It is not without interest, in view of later developments, that a member of the Croat bloc in the Belgrade parliament, Ante Pavelić, lawyer and deputy from the city of Zagreb, founded at this time a revolutionary nationalist organization known as the *Ustasha,* the purpose of which was the creation of an independent Croat state within the territories traditionally belonging to the Croatians. After the death of Radić, leadership of the Croat opposition in Belgrade fell to Dr. Maček.

The Christian Social Party, a prewar Slovene organization, provided the basis for the formation of the Slovene Populist Party under the leadership of Dr. Korošec. The Bosnian Moslems, organized into a political party led by Dr. Spaho, joined several of the coalition cabinets and exerted a considerable influence on Yugoslav politics.

We find it often repeated that the extreme centralization in Yugoslavia was the source of much of its political instability. Svetozar Pribičević, exiled by Alexander and one of his strongest critics, wrote plaintively that "Centralization saps the sources of our national life." The advent of the dictatorship, to last until Alexander's assassination at Marseilles in 1934, constituted another tragic page for the Croatian people. In his proclamation of January 6, 1929, Alexander made his intentions very plain:

> Parliamentary government which has always been my ideal as it was that of my unforgettable father has been so abused by blind party passion, that it prevented every useful development of the state.

The name of the kingdom of Serbs, Croats, and Slovenes was changed to Yugoslavia and the jurisdiction of the provinces was replaced by nine *banovinas*. The dictatorship, to be sure, was not accompanied by the trappings of an official party, mass demonstrations in uniforms, slogans, and the other characteristics of the twentieth-century totalitarian regime in Europe.

The so-called constitutional and electoral reform of 1931 did not alleviate the situation, but merely assured the dictatorship complete control of parliament in the midst of an economic crisis and political unrest that were sapping the strength of the regime. Dr. Maček, the Croatian leader, was sentenced to three years in prison for treason, an act that did not endear the Belgrade regime particularly to the hearts of the Croatian masses. Alexander was assassinated in October, 1934, while on a visit to France.

There was some hope that the Regency, presided over by Prince Paul during the infancy of Peter II, might rally the discordant elements of the nation and provide a new start. Under the guidance of Premier Jevtić, the cabinet included several non-Serbs and Dr. Maček was released from prison before the elections of May, 1935. The regime, in a more liberal spirit than under Alexander permitted the formation of an official opposition, the Croat Peasant's Party, Serbian Democrats, and Moslems joining together for that purpose. This fact indicates substantial progress in that Serbs participated in a political alliance headed by a Croat. Although the antigovernment forces rolled up a very large vote, the anomalies of the electoral law, and possibly the tradition of machinations left over from the dictatorship, gave the government a majority of 303 as against 67 for the opposition.

Milan Stojadinović, designated premier as well as foreign minister, was described as affable and devoted among other things to Rotarianism. He formed a new political combination known as the Yugoslav Radical Union, the main principles of which were loyalty to the monarchy, centralization of the administration, and a gradual, progressive return to parliamentary practices. The Croatians in the cabinet resigned and it was plain that from then on, Croatian support could not be expected for the new government. The dictatorship was continued under Prince Paul who was not, however, comparable to Alexander in the ruthless suppression of all opposition.

Late in 1936, Prince Paul received Dr. Maček and early the next year a meeting was arranged with Premier Stojadinović, the first between the prime minister of Yugoslavia and the Croatian opposition leader since the murder of Radić. One of Maček's lieutenants, Ivan Subašić, became closer to the prince-regent than any Croat politician since the formation of Yugoslavia. The elections of 1938, while returning the Stojadinović government to power with some 58.9 per cent of the vote gave the Croatian-led combination a substantial minority of 40.21 per cent. Through various combinations, the position of Prime Minister Stojadinović became untenable and there was talk of naming Maček premier. This solution was unthinkable in the light of the Croat-Serb tension and a Serbian moderate by the name of Dragiša Cvetković was designated prime minister. Munich had passed and the war clouds were blackening all over Europe. The prince regent hoped to maintain tranquillity through last minute concessions to the minorities, particularly Home Rule for the Croats. The situation in 1939 was singularly favorable for action for Maček was vice-premier and the Croat Peasant's Party with its various adjuncts the strongest political force in opposition. Regionalism was still the most lively force in Yugoslav life as the elections of each year abundantly demonstrated, since in Serbia the Stojadinović machine had triumphed; in Croatia Maček had obtained virtually the total vote, and in Slovenia, Monsignor Korošec was far and away the strongest personality with his clerical party. The Croat leader proposed that this reality be recognized; that the constitution be revamped and the political, cultural, and social structure of each of the three nations or areas form the basis of a reconstructed Yugoslavia. In March, 1939, the Slovaks had cast off the rule of Prague, and this appeared to many Yugoslavs as an omen of what might easily happen in their own country if steps to pacify the Croats were not taken in time.

The result was what is known in Yugoslav political history as the *Sporazum* or agreement. Five days before the war broke out this understanding was entered upon, providing for the constitution of Croatia, Slavonia, Dalmatia, and parts of Bosnia as an autonomous *Banovina*. Internal economy and cultural affairs were to be under provincial control, while foreign affairs, communications, and defense were to remain within the jurisdiction of the central government at Belgrade. Croatia was granted this autonomous charter while the other areas of Yugoslavia were not. The presence of thousands of Serbians within Croatian territory created a special problem as to their status and treatment. The *Sporazum* came at a most difficult moment for the outbreak of the war meant that a large body of Yugoslavs were under arms, parliamentary practices, such as they were, had largely broken down, and a strict censorship prevailed everywhere. The German minority of some 600,000 was being whipped up by the propaganda pouring out of Berlin and the Slovenians were resentful that they had not received the same preferential treatment as the Croatians. The Serbs in turn were bitter that the autonomy charter had come in the form it did and at this particular moment when it appeared to be the consequence of fear on the part of the Belgrade government. In a word, the atmosphere around the understanding was very far from favorable for its effective operation. Had the war not intervened, it is conceivable that similar agreements might have been carried out with other areas and Yugoslavia would have become in reality a confederation of autonomous states.

The war created a supreme crisis for Yugoslavia. There were obviously pro-Axis elements as well as those who favored close association with the Soviet Union. During 1940, the policy of the Yugoslav government was oriented toward neutrality under continuous pressure from the Axis. The Greek resistance to the Italian invasion emphasized the growing importance of Yugoslavia in the approaching conflict in the Balkans. In November, 1940, Hungary and Romania signed the Anti-Comintern Pact, and in February, 1941, Hitler conferred with Premier Cvetković as a prelude to the visit to Vienna in March of the Premier and Foreign Minister Cincar-Marković to sign the Tripartite Pact. Germany occupied at this time, for all practical purposes, Bulgaria and Romania, and had demanded the use of Yugoslav territory for the transportation of troops and materials of war. Yugoslavia was literally caught in a vise as the campaign against Greece took form. Prince Paul's government was indeed faced with a dilemma. The Russo-German Pact was in effect and there was no hope of aid from the Soviet Union; Great Britain was obviously in no position to assist in a practical way, and if the government yielded, it meant German occupation and possible dismemberment of the nation; if it did not yield, occupation was a certainty. On March 25 the decision to sign the pact was taken.

On March 27 the *coup d'état*, organized by a group of officers and Serbian political figures took place in Belgrade eliminating Prince Paul, who took refuge with the British in Greece, and leaving young Peter on the Yugoslav throne. Although Serbian led, many of the other political leaders went along, and the Croatians were assured that the *Sporazum* would not be modified. The leadership of this *volte face* was General Dušan Simović. The new government, although claiming to favor peace and continue negotiations with Germany, was plainly anti-German.

The story of the internal negotiations and intrigue leading to the formation of the new regime under Simović is a further revelation of the complexity of Serbian-Croat relations. The new government was profoundly, even chauvinistically, Serbian. Maček insisted on time to think the problem through in the light of Croatia's interest, for the Croatian deputies had not voted for the pact nor had they been involved in the resignations that succeeded it, and they were gravely concerned with the future of the *Sporazum*. The cabinet that presided over the destinies of Yugoslavia during the few days between the *coup* and the arrival of the German Stukas, was composed of the most diverse elements, with Maček as vice-premier despite his reservations, and Father Anton Kulovec, Slovenian, a second vice-premier. The foreign minister was Momčilo Ninčić, of pronounced pan-Serbian sentiments, who had held the same portfolio under Pašić. Maček consented to entering the government on the basis of a guarantee for Croatian home rule and the promise of Simović that everything possible would be done to avoid war. There were long discussions regarding the possibility of a satisfactory arrangement with the Axis powers to assure Yugoslavia's neutrality. The sterility of all of this as well as the absurdity of the claim that the exit of Prince Paul and the advent of Simović were purely Yugoslav domestic politics, were revealed with brutality on Palm Sunday, April 6, when the Germans attacked Yugoslavia with their full force. Belgrade was ruthlessly bombed and the German forces poured into Yugoslavia across several of its frontiers. The line of retreat to Greece or Albania was cut off so that no repetition of the heroic march of World War I was conceivable. On April 17, the Yugoslav forces were obliged to capitulate in the most complete disorder and confusion. The invasion was a repetition of the tragic experience Europe had known since the fatal first of September when the Hitlerite forces crossed into Poland.

Although the majority of the Yugoslav leaders took refuge in flight, preparatory to setting up the government in exile, Maček decided to remain in Croatia among his own people insisting only that the Croats who served the government abroad stand for the maintenance of the *Sporazum*. During the temporary period of the exiled government's residence in Jerusalem, conflicts arose within the Yugoslav group, with certain of the Pan-Serbians accusing the Croats of betrayal of the army and collaboration in the successful invasion. Others insisted that all Croatians as such were responsible for the excesses of the Ustasha, which had played its part in the demoralization of the Yugoslav forces. The strong undercurrents of Serbianism versus Croatianism were carried over into exile, manifested themselves in London, later reaching the United States among the numerous Yugoslav residents and descendants in this country.

Five days after the capitulation, the Germans and Italians had decided the complex partition of Yugoslavia in eight directions: (1) Germany received part of Slovenia on the basis of racism, claiming that a good portion of the Slovenians were in reality Germanic and hence belonged to the Greater Reich; (2) Italy received southern Slovenia with the capital, Ljubljana, as well as a large part of Dalmatia and most of the Adriatic islands; (3) Albania, then under Italian domination, was increased in size by the annexation of various of the Albanian peopled districts of Yugoslavia; (4) Bulgaria received a very large portion of Yugoslav Macedonia and a portion of eastern Serbia itself; (5) Hungary regained all of the territory north of the Drava-Danube line, lost in 1920; (6) Croatia, Bosnia and Hercegovina, and a part of Dalmatia were made into the independent state of Croatia. The leader of this independent Croatia was to be Ante Pavelić, organizer of the Ustasha; (7) Montenegro was restored as a kingdom and allowed to request an Italian Sovereign. This proposal of personal union never worked out in practice and; (8) Serbia itself and the Banat, to be known as the "Territory of the German Commander-in-Chief in Serbia." In September, 1941, a puppet government was set up in Old Serbia under the guidance of General Milan Nedić.

The problems posed by the collapse and disintegration of Yugoslavia were profound, for there was a question of loyalty and to the government or group considered as representing the authentic national cause. The government in exile claimed to represent the legitimate will of the South Slav peoples; the newly established Croat state claimed to be the culmination of the long process from subjugation through autonomy to independence, while the rising underground movements, to come to a head under the leadership on the one hand of General Mihailović and on the other of Tito and his Partisans, also claimed to express the authentic voice of the South Slavs. The rigors of the occupation in Serbia and the policy of the Ustasha in Croatia created new and profoundly disquieting problems of conscience and of conduct.

The government in exile functioned in London until 1943 when it transferred briefly to Cairo, proclaiming with ardor that the aim of Yugoslavia was to fight on against the Axis in the common cause. On May 12, 1941, it protested against the creation of the independent Croat state. The government adhered to the Atlantic Charter and on January 1, 1942, joined the twenty-six governments in the Declaration of the United Nations. As early as November, 1941, the South Slavs in exile had agreed to the broad line of a union of the Balkan States, a project which merited considerable attention for a brief period and then faded into obscurity, in part because of the jaundiced reaction of the Soviet Union to schemes of this character. On March 18, 1942, a lend-lease agreement was signed between the United States and the Yugoslav government in exile. The United States government, in a communication to Konstantin Fotić, Minister to the United States, expressed appreciation for the struggle of the South Slavs against the Nazi occupation and especially the magnificent resistance of General Draža Mihailović, who had been designated Minister of War in January of 1942. By the autumn of that year the serious conflict between Partisans and Chetnik forces had broken out, to lead to the disastrous betrayal of General Mihailović and the shifting of support to Tito, with the catastrophic results so well known to the world at large.

This cleavage has been the source of the tragedy of Yugoslavia since the period of the war. The versions regarding its nature and scope vary widely. The pro-Tito elements, and especially the communists prior to the break with the Cominform, have taken the customary tack that Mihailović was not fighting the Axis at all, but was a fascist whose main task was to sabotage the work of the Partisans, the authentic defenders of Yugoslav independence and national honor. This stereotyped version of the affair is reflected in Louis Adamič's writings and in the various pamphlets and other documentary sources issued by the Tito government after the liquidation of the opposition.[7]

The calamity that befell contemporary Croatia springs not only

---

[7] The British-Yugoslav Association, Bloomsbury House, London, W.C.1, has been particularly active in the fomenting of this particular mythology, together with devotion to Tito — until the break when he too became a fascist beast and head of a traitorous clique. See such publications as *Yugoslavia Faces the Future,* a report by James Klugman, Betty Wallace, K. Zilliacus, and others. Also *The Trial of Dr. Aloysius Stepinac,* by Betty Wallace, a typical fellow-traveler account of the background and the trial.

from the Ustasha and its political institutions, but also from the grave
consequences of the deliberate choice of the major Allied powers, the
United States and Great Britain, in favor of Tito. Certainly no understanding of the religious crisis that led to the arrest and trial of the
Archbishop of Zagreb is possible without a reference to the curious
procedure whereby Tito achieved power for communism without the
help of the Soviet Union, but thanks to the support of the two major
western states, which, through this policy, foisted on the South Slav
peoples a minority system, hostile in every way to the very things for
which the responsible powers were presumedly fighting. The graphic
story has been told from many angles. It has become clear with the
events of the past few years, that Tito represented at the time of his
accession to authority only a small, fanatical segment of the South Slav
peoples and that in no sense did he belong to any of the traditional
groups with some historical claim to the direction of Yugoslav affairs.
In his remarkable study of this gross deception and ironical turn of
history, David Martin argues that "Tito was created, not by the
political Left but by the political Right, not by the Labor Party
and Roosevelt, but by Churchill, Leopold Amery, Brigadier Fitzroy
MacClean, Seton Watson and the most conservative of the Yugoslav
politicians."[8]

The high points of this epic may be related briefly. On May
4, 1941, Hitler announced that the Yugoslav state had ceased to
exist and six days later Colonel Draža Mihailović, with a small group
of the Yugoslav army, proclaimed the continuation of the struggle
and repudiated the capitulation of Simović. Not until August of
that year did the outside world hear much of the Chetniks and the
ceaseless struggle going on within Yugoslavia. The rebelliousness
that swept Serbia during the summer and autumn of 1941 had as its
center, in so far as a center was visible at all, the Chetniks of
Colonel Mihailović.

Did Mihailović represent a resurrection of the Pan-Serbian idea
and in consequence follow the tradition of those who had held to
this conception of the state rather than a Yugoslav confederation?
If the evidence is not entirely clear on the subject, there is abundant

---

[8] Martin, David, *Ally Betrayed. The Uncensored Story of Tito and Mihailovich,*
New York, 1946, p. 5.

material to show that he did not favor Croatia. One writer claims that:

It should be clearly understood that Mihailović was first of all a Serbian national-ist in political outlook. He believed that Serbia should dominate any future Yugo-slavia and because of the great human sacrifices already endured by the Serbs that no more Serbian blood should be shed through indecisive skirmishes with the enemy. He was convinced that one of the main reasons for Yugoslavia's military collapse was the Croat betrayal of Yugoslavia. To him the Partisan movement was a communist movement, which advocated a federal Yugoslavia. . . .[9]

Despite certain preliminary efforts at collaboration and a unity of action against the Axis enemy, there was no long period during which the Partisans and the Chetniks co-operated for the common cause. There was accusations that Mihailović was more interested in expelling the Partisans than the Nazis and it is clear that until the entrance of the Soviet Union into the war, the communists were extremely discreet in their activity. After that they took full advan-tage of the wave of sympathy for the USSR that swept over the land and their zeal became more and more marked as 1941 wore on. Josip Broz, known as Tito, emerged as the leader of the Partisans. A great deal of mystery surrounds the origin and nationality of Tito. Conscripted into the Austro-Hungarian army in World War I, he was captured by the Russians and took part in the Civil War on the Red side. He became a member of the Yugoslav Committee of the Com-munist International and a leader of the Yugoslav Communist Party. His identity and movements become clear only after he emerges as a member of the Yugoslav Committee. Prior to the events of March 27, when Yugoslavia threw down the challenge to Hitler, the communists had followed the straight party line with refer-ence to Germany and the war. Tito's later insistence, that from the beginning the communists had been the standard bearers of nationalism and the legitimate aspirations of the Yugoslav peoples, has no basis in truth. In the days before June 22, 1941, the Yugoslav communists like their brethren everywhere were busy talking about the imperialist war and the aggressive policies of Great Britain and France. Between Tito and Mihailović there was a clash over strategy as well as over the fundamentals of ideology rendering the civil war quite inevitable. The whole bloody struggle reached its

[9] Wayne S. Vucinich, "The Second World War and Beyond." In *Yugoslavia, op. cit.*, p. 361.

climax in the late spring of 1943 when Partisans and Chetniks were lashing at each other from Montenegro to the Danube. The actual abandonment of Mihailović by the west has been a matter of endless speculation. Some believe that he was let down after reports reached London, from what seemed to be responsible British sources, that were unfavorable to him, although the most common version is that the betrayal was determined at Teheran as a gesture toward the Soviet Union, committed by this time to the hilt to the Tito cause. Some of the impetus toward the betrayal may have come from the irritation felt toward the Yugoslav government in exile of which Mihailović was, after all, the Minister of War. It was evident that the British had decided to abandon Mihailović; the B.B.C. broadcasts minimized his role more and more, and early in 1943 the Partisans were given the almost exclusive credit for achievements in the guerrilla warfare raging in Yugoslavia. By June the shift to Tito was fairly obvious, and in the United States a similar transition had all but been achieved. In October of 1943, Mihailović received his last shipment of supplies. The next few months saw the evolution of things to the point where Churchill was able to say that "Marshal Tito has largely sunk his communistic aspect in his character as a Yugoslav patriot leader." By the time the Quebec Conference took place it was agreed that all personnel attached to Mihailović should be withdrawn. The formal recognition of Tito in November, 1943, was followed by a great strengthening of his cause, thanks to the surrender of the Italians. Henceforth Tito had everything his own way until the end of hostilities.

Politically, the Yalta Conference produced a formula whereby the Yugoslav government was to be broadened along lines similar to those proposed for Poland. Pressure from Washington and London produced the merging of the Tito government and that in exile with six new members added to the existing cabinet, including the Ban of Croatia, Dr. Ivan Subašić. King Peter had acceded to the request that he appeal to his people to join the National Liberation Army and at the same time agree to submit to a plebiscite prior to his own return to Yugoslavia. The whole structure of this first Tito government was a façade of legality behind which the Partisans set up the elements of a permanent regime. In September, 1944, Tito flew to Moscow and concluded an agreement with the Soviet government for the entrance of the Red Army into Yugoslav territory in pursuit of the common enemy and it was understood that the Partisans should retain civil control of the administration in areas under Red occupation. On October 20, Belgrade was "liberated" by combined Soviet and Partisan forces and the following day, Moscow issued a statement to the effect that the Allies were agreed that the Yugoslav peoples should have the right to choose their own government at the conclusion of liberation. Ivan Subašić met with the leader, Ivan Ribar, of the A.V.N.O.J. (The Anti-Fascist Council for the National Liberation of Yugoslavia), the Partisan sponsored parliament or committee, to examine the problem of creating a united Yugoslav government. On January 25, 1945, King Peter redesignated Subašić as Premier under a regency composed of a Serb, a Croat, and a Slovene until the plebiscite should be held. By March the temporary government was installed at Belgrade after some shifting of the personnel of the regency to meet the demands of Tito, who became Minister of Defense in this reshuffling with Subašić as Foreign Minister. During April the federal system envisaged for the component parts of the Yugoslav state was actually set up in Serbia, Croatia, Montenegro, Macedonia, Bosnia, Hercegovina, and Slovenia. On August 3, the National Front met in Belgrade and launched a full dress program for the new Yugoslavia. This organization, which claimed to be not a party but representatives of a group of parties, was under the guidance of Marshal Tito and its statement of aims included insistence on the usual things now associated with the so-called "Popular Democracies." The A.V.N.O.J. was expanded to include a number of political figures who were untainted with Axis collaboration. This organization, now called the Provisional Assembly, prepared the Constituent Assembly which was to provide Yugoslavia with its new basic law. Already there was considerable opposition to the provisional government. Milan Grol, in the Provisional Assembly, insisted on a freer parliamentarianism and real liberty. Several of the Croat members resigned, including Subašić and other representatives of the Croat Peasant's Party. The "elections" of November 11, 1945, for the Constituent Assembly favored Tito heavily. The new gathering abolished the monarchy and declared

Yugoslavia to be henceforth the Federal Peoples Republic of Yugoslavia. The constitution of January 31, 1946, was modeled faithfully and consciously after the Soviet of 1936. In theory it called for a bicameral legislature; in reality the existence of the Presidium solved the question of the supreme authority in the new state. There was the usual provision for the state control of commerce and trade as well as numerous industries. The planning of the nation's economic life came under state direction. The actual functions of government are concentrated in the Presidium. The functions of this body included among other things the following:

1. Convene and adjourn the National Assembly.
2. Fix election dates.
3. Determine if laws agree with the Constitution.
4. Interpret and promulgate the laws as passed.
5. Grant amnesties.
6. Ratify international treaties.
7. Appoint representatives abroad and receive credentials.
8. Appoint special committees within the cabinet.
9. Hold referenda on decisions of the National Assembly or on proposals of the cabinet.
10. Carry out the duties of the National Assembly when that body is not in session, such as appointing ministers, declaring war, and the like.

The various federal republics in theory had their own legislative machinery to operate along similar lines. Needless to say that with Tito in control of the Presidium, any real opportunity for the expression of a dissident opinion was literally impossible, and with the creation of the legal state, the deposition of the monarch, and the liquidation in July of 1946 of General Mihailović, the control of Tito over the destinies of Yugoslavia was absolute.

Tito's jingoistic and recalcitrant mood at the Paris Conference in September, 1946, revealed the broadening chasm between Yugoslavia and the west and the tightening of Tito's hold over the Yugoslav people.

The provisional government, with a few noncommunist figureheads, was Tito's primary concession to the opinion of the Western world. Within the nation, communization was begun with all speed, with the communist party fast forging its usual "State apparatus" so familiar to contemporary readers after the experience of other countries behind the Iron Curtain. It is the old technique, tried over and over again: penetration of the Interior Department, control of the police, pressure on the press and organs of public opinion, threats and terror until the opposition is beaten and harassed, an easy victim for communist toughness and straight arm tactics. The Yugoslav secret police came into being under the name OZNA, modeled down to the last detail on the Soviet pattern. There was the same gigantic domestic espionage system, the same coercion, the same hounding of those who did not give in to the pressure of the regime. R. H. Markham, in his *Tito's Imperial Communism,* recounts how in May of 1945, the vast machinery of communist mass media was already in action with workers' meetings, antifascist rallies, youth conferences, party congresses, and the constant, endless, noisy procedures of mass hysteria. The Belgrade daily *Politika* was able to report, presumably with satisfaction, under date of June 18, 1945, "that the women at an anti-Fascist Congress held in Belgrade suddenly interrupted the chant Ti-to He-ro; Ti-to He-ro by passionately crying, we are Tito's; Tito is ours."[10]

The people's courts were one of the fundamental innovations in the new Tito Yugoslavia. The Commissar for Justice, in 1944, expressed his views on the character of these tribunals in a pithy way: "In our peoples courts, the procedure is simple, short, and quick, with no delays oral or direct." Operating along this line, the courts in Belgrade in one period of three days sentenced 105 persons to death. All, quite naturally, were collaborators.[11]

In this historical résumé there remains as one of the vital elements in this complex mosaic of passions and currents, a word regarding the Ustasha and the period of their rule over Croatia under Axis surveillance. The Ustasha movement had existed for many years, and its leader Ante Pavelić had resided in Italy where presumedly he had received encouragement from the fascist regime. As early as 1932

---

[10] Markham, R. H., *Tito's Imperial Communism,* Chapel Hill, North Carolina, 1947, pp. 191–192.

[11] Quoted from *Politika,* Nov. 26, 1944, in Martin, *op. cit.,* p. 313.

there had been Ustasha incursions in Yugoslav territory and actual fighting in the region of Velebit. The movement was intensely nationalistic, bent on the accomplishment of the complete separation of Croatia and its erection as an independent state. With it went inevitably a bitter opposition to the Serbs and all that Serbia stood for. The carefully nurtured state had scarcely begun its career before the collapse of the Axis. Obviously the period between 1941 and 1945 was extremely abnormal; Partisans and Chetniks operated within Croat territory, and the nascent state was forced to support not only an army of its own, but the Italian and German in addition, for Croatia was in reality an arena of dispute between the two Axis partners. Despite the apparent acquiescence of the Germans in the Italian domination of Croatia to the extent of accepting an Italian prince on the throne, the rivalries were deep and lively. The wedding of Croat and Italian was an impossible thing, especially with the cession to Italy by the Pavelić regime of a large portion of Dalmatia. A Spanish newsman, visiting Croatia at the time, writes of the bitterness that this act had provoked among the populace and how the Dalmatian question had become the issue uppermost in the mind of the citizenry.[12]

With the collapse of the unnatural and superimposed state of Yugoslavia on April 10, 1941, the Croatian people took advantage of the situation to proclaim their own independent state. This proclamation was not a source of unbounded joy to the Axis powers — Germany and Italy.[13] At his trial in Zagreb, Cardinal Stepinac said the following:

> The Croatian nation unanimously declared itself for the Croatian State and I would have been remiss had I not recognized and acknowledged this desire of the Croatian people enslaved by the former Yugoslavia.[14]

Dr. Ante Pavelić, the leader of the movement for a free and independent Croatia, returned from emigration and took charge of the newly formed State within six days of its founding. Despite their antagonism to it the Germans and the Italians made no efforts to

---

[12] Herraiz, Ismael, *Europa a oscuras,* Madrid, 1945, p. 303 f.
[13] See Ciano, Galeazzo, *Diario* (Milan: 950), 6th ed., p. 21 f.
[14] Document D, for details of the relations with the Croat State.

suppress the new State since it served them as propaganda in their oft-made claims that they were fighting for the freedom and liberation of oppressed and enslaved peoples.

A large number of soldiers from German-occupied Serbia withdrew into the mountains with arms and ammunition. Since the Germans were busy withdrawing to the eastern front to fight the Soviet Union they neglected to take or hold Serbian prisoners of war. This withdrawal left Serbia occupied by relatively meager forces.

The newly formed state of Croatia was left virtually defenseless, with no organized army, while the Serbs, on the contrary, were well prepared both with arms and an effective army.

Long before the outbreak of World War II the Chetniks had existed in Yugoslavia. Their purpose was antagonism and hostility to the Croatians in the event of an insurrection. The Serbs were well aware of the growing discontent of the Croatian people and of their desire to assert their rightful independence. Taking advantage of this fact they spread the false belief that the Croatians were responsible for the initial massacres which took place with the upheaval of the Yugoslav government. Facts prove that it was the Serbian Chetniks who committed the atrocities upon the Croatian populace. An American eyewitness, Rev. Theodore Benković, who spent the entire war in Croatia, writes in his book, *The Tragedy of a Nation:*

The match that touched off this smoldering conflagration of hate and revenge was the Cetniks' bestiality perpetrated at Illici and Cim, villages two kilometres from Mostar. . . . Croatia had been declared free April 10, 1941, and on the 13th, 14th and 15th of the same month the terroristic Cetnik bands of Draza Mihailovich began their bestial work. In the villages surrounding Capljina, close by to Mostar, the Cetniks murdered 25 Croat peasants; at the village of Struge by Capljina the Cetniks poured four dum-dum bullets into Franciska Vego who was holding her six month old child in her arms and was surrounded by four of her younger children.

At Illici and Cim the Cetniks burned down to the ground 85 houses, and many of the inhabitants were either killed or seriously wounded. Fra. Leo Petrovich, later my Provincial but then the Vicar of Mostar, together with Don Andrija Majich, the Bishop's Chancellor, were caught in Illici; their hands were bound and with a revolver pointed at their heads, accompanied by constant threats of immediate death, were marched by the Cetniks into Mostar and flung into prison.

Despite frequent talks with the survivors of this Cetnik barbarity, and seeing for myself the ruins of Illici and Cim, I could not, and in the light of subsequent events, bring myself to believe that the Serbs could be guilty of such barbarity; but, all doubt left me as to who were the instigators of this bloody horror when the Croatian Episcopacy in its encyclical letter of March 25, 1945 laid the blame at the doorsteps of the Cetniks and Serb communists. . . .

The atavism displayed by the Cetniks surpasses many a violent chapter in Balkan history. In September of '42 the Cetniks, in the pay of the Italian army, wiped out the village and surroundings of Prozor in central Bosnia, razing to the ground 2400 houses and butchering 1,062 Croatian women, children and old men. In some Croatian villages in Bosnia all over twelve years of age were put to the knife. Not even the partisans committed such heinous crimes as the Cetniks. As a Christmas present to the Croats of the village of Nunich, Dalmatia, the Cetniks sent the barbecued body of their assistant pastor, John Kranjac. In Vrtose, Bosnia, on August 2, 1941, the whole village was destroyed, the inhabitants massacred — the most horrible fate being that of Josip Matijevich, a prosperous business man, and his family of nine. All were beheaded by the Cetniks and their heads fixed on spits were carried about by the Cetniks, while their headless bodies were thrown into the fire.

On September 9, 1941 the Rev. Kresimir Barisich, pastor in Krnjeusa, Bosnia, was captured by the Cetniks, who then proceeded to cut off his ears, amputate his arms and legs and finally hurling the remains of the still living priest into his burning church. Other priest victims of these possessed terrorists were Juraj Gospodnetich, Ilija Tomas, Antun Bakula, Jakov Barisich, and Juraj Mladinov.

Five sisters of the Society of Daughters of Divine Love watched their orphanage at Pale, by Sarajevo, pillaged and destroyed by Cetniks who killed Sr. Berhmana Leidnix, age 80, on the spot. The four remaining sisters, Julia Ivanisevich, Bernadette Banja, Antonia Fabijan, and Kvirina Bajanc, the Cetniks took to their hideout at Gorazda where these sisters were subjected to all kinds of bestial indignities, finally murdered and thrown into the Drina river. This happened during the Christmas days of 1941.[15]

On June 28, 1941, "Vidov dan," a Serbian national holiday, the Serbs living in Croatia revolted in many places, attacking the defenseless Croatian people largely because of their hostility to a free and independent Croat state.

Provoked by this aggression, the Croatian Ustashi retaliated by killing many Serbs living in Croatia and a special group of fanatical Ustashi formed at this time, known to the Croats as "Nastashi" (upstarts), were responsible for numerous crimes committed against the Serbs. Bands of Chetniks and Partisans crossed the borders of the State of Croatia to plunder and kill the Croat Catholics and Moslems alike. It is not recorded that Ustasha or Croatian soldiery set foot

---

[15] Benković, Theodore, *The Tragedy of a Nation*. No date, pp. 34–37.

in Serbia during the last war. The German and Italian armed forces in Croatia at that time purposely refused to end the killings, so that the resulting chaos would give cause to declare the State of Croatia incapable of keeping order. Then after the war, Croatia could be annexed by Germany and Italy.

Within the boundaries of Croatia — a small territory — there were five armies fighting one another — the Croatian army, Ustashi and Domobrans, were fighting for the preservation of the Croatian State; the Chetniks against the Croatian State and for Yugoslavia and Serbian hegemony; the Germans and Italians for their own interests, and the Partisans for a Communist Yugoslavia. In this confusion many more Croatian Catholics and Moslems were probably killed than Serbs. The Catholic Hierarchy in Croatia made unavailing efforts to prevent the bloodshed. In this pastoral letter of March 24, 1945, the Croatian Catholic Bishops said the following:

> Innocent Croatian Blood has been poured out in the course of two world conflagrations in the cities and villages of Croatia, even in the Belgrade Parliament. In Belgrade a concordat, i.e., a most solemn pact between the Holy Apostolic See and the former kingdom of Yugoslavia, was concluded, but it happened that the rights of the Croatian Catholics depended on the whims of the government. In silence we pass over the shameful breaking of promises made to our Croatian leaders. This is not unknown to those who have followed recent events.
>
> When war engulfed our land, the Croatians remained unmoved because they lacked civil liberties and arms while an iniquitous enemy instituted a reign of terror whose one and only purpose was the extinction of the Croatians as a nation. Consequent upon this, and sad to say, some Croatians were found who returned killing for killing. The Bishops of Croatia decried such retaliatory measures.[16]

This in brief is the general backdrop against which the case of the Archbishop of Zagreb, Dr. Aloysius Stepinac, must be understood. His rise to a position of outstanding dignity and importance in the hierarchy coincides with the most difficult years of Yugoslav existence. Ordained in 1930, and made Archbishop in 1937, his public career coincided with the degenerating political situation in Yugoslavia and with the approach of war. It is quite impossible to separate the Archbishop from his background or eliminate the strong currents of Yugoslav history from consideration in treating of his case.

---

[16] Document LXIII.

Chapter II

THE TRIAL OF ARCHBISHOP STEPINAC

THE story of the Church in Tito's Yugoslavia forms the larger background for the trial and condemnation of the Archbishop of Zagreb. The last months of the Independent Croat State were wild and disorderly. The retreat of the German occupiers and the scurrying for refuge of the representatives of the Pavelić government as the Partisans advanced were not conducive to normal religious life. It was not until March, 1945, however, that the open persecution of the Church began. The tension between the communist regime and the ecclesiastical authorities, especially Archbishop Stepinac, became evident just before the end of the war in Europe. Up to that time the Archbishop had not been attacked in the communist controlled press.

The full story of the persecution, not only of the Catholic Church but of religion as such, in Tito's Yugoslavia, would require an entire volume. The trial and conviction of Archbishop Stepinac forms a lurid chapter in this long epic of a heroic struggle against totalitarianism in its most virulent form. It is important, however, to indicate the general lines of the persecution both before and after the trial of the Archbishop of Zagreb. The first formal statement of the disquietude of the hierarchy is best evidenced in the Letter of the Bishops of the Croatian Republic, issued on March 24, 1945. The statement recalls the vicissitudes of the Catholic Church in Croatia and the long *via crucis* to which it was submitted during this century. "From the depth of our soul we protest before God and mankind against the systematic murder and persecution of innocent priests and Catholic faithful, many of whose lives excel in sanctity, upon whom the maddened enemies of the Catholic Church have brought death."[1] The accusation is specifically against those who in the name of the new ideology were bent on the extermination of the faith: "The enemies of the Catholic Church, especially the followers of materialistic communism which the entire Croatian nation rejects . . . have in Croatia exterminated with fire and sword priests and the more outstanding of the faithful." The document repudiates the charge that Bishops, priests, and religious have been guilty of war crimes and deserved punishment. The Bishops express their willingness to have individual cases investigated fully by the impartial representatives of other nations or an international commission. The episcopal conference expressed equal readiness to set up a committee of its own to look into cases in which war criminality was alleged. On the score of Croat approval of the creation of the former independent state, the Bishops indicate their honest conviction that such independence accorded with the will of the overwhelming majority of the Croat people and was the culmination of a thousand years of hope. However, under the new republic, the Bishops recognize that the laws of the state must be respected and obeyed.

The story after 1939 is the epic of Archbishop Stepinac's effort to maintain order and some degree of tranquillity in a Yugoslavia that was first endangered and then ravaged by war. After the arrival of the German occupiers on the morning of April 10, 1941, the Archbishop was faced with the new Independent Croat State, under the Ustasha, and the growing pressure of the pro-Axis elements and the occupying force. His own life merges with that of the struggle of Croatia for existence and the protection of the faith in territories more seriously menaced than ever before in their history.

A short biographical note on Archbishop Aloysius Stepinac may be useful in dealing with the specific problem of the status and position of the Catholic Church in Croatia and the trial of the prelate in September, 1946, for alleged crimes against the Yugoslav state.

Aloysius Stepinac was born of modest peasant stock in Krašić,

---

[1] See Document LXIII, *Encyclical Letter of the Bishops of the Republic of Croatia to the Faithful,* given on March 24, 1945, for the complete text of this episcopal statement. See also Chapter V for further details of Church-State relations under Tito.

near Zagreb, on May 8, 1898, the seventh of eleven children. In 1916, while a student at the minor seminary he was conscripted into the Austro-Hungarian army and fought on the Italian front where he was taken prisoner. After some months in an Italian prisoner of war camp, he was released to join the so-called "Yugoslav Legion," made up of Croat and Slovene prisoners who took advantage of this formality to obtain freedom. He had taken pains to ascertain if this action conformed to the prevailing sentiments of patriotic Croats at the time for it must be emphasized that in accord with the overwhelming majority of his fellow Croats, Aloysius Stepinac believed in Croatia first, in its freedom and independence. The fact of Yugoslav unity might be accepted as a necessary constitutional arrangement with certain external advantages but there was certainly little enthusiasm in the minds of most Croats for the joint enterprise on which they were soon to embark with the Serbs and Slovenes. In 1919 he returned to civilian life and after the completion of his classical studies, entered the University of Zagreb to study agriculture. In 1924 he withdrew to enter the seminary and prepare for the priesthood, spending seven years at the Pontifical German-Hungarian College in Rome where he was ordained on October 25, 1930. At the same time he received the degrees of Doctor of Philosophy and Doctor of Theology. In July, 1931, he was back in Zagreb, assigned to one of the poorest parishes in the city. He founded *Caritas,* an organization to aid and succor the poor and miserable, among whom he had been laboring. A year after this he became the secretary of the then Archbishop of Zagreb, Dr. Ante Bauer. On May 28, 1934, Pope Pius XI nominated him Titular Archbishop of Nicopsis and coadjutor to his ordinary, with right of succession. On December 7, 1937, on the death of Archbishop Bauer, Mons. Stepinac succeeded to the See of Zagreb.

Archbishop Stepinac was arrested on May 17, 1945, and detained in prison for some days. After his release he remained under the close surveillance of the OZNA, the Yugoslav secret police. Two days after his release, Marshal Tito visited Zagreb. The Chief of State received a delegation of the clergy to whom he spoke regarding the attitude of the new Yugoslavia toward the Church and the religious problem. He expressed his general dissatisfaction with the conduct of the clergy and Church during the liberation movement. Without attacking Rome he indicated that he felt the Catholic Church was inclined far too much in favor of Italy and much less favorably to Yugoslavia. It was his feeling that the Church should be more national in spirit and above all that there was real need for a closer collaboration between the Catholics and the Orthodox for the sake of Yugoslav unity. There was an impression that this was a subtle proposal on behalf of a national, separatist church, no longer subject to Rome. Archbishop Stepinac called on Tito during this visit, in the same way and for the same reasons that he had called on Ante Pavelić at the time of the creation of the Independent Croat State. It was with the hope that a satisfactory arrangement might be worked out whereby the vital interests of the Church would be protected and relations between Church and State normalized.

The evidence of increasing State pressure against the Church was clear during the summer of 1945. Commissars were designated to oversee the activities of all schools, institutions, and foundations. The first trials for alleged treason and collaborationism took place during that summer. On July 20, Archbishop Stepinac protested to the head of the Croat Popular Republic, Dr. Bakarić, against State meddling in purely religious matters. To this protest Bakarić never replied formally, although making mention of it before parliament. The Pastoral Letter of September 21, 1945, was the incident that provoked the conflict between the Church and the new Yugoslav state. This Pastoral, signed by all the Bishops of Yugoslavia, and with a note appended specifically assuming collective responsibility for its statements, included precise charges of persecution by the Yugoslav government. The Pastoral disavows any intention of prescribing for Catholics political or social conduct and the only thing on which the hierarchy insisted was that any organization of the nation conform to the universally binding principles of morality. The letter emphasizes that prior to the cessation of hostilities the Belgrade government had pledged its solemn word to respect and honor the freedom of worship, conscience, and private property, an assurance also made provisionally by the Popular Government of Croatia. As a result conversations were held with the civil authorities to the end that a mutually acceptable understanding might be reached. The hierarchy made perfectly plain to the government its position and its interests. The highest government authority was reassuring in its expression of good will and interest in achieving an understanding. Circumstances have demonstrated, however, how vain was the hope that such an agreement could be reached. The Pastoral proceeds then to enumerate exactly the reasons that led the hierarchy to consider the state of affairs as of September, 1945, one of persecution and violence toward the Church.[2] These may be summarized under a number of items. The Bishops protest against the murder of priests and religious, the number of which is constantly increasing. The Bishops assert that according to their knowledge, the statistics on such acts of violence were: 243 dead, 169 in prison and concentration camps, 89 missing, making a total of 501. To that number must be added the death of 19 seminarians, 3 lay brothers, and 4 nuns. These victims were often denied the solace of the last sacraments. Capital punishment was meted out by courts with a rapidity and ruthlessness that surpasses the imagination. The ordinary safeguards in the courts of every civilized country are absent and the defendant rarely has the chance of a normal defense or of the procedures that accompany orthodox judicial practice. There was the case of the Franciscan monastery at Široki Brijeg where 28 of the fathers were put to death with no semblance of a trial. There were unquestionably priests whose nationalist zeal carried them too far and involved them in political action and the whole Church is now suffering the consequence of what at the most were the excesses of a very tiny minority. The number of priests and religious in concentration camps is very large. The Greek-Catholic Bishop Šimrak and Bishop Carević are among those who have either been imprisoned or whose fate is unknown.

The spiritual life of the nation was seriously threatened for parishes bereft of pastors and an official press devoted to virulent attacks on the clergy could not fail to endanger the religious integrity of the people. The Catholic press had totally disappeared and the hundred odd publications before the war had ceased to appear. No refutation or reply to charges and accusations could be made because

---

[2] The complete text of the Pastoral Letter is presented in Document LXX.

there was no instrument by which the Church could respond to its detractors. Seminaries had either been closed or confiscated in Zagreb, Split, Travnik, Sent Vidu, Ljubljana, Maribor, Sinj, and elsewhere.

The Church was hampered at every turn in its work of education. Religious instruction on a voluntary basis was reduced in most cases to an hour a week and in the institutions of higher education, religion was eliminated as contrary to freedom of conscience. A considerable number of important Catholic secondary institutions were closed or taken over by the State, in spite of the expressed wishes of parents with confidence in the excellence and seriousness of the instruction. Catholic institutions of all kinds — hospitals, orphanages, and homes for the aged — were closed down or confiscated, frequently on the accusation of the criminal guilt of those in charge or because the sectarian character of the establishments was such as to make them undesirable.

The State corrupted the young people with anti-religious or at least nonreligious ideas. Every effort was made to hamper compliance with religious duties and precepts, force being often used to induce them to participate in State run and controlled enterprises that revealed what was known as "progressive tendencies." Civil marriage and even the dissolution of Catholic marriages by the civil authority represents another form of affrontery to the Catholic sentiments of the people of Croatia. The great work of *Caritas,* the central charitable organization in Zagreb, was undermined through State supervision which reduced its effectiveness to a minimum. The agrarian reform meant the wholesale expropriation of Church properties. It was certainly not antagonism to a reform in the land system itself that explains the opposition of the Church but the reckless and arbitrary way in which lands devoted to socially beneficial ends were taken or distributed with no thought of compensation. The Church was reduced to literal impotence by the inability to maintain its various works and activities in the face of this program. The sisters in their hospitals and other centers for the care of the sick and needy were harassed and curtailed in their work. Even graves were desecrated in the outbreak of fury against everything that smacked of religion.

The long years of war and the rising persecution under the new

Yugoslavia were producing serious losses among the Catholics. In the one diocese of Banja Luka, the number of Catholics had decreased in less than ten years from 130,000 to 40,000. The concentration camps of Lepoglava and Stara Gradiška were full of Catholics — clergy and laity. The reaction was considerable. It is recorded that among Zagreb university students not more than 200 normally participated in the Easter retreat. In 1946 this number exceeded 4000. On July 10, of that year the annual pilgrimage to the shrine of Marija Bistrica brought together over 100,000 faithful.

The loss among the hierarchy was considerable and serious. The known victims of the Tito regime, besides Archbishop Stepinac himself who was to be tried, were the following:

Mgr. Josip Carević, Titular Bishop of Aristium and retired Bishop of Dubrovnik, missing for some years and believed dead.

Mgr. Janko Simrak, Greek Rite Catholic Bishop of Križevci, died August 9, 1946, the result of maltreatment during many months in prison.

Mgr. Josip Stjepan Garić, O.F.M., Bishop of Banja Luka, died in exile at Graz, Austria, June 30, 1946.

Mgr. Ivan Šarić, Archbishop of Sarajevo. Exiled.

Mgr. Gregory Rožman, Prince Bishop of Ljubljana. In exile.

The story of persecution and oppression does not end in 1946 but has continued in the years that have followed the imprisonment of the Archbishop of Zagreb. In September, 1948, two years after the trial of the Metropolitan of Croatia, Mgr. Peter Cule, Bishop of Moštar, was condemned to eleven and a half years imprisonment, his secretary, Father Matthew Nuić, to eight years, and Fathers Mladen Barbarić and Rufin Šilić to three years and nine months respectively. Three Franciscan nuns, Sisters Crescentia, Melita, and Felicia were given prison terms at the same time of three years, one year, and six months respectively.

The long arm of persecution did not spare those who had undertaken to defend Archbishop Stepinac during his trial. The well-known correspondent of the New York *Times* in Rome, Arnaldo Cortesi, reported under date of April 20, 1947, the story of one of the defense counsel at the trial who escaped to Italy under the name of Blašković, and that Dr. Politeo, principal counsel for the prelate, had been imprisoned for some months after the trial. Dr. Ramljak and Dr. Selaković, involved in the defense also were arrested and remained in prison for a long period of time.[3]

The religious situation in Yugoslavia was investigated in the summer of 1947 by a group of Protestant ministers, invited by the Yugoslav government and the Yugoslav ambassador in the United States, Sava Kosanović. The substance of their report, published in pamphlet form under the title: *Religion in Yugoslavia: A report on conferences with Roman Catholic, Orthodox, Moslem, Jewish, and Protestant leaders and investigations through the medium of religious institutions and documents,* is that religion in Yugoslavia was not threatened by the present government and that the information reaching the public from Yugoslavia was distorted and one sided. Quite naturally this commission found Archbishop Stepinac properly convicted and guilty of the charges that had been made against him.

No more eloquent statement can be found regarding the general problem of religious persecution in Yugoslavia in years following the advent of the communist regime under Tito than that delivered by the Most Reverend Irinej Georgević, Bishop of the Serbian Orthodox diocese of Dalmatia. The statement, released on August 23, 1947, and published in abbreviated form in the New York *Times* constitutes the refutation of those who found religious life in Yugoslavia normal. The view of the Orthodox Bishop, who can hardly be accused of any particular penchant for the Catholic position, is summed up as follows:

The facts of the persecution of the Catholic Church in Yugoslavia are well known in America because of the means of which the Catholic Church disposes. Our own church, alas, has no important international connections and there are very few of our co-religionists in the United States. The facts of the persecution of our church are therefore not so well known here. Though the communist regime has set out to destroy all religion and all belief in God, it would be no exaggeration to say that at the present time the Orthodox Church is being even more severely persecuted than the Catholic.

The figures for the Orthodox clergy follow the same monotonous pattern as the Catholic: 800 to 900 priests in prison; seminaries closed and confiscated, education reorganized and reoriented, and terror applied to those who cling to religion in its institutional form.

---

[3] New York *Times,* May 2, 1947.

As has been indicated, the new Yugoslav regime was not slow in launching its anti-Catholic campaign. The rumblings of the summer of 1945 became thunderous during the autumn. It is curious that in September the Zagreb papers published two photographs showing Archbishop Stepinac, Monsignor Lach, and various Catholic and Orthodox dignitaries in the company of Dr. Bakarić, communist president of Croatia, the Soviet military attaché, and the Partisan commander in Zagreb at a parade celebrating the establishment of the peoples republic of Croatia. This apparent *detente* in the tension between the ecclesiastical and civil authority was purely formal. The reading of the Pastoral Letter of September 21 in all churches led to a literal explosion of anti-Catholic sentiment from the press and other communist organs in the country. The propaganda against the Church and particularly against the Archbishop of Zagreb was stepped up as of that date. On November 4, 1945, the prelate attended the consecration of a church at Zaprešić near Zagreb. His car was attacked with stones and other implements.[4] A priest with him was severely beaten. The Croat Minister of the Interior found no better explanation of the incident than the following:

The attack was begun by the people who opposed the growth of the Church. It reached its climax when an armed priest fired into the people in order to put down the opposition.

The general lines of the indictment that was to be presented a year later against the Archbishop began to take shape in the increasing crescendo of insult and denunciation of the Croat press against the primate. *Vjesnik* published, on December 19, 1945, a photograph of the Archbishop in the company of high officials of the Pavelić government. It described the gathering as a political meeting and depicted the Archbishop saluting the Ustasha flag, arm in air according to the Nazi custom. The paper concluded that this was ample evidence of the strong support accorded the Ustasha. It was afterward revealed that the picture was snapped at the Zagreb fair and the raised arm belonged to a Croat official standing immediately behind the Archbishop.[5]

---

[4] Document LXXI, Letter of the Archbishop to Dr. Bakarić protesting the incident.

[5] See Document LXXII, December 17, 1945, with the Archbishop's refutation.

On December 21, 1945, *Vjesnik* published a letter, allegedly written by Archbishop Stepinac to the Pope in which he asked for a special blessing for the Independent Croat State.

On January 1, 1946, the same newspaper reported that at a Partisan meeting in Zagreb, a "spokesman of the people" asserted that he had been a witness to daily visits to the Archbishop by General Kasche during the German occupation, the purpose of which was to "plot against the people."

Vjesnik appeared on January 19, 1946, with more photographs purporting to show Archbishop Stepinac as the "friend and helper" of the Ustasha and Nazi regimes. The occasion was the group picture taken after Mass at St. Mark's Church on the occasion of the opening of the Croat parliament. The paper studiously avoided all mention of the sermon delivered by the Archbishop at the Mass which was widely interpreted as extremely hostile to the Ustasha.

Vjesnik appeared on January 26, 1946, with the accusation that the Archbishop had failed criminally to intervene on behalf of seven priests condemned to the concentration camp at Jasenovac. The same paper two days later published an anonymous letter stating that the Archbishop had neglected his duty to protect the persecuted and had encouraged crimes against them.

During January the Partisans organized a "peoples demonstration" against the black market in Zagreb. In passing the Archbishop's residence a few of the large crowd, which served as an admirable backdrop, demanded the trial and conviction of the Archbishop for crimes against the people. The impression quite naturally was that this huge mob had gathered for the precise purpose of demanding the Archbishop's trial. The press played up the alleged demand as evidence of the people's invincible will to chastise those who had collaborated with the hated Ustasha during the war.

So violent did the campaign become that Randolph Churchill, writing in the *Daily Telegraph* on January 23, 1946, stated that "the Yugoslav propaganda against the Archbishop has only one purpose, i.e., to prepare his trial."

This prediction was borne out by the events of 1946. On August 30 of that year the trial of His Excellency Gregory Rožman, Bishop of Ljubljana and Dr. Miha Krek, former Vice-Premier and chairman of the Slovene People's Party was held. Both were tried and convicted *in absentia* and were sentenced to eighteen and fifteen years of forced labor respectively, the loss of civil rights, and the confiscation of all property. Incidentally this trial was a precedent for the later one of Archbishop Stepinac. One of the features of the Ljubljana affair, which in due time became a common practice in the courts of Tito's Yugoslavia, was to associate several defendants, some of whom were unquestionably guilty, and create the impression of collective guilt. In the case of Bishop Rožman and Dr. Krek, four other individuals were included, who were charged with treason and who quite possibly may have been culpable.

Another trial ended on September 13 at Varaždin in Croatia where four priests were accused of conspiracy, the center of which was said to be the Franciscan monastery at Čakovec. They were all sentenced to forced labor for varying periods of time.

The major trial that preceded that of the Archbishop and led directly to it, was held in Zagreb on September 9, 1946, when eighteen defendants were accused of collaboration with the Ustasha and the Crusaders. Twelve of them were priests, including Dr. Ivan Šalić, Archbishop Stepinac's secretary, and the rest Franciscans, one of whom was Father Modesto Martinčić, provincial of the Croat province. Dr. Šalić, incidentally, had accompanied the Archbishop on November 4, 1945, when the stoning occurred. He was arrested in December, 1945, and held for nine months before the trial. The major accusation against him was that of providing medical supplies for the Ustasha underground.

The sensational element in the trial was the testimony of Dr. Šalić and Father Martinčić linking Archbishop Stepinac with Ustasha-Crusader activity. Father Martinčić asserted that "the center of all terrorist action and intervention from abroad was the Archbishop." Dr. Šalić had stated that "the Archbishop's palace in Zagreb was the center of Ustasha, Crusader and terrorist action." The testimony advanced further the claim that Archbishop Stepinac had visited Dr. Maček for political purposes and that valuables brought together by the prelate were destined for various terrorist activities. Dr. Šalić at this time used the phrase which was to become famous in connection with the Archbishop's trial. The prelate had stated in a circular letter to the priests of his diocese that his conscience was clear. Dr. Šalić contributed to the discussion the observation: "I think the Archbishop's conscience is not clear." The claim was advanced too that Archbishop Stepinac wanted a Croatia under the Germans, Italians, and Ustasha, that he had invited Eric Lisak, the chief of the Ustasha police, to remain overnight at the palace, and that the Crusader flag had been blessed in the prelate's private oratory.

This testimony naturally cast a different light on the case. The Public Prosecutor claimed that the evidence was piling up that "Stepinac is the immediate accomplice, promotor and collaborator" in the activities of the eighteen accused. The Prosecutor added that "for this reason I have given orders that Stepinac be put in prison and that investigations be initiated against him. When the investigations are complete, I shall indict him for offenses against the people and State." A ten day adjournment was agreed upon so that the Archbishop might be charged jointly with the other defendants. The Belgrade radio announced that Archbishop Stepinac was under arrest.

The atmosphere and events from the moment of arrest to conviction form a commentary on the juridical methods in vogue in the Yugoslav people's democracy. The press and radio were admirably synchronized to pour forth day after day a stream of vilification against the Archbishop. The statement of the Prosecutor that when the investigations were completed he would indict the Archbishop shows clearly enough that the decision had already been made to bring him before the courts regardless of what the investigations actually showed. It is an excellent example of prejudgment before the first steps had been taken to ascertain whether there was sufficient motive for indicting or not. Demonstrations were organized and petitions circulated demanding that the Archbishop be condemned. It was a typical demonstration of the technique of the totalitarian state with all the machinery of mass emotion and mass demonstration at its command. But even the all powerful government was unable to prevent thousands from thronging the churches of Croatia to pray day and night for their Archbishop. The persecution of the clergy became more severe after the primate had been lodged in prison.

Bishop Lach was arrested on a Confirmation tour and imprisoned for a night at Koprivnica while Bishop Bonifačić of Split was forced to turn back at Imotski while on a pastoral visit by the violence of the communists. Bishop Pušić of Hvar was forced to give up his Confirmation tour of the Dalmatian islands because of the increasingly hostile demonstrations against him. On Sunday, September 22, OZNA agents called on parish priests everywhere to forbid them to read the circular letter sent out from the Zagreb chancery office expressing the conviction that the Archbishop was innocent and urging prayers for his intention.

Archbishop Stepinac was arrested at 6 A.M. on *September 18,* the indictment, dated *September 23,* reached him on *the 24th,* and on *the 30th* of the month he was on trial for his life. The defense had exactly six days in which to receive the indictment, prepare the refutation, and examine the evidence advanced by the Prosecution. The latter had had a full year in which to prepare the case, as the newspaper campaigns clearly demonstrated. This is further proved from the argument advanced by the Yugoslav government itself in justifying its action against the Archbishop:

When Archbishop Stepinac was arrested and brought to trial in September, 1946, one argument of the critics ran along these lines: Why did the Yugoslav Government not arrest Archbishop Stepinac immediately after the liberation if his offenses were so grave? If they really had the evidence, why did they wait so long?

The answer is that the Yugoslav Government, far from being motivated by vengeful feelings, made a serious effort to avoid the necessity of taking court action against Archbishop Stepinac. It endeavored earnestly and patiently to reach a *modus vivendi* making possible a settlement of the Stepinac case.

When the War Crimes investigation produced evidence of the Archbishop's complicity in the barbarous regime of Ante Pavelić in puppet Croatia, the Yugoslav Government informed the Vatican of the nature and volume of this evidence and asked that Stepinac be withdrawn. What happened was described by Marshal Tito in an address at Zagreb on October 31, 1946:

"When the Pope's representative to our Government, Bishop Hurley, paid me his first visit I raised the question of Stepinac. 'Have him transferred from Yugoslavia,' I said, 'for otherwise we shall be obliged to place him under arrest.' I warned Bishop Hurley of the course we had to follow. I discussed the matter with him in detail. I acquainted him with Stepinac's many hostile acts toward our country. I gave him a file of documentary evidence of the Archbishop's crimes."[6]

The Archbishop's friends proposed two lawyers to defend him:

---

[6] *The Case of Archbishop Stepinac.* Published by the Embassy of the Federal Peoples Republic of Yugoslavia, Washington, D. C., p. 8.

Dr. Ivo Politeo and Dr. Andrus. The court accepted the first but rejected the second for reasons that were not given. Dr. Katičić was then designated to serve as defense counsel with Dr. Politeo. From the moment of his arrest on September 18 to his conviction on October 11, the Archbishop saw his counsel exactly once, for a single hour, on September 27. Every obstacle was placed in the way of the preparation of the defense. The Archbishop was given no opportunity for the customary consultations, calling of witnesses, and general preparation of the case. Many of his collaborators were subjected to restrictions and vexation making it impossible for them to contribute to the defense of the prelate. Bishop Franjo Salis-Sweis, auxiliary Bishop of Zagreb and Vicar-General of the archdiocese, in charge of its affairs since the Archbishop's arrest, was himself arrested on September 24, the day the indictment was published, although later released. He was arrested again on September 27, the very day on which counsel interviewed the Archbishop. Monsignor Ante Slamić, who directed the chancery office, was arrested and detained until September 28. Canon Stjepan Bakšić, one of the Archbishop's closest associates, was arrested and questioned for some time just before the trial opened.

Archbishop Stepinac was indicted under the "Laws on Crimes against the People and the State," approved August 15, 1945, and amended July 9, 1946. These laws were entirely the product of the new popular democracy in the process of formation in Yugoslavia. They constituted a complete break with the traditional past and rejected outright the usual procedures and guarantees contained in previous legislation. Moreover, the new laws, conceived along strictly political and communist lines, were drafted and put into effect *after* the alleged crimes committed by the Archbishop. In this way the prelate was arrested and tried *ex post facto*, for offenses which were not criminal in the code in existence at the time of their supposed commission.

There are certain precepts of justice which are generally recognized in the entire civilized world. Obviously it is impossible to insist that Yugoslavia conform exactly to the legal procedures of the United States or Great Britain. The federal constitution of Yugoslavia, under Chapter XIII describes the character and functions of the courts in Article 116:

The law courts are independent in the dispensing of justice and mete out justice according to the law.

The courts are separate from the administration in all cases.

Higher courts have within the limits of the law, the right to supervision over lower courts.

Articles 117 and 118 read as follows:

The law courts dispense justice in the name of the people.
Proceedings in the law courts are as a rule public.
The resolutions of a court may be altered only by a competent higher court.
The accused is guaranteed the right of defense before a court.

The basic guarantees universally recognized may be summarized as follows:

1. The right to assistance of counsel. However learned a person may be in other fields, he needs the assistance of legal counsel when confronted with the complexity of a legal defense.

2. The right of sufficient time and opportunity to prepare his defense. It is useless to offer an accused the right to defend if he is unable to avail himself thereof.

3. The right to a fair and impartial court. It is sheer mockery to allow an accused to defend himself before a court which already considers him guilty.

4. The right to present his case in a neutral atmosphere, undisturbed by hostile demonstrations. The average person would be psychologically affected by hostile demonstrations such as hissing or booing from the courtroom audience, so as to affect his ability to conduct his defense.

5. The right to present such witnesses as he, or his counsel, deem essential to his defense, if they are reasonably available. Evidence tendered by the defense may be, of course, excluded if it is "irrelevant, immaterial or incompetent," but, even so, the accused should be permitted to put his witness on the stand so that the court may learn the nature of his testimony.

Despite the meager reference in the Constitution to judicial procedures, it would seem that the guarantee of the right of defense include the conditions cited. It is perfectly clear that Archbishop Stepinac was not given this right and that every obstacle was placed in the way of the preparation of a proper and legitimate defense. The undue haste of the trial constituted a violation of the expressly guaranteed right of defense in the Yugoslav constitution.

The character of the "popular" courts in Tito's Yugoslavia merits a word since the nature of these tribunals is of the utmost importance in judging of the equanimity, impartiality, and objectivity with which the Archbishop's case was heard. The concerted attacks by the Yugoslav press on the Archbishop *before* conviction indicate very clearly that pressure was generated to produce the desired decision. The atmosphere of impartiality and calm so indispensable to the proper trial of a defendant on criminal charges was totally lacking. The evidence of this score is overwhelming:

The Zagreb newspaper *Vjestnik* today denounced Catholic Archbishop Stepinatz as the "Supreme Head of all the dark and bloody crimes committed by pro-fascist bands since allied forces drove the Germans out of Yugoslavia. . . . Stepinatz will answer for the heavy crimes he has committed during the occupation and since Yugoslavia's liberation. He is responsible for four years of collaboration with the enemy. He is responsible for the protection of Ustashi slaughterers, for diplomatic activity before the collapse of the Croat independent state, for the episcopal letter directed against the national liberation struggle and for the anti-national spirit that he propagated as supreme head of the church among his subordinates."

Zagreb papers and the provincial Croat press opened a concerted editorial attack against Archbishop Stepinatz himself. . . . The general Croat press theme today was: "The entire population, with great interest, is awaiting the continuation of the trial of Ustashi criminals before the Supreme Court of Croatia at which time Dr. Stepinatz will appear on the defendant's bench."[7]

The theme of the press attacks on the Archbishop was not that he should be brought to trial for alleged offenses, but that *he was guilty of those offenses* even before the trial had opened and the evidence submitted.

The broad nature of these so-called people's courts may be judged from comments in the Yugoslav press itself. The newspaper *Slobodna Dalmacija* of December 31, 1944, stated:

Instructions as to the work and organization of the courts were given by the Anti-Fascist Council. According to these instructions judgments were not to be given by trained jurists under the complicated laws heretofore in force but are to be made by the best sons of the people, not the dead letter of the written law but by the proper, healthy conception of the people. The judges are to be chosen from the people.

---

[7] New York *Times,* Sept. 23, 1946.

The newspaper *Politika* of November 26, 1944, published the statement of Milan Krujić, trustee for legal affairs of the Anti-Fascist Council of Serbia in which he remarked that in the course of the national liberation struggle the people had swept away the old authority in all its forms including the legal system and had developed their own peoples legal system.

The trial opened on September 30, 1946, in an atmosphere reflecting the typical "mass demonstrations" so much in vogue in the countries under communist domination.

What may be said of the conduct of the judges on the bench? The press dispatches do not say much about this feature of the case, but one or two news items are significant as indicating that the judges, to put it mildly, were eager for a conviction. Under continental practice the judges question the prisoner and the examination may be "thorough and searching." But even so, our sense of fairness suggests that there should be a certain restraint.

Frequently both the president of the court and the prosecution were directing so many questions at him that he was cut off in the middle of a sentence.[8]

This perhaps in itself was a detail. The following exchange is reported in the world press:

A woman witness at the Zagreb trial of Erik Lisak, former Ustashi Colonel and Secretary to Archbishop Stepinatz (*This is an obvious error as Colonel Lisak was never Secretary to the Archbishop.*) showed the court today a piece of rope by which, she said, her daughter was hanged. She demanded that Lisak be hanged by the same rope, the Yugoslav news agency reported.

The court president then asked Archbishop Stepinatz, who is on trial with Lisak on charges of collaboration with the Germans and crimes against the state, whether he still considered that his civic duty had obliged him to attend dinners and banquets with Lisak and "other criminals."

"My conscience is calm," the Archbishop replied, according to the agency.

"You must have a very loose conscience if you could be in the company of such people," the president said.[9]

Extremely sharp questioning in a trial of this sort is to be expected. We are not in position to appraise the guilt or innocence of Colonel Lisak but the incident of the rope is an example of that melodrama and duress so common in Soviet courts, and which is

---

[8] *London Times,* Oct. 2, 1946.
[9] New York *Times,* Oct. 6, 1946.

profoundly repugnant to our sense of justice. The significant point, however, is that the judge brands Lisak as a "criminal" while the trial is still pending. He chides the Archbishop for attending dinners with this "criminal," thus placing him in the same class with Lisak whom he has already pre-judged. He then pre-judges the Archbishop by telling him that he must have a very loose conscience. It will be noted that these observations, according to the press report, were made on the basis of the woman's testimony, with nothing to show that the Archbishop even knew of the alleged offense by Lisak.

These remarks show that this judge considered Archbishop Stepinac guilty before he presented his defense. What is the use of proceeding with a trial before a judge who had already declared from the bench that the accused is guilty?

The atmosphere of the court was determined by the most careful stage setting. The audience was admitted by ticket only with distribution in the hands of the OZNA. The audience was, to put it bluntly, nothing but an organized and synchronized mob. The behavior of the public prosecutor was extremely violent, as may be seen by the reading of the complete text of the indictment in which the extremes of language are most common. The trials began normally at eight in the morning and continued to three or four in the afternoon with a short recess. After October 3, the sessions ran from eight in the morning to eight or nine at night with only a short interruption. There was no time for the defense to examine its position or take account of the testimony as presented by the prosecution. There are the most serious discrepancies between the actual testimony and the published reports. There is no doubt that the original transcription was carefully gone over and in many cases rephrased or parts of it suppressed. There is the specific instance of General Kvaternik who testified that Pavelić and the Ustasha hated Archbishop Stepinac. *Vjesnik* in its printed report of the proceedings of that day, made no mention of this statement at all for the simple reason that it undermined the main contention of the prosecution that Archbishop Stepinac was a close and ardent supporter of the Independent Croat State and the Ustasha. The police allowed no one to take notes outside the official stenographers. The crowd at the trial evidenced again and again their antipathy to

the Archbishop and their entire conformity with the position of
the prosecution:

Most of the spectators hissed when the court read an article describing the
Archbishop's blessing of the Ustashi Crusaders.[10]

The forty-eight year old head of the Roman Church in Yugoslavia accused
of "crimes against the people" and of collaborating with the terroristic Ustashi,
was interrupted many times during his thirty-eight minute defense by jeers from
the audience.[11]

The prosecution was allowed an unlimited number of witnesses,
while the defense was permitted to call only twenty. Fourteen of
the defense witnesses were disqualified by the court whereas those
for the prosecution were uniformly admitted without examination and
could not be cross-examined by the defense. Dr. Politeo tried once to
cross-examine Father Martinčić but was quickly stopped by the
court. The judges, all hostile to Archbishop Stepinac, Zarko Vim-
pulšek, Ante Cireneo, and Ivan Poldrugač, imposed arbitrary rules
again and again to hamper the defense. There was the case of Canon
Penić who was disqualified as a witness because he was a "Fascist."
Nevertheless, three witnesses for the prosecution, former Croat Defense Minister Kvaternik, former Foreign Minister Alajbegović, and
Finance Minister Košak, all awaiting their own trials as Fascists, were
admitted without hesitation as witnesses against Archbishop Stepinac.
Most of the documentary evidence advanced by Dr. Politeo was
ruled out and only a small proportion allowed in the record or in
open court. The time allowances were in line with this obvious
prejudice. On one occasion, Dr. Politeo was accused of unduly
prolonging the trial. He retorted that by actual count, the prosecution
had talked for forty-eight hours and the defense for precisely twenty
minutes.

The fact, of course, that the Archbishop was tried in the company
of various other defendants, some of whom were charged with active
participation in acts of terrorism, confused the situation. It opened
the way to the introduction of testimony quite irrelevant to the
Archbishop's case but which by implication involved him in matters
with which he had no personal connection. Under normal legal

---

[10] New York *Times,* Oct. 1, 1946.
[11] *Ibid.,* Oct. 4, 1946.

practices, several accused are not tried together unless their alleged offenses are connected in time and place.

The Archbishop was denied the privilege of conferring with His Excellency, The Most Reverend Joseph P. Hurley, D.D., Bishop of St. Augustine, Florida, who was present at the trial as acting Papal Nuncio, "despite daily requests since the trial opened."[12] This refusal indicated a distinctly unfriendly attitude on the part of the court. At best, it was petty to refuse this small measure of assistance to an accused on trial for his life. The responsibility for this refusal seems to have been squarely on the court. It was reported in the press that "The prosecutor said today that the question of Bishop Hurley's seeing the defendant was one for the court to decide rather than the prosecution."[13] Therefore, this incident contributes still another detail to the conviction that the court was prejudiced against Archbishop Stepinac from the start.

Another point to mention is that the Archbishop was not a defendant when the trial began. A trial already in progress was interrupted and he was added to the original defendants after evidence involving him had been adduced. In the few days allowed to them, however, the attorneys for Archbishop Stepinac, in addition to preparing their client's defense, had to study the prior record of the trial, which, in itself, must have been a task of some magnitude. This arrangement of adding new defendants while a criminal trial is in progress is unknown to the common law.

The witnesses for the prosecution testified on a wide range of topics. On October 5, fifty-eight of them from Croatia, Slavonia, Dalmatia, Bosnia and Hercegovina testified, for the most part on the accusation of forced conversions. It may be added that only one Zagreb priest was even mentioned in the testimony of this entire company of prosecution witnesses. Fifteen more witnesses were presented on Ustasha crimes and the murder of hostages. Not infrequently the judge would ask: "Was there a priest among those committing the crimes?" The response was always, "Yes, he was there giving the last Sacraments." On October 7, the judges announced that the defense witnesses would be heard. The court excluded the majority of them

---

12 New York *Times,* Oct. 12, 1946.
13 *Ibid.,* Oct. 6, 1946.

on the grounds that they had nothing to contribute to the case, before they were even heard:

These witnesses cannot contribute anything to modify the substance of the indictment. They can only testify regarding details. They might be able to show that Stepinac protected a few isolated Serbs and Jews. But to pretend to base a defense on this would be an intolerable affrontery in a peoples court. The defense witnesses are notorious Fascists and Fascists cannot testify on behalf of Fascists in our country. This would be placing the court and democracy on the level of a country where Fascism and not the people had been victorious. Stepinac supported terrorism . . . his conduct was identical with that of Pavelić. If there were differences it was on the personal level and does not affect the general situation.[14]

No more eloquent testimony could be found of the prejudice and unfairness of the court than this exclusion of a whole body of witnesses and the diatribe against the defendant accompanying it before, let it be emphasized, all the testimony was in and the court had had the opportunity of reaching its conclusions.

Archbishop Stepinac was allowed to speak on the afternoon of October 3 when he addressed the court for about half an hour.[15] The judge responded to his statement by insisting that the prelate restrict himself entirely to the specific, concrete indictment. The verdict was handed down on October 11 with the following sentences:

Archbishop Stepinac	16 years of forced labor
Ivan Šalić	12 years of forced labor
Lambert Margetić, OFM	13 years of forced labor
Col. Eric Lisak	Death by hanging
Pavle Gulin	Death by hanging
Josip Simotsk	14 years of forced labor
Six other Franciscans to varying terms	
Three Franciscans declared not guilty	
Three laymen to various terms of forced labor	

All the forced labor terms were accompanied by the loss of civil rights for a further five years and the confiscation of all property.

World reaction to the trial and condemnation may best be summarized by reference to the public statement on October 11, 1946, of the then Acting Secretary of State of the United States, Dean Acheson:

I have been asked if I would be willing to make some comment or statement

---

[14] Quoted in Fiorello Cavalli, *Il processo dell'Arcivescovo di Zagrabia*, Rome, 1947, pp. 36–37.

[15] See text of address, Document D.

about the trial and conviction of Archbishop Stepinac, and I shall. It necessarily cannot be specific. What I should like to say is that we have for a long time been concerned about civil liberties in Yugoslavia. You will recall at the time we recognized the Government of Yugoslavia, we drew their attention to what we thought was the undesirable situation in that field and reminded them of their undertakings under the United Nations Charter in which all of these matters are specifically dealt with and urged that the matter be rectified as soon as possible. We have since recognition unhappily had to take up a very considerable number of cases with the Yugoslav Government where we have felt that trials of our own citizens were unfairly conducted. It is this aspect of the Archbishop's trial which I am able to say now concerns us. We do not have, of course, a record of the trial, nor have we had a specific report from our Embassy in regard to it. Therefore, our information about it is the same as that you have, which is that which has been conveyed through the press.

It is the civil liberties aspect of the thing which causes us concern: aspects which raise questions as to whether the trial has any implications looking toward the impairment of freedom of religion and of worship; the aspects of it which indicate at least to the reporters who reported it from the spot that the actual conduct of the trial left a great deal to be desired.

You will recall that under the Constitution and law of the United States fairness of trial is guaranteed under the 14th Amendment, and the Supreme Court of the United States has set aside as not being legal procedure at all trials in which the courtroom has been dominated by feelings adverse to the defendant by demonstrations of prejudice. That is deeply inherent in the American system, that the very essence of due process of law is that in trials we shall lean over backward in being fair to the defendant, in the atmosphere in the courtroom, in forbidding demonstrations of spectators, in opportunity of facing and cross-examining witnesses — all these matters seem to us to be absolutely inherent in the matter of a fair trial. It is that aspect of the thing, on which one can have no final evidence until a record and detailed reports are available, which causes us concern and deep worry.[16]

On October 14, 1946, the Holy See excommunicated all those who contributed physically or morally toward the crimes that culminated in the judicial action in which Archbishop Stepinac was "arbitrarily arrested and unjustly sentenced." A declaration issued by the Sacred Congregation listed no names. The text of the excommunication is as follows:

The judicial action whereby the Most Excellent Msgr. Aloysius Stepinac, Archbishop of Zagreb, was arbitrarily arrested and unjustly sentenced by a civil tribunal of Yugoslavia has made a profound impression in the whole Catholic world and in civil society itself.

The Church provides for the defense of sacred pastors and of their freedom

---

[16] *U.S. Interest in Civil Liberties in Yugoslavia,* Department of State Bulletin, Vol. XV, No. 381, p. 725, Oct. 20, 1946.

and dignity above all with three articles of the Code of Canon Law, which provides that excommunication is to be incurred for the very fact in itself by those who:

1. Hale a Bishop, especially their own Bishop, before a lay judge (Canon 2,341).
2. Perform acts of violence against a Bishop or Archbishop (Canon 2,343, Paragraph 3).
3. Directly or indirectly prevent the exercise of ecclesiastical jurisdiction or authority, having recourse for this purpose to any lay authority (Canon 2,334).

All these excommunications are reserved, according to circumstances, simply or specially to the Holy See.

Therefore the Sacred Congregation of the Council, which is charged with the discipline of the Christian clergy and people, not finding in the above crimes any cause that notably decreases their imputability (Canon 2,205, Paragraph 3; Canon 2,229, Paragraph 3) but finding, rather, aggravating causes in them, particularly for the high dignity of the offended person (Canon 2,207), declares that all those who have contributed physically or morally toward the consummation of the above-mentioned crimes or were necessary co-operators in them (Canon 2,209, Paragraph 1-3) have incurred the above-mentioned excommunications, to which they will remain subject until they have obtained absolution from the Apostolic See. F. Cardinal Marmaggi, Prefect; F. Roberti, Secretary.[17]

---

[17] New York *Times*, Oct. 15, 1946.

Chapter III

THE INDICTMENT:
AN ANALYSIS. COLLABORATION WITH THE
GERMANS, ITALIANS, AND USTASHA

THE charges against Archbishop Stepinac are contained in the indictment prepared by the Public Prosecutor of the Peoples Croat Republic and submitted under date of September 23, 1946. The text of this statement with the main lines of the argument is reproduced in English translation as Document A in the Appendix. The main charges have been made available to the English speaking world through the pamphlet published by the Embassy of the Federal Peoples Republic of Yugoslavia in Washington, D. C., in 1946.

The indictment has been broken down in various ways. In this analysis, the following points may be considered as covering the list of charges brought against Archbishop Stepinac:

I. Support of and collaboration with the German, Italian,
   and Ustasha regimes between 1941–1945.

This item includes the accusation of not only moral and material support of the occupation and the ensuing Independent Croat State, known under the initials NDH, but conformity with the ideological content of the program of these regimes, i.e., active sympathy for the principles that guided the action of the occupiers and the satellite regime set up under their auspices. The Archbishop was accused not merely of tolerating the new dispensation, but of supporting it enthusiastically and participating fully in its action and thought, such as anti-Semitism, anti-Serbianism, mass imprisonments, and the like.

II. Directives and consent to support of the regime by
   the Catholic press and organizations.

It was argued that the Archbishop controlled and directed the entire Catholic press of Yugoslavia as well as Croatia and was responsible for the fulsome praise and active support of these publications to the German, Italian, and Ustasha rule.

Catholic societies and especially Catholic Action were accused of collaboration with the occupiers and Ustasha regime at the instigation and direct intervention of the Archbishop.

III. Connivance and approval of the forced conversions of Orthodox and others to Catholicism.

The argument of the Prosecution was that Archbishop Stepinac was directly responsible for the policy of forced conversions, in line with the Ustasha procedure of forcing Serbs and other non-Catholics into religious conformity with what was designated as the religion of the Croat people.

IV. Crimes committed by clergy and other Catholic elements as a result of the designation of Archbishop Stepinac as Apostolic Army Vicar for Pavelić's Ustasha forces and the various other military groups existent in Croatia at the time.

V. Collaboration with fallen Ustasha leaders in 1945, to induce foreign reoccupation of Croatia and the overthrow of the people's government.

Under this item are the allegations that the Archbishop of Zagreb opposed the new Partisan regime, that he aided and abetted the former Ustasha leaders and refused all collaboration with the new government. Under this is also included his alleged relations with Eric Lisak and his concealment of the archives of the Ustasha Foreign Office.

COLLABORATION AND SUPPORT OF THE OCCUPATION AND THE INDEPENDENT CROAT STATE

The expression "collaboration," as constituting criminal conduct, originated during World War II. It is a popular, rather than a legal term, and has no clearly defined meaning. In general, it seems intended to cover such relations between the inhabitants of a country occupied by hostile armies, and the occupying forces, as might be detrimental to their own country. Such traditional and legally defined offenses as treason, rebellion, sedition, espionage, spying, and sabotage would probably be included within the connotation of "collaboration."

In respect to Archbishop Stepinac, the charge of collaboration is complicated by the existence of two distinct elements, the occupying Axis forces and the national uprising of the Croat people which resulted in the proclamation of the Independent State of Croatia.

We should consider briefly the status of this so-called Independent State of Croatia. As has been noted in the chapter on the historical background, for a long time prior to World War II, there had been a strong separatist movement in Croatia. There is no need to go fully into the justice of this sentiment, although it seems to have its roots in real injustice inflicted on the Croat people by the predominant Serbian element. How numerically strong the proponents of separation may have been, we do not know and will probably never learn. It is certain, however, that they represented a substantial portion of the population. The Axis attack in 1941 shattered the existing Yugoslav State and left a political vacuum within the country. The Croatian separatist, through the Ustashi, seized on this to establish an independent state. This development was welcomed by the Axis forces, who were, thereby, spared the necessity of organizing a completely artificial puppet government. It is probable that the organization of the Ustasha government was planned behind the Axis lines in conjunction with Pavelić and other Croatian exiles who had taken refuge in Italy. This was "collaboration" and treason in respect to the Kingdom of Yugoslavia on the part of these Ustashi leaders.

On the other hand, the Croatians were exercising that "right of revolution" which lies at the foundation of so many countries in the world today. International law recognizes that a sovereign state may come into legal existence as the result of successful revolt against the authority of a pre-existing state. Witness the United States. However, before the seceding area can acquire the status of legal sovereignty, the resistance of the parent state must, for all practical purposes, be overcome.

In accordance with the peace preserving rules of international law, recognition of statehood or membership in the family of nations cannot be given until the struggle has ceased or has reached such a condition that the continuance of the separate existence of the insurgent community is assured.[1]

In the case of Croatia, effective armed resistance to the new political entity was offered in the name of the London exile government, until the final defeat of the Axis and Marshal Tito's assumption of power. It was, likewise, at all times clear that the existence of the new state was conditioned on the success of the Axis nations in World War II.

Recognition of the seceding community as sovereign by other states is not essential to the legal status of sovereignty, but it does have evidentiary weight.

There is no doubt that statehood itself is independent of recognition. International law does not say that a state is not in existence as long as it is not recognized, but it takes no notice of it before its recognition.[2]

The Axis powers — Germany, Italy, Hungary, Slovakia, Bulgaria, Romania, and Japan — extended recognition to Croatia. Spain seems to have been the only neutral state to grant recognition. The Holy See did not recognize the independent State of Croatia, but continued to maintain diplomatic relations with the exile government in London.[3]

Another difficulty in the way of allowing a sovereign status to the independent State of Croatia lies in the nature of its relations with Italy.

. . . The Croatians, who had complained bitterly about the oppressive tactics of their brother Slavs, the Serbs, were bound tightly to the Italians by a formal treaty that made the new state no more than a puppet. . . .[4]

The new Croat regime is nothing more than a subservient government which the Axis set up on part of the territory of Yugoslavia occupied in the course of military operations against the latter. It is a well established principle of international law that during a war a belligerent does not acquire sovereignty of enemy territory under military occupation. The action of Germany and Italy in thus disposing of Yugoslav territory by the creation of Croatia can be considered lawful only on the assumption that their war against Yugoslavia was ended by the extinction of the latter.[5]

---

[1] Stowell, *International Law*, ed. 1931, p. 40.

[2] Oppenheim, *International Law*, Fifth Ed., Vol. I, p. 120.

[3] Sereni, Pietro, *American Political Science Review*, "The Status of Croatia in International Law," Dec., 1941.

[4] *Newsweek*, Aug. 26, 1941.

[5] Bordwell, *The Law of War*, 1908, p. 30,

One might consider the independent State of Croatia from one or the other of two viewpoints: as the creation of a national uprising or as a provisional government set up by the Axis occupants with the co-operation of the Ustashi leaders. Definite principles of international law have been evolved governing the conduct of hostile forces occupying an enemy country. An occupying army "may go so far as to establish provisional governments based on new rules of suffrage." However, "He must not attempt to change the Constitution of the country, nor do any act implying a change in the nationality of the people."[6] It is forbidden to compel the inhabitants of occupied territory to swear allegiance to the hostile power."[7] The attempted establishment of the Independent Croat State contemplated both a change in the constitution and a change of nationality, however.

One of the fundamental questions asked by Dr. Politeo, defense counsel, in his argument on behalf of Archbishop Stepinac, was: "What was the occupation and what was the so-called NDH?"[8] It was obviously necessary to establish firmly the nature of the new political order and the exact responsibilities and duties of a citizen under it, especially if he were a citizen charged with vast responsibility as was the case of the Archbishop of Zagreb. The assertion of the Public Prosecutor is challenged that the Independent Croat State did not combine such qualities as to entitle it to consideration as a *state*. The Prosecutor argued that it was not independent but merely an Axis satellite, that it was founded and maintained in bloodshed and violence and the creature of outside influences and that had nothing to do with the Croat people. Whatever may have been the illicit character of the Independent Croat State, these three arguments were not a sound basis for disputing it. Dr. Politeo argued by analogy that the same comments could be made of numerous other so-called "independent" nations. He cited the case of Greece which he dubbed a satellite of Great Britain. He chose to consider Spain as an example of a sanguinary regime and in reply to the argument that existence as a result of outside assistance was

---

[6] *Ibid.*, p. 301.
[7] Annex to Hague Convention, 1907, Article 45.
[8] See Document B, defense statement of Dr. Politeo.

a factor, that the Yugoslavia that came into being in 1919 was in large part the work of the United States, France, and Great Britain. Czechoslovakia in like manner had been created through the disintegration and defeat of the Austro-Hungarian empire and with the direct aid of the Allies in World War I. The Public Prosecutor insisted that the Independent Croat State was "neither independent nor free nor in the least the Croat people's state, but the most infamous Quisling fabrication." There could be discussion whether the Independent Croat State was really a state or simply an occupied country under the fiction of statehood. Dr. Politeo accepted the contention that statehood as such did not exist. A *reality*, however, did exist, namely that the Croat people lived in a territory called Croatia and that for a period of time they were governed or misgoverned, as the case may be, by an institution calling itself the Independent Croat State. That this institution was a mere façade behind which the German and Italian occupiers operated is another thing entirely. The defense counsel argued that this reality was, that the country was under German and Italian supervision and direction, and that for the entire period of the war the Independent Croat State acted only as the agent of the occupier. It became then, without quibbling a question, not of the Independent Croat State but of the practical *control*, direct or indirect, that existed over a part of Yugoslav territory called the NDH. The logical consequence of this agreement regarding the reality of German-Italian control and the fiction of independence is what relation was to prevail between the inhabitants of Croatia and the authority in power.

Perhaps no more fundamental question arises in conjunction with the accusation of collaboration that this one, for the major charges of the prosecution rest on the assumption that contact with the Independent Croat State was *per se* traitorous, antinational, and criminal. The defense insisted that the relations of occupied to occupier are reasonably well defined in International Law and practice and that it is against this background that the action of Archbishop Stepinac must be judged. The defense counsel cites the provisions of the Hague Convention of 1907, Section III, Articles 42 to 56, dealing with the problem of occupied territories wrested from the enemy. Legal power passes in this case into the hands of the occupier and he is empowered to take such measures as are necessary for the maintenance of law and order. The occupier has the right to demand compliance and even obedience from the inhabitants within certain specified areas in accordance with the Hague Convention. Such obedience, Dr. Politeo emphasized, is legal, not necessarily moral.

The question posed is one of the most delicate and serious connected not only with modern warfare, but with the entire problem of postwar Europe. Collaborationism has been used as a term of reprobation with incredible prodigality. In most of the western European countries that knew the tragedy of occupation, hundreds of citizens have been accused, indicted, and sometimes imprisoned for collaboration, whose acts were very different from those of the out and out collaborators or participants in the governments imposed by the invader. What really constitutes collaboration in the case of the ordinary inhabitants is not always easily ascertainable. Dr. Politeo points out that simply because one was not a resistance hero does not make him *ipso facto* a traitor.

It is clearly improper to confuse the Hague denial of allegiance to the occupying power and the obedience to which reference has been made in the defense statement. The Yugoslav courts since 1945 had shown slight respect for the Hague Convention, insisting that since the Germans had obviously not respected it, it was inoperative and had no place in the argument presented in the trials of alleged collaborationists or traitors. Dr. Politeo argued that violation by the Germans did not mean in the least that Serbs and Croats under the occupation might not adhere to the precepts of the Convention in their conduct vis-à-vis the occupier. The plea is made that thousands of innocent Serbs and Croats, whose existence depended on it, were obliged to accommodate their existence to the reality of occupation, and if they behaved in a manner that did not go beyond the limits of the Hague Convention, they could not be accused of willful collaborationism. The place of the Hague Convention in Yugoslav practice is recognized by the fact that the Partisans appealed to this code of law for recognition of their own government once the invader was expelled. In addition to the Hague regulations which prescribe certain conduct in these circumstances and make possible certain essential contacts between occupied and occupier for the maintenance of life, order, and security, in the case of Archbishop Stepinac there is the additional obligation in ecclesiastical law. Pope Gregory XVI proclaimed *Solicitudo Ecclesiarum* on August 5, 1831. It is here provided that the *de facto* recognition of an authority over a given territory does not imply and need not imply *de jure* recognition. When the fundamental spiritual welfare of the people requires it, relations with the authority in power must be maintained, without determining at all the juridical validity of the regime nor its constitutional right to exercise such authority.

The occupation of Croatia was the work of force. But the authority did exist and it could not be argued away on the grounds that it was an usurpation and contrary to the will of the people. It is on the basis of the fact of this power and its force, that the problem of relations between Croatia and the government must be determined. The question for the Church and specifically for Archbishop Stepinac, the highest authority in the Croatian Church, was whether a minimum of relations with the occupiers was not preferable to no relations at all, with the consequent greater evils and more serious threat to the spiritual welfare of the people for whom he was responsible.

Regardless of his personal sentiments, what were Archbishop Stepinac's rights and obligations as a citizen and as Archbishop during the occupation of his country by the Axis and Ustasha forces? As a citizen, Archbishop Stepinac was a member of the peaceful population, as distinguished from the armed forces. The usages of international law have established definite rules for the conduct of the peaceful population and civil officials in an occupied country. It is the duty of the inhabitants to carry on their ordinary pursuits; to behave in an absolutely peaceful manner; to take no part whatever in the hostilities; to refrain from all injurious acts toward the troops or in respect to their operations, and to render strict obedience to the officials of the occupant. Whatever might have been the status of the independent State of Croatia, it was the government ordained by the occupying Axis forces. Archbishop Stepinac, regardless of his personal views on Croatian independence, was, therefore, justified in submitting to its authority.

He was not only a citizen but Archbishop and Metropolitan of Croatia. The tradition of this position required attendance at certain state functions. It is reported that the Archbishop was present at parades and other ceremonies of the Partisan Government during the eighteen-month interval between Marshal Tito's assumption of power and the arrest of the Archbishop. There does not seem to be anything in international law or the laws of war which specifically defines the rights and duties of churchmen during a hostile occupation. It is probable that the situation of an Archbishop under such circumstances might be analogous to that of a civilian local official.

. . . It is generally considered that local officials are under an obligation to remain at their posts. Especially in the large cities the functions of the local government enter so vitally into everyday affairs that their cessation even for a day would seriously impair the life of the community and result in crime and disorder. It is in the interest of the inhabitants that these officials remain, so that in no sense can it be said that they enter the service of the enemy. . . .[9]

Over those who remain in office the occupant has the right of direction, supervision, and dismissal. He may make such orders as he deems necessary for the temporary administration of the territory, and may impose new duties on the officials, provided such duties be not hostile to their government.[10]

From the above, it would seem, therefore, that under international law, Archbishop Stepinac was justified in maintaining such relations with the Ustasha Government as were required by the custom of the country.

On the broad score of collaboration with the occupier and the Ustasha, the argument urged by the communist prosecutor against Archbishop Stepinac contains numerous general references and a large body of detailed allusions. The main allegations may be suggested in the following summary fashion:

1. Archbishop Stepinac collaborated with the Ustasha as revealed in his visit to General Slavko Kvaternik on April 12, 1941, at which time he expressed approval and support for the Independent Croat State.

2. On April 16, 1941, the Archbishop visited Ante Pavelić, head of the new state and known as the Poglavnik or leader, to congratulate him and express loyalty.

3. Archbishop Stepinac signed the Circular Letter of April 28, 1941, urging the faithful to support loyally the new Croat regime.

[9] Bordwell, *op. cit.*, p. 307.
[10] *Ibid.*, p. 309.

4. During the occupation, the Defendant Stepinac helped the occupier, deeming the occasion particularly propitious for enriching the Church and increasing the influence of the higher clergy in the affairs of State.

5. In numerous sermons, Archbishop Stepinac praised the Independent Croat State and urged support of it.

6. The Archbishop sought more active support of the Croat State at the Vatican.

7. His support of the German occupiers was evidenced by his relations with General Glaise von Horstenau.

8. His Christmas message to Croat workers in Germany attests antinational sentiments and co-operation in this criminal action.

9. He aided in maintaining the morale of Croat troops in the Soviet Union and in other forms of collaboration with those supporting the Axis.

Although not specifically included in the indictment of the Public Prosecutor as are the nine points just enumerated, which are taken from the presentation to the court, the accusation that the Archbishop was a firm and unvarying supporter of the Independent Croat State and its German and Italian masters means that he approved the measures and laws put into effect by that regime in line with the ideology of Fascism and National Socialism. The Independent Croat State initiated anti-Semitic legislation within three weeks after the creation of the new state. On May 1, 1941, a law was promulgated distinguishing between Croat *citizens* and Jewish *nationals.* On May 16 of that year the radio sets of Jews and Serbs were confiscated, and on May 22, all Jews and Serbs were dismissed from public office and required to wear special insignia. The Croat legislation regarding Jews was entirely in line with the Nuremberg laws of Nazi Germany.

The general conclusion from this detailed indictment is that Archbishop Stepinac was engaged actively in political affairs, that he welcomed the opportunity for collaboration with the Independent Croat State, and that both personally and for his clergy, urged the liveliest co-operation and support of the new regime. The allegation sums up to this that Catholicism and the Independent Croat State were bound up together and that the Archbishop was one of the main sources of support for it.

Archbishop Stepinac was not a politician, but a churchman as his utterances and whole career attest. At the same time he was a patriotic and loyal Croat. There can be no question that he considered Croatia his fatherland and that he was lukewarm toward the decision of 1919 to join with Serbia in forming Yugoslavia. This conviction or course of action may be open to discussion. Many Yugoslavs may violently disagree with his interpretations of the role and mission of Croatia, but this, it would seem, is a matter of viewpoint and of moral persuasion not certainly a criminal offense. There is a very subtle and delicate problem involved in the attitude of the Archbishop which one cannot pretend to gloss over without consideration. That is his reiterated statement regarding the desirability and necessity for the creation of the Croat nation. It is well to establish a difference here between the Croat nation and the Croat government at any particular moment. The Croat people, in interpreting their own history, are profoundly convinced that despite the vicissitudes that have accompanied their evolution, despite the travail of ten centuries with its occupations, usurpations, and turmoil, the concept of the Croat people as an independent entity has survived. The affirmation of nationhood is one thing; the defense of the particular, immediate government of that nation is another thing entirely. Archbishop Stepinac was undoubtedly in favor of the Croat state and preferred its independence to union with Serbia. In this he shared the opinion and sentiment of a very large proportion of his fellow countrymen. He was equally in favor of the existence of the Croat state as a fact, although the record shows beyond any doubt that in many particulars the functioning of the government of that state, during the brief period of its existence, 1941 to 1945, was very far from what he thought it should be. The Pastoral Letter of March 24, 1945, is clear on his idea of the Croat state.

. . . History testifies that the Croatian people for nearly a thousand years have never renounced their right to nationhood. In like manner, they wish freedom for all other peoples on earth. During World War II, the Croatian people realized their desire and right by establishing their own independent state; cognizant of the will of their people, the Bishops of Croatia assented as was right. No one therefore has the right to accuse any citizen of the Croatian Republic or its Bishops because they acknowledged the will of the Croatian people in what is their right according to both divine and human law.[11]

---

[11] See Document LXIII.

In his courtroom defense speech, Archbishop stated:

Whatever I have said of the right of the Croatian nation to its freedom and independence is in complete accord with the basic principles enunciated by the Allies at Yalta and in the Atlantic Charter.

If, according to these principles, every nation has the right to independence, then why should it be denied to the Croatians? The Holy See has declared that both small nations and national minorities have a right to freedom. Must, then, a Catholic Bishop and Metropolitan maintain total silence on this issue?[12]

A highly difficult question is whether the Bishop's statement, almost at the moment of the collapse of the Pavelić regime, contributed to sedition, treason, or disloyalty to the Yugoslav state as represented by the government in exile in London. In a certain sense the Archbishop as a citizen was in the position of all who accepted the course his people had chosen and whose patriotic aspirations were frustrated by the pressure of adverse events. There is certainly nothing inherently criminal in the Archbishop's preference for an independent Croatia; his conviction that united Yugoslavia was not a workable or satisfactory solution, or his later lack of sympathy with the peculiar form of "popular democracy" that came in with Marshal Tito. Political opposition as such cannot be construed as a crime, and is not, except in those lands where the principle of devotion to class and to the communist party prevails over every other consideration.

It was an instance of loyalty to the Croatian nation against loyalty to the Yugoslav state. He was in somewhat the same position as the patriots had been during the American War for Independence and the citizens of the Confederate States during the Civil War.

During the American War for Independence several Catholic priests took an active part on behalf of the Colonists. Father John Carroll, later the First Archbishop of Baltimore, for instance, was active in the support of the patriot cause. Not only did he speak in its favor, but in company with Benjamin Franklin, Samuel Chase, and Charles Carroll of Carrollton, he went on a mission to Canada in an attempt to persuade the Canadians to join the Colonists in their attempt to overthrow British rule. General George Rogers Clark, who conquered the Northwest Territory for the American cause, received invaluable assistance from Father Peter Gibault, a French

---

[12] Document D.

Catholic priest who urged the French settlers to accept the rule of the American Revolutionists. Had the patriot cause failed the British might have cited both of these prelates for aiding the rebellion.

The Archbishop had a very definite conviction that neither the Church nor the clergy had any business meddling in personal or party politics. This conviction was put into practice by means of the most serious admonitions, over and over again. His insistence on the non-political attitude of the clergy and Church was accompanied by his profound belief in the dignity of man and his complete, Christian sentiment regarding the brotherhood of man, regardless of race or condition. His condemnation of ordinary political activity as a churchman was extended even more vigorously in the case of violence or persecution against anyone. The picture painted by the Public Prosecutor is that of a grand Inquisitor, of an ecclesiastic burning with unholy hatred of all who do not fall within the narrow range of his own fellow Catholic Croats. The very opposite distinguishes the position of Archbishop Stepinac from the beginning of his episcopate; his compassion for those in distress, his hatred of injustice and violence, and his deep concern for wrong, especially if perpetrated by those in high places.

Before examining point by point the nineteen specific accusations made against him, it may be well to take note of his general non-political attitude, with special reference to the complete absence of any element of racism in his make-up. In this connection too it is important to stress his unflinching courage in denouncing publicly the shortcomings and the injustices of the Ustasha government. It may be said unhesitatingly on the basis of the documents and the most irrefutable evidence that Archbishop Stepinac was one of the lone voices in the dark days of 1941–1945 who dared to speak out on behalf of those who suffered or were in misery.

Prior to the advent of Dr. Aloysius Stepinac as Archbishop of Zagreb, his predecessor, Archbishop Ante Bauer issued circular letter, No. 1350 on February 12, 1935, regarding political activity on the part of the clergy:

On May 5 of this year elections for the National Assembly are to take place. As the preparation of electoral lists of candidates has already begun, I announce to my clergy through this letter that I will not permit any active priest to be a candidate on any ticket whatever.

As early as August 10, 1938, Archbishop Stepinac in Circular Letter No. 6348 took the same position:

Since the elections for parliament and various projects relating to them are coming in for more and more discussion, I announce to the clergy of the Archdiocese of Zagreb the following: No priest of this archdiocese, whether active or retired, in no matter what circumstance, may announce his candidacy in these elections, regardless of the parties or groups involved. Consequently, as the elections approach, let no priest apply here for permission to become a candidate for he will not obtain such permission.

Almost a year after the creation of the Independent Croat State, the same problem arose again. It is important to note that the Archbishop does not swerve one inch from the original position. Under date of February 4, 1942, in Circular Letter No. 1722, he informs his clergy in the following terms:

At the request of several priests, the question has been raised if the Circular Letter of February 12, 1935, No. 1350 (*Katolički List,* No. 7, 1935) and of August 10, 1938 (*Katolički List* No. 32, 1938) regarding the participation of priests in elections is still in force. I announce to the clergy of this diocese through this letter, so that they may know what conduct to follow, that the ordinances mentioned are still in force and are constrained to govern themselves accordingly.

The Circular Letter of September 24, 1943, is as explicit as any document can possibly be. It reiterates the absolute prohibition for participation by the clergy in party politics and especially in anything that might menace public order.[13]

That the Archbishop was not guided by any consideration of convenience or the desire to find accommodation with the regime in power is illustrated by his splendid doctrinal statement, issued on September 14, 1944, some months before the end of hostilities and the collapse of the Independent Croat State. The principles enunciated in this document constitute a review of Catholic ideas regarding man and society and form a solid refutation to the accusation that the Archbishop failed to point out the discrepancies between Catholic principles and the political theories of the time:

This Church of Christ gives us our general directives and also sheds light on those questions which trouble the world today and in the chaos of war, a war which would not be if the voice of the teacher had been heeded. The

---

[13] See Document I for complete text of this Circular.

questions are these: (*a*) the freedom and worth of the individual as an independent entity; (*b*) the freedom of and the respect for religion; (*c*) the freedom of and respect for every race and nationality; (*d*) the freedom of and respect for private property as the basis of the personal freedom of the individual and the independence of the family; and, finally (*e*) the freedom of and respect for the right of every nation to its full development and to independence in its national life.[14]

The Archbishop's recommendations are equally precise on this date, and in entire conformity with his councils prior to the establishment of the new regime. He urged his clergy to remain faithful, docile to the teachings of the Church and its supreme authority, and loyal to their duties toward their people regardless of the conditions and adverse circumstances that prevailed.

During the critical year, 1945, with the advent of the Partisan regime, the Archbishop insisted on the same scrupulous abstention from anything that might be interpreted as political action by the clergy. He urged that religious practice be intensified and that every safeguard be sought for the protection of the family and the home. The twelfth point in his Circular Letter, No. 5027/45 of July 6, 1945, is very precise on this matter:

Let preachers in their addresses and sermons avoid absolutely all allusions whatsoever to secular things or conditions, and let them explain only the Gospel and the catechism, that is to say, the doctrine of the Church.[15]

The Archbishop recognized the danger of unwise expression or uninhibited commentary which might lead to complications with the new regime. He therefore added in a footnote to the Letter the following:

The Reverend Clergy are warned to pay close attention to sermons. It would be best to write sermons and deliver them literally or to read them; in this way the text of the sermon can be brought forward at any time if anyone should ask for an account of it. It should be possible to make use of the sermons already prepared by Cezner.[16]

The Archbishop was adamant in his opposition to the clergy in politics during the height of the Ustasha regime. In his letter to Ante

---

[14] See Document II for complete text.

[15] See Document III for full text of this Circular Letter.

[16] *Ibid.* Postscriptum. For further details of the prohibition on political activities by the clergy, see Document XLVI, testimony of various witnesses.

Pavelić, under date of February 8, 1942, on the eve of the convocation of the Croat parliament, the Archbishop reiterated once more his reasons for opposition to any participation by the clergy in political affairs:

> I published a similar letter in 1938, permitting no one to become a candidate or to enter parliament, were it even on the list of the HSS, the Croatian Peasant Party, although there was ill feeling against me because of this.
>
> On the eve of the opening of the Croat parliament, I must, Poglavnik, insist on this point of view. The small good that priests can achieve in politics does not justify me in tolerating the harm, twice as great, to the Church and the nation by the abandonment of their priestly duties, whether these priests are members of the HSS or the Ustashi Movement.[17]

The Archbishop does not limit himself on this occasion to restating the case for nonpolitical activity of the clergy. He asks the head of the Independent Croat State to release the four priests who were serving as Deputies: "I ask you courteously, Poglavnik, to understand with benevolence my point of view, and to relieve four of my priests from their duties as deputies."[18]

The testimony of his own priests is conclusive in proving that political activity and even vigorous support of the regime was forbidden. A hundred and fifty members of the clergy of the Archdiocese of Zagreb signed a joint declaration in September, 1946, regarding the instructions received from the Archbishop. " . . . we state that His Excellency the Archbishop has constantly insisted that his priests avoid all political activity. . . ."[19]

A member of the Catholic clergy who can hardly be suspected of Ustasha sympathies, Monsignor Svetozar Rittig, in a letter dated December 19, 1942, indicates clearly his attitude toward Archbishop Stepinac at that time. Mons. Rittig was a Yugoslav representative at the Paris Conference and later Minister without portfolio in the Croatian government of Partisan Yugoslavia. The report of the seven Protestant clergymen who visited Yugoslavia in 1947 makes the following comment on Mons. Rittig:

> Perhaps the happiest of all these experiences occurred in Zagreb when we met Monsignor Doctor Svetozar Rittig, Papal Chamberlain, a representative of

---

[17] See full text in Document IV.
[18] *Ibid.*
[19] Full text of the statement in Document V.

Yugoslavia at the Paris Peace Conference, and Minister without portfolio in the Croatian government. As a young man he was secretary of the distinguished Roman Catholic leader, Archbishop Strossmayer. During the days of the Austro-Hungarian Empire, he was one of the first and strongest advocates of a Yugoslav state. For many years he was pastor of St. Mark's parish church in Zagreb. . . . When the Italians and Germans set up the quisling Independent State of Croatia, Monsignor Rittig, at the age of seventy, left Zagreb, and from then on served with the Partisan movement. Today he is clearly among the first citizens of the new Yugoslavia.[20]

It is this priest, a strong supporter of the Partisans, who writes to the Archbishop that "your stanch faith in Divine Providence, your prayers, and your sacrifices are a guarantee to all the people and the clergy that we will successfully emerge from this horrible carnage."[21]

The argument of the Public Prosecutor runs from the trivial to the gravest charges. Emphasis was laid on the fact that Archbishop Stepinac paid a visit, on April 12, 1941, to General Slavko Kvaternik, Croat commander-in-chief, and on April 16 to Ante Pavelić, Poglavnik of the Independent Croat State. These visits, as Dr. Politeo showed in his defense, were purely formal and the evidence of their character is that neither at that time nor later, was there any indication that they were the beginning of cordial or even friendly relations between the Archbishop and the head of the State.[22] The following negative facts are adduced to prove that the two visits were of a strictly protocol nature, as behooved the head of the Church:

   I. The Archbishop did not participate in the welcome extended at the Zagreb railroad station on April 13 to Pavelić.

   II. No *Te Deum* was sung at the cathedral on the occasion of the arrival of Pavelić.

   III. Pavelić attended divine services at the cathedral exactly once during the entire four years of his regime. This was in 1943 when the Italians arranged a Requiem for the Duke of Aosta. Pavelić was received at the entrance by a sacristan, not even by a priest and less still by the Archbishop.

---

[20] *Religion in Yugoslavia*, p. 16.

[21] See complete text in Document VI.

[22] The Archbishop explained to the clergy that the visit of April 12 to Kvaternik and of April 16 to Pavelić did not mean that he was in favor of the Ustasha or that he recognized the government of Pavelić, but that, in order to protect religion and the people, relations between the *de facto* state and the Church were necessary. See Document XLVI, Testimony of Dr. Dragutin Hren.

The Circular Letter of April 28, 1941, published in *Katolički List* of April 29, 1941, has been used to demonstrate that the Archbishop urged the faithful to loyalty to the new Independent Croat State. The text presented by the Public Prosecutor is as follows:

Venerable Brethren; There is no one among you who has not been a recent witness to the momentous events in the life of the Croat nation, in which we are all laboring as messengers of Christ's Gospel. These events are the culmination of an ideal long cherished and desired by our people. . . .

Answer, therefore, promptly this appeal of mine in the noble task of conserving and advancing the independent Croat state. . . .

Prove yourselves, Venerable Brethren, now, and fulfill your duty toward the young Croat state.[23]

This Circular Letter, issued eighteen days after the foundation of the Independent Croat State, was the basis of the accusation that the Archbishop had gone far beyond what was necessary to encourage support and loyalty to a particular government then in power in Croatia. There can be no reasonable doubt that the Archbishop prayed for the happiness and success of a government just coming into power. There can be no doubt that he was profoundly concerned about the character and tendency of that government. A careful examination of the whole text and no single part of it reveals clearly these anxieties. Again and again the Archbishop speaks of *Croatia*, rather than of a particular Croatian state. "Speaking to you as the representative of the Church and as pastor of souls, I pray you and exhort you to work and endeavor with all your might that our Croatia may be the country of God. . . ." A little farther on, "Faithful to God and to Christ's Holy Church, our Croatia will achieve that noble task which is the function of our earthly Fatherland. . . . We must everywhere warn and teach that the holy enthusiasm and noble zeal in building the foundation of the new Croat state must be inspired by the fear of God and by love for God's law and His Commandments, for only through God's law and not on false natural principles can the Croat state be solidly erected."

In these phrases we have the essence of the Archbishop's warning regarding the course of the new state. The word of admonition is accompanied by a paragraph which the Public Prosecutor does not quote, but which demonstrates very clearly the anxiety of the Arch-

---

[23] The full text of the Circular Letter is contained in Document VII.

bishop and his conviction that at the beginning of the regime, the role and function of the Church must be clearly understood. The pertinent paragraph is this:

Knowing the men who are today at the helm of the Croat nation, we are deeply convinced that our work will find complete understanding and help. We believe and await that the Church in the newly erected Croat state will be able in complete freedom to preach the sound principles of eternal truth and justice.

In the following paragraph the Archbishop expresses the hope that the head of the Croat state may "have the spirit of wisdom to perform this noble and responsible task."

The most convincing proof that this letter does not represent an endorsement of the Ustasha regime or a pledge of loyalty to it as a state and particular ruling group is the communication of the Yugoslav hierarchy to Marshal Tito, under date of September 22, 1945, in which occur phrases very similar to those contained in the letter of 1941 regarding the Independent Croat State. In the letter to Marshal Tito we find, for example:

We hope for peace and harmony with the state. . . . We declare ourselves to be loyal citizens of the state in which we live, that we will respect its authorities, and are ready to collaborate for its construction. We are persuaded that the wisdom of our statesmen will bring us victory and that through your efforts you will succeed in bringing lasting peace in Yugoslavia.[24]

If the same logic were to be applied to this communication as to the Circular Letter of April 28, 1941, the conclusion would be that the Archbishop of Zagreb and the whole Yugoslav hierarchy had pledged loyalty to communism and had praised the generosity, statesmanship, and guidance of those in charge of the new Federal Yugoslav republic. It is possible to imagine in some distant future, an anti-communist government producing this letter as evidence of "collaborationism" between the Catholic hierarchy of Yugoslavia and the communists.

The nature of the two communications is largely the same. The purpose of both is to appeal for harmony and peace under God's law. Since there is no inherent reason why the Church cannot exist under any regime that respects its freedom, the hierarchy was disposed

---

[24] See Document LXIX for complete text of the communication.

under Pavelić as it was later under Tito to seek the basis of an understanding.

Moreover, the careful reading of the Circular Letter shows nothing that could possibly be construed as an incitement to violence or to crime. In every line there is the prayerful hope that God may grant tranquillity and peace to Croatia and that the new Croat state may function in conformity with God's law and the principles He has made known for the guidance of men in society.

The various accusations of visits to Pavelić or to other Ustasha authorities is gratuitously exploited by the Public Prosecutor as indicative of "a pledge of loyalty" or of adherence to the regime. The Archbishop himself in his own statement asserted that: "I was not *persona grata* to either the Germans or the Ustashi; I was not a Ustasha, nor did I take their oath as did some of the officials of this court whom I see here."[25]

The problem in the Croatia of 1941 was that of the Ustasha as the only constituted authority, for good or for ill. Yugoslavia had ceased to exist for all practical purposes and the only direct contacts possible were with the ruling power in Zagreb.

In an expression of indignation, the Archbishop asked the court and the Prosecutor:

What was my authority? I repeat again: you have been my authority since May 8, 1945, but not before that. . . .

Should I have given allegiance to the authority of the illegal Simović, or — as you call it, the "exiled" — government in London, or to the one in Cairo, yours in the woods or theirs in Zagreb? Is it possible to serve two masters? That is impossible according to Catholic morals, the law of nations, and common sense. We could not ignore the authority here, even if it were Ustasha. . . .[26]

If it is admitted, then, that the Archbishop as the head of the Catholic Church in Croatia was obliged by the nature of his position to maintain a minimum of contact with the regime and with the head of the state and in the light of the documents quoted regarding the participation of clergy in the affairs of state, it becomes evident that the charge the Church was enriched and the higher clergy made powerful as a result of the Pavelić regime is patently absurd. No one in the Croatia of 1941–1945, under German-Italian occupation,

---

[25] See Document D for the Archbishop's statement to the court.
[26] *Ibid.*

burdened with the expenses of the occupation and isolated from the world, with war raging all around was likely to become enriched. Had the Archbishop desired the increase of ecclesiastical influence in the affairs of state, his policy would have been one of constant and enthusiastic collaboration. He himself could easily have attained a position of consequence and perhaps of determining influence in the councils of the Ustasha and the Pavelić government. He preferred to remain aloof with the exception of those cases in which contact was indispensable. It will be demonstrated later that the major portion of the communications as well as contacts of a personal character with the Poglavnik and the Ustasha authorities had as their end protests against Ustasha excesses and appeals for justice for those who had been ill treated. An excellent piece of evidence in this regard is the refusal of Archbishop Stepinac to go to Rome in May, 1941, with a Croat delegation headed by Pavelić, to offer the crown of Croatia to the Duke of Spoleto.

A whole phase of the indictment has to do with the supposed increase in the intimacy of the collaboration, thanks to the approval of the Holy See of the Croat regime. The Public Prosecutor states that "the defendant Stepinac increased his collaboration after the Pope received Pavelić and sent him his special blessings." The assumption on this score as well as in other references to the relations of the Archbishop of Zagreb to the Holy See is that the latter was responsible for pro-Ustasha reports and communications and encouraged the Holy See to look upon the Independent Croat State in a favorable light.

The basic document brought forward by the prosecution regarding the Archbishop's relations with the Vatican on behalf of the Independent Croat State is the alleged report of May 18, 1943. The substance of this report as presented by the Prosecutor was that the Archbishop favored the Ustasha regime; that he detested the Serbs; that he attributed the crimes of the Ustashi to the Chetniks and Serbs, and in general misrepresented the situation in Croatia to the Holy See. Even the Prosecution, in the text of the indictment, is forced to admit the correct attitude of the Holy See toward the whole complex political problem in Croatia. Violent anti-Stepinac publications have stated that the Holy See recognized and supported the Independent Croat State.[27] The very opposite was the case. The Holy See never recognized the Independent Croat State and the visit of Pavelić was in a purely personal capacity. The following statement from the Public Prosecutor is the most eloquent testimony to this:

> The closest collaboration (i.e., with the Ustasha regime) is demonstrated when Stepinac urges the strongest support of the Independent Croat State by the hierarchy, although he knew full well that this Croatian state was not recognized de jure by the Vatican and that the Pope did not receive Pavelić as a sovereign but as a private person. . . .

We may perhaps be allowed to take the word of the Public Prosecutor as to the evident coolness of the Holy See toward the new Croat state. One of the most startling of the contradictions in the formal statement of the Public Prosecutor is that the apparently ardent Ustasha Archbishop was nevertheless encouraged by the Holy See itself "to engage in a more sincere attitude toward the Ustasha authorities."[28] It seems highly doubtful that the prudent Vatican was being urged by the Archbishop of Zagreb to a more enthusiastic position regarding the Ustasha regime, and at the same time the Holy See was urging a "more sincere" attitude on the part of the Archbishop toward that very regime.

The authenticity of the alleged report of May 18, 1943, is open to the most serious question and the internal evidence is overwhelming as to its forged character. The external evidence, and especially the reply of Cardinal Maglione, dated June 17, 1943, furnished strong proof that the document represents either an out and out forgery or a draft prepared by someone which the Archbishop refused to send or regarding the content of which he was ignorant. The document is of the greatest importance because it is used by the Prosecution as evidence of the total subservience of the Archbishop to the Ustasha regime and his constant efforts to enlist the enthusiastic support of the Vatican on behalf of the Pavelić government.

The internal evidence of forgery or falsification would indicate

---

[27] Betty Wallace, *The Trial of Dr. Aloysius Stepinac*. The British-Yugoslav Association, 1947, London, p. 4: "It is significant that the Vatican made haste to recognize the new independent State of Croatia and established diplomatic relations as early as June 6, 1941."

[28] See Indictment, Document A, for these statements.

that the copy read to the court by the Public Prosecutor had in all probability no relation to the original report. Dr. Politeo argued that the copy read to the court was very likely an Ustasha forgery, the aim of which was to create the impression of Vatican support. The content of the report directly contradicts the well-known opinions of the Archbishop. The latter denied completely ever writing such a report. Dr. Politeo acknowledges that mere denial on the part of the defendant does not constitute proof. He proceeds, therefore, to dissect the document to show that from every point of view it is highly improbable that the Archbishop ever wrote it and much less dispatched it to Rome as the expression of his views. In the first place, the report is written in Italian and it was the invariable practice of the Zagreb chancery to draft reports and other communications with the Holy See in Latin. Moreover, the Latin form of these dispatches did not vary and the salutation as well as conclusion always followed the same standard order.[29] The copy as read gives the Archbishop the title of Metropolitan of Croatia and Slavonia which was never used and was incorrect. It is not in the least probable that the Archbishop would sign a document with a title that on no other occasion was ever employed. The copy read by the Public Prosecutor was discovered in the files of the Ustasha Foreign Office which in itself is highly suspicious since no copy of any other report of the Curia was found there nor was any copy found at all in the Archiepiscopal archives, the natural place for such materials to be preserved.

The original of a letter from His Eminence Cardinal Maglione was presented by the defense and dated June 17, 1943, in acknowledgment of the report that Archbishop Stepinac had dispatched to Rome. This reply was evidently made to the authentic report or statement of the Zagreb Metropolitan. The text of this reply shows clearly that the subject matter of the alleged report was totally different from what the prosecution alleged. Cardinal Maglione states that, "I have noted with great interest the ample documentation sent to me by Your Most Reverend Excellency regarding the work carried out by you in favor of the Serbs and Hebrews in

---

[29] On this point the Archbishop's chancery certified to the form that was always used in such correspondence. See Document VIII.

Croatia." The Cardinal adds, "I beg you to continue to keep the Holy See informed in the matter, adding, if possible, some news also regarding the work of the other Croatian Bishops."[30]

Here is very plain proof that the Archbishop had informed the Holy See of the details of his own efforts on behalf of Serbs and Jews suffering persecution at the hands of the Ustasha regime. It is highly improbable as well as impossible for formal proof that he included in this same alleged report eulogistic comments on the very regime against which he was protecting the unfortunate Serbs and Jews. The copy of the alleged report as read was dated May 20, 1943. The Cardinal's reply bore the date of June 17, 1943. The acknowledgment could refer logically only to a report on or about the date of the copy in the hands of the Public Prosecutor.

Furthermore, there is no indication on the copy when the original was sent or by whom. How, then, did this copy come into existence and how explain its presence in the Ustasha files? There is no absolute proof of what happened. The version advanced by the defense was that the chief of the religious affairs of the Ustasha Ministry, Radoslav Glavaš, may very likely have conceived the idea of persuading the Archbishop to sign some such document that would favor the Ustasha regime. It is well to remember that the late spring of 1943 was a critical period for the Axis with the current beginning to turn favorably to the Allies. The reaction in Zagreb Ustasha circles must have been one of panic and fear of the consequences of the inevitable Axis defeat. Nothing was more natural than this grasping at any straw that might strengthen the fragile regime. If a draft of some sort had been prepared by Glavaš, it may have been turned down by others in the foreign office or considered as too risky at the moment. The copy may simply have been filed away in the Archives and the original retained by Glavaš. There is internal evidence here too to allow the supposition that Glavaš may have been the author. The text is full of allusions to Bosnia and its history, a field in which Glavaš was something of a specialist. Moreover, if the Archbishop had had any knowledge of the existence of this document or had supposed that it had been retained in the files of the foreign office, he could very easily have extracted the copy when these files were in storage in his

---

[30] Text of Cardinal Maglione's communication, Document IX.

own palace. The conclusion is that the copy was not drafted by the Archbishop, that he did not send it, and that in all probability it represents an effort on the part of the Ustasha government to compromise the Bishop at a critical turn of affairs for the Independent Croat State. Its value as evidence against the Archbishop is nil.

The Archbishop had frequent contacts with the occupying authorities and with the Ustasha government, and in almost every case the reason for this contact was to protest against injustices or to call attention to excesses for which the government authorities were responsible. These protests were addressed to the Independent Croat State, to the German authorities, and to the Italian Minister. So active was the Archbishop in this respect that the *Völkischer Beobachter,* the official newspaper of the National Socialist regime in Germany, remarked in its edition of November 3, 1943, that "Archbishop Stepinac has protested against mass reprisals and attacked the present regime." These protests on a personal basis and without wide publicity must be taken together with the public sermons in which the prelate attacked the philosophy and ideology of the regime in power, responsible for the various, specific acts which he condemns and in many cases seeks to attenuate.

The Archbishop intervened directly with Minister von Horstenau against the acts of violence of German soldiers and the Black Legion at Odra, Kravarsko, and Pušća.[31] Correspondence with Dr. Mladen Lorković, Croat Minister of the Interior, constituted a similar protest against the excesses of the German soldiery. There is evidence that these *démarches* were sometimes successful.[32]

The Archbishop did not hesitate to protest to the Italian Minister for the excesses of the Italian forces stationed in Croatia. In each case he referred specifically to incidents and places where the soldiery had committed acts which he felt called upon to deplore.[33] The innumerable cases of protection to Jews, Serbs, Slovenes, and other victims constituted one of the principal aspects of the constant solicitude of the Archbishop for those suffering from the rigors of the legislation and the conduct of the occupying forces from the Ustashi.

[31] Document X.
[32] *Ibid.*
[33] Document XII.

The attitude of the Archbishop toward the ideological content of the Ustasha regime and especially toward the racism of the German occupiers is available in his numerous sermons and public addresses from the beginning of the Independent Croat State to the collapse. A selection of the more important of these sermons and addresses will serve to point up the vigorous and courageous way in which Archbishop Stepinac denounced the injustices and anti-Christian character of these doctrines. The Public Prosecutor claimed that the Archbishop had done nothing to modify the essential character of the system then in power. This would imply that at no time did the Archbishop attack more than the blunders or excesses of the system rather than the principles that underlay it. Obviously, as Dr. Politeo points out in his defense, the Archbishop by his courage alone could not bring about the collapse of the whole political order. The most that he could do was to raise his voice against those aspects of it that were anti-Christian, and in his privileged position as teacher and guide of the Catholic people of Croatia, give them very necessary orientation in their own appraisal of the regime. This condemnation of the Archbishop includes not only the Ustasha misdeeds, but the entire ideology of Fascism and Nazism, especially with reference to racism. From 1941 on Archbishop Stepinac repeats over and over again his denunciation of racism, extreme nationalism, and the doctrine that denies the brotherhood of men.

In his sermon at the Zagreb cathedral on the Feast of Christ the King, October 26, 1941, he said:

. . . I wish to draw your attention today to one thing, if you really wish to become true subjects of Christ the King, and that is the love of your neighbor, of the man regardless of what his name may be. In the last ten years, certain theories and atheistic ideologies have succeeded in infecting so much of the world that hate has become, so to speak, the main incentive of all human actions. The danger exists that even those who glory in the name of Catholic, not even to speak of those who glory in a spiritual vocation, may become victims of passion, of hate, and of forgetfulness of the law which is the most beautiful characteristic trait of Christianity, the law of love. . . .

The implications in the sermon, "Jesus Christ, Judge of the World," delivered during the Lenten season, 1942, require very little elaboration. The most significant paragraph was perhaps the following:

What more bitter error than that of the people who hold in their hands the reins of government of peoples and states, but who at every step trample upon justice. It is perhaps that they would escape from You, of Whom it is written, "You will rule them with an iron scepter and You will break them like an earthenware jug." Lord, let no one forget that he cannot escape from Your judgment. Let the powerful and the strong remember that, and let them keep in their souls the awareness of their responsibility before You, Judge of all. Let the proud remember that, and let them humble themselves before You, while there is yet time, that they may not be humbled by You, of Whom it is written, "He will cast down the wicked even to the ground." Let them remember and have patience with those who are unjustly humiliated and persecuted, for the day will come when You will give "to each according to his ways and the fruits of his actions."

Most remarkable was the powerful sermon he delivered on the occasion of the procession of Our Lady of Lourdes, at the end of May, 1942. Some of the noteworthy points touched upon by the Archbishop were:

It would be an absurdity to speak of a new order in the world, no matter what its source, if human personality is not valued in that order, the immortal soul of man, which surpasses all systems and for which nothing can ever be substituted; the soul which has its inalienable rights which no human power can or ought to limit. It would also be an absurdity to think that the Catholic Church could be afraid of any human force in defending the elemental rights of human individuality and the freedom of conscience.[34]

On March 14, 1943, the Archbishop delivered a sermon in the cathedral on the occasion of the anniversary of the Coronation of Pope Pius XII.[35] In this sermon he expressed himself once more with complete clarity against racism and all measures which strike at the fundamental rights of man:

Catholic men and women. Catholic faithful! If you should ask me what we justly regard today to be the immense importance of the Pontificate [of Pius XII] for the human race, I should reply: the defense of that which is today trampled upon, more or less, over the entire world; the defense of the dignity of the human person, the defense of the rights of the family, the defense of the weak.

The statement against racism and the whole notion of racial superiority is unmistakably clear:

Consequently, every man, of whatever race or whatever nation, whether he has studied in the universities of the civilized centers of Europe or hunts his food in the virgin forests of Africa, carries equally on himself the stamp of God the

---

[34] See Document XIII for pertinent text of the sermon.
[35] See Document XIV for text.

Creator and possesses inalienable rights which must not be taken from him nor arbitrarily limited by any human power.

The firm doctrine taught by the Archbishop is not better exemplified than in the sermon delivered at the cathedral of Zagreb on October 25, 1943. The prelate posed the problem by asking:[36]

And what, before God, are the peoples and races of this world? It is worth while to suggest this subject in a time when the theories of class, race and nationality have become the main subjects of discussion among men.

On this basis, the Archbishop proceeded to enumerate the points he wished to make with reference to the subject matter:

The first thing that we affirm is that all nations, without exception, are as nothing before God. . . .

The second thing that we affirm is that all nations and all races have their origin in God. Only one race really exists and that is the Divine race. Its Birth certificate is found in the Book of Genesis. . . .

. . . the third thing that we affirm is that all nations and all races, as reflected in the world today, have the right to lead a life worthy of men and to be treated with the dignity with which one treats a man. All of them without exception, whether they belong to the race of Gypsies or to another, whether they are Negroes or civilized Europeans, whether they are detested Jews or proud Aryans, have the same right to say, "Our Father who art in Heaven!"

. . . the Catholic Church has always condemned, and condemns today as well, every injustice, and every violence committed in the name of the theories of class, race, or nationality.

Lest there be the slightest doubt as to the Archbishop's thesis, he adds that "one cannot efface from the earth Gypsies or Jews because one considers them inferior races. If the principles of racism, which has no foundation, are going to be applied without scruples, does there exist then any security for any nation at all?"

The excerpts from these sermons as well as the more complete text allow for no doubt whatever that Archbishop Stepinac condemned the theories of the "New Order" as propagated in Europe. His barbs were aimed directly and unmistakably at the Nazis and their puppets. On October 31, 1943, he delivered another striking sermon at the conclusion of the procession of Penance in Zagreb, reiterating within a few days of the memorable sermon of the 25th, his convictions regarding racism.

Some ["Officious advisers, of the Right and the Left"] accuse us of not

---

[36] See Document XV for major part of sermon.

raising our voice in time against crimes which have occurred in certain sections of our country. We reply to them first of all, that we are not and that we do not wish to be a political trumpet of any sort, blowing according to the desires and momentary needs of certain parties or individuals. We have always asserted the value in public life of the principles of the Eternal Law of God without regard to whether it concerned Croats, Serbs, Jews, Bohemians, Catholics, Mohammedans, or Orthodox.[37]

On this occasion the Archbishop was obviously concerned at the extremist action of some of his clergy and declared quite plainly that "we are not able to answer any longer for any hothead among the ranks of the clergy." The whole sermon is a crystal clear restatement of Catholic principles and the immutable laws of God which she proclaims.

The Catholic Church knows races and nations only as creatures of God, and, if it esteems one more than others it is because it possesses a more generous heart, not because one has the strongest arm. For it the Negro of Central Africa is as much a man as the European. For it the king in a royal palace is, as a man, exactly the same as the lowest pauper or gypsy in his tent.

The direct denunciation of the rule of force and violence, so prevalent then in Croatia and an integral part of the German drive toward hegemony, is to be found in this excerpt:

The Catholic Church cannot admit that one race or one nation, because it is more numerous or better armed, may do violence to a smaller nation with fewer people. We cannot admit that innocent people may be killed because someone, say a frontier guard, has perhaps killed a soldier, even if he is of a more noble race. The system of shooting hundreds of hostages for a crime, when the person guilty of that crime cannot be found, is a pagan system which only results in evil.

If the Archbishop rejects the New Order in these unequivocal terms, what then does he propose?

. . . The Catholic Church upholds that order which is as old as the Ten Commandments of God. We are not for that order which is written on perishable paper but for that which is written by the hand of the Living God in the consciences of men.

In this magnificent statement, made at the height of the war and when the Ustasha regime was in full force, he condemns not only a vague sort of racism, but the very specific kind as applied to Jews,

---

[37] Document XVI.

Serbs, gypsies, and others. The Archbishop does not merely condemn injustice and violence in broad terms but speaks specifically of the execution of hostages, the burning of villages, the pillaging of homes, and of forced labor, precisely the crimes of which the Nazi were guilty and the reference to whom could not possibly be misunderstood.

That the reference was more than clear may be judged from the instant reaction of the Ustasha government to the Archbishop's sermons. In the publication, *Nova Hrvatska,* Year III, No. 261, of November 6, 1946, Dr. Julije Makanec, Minister of Public Instructions, replied to the Archbishop.[38] The article is one long complaint against the incomprehension of those who do not understand the cause for which the Croat people are fighting. The Archbishop is stigmatized for his failure to grasp the trend of the times and the significance of the issues. He is accused directly of meddling in politics:

> . . . that high ecclesiastical dignitary who has recently, in his sermons, passed beyond the limits of his vocation and begun to meddle in affairs in which he is not competent. He who does not understand the meaning of the political struggle, who has no comprehension of political values, and who does not know how to weigh and evaluate them, will always do best to keep himself aloof from the political sphere, leaving these affairs to those more competent. . . .[39]

The rest of the article is full of innuendoes against the Archbishop with references to "trickery" and the like.[40]

The outspoken sermons of Archbishop Stepinac aroused considerable interest abroad. The British Broadcasting Corporation, on at least four news broadcasts in Serbo-Croatian, addressed to listeners in Yugoslavia, made direct reference to the Archbishop's sermons. Not only did the BBC utilize these statements to the fullest but the Vatican Radio Station likewise reproduced them. This is telling proof that the Vatican fully approved the utterances regarding racism and extreme nationalism and that it was recognized abroad that the ser-

---

[38] See Document XVII for full text of article.

[39] Father Cecelja affirmed that certain Ustashi considered the Archbishop an enemy and that his prohibition of political activity was the reason why only about 15 out of 500 priests were of the Ustasha persuasion and that only about 30 had sympathy for the movement. See Document XLVI, Hren Testimony.

[40] Father Martinčić who testified against the Archbishop on so many points, acknowledged in his interview with the Soviet writer, Ilya Ehrenburg, that the Archbishop had condemned the errors and crimes of Germans and Ustashi in his sermons and that he had "drawn upon himself the hatred and fury of the Ustashi." Document XLVIII.

mons were understood as a "severe and sharp condemnation" of the Ustasha regime. In the 10:15 P.M. broadcast from London in Serbo-Croatian, on July 7, 1943, it was stated that:

In the moral sphere, the Axis has been dealt a heavy blow by the highest moral and spiritual power of the Catholic Church through the medium of the Vatican radio. This blow was directed against Nazism and against its satellites of whom Pavelić is one. . . .[41]

Not once but many times the Vatican reproduced the statements of the Archbishop of Zagreb in his fight against racism and anti-Semitism. The charge that he was ideologically bound to the Ustasha regime and to the Nazi dominators, is clearly based on no substantial evidence. The available documentation reveals that his position was powerfully and consistently the opposite.

The Ustasha Chief of the Section for Press and Cinema, Michael Tolj, Department of Propaganda, Ministry of Public Instruction, was quite aware of the meaning of the Archbishop's words. In a communication to his Ustasha superiors, this functionary calls attention to the character of the broadcasts emanating from London and speaks of the Archbishop's remarks as the "notorious sermon."[42]

The Archbishop's efforts were not merely in the general field of doctrine or feeble protests directed to the occupation authorities on matters of broad principle. His untiring activity on behalf of the distressed and the persecuted, embraced every sector of the population and constitutes the strongest proof in refutation of the accusation that he was indifferent to the plight of the distressed or that he did not extend his efforts to include all who suffered. In this respect the evidence is overwhelming that Archbishop Stepinac aided and succored not only Croats who might have a direct claim on his generosity and assistance but Serbs, Jews, anti-Fascists of every description, and even communists. The full story of this indefatigable anxiety for those in misery cannot as yet be told with the full documentary evidence at hand. We do possess sufficient tangible, positive proof, to show that the Archbishop was the refuge of every type of enemy of the German-Italian occupation and the Ustasha regime. This is a necessary chapter in the long record of devotion and unstinting

[41] See Document XVIII for full text of these statements.
[42] See Document XIX for communication to Dr. Nicholas Mandić.

defense of right and justice which are the outstanding features of Archbishop Stepinac's career under the occupation.

For the sake of clarity, we may divide this effort according to the condition or nationality of the recipients of his aid. They are: (1) Serbs, (2) Jews, (3) Slovenes, and (4) the persecuted and condemned in general.

THE SERBS

A good portion of the evidence under this heading belongs more appropriately to the section of this text concerning the Archbishop's relations to the problem of the forced conversions. There are, however, a number of important cases, selected from among many, that illustrate the conduct of the Archbishop toward the Serbs. On December 29, 1941, Dr. Joseph Ujčić, Catholic Archbishop of Belgrade, addressed a letter to Archbishop Stepinac, asking his intervention to allow the Orthodox Bishop of Gornji Karlovać, Dr. Sava Trlajić, to be released to visit his aged mother in Belgrade.[43] The Archbishop of Zagreb immediately petitioned Pavelić for this favor. On the same date, Archbishop Ujčić informed Archbishop Stepinac that Bogdan Rasković was to visit Zagreb on behalf of Serbian prisoners in various concentration camps.[44] Later Archbishop Ujčić refused, despite pressure from the Russian and Yugoslav communists, to denounce Archbishop Stepinac.

Mr. Rasković expressed his appreciation to the Archbishop of Zagreb for what he had done for the Serbs.

There was the case of Marie Milosavljević, wife of an Orthodox Serb who fled to Serbia at the time of the establishment of the Ustasha regime leaving his wife and five children behind. The wife was falsely accused and haled before the Zagreb court. The children petitioned the Archbishop to intervene on her behalf. The Archbishop went personally to Pavelić regarding the case and finally, on November 18, 1942, the Ministry of Justice sent word that Marie Milosavljević would be able to return home. The children received 500 kuna from the Archbishop and another 1000 from *Caritas*.[45] There was the case

---

[43] Document XX.

[44] Document XXI.

[45] Document XXII. Letter to the Archbishop of appreciation for what he had done, with annotation by Father Laćković, the Secretary.

of the Archbishop's direct intervention with Pavelić on behalf of Stephan Cirić, brother of the Orthodox Bishop, Irenee Cirić. Archbishop Stepinac went to Pavelić several times on behalf of this Serb and despite Pavelić's reluctance it seemed that ultimately the man was released from a concentration camp and allowed to return to Serbia.

In many cases the problem was that of the Orthodox religion of many of the prisoners and inmates of concentration camps. Archbishop Stepinac made no distinction in this respect as is attested by his letter of January 25, 1944, to Dr. Joseph Vragović, Chief of Police of Zagreb, regarding a number of Orthodox who had returned from Italy and were threatened with prosecution before the courts.[46]

The Archbishop made no distinction between those in high and low estate. On July 2, 1942, he communicated with the Most Reverend Mons. Montini at the Secretariate of State of the Holy See regarding two Serbs, Dr. Rajko Gjermanović and Dr. Vittorio Ružić, both imprisoned. His intervention in this case and with the Italian Minister in Zagreb brought about their release.[47]

THE JEWS

The Archbishop's condemnation of anti-Semitism has been demonstrated from his numerous sermons. His action on behalf of the Jews is a no less eloquent testimony of his charity and generosity toward all who suffered persecution. As early as April 23, 1941, Archbishop Stepinac addressed his first communication to the Ustasha government regarding the problem of the Jews.[48] In addition to his general concern for justice and charity toward all, and his recognition that the Croat anti-Semitic legislation was simply the imposition of the Nazi occupier, he was concerned very much that if the unfortunate legislation could not be immediately abrogated the worst flagrant injustices be avoided. Besides the problem of the Jews, as such, there was the more subtle difficulty of those of Jewish race but

---

[46] Document XXIII.
[47] Document XXIV.
[48] Document XXV.

converts to Catholicism. These, quite naturally, came under the jurisdiction of the Archbishop. It is to this point that he addressed his
initial communications.[49] The circumstances of the moment must be
taken into consideration. The argument has been presented, especially
by Dr. Politeo, that Croatia in 1941 was not an independent state. Its
government was a puppet one. Its officials were operating to a
very large extent on sufferance because the real authority, particularly in matters relating to the Jews, was German and it was the
German authorities who determined the nature and effect of the
anti-Jewish laws. In practical terms, the Archbishop was faced with
the problem of doing what he could to relieve suffering and aid the
Jews, safeguard those who had become Christians, and maintain firmly
the Church's doctrinal position on racism. There was a limit to what
he could accomplish materially and practically. Within the realities
of the moment, the Archbishop exerted an extraordinary influence on
behalf of the Jews. It will be noted in the text of the communication
of May 22, 1941, that "We were told that the laws had to be promulgated in that form [making no distinction between religion and race]
for reasons independent of us, but that their practical application
would not be so harsh."[50] Here is the positive proof that the Croat anti-
Jewish legislation was dictated by the Germans. The effectiveness of
the Archbishop's protest, then, was extremely limited, in view of the
inability of the Ustasha government to do more than obey the instructions from Berlin. It would be far too much to expect the Archbishop
of Zagreb to obtain the abolition of the racist laws as 1941 was not
an ideal year in which to bring effective pressure on Adolph Hitler.

The Archbishop was most emphatic in his note of May 22, that
". . . to take away all possibility of existence from members of other
nations or races and to mark them with the stamp of infamy is
a question of humanity and of morals. And moral laws have
application not only for the lives of private individuals but also for

---

[49] When the Nazis occupied Croatia Archbishop Stepinac risked his life to aid
the Jews. With his aid hundreds of Jews were smuggled out of the country and
obtained the repeal of an order that all Jews must wear a yellow tag. He
denounced the Nazi race laws. He worked with the International Red Cross
to rescue Jews in other countries, concealed these victims of racism under his
own roof, and many of his priests did likewise. New York *Times,* Oct. 15, 1946.

[50] Document XXVI.

those who govern states." The episcopal conference of that year expressed itself along the same lines.[51] The letter of the Archbishop to Dr. Andrija Artuković, Minister of the Interior of the Independent Croat State, dated March 7, 1942, is a fair summary of the Archbishop's view:

> I do not think that it can bring us any glory if it is said of us that we have solved the Jewish problem in the most radical way, that is to say, the cruelest. The solution of this question must provide only for the punishment of Jews who have committed crimes, not for persecution of innocent people.[52]

The documents illustrative of the Archbishop's firm stand on this issue are legion. Only a few more need be cited to establish his position and scotch the absurdity that in some manner he sympathized with the anti-Semitic trend of the time and the policy that was foisted on Croatia. In his long letter to Pavelić, dated March 6, 1943, the Archbishop pleads for justice and charity in dealing with the Jews. He argues that these measures perhaps do not come from Pavelić but from other sources. He then adds the significant observation which is the synthesis of his courageous attitude on the problem:

> But if there is here [the anti-Jewish policy] the interference of a foreign power in our internal and political life, I am not afraid if my voice and my protest carry even to the leaders of that power; because the Catholic Church knows no fear of any earthly power, whatever it may be, when it is a question of defending the most basic rights of men.[53]

The Archbishop was dismayed by the irresponsible attitude of the Croatian authorities and the flagrant injustices committed against the innocent. He recalls how in Rome at a conference to deal with refugees, the voice of Croatia was silenced when the Italians refused them the moral right to speak out for the oppressed after their own record in the Independent Croat State.

Archbishop Stepinac was unfailing in his effort to aid individual Jews in need. We have the evidence in his letter of May 8, 1943, to Minister Artuković regarding the petition of the Jewish religious community of Zagreb to aid the Jews still living in the city. The

---

[51] Document XXVII.
[52] Document XXVIII. Under XXIX are other communications illustrating the action of Archbishop Stepinac on the Jewish question.
[53] Document XXX.

Archbishop recommends that the petition be granted in favor of the Jews.[54]

The Archbishop's concern for the welfare of Jews is graphically depicted in the incident that occurred in late March, 1943, when a large number of Jews passed through Zagreb under German surveillance and only the intervention of the Archbishop made it possible for them to receive food and drink.[55]

THE SLOVENES

The Archbishop was accused of negligence of the welfare of the Slovenes and indifference regarding their plight. His compassion and interest embraced them as well as the other nationalities and faiths suffering persecution from the Axis Powers. The evidence is convincing that the Archbishop lent material and spiritual aid to many Slovenes fleeing from the Nazi terror. The episcopal conference of November, 1941, provided for the establishment of a bureau to aid the Slovenes and make available priests of their own tongue for those residing in Croatia.[56] The Slovenes themselves were grateful for the compassion and understanding they found in Archbishop Stepinac.[57]

Through the Office for Slovene Immigrants, the Archbishop made available 50,000 kuna for the Slovenes whose situation was literally desperate. The most notable achievement in this program of aid for the Slovenes was the participation by the Archbishop in the raising of a fund for Slovene relief and especially for anti-Nazi fugitives who were seeking refuge abroad from the terror that reigned in their homeland. We have the testimony to the fact that nearly 6,000,000 kuna were secretly raised in this manner, and the Archbishop was one of the few who was entirely in sympathy with this fund for aid to Slovene fugitives, who were enemies of the Nazi domination.[58]

The Archbishop was instrumental time and again in requesting the government to employ less drastic measures against individuals, and

---

[54] Document XXXI.
[55] Document XXXII.
[56] Document XXXIII contains various documents on the activities of the Archbishop regarding the Slovenes.
[57] Document XXXIII, communication of June 25, 1941, to Archbishop Stepinac.
[58] Document XXXIV.

especially priests. On June 1, 1942, he addressed the Minister of the Interior, Dr. Artuković, on behalf of Father Rihar and his Slovene companions. This letter is typical of the vigor with which the Archbishop called the civil government to task for its policy of suppression and incarceration:

Formerly priests were brought before the court and charges made against them — nearly always because of their pro-Croatian sentiments and activities — but each time the ecclesiastical authorities were notified. After the restoration of the Independent Croat State we have been notified only of the death sentence of Canon Dr. Lončar, although three priests have already been sent to a concentration camp.[59]

The Archbishop protested against the arbitrary arrest of such priests "for such measures harm the reputation of the civil authorities." The Minister of Justice replied that Father Rihar had been sent to the concentration camp because as pastor of Gora Stubica he had refused to celebrate a solemn High Mass on the anniversary of the founding of the Independent Croat State and would not sing a *Te Deum*.[60]

The answer of the Archbishop is the most eloquent refutation of the *canard* that he was the warm supporter of the Ustasha state. Writing to Pavelić on February 24, 1943, he said:

Month after month I have tried to learn the fate of my seven priests who were sent to Jasenovac. All has been in vain. . . .

I must conclude that they were all killed on the assumption that they were anti-national. Why were they not brought before the court? . . .

This is a disgraceful incident and a crime that cries out for vengeance from Heaven. Jasenovac camp itself is a shameful stain on the honor of the Independent State of Croatia.[61]

Even this severe condemnation was not enough. The letter insisted that the "relatives of those who were killed demand satisfaction,

---

[59] Document XXXV. The case of Canon Lončar was the cause of considerable estrangement between the Archbishop of Zagreb and the Pavelić government. This priest had been sent in July, 1941, to protest to the Croat Minister of Justice and Worship, Puk against the policy of incorporating young priests as Ustasha party functionaries. He also protested against the forced conversions of Orthodox. He was well known for his anti-Ustasha sentiments and was later condemned to death. However, after some time he was released from prison and is still alive.

[60] Document XXXV, letter of Dr. Artuković, November 17, 1942.

[61] *Ibid.*

indemnity and the bringing of the murderers to trial. They are the greatest disgrace to Croatia."

This is strong language addressed to the head of the Croat State with which the Archbishop was supposedly the intimate collaborator and one of the most faithful artisans. Directed at Pavelić it is no wonder that General Kvaternik could testify at the trial of the prelate that "Pavelić hated Stepinac." The undaunted courage of the Archbishop in insisting on justice and moderation at all times from all persons is amply verified in this exchange of correspondence regarding a Slovene priest.

AID TO THOSE WHO SUFFERED INJUSTICE

The Archbishop did not limit his compassion to any particular group or tendency as the above evidence demonstrates. He was quite willing to seek justice for communists and appealed to the authorities for clemency in the case of several communists, among them Gamulin, Mohorovičić, Zvonkoa, Kaurić, Tomica Hahn, Jovanovič, Bonaćić, Ilić, Bukovac, Krunić, Bonovećki, and Nemet. The Minister of the Interior under date of August 15, 1944, refused to take action on behalf of Professor Gamulin because of his membership in the Communist Party. The Archbishop had intervened on his behalf in a letter dated July 18, 1944.[62]

The source material from the Zagreb archives reveals the innumerable cases in which the Archbishop sought clemency for those who had been condemned, or persecuted. On August 21, 1944, together with the Apostolic Delegate he appealed to Pavelić for the lives of eleven men sentenced to death.[63]

On August 8, 1944, he appealed for the lives of fifty-four men who had been condemned to the supreme penalty. The Papal Delegate Marcone and the Archbishop had asked for an interview with Pavelić to plead with him to mitigate the sentence. This request was refused. After failure to obtain satisfaction, the Archbishop continued his tireless efforts with the German commander. On October 28, 1944, he

---

[62] Document XXXVI. This letter from the Minister of the Interior and other correspondence regarding known communists on whose behalf the Archbishop intervened are included in the collection of documents.

[63] Document XXXVII.

appealed to General Mirko Gregorić, Commandant of the City of Zagreb, for the lives of eight soldiers condemned to death. On January 23, 1945, he seconded the petition of Dr. Andro Mohorovičić for the life of his son.[64] The list of his petitions became interminable. Part II contains the documentary evidence of a small number of them.[65] Only a fraction of the entire list of persons who solicited and obtained his aid can be given and it is a formidable testimony to the infinite humanity of the Archbishop of Zagreb.[66]

The *Caritas* and various committees represented the principal agencies employed by the Archbishop for his work of assistance and relief. The "Committee to Aid Refugees" dated from 1937 when the Hitler persecutions became violent. The Archbishop served as the intermediary between this organization and the Yugoslav authorities. A summary of the purpose and work of this body is given in Document XL.[67] The report of the Archbishop's secretary to the International Red Cross gives a fairly complete idea of the efforts made in the direction of tangible relief of the persecuted and fugitives.[68]

It was argued that Archbishop Stepinac had evidenced solid support of the Ustasha regime by his approval of the forced labor of Croats in Germany. His messages to the Croats in Germany are cited as evidence of his complacency in their fate. It is evident that there was nothing the Archbishop could do to prevent the fulfillment of the policy of sending these labor battalions to Germany. This formed a part of the Nazi technique during the entire war and was applied to all occupied countries. The Ustasha government was obliged, as

---

[64] *Ibid.*

[65] Document XXXVIII.

[66] Document XXXIX lists some of the persecuted persons on whose behalf the Archbishop intervened. Document XLII further confirms the Archbishop's efforts with the Pavelić government.

[67] Document XL. Memorandum of Miss Theresa Skringer, former secretary of the Committee regarding the work of the "Committee to Aid Refugees," organized by the Archbishop.

[68] Document XLI, report of Father Stephan Lacković to the delegate of the International Red Cross in Croatia, dated September 25, 1943. See XIII for aid to those condemned to concentration camps or driven from homes. Archbishop Stepinac sought further contributions for all Croats interned in Italian concentration camps. The Italian government and Pavelić were not pleased by this activity. Document XLVI, testimony of Dr. Joseph Marić.

Monsignor Rittig in his letter to the Archbishop expresses his admiration for his charities and work of relief. Document VI.

were the others, to accept this fact. The Archbishop exerted his influence to mitigate the consequences of this forced absence from the homeland. His Christmas message of 1941 is full of paternal solicitude for the Croats in German factories, mines, and work camps. There is not a word, not a syllable, in this message that can be construed as an approval of the system. The text reveals the concern of the Archbishop for the spiritual welfare and religious practice of those submitted to temptation and lacking the defenses of a normal home life and community organization. He urges loyalty to Croatia, to be sure, and conduct that will contribute to the best opinion of the Croats abroad. "Appreciate, therefore, even from abroad, your Croatian fatherland but do not despise other nations. And you can honor it in the best way by leading an honest life and doing honest work."[69] A further message from Archbishop Stepinac accompanied the gift of 200 prayer books to the Croat workers and a reiteration of his solicitude for their spiritual welfare. Neither of these documents can be interpreted as political; neither advances a single political argument nor expresses the slightest approval of the system under which Croats were transferred to Germany for labor.

We may conclude that the message of December 18, 1941, to the Croat workers abroad did not constitute what the Public Prosecutor called "an approval of the forced transfer of our people for work in Germany and an invitation to perform this work because it was a religious and patriotic duty," to quote the text of the indictment. The actual text of the two messages proves conclusively that the Archbishop was solicitous for the moral welfare of the workers and expressed the hope that their conduct would accord with their dignity as Croats.

The Public Prosecutor mentions in the indictment numerous minor cases in which it is alleged that the Archbishop collaborated with the German occupiers and the Ustasha regime. These include the alleged incident in which the Archbishop raised his hand in Fascist salute. This has been proved false and the result of a deliberate misrepresentation of a photograph taken at a parade. The charge that the Archbishop took part in the departure ceremonies of the Croat vessels headed for the Black Sea was denied absolutely by the

---

[69] Document XLIII.

Archbishop who stated categorically that he never attended such an affair and knew nothing of it. The argument that he dispatched cigarettes, rosaries, and religious pictures to the Croat troops destined for the Russian front is palpably absurd. Obviously, the Archbishop was concerned that these soldiers be provided with certain of the minor amenities and have suitable religious articles in their possession. He was clearly in no position to stop the Russian campaign or even to prevent the Pavelić government from collaborating with the Nazis in the war. Since the Croat troops were unavoidably obliged to participate in military action against the Soviets, it is incomprehensible that the Archbishop should be charged with providing them these modest gifts.

The evidence is conclusive, then, that the Archbishop felt obliged to deal with the occupying authorities for the protection of the Church and the Croat faithful. He maintained these contacts at a minimum and in almost every case on behalf of the persecuted. His attitude on the principles represented by the Nazi and Fascist occupier is demonstrated by his numerous sermons and public statements. He was concerned exclusively with the protection of religion and the defense of the Church against all authority seeking to impose its will. He insisted that his clergy refrain from politics. In the cases in which priests did not do so, the Archbishop was often unable to do anything about it. Finally, his attitude is best depicted in his constant aid to the distressed, regardless of nationality or religion. Materially and spiritually he spared no efforts to come to the assistance of the victims of the totalitarian regime in Croatia. Although his Croat patriotism was expressed in his hope that an independent Croatia might come into existence and survive, he was pained and disconsolate that the actual form of the Croat state should be a satellite of Germany. The accusation of the Public Prosecutor that Archbishop Stepinac was an enthusiastic supporter of the Ustasha is therefore untrue and contradicted by the evidence, as is the charge that he collaborated closely with the Germans and Italians.

Chapter IV

THE ACTIVITY OF THE CATHOLIC PRESS AND ORGANIZATIONS

T HE second main charge is against the Catholic press, the clergy, and Catholic Action. The accusation, as presented by the Public Prosecutor, asserts that Archbishop Stepinac was responsible for the statements of the Catholic press, the action of the Catholic clergy, and the activities of Catholic Action. As the highest religious authority in Croatia, he consented either actively or by discreet silence to the intemperate utterances of the press and in the dubious conduct of many of his priests and Catholic organizations.

The Public Prosecutor stated in the indictment: "The Catholic press during the occupation was completely dominated by the thought and orientation of the defendant Stepinac who, as president of the episcopal conference and as president of Catholic Action, had supreme control over everything printed in the entire Catholic press of Yugoslavia. In this capacity he influenced the expression of the press and supported whole-heartedly its anti-national attitude."

The counsel for the defense, Dr. Politeo, was most careful in his statement on behalf of the Archbishop to establish a distinction which the Public Prosecutor had either overlooked or deliberately confused; namely, that charges were piled up one on top of the other against the Archbishop of Zagreb with no respect for the plain facts of person and place. In a word, time after time, incidents, acts, and statements were attributed directly or tacitly to Archbishop Stepinac which were in reality those of some other jurisdiction or person. There was no recognition in the indictment of the existence of well-defined ecclesiastical jurisdictions. Dr. Politeo calls this confusion of person and place, "a fundamental fault of the indictment." It forms at the same time one of the salient elements in the defense of the defendant.

The indictment as quoted above speaks of the Archbishop as having "supreme control" over such matters as the press and Catholic Action. The assumption is that anything that happened in all Yugoslavia, *not merely Croatia,* was the direct and personal responsibility of the Archbishop of Zagreb. Dr. Politeo scotches this idea by his assertion that the State is obviously unaware of the facts about "the constitution of the Church and Canon Law." It was necessary to make clear to the court that each Bishop is supreme in his own diocese and that the Archbishop of Zagreb was the supreme authority only within the jurisdiction of that one archdiocese. He had no right to interfere in the affairs of other Croatian dioceses nor was the clergy of these other jurisdictions under his authority in the least. Therefore, he could be accused only of actions that had been taken within his own diocese and none other. This basic fact was not considered by the Public Prosecutor at all, and a large number of the charges brought against specifically Catholic activity refer to occurrences and incidents in other dioceses over which the Archbishop had no control and could have none even if he had so desired. . . . Therefore, the defense claimed that "no one can accuse Archbishop Stepinac of or hold him responsible for what individual priests did in territory belonging to a diocese other than his own of Zagreb."

In his own diocese, he had no authority over the religious orders. "Authority over the Franciscans is exercised by their provincial." Each order was therefore outside the authority of the Ordinary and it was illogical to assume that the Archbishop could be held responsible for their actions. In addition to this, another problem arises. If it is true that once these premises have been established, the responsibility of the Archbishop of Zagreb shrinks considerably, it is equally true that within his own diocese he could not be held guilty for actions of individual priests who violated his instructions or committed acts which were clearly in disaccord with his authority. Criminal responsibility cannot be held collectively. Only if the proof of a conspiracy were advanced in which the Archbishop was a participant, could the action of individual Catholics, lay or clerical, implicate the prelate. Otherwise we are faced with the problem of collective guilt which is precisely the theory of the

Nazis. Just as the latter held collective Jewry responsible for the acts of the individual Jew; just as hostages in Yugoslavia or France were executed for the alleged crime of an individual in a given village or community, so would the prosecution in this case attribute to the Archbishop every treasonable or antinational act of one individual priest or layman, regardless of his actual participation in the act or even his knowledge of it. One of the major weaknesses of the indictment is this insistence on attributing to the Archbishop responsibility for every act of individuals who may have been in many cases under his *authority*, but not necessarily under his *control*.

Moreover, it is necessary to grasp the confused and abnormal situation in Croatia between 1941 and 1945. The impact of the war had produced a certain confusion, both in the minds of men and in their actions. The natural satisfaction of the Croat people that some form of independence had come about was accompanied by the most serious reservations regarding the nature of the new Croat State. The occupier was everywhere and the Nazi terror swept over the country just as it had so many other parts of Europe. Communication was bad, so serious in fact that the ordinary meeting of the episcopal conference was made difficult by the inability to move freely about the land. The breakdown of Yugoslavia led to an outburst of Croatian nationalism. A great many exulted in the disappearance of the dictatorial system they had hated. There was a tendency to give vent to passionate and often intemperate sentiments of exaggerated nationalism. It is not surprising that in this supercharged atmosphere, certain publications and even members of the clergy should go too far. All Catholics were by no means agreed on the excellencies or the defects of the Independent Croat State. There were those who saw in it deliverance from the yoke of Serbia and took pains to say so in public. It is not a simple matter in turbulent times such as those through which Yugoslavia was passing to maintain serenity, equanimity, and absolute objectivity. It was not easy either for the religious authorities to control the utterances and action of the entire clergy and still less of the laity. Political prudence interposed itself very definitely since frequently it was a matter of the lesser evil, the greater aim being the existence of the Church and its power to perform its functions vis-à-vis the faithful.

Let it be added too that the Archbishop of Zagreb had no actual authority as chairman of the episcopal conference. This function as presiding officer gave him no right to intervene in the affairs of the dioceses represented by their Ordinaries at the meetings. Even as Metropolitan of Croatia, his authority over the four suffragan dioceses was strictly limited by the provision of Canon Law and in any event the local Bishop was always primarily responsible for his own diocese.

The Public Prosecutor presents a veritable anthology of extracts from the Catholic press of Croatia to show complicity in the Ustasha regime and collaboration in its criminal acts. "From the beginning to the end of the occupation, this press was directed to the single end of propaganda for Fascism and Ustashism, the glorifying of Hitler and Pavelić, and the praise of the Independent Croat State. This press was distinguished by lies and calumnies against the National Resistance Movement and engaged in inciting religious and racial hatred." Thus far the words of the indictment against the Catholic press. The charges embrace the whole range of the Catholic press: *Andjeo Čuvar, Glasnik sv. Josipa, Crnče, Glasnik sv. Ante, Vrtić,* all publications for children or young people, the larger papers such as *Katolički List, Katolički Tjednik, Vrhbosna,* and *Nedjelja.* The main culprit is *Katolički List,* described by the Prosecutor as "the semi-official paper of the Zagreb archdiocese" and allegedly, "supported the occupier during the entire period of the occupation and expressed itself favorably to the Ustasha." The frequent pictures of Pavelić and the alleged support of this press for the Crusader movement appear to constitute the major crimes adduced by the Public Prosecutor.[1]

There are various important facts to bear in mind in judging the action of the Catholic press in Croatia. A large number of the publications cited by the Public Prosecutor were not under the supervision of the Archbishop and many of them were not even published in his archdiocese. Some were under the direction of the religious orders or communities and were thus not subject to the Archbishop. This was the case of *Andjeo Čuvar,* published by the Franciscans; *Glasnik sv. Ante* by the Franciscans; *Vjesnik Počasne Straze Srca Isusova* by the Third Order; *Glasnik Srca Isusova* by the

---

[1] The problem of the Crusaders, or *Križari,* which play a considerable part in the indictment will be treated later.

Jesuits, and others. *Katolički Tjednik* was published in Sarajevo, another diocese. The papers published in the Zagreb archdiocese were not directly owned or managed by the Archbishop. The Archbishop was in no case the "supreme tactician" as he had been dubbed of the whole Croatian Catholic press. In no single case can it be alleged that the Archbishop was directly responsible for the management, administration, or editorial policy of any publication. The prosecution charged the Archbishop with criminal action, based on the pro-Ustasha statements of many Catholic journals. Such a charge is ridiculous. Under the absolute dictatorship of the Ustasha, the newspapers, Catholic as well as secular, were forced to print what the censors demanded.

It must be borne in mind, too, that the Catholic press suffered from the restrictions of the Ustasha regime. Some hundred Catholic publications existed before the advent of the new order. Within a few months after April, 1941, the number had been reduced to a third. The leading Croat Catholic daily, *Hrvatski Glas*, was itself suppressed. The most frequently quoted, *Katolički List*, was never the semiofficial organ of the Zagreb archdiocese. It published in a special column the official announcements of the Chancery Office of the Archdiocese, but in editorial policy and administration, it was quite independent. As a matter of fact, the Ustasha regime was so ill pleased with this journal that its publication was suspended for a time. At a later date Canon Kolarek, who directed it, was forbidden to sign his name to articles or editorials.

In this connection it is necessary to dwell for a moment on the temper of the times and especially the existence in the independent Croat State not only of a negative censorship but of a positive one. Dr. Politeo has emphasized this in his *plaidoyer* on behalf of the Archbishop. While deploring the eulogistic character of many of the articles in the press, the defense attorney calls attention to the need for judging them and the whole status of the press, "not from the viewpoint of today's conditions, but from that of the situation at the time they were written." Only in this manner can the proper perspective be obtained. The Croat Bureau of Press and Propaganda exerted very heavy pressure on the papers, not only to prevent all criticism of the government, but to step up the praise for the regime and its head. Dr. Politeo continued, "the censorship not only deleted but also inserted words, sentences, and even whole paragraphs by which it often completely changed the whole meaning of the original article." The censor was more than that; he was in many respects the writer of the piece. Canon Kolarek himself explained at the trial exactly how this system operated: He had been criticized for publishing a highly favorable review of one of Pavelić's books. He was accused of contributing through the press to the support of the Poglavnik:

> My name was at the end of the article and I wrote it. I would like to make a remark or two on that point. From the first day the Independent Croat State came into existence, heavy pressure was brought to bear on me. The office of censorship let me know by telephone that my articles were not enthusiastic enough, and that I had failed to understand the situation of the country. My articles were all censored and whole paragraphs were inserted with the greatest liberty. Toward the end of July after the arrest of Mons. Lončar, a number of young priests told me that I was about to be arrested. . . .[2]

Here we have a fairly realistic picture of the state of affairs in Pavelić's Croatia where the rigid control of the press and the destructive censorship left very little leeway for freedom of expression, the Catholic press being submitted to the same control as the rest. Hence the remarkable similarity of expression and even of phraseology that occurs in most of the articles treating of the new regime and its chief.

The problem then posed for the Catholic press was simple. Many of the journals had already gone out of business. Those that survived could not avoid the restrictions imposed by the State. Their editors and directors had no control whatever over the content of articles dealing with political affairs and to refuse such articles was certainly tantamount to suppression. The defense attorney remarks that the public very quickly learned to read between the lines and discern that which had been inserted and that which belonged to the original writer. The total disappearance of the Catholic press would have

---

[2] Document XLVI, Testimony of Dr. Kolarek and Dr. Penić to the effect that the *Katolički List* had been especially censored, that its editors were ordered under threats as to what they were to write, that the censorship was very rigorous in striking out certain words and in inserting others to change the meaning, and that this weekly was twice suspended.

been a very serious blow to the Church in Croatia. Again the problem was one of the impossibility of effective opposition.

To the argument that the Archbishop never gave precise directives to the Catholic press as to its editorial policy, it may be argued that his entire attitude and his public statements constitute directives in themselves. Obviously a small Catholic paper or review could not speak out with the same authority as the Archbishop, lest it be eliminated instantly. It cannot be said that there is any lack of adequate orientation on the part of the Archbishop as to the general line of Catholic thought during those critical years.

The problem of the relations of the members of Catholic Action and of the clergy with the Ustasha is a more delicate point. Here again the problem of collective responsibility enters into consideration. Plainly the Archbishop could not do more than prohibit political activity. The record as already presented shows how consistent his directives were on this subject. If a priest, through extreme nationalism, chose to violate these instructions there was little to prevent it. The Archbishop could exert no more than moral pressure as a restraint. The Ustasha government proclaimed its Catholicism, and professed to consider religion as one of the pillars of the new order. The Ustasha authorities were little likely to respect the Archbishop's expressed wish that his clergy refrain from all active support of the regime. The clergy was, in effect, a potential source of very great popularity for the new state. Membership in Catholic Action and the Ustasha Party had been declared incompatible on December 7, 1941. Many members unquestionably did join the Ustasha. This again was a problem of individual responsibility and could not be ascribed collectively to the Archbishop. Not one shred of evidence exists to prove that the Archbishop ever did anything but discourage political participation by his clergy. Dr. Felice Niedzielski, mentioned frequently at the trial as a leader of Catholic Action who had become an active Ustasha had, in fact, given up the presidency of the youth organizations of Catholic Action two and a half years before entering political life.

The list of priests contained in the Public Prosecutor's List as responsible for Ustasha crimes contains only a very small number belonging to the Zagreb archdiocese. This fact is necessary, first of all, to make clear that the Archbishop had no control over the majority of them, regardless of their activity. They were Vilim Cecelja, Martin Gecina, and Anthony Djurić.[3]

In the second place, the Archbishop was alert to the danger of his own clergy and took action against those of them who overstepped the bounds of propriety in supporting the Ustasha. The following are cases in which such action was taken:

1. The Rev. John Guberina, who was forbidden to celebrate Mass or exercise his priestly functions because of his conduct.[4]

2. Father Zvonko Brekalo, accused by Bozo Lastro, teacher at Banja Luka, of scandalous conduct, assault and general misconduct. The Archbishop demanded an explanation at once, and if the charges were true his suspension.[5]

3. Three priests who had been appointed Ustasha officials were ordered to resign from their posts.[6]

It is important to mention that in some cases priests were designated by the civil authority regardless of the Archbishop's wishes. In these cases there was little he could do. Monsignor Vučetić and Monsignor Vilim Cecelja, pastor of Kustošija, were appointed military vicars by the head of the state. The pressure from the government often extended to requesting additional honors for the government designees.[7]

Father Martinčić, the Franciscan who figured so largely in the adverse testimony during the trial, may be cited as a witness to the Archbishop's desire to avoid politics and keep his priests from engaging in Ustasha activity. In his interview with Ilya Ehrenburg, he states:

Priests could not be punished merely for being Ustashi for that was, during the period of the Independent Croat State, impossible. . . . Rome kept aloof and hoped that priests would have nothing to do with it. . . . Only those Ustashi priests could be punished who, as Ustashi, committed acts which could not be reconciled with their priestly vocation.[8]

The communists alleged that a number of priests were guilty of "criminal" acts, such as:

1. The blessing of Crusader flags by the religious authorities in the Archbishop's palace.

---

[3] Document XLVI.
[4] Document XLIV.
[5] Document XLV.
[6] Document XLVI.
[7] Document XLVII.
[8] Document XLVIII.

2. The use of the crucifix with the dagger and bomb in the taking of the Ustasha oath.

3. The use of prayer books with texts pledging allegiance to the Independent Croat State.

There was very considerable confusion regarding the Crusader movement and the name crops up again and again in the proceedings and publications on the subject of the Archbishop Stepinac trial. The confusion lay in part in the fact that there was an organization known as the *Križari* (Crusader), a nonpolitical body of Croat youth within the Catholic Action organization, founded with the entire approval of the Catholic Hierarchy. In the last year of the Pavelić regime a strongly nationalist and anti-communist movement was established, the members calling themselves the *Križari*. This group, despite the similar name, was a very different organization from the one connected with Catholic Action which antedated it by many years.

The organization *Crusaders* was founded by a layman, Dr. Ivan Merz. After his death, Dr. Ivan Protulipac, a Croatian attorney, well known as anti-Nazi and persecuted by the Ustashi police, served for one year as president of this organization. On January 31, 1946, while a refugee from communism, he was shot in a street of Trieste by an agent of the OZNA, the Yugoslav communist secret police.

As successor of Dr. Protulipac, Dr. Felice Niedzielski, also a young Croatian attorney and patriot, was elected president of the Crusaders. He gave up his post in 1941 to accept a position in the Croatian State administration. He was always ready to aid the persecuted and was even attacked by some Ustashi officials who accused him of defending the Jews and the Serbs. In 1945, he was captured by the Partisans and sentenced to death as a *criminal,* despite an appeal of 850 Serb Orthodox families who declared they had been protected by Dr. Niedzielski and affirmed his innocence. These appeals were in vain: Dr. Niedzielski was executed. He was succeeded as president of the Crusaders by Dr. Leo Znidarčić, also a well-known anti-Nazi and an exemplary young Catholic.

Additional proof that the Crusaders were not a political organization — not to mention an organization of criminals — is furnished by the fact that the spiritual general assistant of the Crusaders was Msgr.

Milan Beluhan, a canon of Zagreb and renowned throughout Croatia as a saintly priest and the firm friend of poor workingmen, including communists. Even the present Yugoslav authorities did not charge him with any "crime." Logically, he should have been condemned first as the "chief criminal" of a "criminal" organization. He is responsible for the organization of the Crusaders as such, not for the private actions of its members.

The blessing of the Crusader banners, that is, the Ustasha version of the Crusaders, is alleged to have taken place in the archiepiscopal palace.

The blessing of the Crusader flag in the archiepiscopal palace was carried out without the consent or approval of the Archbishop. It is claimed that Dr. Šalić and another priest Father Simecki were responsible for this incident in the archiepiscopal palace. The Archbishop learned of it after the event and disapproved of it.[9]

Another item seized upon with great delectation by the prosecution was the ceremony of the Ustasha oath in which the crucifix was accompanied by a dagger and bomb. This has been depicted as in conformity with the Archbishop's views and as receiving his approval. This absurdity may be dismissed very quickly with the quotation of the communication of October 15, 1943, from Archbishop Stepinac to the Military Vicar in which he says:

Since complaints have increased, during the past few days, that oaths are being taken in front of the crucifix with a dagger and a revolver alongside it, thus profaning the sanctity and holiness of the Crucifix, the President of the Episcopal Conference informs you that it is forbidden to administer oaths in front of a dagger and revolver.[10]

The so-called prayer book called *The Croat Soldier* involved the censorship as did most other similar publications. Dr. Slamić, in his testimony, explained how this had come about. The censorship of books was carried out by a special censor who proposed them for approval to the Ordinariate. The publication followed the censor's approval. The Archbishop had no personal knowledge of what was proposed.[11]

---

[9] Document LXXII.
[10] Document XLIX.
[11] Document XLVI, Testimony of Dr. Slamić.

Chapter V

THE FORCED CONVERSIONS

O NE of the most tragic episodes of the Ustashi regime was the attempt at the "forced conversion" of the Serbs living in Croatia. The Serb communities in Croatia retained their old customs and their Orthodox faith. Croatians and Serbians had for long associated religion with race. A Serb had to be Orthodox, a Croatian had to be Catholic. By some quirk of the mind, which is common in dictatorships, Pavelić and his lieutenants hit on the idea that if the Croatian Serbs could be forced to acknowledge the Catholic faith, they would automatically become loyal subjects of the "new" Croatia. The policy of "forced conversions" was instituted whereby pressure was brought on Serb communities to announce their formal acceptance of the Catholic faith. The whole matter is shrouded in a mass of contradictory statements. One version is that whole communities were offered the alternative between "conversion" and death. It appears, also, that numerous Serbs voluntarily asked for admission into the Catholic Church, probably in the hope of thereby conciliating their tyrants. At the same time, frightful massacres of Serbs were being perpetrated which may not have had any relation to the "forced conversions." It is odd that the present government of Yugoslavia should set itself up as the champion of the Orthodox Church. Under international law, however, the hostile occupant is obliged to respect the religious convictions of the peaceful populations.[1] In a sense the Ustashi were agents of the Axis occupants and, hence, made chargeable under this article.

The charge contained in the indictment is most explicit on the

---

[1] Annex to Hague Convention, 1907, Article 46.

matter of the forced conversions. The statement of the Public Prosecutor reads:

The defendant Stepinac was in agreement with the Ustasha threat to the Serbs of Bosnia, Hercegovina and Croatia that unless they accepted Catholicism they would be exterminated. He approved the forced conversions of thousands of Serbs and by this approval encouraged the Ustashi to continue committing these crimes.[2]

The purpose of these forced conversions, according to the indictment, was to widen the cleavage between Croat and Serb, destroy the unity of Croatia and Serbia in the struggle against the occupier, outrage the dignity of the South Slav peoples and extinguish the spirit of resistance among the Serbs of Bosnia, Hercegovina, and Croatia, leading to the final extermination of the Serbs.

If the charge is true that extermination was the aim, it is difficult to imagine why so much would have been made of bringing about conversions. One would think that extermination might be carried out without the preliminaries of conversion and the alleged energies that went into this aspect of the Ustasha program. The indictment cites the cases of persons submitted to the conversions and links them with the massacres, the immediate purpose of which was plunder and confiscation. In the midst of this storm and fury, the episcopal conference met on September 17, 1941, presided over by Archbishop Stepinac. This meeting of the Bishops gave "canonical sanction," to use the expression of the indictment, to the crimes. A committee of three was designated, says the indictment, consisting of Archbishop Stepinac, Bishop Burić of Senj, and Bishop Šimrak, Apostolic Administrator of Križevci. An executive committee under these three was charged directly with the task of promoting the conversions. This was done in accordance with the Sacred Congregation for the Oriental Church and thus it was that "the Vatican and the Catholic hierarchy of Croatia under the leadership of the defendant Stepinac adopted and sanctioned the conversions."

This is the substance of the indictment in the matter of the forced conversions.

The facts of the matter are the exact opposite, as can be demonstrated by the evidence:

---

[2] Document A, The Indictment.

. . . the Catholic Church, as a whole, led by the Archbishop of Zagreb, . . . alone made the evil consummation impossible. The Archbishop spoke publicly and plainly against the forced "conversions" and the persecution which was the alternative to "conversion," and set up ecclesiastical commissions to investigate every case reported. "We call God to witness," he cried, "that we have always been opposed to any compulsory attachment to the Catholic Church. We must declare that the Church has done all in her power to give aid and protection to the Orthodox." It was through the Archbishop's stern condemnation when the Hierarchy met in Zagreb on December 17, 1941, that the endeavor to impose the Catholic faith by the sword ended in failure, so that Pavelić was obliged to accept the presence of Orthodox within his state, and indeed to recognize an official Croat Orthodox Church, with its headquarters in Zagreb.[3]

The Holy Father, in his address to the Sacred Tribunal of the Roman Rota, as reported in the world press, expressed himself as follows:

In a speech delivered at his summer residence Castel Gandolfo, to the Sacred Tribunal of the Roman Rota, which resumes its activities tomorrow, the Pope declared today that Yugoslavia had as long ago as 1942 reported that neither the Holy See nor the Roman Catholic Episcopacy had had any part in the so-called "forced conversions" in Croatia. He categorically rejected the charges made at which he called the "very sad trial" of Archbishop Aloysius Stepinatz that he himself approved such conversions.

The Pope began by explaining what the church means by "freedom of conscience" and by tolerance toward other religious confessions. He dwelled particularly on the article of canon law saying that "nobody must be obliged against his will to embrace the Catholic faith."

Referring directly to Monsignor Stepinatz' trial, the Pope continued: "If, therefore a few days ago, according to news appearing in the press, the public prosecutor in a very sad trial affirmed that the Pope himself had approved the so-called conversions, and moreover — what would be even graver — that he had done so for reasons of national imperialism, we have the right and the duty to reject such a false accusation. In order that our assertion may be duly documented, we consider it fitting to read to you a memorandum of the Secretariat of State, dated January 25, 1942, in reply to a question submitted to it by the Yugoslav legation to the Holy See about the movement of conversion, in which Yugoslavia herself expressly acknowledged that neither the Holy See nor the Catholic Episcopacy in Croatia had had any part whatsoever." The Pope read the memorandum, making it quite clear, that if any forced conversions were occurring in Croatia, they certainly did not have the approval of either the Vatican or the Catholic Hierarchy.[4]

---

[3] *The Tablet*, London, Sept. 28, 1946.
[4] New York *Times*, Oct. 6, 1946.

Before examining the documentary evidence regarding the forced conversions, it may be well to summarize the statement presented to the court by Dr. Katičić, colleague of Dr. Politeo and assigned by the State to the defense of the Archbishop.

In the first place the circumstances of the time must again be taken into account to explain events. Both Dr. Politeo and Dr. Katičić insist again and again on the need for giving special attention to the atmosphere of confusion, terror, and uncertainty that prevailed during those years. The conversion by force of members of the Orthodox faith was a political and not a religious act. This Defense Counsel Katičić asserts is fundamental to an understanding of the procedure. The conclusive proof of the absence of all spiritual motive on the part of the Croat authorities was that the same individuals who brought the conversions about were equally ready to exterminate the converts. After the failure of the policy of forced conversions, these same leaders were quite ready to establish the Croatian Orthodox Church in order to solve what they considered the minority problem of the Serb residents in Croatia. The inevitable conclusion is that the policy was linked with that of the Jewish persecution. It was a deliberate effort to eliminate a minority and especially a minority with strong attachments to Serbia. It was unquestionably part of the larger effort to separate Croatia as completely as possible from Serbia.

The indictment in the matter of the forced conversions rests on two fundamental bases:

1. The participation by numerous priests, under Ustasha guidance, in the conversions, frequently followed by massacres. Abundant testimony to the violent treatment of Serbian Orthodox is introduced to prove this point.

2. The full and avowed approval of the hierarchy and in particular of Archbishop Stepinac in the conversions and his numerous Circular Letters and other statements tending to support and encourage such conversions.

The first point may be dismissed fairly easily. The problem here is not that of individual priests (an infinitesimally small number), some of them suspended by their ordinary, who committed criminal acts. In law, these criminals could be judged only for their own crimes, on an individual basis. The question in the trial of the Archbishop is whether he was responsible, personally and directly, for such crimes. There is a distinction to be made, certainly between actual commission of the grave offenses and the indirect inspiration of those acts. Did the Archbishop of Zagreb so conduct himself, to say the least, that his clergy and the faithful were persuaded that he tacitly approved the policy of forced conversions and contemplated the massacres with tolerance? If the guilt of the Archbishop personally cannot be proved, then the first point is irrelevant. The second point is far more important. This involves Church policy. The question raised is that of the attitude of the Catholic hierarchy, and specifically of Archbishop Stepinac, toward the forced conversions. Did the prelate go along with the politically inspired Croat government policy of eliminating a religious minority or did he undertake to place as many obstacles and safeguards as possible in the way of these arbitrary conversions? The evidence available proves that the Archbishop was not guilty of the charge as formulated by the Public Prosecutor; that he did not tolerate or encourage the conversions, but exerted officially and personally every influence to conteract the evil effects of conversions by force. The documents prove that the hierarchy was fully aware of the responsibility in the matter. The proof is available that the Archbishop was equally aware that the action of the Croat state represented a serious intervention in a field that did not belong to it and which pertained solely to the Church itself.

During 1941 and 1942 a whole series of circular letters was issued in which the conditions of the admission of converts were analyzed and clarified. It was impossible, obviously, to close the door completely to converts. There were cases in which Orthodox sincerely desired to be received into the Catholic Church. It was impossible to announce that no Orthodox, for the simple reason of his religion, could be given instruction or be received. The purpose of these circulars was to lay down the indispensable conditions that must precede such reception. Conversions *en masse* or for purely political reasons had to be combated. The door was left open at the same time for those who honestly sought to inform themselves regarding Catholicism or who contemplated conversion based on conviction.

As early as May 8, 1941, less than a month after the establishment of the Independent Croat State, the Zagreb Chancery issued a circular letter regarding the problem of conversions. It was evident that a number of citizens had appeared desirous of regularizing their marriages or of entering the Catholic Church. The Independent Croat Government had proclaimed with considerable fanfare its support of the Church and to a large degree the impression existed that the state looked with more than normal benevolence on Catholics as against other religious groups. The clergy was informed that the following conditions existed for reception:

1. Reception into the Catholic Church may be permitted only to persons of whom it is sure that they desire to take this step sincerely out of a conviction in the truth of our holy faith and its necessity for the salvation of their souls. Religion is an interior matter of a free conscience and the decision in favor of a religion excludes all dishonest motives.
2. Persons who wish to be received into the Catholic Church must be instructed in the truths of the Catholic religion and ought, during the time of their instruction, to observe the commandments of God and the Church concerning prayer, attendance at divine services, hearing the word of God, abstinence, etc.; in this way these persons are introduced to the practical religious life of the Church.
3. Only persons may enter the Catholic Church who can live according to Catholic principles. Consequently, persons may be received into the Church only on condition that they promise that all children who may be born will be baptized and brought up in the Catholic Church, and that all children already born and still under their authority as parents will enter the Catholic Church.
4. To avoid excessive correspondence with the clergy regarding the conversion of persons asking to be received into the Catholic Church or to have their marriages validated in the Church, it is necessary that the petitions presented be completely detailed, that is to say, that all essential facts be included so that these petitions may immediately be taken into consideration. . . .
5. The clergy in charge of conversions is informed that in these delicate questions of the human soul they must proceed strictly according to the principles of the Catholic Church, careful of its dignity and good name, refusing to admit those who would like to enter the Catholic Church without the correct motives, looking only to the protection of their material interests and their own selfish ends.[5]

These instructions could not be more specific on the conditions necessary for the reception of converts. The fifth point is especially eloquent in insisting on the most scrupulous observance of the

---

[5] Document L.

principles of the Church regarding conversion. The Circular Letter concludes with reference to the large number — several thousands — of Catholics who had apostatized and become Orthodox. It must be remembered that violent as the procedure of the Ustasha government undoubtedly was, it had been preceded for a period of twenty years by the policy of proselytizing on the part of the Yugoslav state on behalf of Orthodoxy. Not infrequently the quest of honors or advantage in the old Yugoslav state had been preceded by conversion to orthodoxy or at least the renunciation of Catholicism. A delicate moral problem was posed with reference to these apostates who sought to return to the Catholic fold. In a word, the whole problem cannot be solved in so simple a fashion as the Public Prosecutor suggested. The matter of conversions was part of the larger problem of the whole Yugoslav atmosphere and the century-old relations of Serbs and Croats. It was historically inevitable, if profoundly deplorable, that under the Ustasha this question should take a violent turn. It must not be overlooked that the passions enkindled at the time had their origins in the twenty years of Serbian-Croat union and in the many centuries of tension between the two South Slav peoples, divided by their religious allegiance.

Under the date of June 11, 1941, in a supplement to *Katolički List,* the rules for reception into the Catholic Church were published in great detail. One of the main problems considered in this communication had to do with marriage. The complications on this score were infinite in the light of mixed marriages between Catholic and Orthodox, invalid marriages, and complications arising out of cases in which one or both of the parties had apostatized and now claimed to wish to return to the Church. The great detail into which the circular enters demonstrates the extreme care of the Archiepiscopal chancery in working toward a solution of these cases. The charge that the hierarchy was eager to collaborate in mass conversions regardless of personal desires or even of the canonical provisions, is absurd. The text of this document reveals the detailed conditions laid down for the reception of new converts or of those who wished to return to the Church.[6]

On November 20, 1941, the Archbishop as president of the episcopal

---

[6] Document LI.

conference wrote to Pavelić a very extensive letter in which the whole problem of the conversions is set forth, and the conditions for the reception of such converts carefully reiterated. This document is further refutation of the charge that Archbishop Stepinac sought to support the Pavelić government in its policy of conversions based on violence.[7]

The contention of this document may be summarized as follows:

1. The Catholic Church alone through the hierarchy has jurisdiction over conversions.
2. "Missionaries" designated by the civil authority have no validity unless the mission and jurisdiction have been approved by the Ordinary.
3. The committee designated by the Croatian Catholic Episcopate has as its function to deal with the State on those matters which have to do with the civil aspect of conversions and the accompanying circumstances.
4. The executive committee named by the Bishops is directly charged with the task of assisting the Bishops in problems arising from conversions from Orthodoxy to Catholicism.

These first items indicate that the three-man committee of Bishops and the executive committee designated by them had as their function those aspects of the question of conversion that were of legitimate concern to the state. There were such questions obviously. Conversion produced difficulties regarding marriage, property, and in some cases the ecclesiastical holdings of the Orthodox. It was plainly necessary to have an authorized and fully qualified committee of the Croat hierarchy to deal with these matters. It must be remembered that despite the forced conversions, there were frequent normal, legitimate conversions, both of persons from Orthodoxy and of those who had at one time or another left the Church. The executive committee was charged with responsibility in the matter. This step does not prove at all the contention of the Public Prosecutor that the committee was set up to collaborate with the government in *promoting* the conversions. It was set up to *supervise* conversions, examine their validity, and prevent invalid conversions.

---

[7] Document LII.

The greatest insistence was made by the Bishop's conference on the fact that converts would be received only if they so petitioned "without any constraint, completely free, led by an interior conviction of the truth of the Catholic faith, and . . . have entirely fulfilled the ecclesiastical regulations." No greater safeguards against arbitrary conversions could be made. These were laid down formally as conditions *sine qua non* to the reception of converts.

The Archbishop's letter to Pavelić calls attention specifically to the fact that "local authorities are forbidden to interfere in these questions. In the spiritual work of the Church, no lay organization, nor the Ustashi may interfere, for that could only harm the cause of morality."[8] The Archbishop's letter refers specifically to the use of violence by the Ustasha officialdom against the Orthodox. In the hope that Pavelić would rectify the errors committed to date, the Archbishop stated that "we realize that these acts were a political reaction" and that "in the future the activities of these irresponsible elements be eliminated."

The Bishop of Mostar, His Excellency Mons. Aloysius Mišić, is quoted as expressing the view that the interference of the State in matters of conversions through instructions to its officials was not conducive to the best results: "As a matter of fact, according to general indications, these instructions are not of a sort to serve the general welfare of the Church or even that of the State."

Archbishop Stepinac himself was most severe in his comment on the activity of the State in this regard: "Unhappily the authorities by their extreme views are, without perhaps intending to, placing obstacles in the way of the Croatian and Catholic cause."

The Archbishop concludes in this long letter to Pavelić that the policy of conversions has produced these results because they were not entrusted to "the authority to which alone, according to Divine Law and canonical regulations, it ought to have been entrusted; that is to say the Croatian Catholic Bishops who alone are called to give to this work for souls an apostolic character of holiness and charity." The prelate then reviews the numerous errors committed by the meddling of the civil authority in the conversions. The final appeal of the Archbishop to Pavelić was couched in these terms:

---

[8] *Ibid.* Point (*d*) confirming previous letter to the government on July 30, 1941.

No one can deny that these terrible acts of violence and cruelty have been taking place, for you yourself, Poglavnik, have publicly condemned those which the Ustashi have committed. . . .

The Croat nation has been proud of its thousand year old culture and its Christian tradition. That is why we wait for it to show in practice, now that it has achieved its freedom, a greater nobility and humanity than that displayed by its former rulers.

Dr. Katičić in his statement for the defense called attention to the fact that the instructions of the episcopal conference as well as the numerous circular letters of the Zagreb Curia, produced their effect among a great many of the clergy. "Here is the letter of the chief district officer of Požega, Velika Župa Livac Zapolje, in which the clergy was severely attacked for not doing its duty, for showing criminal negligence" in not collaborating more vigorously with the officials in the conversion of the Orthodox.[9] The reply of the Vicar-General, Dr. Salis, is very plain on this matter and reiterates the position taken by the hierarchy in the circular letters:

The Church authorities, on the subject of conversions from the Orthodox and other religions, act according to the laws and rules of the Church. The Church forces no one to embrace the Catholic religion, but when someone comes to the representatives of the Church, they instruct him with the greatest zeal and if he shows that he is embracing the Catholic religion with good intentions, they welcome him.[10]

The Archbishop and the Curia made constant efforts to halt the evil consequence of the persecution and massacres of the innocent. A few examples of this conduct will suffice to show the attitude and reaction of the Archbishop to the hundreds of requests that came to him. On July 20, 1941, to pick a date early in the existence of the violence, several priests petitioned the Archbishop to intervene to stop the deportation of Orthodox inhabitants converted to Catholicism. The memorandum was sent to Pavelić with the Archbishop's recommendation on July 24.[11]

The long statement of Father Augustin Kralj, pastor at Crkveni Bok-Sunja, dated October 16, 1942, related the experiences of a number of deportees and begged that something be done to stop this

---

[9] Document C; and see Document LIII for letter quoted.
[10] *Ibid.* Reply of Vicar-General Salis, Feb. 8, 1942.
[11] Document LIV.

procedure. The Archbishop himself transmitted the report to Pavelić.[12]
The statement of Father Žužek, Pastor of Glina, as to his personal
experiences with the Ustashi terrorists, reveals also the degree to
which the Archbishop was looked upon as the protector of those
who were suffering injustice.[13] The Archbishop intervened again and
again with Pavelić — thus explaining his somewhat frequent contacts
with the head of the State — to the end that relief might be made
available to many of the unfortunates.[14] The Archbishop protested
against violence to Orthodox property and the destruction of their
churches as is shown in the reply of the Ministry of the Interior
under date of February 13, 1942.[15]

Two documents of significance summarize the attitude of the
Archbishop during the period of Ustasha rule. A number of his
associates stated, in connection with the trial, that when under
pressure from the government the problem of conversions came
up "the Archbishop, Dr. Aloysius Stepinac, in reply adopted a
policy regarding reception into the Church in strict accordance
with practices of the Church."[16]

Dr. Katičić analyzes the Archbishop's relations to these events
by showing that in many ways the Metropolitan was the victim of a
series of *faits accomplis*. "The acts of violence and the movement
for rebaptism (as it was mistakenly called) grew like an avalanche.
The people begged ceaselessly to be admitted into the Catholic
Church." At no time was violence exerted by the Archbishop or by
anyone with his consent. No one scrap of proof can be adduced to
indicate even the remotest responsibility of the Archbishop for the
incidents of violence that were terrorizing the land.

Dr. Katičić made a very strong point when he replied to the
Public Prosecutor's argument that the committee appointed by the
episcopal conference in November, 1941, was responsible for the
forced conversions. From the text of the Prosecutor's indictment
it is plain that the designation of the committee of three Bishops
and the executive committee under them was allegedly the instrument

---

12 Document LV.
13 Document LVI.
14 Document LVII.
15 Document LVIII.
16 Document LIX.

for the work of conversion. The Prosecutor presents the argument that instructions were given for the speedy and expeditious conversion of non-Catholics, the presumed direct consequence of the existence of the committee. The counsel for the defense insists that after very considerable examination of the record and the sources, he has come to the conclusion that this committee never did a thing; that it very probably never even met. If the committee did no work, then certainly the Archbishop could scarcely be responsible for acts or incidents supposedly flowing from its activity.

The Archbishop himself stated at his trial that,

> The guilt for the rebaptism of Serbs is ascribed to me. This is a misleading expression, for he who is once baptized, need not be re-baptized. The question concerns change of religions, and of this I shall not speak in detail, except to state that my conscience is clear and that history shall one day render its judgment in this matter.
>
> It is a fact that I had to remove pastors, for they stood in danger of death from the Orthodox. The Serbs wanted to kill these priests because they refused them admission into the Church. It is a fact that during the war the Church had to find its way through countless difficulties. There was a desire to aid as far as it was at all possible the Serbian people.
>
> The honorable judge has produced evidence showing that I sought an abandoned Orthodox monastery (once belonging to our own Pauline Fathers) in Orahovica to lodge Trappists whom the Germans had driven away from Reichburg. It was my duty to aid my brother Slovenes, whom the Hitlerites had banished, to find temporary shelter.[17]

A few additional facts and summary may be presented to support the contention of the Archbishop's innocence in the matter of the forced conversions:

a) Under the pressure of the Croat state policy, masses of Serb-Orthodox in Croatia asked for admission into the Catholic Church. They urged and forced the Catholic priests to receive them. They declared they had a right intention. There is no doubt of the right intention of many who were admitted into the Catholic Church, especially of 200,000 former Catholics, who — for political reasons — passed into the Orthodox Church, and were re-admitted into the Catholic Church.

b) Archbishop Stepinac protested strongly against any meddling of the Pavelić regime in conversions of the Orthodox Serbs.

In point of fact, the Croatian Bishops set up an Ecclesiastical Commission of Bishops and other priests, not to promote "forced conversions," as the communist accusations charged the Archbishop, but on the contrary, to protect the

---

[17] Document D.

freedom from all coercion and to examine if there was right intention on the part of those who were applicants.

c) The Holy See was informed of these conversions. The general Canon Law and the special norms, issued by the Holy See in order to protect the liberty of the Orthodox asking for admission into the Catholic Church, were strictly observed by Church authorities in Croatia.

The Holy Father said before the Sacred Roman Rota that the Croatian Bishops had no part in so-called "forced conversions" of the Orthodox in Croatia. In order to prove the innocence of the Croatian Bishops, and specially of the Archbishop of Zagreb, the Holy Father read to the members of the Rota an official document sent to the Holy See by the Yugoslav Legation (which was accredited to the Holy See) stating that the conduct of the Croatian Bishops has been correct and in accordance with Canon Law concerning the matter of conversion to the Catholic faith.[18]

d) If anything happened contrary to these ecclesiastical laws and orders, it happened without knowledge of the Bishops and against their strict orders. If any priest has made an error in this matter, he was censured or suspended, as announced in the joint Pastoral of the Croatian Bishops on March 24, 1945. When the Yugoslav prosecutor at the trial of the Archbishop produced a "document" allegedly addressed to the Pope, stating that the conversions were justified, the Archbishop denied the authorship of this "document" since it was not signed or sealed. The Secretary of the Vatican State did the same. I have read this "document" in the Yugoslav papers and found it naïve and a malicious falsehood.

e) In his sermon delivered at the cathedral of Zagreb on June 29, 1942, the Archbishop publicly stated that by admitting the Orthodox into the Catholic Church, he was guided only by supernatural motives and by Christian charity to help all who were endangered and asked for protection.

As a result of the Archbishop's interventions, the campaign for conversions of the Orthodox made by the state authorities in Croatia stopped and the Pavelić regime was compelled to recognize an "Independent Orthodox Church in Croatia."

At the end of 1941, a high official of the Serbian government in Belgrade visited Archbishop Stepinac. He expressed gratitude in the name of the Serbs for all efforts of the Archbishop to save the Serbs in Croatia. Had they all embraced the Catholic faith that would not matter, he said.[19]

---

[18] *Osservatore Romano*, Oct. 7–8, 1946.

[19] Statement of Father Stephen Lacković, former secretary to Archbishop Stepinac.

Chapter VI

THE QUESTION OF THE MILITARY VICARIATE

THE indictment as presented by the Public Prosecutor states that "at the beginning of 1942, the Vatican appointed the defendant Stepinac as military apostolic vicar to Pavelić's Ustasha and Croat Home Army. The defendant Stepinac accepted this appointment and designated as his substitutes the well-known Ustasha priest Stipe Vučetić and Vilim Cecelja. So the defendant Stepinac became officially the supreme military chaplain of Pavelić's army and under him were all the military chaplains in the Ustasha and Croat Home Army, who were the instigators of crimes and criminals themselves."

Following on this general accusation is a list of priests who allegedly acted in a criminal fashion as army chaplains. The list includes at the top, the well-known name of Miroslav Filipović (error for Timoslav), late director of the Jasenovac camp and responsible for the mass massacre of February 7, 1942, in the villages of Drakulići, Saragovac, and Motika in which 1300 men, women, and children were killed. Others so listed included Zvonimir Brekalo, Ustasha captain and chaplain of Jasenovac troops, Joseph Vukelić, who is alleged to have participated as chaplain in the numerous burnings in Banija, John Miletić, and others.

There is no doubt that *if* these priests took part as officers in the Croat army in massacres and pillage, if Archbishop Stepinac as Military Vicar had knowledge of these acts and did nothing about them, the accusation would be extremely grave. It was not demonstrated by the Public Prosecutor that the Archbishop was responsible for the conduct of these priests. It is demonstrable that he took action against them in cases when their conduct was such as to merit chastisement.[1]

The collective letter of the hierarchy on March 24, 1945, stated the position clearly:

If any priest, a rare occurrence, has injured others in their rights, we shall not hesitate to impose ecclesiastical sanction against him even to deprive him of his sacerdotal or religious status.[2]

A very vital point in the discussion of the Archbishop as Military Vicar is the fact that he was granted these faculties, but without the title, prior to the outbreak of war between Yugoslavia and the Axis and long before the Pavelić regime came into existence. In fact, he was the Military Vicar for all Catholics in the regular Royal Yugoslav Army and not the Ustasha. This is proved by the communication dated November 20, 1940, regarding the designation.[3]

In his speech of defense, the Archbishop did not deny that he had taken measures for the spiritual care of Croatian soldiers. He said:

When the war between Yugoslavia and Germany neared its end, I extended spiritual aid to the Catholic soldiers of the former Yugoslav army and of the newly created independent State of Croatia. If, therefore, the state had fallen, but the soldiers still remained, I felt obliged to concern myself with this situation.

It is suggested that the above constituted a perfect defense on this count. Whatever might have been the political views of Archbishop Stepinac, he was a shepherd of souls. He was responsible for the spiritual care of men who served in the Croatian forces, whether by enlistment or conscription. He could not let them live and die without the ministrations of the Church. Nor should it be overlooked that his concern for the spiritual welfare of all Yugoslav Catholics during the war extended to those engaged with the Partisans as well. The Archbishop did not take jurisdiction away from the priests Victor Merz and Auguste Stanzer who joined the Partisans. He explicitly gave his permission to Jean Kokot, pastor of Sv. Klara, who asked leave to join the Partisans.[4]

---

[1] Timoslav Filipović was expelled from the Franciscans as indicated and deprived of his sacerdotal functions. Father Brekalo was also removed upon request of the Archbishop to Mons. Cecelja.

[2] Document LXIII.

[3] Document LX.

[4] Document XLVI, Testimony of Dr. Dragutin Hren.

There is no evidence whatsoever to prove that the Archbishop was responsible for the individual acts of violence in which a few priests engaged. The trial was not directed to proving that a given priest at a given moment had committed crimes punishable by law. The trial was that of the Archbishop of Zagreb and the mere listing of names, particularly of priests who were not under the Archbishop's authority or had already been suspended, proves absolutely nothing. The link between the Archbishop and the guilty priest in a particular case was not demonstrated and could not be demonstrated. That the number of priests guilty of these outrages was not large may be seen from the communication of Colonel Vujanić, dated September 18, 1941, in which it is noted that only a small number of the clergy seemed suitable for service as chaplains.[5]

Dr. Katičić pointed out on this point that the Archbishop had practically no powers over chaplains and that the real authority rested directly with the Ministry.

There is therefore no solid or substantial proof that Archbishop Stepinac was guilty of personal responsibility for the excesses of any military chaplain. The proof is overwhelming that he removed those proved unworthy, and condemned action that was not strictly spiritual in character.

---

[5] Document LXI.

Chapter VII

CONSPIRACY AGAINST CONSTITUTED AUTHORITY

THE last charge against the Archbishop embraces a number of aspects. The Public Prosecutor asserted that "just before the collapse of the Independent Croat State, the defendant Stepinac, in agreement with Pavelić and for the purposes of concealment, hid the files of the Ministry of Foreign Affairs and the personal documents of the Poglavnik in the archiepiscopal palace." This charge in and of itself seems trivial enough. The Public Prosecutor links it up with the alleged intent of the Archbishop to collaborate in efforts for the restoration of the former regime and the undermining of the new Partisan administration. The Public Prosecutor marshals his so-called evidence in the following manner:

1. Early in the spring of 1945, the Yugoslav army freed our country of the occupier. Pavelić, Maček, Stepinac and the rest of the anti-national elements foresaw the defeat of the German occupier. They forged plans for the reoccupation of the country by some other foreign power, thus evidencing their willingness to overthrow the people's authority.

2. Archbishop Stepinac collaborated with the representatives of the so-called National Committee of Slovenia, the traitorous organization of Rupnik and Rožman.

3. The Archbishop submitted a memorandum to Pavelić, dated April 21, 1945, suggesting the unification of the military under Mihailović, Pavelić and Rupnik and the formation of a central political body for all Yugoslavia.

4. The defendant Stepinac has attacked the people's authorities and the just sentences of the courts against Ustasha priests and other war criminals.

134

5. He had alleged that this was a persecution of the Church.
6. The defendant Stepinac received in the archiepiscopal palace on September 15, 1945, the Ustasha colonel and former director of Public Order, Eric Lisak and on September 17 and October 3, 1945, received two letters from the Ustasha Colonel, Moškov.
7. The defendant Stepinac received an émigré student and the spy Lela Sofijanec.
8. He approved and concealed the terrorist activity of his secretary, Ivan Šalić.

The refutation of these arguments involves the whole attitude of Archbishop Stepinac toward the Tito regime and his constant effort to arrive at a satisfactory agreement for the welfare of the Church and the Catholic people of Croatia. The evidence is quite clear that the Archbishop was the very opposite of the conspirator, terrorist, and murderer that he was depicted by the Public Prosecutor.

The first point regarding the alleged concealment of the archives of the Croat Foreign Ministry can be answered very briefly. The brochure of the Yugoslav Embassy in Washington on the case of Archbishop Stepinac uses the word *buried* to describe this incident.[1] The facts of the case are these. The documents were preserved in the archiepiscopal palace, not concealed. The arrangement was between Foreign Minister Alajbegović of the Independent Croat State and the Archbishop. The former had requested the prelate to take these historically important documents, most of which had already been published, and keep them in the archiepiscopal palace, since it was considered safer than the ministry office during the fighting between Partisans and Croats. There was the possibility of bombardment and it was deemed safer to have them there. Alajbegović himself, a witness called by the prosecution, testified that there was no agreement at all between Archbishop Stepinac and Pavelić. Within a month after the entrance of the Partisans into Zagreb, and as soon as the Archbishop himself had been released from temporary imprisonment, he informed Dr. Bakarić, the new Partisan head of Croatia of the presence of the documents in the palace. This is attested by the exchange of letters between the Archbishop, under

---

[1] *The Case of Archbishop Stepinac, op. cit.*, p. 81.

date of June 6, 1945, and the Commission for Religious Affairs of the new Croatian Government.[2]

The accusation regarding the participation by Archbishop Stepinac in a plot involving Pavelić, Rupnik, and Bishop Rožman is based on nothing but the assertion. Bishop Rožman himself at a later date declared that he had maintained contact with Archbishop Stepinac, as was quite natural between the Slovene and Croat sees. Dean Skerbec had indeed been sent to Zagreb to establish and maintain this liaison. The interests of the Church in both countries were severely menaced in the closing days of the Ustasha regime. It was inevitable that the religious leaders of the area co-ordinate their activity to some degree. If any sort of plot for the restoration of the old regime were proposed, there is not a shred of proof that Archbishop Stepinac did anything but refuse to countenance it. If he is guilty at all, it is the guilt of passivity, as Dr. Politeo points out. One cannot very well condemn a man because someone proposes something to him and he rejects it. Moreover, the testimony of Dr. Alajbegović was conclusive that Archbishop Stepinac could very easily have exercised supreme authority in Croatia if he had wished since Pavelić urged the regency on him. In short, if the Archbishop were the inveterate plotter depicted by the Prosecution and overwhelmingly desirous of defending the Ustasha state, he had an exceptional opportunity when Pavelić himself suggested he assume the direction of affairs at the time of the collapse. That the Archbishop did not do so and flatly refused to have anything to do with such a scheme is evidence of his point of view and conviction that his place was not in politics. Dr. Politeo insists that three reasons motivated the Archbishop's action on this score:

I. He was convinced that it was not his business to take part in politics.
II. He did not wish to accept anything from Pavelić.
III. The new authority must come from the Croat people and not from Pavelić or the Ustasha.

Dr. Alajbegović explained that the great prestige of the Archbishop and the reason that a regency under his guidance seemed desirable,

---

[2] Document LXII.

was derived from his attitude during the four years of occupation and his well-known hostility to every form of violence or coercion.

It goes without saying that the situation of Croatia was particularly critical in those spring days of 1945 when the Partisans were advancing and the German and Ustasha forces were obliged to abandon the country. The Archbishop was eager to do everything possible to preserve the city from destruction and save Croatian lives. It is true that he visited Dr. Maček at his house. It must be mentioned, however, that Dr. Maček was at the time under house arrest and that it was possible to gain admittance to him only by Ustasha authority. Therefore the Archbishop went with General Moškov, an Ustasha officer. The latter was the only one who had the keys to Maček's house. The Archbishop had denied that he discussed plans for flight, but that he went to obtain the support of Maček on behalf of the population. Obviously, if Archbishop Stepinac had wished to flee he could have done so long before the arrival of the Partisans. The fact that he remained in Zagreb without taking measures of any kind for his own protection or safety would indicate that he was not fearful of the consequences of the "criminal acts" of which the Prosecution constantly speaks.

The Prosecutor presents a picture of the Archbishop during the spring of 1945 as engaged in constant conspiracy and plotting against the inevitable triumph of the peoples' government under the Partisans. The archiepiscopal palace, according to this version, was the center of unceasing cloak and dagger activity. The substance of the accusation on this score consists of these facts:

1. Visit of Eric Lisak, former chief of the Ustasha security police.
2. Visit of Lela Sofijanec.
3. Visit of an émigré Ustasha student from Salzburg.
4. Reception of two letters from Ustasha General Moškov.

This is the sum total of the acts for which the Archbishop is accused of hostility to the people and conspiracy against the new regime after the liberation. The absolute triviality of these charges is demonstrated by the testimony of various witnesses: Bishop Lach, Dr. Franolić, Lisak himself, Dr. Šalić, and the Archbishop. It is true that Archbishop Stepinac received Lisak, but not as such. On September 24, 1945, according to the most complete evidence available, a certain Petrović presented himself at the Archbishop's palace. Between the Archbishop and Dr. Šalić there is a slight difference in the version. According to the former he did not recognize him as Lisak until he had put on his glasses and was in front of him. According to the latter, the Archbishop was told it was Lisak at the moment of entering the study to receive him. Dr. Politeo points out: "The Archbishop had already consented to receive Petrović and had come to the room where Petrović was waiting and, at the last moment, when he reached the door of that room, he learned, according to the testimony of Šalić, that Petrović was not Petrović, but Lisak." The Archbishop was probably startled, but he had promised to see the man and did. The interview lasted a few moments. Both the Archbishop and Lisak are in fundamental agreement in their respective statements on what transpired, which in itself gives considerable credence to the veracity of the testimony. Lisak did all the talking and on his departure, the Archbishop gave instructions that he was not to be admitted again. The facts that are available indicate then that (*a*) Lisak came uninvited, (*b*) that he came under a false name, (*c*) that the Archbishop did not know until the last minute that Petrović was Lisak, and (*d*) that after this brief encounter the Archbishop broke off relations with him and there was no further contact.

The Lisak case is a trivial incident without political significance. Lela Sofijanec and that the Ustasha student from Salzburg represented two of the innumerable visitors to the Archiepiscopal palace. Day after day people came to see the Archbishop, obtain aid from him or pour out their stories. It was impossible for him to recall every individual and much less avoid the reception of persons whose intentions were sometimes political. In the case of the Salzburg refugee, the Archbishop asserted that as soon as this person began to talk politics he insisted that he leave. The incident of the Moškov letters is the same. After all no one has control over what correspondence will be sent him through the mails. The recipient can hardly be held responsible for the content of letters which he did not solicit and which came to him unrequested. These letters were not addressed to the Archbishop but to his secretary, Father Lacković. There is no evidence that the Archbishop ever bothered to read them, and much less that he acted in accordance with any suggestions contained therein.

The Prosecutor's case was based largely on attributing to the Archbishop the actions of others. In the final days of the Independent Croat State its leaders moved heaven and earth to seek protection and save something before the final collapse. That some of them hoped to entice the Archbishop into giving support to schemes directed to that end also admits of no doubt. Letters and visits were easy, but the fact remains that no proof has been advanced to show that in any single case the Archbishop responded to these advances or committed himself. No letter *from* the Archbishop to anyone has been presented to prove this. All the evidence rests on the fragile foundation of casual visitors and unsolicited letters.

Archbishop Stepinac devoted his energies to working out a satisfactory arrangement between the Church and the new government of Yugoslavia, under Marshal Tito. Reference has been made, in the section on the attitude of the Archbishop of Zagreb to the new state, to the visit of the prelate to Marshal Tito and the various contacts with Dr. Bakarić, head of the new Croatian state. The authorities of Partisan Yugoslavia proposed that the Archbishop and clergy visit Marshal Tito on the occasion of his presence in Zagreb. This interview gave rise to an exchange of views between the ecclesiastical authorities and the head of the State. It is significant that Archbishop Stepinac was willing to have this exchange of views occur. If at a later date Tito's Yugoslavia should give way to some anti-communist regime, it is highly probable that Archbishop Stepinac and his associates will be accused of having gone to a meeting with Tito and collaborated with his government. The Archbishop, in line with his often repeated policy, was eager to work out a solution if this could be humanly done with whatever government happened to be in power.[3] It is not without significance that this interview was carried out while Archbishop Stepinac languished in prison. After this encounter, the Archbishop was released. Two days later, on June 4, Archbishop Stepinac met with Marshal Tito.[4]

---

[3] Document LXIV. Note on the meeting of the higher clergy with the Marshal of Yugoslavia, Joseph Broz Tito, on June 2, 1945.

[4] Document LXV.

The Archbishop was outspoken in the discussion on this occasion, emphasizing the position of the Church and his sincere desire for harmonious relations with the State. The development of events in the new Yugoslavia soon proved that the hope which Marshal Tito had given at the meeting early in June was not to be realized. On that occasion he had indicated a willingness to proceed by judicial methods and with the greatest care to avoid punishment of the innocent. On July 21, 1945, Archbishop Stepinac wrote Dr. Vladimir Bakarić, President of the People's Republic of Croatia, regarding the numerous cases of death sentences against priests and nuns either executed or pending. The names of these condemned constitute a tragic balance of persecution and violence. This list included:

Kerubin Šegvić
Sjepan Kramer
Sister Blanda Stipetić
Sister Panika Splajt
Matija Kranjčić, pastor at Ozalj
Rikard Ribić, Franciscan
Beato Bukinac, teacher at Karlovac
Stjepan Pavunić, pastor of Koprivnica
Michael Kanoti, pastor of Varaždin
Josip Kalajdžić, pastor of Biskupec
Peter Kovaćić, pastor of Zagreb
Dr. Guberina, priest of diocese of Šibenik

The Archbishop reproached the President for the manner in which these priests and religious were condemned to death. The absence of an adequate opportunity for defense and the nonpublic character of the trials, most of them military, which had passed the sentences, with an alarming lack of the ordinary precautions for the accused. The Archbishop called attention to the fact that the aged Father Šegvić had been condemned because he had written that the Croats were of Gothic origin. The prelate admitted that such a theory might well be thoroughly unsound but hardly sufficient reason for condemnation to the supreme penalty. The long letter examines in detail the grave defects in the Tito administered justice.[5] The Archbishop's strictures include the concentration camps, the limitations on the Catholic press, and various incidents that had occurred by virtue of the action of the Partisan government. Despite Marshal Tito's

---

[5] Document LXVI.

statements to the clergy regarding the importance of respect for the religious convictions of the people, the Archbishop expressed grave concern regarding the status of religious instruction and its reduction or elimination in the schools. Dr. Bakarić replied on July 26, 1945, recognizing that on some points the Archbishop was correct, on others he believed him to be ill-informed or was in disagreement with his views. The Archbishop insisted just as he did in Ustasha days on the ardent desire of the Church to refrain from any political activity.

The reply of Dr. Bakarić was in the form of a speech to the Sabor[6] in which he took up some of the points raised in the Archbishop's letter and added others, notable among them that Archbishop Stepinac was involved in passing information to the British and was responsible for the organization of enemies of the regime. The tone of this address was a sharp and provocative attack on the Archbishop, the precursor, let it be stated, to more and violent aggression against his person.

On August 11, 1945, the Archbishop again addressed Dr. Bakarić regarding the education problem and religious instructions in the schools. The main points raised by the prelate were:[7]

1. That in state schools religious instruction be given two hours a week.
2. Students regularly enrolled in these courses be subject to the normal control of all registered students.
3. In the curriculum, the same place be given to religion as had always been accorded it.
4. The students in the religious courses be allowed to perform their religious duties.
5. That Catholic high schools be allowed as up to the present time.
6. That ecclesiastical seminaries be allowed to function.

On August 17, 1945, the Archbishop addressed a long memorandum to Marshal Tito, Dr. Bakarić, and the Commission for Religious Affairs in which he took up certain of the problems outstanding between the Church and the government.

Much has been said in the attacks on Archbishop Stepinac that

---

[6] Sabor (Croatian for assembly or congress).
[7] Document LXVII.

he was the enemy of the proposed agrarian reform and consequently the ally of "reaction." This document explains in part his position on this extremely important question. Marshal Tito had promised during his visit to Zagreb in June that all matters likely to produce disagreement between the State and the Church would be worked out amicably. "I expressed my hope, based on the promise of the President of the Federal Government, Marshal of Yugoslavia Josip Broz, made to the representatives of the Zagreb clergy and to me personally, that all questions touching on the relations between Church and State would be worked out by agreement and that, in the question of agrarian reform, the Church would be given a chance to examine the proposed law. Had this been done, it would have been possible to come to an agreement with the Church and draft a statute more just and complete than that now presented to the Provisional Popular Assembly."[8]

This statement indicates clearly that Archbishop Stepinac was concerned with full Church participation in the study of the question, a logical position, since Church lands and properties were involved. He does not on this occasion or on any other decry the need for agrarian reform; he merely urges that an arrangement be made whereby the Church shall take part in the discussions and a better and more complete piece of legislation be presented to the assembly. This is far from out and out opposition to agrarian reform *per se*. The Archbishop explains in detail the effect on the Church of the reform. He points out in detail the status of the Church regarding property and especially large property holdings. The patent injustice of many of the provisions of the proposed law may be seen in the fact that "the agrarian reform passed in Poland and Hungary, occupied at the time by Soviet troops, left to the Catholic Church far more land for the support of its priests and religious and ecclesiastical institutions than is proposed here at home. Is it not proper to conclude that in Yugoslavia the new agrarian reform seeks to strike a blow against the Church and make it impossible for it to carry on its normal activity?"

The point against which the Archbishop protests is that Marshal Tito had promised to work out an agreement and that "unilateral

---

[8] Document LXVIII.

agrarian reform conceived in a spirit hostile to the Church, such as is now before the Provisional Popular Assembly, would, in the event of approval, be a new proof that in this nation the Catholic Church, despite all the assurances of religious freedom and respect for private property, has been deprived of all its rights." In a further letter to Marshal Tito and an address to the President of the Provisional Popular Assembly at Belgrade, the Archbishop elaborates and reiterates his position on the agrarian reform.[9]

The Archbishop was given no information by the government nor even kept *au courant* of what was proposed in the new law. He expresses his concern several times that his source of information was the daily press. In view of the fact that the law as it was then conceived would destroy Church property and make impossible the sustenance of numerous communities, and even dioceses, the Archbishop continued his efforts to place the question on the plane to which Marshal Tito had consented in June, 1945. Hence the telegram of August 21, 1945.

Marshal Tito's reply of September 1, 1945, typifies the communist approach to the problem. The deputies in the Provisional Popular Assembly were not responsible for the inclusion of church lands in the law. It was "the result of the state of mind of the peasant masses." Marshal Tito complained that he had not received the results of the episcopal conference and hence was deprived of certain directives that would make possible an understanding with the Church. On September 13, 1945, the Archbishop addressed another long letter to the Marshal setting forth the position of the church on the agrarian reform. "I consider it my duty . . . to request a revision of the agrarian reform law. The Catholic Church cannot recognize as just the outright confiscation without indemnity of the properties it has legally acquired. The Church cannot accept the minimum amounts of its possessions left to it, for this minimum is far from enough to satisfy the just and proven needs of its priests, religious and institutions."

The episcopal conference, held September 17 to 22, 1945, transmitted an address to Marshal Tito in which are listed the various forms of religious persecution then transpiring.

---

[9] *Ibid.*

The letter to Marshal Tito, with the same essential points contained in the Pastoral Letter of September 21, was dated the 22nd.[10] This was unquestionably the turning point in Church-State relations in Yugoslavia. The pastoral of September 21, 1945, was seized upon as the expression of hostility to the new state and received by the government very much as a declaration of war.[11] The ecclesiastical authorities took advantage of the invitation of the government to private citizens and institutions, to express its views on the proposed constitution. Three basic problems merited attention in this petition:

I. The separation of Church and State.

II. Obligatory civil marriage.

III. Separation of schools from the Church.

The statement analyzes the problem of Church and State and applies the general principles of the Catholic Church to the particular reality of Yugoslavia. The position of the hierarchy on the three points under discussion is stated fully in the text as reproduced in the appropriate Document in the Appendix.

On November 24, 1945, the Archbishop protested most strongly to Marshal Tito for the appraisal he had made of the status of State-Church relations.

By this time it was clear that the drive for the communization of Yugoslavia was so strong that there was neither the intention to reach, nor interest in reaching, a peaceful agreement with the ecclesiastical authorities. The position of both sides was drawn. Archbishop Stepinac had appealed again and again to the early statements of Marshal Tito regarding the possibility of arriving at a satisfactory understanding. The measures of an anti-Church and anti-Catholic nature now being put into effect made it increasingly difficult to maintain the dialogue between the two parties in conflict. It was inevitable and entirely foreseeable that the new regime would ultimately feel that so powerful a figure as the Archbishop of Zagreb must be eliminated. It was equally clear that the Archbishop, who had stood firmly against Ustasha and Nazi pressure, could not and would not recede from the position of principle to which he clung with courageous and unfailing devotion.

---

10 Document LXIX.
11 Document LXX full text of Pastoral Letter.

Chapter VIII

THE PERSECUTION OF THE CHURCH IN YUGOSLAVIA

THE systematic persecution of religion in Yugoslavia has not ceased since the trial and conviction of the Archbishop of Zagreb in 1946. The idea that action against the Catholic Church was the result of politics and aimed at restraining the ecclesiastical authority from intervention in the political life of the nation, is demonstrated as false in the light of the tragic and uninterrupted continuation of the most violent persecution against the Church as an institution, its clergy and hierarchy, and everything that smacks of the spiritual or supernatural.

In the communication of the Holy See to the Yugoslav government, under date of December 15, 1952, a detailed analysis was made of the more recent evidences of antireligious activity on the part of the Yugoslav government and the communist party of the various federal republics. In Slovenia and Croatia, where Catholics constitute an overwhelming majority, the controlled press has been singularly virulent in its denunciation of all forms of religious manifestation. On February 9, 1952, *Slovenski Poročevalec* of Ljubljana published a circular addressed to the various sections of the Slovene communist party in which it was stated: "During the school year, everything must be done to make the children understand, on the basis of scientific reason, the negative and reactionary influence of religion and obscurantism." This circular bore the signature of Edvard Kardelj, Vice-President of the Council of State and Minister of Foreign Affairs of Yugoslavia. *Borba*, Yugoslavia's leading newspaper, reported on November 7, 1952, a speech delivered by Aleksander Ranković, Minister of the Interior, who declared before the sixth congress of the Yugoslav communist party the necessity of carrying on the struggle against "bourgeois, clerical and cominformist ideas." *Vjesnik* of Zagreb (November 9, 1952), contained an article by Marko Kostrenčić: "The morality of Christ must be rejected because it is unworthy and condemns man to a vegetative existence. Christian morality is a stimulus to the commission of the most spectacular crimes."

Nova Makedonija of Skoplje (March 2, 1952) asserted that "Our party has never been indifferent to the religious question and the Church. Today it is necessary to organize a systematic ideological war . . . to destroy all religious convictions, all prejudices and all spiritual traditions." *Borba,* under date of March 1, 1952, reports that the central committee of the Macedonian communist party approved a resolution calling for increased activity among the workers to "liberate them from the influence of religion and mysticism." *Oslobodjenje* of Sarajevo (September 13, 1952) informed its readers that at the meetings of the local communist party in Foča and Kiseljak, attention had been called to the fact that a number of party members still believed that they could attend religious services because it is permitted under the constitution. "They fail to understand that party members should be the torchbearers of progress and the first in the struggle against superstition, backwardness, and the remnants of reaction." Marshal Tito, in an address reported in *Borba* for April 30, 1952, stated: "I know that abroad we are reproached for separating our young people from god (*sic*) and the church. But we cannot allow that people practice superstition. We must carry on unceasingly the struggle against it."

At the time that the Tito regime came into power in Yugoslavia there were 152 Catholic papers — newspapers, reviews, parish bulletins, and the like. There were over twenty important Catholic publishing houses. Almost all this publishing activity has now ceased. For some time the only publications to survive were *Verski List* of Maribor, *Oznanilo* in Ljubljana, and *Gore Srca* in Zagreb. All three have since disappeared. The Catholic press is represented today by *Vjesnik,* a monthly bulletin for the clergy, published at Djakovo, and *Blagovest,* a monthly review published in Belgrade and which is faced by constant difficulties. More recently a small monthly sheet

called *Družina* has appeared at Nova Gorica under the auspices of
the apostolic administrator. None of these journals is free to refute
any of the calumnies against the Church, the clergy, or the Bishops.
Any effort to demonstrate the falsity of the government's charges
would bring about instant suspension. The publication of religious
books of any kind is practically impossible because of the innumerable ways, aside from direct confiscation, which the state employs
to obstruct it.

All Catholic schools have been closed. In the State schools, which
now enjoy a monopoly, there is no religious instruction of any kind
and materialistic atheism is obligatory. *Vjesnik* of Zagreb (February
22, 1952) reported that numerous students had been expelled from
institutions because of "religious offenses," that is, because they were
absent from classes on Christmas day. Thirty-two students were
expelled in Maribor during the early part of 1952 because they still
went to church.

The persecution of the clergy goes on unceasingly. Arrests take
place constantly. The clergy has been reduced to the most abject
poverty. The application of the agrarian reform in the case of
religious communities has been extremely rigorous, going far beyond
the actual letter of the law in many cases. The cases of individual
persecution are so numerous as to defy recounting in these pages.
There was the case of Father Čekada, from Zenica, who was sentenced
to six years of forced labor. This courageous priest had saved some 120
Greek Orthodox civilians from death and concentration camps. Despite
this heroic record on behalf of the Serbs, Father Čekada was condemned because, it was argued, "unless he had been friendly to
the German occupier he would have been unable to save any of
these people and is therefore to be sent to prison as a collaborationist." Titoist concentration camps are filled with priests and religious. Many of them in the Catholic areas are in the Stara Gradiška
camp in Croatia. A former inmate of this camp, a Croatian priest
who managed to escape in 1947, has described the life there for the
members of the clergy (published in *Hrvastski Dom,* Brussels,
May, 1947):

In the concentration camp at Stara Gradiška there are approximately eighty
priests and they are obliged to perform the foulest of tasks. They are responsible

for cleaning the latrines and must do so with their hands. Every day they appear before the director of the camp to receive instructions for the day and this is an occasion to insult them. The commander of the work battalion forces the priests to use a daily password as they move about and this is invariably a blasphemy of some sort. The priests refuse to make use of the expression and are severely punished for insubordination. One form of punishment is to inscribe communist slogans on the walls.

The idea that all of this terminated with the Cominform-Tito split is inaccurate. The religious persecution has not ended and there is no indication that it will end as long as the present regime remains in power. The tragedy is that with the support of the West Tito is able to present himself to his own people in the guise of one whose power and influence are so great that he can resist the enormous pressure of the Soviet Union and at the same time receive favors from the West, which is obliged thus to pay homage to his strength.

Only a few cases will suffice to demonstrate how the persecution continues to operate. The Apostolic Administrator of the Banja Luka diocese, Dr. Smiljan Čekada, was advised in March, 1951, that the "people's authority" of Bosnia and Hercegovina instructed him to leave the territory of the republic within twenty-four hours. He had been Bishop of Skoplje and had been ousted from this post. The former Bishop of Banja Luka, Dr. Josip Garič, died in exile, expelled likewise by the Tito government. The case of the Bishop of Mostar, Dr. Peter Čule, is particularly tragic. He was condemned to eleven years imprisonment and, until recently, was lodged in the prison at Zenica, where he was treated exactly as a common criminal. The communists undertook to "re-educate" him by forcing him to learn the trade of carpenter. In May, 1951, he was transferred, with a large number of others, to the prison of Sremska Mitrovica. On May 27, at the Slavkovci station near Vinkovci, the train on which he was being transported was wrecked and Bishop Čule was badly hurt. It is noteworthy that an Orthodox Bishop, Dr. Nastić, was gravely injured. The presence of Catholic and Orthodox clergy and prelates in the same prisoner train demonstrates that the persecution is by no means limited to Roman Catholics but extends to Orthodox as well.

In June, 1951, a trial was staged in which sixteen seminary students and their professor were charged with "illegal terrorist organization in the Kaptol seminary." On the flimsiest of evidence, the students were condemned to prison terms running as high as thirteen years. The temporary administrator of the diocese of Zagreb, Dr. Salis Sevis, was accused of gross negligence for allowing this sort of "anti-state activity" in his seminaries. In the Maribor district of Slovenia, the confirmation trip of Bishop Držečnik, in the spring of 1952, was marred by the fact that the government accused the prelate of "provoking hostile demonstrations" and arrested numerous persons involved in processions. The Bishop's identity card was taken from him and he was unable to continue his travels. The Premier of Slovenia attacked the Church on this occasion and reiterated the usual accusation that it was responsible for "clerical reaction." The Minister of the Interior of Slovenia, Boris Kraijger, stated in public that "There is no retreat for us in spite of the ardent wishes of the Soviet Union and the Vatican, the policy of both being identical toward the new Yugoslavia."

The campaign against vocations has reached astonishing heights. Parents of seminarians are the victims of every conceivable pressure, especially the increase of taxation, which is particularly harsh on peasant families. In Yugoslavia today, the crisis is acute because of the absence of clergy. In the entire country there are seventeen Catholic dioceses. Only six Bishops are actually engaged more or less normally in the discharge of their duties (Senj, Split, Hvar, Krk, Dubrovnik and Subotica). The Bishop of Mostar is in prison and the Archbishop of Sarajevo is living in exile abroad.

In four dioceses, temporary apostolic administrators are in charge (Djakovo, Banja Luka, Rijeka and Poreč-Pulj). In the Zagreb arch-diocese the number of priests has decreased by 241 and over 70 parishes have no priest at all. Thirteen monasteries and eighty-nine convents have been closed. In the Mostar diocese, ten priests and ninety-four religious disappeared and of the Franciscan community of forty-two, only six remain. The diocese of Split lost seventy-seven priests and Dubrovnik fifty-three. A very large percentage of the Catholic clergy in Yugoslavia, both secular and regular, has been eliminated either through imprisonment, death, or exile.

In Slovenia, Bosnia, and Hercegovina women's religious communities have been dissolved. Catholic organizations of all kinds, for whatever purpose they may exist, have virtually disappeared from Yugoslavia. Church buildings have been turned to other uses as is the case of the ancient church of the Teutonic Order in Ljubljana, which has been given over to the Old Catholics, a sect that has almost no following in the locality. The Church of The Most Holy Redeemer in Rijeka has been destroyed; the Church of Our Lady of Ptujiska Gora has been converted into a museum against the protest of the ecclesiastical authorities. Permission is never given for construction of new churches and very rarely for necessary repairs of those existing. The circular of January 31, 1952, in Croatia not only forbade all religious instruction in schools but made it impossible to bring children together for the catechism even in parishes or in private homes. In Bosnia and Hercegovina, all religious instruction is forbidden under the fallacious pretext that the Church and State are separate and that everything worth teaching is already contained in the regular school programs. The faithful are constantly victims of persecution if they frequent the Sacraments. *Ljudska pravica* of Ljubljana (September 13, 1952) threatened a midwife with dismissal from the public health service for suggesting to a patient that her child be baptized. Father Peter Berissa, parish priest of Djakovica, was condemned to thirty months' imprisonment on October 24, 1952, for attempting to regularize a marriage in his parish of a couple who had not been married in the church.

Reports reaching the West are sufficiently frequent to indicate that the religious persecution goes on despite the increasingly close relations between Tito's regime, the western European states, and the United States. The New York *Times* (October 9, 1952) published a long report under the title "Yugoslavs renew Church struggle." The cause for the renewal of the persecution was the decision of the Bishops' conference of September 23–26, 1952, in which the Yugoslav hierarchy had protested against the fictitious "priests associations" that the Tito government was encouraging. The government used every form of propaganda to counteract the statement of the Bishops against the state sponsored ecclesiastical organization. The most extraordinary thing was that the major argument of the Yugoslav state was that any impediment placed against priest participation in this association constituted a denial of the freedom of association and was a violation of the Bill of Human Rights of the United Nations.

At the Bishops' meeting, to which reference has just been made, the Hierarchy addressed a collective letter to Marshal Tito in which it reiterated the intense dissatisfaction of the ecclesiastical authorities with the state of affairs prevailing in the country. This document forms an excellent summary of the basic charges which can be leveled against the Yugoslav regime and its policy of religious persecution.

On November 1, 1952 the Yugoslav government addressed a communication to the Holy See protesting against the decision of the Bishops to forbid membership of the clergy in the state supported clerical associations. On December 3, 1952, the name of the Most Reverend Aloysius Stepinac, Archbishop of Zagreb, was among those designated for elevation to the College of Cardinals. On December 15, the Holy See replied to the Yugoslav note, with a full statement of the disabilities under which the Church was operating.[1]

This note was returned unopened. On December 17, 1952, diplomatic relations were broken between Yugoslavia and the Holy See.

Early in January, 1953, Marshal Tito received seven members of the Bishops' conference to discuss the basis of a Church-State agreement. It has long been Tito's thesis that the only difficulty in the way of an agreement was the interference of a Vatican, dominated by the Italian enemies of Yugoslavia. Once this impediment were removed, there would be no major obstacle in settling all outstanding points at issue. The official Yugoslav attitude was expressed by Marshal Tito in a speech at Smederevska Palanka on December 16, 1952:

The Vatican is pursuing an Imperialist policy. The Vatican and Italian policies complement one another. The Italian government is contributing to Vatican domination by spreading reaction in the world, while the Vatican helps the Italian Imperialist aspirations toward Yugoslavia and others.

---

[1] *Osservatore Romano,* Jan. 14, 1953, for the full text in French and Italian of the notes exchanged.

The Vatican has insulted Yugoslavia by appointing the war criminal Stepinac as Cardinal and wishes to present him with the Cardinal's hat. The man is a political bishop. He served in the arrangement between Alexander Karageorgevic and the Vatican on the occasion of the Concordat agreement and became a Bishop overnight. He did not become a bishop because of his holiness or great services: it was a matter of politics at that time, as it is today. However, they will not see Stepinac installed in Zagreb.[2]

---

[2] See Michael Derrick, *Tito and the Catholic Church* (London, 1953), p. 16, in which this and other texts are reproduced.

Part II :: DOCUMENTS

INTRODUCTION TO DOCUMENTS

T
HE documents and *pièces justificatives* presented here represent a variety of sources testifying to the conduct and attitude of Archbishop Aloysius Stepinac during the critical years of the Independent Croat State, the occupation, and final communist control. In their presentation little attempt has been made to embellish, polish, or otherwise transform them into more attractive literary pieces.

It is important to understand that these documents do not fully illustrate the whole situation in Croatia during the period covered. They picture rather shortcomings and negative aspects of conditions prevailing in the Croat Independent State. This results from the very nature of these particular documents, the purpose of which is to prove that Cardinal Stepinac is innocent of the crimes for which the Communist controlled court condemned him as a war criminal and Nazi collaborator. The archives of the Croat State, were they available now, would undoubtedly show that there were also positive and beneficial results for the Croat people.

Many items in Dr. Politeo's defense of Cardinal Stepinac are to be understood as dictated by a desire to placate the Communist authorities. His unfavorable references to Bishop Šimrak, for instance, are entirely biased. Bishop Šimrak was a devout son of the Catholic Church, a renowned Croat patriot, and an outstanding member of the Catholic hierarchy in Croatia. Dr. Politeo himself was imprisoned by the Communists after the imprisonment of Cardinal Stepinac, despite the fact that he placed a good deal of blame on the authorities of the Croat State as a means of creating a measure of favor for his client in the communist court.

A word is in place here also regarding the two priests who took part in the trial of Archbishop Stepinac — Father Modestus Martinčić,

Franciscan provincial from Zagreb, and Father Ivan Šalić, the Archbishop's secretary. Both priests made accusations against the Archbishop and talked about crimes which Archbishop Stepinac had never committed. Before the trial both priests had been subjected to rigorous treatment in jail. Like Cardinal Mindszenty, their physical and mental condition were such that they repeated about what their torturers wanted them to say. Father Martinčić and Father Šalić, both prominent and devout priests, were so weak and broken in court that their closest friends could hardly recognize them. Hence, no credence can be given to their testimony against the Archbishop.

The "logic" of the order of presentation of the documents is the "logic" of the indictment against the Archbishop. No really satisfactory arrangement of such a heterogeneous collection of sources is possible — if ordered chronologically, or by subject matter, reference to them as each item of the indictment is considered poses something of a problem. It has seemed preferable to marshal this array of "witnesses" exactly as the prosecutor deployed his forces in challenging the prelate's integrity and loyalty. As each item in the accusation is considered, the appropriate materials throwing light on that particular point are brought forward. To simplify somewhat this bewildering jungle of pastorals, circular letters, sermons, correspondence, and petitions, the following broad divisions are suggested:

Organization of Documents

  I. The Trial
    A. Indictment
    B. Address of Politeo
    C. Address of Katičić
    D. Statement of Archbishop Stepinac
  II. Collaboration With the Independent Croat State; the Germans and Italians. The Clergy in Politics. I–XLIX
  III. The "Forced Conversions." L–LIX
  IV. The Military Vicariate. LX–LXIII
  V. Conspiracy Against the New Authority and Relations With It. LXIV–LXXIII

I. THE TRIAL

DOCUMENT A

PUBLIC PROSECUTOR OF THE POPULAR CROAT REPUBLIC
ZAGREB, September 23, 1946

To the Supreme Court of the Popular Croat Republic
On the basis of Article 13, paragraph 2 of the *Law on Criminal Activities against the People and the State,*

I submit

THE INDICTMENT

against:

Dr. Aloysius Stepinac, born on May 8, 1898, in Krašić of the late Joseph Stepinac and Barbara Penić, a Croat citizen, Archbishop of Zagreb and President of the Episcopal Conferences, at present under arrest.

The German and Italian imperialists, in their plans for world power and the enslavement of other peoples, began long before 1941 to prepare the occupation of Yugoslavia along with the other European countries through the exploitation of the national and religious antagonisms which have existed among the peoples of Yugoslavia. The old Yugoslav governing cliques by their policy instigated the continuation of those antagonisms. The fascist exploitation of such animosities in various parts of Europe consisted in the discovery of Quisling leaders, the erection of a puppet government, the economic and political subjugation of the nation, and finally its emergence as a "free," "independent," and "allied" country within the framework of the new European order.

Thus it was that the Germans and Italians, long before the actual occupation, incited the Croats against the Serbs and vice versa, organized a Fifth Column, weakened the power of resistance of the nation, and encouraged their agent Pavelić and a small number of Ustasha bands, who, having emigrated abroad, had been maintained and trained for years for sabotage against Yugoslavia. Once the aggression was unleashed, they were introduced into the country where they formed the nucleus of the Ustasha terrorist occupation force. With the pretense of carrying out the age-old longing of the Croat people for independence, the occupier dismembered Yugoslavia and created the so-called independent Croat state, which was neither independent nor free nor in the least the Croat people's state, but the most infamous Quisling fabrication. Its administrative machinery was placed under the direction of the Fascist agent, the sanguinary Pavelić, a most repugnant specimen of terrorism and an agent of the Gestapo.

The occupier could not hope, with the aid of the few Ustasha imported from abroad and the small number of their sympathizers in Croatia, to carry out the plan of subjugation and organize the military and administrative machinery to enslave the Croat people, incorporate them into the war program, and render all resistance impossible. Certain antinational groups among the Croat Peasants Party (HSS) under Maček and pro-Ustasha clergy under Stepinac have made common cause with the occupier. Caring only for their own interests, devoted to their narrow cliquish aims, partisans of every antinational combination or regime, aloof and hostile toward the interests and destiny of the whole nation, they have become willing collaborators. Thus it was that Maček, in agreement with Gestapo agent Wesemayer and "Field Marshal" Slavko Kvaternik, under date of April 10, 1941, called on the Croat people to obey and collaborate loyally with the occupier. The following appeal was issued in this sense:

Croat people! Colonel Slavko Kvaternik, the leader of the nationalist movement in the country, proclaimed today a free and independent Croat state, to include the historic and ethnographic territory of Croatia, and assumed authority over this state. I appeal to the Croat people to obey the new government and call upon all members of the Croat Peasants Party in the administration as well as district councilors and municipal officials to collaborate loyally with the new government.

At the same time Maček put the administrative machinery of Croatia at the disposal of the occupier and Pavelić. In addition, Maček made available to the new state his semimilitary organization, called the *Gradjanska i seljačka zaštita* (Civil and Peasant Protection). The accused Stepinac paid a visit to "Field Marshal" Slavko Kvaternik on April 12, 1941, and on the 16th of that month to Pavelić. On April 28, 1941, the following official circular letter was issued to the clergy of the Archdiocese of Zagreb, containing among others the following passages:

Venerable Brethren! There is no one among you who has not been a witness to the momentous events in the life of the Croat nation, in which we are all laboring as messengers of Christ's Gospel. These events have culminated for our people in an ideal which they have long cherished and desired.

A little further it is stated:

Answer therefore promptly this appeal of mine for the noble work of conserving and advancing the independent Croat state.

And still further:

Prove yourselves, Venerable Brethren, now and fulfill your duty toward the young Croat state.

On June 26, 1941, the defendant Stepinac led the Catholic hierarchy in an audience with Pavelić and in his speech of greeting offered the sincere and loyal collaboration to the state, in his own name and that of his clergy. That help and collaboration developed and assumed different forms during the war and the liberation campaign in this country, according to instructions from the Vatican. There is one central line, however, that is constant and persistent. It is the opposition to the campaign for the liberation of our nation and once this liberation is achieved it incites co-operation with the "Crusader" terrorist bands in the country in their crimes against the life, property, security, and freedom of our people.

After the German and Italian occupiers plundered and dismembered Yugoslavia and in Croatia, Bosnia, and Hercegovina the Ustasha initiated mass massacres, the peoples of Yugoslavia, among them the Croats, reacted in a military uprising for their freedom, independence, and existence. The leadership of this national resistance reacted against the religious and national hatreds that divided the country. The liberation policy carried with it that of the national equality of all sectors of Yugoslavia and its mission was defined as the single and supreme one of the struggle against the occupier under the banner of fraternity and unity. For four years this struggle was carried on in a superhuman battle against the occupiers and their domestic accomplices. As the national resistance became stronger and its success closer with the victory of the peoples of Yugoslavia, the traitorous and Quisling elements collaborated more closely, both in Yugoslavia and the Croat state, for the purpose of stamping out the foci of resistance and supporting the occupier. The defendant Stepinac with a considerable portion of his Catholic clergy helped the occupier, deeming the opportunity particularly propitious for the enrichment of the Church, and the increase of influence of the higher clergy in the affairs of the NDH [Independent Croat State]. The defendant Stepinac worked consistently against the interests and efforts of the people, who had arisen to expel the occupier and domestic traitors from the country and insure a better and happier future. The defendant Stepinac increased his collaboration with the Ustasha government after the Pope received Pavelić in audience, and sent him his special blessing. This collaboration increased after the Vatican Secretary of State Maglione stated that the "Ustasha successes in Bosnia had been well received in Roman circles." The Secretary of State urged Stepinac to assume a more loyal attitude toward the Ustasha authorities. After the entry of German troops into Zagreb, Stepinac led the Catholic episcopate in an audience to the bloody Pavelić, offering him his sincere and loyal collaboration. He personally accepted the post of apostolic military vicar in the Pavelić army, appointing as his subordinates known Ustasha priests who in turn designated the army chaplains. His attitude was such that many priests engaged in Ustasha terrorist activities as organizers and participants in the Ustasha crimes against our people. The period of the infamous Pavelić terrorism against the Serbs in Bosnia, Croatia, and Hercegovina, the end of which was to destroy the spirit and soul of the resistance, was seized upon by the defendant Stepinac as an excellent opportunity for the forced conversions. The purpose of these conversions was to strengthen popish interests in the Balkans, and extend the influence of Italian imperialism. He must have known that the forced conversions of Serbs was made possible only by the strongest of Ustasha methods. He was responsible for circular letters and other communications to his clergy — against the protest of some of them — approving the conversions in spite of the fact that the policy is contrary to canon law and all moral and ethical principles. The forced conversions represent a form of approval of the Ustasha crimes in Bosnia, Hercegovina, and Croatia against the Serbs. Frequently these instructions were the basis for making the mass conversions nothing but massacres, at the instigation of Ustasha priests and Ustasha murderers. The defendant Stepinac, through explicit approval and general attitude, toward the various clerico-fascist organizations, such as the "Great Crusader Brotherhood" and the "Great Crusader Sisterhood," encouraged their members to seek positions in the Quisling Croat state. In like manner he was responsible for the attitude of the Catholic press, encouraging praise of Hitler, camouflaging the occupation of our country, and glorifying the sanguinary Pavelić and Ustasha as Croat patriots and liberators. He depicted the NDH as the authentic expression of the Croat people and incited this people to religious and racial hatred as well as maligning and defaming the campaign of the people of Yugoslavia toward liberation with the most repugnant lies and calumnies.

The defendant Stepinac realizes that this conduct is possible only in such a state as the so-called independent Croatia. Therefore, he defended this state right up to the moment of its collapse and the defeat of the German fascists. At the moment of the liberation of our country, Stepinac, under the cloak of religious and ecclesiastical activity, and of Croat patriotism, encouraged the defeated Ustasha leaders, then in hiding, to avoid answering for their crimes before the national authorities. Prior to the liberation, Pavelić, Maček, and Stepinac explored the possibility that after the liberation, the NDH might be restored through the intervention of foreign imperialist interests. They were encouraged in this hope by the propaganda of the international reactionaries, the repercussions of which were favored all over the country by Stepinac and the organized activity of Šalić and collaborators. Stepinac has directly encouraged organizations many of whose members are now before the tribunals. These organizations have in turn helped the so-called crusader groups which up to now committed many crimes and atrocities against our citizens. All of this is part of the plot to restore the old regime with the assistance of the new imperialist masters.

The Yugoslav peoples defeated the occupier, destroyed the Quisling states, Nedić's Serbia and Pavelić's Croatia, restored the truly democratic popular regime and created a common state of equal nations, the Federal Popular Republic of Yugoslavia. The defendant Stepinac played an active part in achieving the ends of international reaction against the people, the government, and democratic institutions, with no consideration for the interests of the nation, the will of its citizens, the true freedom of religion and the Church. In doing this he abused his position as the highest Catholic functionary in Yugoslavia. All of these efforts have been vain because they were smashed against the invincible will of our peoples who are now engaged in the reconstruction of their national state and are defending democratic institutions through the Federal Popular Republic of Yugoslavia.

With these ideas in mind, I accuse Dr. Aloysius Stepinac of the following criminal acts:

I. During the war and enemy occupation, he collaborated with this enemy politically, extending aid to the occupiers and their Ustasha agent.

a) On April 12, 1941, while the battle was still raging against the German and Italian invaders, the Croat Metropolitan visited "Field Marshal" Slavko Kvaternik to congratulate him on the creation of the Independent Croat State. On April 16 he paid an official visit to the sanguinary Pavelić. During the very first days of the occupation he offered supper at the Archbishop's residence to a group of Ustasha émigrés and was photographed with them. On April 28 he issued a circular letter to the clergy of the Zagreb archdiocese in which he appeals for collaboration and urges the faithful to give all support to the NDH. On June 26, 1941, as chairman of the episcopal conferences, and during one of these gatherings to study the best method of collaboration with the Ustasha authorities, he led the hierarchy in special audience before Pavelić and on this occasion greeted the fascist agent as the head of the state and promised him sincere and loyal collaboration.

Thus the defendant, even during the first days of the occupation, helped the occupier and the Ustasha, undertook to collaborate with them and called on the clergy for such collaboration, an attitude which hundreds of the priests actively assumed. He was responsible for thus misleading many priests and faithful into treason against their country and the commission of war crimes. This collaborationist attitude, activity, and open statements of the defendant Stepinac confirmed the Ustasha priests in their treason and incited to action many others who were unfriendly to the people. Priests were urged to take part in disarming the Yugoslav army, to accept responsibility for assisting in the organization of the Ustasha authority and co-operating with the various Ustasha military organizations and militia. The following priests are known to have collaborated in this fashion:

Father Vilim Cecelja in Vrapče
Friar Didak Corić in Jaska
Father Vilim Nikšić in Ogulin
Father Dragutin Marjanović in Slav Brod
Father Martin Gecina in Rečica
Father Mate Moguš in Udbina
Father Antun Djurić in Dvorna Uni
Father Josip Astaloš in Dalj
Friar Petar Berković in Drniš
Friar Ivan Hrstić in Sinj
Friar Stanko Milanović in Imotski
Father Tomas in Capljina
Father Vrdoljak in Capljina
Friar Srećko Perić in Livno
Father Božo Bralo in Sarajevo

Friar Radoslav Glavaš and other Franciscans in Široki Brijeg
Friar Velimir Šimić in Kotar
Friar Karlo Grbavac in Duvno district
Friar Mijo Čuić
Father Ante Klaić in Bos Šamac district
Friar Emanuel Rajić in Gornji Vakuf district
Father Ivan Miletić in Višegrad
Father Dragutin Kamber in Doboj district
Father Županjčić in Bos Gradiška
and many other priests.

b) The Catholic press during the occupation was completely dominated by the thought and orientation of the defendant Stepinac, who, as president of the episcopal conference and as president of *Catholic Action,* had supreme control over everything printed in the entire Catholic press of Yugoslavia. In this capacity he influenced the expression of the press and supported wholeheartedly its antinational attitude.

The Catholic press, even before the war, engaged in propaganda for Fascism and other antinational causes. From the beginning to the end of the occupation this press was directed to the single end of propaganda for Fascism and Ustashism, the glorifying of Hitler and Pavelić, and the praise of the NDH as the Croat state. This press was distinguished by lies and calumnies against the National Resistance Movement and engaged in inciting national, religious, and racial hatred. The extent of this press campaign may be judged even in the publications devoted to children and the young people, such as *Andjeo Čuvar, Glasnik sv. Josipa, Crnče, Glasnik sv. Ante, Vrtić,* and others, which included pictures of Pavelić, eulogizing him and his Ustasha as God's missionaries and the agents of divine justice and providence. In this way the children's minds were abominably poisoned.

In addition to these children's publications, the ordinary press for adults, daily newspapers, weekly sheets, and semiofficial journals, such as *Katolički List, Katolički Tjednik, Vrhbosna,* and *Nedjelja,* persistently and constantly diffused the propaganda of Fascism and

Ustashism, defended the occupier and the NDH and incited people to opposition to the National Resistance Movement and the Allies. Examples of this can be found on almost every page of this press during the war and the occupation. Here are some specific examples:

Andjeo Čuvar, issue of December 4, 1943, in a report entitled "John of the Third Company," written by Lieutenant Martin Fuček, recounts an incident glorifying the Croat Resistance:

We had a good supper, beans with meat, and my uncle Mile asked if I would accompany him into the bunker. Why not? The Lieutenant gave me his revolver and we went to the bunker. I warmed myself and listened, when suddenly the guards shouted, "Enemy." Shooting began while I was in the bunker but I was not afraid — we repelled the enemy. You are aware, Lieutenant, that I serve your soldiers on every occasion. I bring them postcards, take their mail to the post office, buy them matches, pencils and all they need. You're not angry with me. No. John, come with us for you are a true soldier. You were in the bunker — you fought — you have the right to come.

Glasnik sv. Ante, Nos. 5–6, June, 1941, p. 112 says:

The Jews in Croatia number more than 30,000. In Zagreb itself there are 12,000. In the poorer areas such as Hercegovina, Lika, Gorski, Kotar, Dalmatia, Zagora and some of the Dalmatian Islands, there are no Jews, because there is no chance for them to exploit. Poglavnik has announced that the Jewish question would be solved in a radical way.

Vjesnik počasne straže Srca Isusova, Nos. 5–6, 1941, p. 98, in an article entitled "Flag of Croatia — Heart of Jesus," asserting that the NDH is the work of God, says:

Then this golden freedom appeared. In the early spring, on the eve of the Resurrection of Christ, the Croat people experienced their own resurrection. His son came and gave back freedom and the ancient rights. This is God's work, and since the Lord accomplished it, it is wonderful in our eyes.

Nedjelja, No. 26, of July 6, 1941, p. 2, in an article entitled "Christ and Croatia," deals with Christ and the Ustasha as well as Christ and the Croats. It asserts that they come down in history together and that Christ is the leader of the Ustasha movement. "The Ustasha Croatia will be Christ's, ours and nobody else's. The entire Croat nation, from our dear Poglavnik to the smallest child felt the hand of Christ during these days."

Dr. Felice Niedzielski, whom Stepinac praises for his Crusader work, ends an article called "The Life and the Work of Poglavnik, Dr. Ante Pavelić," published in *Nedjelja,* No. 15, April 26, 1941, p. 5, with these words:

Glory be to God, our gratitude to Adolph Hitler and unlimited love and loyalty to Poglavnik, Dr. Ante Pavelić.

The whole tenor of the article is fulsome praise of the social program of Hitler and Pavelić.

Glasnik Srca Isusova, No. 6, 1941, p. 154 states that this monthly review considers itself quite removed from politics but that it is not antinational. It is Croat and because it is, welcomes the NDH and its ruler. The article concludes with the following expression:

NDH has, in the person of Poglavnik Dr. Ante Pavelić, once more its sovereign ruler of its own race. Great European states, such as Germany, Italy and others have recognized its independence. The best sons of our country have rallied around Poglavnik whose sufferings and tribulations have prepared him for his great task. It is their purpose to build on the basis of Croat honesty and the principles of the Gospel the new Croat state and to lead our dear country to a better and more glorious future. *Glasnik Srca Isusova* wishes them God's blessing in abundance in this great and difficult task.

Nedjelja, No. 22, of June 15, 1941, p. 1 inserts an article in praise of the German occupying soldier, depicted as a warrior and a gentleman, with the comment that the ordinary young peasant from Bavaria or the Tyrol always behaves in the gentlemanly manner of their superiors.

In the review *Sanctuary of St. Anthony,* published by the monastery of the Conventual Franciscans in Zagreb, the exclusive aim of which is supposed to be devotion to St. Anthony, we find on examining the numbers issued during the occupation, the following: During 1941, in No. 5 a photograph of Pavelić and a word of welcome to the NDH; in No. 9 a portrait of Pavelić; in No. 10 another photograph of Pavelić and of Budak as well as the picture of a group of Ustasha under the title, "bodyguard of our great Poglavnik, the renewer of NDH"; in No. 11 another picture of Pavelić with the phrase "Our great Poglavnik among his people." During 1942, in No. 1, in the leading article, "The first Christmas in free Croatia," the Ustasha is glorified with pictures of Ustashi and priests at the St. Francis Hospital on Sv. Duh in Zagreb. No. 2 contains the picture of Pavelić and his closest collaborators under the title, "Our great Poglavnik among the most faithful"; No. 4, in addition to another picture of Pavelić, includes a leading article "From Resurrection to Resurrection" in which NDH is highly praised. The same number describes the Ustasha chapel on Lipari with an article by Father Aljinović on the festivity of St. Anthony, with photographs of Ustasha participants. The picture of Pavelić appears with some of his Ustashi, under the title "Our great Poglavnik visits his people." Nos. 3–4, in 1943, produce the photograph of Pavelić and an article on the NDH. Nos. 5–6 publish a poem called *Prayer* with Pavelić's picture. In Nos. 1–4 for the year 1945, Pavelić's picture is again published against the map of Croatia and the text, "The achievement of our national freedom and independence is the voice of the entire nation and therefore is the voice of God and this, God's work, nobody must destroy."

Katolički List, semiofficial paper of the Zagreb archdiocese, supported the occupier during the entire period of the occupation and expressed itself favorably on the Ustasha. It includes various reports on the activity of the highest ecclesiastical functionaries, along pro-Ustasha lines.

For example, this paper inserts in No. 16, of April 21, 1941, p. 185, in addition to the report of the entry of German troops into Zagreb and the proclamation of the NDH, this comment:

These events have marked the foundation of NDH. The Croat state is now a fact. Our forefathers carried this ideal hidden for centuries until Providence permitted it in the year of our great national Jubilee. The Catholic Church, which has led the Croat nation spiritually through 1300 years of difficulty, accompanies with rejoicing and delight the whole Croat people in this moment of its reconstruction and political independence.

In the following number the lead article stated that:

with sincere joy and pleasure we welcome the foundation of the NDH. Our gratitude is particularly due to those self-sacrificing fighters who, under the leadership of Ustasha Poglavnik Dr. Ante Pavelić, prepared the way for the proclamation of NDH. Our grateful memory contemplates the twelve years of laborious activity of Poglavnik, characterized by self-denial but who, with unshaken belief, achieved the event after eight centuries of waiting. His vision made possible a clear understanding of the dynamics of the new European Order and thus made possible the historic Holy Thursday, 1941. We realize that the new Croat state cannot be erected without great sacrifices such as every nation must undergo and as indicated by Poglavnik in his great address on Saint Mark's Place. We appreciate the sacrifice of those who fell victim to the idea of the new Croat state. May these sacrifices be the pledge of the durability and the solidity of our nation's independence.

In issue No. 41, in 1941, there is a leading article entitled, "The Independent Croat State," written by the editor-in-chief, Canon Janko Penić. Here too is a photograph of Pavelić and among other things it is stated that "Pavelić achieved the aim of our entire national history in a half year." It is stated further that:

Poglavnik restored to the Catholic Church her traditional, divine authority, which had suffered so greatly in the former Yugoslavia. Poglavnik devotes a great deal of attention to the problems of religion and morality. The independent Croat state is a young institution. It is in the process of building and must evolve. Every development requires strength, and the construction labor and effort. It is the duty of all of us to contribute to this development with our utmost ability. To this end, he is entitled to demand sacrifices for the sake of the nation. Only our selfless work and manifold sacrifices will bring lasting freedom and complete prosperity to the independent Croat state.

In No. 25, of June 25, 1941, p. 296, *Katolički List* welcomed the German aggression against the Soviet Union enthusiastically and full of the conviction that victory would favor the aggressor, wrote:

Together with all the civilized, Christian world, we welcome this necessary operation on the body of mankind, convinced as we are that the German Army will succeed in extracting the poisoned tooth by which the Comintern has polluted the healthy organism of human society. When that is accomplished the world will breathe more freely because the terrifying specter that has haunted humanity for twenty years will disappear.

In issue No. 44, of 1941, *Katolički List* denounces the Jews in terms quite comparable to those employed by the Nazi.

In issue 4 for 1942, p. 45, we read under the title of Ecclesiastical News that:

the members of Poglavnik's Body Guard of the Croat Home Army[1] and the military police have thoroughly eliminated communist nests in the region south of Kupa, especially in the area of Borić. On St. Silvester's Day, Poglavnik himself, accompanied by Lisak visited this area south of Kupa where evidence of the recent fighting is still visible and was very much impressed by the spirit and sacrifice of the Croat soldiery engaged in these encounters.

The entire press under the control of Stepinac invariably notes the activity of the clergy and the clerico-fascist organizations on behalf of the occupier and the Ustasha, and engages consistently in calumny against the National Resistance Movement and the real fighters for the freedom of Croatia and the other parts of Yugoslavia. Under the false slogan of an "anticommunist campaign" the

---

[1] The Croatian word is *Domobranstvo*, the name given by the new Croat State to the regular army. The purpose of the name was to stress the Army's duty to protect its homeland (*Domobranstvo* and *Domovina* — homeland).

claims of the Nazi propagandists and the foreign reactionary press were accepted without question. The accused Stepinac seeks to depict the national resistance campaign against the occupier and the local traitors as civil war and reciprocal extermination. The conclusion is that the accused Stepinac, responsible for the writings in the Catholic press, supported the occupier and the Ustasha in their attempt to destroy national resistance.

c) In like manner, various organizations affiliated with "Catholic Action" and presided over by the accused Stepinac followed the appeal of the latter for collaboration with the Ustasha and became the nucleus of its support. These organizations were particularly the ones known as the "Great Crusader Brotherhood," the "Great Crusader Sisterhood," and "Domagoj." Members of these organizations took part in disarming the Yugoslav army. Many of them became officials in the administrative organization of the Ustasha.[2] From their ranks came many of the officers in Pavelić's army. Many of the chaplains of the crusader groups volunteered their services to the Ustasha and regular forces. The president of the "Great Crusader Brotherhood," Dr. Felix Niedzielski was designated vice-chairman and administrative director of Ustasha youth.[3] The most eloquent testimony to the character and activity of the Crusader organizations are their acts and the frequent articles in their weekly paper, *Nedjelja*. This publication, in the issue of August 10, 1941, under the title, "Crusadism in the Independent Croat State," said:

It is important to make mention of the men who are today in responsible posts because they have come up through the Crusader organizations.

It further adds:

Just as we strongly believe in God, so we believe in our Poglavnik. . . . Justice is being carried out and our enemies are being crushed.

The defendant Stepinac approved and supported the activity of the Crusader organizations. Stepinac and the secretary of the Papal Delegate, Massucci, received on March 7, 1941, the representatives of the Crusaders' conference, approving and blessing the antinational aims of their program. It was out of the provincial Crusader groups, as for example that of Gospić, whose leader was the Ustasha Jurica Frković, that many of the organizers of the massacres of Serbs came.

---

[2] The Croat terms are: *Tabor, Logor, stožer,* and *povjereništvo.*

[3] Here again the Croat term *Župan* may be rendered "governor."

d) The defendant Stepinac abused the character of the religious holidays, converting them into political rallies for sanguinary Pavelić and his Ustasha bands. This is perfectly clear from the work of the organizations and from the sermons delivered on those occasions. *Hrvatski glas* of July 15, 1941, explains the meaning of the five candles carried in the procession of Marija Bistrica by saying that "two of them are as a token of gratitude for the happy return of our Poglavnik; the next two for the Poglavnik's collaborators, and the last one with the Poglavnik's picture as an expression of our hope for his health and well-being. On the occasion of the pilgrimage to Marija Bistrica in 1942, the defendant Stepinac said:

Let us pray for those too who left the country and sometimes seek to advise the Catholic Church for whom it should or should not pray. We know that it is our apostolic duty to urge the faithful that they pray for all men, particularly for those charged with the responsibilities of government and especially for the head of the state.

In his sermon on the same occasion in 1944 when it was clear to everyone that the Ustasha was nothing but the Gestapo's arm and the Quisling creation called the NDH was very close to collapse, the defendant Stepinac, seeking to give support to Ustashism, identifies the Ustasha with the Croat people and service to the occupier with the defense of the state's independence. He said:

Is it to be considered a crime as terror hits our country that the Croat people longs for freedom as it has for centuries and defends today at tremendous sacrifice the nation's independence?

Even at this late date, the Marija Bistrica pilgrimage is used to revive Ustashism and undermine the structure of our republic.

e) From 1941 on, until the Liberation came, the defendant Stepinac celebrated a solemn Mass every April 10 in honor of the NDH. The feast of St. Anthony became invariably an expression of praise for the criminal Pavelić. Stepinac ordered his clergy in his circular letters to celebrate solemn Mass for the intention of Pavelić and the NDH! In such a letter dated June 11, 1941, he said among other things:

The feast day of Poglavnik, Dr. Ante Pavelić, chief of the Croat State falls on June 13. I appeal to the clergy on this occasion to celebrate a *Te Deum* after the High Mass on Sunday next, June 14. It will be appropriate to invite the authorities and schools to this ceremony. In Zagreb the Mass will be celebrated on the feast day itself in the cathedral. On this occasion, the people are invited to offer their prayers to God for the intention of the Independent Croat State, the Poglavnik and for the return of peace to the world, to the end that Croatia may be more prosperous for the temporal and eternal profit of her children.

The Ustasha parliament was opened on February 23, 1942. The defendant Stepinac joined in evidencing his approval of this deception of the Croat people. On this occasion, in the company of the Canons of the Zagreb chapter, the secular and regular clergy, Stepinac awaited the arrival of Pavelić and the members of the Ustasha parliament at the entrance of the cathedral, welcoming them with a speech later reproduced in all the Ustasha and Catholic press, in a part of which he said:

Poglavnik! At this moment the Croat parliament, this ancient symbol of the Croat State, is meeting with you as head of the Croat State, to ask God's blessing for its work. I cannot fail to speak as a representative of God's church.

The defendant Stepinac expressed his solidarity with the German and Italian occupiers in every possible way: official concerts, festivities, congratulations, and expressions of good will. He was present for the opening of the university week for German and Croat students in the presence of the Ustasha authorities and German generals, among them General Glaise von Horstenau. He was present at the opening of *Zagrebački Zbor* with German, Italian, and Ustasha functionaries. He took part in the official anniversary of the March on Rome. These are only a few of the cases in which the defendant Stepinac, publicly and officially, in flagrant contradiction with his office of Archbishop of Zagreb and Metropolitan, did willfully collaborate in every way with the occupier and the Ustasha.

The defendant Stepinac was in agreement with the Ustasha threat to the Serbs of Bosnia, Hercegovina, and Croatia that unless they accepted Catholicism they would be exterminated. He approved the forced conversions of thousands of Serbs and by this approval encouraged the Ustashi to continue committing these crimes.

It is well known that many of the so-called "converts" were later murdered and that many of those who came together for conversion were massacred instead.

The purpose of these "conversions" was to widen the cleavage between Serb and Croat; destroy their unity in the struggle against the occupier; outrage the dignity of the Yugoslav people, and extinguish the spirit of resistance among the Serbs in Croatia, Bosnia, and Hercegovina. The ultimate aim was simply the extermination of this people.

The story of how these conversions were actually carried out is confirmed by such persons as Steve Vujaković, Dušan Obradović, Mirko Vujanić, Nena Begović, and George Vujaković of Pobrdan who state:

We, the undersigned, recall quite well the conversion of Serbs in the village of Staza, Sunja District, to which we had been invited by the Ustasha authorities under local chief Krznarić and in accordance with the orders of the parish priest Orlić and curate Dionysius Juričev. They compelled us to receive instruction in the catechetical school and after a few days Dionysius Juričev spoke to the people and in his speech threatened the Serbs in this fashion: none but Croats can live in this country, because it is Croatia and we know how to deal with anyone who refuses to be converted. I have helped get rid of everyone from the small child to the old man in certain other parts of the country. I shall do it here because it is no sin to kill a child of seven years if it constitutes an obstacle to our Ustasha movement. We are to be all Croats now and when we are strong enough we will destroy the others. Do not think because I am in priest's garments than I will fail to use a machine gun to exterminate everyone opposed to the Ustasha state and its authorities.

On pretext of the "conversions" the Ustasha killed thousands of Serbs and plundered their properties, private and ecclesiastical. We may take as an example the case that occurred on April 26, 1941, in Grubišno Polje where the priest Peter Sivjanović called the Serbs together to force their conversion to Catholicism. He was extremely active in propagandizing for this purpose outside the church. He advanced as the principal reason for their conversion the chance to save their lives. With bribes he managed to convert to Catholicism some hundred Serbs who were later massacred. There is the case in the village of Stikada, Gračac District, described by Jovan Trbojević in the following words:

The massacre in the village of Stikada was carried out by Ustashi from Gudura with the full support of the Roman Catholic parish priest of Gračac, Father Morber. On the day of the massacre the above-mentioned priest came by car to Stikada and called the local people to meet near a swamp because conversion is necessary, after which no Serbs will be persecuted. The Serbs believed the parish priest and gathered together at the place mentioned. Some who did not come were brought by force. Some of the Serbs managed to save their lives by escaping from the village, apparently with some premonition of what was in the offing. When all the Serbs available were together, the Ustashi from Gudura, heavily armed, proceeded to massacre them. Some were killed with axes, as the exhumation authorized by the Italians in 1942 proved since a number of skulls were revealed as opened with a blunt instrument. Others were buried in an upright position.

During the period of the forced conversions, the plenary conference of the Catholic bishops met on November 17, 1941, presided over by the defendant Stepinac. The defendant, together with the other bishops, not only did not condemn the conversions but gave this repugnant war crime the canonical sanction of their approval. This plenary conference designated the so-called committee of three: the accused Stepinac, Victor Burić, Bishop of Senj, and Janko Šimrak, Apostolic Administrator of the diocese of Križevci. This committee was charged with the solution of difficulties arising out of the conversions in consultation and agreement with the Ustasha Minister of Justice and Worship. An executive committee under the direction of these three was also designated to deal directly with the conversions. The conference issued resolution 253/41, by which instructions on conversions are given in the light of the provisions of the Sacred Congregation for the Oriental Church. Thus the Vatican and the Catholic Hierarchy of Croatia, under the leadership of the defendant Stepinac, adopted and sanctioned the conversions. When the resolution speaks of these "conversions" as the consequence of free will and internal conviction only, it was a form of scandalous hypocrisy and bitter irony in the light of the fate of the persecuted Serbs. As if this were not sufficient, and in order to exploit the difficult situation of the Serbs, he issued a circular letter (September 26, 1941, No. 15964/41) asking that the lesser clergy speed the conversions and that "these conversions be carried out more quickly and without obstructions."

At the beginning of 1942 the Vatican appointed the defendant Stepinac as military apostolic vicar to Pavelić's Ustasha and Croat Home Army. The defendant Stepinac accepted this appointment and named as his substitutes the well-known Ustasha priests, Stipe Vučetić and Vilim Cecelja. So the defendant Stepinac became officially the supreme military chaplain of Pavelić's army and under him were all the military chaplains in the Ustasha and Croat Home Army who were the instigators of crimes and active criminals themselves. Here are some specific examples of how the military chaplains acted:

Friar Miroslav Filipović, Ustasha captain and chaplain of the PTS (Pavelić's body guard) later director of the Jasenovac camp, carried out on February 7, 1942, a mass massacre in the villages of Drakulići, Sargovac, and Motika, in which about 1300 men, women, and children were killed. As director of the Jasenovac camp he ordered the murder of about 40,000 persons, and took part personally in the massacre.

Zvonimir Brekalo, Ustasha captain and chaplain of troops at Jasenovac, together with Čulina, Cvitan, and Lipovac, chaplains in the same camp, ill-treated and killed many of the camp's inmates.

Joseph Vukelić, chaplain, took part with his troops in the frequent plundering and burning of villages and the massacre of the population of Banija.

John Miletić, priest and chaplain in Višegrad, at the invitation of Ustasha officer Gavez, "went among his soldiers to console the tired, comfort the low in spirit and raise morale. He took a machine gun in his hands and sowed death among the Serbian partisans." So writes the priest Eugen Beluhan of his confrere in *Hrvatski Narod*.

Joseph Bujanović, chaplain and acting administrative head in Gospić,[4] liquidated the remaining Serbs in that community and participated with the Ustashi in killing people and burning villages in Lika.

Friar Dionysius Juričev, Ustasha captain, chaplain of Pavelić's guard, chief of the religious affairs department of the so-called *Ponova*, which was in charge of the "Serb conversions," was killed in combat against the National Resistance Army at the village of Dicma.

Many priests entered the enemy intelligence service, provided the enemy with information on the status and movements of the National Resistance Army (NOV) and denounced the patriots to the occupier and the Ustasha authorities. Some of the priests guilty of this type of activity are: Ivan Nikšić, Friar Ilija Božić, Friar Borivoj Mioč, Friar Bono Grebenarović, Friar Božo Bralić, Friar Marijan Stašić, Friar Ciprijan Lisica, Father Matija Crnković, Friar Krsto Kržanić, Father Krsto Jelinić, Vendelin Gasman, Ljubo Grgić, Rikard Ribić, Miroslav Buzuk, and others.

The defendant Stepinac employed other methods to encourage the Ustasha criminal spirit and attitude in Pavelić's army and the general war effort of the German occupier. On December 18, 1941, the defendant Stepinac in a "Christmas message from the Archbishop of Zagreb to Croat men and women workers in Germany," expressed approval of the arrangement whereby our people were

---

[4] The Croat designation for the temporary function of this priest is *velikei Župan*.

submitted to slave labor in Germany, inviting them to work diligently as this was their religious and patriotic duty.

When a collection was taken up for the Ustasha legion on the eastern front, the defendant Stepinac made his contribution in the form of cigarettes, rosary beads, medals, and magazines, thus undertaking to raise the morale of the Ustasha bands in the struggle against the fraternal Soviet Union.

The defendant Stepinac attended the farewell of the Ustasha navy, dispatched into the Black Sea under German command to participate in the fighting against the Soviet Union and commit crimes against the civilian population. His presence gave approval to this criminal decision and aided recruitment for the enemy armed forces.

The defendant Stepinac, as president of the Curia, approved on February 10, 1944, the prayer book called "Croat Soldier," which the Ustasha Lieutenant Colonel, Vilim Cecelja, had composed and in which it is asserted that it is a religious duty to render service to the occupier and loyalty to Pavelić and in which known Ustasha criminals such as Jure Francetić and others are praised.

During the years 1944–45, just before the collapse of Hitlerite Germany and her satellites, when the Ustasha also was at the end of its rope, the defendant Stepinac undertook conversations with Pavelić and Maček as well as with the traitors to the Serb and Slovene peoples, Mihailović, Rupnik, and Rožman, for the purpose of forming an alliance of all the people's enemies for the restoration of the old order. They sought military intervention from abroad and the occupation of our country by foreign imperialists, hoping that as a miserable minority they might save the Quisling creation of the Independent Croat State or in other ways prevent the full victory of our country. He was engaged in this activity at the very moment that the last remnants of Yugoslavia were being freed and when already a large portion of the nation was re-established under democratic authority through its supreme legislative and executive bodies. Some of the specific acts of Stepinac in this situation were:

a) In his speech delivered on July 7, 1944, to the members of the *Domagoj*, he said:

Croatia is passing today through a most difficult time. The situation may very well grow worse. We must retain our optimism and believe that Croatia will endure and that no one can destroy her. The Croat people are deeply moved by this spectacle. It wills that the state shall be preserved. All movements contrary to the Croat nation and its independence must be discouraged. Everyone must make increased sacrifices for the defense and reconstruction of the state.

b) In his speech to the university students on March 18, 1945, he protests against peace and incites to further bloodshed. He calumniated the popular government and justice in the following words:

Does peace mean that a single social class shall seize power by force and slowly strangle the other social classes who may perhaps be the majority? Does peace mean that there is impunity to slaughter the intellectuals, priests and the citizenry with different political convictions? Does it mean that for such slaughters no responsibility shall be fixed? Does peace mean that the work of the Church is to be made impossible with the pretext that the Church has nothing to do with politics?

During the second half of March, 1945, the Ustasha government, now in its death throes, arranged a bishops' conference for the purpose of obtaining the aid of the Catholic hierarchy in saving the remnants of the Croat State and the protection of Ustasha war criminals faced with the prospect of trial before the people's courts. To this end, Mandić, president of the Ustasha government, on instructions from Pavelić, charged the director of Ustasha propaganda, Ivo Bogdan, with the task of drawing up the bishop's pastoral letter. A suggested draft was delivered to Bishop Janko Šimrak who put it in final form. The letter incorporated the political ideas of Pavelić, of Bogdan, and, of course, those of a more strictly religious character. The final text was submitted to Pavelić, who approved it and ordered it printed. This was the origin of the letter of the Croat hierarchy, of whose episcopal conference the defendant Stepinac was the head and which was issued on March 24, 1945. Here is a part of the text containing Ustasha slanders couched in ecclesiastical language:

False witnesses have risen to accuse the Croat ecclesiastical authorities, with their clergy and most devoted faithful of guilt in the present bloodshed in Croatia. We decry the recent tendency of those who have begun systematic propaganda to incite irresponsible and ill-intentioned feeling against war criminals, but whose real aim is the extinction of the greater part of the Croats, especially priests and Catholic intellectuals, depriving them in some cases of their life and in others villifying their characters.

In exceptional cases, if an erring priest sinned against his neighbor, we did not shrink from imposing ecclesiastical sanctions on him, even to the extent of excluding him from his priestly functions. But today we protest before God and world public opinion against the systematic killing and ill-treatment of innocent Croat Catholic priests and faithful, many of whom lived holy lives. Their lives were often forfeited by the acts of those who hate the Catholic Church, with illegal sentences based on fictitious charges.

History bears witness to the tenacity of the Croat nation through 1300 years of history. This persistent adherence to freedom and independence has never excluded a similar wish for every other nation. When this ideal was more fully realized during World War II the Croat Catholic bishops respected this evidence of the national will. No one has the right to condemn a citizen of the Croat state, and especially the Croat bishops for respecting this inflexible will of the Croat people, since it is a right sanctioned by Divine and human law.

It must be pointed out that no other religious organization replied to Pavelić's appeal for partisan letters. The Franciscan provincials of Zagreb and Bosnia refused to engage in public defense of the NDH along the lines demanded by Pavelić.

Just before the collapse of the NDH the defendant Stepinac, in agreement with Pavelić and for the purpose of concealment, hid the files of the Ministry of Foreign Affairs and the personal documents of the Poglavnik in the archiepiscopal palace. The accused Stepinac hid in addition the records of Pavelić's speeches, both during the period of exile spent in Italy and after his return to Croatia. These records were carefully stored in the archives of the archiepiscopal curia in Zagreb.

Early in the spring of 1945, the Yugoslav army freed our country of the occupier. Pavelić, Maček, Stepinac, and the rest of the anti-national group foresaw clearly the defeat of the German occupier. They proceeded to forge plans for a reoccupation of the country by some other foreign power, evidencing in this manner their willingness to overthrow the people's authority re-established in a large part of Yugoslavia.

The Ustasha government was desperate. It forwarded a memorandum to the Allied Headquarters for the Mediterranean area, requesting occupation. Still earlier, the representatives of the so-called national committee of Slovenia, the traitorous organization of Rupnik and Rožman, submitted a memorandum to Pavelić on April 12, 1945, suggesting the unification of all the military under Mihailović, Pavelić, and Rupnik, and the formation of a central political body for all Yugoslavia. The situation in the country was depicted to the Allies as one of civil war, thus making indispensable the latter's intervention. Contact with the Anglo-American armies was necessary to achieve this end. According to plans, Maček was to become the dominant political figure in Croatia and it was proposed that the occupiers transmit power to him and to King Peter.

The defendant Stepinac was active in these negotiations, had contact with Pavelić, consulted with Pavelić's representatives Alajbegović, Edo Bulat, and others. In compliance with this purpose, he visited Maček in the company of Moškov. Pavelić also visited Maček for similar consultations.

Ustasha minister Vrančić flew with the above-mentioned memorandum of the Ustasha government to Allied Headquarters where he was arrested and interned.

All this activity is entirely in line with the evil purposes of international reaction which then as now attacks the new Yugoslavia with unequaled fury, demanding the occupation of the country, spreading false rumors of disorder and chaos, and predicting intervention and the collapse of the new state.

This activity on the part of the defendant Stepinac produced a certain amount of confusion among the ill-informed, a number of whom, under the compulsion of Ustasha terror and propaganda, fled abroad. Many of these who sought refuge in Slovenia with the remnants of the defeated Germans and Ustasha, returned to their homes. Our country and its army destroyed these sinister plans which were the work of a handful of conspirators, despised as traitors and cast out by their own people.

The defendant Stepinac, who remained after the liberation, supported systematically the hope that the "regime" (as he called it) in the Federal Peoples Republic of Yugoslavia, would soon be changed, that Maček would return to Croatia, King Peter to Serbia, and that ultimately the Ustasha would be restored. The defendant Stepinac has continued to attack the popular authorities and the just sentences of the popular courts against Ustasha priests and other war criminals. He has claimed in this connection that it is a matter of the persecution of the clergy, the Church, and religion, and the extermination of the Croat people. Encouraged by this attitude and statements many Ustasha priests as well as those who sympathize with the movement have met together to organize the Ustasha again. Hiding from the public authority, they have carried out propaganda, incited the murder of citizens, and encouraged the plunder of their property.

The defendant Stepinac received in the archiepiscopal palace on September 19, 1945, the Ustasha colonel and former director of public order, Eric Lisak, and on September 17 and October 3, 1945, he received two letters from the Ustasha colonel and commander of the PTS, Ante Moškov. Both Lisak and Moškov arrived at the moment of Stepinac's greatest activity in the direction indicated.

They came to organize and rehabilitate the scattered Crusader groups. Stepinac received an émigré Ustasha student on November 8, 1945, who brought him from Salzburg the pledge of the Ustasha intellectuals in the struggle for the liberation of the Croat people. He received the spy Lela Sofijanec who frequently came and went illicitly from Trieste with messages. He approved the terrorist activity of his secretary, Ivan Šalić and of Josip Simečki. These men, encouraged by the attitude of the defendant Stepinac, in collaboration with Dr. Pavao Gulin and Josip Crnković set up a small terrorist organization affiliated with similar groups all over the country.

Just before the elections for the Constituent Assembly, when the people's enemies were striving by every means to provoke confusion with the nebulous hope of an imminent change, although aware that the elections would reveal the real will and mind of our peoples, the Catholic hierarchy of Yugoslavia, at the bishop's conference presided over by the defendant Stepinac, issued the pastoral letter of September 20, 1945. This communication misrepresented the situation in our country and encouraged the Ustasha and other traitors to commit further crimes. In this letter, full of lies and calumnies against our Republic, it is stated among other things that the Ustasha priests as well as other war criminals who had been tried by our people's courts were innocent, their only crime being a different political opinion. An example of how far the letter goes in perpetrating lies of this nature is the assertion that the well-known Ustasha criminal Franciscans at Široki — Brijeg were "almost all known enemies of the fascist ideology." The Pastoral Letter further states that the Catholic Church is exposed to persecution in our nation. This and similar lies and calumnies against our Republic are impertinent provocations of the Yugoslav people and an incitement to national and religious hatred. It is an encouragement to our enemies both within and without the country and particularly to Ustasha guerrillas who call themselves "crusaders." It contributes to their terrorist activities against the life and property of our citizens.

The defendant Stepinac, with the aid of Ustasha priests and Ustasha families, has collected false information regarding alleged murders in camps and prisons, and in the same way he brought together inaccurate information regarding the elections for the Constituent Assembly of the Federal Peoples Republic of Yugoslavia. This information has been dispatched abroad to feed the campaign of lies and calumnies against our country.

The Archbishop's house and especially the secretary's office became a refuge for Ustashi and their families as well as for traitors and enemies of the people. False information regarding the situation inside the country and abroad encourages them to expect the collapse of our Republic and the imminent "restoration of the old order." The Ustashi and their collaborators are the agents for the spread of these falsehoods. The accused Stepinac, in the light of his anti-national position, makes his palace the center for the diffusion of such lies and calumnies against our Fatherland, the Federal Peoples Republic of Yugoslavia. By this activity, the defendant Stepinac committed the following criminal acts:

1. Against the Criminal Code, Articles 2 and 3, Point 6. Crimes against the people and the state.
2. Articles 2 and 3, Point 3.
3. Articles 2 and 3, Point 4.

Acts classified under these numbers fall within the scope of the Articles of the Criminal Code as indicated.

By hiding the Ustasha archives, thus concealing evidence of Ustasha crimes, the defendant committed a criminal act against procedure in addition to the accusation under Article 3, Point 6. The defendant is also guilty of calumny against the people's authorities.

All of the above-stated criminal acts from the Code of Crime against the People and the State are punishable according to Article 4 of the same Code.

I submit to the Court the following Proposal:
1. That the Supreme Court of the Popular Republic of Croatia, in conformity with the oral proposal made at the session on September 11, 1946, in the action against Eric Lisak, Ivan Šalić, and others, agree to proceed against the defendant Stepinac at the same time as against the defendants Lisak, Šalić, and others.
2. That the Supreme Court of the Popular Republic of Croatia fix the date of a public trial, allow the defendant to be present, convoke the defense and the undersigned Public Prosecutor.
3. That the charges as here listed be presented as the bill of indictment.
4. That after the final session and the evaluation of the evidence, sentence be passed in accordance with the law.

Explanation

The most difficult days in the history of the component peoples of Yugoslavia came with the occupation of our country by the German and Italian imperialists. The German aggression against the Soviet Union revealed the clear outline of German imperialism, the purpose of which was to plunder the world, deprive people of their freedom, and subjugate and destroy small nations.

Strong in their power and hatred the German and Italian occupiers invaded our country and with the help of domestic traitors began, with fire and sword, the extermination of our people.

The campaign initiated by the Soviet Union against the fascist aggressors won the popular masses to our cause in the holy war of liberation, victory in which assures people a true freedom and a better life. The people of Yugoslavia rose up courageously. All progressive people, all who love freedom and their homeland, aided in this campaign and pledged everything to it. Peasants, workers, the intellectuals, the young people, all felt that the existence of our peoples depended on this effort. They accepted it as the only road to salvation. Despite the tremendous advantage of the occupiers, the terrible crimes and terrorism of the domestic traitors, our people, with supreme faith in the Soviet Union as well as Britain and America, suffered the consequences of this campaign from start to finish and witnessed the liberation of their land at the same time that their Allies slew the fascist dragon.

The former governing cliques, their public and secret collaborators; all those who stood aloof from the people and supported every anti-national regime; all those who plundered and oppressed the people and were moved by hatred of them, realized fully that the campaign that had been initiated would destroy them when the people's victory was achieved. They appreciated that only the occupier could defend their position against the powerful people's movement. Therefore they supported the occupier against the National Resistance Movement and fought with every means at their disposal — from the bestial Ustasha crimes to the demoralizing propaganda of Maček's adherents.

The defendant Stepinac played a very considerable part in the support of the occupier, motivated by his fanatical hatred of everything that is progressive, popular, and democratic. He has been blind in his refusal to appreciate the transformation in the strength of the people's state, the Federal Peoples Republic of Yugoslavia. He was dazzled with the promises of international reaction. He persuaded many to form small terrorist crusader groups in the country which, during their existence from the autumn of 1945, committed numerous crimes against the citizenry.

From the first day of the occupation the defendant Stepinac supported the occupier and Pavelić, representing the Quisling Croat state as God's work, "antemurale Christianitatis," whose orders also were a reflection of the will of God. We quote below the most significant part of a leading article of Dr. Vilim Nuk in *Katolički List,* dated June 11, 1941.

We may begin with two invaluable statements of our leaders in political and religious life. The provisional substitute for the Poglavnik, Field Marshal Slavko Kvaternik, began his radio address to the Croat State as follows: Croat people. God's Providence and the will of our Allies combined with the laborious struggle of centuries and the great efforts of our Poglavnik, Dr. Ante Pavelić, aided by the Ustasha movement inside and outside the country, made possible today, on the eve of the Resurrection of the Son of God, the reestablishment of our independent, Croat state.

The Archbishop of Zagreb, His Excellency Dr. Stepinac, in his circular letter to the clergy on April 28, 1945 (*Katolički List,* No. 17), wrote as follows:

Who can blame us when, as spiritual pastors, we join in the expression of the national joy and enthusiasm; when, with deep emotion and warm gratitude, we turn our hearts to the majesty of God? For no matter how complex the web of contemporary events, . . . the hand of God is plainly visible. A Domino factum est istud et est mirabile in oculis nostris (Ps. 117:23).

These two statements undoubtedly spring from the hearts of those who uttered them. They are not mere slogans but the expression of the deepest conviction of the moment. Do I have to prove, then, that Divine Providence restored an independent and sovereign state to the Croatian people which was destined to fulfill its mission as the "antemurale Christianitatis" in the new era of European history? Does not this circular letter of Stepinac speak for itself? The comments on it in the leading article of the semiofficial paper of the Zagreb archdiocese, accompanied by numerous statements of the accused Stepinac of loyalty to the Ustasha and Pavelić, constitute sufficient proof of how he led the clergy and how closely he was attached to the occupier and the NDH.

The defendant Stepinac became an even more resolute Ustashi

and stanch defender of the NDH in 1944. This is clearly evidenced in his statement to the university students when he asserted:

The Croat people has bled for its independence and will preserve it. Every movement against the Croat nation and its independence must be discouraged. Everyone must make the greatest effort toward the defense and reconstruction of the state.

The defendant Stepinac never deviates from this line. In his pastoral letters and circulars, culminating in that of September, 1945, he develops this same thought, inciting the faithful to antinational action and a crusade of terrorism after liberation came.

From all the material available, it is clear that he did not yield in his devotion to Ustashism from the beginning to the end. On the contrary he became an even more violent enemy of the people, defender of the Ustasha and the NDH. He became the instigator of new Ustasha crimes and treason on a still bigger scale as the people's victory approached. Even when NDH was dead and buried, the defendant Stepinac remained its defender, urging his priests and faithful on in the adventure of Ustasha-crusader terrorism and dishonored the Church with his own crimes and those of his priests.

It is not necessary to prove specifically the guilt of the defendant Stepinac during the occupation. From a series of written and oral statements and documents, it is clear that the accused Stepinac conceived the destiny of the Church as bound up with that of the Independent Croat State. It was this conception that made it possible for so many of the Catholic priests to take part in its achievement and collaborate with its organizations, its local administration, and militia, through the methods of forced conversions, murder, plunder, and burnings. Here is a passage from Stepinac's report to the Pope:

In the course of things, unless God determines otherwise, the progress of Catholicism is closely bound up with that of the Croat state. Its existence is her existence; its salvation is her salvation.

The guilt of the defendant Stepinac as the organizer of the forced conversions of the Serbs in Croatia, Bosnia, and Hercegovina is completely proved. These "conversions" form a part of the worst Ustasha atrocities. Everyone was aware at the time that the Ustasha as a whole and especially the Ustasha priests, threatened the Serbs that if they did not accept conversion, they would be assassinated, sent into concentration camps, or at least, expelled from their homes. No one believed at the time, since it was clear to all, that neither

Pavelić nor the Ustasha were interested in religion at all but in terrorism against the Serb people. Everyone was aware that even conversion did not save the people from massacre and that many who came to the Ustasha were deceived as the mass murders at Glina, Stikada, and elsewhere amply prove. Everyone was aware then, of what the defendant Stepinac pretends not to know, that no one was converted of his own free will, but solely under pressure of a Ustasha knife at his throat. Referring to this situation, Janko Šimrak, Bishop of Križevci, says in a text of May 22, 1945:

> The NDH authority ordered all Orthodox to be converted to Catholicism. If they refused they were threatened with the concentration camp. After that the people were frightened and many came over to the Latin rite. We received them *en masse* without any preliminary formalities.

When some priests wanted to receive converts only after evidence of free will and in conformity with the canonical formalities, and when certain functionaries sabotaged the conversions, the Ministry of the Interior of the NDH, in the Circular No. 34238 MUP/41 of September 16, 1941, ordered conversions to be made as speedily as possible and with no regard to formalities. Vicar-General Lach sent the following circular (No. 15964/41, September 26, 1941) to the clergy:

> The required religious rites are to be performed speedily and without regard to obstacles. . . . In cases where the public authority fails to carry out the purposes of the circular letter [the one of the Ministry of the Interior], information regarding such lack of cooperation shall be transmitted to the Ministry so that the appropriate measures may be taken.

In support of the organization of these crimes, a set of resolutions was drawn up on November 17, 1941, by the plenary conference of the so-called Croat Catholic hierarchy and issued by the president of the episcopal conference of Zagreb, the defendant Stepinac. This document bears the number 253/41. Point 8 of these resolutions says that only persons can be received into the Catholic Church who evidence this desire of their own free will. At the time of the Ustasha violence and terror this meant absolutely nothing. It was an abuse of canon law and a travesty on the Church to pretend to camouflage the bloody truth in this manner. It meant a tacit instigation of the Ustasha criminals to continue their nefarious work.

Today the defendant Stepinac speaks once more of free will. He states that the converts manifested their free will and that the rumors of forced conversions are mere tales and that at the present time it is not possible to say with certainty how many of these converts remained within the Catholic fold.

The lies with which the defendant Stepinac replied to the questions asked of him in the preliminary hearing and the impertinence of manner with which he retorted testify to the fact that even now he defends insolently the Ustasha crimes. His attitude is unchanged after the declarations of Mandić, Budak, and others. It is plain that Stepinac is more Ustasha than the Ustasha ministers themselves.

It is very clear too for whom these crimes were committed and how after the defeat of fascism in our country, the Pope's and Italy's imperialistic designs were shattered, from the text of the report submitted by the defendant Stepinac to the Pope on May 18, 1943, in which he said:

The young Croat state, erected amidst the greatest century-long difficulties, fighting desperately for its existence, shows at every step its desire to remain faithful to its glorious Catholic traditions and to ensure a better and brighter future for the Catholic Church in this part of the world. Thousands of the best Croat faithful are ready to give their lives with joy in order to prevent the loss or even the serious diminution of Catholic influence in Croatia. In the event of defeat the loss would involve some 240,000 Orthodox Serbs and the entire Catholic population of this territory.

The defendant Stepinac declared during the questioning in his own defense that the Pope approved his attitude and that of the hierarchy toward the forced conversions. This defense on the part of the defendant Stepinac means simply that a crime remains a crime even if the Pope approves and blesses that action and that Stepinac must answer for this offense before the people's court.

The defendant Stepinac was appointed by the Pope Military Vicar, *sine titulo*, in Pavelić's army. The kind of Military Vicar he proved to be may be judged by the term *sine titulo* which would indicate that the NDH did not exist *de jure* and therefore Pavelić's Ustasha and the Croat Home Army bands were not even recognized as a legal fighting force. Stepinac appointed as his representatives the well-known Ustasha priests Vučetić and Cecelja.

The military chaplains were well selected Ustasha priests whose job was to turn fanatical, backward, misled, and primitive men into the perpetrators of the Ustasha crimes. Therefore the candidates for military chaplaincies had to submit their applications through the ordinary ecclesiastical channels to the appropriate Ustasha bureaus which issued the final certificate of their moral and patriotic integrity.

On the application form are various questions such as these: Were you a Ustasha before April 10, 1941? Have you taken the Ustasha oath? When and where? Full information regarding the various services and opportunities under the Ministry of War was published in the semiofficial paper of the Zagreb archdiocese, *Katolički List*. On page 499 of this publication, in 1944, Bishop Lach, as vicar-general proposed that "a friendly response be given to the requests of the military authorities so that there may be harmony and good relations between the Croat ecclesiastical and military jurisdictions. This will have a salutary effect on the young Croat army. Pavelić devoted special attention to the problem of the military chaplains, fully aware that they were the primary source of the Ustasha poison. The first military chaplains took the oath before Pavelić. Kvaternik made a speech and in praising Pavelić's crimes, he stated that "in this work these priests are helping you." On the same occasion, Pavelić addressed them and in expressing his gratitude, indicated how the military chaplains were to spread the "Ustasha spirit and morale in the army." His words were as follows:

I am sure that the future generations will be indebted to you because you have instilled in the first Croat army a healthy spirit, sentiment of respect, awe before God and courage and fortitude against foreign and domestic enemies.

The character of the military chaplain may be judged from a typical excerpt from the address of Ustasha Chaplain, Captain Šabi, at Zagreb on November 12, 1942, to a group of recruits entering the transport service of the army:

I am convinced you appreciate fully the seriousness of this hour in which we live. Life today is a struggle. By taking the Ustasha oath, you remain a Ustasha until death. As examples which will keep you steadfast in your devotion to Poglavnik and the nation, I hold up the rare constancy and readiness of those unflinching fighters and heroes from Lipari and Janka Pusta who revealed such strength and intrepidity. Be proud to take the Ustasha oath for in so doing you become a member of the great Poglavnik, brothers of those Ustashi who saved the honor of the Croat people and the Croat name and who, with gun, bomb and dagger appeared when our enemies least expected them.

The following passage is from the speech of Father Filipović:

Ustashi brethren. We know from experience that our word cannot be broken. When we swore fealty to the head of the state, the glorious Poglavnik and our beloved NDH, we knew what to expect and what will befall us if we disobey.

The oath is taken in accordance with the ritual prescribed in the "Ustasha Regulations," paragraph 9, Article 8, which reads: "The oath is taken before a crucifix or the Koran and two candles, before which lie a dagger, a bomb and a revolver."

The defendant Stepinac knew perfectly well what the military chaplains were doing, as he admitted during the interrogation when he acknowledged receiving reports from Vučetić and Cecelja.

A characteristic statement is that of a chaplain, Ustasha Colonel Joseph Vukelić, which he made before the appropriate judicial authorities on August 21, 1945:

I am aware that the Ustasha committed many misdeeds and burned several villages in Banija. I know that they committed murders in the company of their allies the Croat Home Army. I remember that on February 23, 1945, in some of the Banija villages, about 400 of the Croat Home Army burned many houses and killed a number of people. These troops came from Petrinja. I did not protest against this massacre and burning, because others, including Stepinac, did not protest. I participated personally in this action with the troops because it was my duty.

The guilt of the defendant Stepinac is further proved by the fact that he occupied a leading position as president of the Bishops' conference and imposed his will on the entire hierarchy. Many of the communications authorized by his signature are nothing more than pious versions of ordinary Ustasha-fascist pamphlets.

The defendant is fond of asserting that he is above politics and that he looks at things from the point of view of the Church and her supernational mission. He asserts that as early as 1935 he forbade the clergy taking part in politics. This is nothing short of an attempt to hide his own crimes with artificially generated fog, to provoke discussions about the persecution of the Church, and to avoid responsibility before the people's court for his concrete criminal acts.

He is fond of speaking of the eternal character of the Church. He also spoke of the "eternity" of NDH and accompanied this impertinence with a defense of war criminals, attacks on the men and women heroes of the struggle for liberation, and contempt for the people's authority and courts.

He headed the whole ecclesiastical organization, from the first day of the occupation to the moment of liberation, in direct opposition to the people and its struggle. After the collapse of the Quisling Pavelić and the disappearance of Maček's Peasant Party under the blows of our army, the defendant Stepinac with his Ustasha priests and friends remain in the country as avowed enemies of the people and the new state. Stepinac undertakes to carry the Church with him in this antinational position.

The conspiratorial talks of Pavelić, Maček, and Stepinac on the eve of the national liberation were followed by an arrangement whereby the defendant Stepinac would assume power until the new occupation of our country and the return of Maček and Pavelić which they fondly believed was soon to follow. Stepinac became the leading Quisling in the country. The enemies of the people gathered about him. These included smugglers and black marketeers, Ustasha wives and widows, and the crusader criminals in hiding.

The defendant Stepinac became blind from hatred of the people, its government, and the Federal Peoples Republic of Yugoslavia. He was quite unable to understand the tremendous power of the people and the Republic. So blind did he become from sympathy for the Ustasha and the crusader criminals that when questioned about what happened at Jasenovac and what the crusaders are, he replied that he knew nothing because he had not been a witness to anything and secondhand information is always unreliable.

Truth and reality mean nothing to him. Ustasha lies and information collected by their spies regarding the situation and the prospects for the Constituent Assembly are for him from authentic sources, to be believed and transmitted abroad to provide "reports" on what is going on in Yugoslavia. He in his blindness does not see the defeat of Fascism in the world or the victory of democracy. He believes in the return and restoration of the NDH through foreign intervention. This is the reason why he is so impertinent and impudent in spite of the fact that he speaks so little. He held no episcopal conference in the days of the Independent Croat State without the approval of the Ustasha. No pastoral letter was ever issued without the agreement, censure, and often the expressed order of Pavelić. The closest collaboration is demonstrated when Stepinac urges the strongest support of the Independent Croat State by the hierarchy, although he knew full well that this Croatian state was not recognized *de jure* by the Vatican and that the Pope did not receive Pavelić as a sovereign but as a private person and that many ecclesiastics have complained that they were humiliated in Rome. These ecclesiastics bear the blame in Rome for the crimes committed in Bosnia, Hercegovina, and Croatia. The defendant Stepinac spends his time justifying the Ustasha to the Pope. On his insistence, the Pope acknowledges Pavelić and the Ustasha by employing such expressions as *"antemurale Christianitatis"* and the "Wall of the Drina."

The defendant Stepinac emphasizes that he is bent on establishing normal relations between the Church and the State. In this the defendant Stepinac is criminally insincere because his idea of a state is the Independent Croat State. He demands that war criminals go unpunished. He opposes the people's courts and the people's authority. He is opposed to a better life for the workers and peasants. He claims that the people supported him. Suppose we examine the situation to see if this is true. One recalls the Bistrica pilgrimage during which a handful of Ustasha bandits and fascist *agents provocateurs* incited the peaceful people to acclaim Pavelić and the Ustasha. The defendant Stepinac considers this the support of the people. At the end of the pilgrimage, instead of unmasking the Ustasha criminals who compromised the religious character of the pilgrimage, he delivered a speech in which he attacked the people's authorities. Instead of discouraging the excesses of the *provocateurs*, he egged them on to further antinational activity. This "pilgrimage" and the attitude of Stepinac was a clear sign to the Ustasha priests and all pro-Fascists as to the course they were properly to follow. Many priests were thus encouraged to commit crimes against the people. Many of these criminals were brought before the courts, the charges proved, and their guilt established.

If the defendant Stepinac, as Archbishop and the most responsible ecclesiastical authority, had really been concerned with the integrity of the Church and the priestly vocation, he would defend it in the company of the people's authorities and purge the clergy of its criminal elements. But what did the defendant Stepinac do? He despises truth and documentary evidence. He attacks the people's government and courts and claims that they try and persecute priests without any reason. He sees in the prosecution of criminals, the persecution of the Church. In the abolition of some of the confessional schools he sees an attack on religion and freedom, despite the fact that these schools were fascist educational centers. In a word, the freedom of the Church, religion, and teaching, mean to him freedom to commit crimes against the people, hinder and hamper the progress of the people. All of this is done under the guise of the defense of religion, thus seriously compromising the Church itself.

Lisak visited him and was received. He received correspondence from Maček. He was the recipient of the "oath" of the Ustasha intellectuals in Austria, assuring him of their zeal for a struggle to the finish. He received communications from crusaders in hiding. He receives the spy Lela Sofijanec and had contacts with Trieste. On his orders, his secretary Šalić examined the trustworthiness of the accused Gulin, a representative of Moškov. On his orders, the defendant Šalić received the defendant Lisak and gave him Stepinac's answer He utilized the services of the parish priest Kolesarić to transmit information to the defendant Simečki not to return to Zagreb for fear of the authorities who are searching for him for terrorist crusader activities. The defendant Stepinac participated directly in the work of these terrorist organizations, whose headquarters is the archiepiscopal palace.

He is fully aware of the blessing of the crusader's flags. He appreciates the significance of this act and his only concern is to urge caution on Šalić and Simečki. He is no longer an archbishop but an ordinary terrorist conspirator. This was perfectly known by the Ustasha priests, by all the clergy, and the entire people. Those who did not believe in the strength of the people's cause, or who lacked the will to join with the people were inevitably influenced by the defendant Stepinac. The deserters wandering about the forests, the Ustasha émigrés abroad maintained hope for the future because of the attitude of the defendant Stepinac.

Everyone is aware that the defendant Šalić is the Archbishop's secretary and that the contacts with the crusaders would have been impossible without the tacit consent and even the initiative of the defendant Stepinac.

The Pastoral Letter of 1945 was carried by priests to the crusaders in hiding so that it is perfectly clear what its purpose was. If you analyze the Archbishop's statement in the preliminary questioning, you will observe that he is willing to accept responsibility if the Pastoral Letter gave scandal to any priest. However, when Šalić sends Ustashi with the document to take it to those in hiding, the Archbishop disclaims any responsibility.

In other words, his reasoning runs something like this. The Pastoral Letter favored the terrorist activity of the crusaders. Šalić and the Ustasha priests aided and supported the terrorists. This does not concern the defendant Stepinac in the least. He asserts constantly that according to his conscience — and he appeals to it frequently — these same priests are now the innocent victims of persecution and that this is a persecution of the Church and religion.

The defendant is, in reality, the major instigator of all this. He announces in the Pastoral Letter in the autumn of 1945 that he is the rallying point of the people's enemies.

Šalić's central group is formed at this time and to it are linked the crusader and other organizations throughout the country. Lisak and Moškov arrive. Ustashi come individually and in groups from abroad. Terrorist crusader organizations are founded under the leadership of the Ustasha priests. Several instances of this can be given, with place and name:

Slavonski Brod	— Slavko Bajković, Vendelin Kristek, Josip Haubrih (all priests)
Varaždin	— Dragutin Gazivoda, Josip Lukša, Friar Ivan Kolenko
Klanjec	— Bast
Osijek	— Gilbert Djerkeš, Kerubin Posavec
Karlovac	— Ivan Sudić
Sinj	— Mato Džakula, Friar Bernardin Medvid
Bjelovar	— Josip Sukner
Knin	— Friar Ivan Samardžija
Sarajevo	— Ivan Condrić
Tuzla	— Friar Ljudevit Josić

Nevertheless the defendant Stepinac claims in the preliminary hearing that his conscience is clear and that every priest must answer for himself. He is deaf to the repeated declarations of these priests, more or less sincerely repentant before the people's courts, when they affirm that only the Archbishop's attitude, the Pastoral Letter, and sometimes the threat of a transfer, induced them to commit crimes against the people.

It is to be noted that after the arrest of Lisak, Šalić, and their group and after their center was destroyed, the activity of the Ustasha crusader groups throughout the country has visibly lessened. The close tie-in with the clergy has also been weakened.

The defendant Stepinac is perfectly aware that in the Independent Croat State there were about 150 military chaplains, well selected by the Ustasha. There were more than 30 priests who were mostly assuredly Gestapo spies, UNS [Ustasha police], and a great many more priests were Ustasha functionaries of one kind or another. A large number have been active crusader organizers in 1945. This is true despite the assertion of the defendant Stepinac in his letter of March, 1945, that these are "innocent Croat Catholic priests, a great many of whom lived lives approaching sanctity."

In the same passage the defendant Stepinac asserts that these criminals were convicted by irresponsible sentences based on the fiction of guilt.

When the defendant Stepinac stated today in the preliminary hearing that God will be the judge of Pavelić, Kvaternik, Luburić, and other criminals, it is merely a subterfuge to camouflage their crimes in the commission of which he collaborated.

This is simply an effort on his part to deny the people's courts the right to judge war criminals and the right of our people, as of all freedom loving people, to bring before the tribunals the Fascists and Quislings responsible for the war.

The defendant asserts in the preliminary hearings that no court in any other country would be competent to judge him and his priests according to natural, international, or divine law. But the defendant Stepinac must explain that in no other country have so many priests been war criminals as in Yugoslavia. Furthermore, Stepinac has overlooked the decision of the Allies to prosecute war criminals. Moreover, our nation was victorious in the war, the people created the authority of the new state, and it has been recognized by the Allies and the Vatican itself. Our people, regardless of what is done elsewhere, is entirely competent in this respect and has the right to summon to the people's court all those who must answer for their activity at the time when we were engaged in the struggle against the German and Italian imperialists and in the forging of a destiny of our own.

To conceal his guilt for criminal acts and foist this guilt on others, the defendant Stepinac, a calumniator attacking our state and the people's courts, states that in the conflict between the Church and the State in its ideological form, he clings to religious and canonical principles. From the content of this indictment, with proof and the statements of many Ustasha priests, particularly the defendant provincial Martinčić, it is clear that their criminal acts had nothing to do with canonical, religious, or ecclesiastical criteria. They were criminal acts against the people, its political freedom, personal liberty, and property rights.

In conclusion, there can be no question of the persecution of the Catholic Church, her priests, or her faithful. It is a question solely of the persecution in criminal law of the defendant Stepinac who, as a simple traitor to our people, supported the occupier and with Pavelić and the Ustasha collaborated against the National Resistance

Movement. He incited the people to civil war and a fratricidal struggle and after the liberation continued to incite, aid, encourage, and support the former Ustasha regime who, under the guise of crusaders, continued to commit crimes.

Therefore our whole people, eager for peace, work, progress, and freedom demands that the defendant Stepinac, with the other defendants be punished as they deserve.

Death to Fascism! Freedom to the People!

Public Prosecutor of the Popular Croat Republic
JAKOV BLAŽEVIĆ

DOCUMENT B

Address of the lawyer, Dr. Ivo Politeo, as attorney for the defense of Archbishop Dr. Aloysius Stepinac before the Special Council of the People's Supreme Court at the proceedings of October the eighth, nineteen hundred and forty-six in Zagreb

Judges of the People's Supreme Court! Sixteen years ago, at a time when Fascism had reached the peak of its power and our Fiume belonged to Italy, the Italian police of that city arrested a young Croatian engineer who was suspected of having committed certain political crimes. Once arrested, he was taken to Rome, to the Regina Coeli prison. His old father, also a Croatian from Fiume, not having had any news of his son's fate for a long time, came to see me, asking me to go to Rome and there, in so far as I was able as a foreign lawyer, to inquire about the prisoner and take what steps I could on his behalf. I went. Since, as a foreigner, I was not acquainted with conditions in the city of Rome, I asked a local attorney to give me legal aid and to collaborate with me in this case. But the Italian lawyer replied to me, "Colleague, I am a Fascist and, according to Fascist principles, I cannot defend anyone suspected of having sinned against the state or the Fascist government."

Such were conditions in the Italy of that time — but such are not and such must not be the conditions in the Yugoslavia of today. Since every day we use the words, "Death to Fascism," they should also mean death to all fascist principles, and even to that principle which was expressed by the Italian lawyer mentioned above. It has never even been necessary for us democratic and free thinking Croatian lawyers to kill Fascism, for its principles were never palatable to us nor were we contaminated by them. From the very beginning of our careers as lawyers — and for many of us well before that — we were conscious of our duty to undertake the defense of the accused without regard to the kind or the degree of the charges brought against him since, by not undertaking his defense, we would deprive him of necessary legal assistance and expose him to the danger of being either falsely convicted or, if actually guilty, of being punished too severely; in effect of being the victim of errors against which no public prosecutor or judge can ever, by himself, be forearmed. Therefore, in assisting the accused in his defense, we at the same time assist the court, seeking along with it the factual truth, the applicable provision of the law, and its correct judicial interpretation; for all these things are necessary in order to come to a just verdict. We must not retreat before the claims of an indictment if we are convinced that they are false in whole or in part.

My client, Archbishop Dr. Aloysius Stepinac, is accused of having committed crimes against the people and against the state. As for his defense, I will try with all my power to base it only on these principles, namely, on the truth, on the law, and on its correct judicial interpretation, that is to say, on justice. I must, however, admit that this defense is very difficult for me. But the difficulty does not consist in the weight of the material arguments; it consists rather, in the first place, in the fullness of authority which the public prosecutor has today urged for his indictment, and then in the attitude which our newspapers and the rest of the press have stirred up among a part of the public by constantly writing against the Archbishop without giving him a chance to defend himself in the same papers. Finally, the defense has been made hard for me even by my client who, according to his resolution, said that he would not defend himself and that consequently he would keep silent, but who, obstinately questioned, has been led against his will to the necessity of partially interrupting his silence and even of challenging certain questions. This manner of replying in part and in part of refusing to reply has been interpreted by some to his disadvantage as if, in certain questions to which he did not reply, he could not reply without harming his case or else did not know how to reply. This interpretation is, however, completely erroneous. If Archbishop Stepinac had, instead of keeping silent, responded to the various questions, each of his replies would have been to his advantage, for the truth is his best defense.

But let us look at the actual case; at the indictment.

The indictment has divided the actions with which Archbishop Stepinac is charged into three periods: his actions during the occupation, his actions immediately before the collapse of the so-called NDH, and, finally, his actions after the liberation. This division is quite correct. What is not correct, however, is the fact that the indictment makes no further division or distinction concerning persons or places. Instead of making such divisions and distinctions, it confuses the actions of Archbishop Stepinac with the actions of other persons in other places. This manner of confusing the activities of Archbishop Stepinac with the activities of completely different people and with what was done in places outside of his own diocese, the Archdiocese of Zagreb; this imputation of responsibility and guilt to Archbishop Stepinac for what was done by other persons in other places is a fundamental fault of the indictment and at the same time, in general, the main defense against a considerable part of the charges. In the course of further explanation I will speak of these things in greater detail.

Before going on to the charges having to do with the period of the occupation, I am going to sketch in a few short lines the past history of my client and his activities before the occupation. Let us see what he was upon entering this period.

At the time of World War I, Archbishop Stepinac enlisted in the Austro-Hungarian army, his high school studies having been completed. He was sent to the Italian front where he was captured and made a prisoner of war. Along with a great many other Croatian prisoners, he signed his name to a list of volunteers to fight against the Austro-Hungarian monarchy and thus became a Yugoslav volunteer and, as such, he was sent to the Salonika front. In 1937 he accepted a post on the Committee for Aid to Refugees and with this committee morally and materially aided anti-Fascists who, in flight from Hitlerite persecution, had left their own countries, Czechoslovakia, Poland, Austria, etc. For this activity of his, which lasted up to and during the occupation, I will later introduce proofs; for the moment, as an example, I will mention only the former refugee and present Minister of Justice in Austria, Dr. Gere. In 1938 Archbishop Stepinac publicly voted for Dr. Maček, the leader of the Yugoslav democratic opposition, or, as he himself says, for the Croatian people.

With such a background and with the attitude of a fighter for liberation from the German-Magyar yoke, for the Yugoslav community, for the Croatian people and for their independence, for democracy, for the anti-Fascists and against Fascism and Nazism — Archbishop Stepinac entered into the period of the occupation. Can it be thought that such a man as Stepinac would belie his whole past under the occupation and collaborate with the enemy?

If we wish to judge correctly the activities of Archbishop Stepinac during the occupation, we must first of all clarify the questions, *what was the occupation and what was the so-called NDH?* As to the latter, the public prosecutor said in his speech yesterday that the NDH was not a state. I agree with that conception but I do not agree with criteria cited by the prosecutor to support his thesis. He said first that the NDH was not a state because it was not independent. But we read every day in our newspapers that this quality of independence is also lacking in Greece, which is a satellite of Great Britain, and yet Greece is taking part in the Peace Conference in Paris as a recognized state. The prosecutor cited as his second criterion the bloody regime of the NDH. How many things have we read of the bloody regime in Spain, yet no one doubts its status as a state! Finally, the public prosecutor condemned the NDH as having been created by the help of others, that is to say by the Germans and by the Italians. This latter fact is true. Was not, however, prewar Yugoslavia also, in major part, itself brought into being by the aid of others, France, Great Britain, and the United States of America, which defeated the Austro-Hungarian monarchy and liberated Serbia? In a like manner, the Czechoslovak Republic was also created by the aid of other nations, and no one ever thought of challenging the status of either Yugoslavia or Czechoslovakia as a state. No, the NDH was not a state, although it did exist; according to legal authorities who have applied to it the accepted definition of a state — the prerequisites of which are people, territory, and power.

No, the NDH was not a state, not for the reasons cited by the public prosecutor, but rather for this reason: *That the territory of the Yugoslav state was under the military occupation of the Germans and the Italians, and that their occupation forces, during the whole of the war, kept this territory under their control for all practical purposes and that they exercised their will and their power through the Ustasha government which only acted as their agent.*

It is a question, then, not of the NDH state, but of the practical control, direct or indirect, exercised by the occupying powers over a part of Yugoslav territory called the NDH.

Consequently it is necessary to ask ourselves this: What were the legal relations which, as a result of the occupation, prevailed between the occupying powers and the inhabitants of the occupied territory?

The answer to that question is given us by the legal provisions of the Hague Convention of 1907 and, in particular, by those of articles 42–56 of Section III, dealing with military power on territory taken from the enemy. According to this source, all legal power passes into the hands of the invader who — this is explicit — has the right and the power to take any measures for the maintenance of public order and public life. The invader, it is true, must observe the laws of the country, but only in the case where he is not hindered from doing so by some unavoidable, compelling obstacle. He has the power to demand obedience from the inhabitants within the limits and with the exceptions provided by the Hague Convention. Consequently the inhabitants are obliged to obey him within the prescribed limits. It goes without saying that this obedience is only *legal,* and if anyone does not *wish* to obey, he may refuse obedience; but he does so on his own responsibility and at his own peril. In fact, hundreds of thousands of Croats and Serbs did refuse to obey and took to the forests so that there they might fight, their weapons in their hands, against the invader for the liberation of their enslaved country. For this we all render them honor and praise. But not everyone is made to become a hero and, if a person has not been one, he does not by that sole fact become a traitor, a collaborator with the enemy, or, least of all, a war criminal. Moreover, we are here examining only the recognized international legal rules which, in so far as they were authoritative and in force, consequently excused Archbishop Stepinac for doing what, in fact, he did do and of which he now stands accused.

It is true, as the public prosecutor said in his speech yesterday evening, quoting a writer on international law, that the inhabitants of occupied territory do not owe allegiance to the occupying power. It is true that, according to the Hague Convention, they cannot be forced to swear allegiance to the invader (Art. 45). But there is a difference between allegiance and the obedience which we have just described.

In the various political trials which have taken place since the liberation, we lawyers have tried several times to appeal to the Hague Convention in order to excuse legally, by means of these international juridical rules, not all but at least some of political and economic collaboration. However, the courts have each time refused to allow such a defense on our part, stating that the Germans did not observe the Hague Convention so far as we were concerned and that we could have the recourse of taking that convention into consideration. For myself I understand and approve such a statement with reference to the *Germans, the invaders,* but it is completely *incomprehensible to me in regard to members of our own nation,* the victims of the invaders, in regard to Serbs and Croats who observed or were ready to observe the Hague Convention. How can it be that revenge should be taken on *them* for the crimes of others, of the Germans, who violated the Hague Convention? Does it conform to logic or justice that these innocent persons among our own people should atone for the crimes of the German invaders? Here, naturally, we are not considering the cases of those persons who, *of their own free will,* collaborated with the invaders *beyond the limits prescribed by the Hague Convention.* Their collaboration is criminal and they do not have the right to appeal to the said convention.

In conformity with all the experience that I have acquired in practicing before the courts up to the present time, I today again appeal to the Hague Convention, and the more so since it is precisely on the basis of the Hague Convention that our allies demanded that the Germans and the Italians recognize the Partisans, the people's army of liberation, as a regular army.

Besides the Hague Convention as a body of rules having the force of law between states, there also exist ecclesiastical rules which give to the relations of Archbishop Stepinac with the occupying forces, and therefore with the so-called Ustashi government which was their agent, a completely different significance from that which is stated in the indictment. It is a question of the Constitution, "*Solicitudo Ecclesiarum,*" proclaimed by Pope Gregory XVI on August 5, 1831. Because of the difficult Latin style in which the Constitution is written, I do not wish to quote from it literally. I am only going to give a résumé of its thought, but so that my summary may be checked, I am putting the complete text of the Constitution at the court's disposal. This Constitution, then, says that, at the time of a revolution, in the fight for power, one must not take the *de facto* recognition of a state or a government by the representatives of the Church to be a *de jure* recognition, and one must not conclude from this that anyone's prior rights have ceased to exist. If, then, in order to insure the eternal spiritual well-being of the nation, the representa-

tives of the Church establish relations with persons who, *de facto,*
hold power, this is to be regarded as done on the condition that, as
a result of these relations, no previously held legitimate rights will
be violated. The accused, Dr. Stepinac, as Archbishop, as the highest
representative of the Church, at least in his own diocese, was obliged
to make his conduct toward the occupying forces conform to this
constitution.

But even if there were not all these legal rules which we have
just mentioned, there would incontestably remain the *actual fact of
the occupation* which, as such, alone held *power* and possessed the
means of applying *force,* and its power was not that of just any
invader, but of an invader as inhuman as the Germans and their
Ustashi agents. Arbitrary power and force of this kind exclude the
voluntary character of the actions of those to whom they are applied
or who are at every moment threatened by their application — they
exclude, therefore, that condition without which, according to the
laws of all civilized peoples, one cannot commit a punishable offense.
Moreover, all inhabitants of occupied territory, with the exception
of those who sought refuge in the forests, lived under this arbitrary
power and threat of force. Under this threat judges heard cases and
pronounced sentences, in the name of the "Independent State of
Croatia" — under this threat administrative employees conducted their
affairs; under this threat citizens had recourse to the courts and
administrative agencies; under this threat taxes were paid, money was
circulated; under this threat workmen worked in the mines, in the
factories, and at their trades. Again, I repeat, with the exception of
those who had fled to the forests, each person conducted himself
as his profession and his state and position in life required, at least
in that part of his activity that was *public.* If, then, millions of people
who lived under the occupation are not reproached for their way of
acting and for their relations with the occupying power, it is not
logical, especially considering his eminent position, to reproach Archbishop Stepinac for his relations with that authority, which were
kept at a minimum, limited to what was strictly necessary in order
to avoid, in the greatest measure possible, the worst evils for the
people and the Church. (Laughter in the courtroom.)

Those who laugh now kept silent then; if they were in Zagreb,
they quietly walked the streets without protesting against the soldiers
of the invader or the Ustashi, and — to use the words of the Comrade
President of the Court — they put their laughter in their pockets.

But he who did not keep silent and who publicly protested, was Archbishop Stepinac! I would like to see him who, on occupied territory — not from outside it — right before the occupation forces and the Ustashi, protested so openly, so strongly, and so frequently against all the acts of violence of the invaders and the Ustashi! Consequently let them not boast today or turn in derision on one who showed himself in action to be much more heroic than themselves.

To deny this power and this threat of force, to belittle it or not to admit it means to deceive oneself, to deny the occupation in general, and especially to present it as less cruel than it was, the cruelist occupation of all. To deny this power and this threat of force means to show the occupation forces and the Ustashi as rightful masters who took from the persons under occupation only what those persons voluntarily gave them. These are the absurd conclusions and contradictions to which one is led by making crimes of acts that under the occupation were unavoidable or which could have been avoided only at the price of one's life or by the greatest sacrifices.

Consequently, at the time when Archbishop Stepinac, on April 12, 1941, paid a visit to the so-called Commander-in-Chief, Kvaternik, and, on April 16, to the so-called Poglavnik, Pavelić, he did what his position required and what others did in an analogous fashion according to their positions. If one compares these situations, they are the same. And if others are not reproached for similar acts, why is it that only Archbishop Stepinac is reproached and, what is more, told that his actions were a crime? When these two visits are mentioned, why is it not stated that Archbishop Stepinac *did not* take part on April 13 in the welcome given to Pavelić at the railway station where, alas, to their shame, the citizens of Zagreb went en masse? Why is it not said that he did not sing a *Te Deum* following the arrival of Pavelić? Why is it not recalled that Pavelić, because of the Archbishop's attitude toward him, went only once to divine services at the Cathedral during the four years of the occupation, and that in 1943 when the Italians had a requiem sung for the Duke of Aosta, he was received at the entrance not by the Archbishop or any other member of the clergy, but by the sacristan? Was it by this way of acting toward the so-called chief of state that the Archbishop, as is charged, recognized, supported, and collaborated with him?

During the trial a passage was read from the circular letter sent to the clergy of the Archdiocese of Zagreb on April 28, eighteen days after the foundation of the so-called NDH. It is now necessary to quote still other passages from the same circular letter, and particularly the following: "I ask and beg you to make every effort so that our *Croatia* (not, note, the NDH) may be a country dedicated to God, for it is only thus that it can perform its two essential tasks, which it must perform as a state, to the profit of its members." And next, "Everywhere we must preach and teach that the sacred spirit and noble enthusiasm for the building of the new Croatian state (again not NDH) must be entered into by the fear of God and by a love for the law of God and His Commandments, since it is only upon the Divine Law, and not on the false principles of this world, that the Croatian state can be built on a solid foundation." What the Archbishop understood as the Divine Law and Commandments, was it not basically the same as what is expressed by the noblest principles of all truly civilized peoples, of all civilized humanity? Does appealing to the Divine Law and Commandments mean collaborating with the enemy, inciting the occupation forces and the Ustashi to their crimes? What a blessing if those who committed those crimes had heeded the Archbishop's appeal! It would be indeed difficult to find anyone who, perceiving the reality and not merely the form, would not make that appeal to the NDH. It was not the fault of Archbishop Stepinac if, contrary to his words, his will, and his efforts, affairs took a bad turn. It was not in his power to do anything more than to speak, to make appeals, to blame, to stigmatize, to turn people away from and save them from the worst evils. Even those whose power lay in their weapons and in every sort of material means succeeded only after four to six years in defeating Hitler and his accomplices, and in finally putting an end to their crimes.

A considerable part of the indictment deals with what various priests did during the period of the so-called NDH, and Archbishop Stepinac is accused of responsibility for their acts and of guilt because of them. Such an accusation is proof of ignorance of the constitution of the Church and of Canon Law. It is based on the erroneous notion that an archbishop has power over all other bishops. According to canon 273, however, an archbishop has in his own diocese the same rights and obligations that any other bishop has in his own diocese. Each bishop is as ordinary, completely autonomous in his own diocese, and an archbishop has no right to interfere in his local affairs. Accordingly, the priests of other dioceses are in no way subject to an archbishop nor are they dependent on him. The archbishop cannot in any way exercise any authority over their actions. Consequently, even without mentioning the fact that one person cannot be responsible for the actions of another, no one can accuse Archbishop Stepinac of, or hold him responsible for, what individual priests did in territory belonging to a diocese other than his own Diocese of Zagreb. And even in his own Diocese he has no power over the members of the religious communities. Authority over the Franciscans is exercised by their Provincial, the accused, Modesto Martinčić, who, moreover, in a most un-Christian manner, tried to place the blame for his own crimes on the Archbishop, although he could not prove that during the occupation he had done anything at all comparable to the noble, energetic, and redeeming work of Archbishop Stepinac. There are only a very few priests, specifically those of the Archdiocese of Zagreb, for whose actions the Archbishop could be held responsible; and even concerning those priests it cannot be shown that they committed any crimes whatever instigated or incited by the Archbishop. Everything that the Archbishop directly or indirectly urged on the priests under his authority by either his words or his actions was good, moral, and in conformity with Christian doctrine; and if any individual priest strayed from this path constantly pointed out to him, it is clear that his crime cannot be attributed to the Archbishop but only to the individual himself. If any priest carried on propaganda for the Ustasha ideology, certainly he had not learned it from Archbishop Stepinac who rejected these ideas. If any priest forgot not only that he was a priest but that he was a man committing acts of violence against the Croatian or Serbian people, this cannot be attributed to Archbishop Stepinac who by his words and deeds is a living condemnation and contradiction of that kind of conduct.

Like the priests, the *Catholic press* is also among the responsibilities for which, according to the indictment, the Archbishop must answer. Most of the periodicals from which passages are quoted in the indictment as proofs against Archbishop Stepinac were published in other dioceses or belonged to the religious. Thus, for example, *Andjeo Čuvar* was Franciscan, *Glasnik sv. Ante* was put out by the Conventuals, *Vjesnik počasne straže Srca Isusova* by the Third Order, *Glasnik Srca Isusova* was Jesuit, *Katolički tjednik* was published in Sarajevo, etc. But even the periodicals published inside the Archdiocese of Zagreb could not be identified with Archbishop Stepinac since he was neither their proprietor, publisher, editor, nor, least of all, their *tactical adviser*. However, it is precisely on the grounds of the alleged activity of the accused, Archbishop Stepinac, as *supreme tactician* of the writing of the whole Catholic press that the indictment fixes criminal responsibility. But of what did this activity as supreme tactician consist? The public prosecutor has not shown us. Did it, perhaps, consist in the fact that the accused was Archbishop of Zagreb? But how does that fact show that Archbishop Stepinac also set the policy of the Catholic press? If by setting policy, directives and instructions given to the press are understood, then these latter — and then only indirectly — can be found only in circular letters, pastoral letters, and sermons — from which I will quote in a moment — but there is no trace there of anything that could lead any author into criminal writing. The public prosecutor has not been able to show the contrary from other directives since, quite simply, they do not exist. Moreover the role of tactician is understood as positive and active. Yet even if, *dato non concesso,* his action is interpreted as negligence, that is, for not having, in a specific, particular, and direct fashion, warned the various editors or writers that they must not write in a certain way, such negative action could not be considered criminal, because, without taking into consideration the fact that he was under no legal obligation to do this, it would not have been physically possible to supervise such a great number of periodicals. In addition, the prosecutor has here publicly declared that he would not prosecute the Archbishop on account of his passivity, but rather on account of his activity. But is neglect to supervise, perhaps an obligation, and to forbid an activity? Is this not passive? How, then, can Archbishop Stepinac be required to bear responsibility for negligence, a passive attitude, not even to mention that no activity in this matter existed or was proved.

Although as a result of my explanation concerning the Catholic press a very precise distinction has been established between Archbishop Stepinac, who was not responsible, and the writers and editors who were responsible, I would like also, *per superfluum,* to say a few words on the subject of the Catholic press. The passages which the public prosecutor has quoted from it are truly distressing. Their deplorable character does not, it is true, disappear but it is lessened if the various articles are examined, *not* from the viewpoint of *today's* conditions, but *from the viewpoint of conditions at the time they were written.* Only in this way can a true picture be presented. The time when these articles were written was during the occupation when special pressure was put on the press, and it was directed, manipulated, and dictated to by the occupation authorities and the Ustashi, especially by the Bureau of the Press and Propaganda. There existed a preventive censorship that was more than normally severe. The censorship not only deleted, but it also inserted words, sentences, and even whole paragraphs by which it often completely changed the original sense of an article. The censor was more than a censor; often he was also a writer, dictating the kind of writing allowed, and whole articles were sent to editors with orders to publish them. The people knew all this and did not take seriously this enslaved, standardized press which, for that very reason, was unable to influence the people as much as its official Ustashi controllers would have liked. As everywhere under such circumstances, people learned to read between the lines and to distinguish what had been dictated from what the writer had really meant, in effect, from what had escaped the censor.

Yesterday the public prosecutor stigmatized the Ustashi, and rightfully so, because they had — exactly as the Germans and the Italians — introduced the concept of *collective criminal responsibility*. But, I ask, is it not something like applying *collective responsibility* when the public prosecutor accuses one person, Archbishop Stepinac, of what other persons did; other priests as well as the writers and editors of the Catholic press? Is that not the negation of *individual responsibility*, alone legitimate, which is the only responsibility admitted by our criminal laws? Today in our country a son is not responsible for the crimes of his father, nor the father for those of his son, nor, in general, any member of a family for those of another member of the same family. This is perfectly sound. If this is true for a family, which represents a small social unit bound together by very close ties, where by reason of such close ties one could justly presume a greater or lesser degree of collaboration by members of the family in the crime of another one of its members — how, then, can one presume and charge that there was such collaboration on the part of the Archbishop for the members of so large and numerous a community, separated by time and space, bound together principally by Christian doctrine and by their vocations, as the clergy and the Catholic press of one, and even many, dioceses? There is hardly a man whom one cannot, on the basis of this conception of collective responsibility, accuse and punish.

And now let us examine certain aspects of the positive activity of the accused, Archbishop Stepinac; let us see what he said and what he taught, to what ends he urged not only his clergy but also all the faithful, Croats and Serbs, all those who were reached by his words or his influence. Although the *public* activity of a bishop is best shown by his *sermons,* I am going to quote here only a few particularly striking passages because I have neither the time nor the physical stamina to quote them all. Listen then!

On the Feast of Christ the King, October 26, 1941, Archbishop Stepinac said among other things,

> . . . I would like to draw your attention today to one thing if you really want to be true subjects of Christ the king, and that is to *love for your neighbor, love for the man himself regardless of what his name may be.* Within the past ten years certain theories and atheistic ideologies have succeeded in infecting so much of the world that hate has become, so to speak, the main incentive for all human action. The danger exists that *even those who glory in the name of Catholic, not even to mention those who glory in a priestly vocation,* may become victims of passion, of hate, and may forget that law which is the most beautiful characteristic trait of Christianity, the law of love. . . .

Is this not a clear allusion to Pavelić and to the Ustashi, who boasted of being Catholic but who acted in a most un-Catholic fashion; an allusion to the misled priests who followed the example of the criminal Ustashi? Are words of this sort an instigation to crime, directives, and tactics for criminal writings in the Catholic press? Do they constitute collaboration with the occupation forces? These words were spoken in the sixth month of the occupation.

In his sermon on the occasion of the procession of Our Lady of Lourdes toward the end of May, 1942, he said, "Do you think there is only one illusory dignity of this sort in the world?" Everyone understood that these words referred to Hitler and his satellites, including Pavelić. Then, "It would be absurd to speak of *a new order in the world, no matter what its source,* if in that new order were not valued human individuality, the human immortal soul . . . , which has its inalienable rights that no *human power* can or ought to limit. And it would also be absurd even to think that the Catholic Church would be afraid of any *human force* in *defending human individuality and the freedom of conscience.*" I would like to find one who, in occupied Zagreb when the power of the occupation forces was at its height, in the midst of the forest of German and Ustashi bayonettes and completely unarmed, would so publicly and valiantly have held his head so high before Hitler who was then all powerful, before Mussolini who was somewhat less powerful, and before Pavelić who was still less powerful.

And here are the Archbishop's words from the sermon given a month later on June 29, 1942, in the cathedral on the Feast of Sts. Peter and Paul. "We cannot be Catholics in church, and in the streets attack like pagans the orders of the Vicar of Christ given for the purpose of public welfare because, perhaps, they do not suit our personal taste. We cannot today because it suits us praise the Holy Father, and tomorrow in the newspapers cross out in red pencil his words and his sermons, given for the sole purpose of leading men to God."

On the Feast of Christ the King, October 25, 1942, the Archbishop said in his sermon, "How then must we judge individuals who arrogantly behave as if God no longer existed on the earth . . . ?" It was immediately clear to the thousands who heard this sermon that this was a reference to the Führer, to the Duce, and to the Poglavnik, that it was they who had behaved so arrogantly.

But in this same sermon the Archbishop goes even further.

All nations and all races have their origin from God. . . . Each nation and each race that is found on the earth today has the right to live in a manner worthy of men and to be treated in a manner worthy of men. They all, without exception, whether they belong to the race of Gypsies or to some other race, whether they are Negroes or civilized Europeans, whether they are hated Jews or proud Aryans, have the equal right to say, "Our Father Who art in heaven!" . . . That is why the Catholic Church has always condemned and condemns today all injustice and all violence whether committed in the name of theories of class, race, or nationality. One cannot exterminate the intellectual class from the earth. One cannot exterminate from the face of the earth the Gypsies or the Jews because one considers them inferior races. . . .

These words loudly proclaim his condemnation of Jasenovac, Jadovan, Dachau, Auschwitz, and all the acts of violence committed by Hitler and by Pavelić, but this condemnation especially concerned *racism*. And what is more, it was from this racism, which as a science divided the races into superior races and inferior races and declared the Germans to be the highest race, that Hitler deduced the right of the Germans, as the "Herrenvolk," to rule the whole world. It was, then, a condemnation of all violence and of all the means by which such violence was committed.

The public prosecutor said that Archbishop Stepinac had only been for the *modification* of the system but that he had not been against the system as such. Even if my quotations up to this point were not proofs against such an accusation, we would certainly find this proof in the following words with which the Archbishop ended his sermon in the cathedral on the occasion of the procession of penance on October 31, 1943.

Finally I appreciate the question in the minds of the thousands of you who are listening to me; what then is the social order which the Catholic Church supports, for all the world is fighting for a *new social order,* that is, to say it parenthetically, the "Neue Ordnung." *Condemning all injustices, all murders of innocent people, all burnings of peaceful villages, all destruction of the means of livelihood of the poor, sorrowing for the miseries and the sadness of all who today suffer unjustly, we answer this: the Catholic Church upholds that order which is as old as the Ten Commandments of God. We are for that social order which is written not on paper that will fall into dust but which is written by the hand of the living God in the souls of men.*

In effect, according to these words, there is no more need to show that Archbishop Stepinac was against the regime and only in favor of certain modifications. In any case, he was not in a position to overthrow this system by his courage alone, but by his courage in fighting it, and by his authority, he succeeded, after doing all that was in his power to do, in *modifying its practices.* And he succeeded to the greatest possible extent. Thousands upon thousands of Jews, Serbs, Croats, Slovenes, activists, communists, anti-Fascists, and, in general, all sorts of men of various religions, nationalities, or political convictions owe their lives to the efforts of the Archbishop. Who, in this desperate situation, did not recognize such a modification as the maximum success it was possible to achieve under the circumstances? In that alliance of states and peoples, of millions of men, not one of whom could have done anything alone, but in unity, finally, defeated Hitler and his satellites, the acts of Archbishop Stepinac were a most valuable contribution.

Why quote more passages from the sermons of the Archbishop? They are well known to the people of Zagreb who had the misfortune to be in the city during the occupation; these sermons were for them, in those hard times, the chief consolation, a firm support in their resistance, a hope for the fall of Ustashism and Fascism, a hope for a better future in a time not too far off. The faithful crowded the church to listen to these sermons and many came only to hear them. These sermons were repeated, printed, copied, retold, and circulated in thousands and thousands of copies among the people and even reached liberated territory. Spoken in public, they became an underground press, a successful method of propaganda against the Ustashi, and a supplement to the opposition press.

When the activity of Archbishop Stepinac is considered in the light
of these numerous sermons, all that is contained in the indictment
against the accused loses the collaborationist character which is
attributed to it and disappears in the light of the anti-Ustashi activity
of the Archbishop. What, for example, did the visit to Pavelić and
Kvaternik at the beginning of the occupation mean? Nothing more
than an inevitable but ordinary and conventional courtesy such as
are called "konventionelle lugen," without which the Archbishop
would never have had the chance to rescue the persons whose lives
he saved or to do so much good during the occupation. Through
such courtesy he in no way sacrificed his goal or his good works.
For example, we now see at the Peace Conference what bitter conflicts, not only of an ideological but even of a purely personal nature,
take place among the delegates from the various countries. But when
one delegate invites the others to a banquet, they all act toward each
other as if they were not enemies at all. Does anyone take these
courtesies for proof that disagreements have ceased, that each recognizes the viewpoint of his adversary, or that each will abandon the
position he has held up to then? It is somewhat similar to the
various notes of protest between countries and to the replies to those
protests which we have so often read, especially in recent times.
They reflect opposition, contain bitter criticism, but they begin
and end with words of the greatest politeness and cordiality. Courtesy
frequently does not reveal the true nature of a situation and, hence,
is not always a proof of its character.

Yes, Archbishop Stepinac was in contact with Pavelić from time
to time. But, excluding rare conventional courtesies their purpose
was to intervene on behalf of the persecuted, and put an end to
Ustashi crimes. They were in no way acts of collaboration or co-operation — for he actually acted against them; but rather acts of opposition. The public prosecutor himself, on page 3 of his indictment,
quotes the Vatican Secretary of State, Cardinal Maglione, who in
1942 had recommended to the Archbishop, in the interests of the
Church, the adoption of "a more adroit and more cordial attitude
toward the Ustashi authorities." During the trial itself we have heard
from the mouths of the so-called Marshal and Commander-in-Chief
Kvaternik — who was brought in as a witness by the public prosecutor, not by me — that Archbishop Stepinac had constantly been "the
object of Pavelić's hatred." This hatred was such that, for example,
Pavelić — despite the several banquets spoken of by the prosecutor —

never entered the archiepiscopal palace. This hatred was no secret for it was known by all Zagreb, and only yesterday we heard further proof of this hatred from the testimony of several witnesses, most important of whom were Canon Dr. Hren and Dr. Lončar, whose anti-Ustashi sentiments and whose veracity have been acknowledged by the prosecutor himself. These witnesses, who belonged to the group of men closest to the Archbishop, gave us so many details concerning his thought and his work that they preclude any possibility whatever of any support having been given to the Ustashi regime or to the occupation forces.

The reputation of the Archbishop, in direct contradiction to what is stated in the indictment, became known to the Allies. I have placed before the court the record of several news broadcasts from London in the years 1942 and 1943 in which the Archbishop's anti-Ustashi attitude was repeated along with the favorable reaction to his sermons there. I also introduced a news report from the Propaganda Ministry of the Ustashi regime in which the authorities were warned how the Allies were profiting from the Archbishop's sermons against the Ustashi government. Among those documents, which I presented to the court but which were not read, was a letter from Monsignor Rittig, written toward the end of December, 1943, in which he acknowledged the Archbishop's arduous and painful work and his delicate situation; the great sacrifices he had made for the people, and especially his gifts to the people from the Croatian seaboard, and who, in sending the Archbishop Christmas wishes expressed the hope that he would successfully pass between his Scylla and Charybdis. Would Dr. Rittig, who was very well informed and very friendly toward the NOP, have written in such a manner if he had had the least suspicion of the Archbishop's loyalty or of his work on the people's behalf?

How troublesome the Archbishop was to the Ustashi government and how much this regime felt itself attacked by his sermon of October 31, 1943, at the end of the already mentioned procession of penance may be seen in the manner in which the authorities reacted to it. One of the officials, the so-called Minister, Dr. Julije Makanec, wrote an article under his own name, printed in the Ustashi publication *Hrvatska Narod* on November 7, 1943, in which he violently attacked Archbishop Stepinac, ridiculed him, and warned him not to meddle in politics. The political activity of the Archbishop to date had consisted of condemning Ustashi acts of violence. The Archbishop has been reproached for having attended Benedic-

tion at St. Mark's Church on February 23, 1942, before the opening
of the so-called Hrvatski Sabor (the Croatian Parliament) of the
Ustashi. We have heard witnesses who stated that it was only with
the greatest difficulty that the Archbishop was persuaded to perform
this act. Only a part of his sermon given on that occasion has been
read here, but the principal part of it containing the clear intention
of the Archbishop was not read. That part says:

Let it [the Parliament] pass honest laws which will not be contrary to Divine
law so that it may assure the blessing of God the Creator. . . . Let it pass *just*
laws: where there are equal burdens, let there be also equal rights. Let it pass
possible laws, let it not burden the people with a load they cannot carry. . . .
Let the Eternal Judge who governs the fate of peoples be built into the
foundations of the Croatian Parliament and let Him as well impress into the
hearts of all your co-workers a profound *sense of responsibility* so that they may
successfully assist you, the leader of the Independent State of Croatia, in the
reconstruction and reformation of our beloved fatherland on the eternal foundations of the *principles of the gospels of Christ.*

On that particular occasion he was not able to avoid calling
Pavelić the leader of the NDH, but he clearly reproached him for
the dishonest and unjust laws he had decreed up to that time and
for his irresponsibility. Pavelić grasped this meaning very well with
the result that — according to the statements of two of the witnesses
we have heard — after the sermon he was irate and said to his
retinue, "What! Does this greenhorn [that is to say, the Archbishop]
propose to give me lessons in politics!" According to the statements
of witnesses, the relations between the Archbishop and Pavelić, bad
up to then, became, as a result of this, still worse. I must also emphasize that this Parliament was not a real one, so that the Archbishop
had no right to reprimand it — save from the point of view of principle
— because its members were appointed and not elected. But this
so-called Parliament had the future before it and many people hoped,
although they were completely mistaken, that through it it would be
possible to restrain the arbitrary power of Pavelić and the excesses
of the Ustashi. This Parliament, moreover, whatever it may have
been, did realize up to a certain point the hopes of these well-
meaning persons. Within it a strong opposition began to form, and
for that reason Pavelić ceased convoking it soon after it had met a
few times. Another reason for this was that two members of Parliament, Dr. V. Prebeg and Dr. Ljubić from Banjaluka, had demanded
an explanation of the imprisonment of Dr. Maček. I remark once again

that the Archbishop had forbidden four of his priests who were nominated for Parliament to become members of it. Proof for this is in the Archbishop's letter of February 8, 1942 which has been presented to the court.

The Archbishop's communication to Pavelić written on March 8, 1943, at the moment of the intensified persecutions of the Jews, has been read here. In that letter he openly rebuked Pavelić for persecuting Catholics because of their Jewish wives, while not applying this so-called Aryan law to himself and to the members of his government. (That is to say to Pavelić, and his so-called Minister, Žanić, both of whom were married to Jewesses.) Then, clearly alluding to the Germans, he wrote in this letter, *"But if any foreign power interferes in our internal national life or in our politics, then I will not be afraid if my voice and my protests reach the rulers of that foreign power,* for the Catholic Church knows no fears of any worldly power, whatever it may be, when it is a question of *defending the most basic rights of men."*

Let us examine the Archbishop's attitude toward the German occupation forces.

In Zagreb the Germans were represented by two men, Kasche and General Glaise von Horstenau. Kasche, a former glassware salesman, was the Reich's ambassador to the so-called Ustashi government. He was a member of the Nazi party and a fervent partisan of the Ustashi. General von Horstenau, on the contrary, as a secret enemy of the Nazi (after the attempted assassination of Hitler he was removed from Zagreb), detested the crimes of the Ustashi, and in attempting to restrain them found himself in continual conflict with Kasche. General von Horstenau was an Austrian officer of the old school, an enemy of the Prussian "Junkers," and a respected specialist in the field of military science; he had been made a doctor *honoris causa* by the University of Vienna. The differences between these two Germans were generally known in Zagreb and various anecdotes about them were current around the city. During the time of the occupation the Archbishop met with Kasche about three times, and then only on courtesy occasions. With Von Horstenau he was in contact somewhat more frequently, *but only for the purpose of intervening on the behalf of those who were persecuted by either the Ustashi or the German soldiers.* Most of these interventions were successful. There are even communists in Zagreb who owe their lives to the protection of General von Horstenau. In the course of the trial several letters were read which prove the Archbishop's success when he asked for protection for certain persons from Von Horstenau. A witness was also questioned here who said that Von Horstenau had prevented, through the Archbishop's intervention, acts of violence on the part of the German militia in several villages around Jaska. Even the accused Marić himself spoke of this. Let him who has truly worked for the benefit of the others answer whether guilty collaboration consists of saving people's lives or whether it would have been better for the Archbishop to have refused even the least contact with Von Horstenau and to have abandoned those persons to their fate.

While relations between the Archbishop and Von Horstenau were rare and were undertaken only for the noble purpose of saving Croatian and Serbian lives, for the most part those of anti-Fascists, relations with the *Italians* hardly existed at all. They are described in the letters presented to the court by me, especially by that one sent by the Archbishop to the so-called Italian Ambassador, Casertano, on March 27, 1943. It is known that Casertano, together with Pavelić, detested the Archbishop and wanted him removed from Croatia.

During the trial the prosecutor read a very long report, an alleged report of the Archbishop to the Holy See, dated May 18, 1943, according to which it is possible to conclude that the Archbishop was working for the Ustashi regime, that he hated the Serbs, that he falsely informed the Holy Father as to the situation in the NDH, and that he attributed the crimes of the Ustashi and Chetniks to the Partisans. I am sure that the reading of this alleged report of the Archbishop, especially accompanied as it was by the remarks of the prosecutor, created a bad impression. The prosecutor has given to this report a special importance by considering it to be authentic, or, to speak more exactly, by considering *his copy, which is the only one in existence,* to be a true copy of an original report which, he probably concluded, had been sent to the Pope by the Archbishop. I too attribute a special importance to this report but I have compelling reasons for not considering it authentic, but a Ustashi forgery or, at least, a Ustashi composition which was never used by the Archbishop. One reason for such an opinion on my part is the total contradiction of this copy of the alleged report to all the opinions and actions of the Archbishop. Another reason is the fact that the Archbishop, on hearing the first passages read by the prosecutor during the trial, denied authorship. The statements of the defendant are not sufficient for me as attorney for the defense, but they are, nevertheless, an indication when one is seeking the truth and trying to prove it. Besides, I believe the Archbishop. I am convinced that this report is apocryphal for the following reasons:

1. The copy of the alleged original report is written in *Italian* while all the other reports that the Archbishop sent to the Holy See were written in Latin.

2. The copy read by the prosecutor was found in the archives of the *Ustashi Ministry of Foreign Affairs* but the Archbishop never sent copies of his reports to that Ministry. As a matter of fact, not one copy of any other report of the Archbishop was found in these archives. Nor was a copy of this allegedly criminal report found in the archives of the Archdiocese where otherwise all first drafts or copies of all reports sent to the Holy Father are kept.

3. I presented to the court the original of a letter from the Secretary of State of the Vatican, Cardinal Maglione, sent on June 17, 1943, in which he acknowledges receipt of the Archbishop's report and also indicated its subject matter — *that the Archbishop described in his report the activities which he had undertaken on behalf of the Jews and Serbs in Croatia.* The copy of the report cited in the indictment bears the date, May 20, 1943; the letter from Cardinal Maglione is dated June 17, 1943. The only report, therefore, which the Archbishop could have sent to the Holy Father at that time could only have had the subject matter which Cardinal Maglione indicated in his letter. *And the subject matter of that report, as affirmed by the Cardinal, was in complete contradiction to the subject matter of the copy with which the prosecutor rebuked the Archbishop.*

4. All the reports of the bishops are written in a formalized Latin style: This style is especially marked at the beginning and at the end of reports. The formula with which all such reports begin is as follows:

Beatissime Pater: Aloisius Stepinac, Archiepiscopus Zagrebiensis, ad pedes Sanctitatis Vestrae humillime provolutus, ea quae sequentur exponit.

Then follows the subject matter of the report.
The formula at the end is the following:

Et deus, et. . . .

ALOISIUS STEPINAC,
Archiepiscopus Zagrebiensis

We have all heard, on the contrary, that the beginning and the end of the copy read by the prosecutor were formulated in a very different fashion, which obviously eliminates the Archbishop as the author of the original, supposing that an original exists. And the style of all the rest of the content of the copy does not correspond at all to the style of the Curia, which was well known to the Archbishop. The subject matter of the copy is very extended and speaks of things about which the Archbishop, for the most part, could have known nothing.

5. It is nowhere noted on the copy whether the original had been sent, when, by whom, how, nor does one find any data concerning these things in the archives of the Ustashi ministry concerned.

6. In the text of the copy the Archbishop is spoken of as Metropoleta de Croatiae et *Slavoniae,* which latter the Archbishop is not nor has he ever anywhere referred to himself as such.

In view of these compelling reasons I cannot and I must not accept the statement of the prosecutor as to the authenticity of this copy; on the contrary, I am obliged, at least until stronger counter-proofs are presented, to consider this copy a Ustashi forgery or an attempt at forgery. In the face of such strong proof no court could admit this allegedly incriminating text as evidence against the Archbishop. Confronted with such compelling reasons, the prosecutor relies in vain on the testimony of Rušinović, the representative of the so-called NDH in Rome at that time, but all his testimony relates to the year 1942, and it is clear that it can bear no relation to the Archbishop's alleged report in 1943. Confronted with these reasons, the prosecutor relies in vain on Prince Lobković, Papal Chamberlain in Rome and at the same time a representative of the Ustashi government. The prosecutor cannot pin his faith on Ustashi "diplomats" — those dilettanti in diplomacy — who themselves complained that everyone scorned them, and whose lack of success led them to play loosely with the truth. Furthermore, when one analyzes their testimony closely, it is plain that the Archbishop adroitly side-stepped their lies, according to which they either erroneously thought they had been successful or by which they purposely represented themselves as having been successful.

It is incredible — and it would have been ridiculous and naïve on the part of the Archbishop — to count on, and still less desire that the Holy See do anything on behalf of the NDH. This episode occurred when it had become abundantly clear that Hitler and his satellites would lose the war and that, consequently, the ruin of his creature, the NDH, was inevitable. This was in May, a long time after the Americans had landed in Africa, after the Germans had been beaten at Stalingrad and had been forced to retreat, when Africa — due to the total defeat of Rommel's army — had been completely cleared of German and Italian forces, when the Anglo-Americans were getting ready to invade the so-called "Festung Europa" — and when they were preparing to land in Sicily. How, then, can one think that the Archbishop, who until then had been an enemy of the so-called NDH and who had sent only unfavorable reports concerning it to the Pope, would suddenly, at that particular time, at the least favorable moment, with a complete reversal of the war situation and with the future clearly visible, have changed the attitude toward the NDH that he had held up to that time? How could he have modified his opinion and how could he have now taken up the cause of the NDH? Remember that his two most fervent sermons against Hitler and against the Ustashi were delivered in 1943. The Pope had not recognized the NDH before; how then could he have been persuaded to do so at a time like that? Rome was especially well informed and the Archbishop, devoted to the Holy See, conformed to its commands rather than it to his own will. Even supposing that his alleged report was authentic, it could have had no effect on the NDH.

After citing these irrefutable proofs against the authenticity of the copy of the alleged report, it should not be necessary nor do I feel myself obliged to explain how this Ustashi forgery was concocted. I will only mention that means which ecclesiastical circles here presume to have been employed. The chief of the Religion Section of the Ustashi Ministry was the well-known Ustasha, Brother Radoslav Glavaš. Probably the idea occurred to him of persuading the Archbishop to present such a report; he composed it himself and told the officials at the so-called Ministry of Foreign Affairs about it. Then either the people at the Ministry did not accept his proposal or his attempt to persuade the Archbishop did not succeed — or perhaps he had already felt that it could not succeed — at any rate, the copy remained in the archives of the Ministry of Foreign Affairs and the unsigned original was kept by Glavaš. This supposition is, moreover, strengthened by the nature of the subject matter of the copy for in it is a great deal of historical material concerning Bosnia, and Glavaš had been a great student of Bosnian history as a result of which he was considered a better historian than theologian. Still another thing;

if the Archbishop were the type of person he is said to be by the prosecutor and if he actually were the author of the alleged report, he could very easily have stolen the copy out of the archives of the Ustashi Ministry of Foreign Affairs when they were kept at his palace. But Archbishop Stepinac is capable neither of such a theft nor of presenting such a report. He is sincere and has no reason to fear truth.

With this, Section No. 1 of the Indictment is finished. As to Sections Nos. 2 and 3, which concern the so-called conversions and the military vicariate, my colleague, Dr. Natko Katičić has handled these matters and will speak of them himself. So I will go immediately to Section No. 4. This deals with the charges against the Archbishop for his activities in the last half of 1944 and the beginning of 1945, hence with the period immediately before the fall of the NDH.

In Section No. 4, the Indictment cites first the Archbishop's speech given, so it says, to the "Domagojevci" on July 7, 1944. Despite the fact that I have searched a long time for a copy of this speech, I have not been able to find one, and, therefore, I cannot say whether or not it was made. But if this speech really was made, which nowhere mentions the Independent State of Croatia but rather the state of the Croat people who undoubtedly have the right to have their own state — today they have their Croat Republic — then I can explain it as a reply to the well-known continual threats of the Chetnik's that they would wipe out the whole Croat people and thus prevent them from establishing their own state.

The passage from the speech given to the university students on March 18, 1945, which is regarded as criminal is that one which is directed against the dictatorship of the proletariat. But some of our allies, the western democracies, were also against this; was it, then, a crime for the Archbishop, especially at that time? The indictment, moreover, did not cite the sentence coming immediately before the passage it calls criminal. This I am going to quote myself. It says, "Does it mean peace when great states and nations impose their wills on small peoples by force of arms and then declare to the whole world, 'We are in agreement'?" Is there not expressed in this sentence the same attitude that is today represented by the Yugoslav delegation to the Peace Conference in Paris when it opposes the four great powers, the Big Four, who are imposing upon us a provision in the peace treaty that the delegation does not like; when it fights with all its might against the tearing away from Yugoslavia, from its living body, of Trieste and a considerable part of Croatian-Slovenian Istria and Gorizia? Why was not the Archbishop's speech to the university students interpreted according to this sentence and, perhaps even according to the rest of its content, and not in the light of the single passage dubbed as criminal?

We now come to the allegedly criminal letter of the Episcopal Conference of March 24, 1945. I do not deny that a certain relation existed between the Ustashi government and the Episcopal Conference, but I do dispute the fact that the Ustashi government had any connection with the letter, and in so far as any connection actually existed, the Archbishop did not know of it or approve of it. The relation between the Ustashi and the Episcopal Conference existed in so far as the Archbishop had consented to Canki's proposal that the Ustashi government offer it technical assistance so that the Conference could meet at a time of serious communication difficulties. It was Canki himself who made that statement and who also said that the Conference had been convened at the desire and on the initiative of the Archbishop. I believe more in the statements of Canki than in the contrary statements of Mandić and Bishop Šimrak, for old Mandić, at the end of his physical and mental powers despite the fact that he was President of the Government, was very badly informed and without any influence on the activities of the Ustashi regime, while Šimrak was a Trojan horse used by the Ustashi, and especially by Bogdan, to insinuate into the letter of the Episcopal Conference the meaning they wanted. If Bogdan was in contact with Šimrak, and if he gave him a first draft for the Conference's letter so that he might secretly introduce it into the Conference, that is not the fault of the Archbishop because these behind-the-scenes meetings between Bogdan and Šimrak were not known to him and besides, we have here recognized the Archbishop as a man to whom the Ustashi could not dictate. Furthermore the prosecutor himself admitted that, in addition to Bogdan's first draft, there were three others, including Canki's, and that the text of the episcopal letter was closest not to the first draft of Bogdan-Šimrak, but rather to that of Canki. That, therefore, is a proof that Bogdan and Šimrak did not succeed. I have not read any of these first drafts, not even Canki's, so that I cannot judge of the alleged similarity of these drafts to the actual text of the episcopal letter. But even if this similarity existed, it would not be a proof that the Ustashi government imposed its text on the Conference, because Canki was the Minister of Justice and Religion in that government who, by nature of his jurisdiction, came in contact with the Archbishop several times and it is not impossible that they exchanged views on the subject of the Conference, that is to say on the allegedly systematic torturing and murdering of Croatian priests and faithful. It is not impossible that Canki gave information to the Archbishop on this subject and at that time there were also many similar reports by refugees who were fleeing from liberated regions. In those days the Ustashi press abounded in the most exaggerated reports of the massacres of priests and faithful. A week before the Episcopal Conference a ceremony was held by the government to commemorate murdered priests; on that occasion the then Rector of the Croatian University, Horvat, gave a lengthy speech on the subject. If the Archbishop believed these reports, if he succumbed to such propaganda, if he convened the Episcopal Conference at that time, and if he published, together with the other bishops, the allegedly criminal episcopal letter, that can be considered as his mistake, but not as his crime. The Archbishop could not have prevented the Ustashi government from exploiting the episcopal letter for its own purposes and even from falsifying it. (In the text of the episcopal letter was written "Hrvatska" which the Ustashi changed to "Nezavisna Država Hrvatska.")

Next it is considered a crime that the Archbishop hid the archives of the Ustashi Ministry of Foreign Affairs in his palace by arrangement with Pavelić. The former Ustashi Foreign Minister, Alajbegović, a witness called by the prosecutor, stated here that there was no agreement made between Pavelić and Stepinac and that it was he himself. Alajbegović, who had requested the Archbishop to provide shelter for the archives from the danger of bombing and not for the purpose of hiding them. In effect, the Archbishop did not hide them, for by the beginning of June, 1945, he had already informed the people's authorities of this situation on his own initiative, which I can prove by the original of the certificate of the Religion Commission of June 13, 1945. I have also brought the pro-memoria of the Archiepiscopal Secretariate of June 6, 1945, as proof that the Archbishop had also notified the President of the NRH Government, Dr. Bakarić, of all that was kept at his palace. Of the phonograph records of Pavelić's speeches the Archbishop knew nothing, as has been confirmed by the codefendant Šalić who had notified the government of them.

It is incomprehensible — at least from a juridical point of view —

how the indictment can make Archbishop Stepinac responsible for the attempts of Pavelić, Rupnik, and Rožman to save themselves during the last hours of the occupation. If these persons did make such a plan involving Stepinac and if they did propose the plan to him, how can he be guilty of their actions? It is certain that he did not enter into their plot and that, in so far as they urged him, he *refused.* He refused, not after discussions, but *at the beginning.* In this instance there is no *activity* on Stepinac's part, as the indictment states, but only *passivity.* Yes, the regency was offered to the Archbishop by Pavelić, the opportunity to take power, but he immediately refused it, first because of his principle not to take any part in secular affairs, second because he did not want to accept anything from Pavelić, and third because he held the democratic point of view that power must come from the people and not Pavelić or the Ustashi. The witness, Alajbegović, also stated exactly why it was that Archbishop Stepinac had been proposed as regent. It was because of his great authority over the people and the fact that to a very great extent he enjoyed their confidence. But the Archbishop merited this authority and confidence precisely because of his correctly hostile attitude toward the occupation forces during the four years of their sway. Immediately before the liberation the danger of massacres existed, not in all cases by the NOV but also from the German army, for it appeared that it intended to defend Zagreb, and from the Ustashi who had threatened that before their retreat they would kill 40,000 Zagreb citizens. (And, in part, they carried out this horrible threat.) Impelled by the desire to save Zagreb from such massacres, the Archbishop took advantage of the invitations of Bulak and Alajbegović to see Maček. He went to the home of Dr. Maček accompanied by the Ustashi General Moškov — without him he could not have gone at all, for Dr. Maček had been put under house arrest and it was Moškov who had the keys to his lodging. Here again, as always, we find the Archbishop engaged in an activity that was designed to assist and to save the people, to prevent greater disasters in so far as was possible under the circumstances. The Archbishop denies that Maček told him that he was going to escape; he affirms, on the contrary, that he told him that he would remain in Zagreb. In any case, Archbishop Stepinac remained in Zagreb and, after having done everything possible to avoid the massacres, he awaited the liberation with a clear conscience.

And the liberation came on May 8, 1945. Therefore we now come to section No. 5 of the indictment which contains the charges against Archbishop Stepinac in the period *following the liberation* under the new Yugoslavia.

Here Archbishop Stepinac is described as the most active enemy of the people and the state; as the motivating power behind all the acts of the "Križari" and the Ustashi and behind other terroristic activities; as the executive of a systematic plan of action for the return of Maček, the Ustashi, the reaction, and King Peter. And what is introduced as proof of all those appalling charges?

The fact is cited that, about five months after the liberation, the Archbishop received Lisak, Lela Sofijanec, an emigrant Ustashi student from Salzburg, and two short letters or notes from the Ustashi General Moškov, and also the fact that he took part in the Bishops' Conference which published on September 20 the letter known as the episcopal letter of September 20, 1945.

These are all the proofs introduced concerning all the acts with which the Archbishop has been charged and from which have been deduced his alleged activities against the state and the people.

Actually it should not be necessary to analyze these few minor facts, since one can see at once that they cannot possibly prove such grave accusations. But I would like to go over them in some detail.

It is incontestable that Archbishop Stepinac received Lisak, the first of the accused, on September 24, 1945, but it is also incontestable that he did not receive him as Lisak, but as an unknown person named Petrović. On this point all testimony is in agreement; that of Dr. Franolić, of Bishop Lach, of Ostojčić, of Lisak, of the codefendant Salić, and of the Archbishop himself. There exists only a very slight shade of difference between the statement of Šalić and that of the Archbishop. While the Archbishop says that he recognized the so-called Petrović as Lisak only at the moment the man was already before him and he had put on his glasses, Šalić says that immediately before the Archbishop came into the room where the so-called Petrović was waiting, he, Šalić, had said to the Archbishop that he had recognized him as Lisak. I believe the Archbishop and I think that Šalić is mistaken. But even if Šalić's statement were true, it would still not be a proof that the Archbishop *had really wanted to receive Lisak*. The difference is only the matter of a few seconds. The Archbishop had already consented to receive Petrović and had come to the room where Petrović was waiting and, at the last moment, when he had reached the door of the room, he learned, according to the testimony of Šalić, that Petrović was not Petrović, but Lisak. It can happen to any man that after such a surprise he might do something that he would certainly not do if he had not been startled. Thus it was with Archbishop Stepinac. If what Šalić says is true, then the *willingness of the Archbishop to receive Lisak cannot* be seen in his sudden resolution by the door to receive a man who was waiting to see him. One can, perhaps, perceive that despite the Archbishop's distress, and due to his well-known charity and courtesy, he would not refuse a man to whom he had made a promise because of the man's false claim. They spoke for twenty or thirty minutes. What they spoke about we know only from the testimony of the two participants. Their statements are in essential agreement. According to these statements it was only Lisak who spoke, while the Archbishop kept silent, interrupting his silence only to ask two questions; what had become of the children of the refugees abroad, and what had become of the priest, Father Tiso, former President of Slovakia. Lisak explicitly told the Archbishop that he had not come for the purpose of any political or terroristic action, because there had already been enough violence. One can believe this because Archbishop Stepinac expressed his displeasure that Lisak had come to his palace and ordered Salić never to receive him again.

It is, then, incontestable that Lisak came uninvited, that he slid into the Archbishop's palace under a false name, that the Archbishop did not know until the last minute that Petrović was Lisak, that after a short interview with Lisak he broke off all relations with him, that he explicitly expressed his regret that he had let himself be deceived and had thus received him, and that from this forced interview there followed no results. What occurred at the Archbishop's palace concerning Lisak could have happened to anyone. It all happened against the will of the Archbishop.

In the question of the reception of Lisak by the Archbishop, I am reminded of the scenes from Victor Hugo's *Les Misérables* in which the good French bishop received the prisoner, Jean Valjean, and in which he pays a visit to the home of the old revolutionary, member of the Convention, an atheist who lives completely alone and whom everyone avoids. No reader sees in this an understanding of a Catholic bishop with a criminal any more than were the relations of Christ with Mary Magdalen and later, upon the cross, with the good thief — detestable. Even had the Archbishop of Zagreb received

Lisak knowing that he was Lisak, should he be judged differently
than Hugo's bishop? But to the Archbishop of Zagreb politics,
conspiracies, and intrigues were repugnant, and everything which
could at any time harm the Church or the State, and that is why
he did not want to receive Lisak when, tricked by him, he did
receive him and why he ordered that he never again be received.

And Lela Sofijanec? So many thousands of men and women have
been at the Archbishop's palace that he could not possibly remember
them all, despite an excellent memory. He recalls only one woman
who came from Trieste with some rosaries. He also remembers an
immigrant student from Salzburg and only because he started talking
politics whereupon the Archbishop immediately insisted he cease.

As I have said, what happened to the Archbishop in these cases
could have happened to anyone. The Archbishop is not guilty of
the fact that the Ustashi and various immigrants deluded themselves
on the subject of the Archbishop's attitude, of the fact that, in
their error and in their despair concerning their situation, they sought
to draw near to the prelate. Such attempts are *their own* acts, not
the Archbishop's. The only accusation which is lodged against the
Archbishop is based on *his own acts*. And is that accusation punishable? It is not really a proof that he did not wish to have and did
not have any connection with anyone's illegal actions?

The facts regarding Moškov's letters or notes are similar. They
were not even addressed to the Archbishop; this can be seen from
their salutations (Stephano — hence to Lacković!) and from the
testimony of Dr. Gurin. Even when, in spite of that, they were
forwarded to the Archbishop, after reading only the first few lines
he stopped and threw them into the wastebasket. To whom among
us could it not happen that Moškov, Pavelić, Luburić, or others of
their ilk might send us letters, and even letters with criminal content,
with contents different from those of the innocent letters from Moškov?
Would this incriminate us? What is important is the way in which
the Archbishop reacted to Moškov's notes. Into the wastebasket!

And now I ask, how can anyone on the basis of these three unwanted visits, or these letters, equally unwanted, and, in general,
on *the actions of others* build up a case proving the collaboration of
the Archbishop with the "Križari," the terrorists, with the reaction
at home and abroad? If it is admitted that such a case may be
constructed, no one of us is secure against a similar charge and
conviction.

The last charge of section No. 5 and the final point in the indictment is a more serious matter. It concerns the *pastoral letter of the Episcopal Conference of September 20, 1945*. This at least is the work of the Archbishop, but it is not only his, it is also the work of the other seventeen bishops of Yugoslavia, who all signed it with the special note that the whole Episcopate of Yugoslavia assumed responsibility for it. Let us take a look at this pastoral letter.

First the bishops express in it their thanks to God that finally the tragic, fratricidal war is over. Consequently Archbishop Stepinac together with the other bishops thereby confirms the principle of the *fraternity* of the several Yugoslav peoples.

What impelled the bishops to publish this pastoral letter? The letter gives us this specific answer: concern for the spiritual welfare of all the faithful! For what purpose was it published? The letter's reply: so that postwar conditions in our country may become normal as soon as possible.

But in what did the bishops see abnormal conditions in postwar Yugoslavia? In the fact that the points of conflict between the Church and State remain unsettled.

In the numerous convictions of so many innocent priests, condemned even to death without a chance to defend themselves.

In the suppression of the Catholic press.

In the fact that the use of seminaries has been made impossible.

In the announced suppression of private Catholic secondary schools.

In the closing of most of the Catholic boarding schools.

In the manner of teaching religion in the secondary schools.

In the obstacles put in the way of the performance of religious duties.

In obligatory civil marriage.

In the fact that "*Caritas*" was put under the surveillance of state representatives.

In the way in which agrarian reform was carried out in relation to the Church.

In the difficulties that have been made for the orders of nuns.

In the treatment accorded certain cemeteries.

In the treatment accorded to prisoners in concentration camps.

In the propagation of a materialistic and atheistic spirit.

Certain facts in relation to the above-listed objections are true, as for example those which concern the suppression of the Catholic press, obligatory civil marriage, the naming of state delegates to oversee *"Caritas,"* etc. It is another question to ask whether the objections to these facts are justified and well founded. This is a question of opinion, of one's point of view, and that, in itself, is not a crime. The state may be of the opinion that, for example, civil marriage can be regulated only in the way in which it has been regulated, but the representatives of the Church are free to hold another opinion. Even if the objection of the bishops on the subject of civil marriage seems reactionary and contrary to the principle of the freedom of conscience, the matter nevertheless appears in another aspect after we have heard here at the trial the statement of the Archbishop. For he expressed here his opinion that civil marriage could have been regulated as it is, for example, in the United States, that is to say to allow each person the freedom to be married either in church or before a civil magistrate, and to oblige those who take charge of church records to notify the state record keepers of the marriage. Whether the suppression of the Catholic press is justified is another question, but one can understand that the bishops have an opinion on this matter different from that of the public prosecutor. These complaints, then, are things on which persons can have different opinions, which they can discuss, and upon which they can, in view of the freedom of the press, publicly express their opinions without committing a crime. What must be regarded as false are, for example, the statements that innocent priests have been killed, the statements on the subjects of the concentration camps, and the graves. I, at least, do not know how to introduce any proof for these things and one ought not to state what he cannot prove. But from what the Archbishop has said here, it can none the less be seen that on these subjects the Archbishop did receive such information, which served him as the basis for those parts of the pastoral letter composed by him and the other bishops. The Archbishop, therefore, did not write these things knowing them to be false and with the intention of slander. His fault consists in accepting false information, as though it were the truth.

Such a fault, however, is not deceit. If the authors of the pastoral letter arrived at, let us say, a false conclusion; at a conclusion which was not true, which was reached on the basis of facts which were in part true and in part false; and the conclusion that "the present situation of the Catholic Church in Yugoslavia can, in our opinion, only be characterized as one of open persecution of the Church," then that conclusion, like any other conclusion, must be considered from a *subjective* point of view. For it is only an *opinion*, and an opinion — even one that is false from an objective point of view — ought not always to be judged blameworthy. As to what specifically concerns the death sentences of the priests, who can say that all sentences are infallible? Every sentence is the expression of the conclusions of the court which pronounced it, but these conclusions may vary according to the personality of the judge, according to his disposition at the time of the trial, or according to still other circumstances. Does it not happen that different counselors before the same tribunal obtain different answers to the same question? Is not the administration of justice in every country full, more or less, of contradictory verdicts? Why, then, cannot someone doubt whether these sentences are well founded and infallible, especially if he has information on the subject which may, perhaps, be false but which he regards as true? Such suspicions, moreover, arise most frequently in times of revolution when sentences are not pronounced as calmly, deliberately, or prudently as in times of peace. Furthermore, the law itself presupposes the fallibility even of valid verdicts and for the purpose of correcting them puts at our disposal various means for their revision: the appeal of the prosecutor and pardon. Criticism of sentences in itself, made on the basis of honest doubts and with the intention of making them better in the future, is not, then, to be condemned.

When Archbishop Stepinac, together with the other seventeen bishops, clearly stated, toward the end of the pastoral letter, the demands of the Church — except for the general demand on the subject of the complete freedom of the human person and of his inalienable rights — and when he designated these demands as the basis for the normal arrangement of things in our country and for the realization of a lasting peace, that could not have had and in fact did not have anything to do with the "Križari," nor with those who were deserters, nor with the Ustashi, nor with our enemies from either within or without the country, and for that reason I consider unsound the charges made in the indictment concerning these points.

The pastoral letter, despite all its admitted inaccuracies and exaggerations, is not, however, of such a nature that it could lead or — as has been said several times in the course of the trial — push anyone along a false path or into any activity directed against the state. The codefendant, the Franciscan Provincial, Brother Modesto

Martinčić, it is true, has tried in a most un-Christian manner to exonerate himself by testifying to the bad influence the pastoral letter had on him; but it must not be forgotten that he committed his crimes a long time *before* the publication of the pastoral letter and during the occupation he demonstrated nothing that resembled the charitable activities, aid to the persecuted, or the antioccupation attitude of Archbishop Stepinac, and that it was I who finally presented during the trial his own irrefutable admission in writing that he had not even read the pastoral letter two months after its publication but that according to what he had heard of it, it did not lead to any political action.

Judges of the People's Supreme Court! When one judges the pastoral letter and many other things, one must keep in mind the fact that Archbishop Stepinac is the highest representative of the Catholic Church and the Catholic religion in Croatia and, indeed, in all Yugoslavia. And what the Catholic religion means to the people of Croatia and to what an extent they are attached to it, the following example of the late Stjepan Radić will show us. When the deceased leader of the Croatian people, who had the best knowledge of their soul, held his meetings, he began them with the salutation, "Praise be to Jesus Christ and to Mary!" and if, during his speech, the church clock began to ring the Angelus, he took off his hat to pray and all the men who were attending the meeting — there were sometimes tens of thousands — followed his example. That is why one can still say today that the Archbishop, whenever he is acting for the interests of the Church and the Catholic religion, has behind him the overwhelming majority of the Croatian people. One cannot forget that fact.

Nor must one pass over the passage from the pastoral letter of September 20, 1945, in which it is stated that the bishops do not at all want to provoke a clash with the new government, but that on the contrary they seek an agreement and that toward that end they have already tried several times — the Archbishop says fifteen — to inform the proper authorities in writing of the point of view of the Catholic Church. That it is the Holy See which, in the last analysis, will decide on all questions which concern both Church and State. I again add the statement of the Archbishop that he personally spoke of all these things with the President of the Federal Government, Marshal Tito, and with the President of the NRH, Dr. Bakarić, in his audience with them immediately after the liberation.

So much for the pastoral letter of September 20, 1945.

Before finishing, I would like to again review certain details of the trial.

In the course of the trial, I relied among other things on the well-known speech of the President of the Croatian Government, Dr. Bakarić, delivered to the People's Assembly on March 24, 1946, in which the President explicitly admitted that *the high officials and the clergy had not taken the part of the Germans or the NDH up to the beginning of 1945*. To that argument the public prosecutor replied that the President had then known nothing of certain documents drawn from the archives of the Ministry of Foreign Affairs. For myself, in any case, I could not imagine that the President had not known of these documents from the archives by March, 1946, from the archives which the government had already received in June of the year before (1945), but, in spite of all that, I loyally accepted the reply of the prosecutor in matters concerning Dr. Bakarić. But I must also reply to the public prosecutor that he has based his indictment on charges, *on facts which he had not learned solely from the archives* but which were known to him from other sources. The prosecutor has produced documents drawn from the archives *apart from the indictment only during the course of the trial*, but I have today produced, I believe, sufficiently strong reasons against the authenticity of these documents. Therefore, my appeal to the speech of the President, Dr. Bakarić continues to have value on the subject of the charges in the indictment which relate *to the time up to the beginning of 1945*, and that is the period in which the charges are most numerous.

The public prosecutor has said several times in the course of the trial that Archbishop Stepinac has lied, and once he even flung the word *liar* at him. This is a serious charge that is made only against a man who has *deliberately* told an untruth. To confirm this grave charge the prosecutor cited the Archbishop's public reply on December 17, 1945, to the statement of the President, Dr. Bakarić, that was published in the daily press. He asserted that the Archbishop had lied in this reply when he wrote that Lisak had not visited his palace. He who carefully reads the Archbishop's reply will see that the Archbishop did not say that. Nowhere in this reply did he state that Lisak had not been to his palace. I have brought a copy of the December 17, 1945, issue of *Vjesnik*, the newspaper of the Popular Front, as proof that others also understood the Archbishop's reply

correctly and not in the way in which the prosecutor interpreted it —
Vjesnik published a whole article against Archbishop Stepinac in
which the author interpreted the Archbishop's reply as having admitted that Lisak had been at his residence. And with the Archbishop's
admission, with his statement that Lisak had been at his residence,
the author condemned him throughout.

When it is a question of newspapers, I must mention again that
another Zagreb paper, the *Narodini List,* published two articles
against the Archbishop signed by a certain J. R. In these articles
the Archbishop was accused of not lifting a finger on behalf of the
five Slovenian priests imprisoned and finally killed in the concentration camp at Jasenovac, prominent among whom was Father Rikar.
It was asserted that Rikar was so indignant at the alleged negligence
of the Archbishop that just before being shot he had given his
breviary to the author of these articles along with an ironic message
for the Archbishop, asking the author to take his breviary to the
Archbishop as a sign of his gratitude for his intervention. Without
taking account of the fact that the author of these defamatory articles
did not carry out the last request of the late Father Rikar, that he
sent neither the breviary nor the message to Archbishop Stepinac,
that he did not even in his article take into consideration the well-
known state of mind of nearly all prisoners, that is to say that they
wanted the whole world to take action on their behalf and that
they thought that no one cared for them; I have this to say: in the
course of the trial I have submitted four documents to the court
which irrefutably prove that the Archbishop took strong and frequent
action on behalf of the five Slovenian priests, and especially on behalf
of Father Rikar, and, that when he learned of the failure of his
actions and of the death of the latter, he sent a very severe letter
to Pavelić, in which he rebuked Pavelić — among other things — for
this incident, which he said was — I quote literally — "*a disgraceful
incident and a crime that cries out for vengeance from heaven. Jasenovac camp itself is a shameful stain on the honor of the NDH!*"
Narodini List did not publish the correction that was sent to it and
in this way it let the public believe similar lies against Archbishop
Stepinac. The Archbishop, moreover, has never been given the chance
to defend himself in the newspapers against the attacks directed
against him and published in those same papers.

In the same way I, that is to say the defense of Archbishop Stepinac,
have not been given the chance during his trial to introduce proofs

to refute and to completely demolish what the prosecutor has said here against the Archbishop *in relation to the activities of "Caritas."* It is well known throughout all Zagreb, and also outside of Zagreb, how many charities the Archbishop has accorded to the poor without taking account of their religion, nationality, or political opinions; how many children he has saved, especially children of the Orthodox and those of Partisans — about 7000 from Kozara! — and how many noble anti-Fascist citizens he has brought together in this institution. The devoted work performed by the Archbishop through *"Caritas,"* of which he could rightly be proud were he not so modest, has spread his renown and his glory as much as have his sermons and his opposition to the occupation forces. Despite this work, recognized by all, friends and enemies alike, the prosecutor has tried in this trial by means of several statements of the late director of *"Caritas,"* Dumić, to present it, and thereby the Archbishop, in the worst possible light. I, on the contrary, have proposed several witnesses to prove that these statements were made by Dumić, now the late Dumić, a short time before his death when he was in a state in which he was not accountable for what he said, and that he had retracted these statements at the time when he was in full possession of his faculties; then I proposed a large amount of material proofs, both documents and witnesses, which should have shown the work of *"Caritas"* and of the Archbishop in the best, the most just, and the truest light, and thus refute all the statements and so-called proofs of the prosecutor — but my proofs were not admitted. That will do no harm among the people who are informed, who had the chance during the occupation to follow the Archbishop's work closely, but I do consider this nonadmission of proofs as an essential omission of the court, the more so because this court is a court of first instance and of final appeal, above which there is no further appeal, no court where one can, by means of judicial remedies, refute all the omissions in procedure.

I think that this indictment is also, in part, a consequence of the prejudgments made concerning the Archbishop before the final liberation. The Partisans, it is true, kept in communication with occupied territory, but along with exact information, also received a good deal of false information. The forest represents the heroic armed resistance of our people against the occupation forces, but the men who fought had neither the opportunity nor the time to learn to know the Archbishop as the hundreds of thousands of citizens of occupied Zagreb learned to know him. It is difficult — it is completely impossible — to mar or to tarnish the lofty and luminous idea of their Archbishop that is held by the hundreds and hundreds of thousands of the Croatian people in Zagreb and beyond it. Nor can this trial succeed in doing it.

Among other things, the prosecutor said that the Archbishop is immodest and a megalomaniac. To tell the truth the Archbishop is a living refutation of these weaknesses. It is well known, for example, how many times he sought to escape becoming an Archbishop. We have heard here how he has refused all the honors that have been offered him, the regency, the chance to take power — not only because of his principle that secular things are incompatible with his status as a priest, but also out of modesty. His entourage know best how he avoided ceremony and festivities, how disagreeable it was to him to show himself in public, how friendly his conduct was to the poorest people, and that he led a modest, even an ascetic, life. Even his greatest enemies were not able to reproach him with anything concerning his life as a priest. Would such a man be a criminal?

I am going to mention one more detail on this subject, but it is characteristic. When we visited him in prison before the trial, we his defenders, he told us that he had not read any of the news in the papers about the trial of Šalić. We believed him, and those closest to him affirmed it. Only a man who has a clear and tranquil conscience can act in that fashion. If he had felt even a little guilty, would he not have read the reports, at least to enable himself to make his future statements consistent with the testimony of Šalić and the others, and thus to avoid important differences in these statements?

The Archbishop has publicly declared in his interrogation and here that he recognizes the people's courts, that he does not claim for himself any extraterritoriality, that he recognizes the Constitution in so far as it is not in contradiction to the moral principles of the Church, and that, in general, he recognizes the people's government and wants an agreement between the Church and the State. This is further proof that he is incapable of committing crimes against the people and against the State.

In summing all this up in an objective manner, especially the matter of proofs, which I have here cited only in part but whose other part is also known to the court without my citing it, my conscience does not permit me to agree with the final plea of the prosecutor. In the past few days the newspapers have published numerous telegrams in which the conviction of Archbishop Stepinac has been demanded. The prosecutor has here referred to those telegrams. On my part I oppose them not only with the statement of 150 priests from Zagreb, which I presented to the court and which refutes the accusations against the Archbishop, but also with the prayers of thousands and thousands of the Croatian faithful, who in the churches and in their homes have been ceaselessly praying for days, and are still praying at this moment, convinced of the innocence of their Archbishop, praying to God for his acquittal as the most just decision. And I, as lawyer for his defense, propose to the People's Supreme Court that it dismiss the charges against the defendant, Archbishop Dr. Aloysius Stepinac.

DOCUMENT C

Address of the Assistant Counsel for the Defense, Dr. N. Katičić,
Delivered on October 8, 1946

After the address of the attorney for the defense, Dr. J. Politeo, who had reviewed the political part of the accusation and who, at the same time, had delivered the final plea of the defense for the acquittal of the accused, the other defense attorney, Dr. N. Katičić, spoke as follows (in an abridged form, taken from prepared notes):

I speak as an appointed attorney for the defense, according to official order, on behalf of Dr. Aloysius Stepinac, Archbishop of Zagreb. I will speak on sections No. 2 and No. 3 of the indictment and I will limit myself to this subject.

I have, therefore, concerned myself with the acts of violence committed in relation to the so-called "rebaptisms" of the Orthodox.

We all remember the frightful events that took place, and the moving scene that was described here a moment ago has recalled them to our memories. Those events were the greatest of misfortunes not only for those who went to their death, but also for the living among whom remain hate and poisonous rancor. Those violent deeds were crimes which spread discord between the Croatian and the Serbian peoples, and were profitable only for the occupation, whose agent unanimously stimulated and encouraged them without any feeling for our peoples.

As defense attorney by official order, and because the defendant has not accepted any defense for reasons of principle, and since consequently I could receive from him neither assistance nor cooperation, I must take special care to place before you the facts and to explain to you the reasons and points of view which give support to the defense, the more so since the prosecution has already tried to show you all that is contrary to them.

The question that is posed is: how did the above events reflect the work of Archbishop Stepinac and what was his attitude toward them? Because when an indictment for a crime is drawn up, it is first necessary to ask the questions: has he who is charged with crime actually committed it, what was in his mind, what was his intention?

To reply, it is necessary, before all, to consider the history of the events connected with the so-called "rebaptisms" and, to that end, I shall divide them into four parts.

1. When the NDH was founded, a violent terror arose. Various acts of violence were committed. In some places, priests were involved who were, however, cast out of the Church and their spiritual and frequently their personal ties to it were cut. There took place among them the same cleavage as among all classes of our society; those who were in favor of the terror and those who bitterly opposed it.

This flood of terror immediately gave rise to the problem of the so-called "rebaptisms," and it was the terror's partisans who began to put pressure on the Orthodox to force them to accept the Catholic religion.

These acts were not religious in character. No spiritual reasons gave meaning to these acts of violence. This is irrefutable and is best demonstrated by the fact that the very men who first committed these acts designed to make the Orthodox embrace the Catholic religion, continued to persecute the "rebaptized," later founded the Croatian Orthodox Church. Therefore the motivation was not at all religious.

2. How did the Church react to this situation? By means proper to it, by a tested method founded on very long experience; it withdrew into canon law and thereby hesitated in this matter and delayed in an effort to gain time. From May, 1941, until 1942, a great many circular letters were issued, one after another, in which the rules concerning admission of the "rebaptized" into the Catholic Church were analyzed and clarified. For admission it was necessary to petition the approval of the superior spiritual authorities; religious instruction was prescribed, and it was only then that reception into the Church followed. From the beginning of this procedure to the

end it was necessary that the greatest possible amount of time elapse. The goal was to establish in this way a more peaceful situation and to remove opportunities for the acts of violence committed by the other side. I am going to cite several examples which will show that this procedure was followed.

Here is the letter of the chief district officer of Požega, Velika Župa Livac Zapolje, in which the clergy was severely attacked for not doing its duty, for showing criminal negligence, for not making its rounds among the Orthodox who wanted to enter the Catholic Church, and for waiting "until the Serbs should agree with them and send their carriages for them," for excusing themselves as being too busy with other work, and, what is worse, for saying to the "rebaptized" that the Church did not show the least pleasure because they had entered it. At the time of this complaint, the Archiepiscopal Court in Zagreb replied to Velika Župa saying that the clergy was certainly correct and that probably they were not able to do their official duty in specific cases, that there did not yet exist any formal charges, but that it would, however, investigate the matter and if it seemed that there were any faults on the part of the clergy that they would be called to account. This is the typical way in which, at that time, individuals and the authorities resolutely hesitated in this matter and in which they opposed the pressure brought to bear on them.

Next is a very interesting document which was contributed by the prosecution. It is a letter from the Ustashi priest Kamber written to Pavelić in 1941 in which the priest complains that the process for "rebaptism" is too complicated, that it takes a long time, that petitions are sometimes kept for three months in the bishops' offices, and requests that this procedure be modified.

It is the same with the question of the acceptance of Orthodox churches and property. At that time a request was sent to the Vatican, whence came, after a considerable period of time, a reply giving an explanation of the canonical rule on the matter. The parish bureaus were then notified that Orthodox churches must not be accepted except in the case when all of its members or a large majority of them enter the Catholic Church, and that no transfers at all were to be made at the registry offices.

Such a tactic of procrastination would without doubt have been very good for the re-establishment of more normal conditions. One would suppose that the Ustashi would have contented themselves with the fact that the process of "rebaptism" was at least beginning and that they would have left the people in peace. In this question, however, one must consider things from the perspective of that time. Acts of violence had already occurred here and there in isolated instances, although none the less frightful for that, but it was believed that they would not be repeated. And even if they had been repeated in a few places, it was not really considered probable that such incidents would continue; it was believed, moreover, that tempers would cool and that with the passage of time there would be introduced some kind of order, and that is why the Church properly hesitated in the procedure concerning conversions. There were also other reasons. Thus, for example, in the beginning, several agencies were established by the Ustashi, such as Ponova (the Renewal), which was in charge of matters relating to the so-called "rebaptism" and which, in a completely arbitrary fashion, without any authorization on the part of the Church, and without any jurisdiction, sent out priests and missionaries on its own authority. By insisting upon regulating this procedure according to strict canonical rule the Church was able to overcome such arbitrary procedures and to curb priests who had not been authorized. It was hoped that "conversions" would be carried out in a more peaceful and humane fashion with the least possible bitterness until the time when, in the words of Canon Lončar, "all the Orthodox will return to their Orthodox Church."

But now the prosecution asserts that all that I have just described means nothing, that it was only a form of deceit by which the Church expressed its agreement with the acts of violence committed against the Serbs. One can hold to the assertion of the prosecution, one can accept what I have said, but one can only be guided by truth as based on proofs and facts. My assertion is supported by the following:

First, it is especially demonstrated by what has been mentioned above with reference to the dilatory tactics of the Church in this matter, which clearly proves that it did not act with the intention of exploiting the Serbs, but that it hesitated and procrastinated so that a more peaceful situation might be brought about.

Second, common sense confirms it. Why suppose that someone wants to achieve an evil end by means of a certain act when the very facts show that he desires a good end? Besides the few priests guilty of committing acts of violence and who were expelled from the Church, there is a legion of brave, honest, and judicious priests who remained at their posts and filled them loyally, who remain there today and whom the people hold in high esteem. It is necessary to insist on the fact that of all the priests in the Archdiocese, only a completely insignificant number were in the ranks of the Ustashi or showed sympathy for them. It is necessary to note that out of more than fifty witnesses questioned here about the acts of violence in relation to the "rebaptisms" there were only a negligible number of cases involving the territory of the Zagreb Archdiocese, and still fewer cases that involved priests who belonged to that Archdiocese. Can anyone imagine that these men would suddenly go mad and become avid for thousands of converts, whose conversions they knew, in any case, did not have a religious basis, and who would, they knew, return to their own religion as soon as it was possible for them to do so? That would be contrary to common sense, and it is the reason why it was perfectly natural for the Church to wish to avoid these conversions, and not to take advantage of sheer violence so that the Orthodox would accept as quickly as possible the Catholic religion.

Thirdly, my assertion is proved by the reaction of the Archbishop himself who revolted against this violence, and who held back and calmed his priests, who sent Canon Dr. Lončar to protest against them, and who, as we have heard him, stated that he did not want converts except as they became Catholic by their own free will, after having made their decision to do so freely.

For all these reasons one must believe that the Church acted in this manner and for these reasons as I have described them.

3. While waiting the terror increased. It happened that the methods of procrastination were not sufficient. Heads fell. The people invaded the Church, crying and pleading, open your doors to us. In effect, chaos had taken the upper hand. Zagreb was isolated, the country-side was plunged into a sea of disorder, communications with many parishes were lacking. The methods which the Church had favored became less and less adequate. Rebaptisms took place and were bound to take place in greater and greater numbers; it was only this that brought any security; the door had to be opened. That the Church, none the less, conducted itself correctly and that it had to adapt itself to this development is clearly shown in the circular letter of March 2, 1942, on the procedure for conversions, in which it was stated that the principal motive for conversion ought to be a conviction of the rightness of the Catholic religion, but that if there

were secondary motives, in so far as they were not dishonorable, they would not be an obstacle to conversion. That is the meaning of opening the door — so that the unfortunate might be able to find protection.

4. The whole movement concerning "rebaptism" stopped suddenly (in 1942). The reasons for that lay in the political and moral failure of those who had committed acts of violence and also in the growing progress of the fight for the liberation of the people. Soon all this will be only an episode on which history will render its verdict.

What, then, was the attitude taken by Archbishop Stepinac toward the events that we have just considered?

(Ad 1). As in the case of the entire Church, he was placed before a *fait accompli*. These events, the acts of violence and the movement for "rebaptism," developed like an avalanche. The people begged ceaselessly to be admitted into the Catholic Church. One could not foresee any change that could come quickly, but he, as well as the others, believed and had to believe that these frightful scenes would not repeat themselves, that it would be possible effectively to calm and help the people.

(Ad 2 and 3). If we do not know directly the opinion of the Archbishop, we must conclude from all these events that his intentions were the same as the previously described intentions of the Church in general: to help the people, to pray for time, but not to exploit them. At no time was any violence exercised either by himself or by anyone else with his consent. By regulations, by the organization of the processes of conversion, it was necessary to find a peaceful solution. It was also at this time, in the fall of 1941, that the Episcopal Conference took place along with the establishment of the Committee of Three to watch over the conversions, of which the Archbishop was the president.

I took great pains to examine all the pertinent material, but I was able to find no trace of any proof that this committee ever did any work. This committee did no work at all. Judges of the People's Court! You must pay great attention to this fact, because if this committee did no work, then it cannot be asserted — as it was in the indictment — that the Archbishop as head of this committee was basically guilty of forced "rebaptism." In any case, the Archbishop, by joining this committee took on a certain responsibility, but if one takes into account the fact that the committee did no work, this responsibility was no greater than that which he had already had before his joining, because aside from the responsibility which every individual priest has for his actions, he always had as well the responsibility of the authority of a bishop. That is why the examination of this fact must be particularly thorough. It is up to you to evaluate, to judge, and I am sure that you will not find, as I have not found myself, that the Committee of Three did any significant work.

But if this committee did no work, and if one cannot assert along with the indictment that it was the basis of all activity relating to the "rebaptism of the Serbs," then one must conclude, on the contrary, that all the actions of the Archbishop in relation to the foundation of this committee, and all his work in general, had the same character as the actions of the Church that have been previously described: hesitation, procrastination, and care, but not at all the exploitation of the violences committed against the Serbs.

(Ad 3 and 4). At the same time that the terror and the persecution grew greater and greater, the need for more effective aid presented itself. It was no longer a question of the application of canonical rules, it was necessary to save lives; aid became a duty. The Archbishop offered this aid in so far as he was able — to those who were not "rebaptized" just the same as to those who were "rebaptized."

It is I myself who assert that the action for the forced "rebaptism" of the Serbs was no act of charity toward the Serbs, but was directed against them. But the reaction of the Archbishop to these forced conversions meant help and rescue, even if the person saved kept his life and freedom only for as long a time as it took him to gather his belongings and join the army for the liberation of the people. And the part that was played in this rescue by any Catholic priest, by Archbishop Stepinac himself, or by the organization of the Church under his general direction, must be recognized and approved as being good.

During the course of the trial I was greatly interested in ascertaining the approximate number of Serbs whose lives were saved, some for the time being and a great many permanently, by their conversion to the Catholic religion. I was not able to learn this number. But I am eager to know it, for I want as a Croatian to be proud of the rescue work that a compatriot performed so abundantly on behalf of the persecuted and suffering in the most difficult of times.

On this subject I must insist on one point. In those terrible times difficult conflicts of conscience presented themselves, so difficult that one could scarcely hope to solve them. Perhaps it is not for me to speak here of the anguish that took place in the hearts of the men of the Church. It was, however, necessary to solve those conflicts, and it was necessary to base their solution on that which was most valuable: canon law or men's lives. Even the least important men had to solve such conflicts. I knew a Franciscan in Bosnia who, in the most terrible circumstances, when he had to receive "converts," did it in this way. He said, "I baptize thee, and you are going to continue to believe as you have up to now. And when the time comes, you will make your decision freely." I believe that this brother had resolved this conflict in his conscience well and had nothing for which to reproach himself.

When we consider what was in the mind of Archbishop Stepinac, and what his purposes were in the matter of the "rebaptisms," we conclude:

He was conscious of the fact that forced conversions neither could be supported nor approved by the Church or by himself under any circumstances.

He was conscious of the fact that he accepted the Orthodox into the Catholic religion for the purpose of helping them, often of saving their lives.

He had the intention of attaining such a result, and many reasons to await such with confidence, and if other results occurred on occasion because of terrorism his intention remained.

That is what was in his mind, and in forming a judgment, the conflict of values which he had to resolve will become clear to you. In the recent past it was often impossible not to choose a lesser evil in order to obtain a greater good. It is necessary to put that in the balance, and it will show that the Archbishop chose the way which, according to men's judgment, had to be and was the best.

As to what concerns the Military Vicariate (section No. 3 of the indictment), I would like to remind you, and I ask you to verify this, that the Archbishop only received the appointment as Military Vicar a month after the Ustashi government had already appointed Vučetić and Cecelja as Vicars. It was absolutely impossible to remove them. As I have been able to prove, the Archbishop as Military Vicar had, in fact, no powers except to have priests suspended whom he had learned had conducted themselves unworthily. All effective influence belonged to the Ministry and to other agencies. The chaos that I described before was especially prevalent in this Ministry so that

I was not able to ascertain, and it is not recorded anywhere, who the persons were who were validly appointed military Chaplains, and especially if they were also the persons cited under this section of the indictment. But, in any case, do not forget that he was a good Vicar in the true sense of the word, a good pastor who worked for innumerable soldiers and officers, and for the persecuted and imprisoned whom he saved even from death sentences.

I hesitate to insist on the matter and will only mention in passing how much charity was dispensed by Archbishop Stepinac, the people without number whom he aided and saved, because all are aware of these things and I am sure that he would not wish me to speak of them, as he did these things out of his great generosity and his duty and not to reap any profit from them.

I ask you to bear in mind all these facts and all these conclusions when you pass judgment, and, on the basis of all that has been shown you, to reach a just verdict.

DOCUMENT D

ARCHBISHOP STEPINAC'S REPLY
AT THE TRIAL

To all charges brought against me here, I answer that my conscience is in every way clear (even though the public here present ridicule this statement), and I seek neither to defend myself nor appeal against the verdict.

For my convictions I am able to bear not only ridicule, hatred, and humiliation, but — because my conscience is clear — I am ready at any moment to die.

Hundreds of times during the trial I have been called "the defendant Stepinac." There is no one so naïve as not to know that with the "defendant Stepinac" here on the bench sits the Archbishop of Zagreb, the Metropolitan, and the head of the Catholic Church in Yugoslavia.

You yourselves have many times appealed to the accused priests present to acknowledge that only Stepinac is guilty for their, the people's, and the clergy's attitude. Stepinac, the man, cannot wield such influence, only Stepinac, the Archbishop.

For seventeen months a campaign has been waged against me,

publicly and in the press; and for twelve months I suffered actual house arrest in the Archbishop's palace.

The guilt for the rebaptism of Serbs is ascribed to me. That is a misleading expression, for he who is once baptized, need not be rebaptized. The question concerns change of religions, and of this I shall not speak in detail, except to state that my conscience is clear and that history shall one day render its judgment in this matter.

It is a fact that I was obliged to remove pastors, for they stood in danger of death from the Orthodox. The Serbs wanted to kill these priests because they refused them admission into the Church. It is a fact that during the war the Church had to find its way through countless difficulties. There was a desire to aid as far as it was at all possible the Serbian people.

The honorable judge has produced evidence showing that I sought an abandoned Orthodox monastery (once belonging to our own Pauline Fathers) in Orahovica to lodge Trappists whom the Germans had driven away from Reichburg. It was my duty to aid my brother Slovenes, whom the Hitlerites had banished, to find temporary shelter.

Because I was the Military Ordinary, grave criminality is imputed to me. The honorable judge asked me if I did not consider myself a traitor to Yugoslavia because in this matter I sought an understanding with the independent State of Croatia.

I was the Military Ordinary in the former Yugoslavia. I labored during those eight to nine years to bring about a definite solution of the religious problem. This question was finally solved through the Yugoslav Concordat, which was agreed upon after great difficulties, solemnly ratified in parliament, but then shelved.

When the war between Yugoslavia and Germany neared its end, I extended spiritual aid to the Catholic soldiers of the former Yugoslav army and of the newly created independent State of Croatia. If, therefore, the state had fallen, but the soldiers still remained, I felt obliged to concern myself with this situation.

I was not *persona grata* to either the Germans or the Ustashi; I was not a Ustasha, nor did I take their oath as did some of the officials of this court whom I see here. The Croatian nation unanimously declared itself for the Croatian State and I would have been remiss had I not recognized and acknowledged this desire of the Croatian people enslaved by the former Yugoslavia.

I have said that Croatians were not allowed to advance in the army or to enter the diplomatic corps unless they changed their religion or married a nonbeliever. That is the factual basis and background of my pastorals and sermons.

Whatever I have said of the right of the Croatian nation to its freedom and independence is in complete accord with the basic principles enunciated by the Allies at Yalta and in the Atlantic Charter.

If, according to these principles, every nation has the right to independence, then why should it be denied to the Croatians? The Holy See has declared that both small nations and national minorities have a right to freedom. Must, then, a Catholic Bishop and Metropolitan maintain total silence on this issue? If fall we must, then we fall because we have done our duty.

Do not think that the Croatian nation is pleased with this trial, or that if given an opportunity to express themselves I would suffer as a result. I have honored and respected the will of my people, and I shall continue to do so.

You accuse me as an enemy of the State and the people's authority. I acknowledge your authority. What was my authority? I repeat again: you have been my authority since May 8, 1945, but not before that. Where is it possible in the world to obey two authorities: you in the woods; they in Zagreb?

Should I have given allegiance to the authority of the illegal Simović, or — as you call it, the "exiled" — government in London, to the one in Cairo, yours in the woods or theirs in Zagreb? Is it possible to serve two masters? That is impossible, according to Catholic morals, the law of nations, and common sense. We could not ignore the authority here, even if it were Ustasha. It was here. You have a right to call me to account for action since May 8, 1945.

As to my so-called acts of terrorism, you have no proof, nor can anyone believe you. If Lisak, Lela Sofijanec, and others came to me under assumed names, if I received a letter which I never read, and if it be a crime for men to come to me, I shall accept the verdict with equanimity.

It does not trouble my conscience to have issued a certificate of free movement to the Rev. Marić, for I did not do so with the purpose of creating difficulties, and if this be guilt I would leave this world with my soul at peace.

Whether you believe me or not, does not matter. The accused Archbishop of Zagreb knows not only how to suffer but also to die for his convictions.

President Bakarić [of Croatia] himself acknowledged to the Rev.

Milanović: "We are convinced that the Archbishop stands behind these acts, but we have no proof." That, for me, is sufficient acknowledgment.

And now, what is the essence of our controversy and our vicissitudes, and why has not a peaceful solution been reached? The state prosecutor has many times affirmed that nowhere else is there such freedom of conscience as in this state. I am free to demonstrate the contrary.

Before all, I repeat: 260 to 270 priests have been killed by the National Liberation Movement. In no civilized state in the world would so many priests be punished for such crimes as have been imputed to them. For example, the pastor of Slatina, the Rev. Burger, as a member of the Kultur bund, should have been sentenced, say, to eight years imprisonment; but no, you killed him because he, in fulfillment of his duty as dean, had saved the sacred vessels of a national shrine.

The Rev. Povoljnjak was, without benefit of trial, murdered like a dog in the streets. And the same has been the fate of accused Sisters. In no other civilized state would death have been meted out; only, at the most, a prison sentence.

You have made a fatal mistake in murdering priests. The people will not forgive you for that. Such is your "freedom."

Our Catholic schools, built at the cost of great sacrifices, have been taken away from us. If I had not received seven carloads of foodstuff from America, we could not have done anything for the children of our poor peasant folk.

With force you took away all the seminary property. You have done nothing less than what the Gestapo did in seizing the seminary at Mokrica. We are not against agrarian reforms — the Holy See has issued many encyclicals on the social question — but they should have been carried out in agreement with the Holy See.

Our orphanages have been rendered useless. Our printing presses have been silenced, and I am not sure if one still exists. We have no publications today, although they have been violently attacked here.

Is it not manifestly scandalous to insist that nowhere does the Church enjoy such "freedom" as here?

The Dominicans were unable to publish a spiritual book, translated by me from the French, to be printed at a cost of 75,000 dinars. Is this freedom of the press?

The St. Jerome Society has ceased to exist. It is a grave offense against the people to treat their greatest and oldest cultural institution in this manner. You have reproached me for the work of my "*Caritas.*" But I say to you: "*Caritas*" has performed untold services for our people and your children.

There is the question of religious instruction in the schools. You have laid down the rule: In the higher grades of the secondary schools religious instruction is forbidden, and in the lower grades it is discretionary.

How can you give to children the right to determine for themselves when they have not grown up, while those in the higher grades who have the right to vote are not allowed freedom of choice in this regard?

Our nursing Sisters in the Catholic hospitals must bear untold miseries and hardships.

Against the overwhelming opposition of the people you have introduced civil marriage. Why did you not interpret this freedom in accordance with the spirit of society in America, for example, where one is free to choose either civil or religious marriage?

We do not deny to you some degree of control over marriage. But it grievously pains our people when they must first enter a civil before a religious marriage. If you had turned to us, we would have given you suggestions on this matter.

The buildings of some of the religious in Bačka have been confiscated. Some churches in Split (I do not know whether it still holds true) have been converted into warehouses. Church lands have been seized without any agreement with the Holy See. You have witnessed how the people, in the face of your agrarian reforms, refuse to take these lands.

No, the material question is the least of our concerns. The tragic thing is this: not one priest or bishop is today certain of his life day or night. Bishop Srebrnić was attacked in Šušak by youngsters at the instigation of responsible persons. For three hours they tormented him and invaded his quarters while your police and militia looked on.

I myself suffered a similar experience in Zaprešić when I was attacked with rocks and revolvers. Bishop Lach, when he was on a Confirmation tour across the Drave, and even though his mission was known, was turned back and held the whole night in the prison at Koprivnica. In fact, your own men who were in the woods came to me and declared: "This is unbecoming conduct. We shall protest to the authorities."

Rocks were hurled through the window of the house where Bishop Burić was staying while on a Confirmation tour. Bishop Pušić, as I heard, was recently the target of rotten apples and eggs.

Such "freedom" we hold to be an illusion. We do not wish to exist like outlawed bandits. We shall fight, by all just means, for our rights — and here in this state.

I would add — so that you may understand why we fight — three or four more examples of your "freedom." In the classrooms it is officially taught — in defiance of all historical proofs — that Jesus Christ never existed. Know you, then: Jesus Christ is God. For Him we are ready to die. And today, you teach that He never actually lived. If a teacher dared to teach the contrary, he would certainly be expelled.

I tell you, Mr. Prosecutor, that under such conditions the Church is not free, but will be slowly annihilated.

Christ is the foundation of Christianity. You express concern for the Orthodox Serbs. I ask you: how can you conceive of Orthodoxy without Christ? How can you conceive of the Catholic Church without Christ? It is an utter absurdity.

In the schoolbooks it is stated that the Mother of God was an adulteress. Are you unaware that for both Catholics and Orthodox the Mother of God is holy?

You have proclaimed, as official doctrine, that man descends from the apes. That perhaps may satisfy the ambition of some. But why decree that as an official theory when no scholar of reputation holds it to be valid?

According to your reviews, materialism is the only acceptable system and that implies the elimination of God and Christianity. If there is nothing but matter — then thank you for your "freedom."

One of your men of influence once boasted: There is no one in this State whom we could not bring to court and sentence.

To these outrageous charges whereby you place us among murderers and associates of terrorists, I say to you that not all the evil committed in the former independent State of Croatia was the work of the Demobrani or the Ustashi.

Let no one think I want conflict. Let the present authorities come to an understanding with the Holy See. The Church does not recognize dictatorship, but she is not against honest understandings. If that could be achieved, then the Bishops will know what is their duty and there will be no need to seek out priests to point out their [the Bishops'] guilt, as was done here.

Finally, I want to say a few words to the communist party, which, in reality is my accuser. If you think I have taken the present stand because of material things, you are wrong, for we have remained firm, even after you have made us poor.

We are not against workers obtaining greater rights in the factories, for this is in line with the Papal Encyclicals. Nor are we against reforms. But let us make it plain to the leaders of communism: if there shall be freedom to diffuse materialism, then let us have the right to confess and propagate our principles. Catholics have died and will die for that right.

I conclude: With good will, an understanding can come about. The initiative lies with the present authorities. Neither I nor the hierarchy are the ones to enter into this basic agreement. That is a matter between the State and the Holy See.

As to myself and as to the verdict, I seek no mercy. My conscience is clear!

II. COLLABORATION WITH THE INDEPENDENT CROAT STATE; THE GERMANS AND ITALIANS. THE CLERGY IN POLITICS

DOCUMENT I

Circular Letter to the Secular Clergy and to the Religious of the Archdiocese of Zagreb

ZAGREB, September 24, 1943

No. 8614/43

REVEREND BROTHERS:

The distressing state of the world in general and especially of our own country, subjected to such painful trials, compels me to draw your attention over and over again, in a most serious fashion, to the point of view of Holy Church and to ask you to reconcile entirely your opinions and actions as priests with its commands, which have been stressed so many times on such diverse occasions.

The great Pope Leo XIII in his Encyclical of September 2, 1893, emphasized that, "The greatest intelligence and prudence are necessary so that the bearers of Holy Writ may not forget seriousness and the true path and that it may not seem that they care more for that which is human than for that which is Divine" (III. N. 62. Op. 40).

Several directives and regulations have been published with special reference to the public activity of the clergy. For example, when a few persons made strenuous efforts during the persecutions in Mexico to bring together Mexican Catholics into a strong political party that might resist these attacks, Pope Pius XI, on February 11, 1926, firmly ordered Mexican priests *to refrain from all active participation in any political party whatever* (AAS, 1926, 178).

In the concordats concluded between the Holy See on the one hand and Italy and Germany on the other, Pius XI commanded priests and religious to refrain from membership or support of any political party (AAS, 1929, 233; 1933, 107).

The ecclesiastical code especially forbids priests from taking part in any disturbance whatever of public order, *"ne ordinis publici per-turbationibus opem quoque modo ferant"* (Can. 141, No. 1).

It is necessary that we keep always in mind what Pius XI said on September 19, 1924, concerning the political and social work of priests, "Priests in performing the work that Divine Grace has designed for them, that is to say, work for the glory of God and the salvation of souls, take part in the most exalted way in the work for the social and political welfare of all."

Our holy duty is to conduct ourselves in everything and to think only as *"ministri Christi et dispensatores mysteriorum Dei"* (1 Cor. 4:1), to preach only of Jesus Crucified and His Holy Gospel (Can. 1347, No. 2), and to leave *"negotia saecularia"* to others; according to the inspired words of St. Paul, *"Nemo militans Dei implicat se negotiis saecularibus"* (2 Tim. 2:4).

Reverend brothers, I have considered it my obligation as Arch-bishop to draw your attention to these things and I hope that this exhortation will be understood in the spirit of the words quoted from St. Paul.

Our position and the very grave situation in our beloved fatherland of Croatia demands this of us.

ALOYSIUS
Archbishop of Zagreb

DOCUMENT II

Circular Letter to All the Priests of the Archdiocese of Zagreb

Ordinariate of Zagreb
No. 6920/1944

REVEREND BROTHERS:

For the past few months world events have been developing with the speed of lightning. The frontiers of states; the governments of nations; the social conditions in the world; the principles and precepts of world systems with their intellectual, social, and political maxims, all have an uncertain future and are all subject to change since they are, according to their nature and form, temporal and human, hence ephemeral.

Only one institution is eternal and imperishable in its existence, in its precepts, and in its judgment of the world; this because it is of divine origin and guided by the Holy Ghost. It is the Church of Christ and its doctrine. Its one divine Founder has said of it, ". . . the gates of hell shall not prevail against it" (Mt. 16:18).

Although its mission does not consist in establishing the forms of states, directly determining their social intercourse, or judging the controversies of their subjects, its doctrine is of such a nature that it provides the principle and imperishable maxims concerning all phases of human society. It is necessary to warn everyone who seeks new ways to correct and regenerate humanity that the great Pope Leo XIII was right in saying, "If one is looking for the way to save human society he must know that it is to be found only in the Christian regeneration of public and private life. One should know the axiom that each society must return to its original sources if it wishes to attain spiritual renewal" (Leo XIII, 1891, 12, 40). It is necessary, then, that society return to God and His commandments, for, as the Church is a divine institution, it consequently has the same Creator as human society; but beyond that, it is according to the divine order, the guardian and teacher of divine knowledge. The code strongly emphasizes that, "The Church has the right and duty, independent of any civil power whatever, to teach the knowledge of the Gospels to all nations. All are obliged, according to Divine Law, to acquire that knowledge and to embrace the true Church of God" (Can. 1322, No. 2).

It is for this reason that the Church has precisely and irrevocably stated its opposition to every doctrine and theory contrary to its teaching.

In effect, the first and most important end of the coming of Christ and His Church is the salvation of souls for eternal life, but His doctrine is so full of life that it is a rich source even for the temporal existence of men, individual, social, and political.

The Church of Christ gives us our general directives and also sheds light on those questions which trouble the world today and in the chaos of war, a war which would not be if the voice of the Teacher had been heeded. The questions are these: (*a*) the freedom and worth of the individual as an independent entity; (*b*) the freedom of and the respect for religion; (*c*) the freedom of and respect for every race and nationality; (*d*) the freedom of and respect for private property as the basis of the personal freedom of the individual and the independence of the family; and, finally (*e*) the freedom of and respect for the right of every nation to its full development and to independence in its national life.

1. The freedom of and respect for the individuality of man find a solid foundation in the doctrine of Christ: "Every man has a soul which the world cannot kill" (Mt. 10:28); "The soul of a man is more valuable than the whole world" (Mt. 16:26); "There is nothing that man should give in exchange for his soul" (Mt. 16:27); "Man through his soul is the image of God" (Gen. 1:26), because he has intelligence and free will. Therefore he is a person. It is here that one finds his worth and inalienable dignity. And for this reason any treatment of a man as if he were not a man is against Divine Law.

To subject man to any power that makes him a slave, a machine, or a dependent and integral organ of the machinery of any organization or world view is not in harmony with the Divine Law, but is rather violence and the worst tyranny.

2. The natural law, the religious sentiment common to human nature, and Divine Revelation irrefutably call for the freedom of and the esteem for the Christian religion. That is why Holy Scripture calls insane anyone who is opposed to it. "The fool has said in his heart: There is no God" (Ps. 13:1). The eternal salvation of the soul requires this. "He that believeth in the Son, has life everlasting; but he that believeth not the Son, shall not see life; but the wrath of God abideth on him" (Jn. 3:36). The prosperity and progress of every nation also call for this freedom. "Religion is the source of the prosperity and greatness of a nation and the main foundation of every well-organized society" (Leo XIII, 1898, 32, 6). Human society in general requires this freedom. "The Revelation of God guides individual families and even the whole of human society towards the highest degree of prosperity" (Pius X, 1904, 3, 45).

3. It is revealed Divine Truth that teaches the freedom of and the respect for every individual and class, every race and nationality because, "God is the Father of all" (Mt. 6:6–15). We are all sons of God through faith in Jesus Christ (Gal. 3:26). We are brothers since we are all children of one Father, we are free because we are freed from the slavery of sin, we are all equal, formerly as slaves and now as children of God and heirs to the heavenly Kingdom. "There is neither Jew nor Greek; there is neither bond nor free; there is neither male nor female. For you are all one in Christ Jesus" (Gal. 3:28).

Although we must love all men and all nations, it is, however, our special obligation to love our blood brothers. Our divine Master gives us an example of this, who cried for love of His Jewish people when He foresaw in His mind the destruction of Jerusalem and the bitter exile of all of His people (Lk. 19:41–44). And His apostle, the great St. Paul, serves us as a similar example, he who deplored from the depths of his soul the apostasy and the denial of the Lord by his people of Israel (Rom. 9:2–5).

Consequently the love of one's own nation, work and service in its national development, represent not only one's right and duty under the natural law, but the positive commandment of God and Christian virtue.

4. Despite all this, it must not be forgotten that in every state national minorities also have the natural and inalienable right to life and to growth. This principle has its basis not only in the order of the natural law, but also in the eternal truths of the Gospel. "Thou shalt love thy neighbor as thyself" (Mt. 22:39). "All things therefore whatsoever you would that men should do to you, do you also to them. For this is the law and the prophets" (Mt. 7:12). The sins against this principle are judged according to the severe words of God, "Woe to him that buildeth up his house by injustice" (Jer. 22:13). And again, "The voice of thy brother's blood crieth to me from the earth" (Gen. 4:10). And so it is entirely understandable that Pius XI has called hypernationalism, which thinks only of its own nation without regard for the rights of others, the worst heresy of the twentieth century and an apostasy from religion. It is, in truth, a brutal violence to the commandment of Christ, "These things I command you, that you shall love one another" (Jn. 15:17).

Indeed all the theories of other kinds of morality, such as the morals of commerce, of war, politics, and nationalism, are false and unrealizable. The will of God as the supreme and definitive foundation of the true and just moral law is always and everywhere one and the same.

5. The natural law and Divine Truth demand the freedom of and the respect for private property with these words, "Ananias, why hath Satan tempted thy heart, that thou should lie to the Holy Ghost, and by fraud keep part of the price of the land? Whilst it remained, did it not remain to thee? And after it was sold, was it not in thy power?" (Acts 5:3–4.) Holy Scripture speaks also of the property of the first Christians, ". . . (Peter) came to the house of Mary the mother of John, who was surnamed Mark" (Acts 12:12). In emphasizing that the principles of private property must not be violated, Scripture speaks of mutual aid and care for the poor (Acts 4:32).

In agreement with this Pius XI says that private property has two ends and two natures: private and social, that is to say, that on the one hand it enables individuals to take care of themselves and of their families, and on the other hand it enables them to help the destitute of human society (*Quadragesimo anno*).

In the possession of private property in any form, whether its possessor is a physical or legal person, no one is an arbitrary or absolute master, but must be governed according to Divine Law. No one is permitted to abuse it himself or to keep others from acquiring and exercising their own property rights. Christ and His apostles resolutely taught, as well as the Church and its authorities: "Take heed and beware of all covetousness; for a man's life doth not consist in the abundance of things which he possesseth" (Lk. 12:15, 20–21). And again, "For the desire of money is the root of all evil; which some coveting have erred from the faith, and have entangled themselves in many sorrows" (1 Tim. 6:10).

Private property, then, which finds its origin and its source in the positive law of God is permitted and morally good and one cannot, on principle, in any way judge it to be harmful to the community. It becomes this only when it is in the hands of atheists without the sense of Christian charity and justice.

Reverend brothers, I have several times emphasized the doctrines of the Church, in my sermons and in my letters. I have, moreover, reprimanded and condemned, not only privately but also in public, all errors and transgressions against the principles of the Church no matter what commandment of God they concerned. But I have especially condemned those transgressions which relate to the great law of Christian charity toward one's neighbors.

Now, as we approach troubled and uncertain times, I consider it my duty as Archbishop once again to draw your attention to these matters, especially when a great many priests are asking me for instructions and counsel. In thinking of all that I have just said, I ask you particularly, reverend brothers:

1. That the doctrine of the Church become more alive for us under wartime conditions, waged by the different modern theories, because in this chaos and conflict of diverse ideologies our uninformed faithful and even priests are easily led astray.

2. That individual priests allude to nothing in their writings, in their sermons, or by their actions which relate to things on which the Church alone and its highest authorities have the right and the duty to speak with competence and to pass judgment.

3. I warn you that it is only the Holy See and the Hierarchy which have the right to intervene in the relations that exist between the authorities of the Church and those of the State, and that other ecclesiastics must confine themselves strictly to preaching the Gospel, occupying themselves with spiritual work and the salvation of immortal souls, and leave *"negotia saecularia"* to others according to the words of St. Paul, "Nemo militans Dei implicat se negotiis saecularibus" (2 Tim. 2:4). Pius XI said it well, "Priests in performing the work for which Divine Grace has destined them, that is to say for the glory of God and the salvation of souls, take part in the work for community welfare, social and political" (Pius XI, September 19, 1924).

4. I warmly recommend to your heart and to your conscience that each one of you remain at his post and that this be a consolation and of spiritual utility to each one himself and to the people who trust in him; do this if there is no particular and personal reason or especially clear indication that it would be better to go into hiding.

5. I command that all sacred vessels, vestments, and other objects of value be put immediately into a safe place in those regions and villages where it is dangerous or difficult to keep them where they are now.

6. Remember always that the Church has the right and duty that God has given it to teach the Gospel truths and to lead its people to the salvation of their souls, no matter what temporal or civil conditions are found in the world (Can. 1322, No. 2).

7. It is self-evident that each priest of the Diocese of Zagreb, or who has been received in the Diocese of Zagreb, has over the whole of the Diocese of Zagreb this jurisdiction, which he has obtained until it shall be taken from him. If the jurisdiction obtained by any priest has expired, and if he has not been able to ask for an extension because of unusual circumstances, I grant to him such an extension through this letter until such time as he will be able to ask for it.

Keep present in your minds in these terrible days the words, "Your protection is in the name of the Lord, who created heaven and earth" (Ps.). I send you all my Archiepiscopal blessing.

> Zagreb, for the exaltation of the Holy Cross,
> September 14, 1944.
> THE ARCHBISHOP

DOCUMENT III

*Circular Letter on the Point of View of the Clergy in
Today's Troubled Times*

No. 5027/45

REVEREND BROTHER PRIESTS:

We have entered into the new conditions of the postwar period beset by anxiety, not only for ourselves, but also for those whose obligation is the reconstruction of our modern society, which has been destroyed by the war and invaded by the new spirit. That is why great patience is required, as well as unceasing prayers addressed to our heavenly Father, that He may not permit His earthly family to be subjected to trials beyond their endurance, but that He may direct, by the hand of God, both leaders and subjects on the road of truth, repentance, and peace. And we, in no matter what circumstances, place all our trust in the hands of God because, "Our protection is in the name of the Lord, who created heaven and earth."

Having firm trust in God, let us hold high our conscience and our honor as priests, let us arouse in our people a lively faith and an unshakable devotion to the Holy Roman Catholic Church. And, in accordance with this, let us strive with the greatest zeal:

1. To have our Catholic families, every evening, pray together in their homes, in front of the statue or the picture of the Blessed Virgin, in honor of the Sacred and Immaculate Heart of Mary, together with all their other customary prayers: one Pater Noster, Ave Maria, and Credo to preserve the holy faith of all the members of the household, no matter where they may be, and, when it is possible, to also say the holy Rosary.

2. That the faithful who recite the holy Rosary make each day a resolution to offer a decade for the intention mentioned above.

3. In public devotions it is necessary each time to say with the people, "the prayer for all Christians," taken from the Litany of the Blessed Virgin, but one must say in a loud and clear voice before this prayer, "Let us pray for the welfare of our Holy Roman Catholic Church, as well as for the perseverance and firmness in the Holy Faith of all the faithful."

4. That the faithful, on Sundays and holy days, read in their homes the catechism from the book *Kruh nebski* (*Bread of Heaven*) or *Spasi dušu svoju* (*Save Your Soul*), especially Chapter VI, "The Christian Doctrine of Man."

5. It is necessary to remind all the faithful frequently that they may neither read nor buy books or pamphlets which speak against God, against holy religion, or against the Catholic Church.

6. Often it is necessary to speak to parents so that they may be more attentive and endeavor most conscientiously to see to it that the conduct of their children is moral, that they say each day their morning and evening prayers, grace before and after meals, that they attend Holy Mass on Sundays and holydays, that they attend Christian instruction at Church, and that they receive the holy sacraments frequently.

7. Religious instruction in the schools has not been suppressed, but parents may vote whether they wish or do not wish their children to have such instruction, and the future of this part of the program in the school depends on the outcome of the vote. Let the priests be on their guard in this controversy and let them not trouble themselves with a few obstinate people who would wish otherwise.

8. Let us recommend above all devotion and religious instructions in the parish churches, or before the crucifix and statues of each village, and thus maintain relations with the faithful; special and most affectionate attention must be devoted to children and through them relations established with the parents.

9. Let us particularly recommend to the faithful the saying of the holy Rosary at public meetings and public devotions as well as in private prayers.

10. Let priests perform only, strictly and with zeal, their pastoral duties, that is to say, the work for the honor and glory of God and the salvation of souls, because it is thus that they take part, in the most exalted manner, in the work for community prosperity, social and political (Pius XI, "Il fermo proposito").

11. *Let preachers in their addresses and sermons avoid absolutely all allusions whatsoever to secular things or conditions, and let them explain only the Gospel and the catechism, that is to say, the doctrine of the Church.*

12. Please inform this Ordinariate immediately of all hostile actions against dogma, religious instruction, or the persons of the clergy, as well as the seizure of objects or property belonging to the Church or the deprivation of the freedom of any priest so that appropriate steps may be taken with the competent authorities.

Brother priests, let us not lose courage whatever happens to us, because despite the trials and dangers that overtake us, the Lord is beside us. That is why in our daily prayers, and above all at holy Mass and in reading our breviary, we beg God that He will shorten these days and that the Sun of Divine Mercy will shine upon us and upon our faithful. Let the Word of God give us courage in all things, that Word which says clearly that for him who puts his trust in God, *"In Te Domine, speravi, non confundar in aeternum."*

DR. ALOYSIUS STEPINAC, *Archbishop*

Zagreb, July 6, 1945

P.S. The reverend clergy are warned to pay close attention to sermons. It would be best to write sermons and give them literally or to read them; in this way the text of the sermon can be brought forward at any time if anyone should ask for an account of it. It should be possible to make use of the sermons already prepared by Cezner.

DOCUMENT IV

Letter of Archbishop Stepinac to Ante Pavelić, February 8, 1942, Regarding the Clergy in Politics

POGLAVNIK:[1]

I feel myself obliged to address you as head of the Independent State of Croatia to clear up certain questions relating to the convocation of the Croatian Parliament.

During the past few days several priests have asked me if I would persist in my decision to exclude priests from political activity in the light of my circular letters to the clergy in 1935 and 1938. I replied that these letters were still in force for priests holding an ecclesiastical post.

Here is the problem. Just after World War I, I had the opportunity, although young and a layman, to note the unfavorable reaction to the Catholic Church caused by priests who appeared on the electoral lists of the various parties disputing power. This was not surprising, for a priest who had declared himself an active member of a political group could never as a politician be a consistent defender of the ideals of the Church, however honest and dignified he was otherwise.

---

[1] Leader, chief — the title assumed by Ante Pavelić and equivalent to *Duce* or *Führer*.

Again I remember well the peasants in my own district who, even before the great war, fractured the skull of a parish priest who in the elections had defended the cause of a party which did not merit their support. This is not the only case of its kind. What is worse is that among priests belonging to different political parties, there was sometimes such hatred that for years they would not speak to each other, though formerly they had been the best of friends; all this to the great scandal of the people. The situation became more serious if they neglected their official duties because of political activity. They lost hours, even entire days, in discussions that led nowhere, and abandoned their schools, their sermons, the catechism, visits to the sick, and many other duties. All their political activity led to little good and much harm to the Church and to the country.

Things became worse after World War I. Priests threw themselves into politics, joining the numerous parties, from those on the Right, through the Peasant Party, the Popular Democratic and Radical parties, and even the National Yugoslav Party and the Yugoslav Radical Union; all that to the great detriment of the Church and the nation.

That is why, on becoming Archbishop, I resolved to put an end to all these abuses. The first to be dealt with was the pastor of Bednja, Matica, a former member of the HSS, the Croatian Peasant Party, and then a minister in the cabinet of Zivković. I notified him to resign either his post as minister or his pastorate. He preferred the post of minister and I removed him as pastor. Today he probably realizes that the right was on my side.

On the eve of the elections in the year 1935, I sent the clergy a circular letter in which I forbade them, under threat of canonical discipline, to become candidates on any party's list so long as they held an ecclesiastical post. A certain priest hesitated and asked whether, despite the prohibition, he could become a candidate. I let him know that he could do so, but that on the very same day he would lose his parish.

I published a similar letter in 1938, permitting no one to become a candidate or to enter Parliament, were it even on the list of the HSS, the Croatian Peasant Party, although there was ill feeling against me because of this.

On the eve of the opening of the Croat Parliament, I must, Poglavnik, insist on this point of view. The small good that priests can achieve in politics does not justify me in tolerating the harm, twice as great, to the Church and the nation by the abandonment of their priestly duties, whether these priests are members of the HSS or of the Ustashi Movement.

Times have changed completely. The population has become unruly, the scourge of birth control decimates their ranks, the people are weighed down with sin and vices of every sort, and there are so few priests. In my archdiocese the loss of one priest is a severe blow, because we have a thousand priests too few to administer our parishes. But even in theory, a priest cannot accept responsibility for political acts. It is the Apostle Paul himself who says: "No one who fights (for God) involves himself in the affairs of this life so that he may please the Master — Christ." Ecclesiastical law confirms this when it exhorts priests, "senatorum aut oratorum legibus ferendis, quos deputatus vocant, munus ne sollicitent neve accepent." This is the opinion of every true and faithful Catholic, who expects priests to care for souls and not involve themselves in political debates. This principle is emphasized in nearly every modern concordat, and that usually on the initiative and request of the secular authority.

I ask you courteously, Poglavnik, to understand with benevolence my point of view, and to relieve four of my priests from their duties as deputies. Superhuman efforts are demanded every day of my priests in the spiritual care of the people; I am sure each of them will give me thanks for delivering him from this added responsibility.

If, however, some should find fault with my point of view, which is completely in accord with the spirit of the Catholic Church, I prefer unjustified reproaches rather than abandon the true interests of the Church and the nation.

Please accept, Poglavnik, my most sincere good wishes.

THE ARCHBISHOP OF ZAGREB

Zagreb, February 8, 1942

DOCUMENT V

Declaration Signed by 150 Priests, Dated September 24, 1946,
Regarding the Archbishop's Prohibition on Political
Activities of the Clergy

On the occasion of the arrest of His Excellency the Archbishop, Dr. Aloysius Stepinac, and on the occasion of the charges made against him, we, the undersigned priests and religious of Zagreb, declare:

1. Never has His Excellency the Archbishop, Dr. Aloysius Stepinac, given to any among us, either in writing or orally, any instructions or incentives to any kind of illegal or terroristic political activity, nor have we ever noted or found in his actions toward us any motive whatever for such activity.

2. On the contrary we state that His Excellency the Archbishop has constantly insisted that his priests avoid all political activity and that by virtue of ecclesiastical regulations limit their work to the purely religious sphere. As proof we quote the circular letters of (a) August 10, 1938, No. 6347, (b) February 4, 1942, No. 1722, (c) September 24, 1943, No. 8614, (d) September 14, 1944, No. 6920, and (e) July 6, 1945, No. 5027.

3. If any priest, contrary to the clear instructions of his archbishop, concerns himself with illegal activity, he alone must bear full responsibility for it and he commits a grave injustice if he attempts to cast the responsibility for his crime on his ecclesiastical superior.

Following are the signatures of 150 priests

Zagreb, September 24, 1946

DOCUMENT VI

Letter of Monsignor Svetozar Rittig in Praise of Archbishop Stepinac's Aid to the Victims of the War and Injustice

MONSIGNOR ARCHBISHOP:

I pray you to accept my most humble good wishes and fervent prayers that, the occasion of the approaching feasts of the Infant Jesus, sole Saviour of the world, He may accord to your Excellency the heavenly gifts of wisdom and strength, so that you may successfully surmount difficulties and terrible trials such as our venerable archdiocese, throughout all its long history, has never had to endure. We all raise our hands to heaven in union with you that you may not falter under the burden of your high office, which is, moreover, true martyrdom, and that you may safely steer the ship of our archdiocese and of the whole Catholic Church in Croatia between the whirlpools and rocks of Scylla and Charybdis. Your stanch faith in Divine Providence, your prayers, and your sacrifices are a guarantee to all the people and the clergy that we will successfully emerge from this horrible carnage. The Infant Jesus and the Name of Jesus are, with us, as in ancient times, honored and praised!

We read that you have received from all parts of the depressed regions letters of thanks for your noble initiative in aiding the starved and miserable orphans. For your satisfaction and consolation, I too am able to write you from these regions how much you have eased the struggle for the bare necessities of life for the fugitive Poles here, for they are suffering even more than our own poor who still get some small crumbs of nourishment from their relatives and some employment, while the Poles have no one outside of high heaven above their heads and the aid of the Holy Father, sent through his intermediary, the Bishop of Senj.

I ask your episcopal blessing for me and for my work.

Yours very sincerely in Our Lord,
SVETOZAR RITTIG

Hrv. Selce, December 19, 1942

DOCUMENT VII

Circular Letter to the Venerable Clergy of Zagreb Archdiocese
(*Published in* Katolički List, Zagreb, *April 29, 1941*)

VENERABLE BRETHREN:

There is no one among you who has not been a recent witness to the momentous events in the life of the Croat nation, in which we are all laboring as messengers of Christ's Gospel. These events are the culmination of an ideal long cherished and desired by our people. This is a time when the tongue speaks no more, but only the sense of heritage and community in the country in which we saw first God's light and with the people from whom we descend. It must be stated that in our veins too the blood coursed more strongly and the heart in our bosom beat faster. No reasonable person can condemn and no honest one can cast blame, because the love toward one's own people is inscribed in the human heart by God and is His commandment.

And who can blame us, when we as spiritual pastors contribute to the national joy and enthusiasm, when we turn our hearts full of deep emotion and warm gratitude to the Majesty of God? For, however complicated is the web of contemporary events; however heterogeneous the factors which influence the course of affairs, it is easy to see the hand of God at work. *"A Domino factum est istud et est mirabile in oculis nostris"* (Ps. 117:23).

Today from this ancient castle, in the shadow of this old cathedral, this silent witness to our Croat history, I speak to you not only as a son of the Croat people, but even more as the representative of Holy Church. I speak to you as the representative of that divine institution which has sprung from eternity and the end of which is in eternity in the full sense of the word. As a representative of that Church which is *"firmamentum et columna veritatis"* (1 Tim. 3:15) and which was not afraid to speak the truth through my mouth, when it was necessary, although unfortunately her voice remained frequently "a voice crying in the wilderness" (Jn. 1:23).

As the representative of the Church and as pastor of souls, I pray and exhort you to work with all your might that our Croatia may be the country of God, because only in that way will she be able to fulfill the essential tasks for the benefit of her members.

Faithful to God and to Christ's Holy Church, our Croatia will achieve that noble mission which is the function of our earthly Fatherland of promoting the supernatural interests of its members. Faithful to God and to the Church she will show her belief that the final aim of all human strife is eternity, where our true home is. In respect for religious and moral values she will prove her belief that the earthly home is a true mother only when she teaches us to pray and to "give to God what is God's," and that she is a solicitous mother in our life only when she directs our steps on the roads which lead to God and when she casts aside tribulations from the souls which God created for Himself.

Faithful to God and to the Church, our Croatia will not only perform its duty in the promotion of the supernatural destiny of the Croat people, but will erect a solid foundation of sound progress in the natural order. The Church, which has already seen two thousand years of changes in the world's history, is the historical witness of how *"regnum de gente in gentem transfertur propter injustitias et injurias et contumelias et diversos dolos"* (Ecclus. 10:8). We must therefore regard as our supreme duty, in these crucial times in the history of our nation, to spiritualize our whole national being with deep insight in eternity. We must warn and teach that the holy enthusiasm and noble zeal in building the foundations of the new Croat state must be inspired by the fear of God and by love of God's law and His commandments, for only through God's law and not on false natural principles can the Croat state be solidly established.

Answer, therefore, promptly this appeal of mine in the noble task of conserving and advancing the independent Croat state.

Knowing the men who are today at the helm of the Croat nation, we are deeply convinced that our efforts will find understanding and assistance. We believe and expect that the Church in the newly erected Croat state will be able in complete freedom to preach the principles of eternal Truth and Justice. She will therefore fulfill the words of Holy Scripture: *"Verbum Dei non est alligatum"* (2 Tim. 2:9). And she will regard as her holy duty *"opportune, importune, arguere, increpare, obsecrare in omni patientia et doctrina et cum omni apostolica libertate"* (cf. 2 Tim. 4:2).

May God grant that this shall come to pass. And that it may be so, I appeal to you, venerable brother priests, that you do not cease exhorting to prayer the faithful entrusted to you, and that you yourselves at God's altar raise up your hands the more to the "Father of Lights," from whom descends every good gift and every perfect endowment (James 1:17), that the Chief of the Croat State may have the spirit of wisdom in order to fulfill this noble and responsible office for the Glory of God and for the salvation of the people in justice and truth; so that the Croat people may be people of God, attached to Christ and to His Church, founded on the rock of Peter! It may be that prayer seems to the world a superfluous thing; we regard it as the most vital thing in life, for "when the Lord does not keep the city, in vain he watches who keeps it" (Ps. 12:1).

The Church of God has never wasted herself on empty slogans, and has never failed in the patient work on which are laid the foundations for the happy future of individuals, of nations, and of states. Prove yourselves, venerable brethren, now, and fulfill your duty toward the young Croat State.

I have decided that on Sunday, May 4 of this year, a solemn *Te Deum* will be held in all parish churches, on which occasion the parochial officers should invite the local authorities and the faithful. I hope the fulfillment of this request will be possible on the date suggested. But in the event communication difficulties prevent the *Te Deum* may be transferred to the first free day. As regards Zagreb Cathedral, I shall check the date in conformity with the public authorities.

ALOYSIUS, *Archbishop*

Zagreb, April 28, 1941

DOCUMENT VIII

*Statement of the Zagreb Chancery With Reference to the Latin
Forms Used by Archbishop Stepinac in Correspondence
With the Holy See*

Archiepiscopal Ordinariate of Zagreb
No. 6180/46

Statement,

by which it is certified and declared that the reports of the Archiepiscopal Ordinariate of Zagreb and of His Excellency, Monsignor, the Archbishop, sent to Rome are regularly written in the Latin language. And that the salutations of letters written to the Holy Father are as follows:

"Beatissime Pater!

"Aloisius Stepinac, archiepiscopus Zagrebiensis, ante pedes Sanctitatis Vestrae provolutus, ea, quae sequuntur humillime exponit."

Next follows the content of the message and at the end is placed the following conclusion:

"Et Deus, etc. . . . .

"Zagrebiae, die . . ."

ALOISIUS STEPINAC
Archiepiscopus Zagrebiensis

DOCUMENT IX

Letter of Cardinal Maglione to Archbishop Stepinac

State Secretariat
of His Holiness
No. 37773/43
to be cited in the reply

THE VATICAN
June 17, 1943

MOST REVEREND EXCELLENCY:

I have noted with great interest the abundant documentation sent to me by your Most Reverend Excellency regarding the work carried out by you in favor of the Serbs and Hebrews in Croatia.

In thanking you heartily, I beg you to continue to keep the Holy See informed in the matter adding, if possible, some news also regarding the work of the other Croatian Bishops.

I take this opportunity to reiterate my sentiments of particular and sincere esteem,

> *Of Your Most Reverend Excellency Servant,*
> L. CARD. MAGLIONE

To His Most Reverend Excellency
Monsignor Luigi Stepinac
Archbishop of Zagreb

DOCUMENT X

Letter of Archbishop Stepinac to Glaise von Horstenau,
German Minister in Zagreb and Related Correspondence
Regarding Excesses of German Troops

ZAGREB, January 3, 1944

To His Excellency, Dr. C. Edmund Glaise von Horstenau,
Minister

EXCELLENCY:

I have the honor to address the following request to you:

About eight days ago the vicar of the parish of Kravarsko, near Velika Gorica, Francis Genc, was arrested and taken away, with twenty men from the same place, by individuals belonging to the German Army. At the moment, they are all at Sisak, detained by the German police.

As regards the vicar, Genc, I can assure you that he is one of the best of my younger clergy. I have also received favorable information concerning the peasants arrested with him.

I earnestly beg Your Excellency to take measures to release the above mentioned persons as soon as possible, especially the vicar, Genc, since the parish of Kravarsko is without its pastor during the Christmas season, when there is an especially large amount of pastoral work.

Accept, Excellency, the expression of my highest esteem.

> Very truly yours,
> THE ARCHBISHOP OF ZAGREB

P.S. I have just this minute learned that the theologian, John Premenić, a seminarian from Zagreb, was also taken away from the

village of Vrbovo, in the vicinity of Velika Gorica, a few days ago
by the German Army. I am not presently informed of the place of
his imprisonment.

ZAGREB, January 11, 1944

To His Excellency, Dr. C. Edmund Glaise von Horstenau

EXCELLENCY:

With reference to our conversation of last night, I have the honor
of sending you a list of the persons in the parish of Kravarsko, who
were arrested, in the hope that the return of these people to their
homes can be arranged.

Is there no way to avoid the rape of women and the murder of
an old peasant who wished to defend the honor of his granddaughter?
The people have been plunged into black despair.

I pray your Excellency to accept my best wishes.

DR. ALOYSIUS STEPINAC
Archbishop of Zagreb

This letter was sent, together with the list of the parishioners who
were taken to Germany on January 11, 1944 — by me personally.

ŠALIĆ
Secretary to the Archbishop

ZAGREB, February 7, 1944

Independent State of Croatia
Minister of the Interior

EXCELLENCY:

In regard to your letter of January twenty-third of this year, I
regret not replying sooner, but wished first to gather all pertinent
information.

I have communicated the details of the affair to the plenipotentiary
German General in Croatia, Glaise von Horstenau, as well as to
Minister, Mr. Siegfried Kasche. The German general had already
been brought up to date on the matter by yourself.

At the same time I ordered our liaison officer with the division,
Krčelić, to examine the case, and I am taking the liberty of enclosing
a copy of his report.

I am pleased to state that the Croatian government has asked,
again and again, through the medium of the competent German

authorities, for the removal of this army division from the territory of the Independent State of Croatia. It is to be hoped that this request will be granted.

Please, Excellency, accept at this time the expression of my most respectful good wishes.

Za dom Spremni! Hail Ustashi: ready in the service of the Fatherland.

Dr. M. Lorković

Enclosed documents: one
To His Excellency, Dr. Aloysius Stepinac
Archbishop of Zagreb, Zagreb

Zagreb, February 11, 1944

Mr. Minister:

I have the honor, Mr. Minister, to acknowledge the receipt of the two letters received from you: one on the subject of the permission granted a priest to visit the prison on Savska Cesta Street, as well as that which concerns the incidents in the parish of Odra and vicinity.

Even if the first report of what happened in the parish of Odra, written very probably in a great hurry and in fear of the troops, was not entirely correct as to the number of soldiers who had violated a woman, there can be no doubt that the incident actually occurred, since a new report incontestably proves it. The name of the informant remains temporarily unknown since eventual persecution is feared. There have been several cases of rape of this sort.

A few days ago, my dear Minister, I was myself a witness to a similar incident on my property at Brestovica, where a soldier seized a woman, dragged her about, and, against the protests of some workers and masons who were engaged in the construction of a convent at that place, fired several shots into the air to frighten the persons present. After that, the German officer who was in command intervened and would have shot him on the spot if he had succeeded in raping the woman. I rejoice, however, in your news that this division will soon leave Croatia.

Please accept, Mr. Minister, on this occasion, the expression of my most respectful good wishes.

The Archbishop of Zagreb

Dr. Mladen Lorković
Minister of the Interior, Zagreb

DOCUMENT XI

Note Regarding Certain Incidents in Pušća of German Excesses

ARCHIEPISCOPAL ORDINARIATE OF ZAGREB

In the village of Hruševica, in the commune of Pušća, in the district of Hrvatsko Zagorje, a serious incident occurred on the twenty-third of this month:

Some legionnaires of the Black Legion, several of whom were drunk, entered the village, chased all the inhabitants out of some eighty houses, to which they then set fire. They shot and robbed a number of persons on the spot while they were conducting more than fifty men to Zagreb to the prison on Runjaninova Street.

Among the victims were the following:

Stephen Horvat, born in 1901, and his son Nicholas, born in 1929.

Stephen Perički, born in 1877, one of whose sons serves with the Ustashi and whose grandson fell as a soldier on the field of honor.

The wives and children of these unhappy families ask that they be returned to their homes.

Let only those be kept in prison against whom there is some proof of criminal action.

On December 29, 1944, His Excellency, the Ordinary, intervened. The liberation of the persons listed was promised.

STEPHEN LACKOVIĆ

DOCUMENT XII

Letter of Archbishop Stepinac to the Italian Minister,
Raffaello Cavaliere Casertano, Regarding the Excesses
of Italian Troops

To His Excellency
Raffaello Cavaliere Casertano,
Italian Minister in Zagreb

EXCELLENCY:

With reference to my letter to you of February 6 last, sent to Your Excellency for the purpose of informing you of the excesses of Italian troops, who, in certain villages of my Archdiocese have dishonored the Italian army, I wish to transmit sworn statements regarding these acts. This is proof that my letter was not written in undue haste or as the result of nervousness, but was the consequence of the facts, all of which have been fully confirmed.

Excellency, these excesses as well as the treatment of Croats interned in concentration camps in Italy are obstacles to the real friendship of Croatia and Italy. The Italian authorities have promised to repatriate the internees in Italy, a policy which fills our hearts with joy and satisfaction. I hope that the Italian military authorities in Croatia, on the request of Your Excellency, have ceased and will cease acts such as those described in this report.

This state of affairs has a religious as well as a political and national aspect. Natural law is involved which should be respected in conscience by all. There is the special factor that the Italian people is profoundly Catholic and has the great fortune to have the Vicar of Christ in its capital. This makes all the more repugnant outrages and scandal on the part of those belonging to the noble and Catholic Italian people, especially when these acts are offensive to the rights of Croats living in occupied or annexed territory.

It is to be observed that in Croat territory annexed by Italy, there is a steady decline in religious life and a certain tendency to pass from Catholicism to the schismatics. The responsibility and guilt for this situation, before God and posterity, will be Catholic Italy's.

The religious character of the problem obliges me, as responsible for the religious welfare of Croatia, to write Your Excellency in this vein. I hope Your Excellency will take these comments in the proper spirit. I write not as a diplomat or as a politician but as the representative of the Catholic Church which must preach always and everywhere Truth, Goodness, Justice, and Peace. I trust that Your Excellency has observed that I have striven to defend the rights of others as well as those of our own, without distinction. I do so now and will always in the future defend the rights of my people who for thirteen centuries on this Adriatic coast have contributed much to the common Christian civilization of Italy and Croatia.

I am always ready to discuss these matters of common interest and justice with Your Excellency personally.

With the expression of the greatest esteem, I am,

ARCHBISHOP OF ZAGREB

DOCUMENT XIII

*Sermon at the Procession of Our Lady of Lourdes
at Zagreb at the End of May in 1942*

Regina Pacis, ora pro nobis!

BROTHERS:

It was a great joy that filled the patriarch Noah when the dove returned, after a long time, with an olive leaf in its beak as a sign that the water had gone down and that the punishment of the deluge was coming to an end; that heaven had reconciled itself anew with the earth. An even greater joy filled the shepherds that holy night of Christmas Eve when the song of the angels announced that a barrier had been placed before the deluge of human sins and passions, because the Blessed Virgin, not far from them, in a stable in Bethlehem, held in her arms the true olive branch of peace, the infant Jesus, Son of God, who came into the world to reconcile man with God. But I do not know if they awaited the messenger of peace from heaven more eagerly than the people of our day await him. The flood of unbridled passions of hate and vengeance draws near to its zenith. All of us who believe in God, who believe that He alone is the Absolute Master of all that takes place on the earth, encouraged by the voice of the Supreme Shepherd of the Church, Pope Pius XII, pray during the month of May for peace between men, and today, at the end of May, lift our arms and our eyes to heaven and sigh with a penitent heart with the poet of the Old Testament, *"ostende faciem tuam et salvi erimus!"* Show us thy face, and we shall be saved (Ps. 79:4).

Yes, it is true, when man contemplates what transpires today over the entire globe, that he may be tempted to abandon himself to despair and to ask sadly of the Lord, who is in heaven, as the poet of the Old Testament, "O Lord God of hosts, how long wilt Thou be angry against the prayers of Thy servant? How long wilt Thou feed us with the bread of tears: and give us for our drink tears in measure?" (Ps. 79:5-6.) But guard us, Lord, from this rash thought, from charging You with even the least injustice toward us. For it is not necessary to search long to find the source of all the evils on earth. Neither is it necessary to ask for long, when will they cease? But, for him who knows who is God and who is man; for him who knows what God has done for man, and what the conduct of man toward God has been; for him who knows how God regards the mutual relations of men, and how men conduct themselves toward one another; for him who knows what God wishes from each individual, and in what way a great many individuals live; for him the answer is easy to find — the answer to the question, when will the days of trial for all humanity be shortened? That will be when men recognize God for what He is, and when they will render unto Him the honor they owe Him; it will be when one will see in each neighbor what he really is, a child of God; it will be when the proud will no longer think they can do everything they desire to do, as if they were responsible to no one, but when they will strike their breasts and sigh, "Lord, have pity on me, a sinner." Then, and only then, will a true peace be achieved among families, nations, and states; peace throughout the whole world. If this should, perhaps, seem bizarre, or even ridiculous, to those who think that only force can bring peace, we reply to him with St. Augustine, by recalling what is necessary for a durable peace. Peace, says St. Augustine, is the stability of order. And what does true order demand? It demands first and above all that man, each man without exception, confess everywhere and in all places his wretchedness and weakness, as well as the greatness and omnipotence of God. *"Afferte Domino gloriam et honorem, afferte Domino gloriam nomini ejus,"* says the Psalmist. "Bring to the Lord glory and honor; bring to the Lord glory to his name" (Ps. 28:2). And we must not do this only by pronouncing His name on our lips, and treading the path of His laws, but, in truth, with our whole hearts and souls, with our whole life. Does man today do this? Since he has succeeded after so much labor in projecting himself into the skies in an airplane; since he has succeeded, after much ingenious work, in diving for hours under the sea; since he has succeeded, after much hard work, in finding a cure for this and that disease; since he has succeeded in inventing a more perfect telescope to contemplate the starry sky, he has inflated himself and raised his head, thinking he has no more need of God; he thinks that he is self-sufficient.

Give him but a little and he will take the Creator of the universe for his equal, or perhaps, for someone who is even inferior, and whom he may mock at his own good pleasure. There are many today who resemble a certain vain writer who thought himself such a genius that he could not find his equal on the earth. And one day one of his acquaintances, having found him seated in a garden and plunged in thought, made fun of him in this witty fashion.

"What are you thinking about?" he asked him.

"About death," replied the writer, "and about what I am going to say to God when I see Him face to face."

"But that is easy," replied the other. "You will say to Him, 'my dear colleague.'"

Do you think that there is but one infatuated fool of this sort in the world? So many merit the words of Holy Scripture, *"Deis superbis resistit."* "God resisteth the proud" (James 4:6). He did not spare Lucifer, the superb, when sought to appropriate to himself the honor of God, but in punishment He hurled him as a thunderbolt into the depths of hell as deeply as he had been raised high in honor; said Christ, "I saw Satan like lightning falling from heaven" (Lk. 10:18).

He did not save the first-born of the human race, Adam and Eve, when they obeyed not the Voice of God, but that of the serpent seducer and ate of the forbidden fruit. He struck down King Balthasar in the midst of a banquet when he dared mock the true God. He humbled Napoleon when he was at the peak of his power. It would never be difficult for Him, should He wish, to strike down today all human vainglory which thinks it can trifle with God. *"Deus non irridetur."* "God is not mocked" (Gal. 6:7), says the Apostle. Hence the first rule, if we wish to see better days, days of peace, is to render to God the honor which we owe Him and to humble ourselves before Him. The stability of order, then, true peace, demands a just relation with our neighbors. Jesus Christ has shown this at its best in the parable of the Good Samaritan, who poured oil and wine on the wounds of the injured man whom he met with on his journey, without regard for the origin of the sufferer, or for other circumstances, but only out of regard for human suffering and human nature. Jesus Christ also showed this relation very clearly by His words on the Cross when He prayed for His tormentors, "Father, forgive them, for they know not what they do" (Lk. 23:24).

Yes, the true relation with our neighbor demands that we see in him a man, not a wild beast; the child of God, as we are ourselves; our brother, whom we must love because we all must pray together, "Our Father, who art in heaven" (Mt. 6:9). *It would be an absurdity to speak of a new order in the world, no matter what its source, if human personality is not valued in that order, the immortal soul of man, which surpasses all systems and for which nothing can ever be substituted; the soul which has its inalienable rights which no human power can or ought to limit. It would also be an absurdity to think that the Catholic Church could be afraid of any human force in defending the elemental rights of the human personality and the freedom of conscience.*

Now, it is true that there are many in our day who mock the Church because it exalts the law of Christian charity, which they take for weakness. Pope Pius XII once replied very effectually to that objection, "Yes, weakness! But the weakness of God, for God is Charity. Charity is the force of Christ. Charity is the force of His Church by which it takes the road to a place which no other human force can penetrate — to the human heart — where it gives to the weak, the poor, the dying, the unhappy solace and comfort which no medicine nor surgery can ever give" (*Osservatore Romano*, December 14, 1941).

Yes, without this charity all would crumble, nothing solid could be built; without it all freezes and grows numb; but there, where it reigns, comes force and warmth which can carry even the heaviest burdens of human life across all barriers, like a locomotive, red with fire, pulling hundreds of cars in succession by its power and drive.

The stability of order demands, finally, that man follow the true path with regard to himself. Otherwise one cannot speak of a durable peace in human society. "*Unde bella et lites in vobis?*" asks the Apostle. "From whence are wars and contentions among you? Are they not from your concupiscences, which war in your members?" (James 4:1.) Is it not an absurdity for one to speak of the reform of human society, of peace among men, while at the same time he is the plaything of his passions, takes from another his legitimate spouse and lives as an adulterer; robs his neighbor of property acquired in a just manner to satisfy his avarice; and neglects all the laws of God and the state and who regards his tyranny as in the interest of the community and of the whole state? Have the words of Christ, "Render therefore to Caesar the things that are Caesar's; and to God, the things that are God's" (Mt. 22:21) no meaning today?

The whole world, as I have said, yearns after peace and is impatient for the moment when the olive branch of peace will appear on the horizon of the human community bleeding from a thousand wounds.

The Mother of God, the Most Blessed Virgin, carried in her arms the true Olive Branch of Peace, the Author of peace on earth, Jesus Christ, when the angels, the holy night of Christmas Eve, took pride in singing, "Glory to God in the Highest, and on earth peace to men of good will." All of us come to the Mother of God, following the counsel of St. Peter, and at the end of May we pray, hands joined together and eyes upraised, "Queen of peace, pray for us."

Who can doubt her maternal protection and her aid, when she herself invites us through the mouth of the psalmist, "Come, my sons, listen to me, I will teach you the fear of God" (Ps. 33:32). And what is that truth and what are those counsels necessary to gain the desired peace for humanity? They are very simple. "Turn away from evil and do good: seek after peace and pursue it" (Ps. 33:15). We shall gain peace with God when we know Him for what He is, rendering Him the honor that is due Him, "Be converted to me, and you shall be saved: for I am God, and there is no other" (Isa. 45:22). Peace with your neighbor, recognizing in all men the children "of your Father who is in heaven, who maketh his sun to rise upon the good, and bad, and raineth upon the just and the unjust" (Mt. 5:45). Peace in our own soul, by curbing in the future the wicked concupiscence which is in us, and for that which was evil in the past, striking our breasts, crying with the repentant publican, "O God, be merciful to me a sinner" (Lk. 18:13). That is the path that leads to true and durable peace in the world!

Mother of God, Queen of Peace, pray for us and procure us peace from God as soon as possible!

DOCUMENT XIV

The Sermon of the Archbishop in the Cathedral on the Anniversary of the Coronation of Pope Pius XII, March 14, 1943

"And thou, being once converted, confirm thy brethren" (Lk. 22:32).

CATHOLIC MEN AND WOMEN, CATHOLIC YOUTH, MY BELOVED FAITHFUL!

During the Last Supper while the Apostles like weak men were quarreling among themselves about who would be the greatest among them, Jesus Christ addressed the following words to Simon Peter: "Simon, Simon, behold Satan has desired to have you, that he may sift you as wheat: But I have prayed for thee, that thy faith fail not; and thou, being once converted, confirm thy brethren." He said to Him, "Lord, I am ready to go with thee, both into prison and to death." But He said, "I say to thee, Peter, the cock shall not crow this day, till thou thrice deniest that thou knowest me" (Lk. 22:31-34).

And truly! Peter, through human weakness, denied knowing Jesus during His bitter passion. God allowed this in order to deliver Peter from his pride and to affirm humility in him. But there is one thing that Peter did not do! He did not conceal nor abandon his belief that Jesus Christ was the true and living God, that He was the Saviour of the world. On account of this, we should not be astonished, if we read in Holy Scripture how St. Peter appeared as master of the truths that the Son of God had revealed and how he taught them to the Apostles that he might continue to reveal them to the world. This was shown best when the first Council was assembled at Jerusalem, under the leadership of Peter, to resolve the difficulties presented by the narrow criteria of certain individuals who did not yet understand that Christianity was, in its essence, above all nationality; that it did not separate people, but that it reunited them in one great family and in one great community of love and mutual respect. St. Peter appeared, as chief of the Apostles, against the destroyers of that great family of Christians into which all nations must enter. This, because St. Peter was destined, according to the order of God, to be the infallible teacher of the faith; in the words of the holy Council of the Vatican, "This doctrine of the apostles has been accepted by all the venerable Fathers, and the holy faithful Teachers have respected it and followed it, absolutely convinced that the Throne of Peter keeps itself free from all error in accordance with the Divine promise of the Lord our Saviour given to the chief of His disciples, 'I have prayed for thee, that thy faith fail not: and thou, being more convinced, confirm thy brethren'" (DB, 1836).

My dear faithful today we fix our eyes on that rock of solid principles in the midst of the raging sea of the opinions of men; we fix our eyes on that lamp of truth in the midst of the shadows and the lies of false doctrines; we direct our vision toward that home of love and of peace among men, peoples, and states from this hell of hate into which humanity has fallen. The devil has sought according to the words of Christ to sift the Apostles like wheat, that is to say, to kill in them their faith in Christ. But Christ prayed that the faith of Peter might not be weakened, but that he, after being convinced, might confirm his brothers. Over the centuries Satan has tried constantly to uproot from the hearts and souls of men all belief in the One God, and along with faith in God, all principles of morality, honesty, true civil order, and, in place of them, establish throughout the world the triumph of lies, hypocrisy, and hate. The eyes of all mankind looked during centuries, and today look more than ever, toward the throne of Peter to hear from it these words of truth, of consolation, and of salvation.

Catholic men and women, Catholic faithful! If you should ask me what we justly regard today to be the immense importance of the Pontificate for the human race, I should reply: the defense of that which is trampled upon, more or less, over the entire world; the defense of the dignity of the human person, the defense of the rights of the family, the defense of the weak.

Yes! It is without doubt one of the gravest errors of our times that the dignity and merit of the human person has fallen so low. When the value of money fell — the world had already accustomed itself to that in the last war — no one saw anything extraordinary in it. The world had also accustomed itself to the failure of so many other material values. But the mind of normal man can reconcile itself to the collapse of the dignity of the human person, to the fall of the value of man. Because, whether he believes in a personal God or not, each one, and even the worshiper of materialism, feels in the depths of his soul — and confesses it by his whole life — that he is not and cannot be the same thing as his dog; that he is not and cannot be the same thing as a small cog in a machine; that he is not and cannot be the same thing as a soap bubble that a playful child breaks in the air with a straw. Each one, and even this idolater when he rages most against God, feels in the depths of his soul the significance of the words, "*ad majora natus sum!*" I am, however, born for something higher. And he who has kept the faith best, he who carries in his soul the invincible realization of the existence of God the Creator, knows that man is never the chance effect of a nebulous, pantheistic evolution; but rather the work of the will of God who said, "Let us make man to our image and likeness" (Gen. 1:26). Consequently, every man, of whatever race or nation, whether he has studied in the universities of the civilized centers of Europe or hunts his food in the virgin forests of Africa, carries equally on himself the stamp of God the Creator and possesses inalienable rights which must not be taken from him nor arbitrarily limited by any human power. Each of them has the right to marriage, the right of physical life, the right to the life of the soul, the right to a religious education, the right to use material goods in so far as not contrary to just laws which protect the interests of the whole community; and many other rights. Every violation of these rights of the human person can only have evil consequences. And if today we sigh so much after peace, I repeat the words of Pope Pius XII, who gloriously rules the Church, which appear in his message of last Christmas, "Let him who wishes that the star of peace appear, as it did in earlier times to the Wise Men, and that it may remain above human society, contribute, on his part, in rendering to the human person the dignity that God has given it since the beginning of time" (*Osservatore Romano,* 1942, No. 300, p. 2).

The Pontificate is today a solid bulwark in the defense of the family and its sanctity. The full meaning of this can only be grasped by witnessing the tears of those who are in danger of the destruction of their families. This past week we have seen such tears and listened to the sobs even of stalwart men, and the cries of women without assistance, over whom this danger hung, for the sole reason that the sanctity of their families did not conform to the theories of racism. We, as representatives of the Church, could not and should not keep silent without betraying our mission. We repeat the words of Jesus Christ Himself, "What therefore God hath joined together, let no man put asunder." And today we proclaim it in public as well. No one denies the right of the secular authority to punish proved crimes. It has that right and that duty. But no one gives to human authority the right to violate the sanctity of the family or of a marriage which has been concluded on the foundation of the natural and positive law of God.

In any case it would be false to think that the Catholic Church would approve of measures which violate the elementary rights of man. There is still another reason why the Church cannot do so, because by such measures more and more individuals are driven into the ranks of the enemies of the present government because they cannot suffer — despite the best will — their families to be destroyed and annihilated, while they are conscientiously doing their duty to the state, on the battlefields, and elsewhere, where they strive to be trustworthy and useful citizens of the community in which they live. The great Pope Pius XII emphasized in his Christmas message, "Let him who wishes that the star of peace shine above human society repel any form of materialism which considers the nation only a mass of individuals — broken up and without any interior bond — to be arbitrarily dominated" (*Osservatore Romano, ibid.*).

As in the case of the doctrines on the natural law and on the equality of all men, the popes have not been indifferent to the question of nationality; rather have they always exalted the praiseworthy and noble qualities of individual nations and defended their rights if they were exposed to danger. But they have never considered them through the narrow prism of human passions, which makes of one's own nation an idol before which all must prostrate themselves; but instead through the prism of the Gospels which sees in these nations only the work of God the Creator with the fixed purpose of serving the glory of God as well as the national community. Only when considered in this way, does the Christmas message of Pope Pius XII ring true: "Within the scope of the new social order, based on moral principles, there is no place for the violation of the liberty, inviolability or security of other nations, no matter what their territorial extent or their capacity for defense. If it is inevitable that large states because of their greater capacities and power dictate conditions in the establishment of economic groups between themselves and smaller and weaker nations, the rights of the smaller and weaker nations are, nevertheless, incontestable, according to the common good which does not distinguish their rights from the rights of larger nations: the right to liberty in their political domain; the right to guard actively their neutrality in quarrels between states, which right belongs to them by natural and national law; the right to defend their economic development. It is only in this way that they will be able to achieve — in the interest of the common good — the material and spiritual prosperity of a true nation" (*Osservatore Romano*, 1941).

Only if viewed through the Gospels, as in the declaration of Pope Pius XII now gloriously reigning, can it be seen that, "In the realm of the new order, founded on moral principles, there is no place for open or disguised pressure on the cultural particularities or languages of national minorities, nor place for the obstruction or denial of their economic possibilities, and no one may limit or make impossible their natural expansion. The more the competent authorities conscientiously respect the rights of minorities, the more they are able to exact from the members of minorities an honest performance of their duties as citizens which are common to other citizens" (*Osservatore Romano*, 1941).

The popes of Rome have taken this position in the past, and the present Pope, Pius XII, takes this same view of our nation. If other peoples accept this doctrine the Croatian people will secure all the rights which belong to them in accordance with the natural and Divine Law. If our people will observe this same doctrine, taught from the Throne of Peter, they will be happy and blest by God, because it is only truth and justice which can, in the last analysis, save individuals and peoples.

My dear faithful, Catholic men and women! It is said that above the entrance of the main hall at the University of Uppsala is written in golden letters, "To think freely is a great thing, but to think justly is yet a greater thing." Yes, the intelligence of man is only too liable to error and it needs someone to correct it if, unhappily, it should stray from the way of truth.

And almighty God rendered an enormous service to humanity in giving to it an infallible teacher in questions of faith and morals. That is the Pope! We regard in him the deputy of Christ on earth, and we pray today, on the occasion of the fourth anniversary of his coronation, that God may protect him, grant him a long and happy life, and that He will not abandon him to the will of his enemies.

DOCUMENT XV

Sermon Delivered in Zagreb, October 25, 1943

Christ, You are the King of centuries, You are the Prince of all peoples.
You are the Sole Judge of all minds and of all hearts (Hymn I, Vesp. *Christi Regis*).

CATHOLIC MEN AND WOMEN, CATHOLIC FAITHFUL!

When we look about us in this world, and when we consider what goes on around us, we conclude that all that is created on this earth is subject to change. There are the vegetable and mineral kingdoms which are subject to change. There are the seasons which are subject to change. There is the firmament and the depths of the sea which are subject to change. And there is man who is also subject to change. On leaving his crib, where his mother's hands had put him, he learns to walk; from the age of a little boy he grows to adolescence; from the age of adolescence he grows to manhood, only to find himself in a short time a weak old man at the edge of the tomb, to become again the dust from which he was made. And human power is also changing on earth. Today millions tremble before individuals whose names will evoke no memory tomorrow.

There exists one power which knows no end, which knows no rival, which knows no fear, and which knows no change. That is the Royal Power of Jesus Christ, Son of God, of whom the Apostle said, "Jesus Christ, yesterday, and today, and the same forever!" (Hebr. 13:8.)

It is to this immortal King that the Church sings today from the canticles, "Christ, You are the King of centuries, You are the Prince of all peoples, You are the Sole Judge of all minds and hearts." It is to this "King of kings, and Lord of lords" (Apoc. 19:16) that we have come today, to adore Him, full of a lively faith, of profound humility, and with hearts full of repentance.

Let us reflect on His royal power and on our relations with Him both as individuals and nations. If individuals and peoples were conscious of what they really are before God, and of what their functions were, there would be less misery on earth and more happiness.

What are we as individuals? As individuals we resemble Lazarus in his tomb. He would have stayed for all eternity in this darkness if the Light of the World, Jesus Christ, had not bent over his tomb and if He had not said, "Lazarus, come forth" (Jn. 11:43). Each of us is nothingness and would have remained so eternally if the love of God and the power of God had not called him to life and if it had not maintained him in life. All men of good will join with St. Paul the Apostle, "By the grace of God, I am what I am" (1 Cor. 15:10).

How, then, must we judge those individuals who raise their heads proudly as if God no longer existed on the earth and as if the law of the Gospels were superfluous? We ought to say to them that which Christ said to the unfaithful city of Capharnaum, "And you, Capharnaum, will you raise yourself to the sky? You will descend into hell" (Mt. 21:23).

And what, before God, are the peoples and races of this world? It is worth while to suggest this subject at a time when the theories of class, race, and nationality have become the main topics of discussion among men.

The first thing that we affirm is that all nations, without exception, are as nothing before God. "All nations are before him as if they had no being at all," says the prophet, "and are counted to him as nothing, and vanity" (Isa. 40:17). These words of the prophet have already found their affirmation many times in the history of the world, when the Divine Hand, for various reasons, has swept individual nations from the face of the earth. It is, moreover, in the act of doing that today to every nation, if as nations they do not conform to the laws given by God, because "The Lord made the little and the great" (Wisd. 6:8).

The second thing that we affirm is that all nations and all races have their origin in God. Only one race really exists and that is the divine race. Its birth certificate is found in the book of Genesis, when the Divine Hand formed the first man from earthly clay and breathed into him the spirit of life (Gen. 2:7). He made him as well a woman, blessed them saying, "Increase and multiply, and fill the earth" (Gen. 1:28). Among all who belong to that race, entrance into the world and their departure from it is the same and will remain the same until the end of time, for it is written by the Divine Hand for all, "For dust thou art and unto dust thou shalt return" (Gen. 3:19). Those who belong to the race may have a greater or lesser culture, may be white or black, separated by oceans, live at the North or the South pole, but they remain essentially the race which comes from God and which must serve God according to the norms of the divine natural and positive law, written in the hearts and in the souls of men and revealed by the Son of God, Jesus Christ, Prince of all peoples.

But why, then, the different nations? What is their function? They are all here, without exception, for the glory of God. Because, even if God is in Himself a simple being, for us men His greatness and His beauty are made more evident by the diversity of created things. How much God ought to be admired in the creation of the vegetable kingdom with colors so varied! The mineral kingdom so diverse! The animal kingdom so diversified! The enormous number of stars in the sky! The immense oceans! But does not His greatness manifest itself in an extraordinary manner, as well as His wisdom and His power, by the fact that He created such a great number of peoples on the earth, with such different languages? This diversity of languages and peoples can lead to much rivalry among nations and much cultural progress, as life is much more animated in families where there are many children!

Finally, nationality as such can be a strong factor in resisting the moral decadence which springs from and is propagated by another nation. God, therefore, had great and wise reasons when He created diversity among peoples and when He gave the commandment of sincere love for one's own nation to the hearts and souls of men.

But this diversity must not become a source of mutual destruction. For the third thing that we affirm is that all nations and all races, as reflected in the world today have the right to lead a life worthy of men and to be treated with the dignity with which one treats a man. All of them without exception, whether they belong to the race of Gypsies or to another, whether they are Negroes or civilized Europeans, whether they are detested Jews or proud Aryans, have the same right to say, "Our Father, who art in Heaven" (Mt. 6:9). And if God has given this right to all, what is the human power that can deny it? All nations, no matter what their names, have the same duty: to beat their breasts and to say, "And forgive us our trespasses as we forgive those who trespass against us" (Mt. 6:12).

That is why the Catholic Church has always condemned, and condemns today as well, every injustice and every violence committed in the name of the theories of class, race, or nationality. One cannot exterminate intellectuals from the face of the earth because it may be agreeable to the working class, as Bolshevism has taught and done. One cannot extinguish from the face of the earth Gypsies or Jews because one considers them inferior races. If the racist theories, which have no foundation, are to be applied without scruples, is there any security for any nation at all? The Catholic Church had the courage in the very recent past, as it always has when it is necessary to lift its voice against the secret work of international Freemasonry, against the moral deprivation of our youth by the unscrupulous press, against crimes of abortion practiced by those who, without conscience, are eager only for material gains. It had the courage to defend our Croatian national rights, and to hurl that word of defense before crowned heads. It would be unfaithful to its duty if it did not raise its voice today, with the same energy, in defense of all those who suffer from injustices, without consideration of the race to which they belong. No one has the right to kill or harm in any way those who belong to another race or another nation. That can be done only by the legitimate authorities, if they had proved the crime of an individual and if the crime merits such punishment.

These things, moreover, are those which look to the interests, justly understood, and the love, well comprehended, of one's own country which are and remain for a Catholic not empty words but the moral duty for which he is responsible to God.

Catholic men and women! Faithful Catholics! Today is the feast of Christ the King. Not a king whose power lasts for today and tomorrow, but the feast of the Prince of princes! And of this Prince it is written, "For the nation and the kingdom that will not serve Thee, shall perish, such nations will be totally laid waste" (Isa. 60:12). This is what history has shown many times. It will show it again if the present-day nations reject the law of the Gospels and if they should repel Christ.

Your duty is to work in such a way that the spirit of the true Gospel may be introduced into our public and private life. For in the Gospels man is closest to God, and, so to speak, only in the Gospels can the human person find fulfillment. God has placed man as the crown and master of all creation. "Increase and multiply, and fill the earth, and subdue it, and rule over the fishes of the sea, and the fowls of the air, and all living creatures that move upon the earth" (Gen. 1:28). And that human personality, which our modern age has degraded to the rank of slave to creatures, must become again the center around which all creation revolves according to the plan laid down by the Creator of the world. Because the least human being, whatever his name, to whatever race or nation he belongs, carries upon himself the imprint of the living God, an immortal soul.

One of the reasons that impelled Christopher Columbus, convinced that he would find land beyond the sea, was the desire to lead new nations to Christ. After his return, when he was questioned about the new countries, he described the wealth and the marvels of the new world with enthusiasm. But he concluded his description with the words, "India" — for he thought that America was India — "India is beautiful and rich, but the most beautiful jewel of India is the souls of the Indians." Yes! That is the most beautiful jewel of every man, for which, when it was lost and in order to restore it, the Son of God, Jesus Christ Himself, descended from heaven, to give up not only all that He had, but even to give His own life on the cross to redeem this jewel — the soul of man — from the mire of sin, to pick it up, and to save it.

Catholic men and women! Catholic faithful! It often happens, as a man walks across fields and climbs mountains, that he treads upon jewels or upon gold which is hidden underfoot, and of which he has no inkling. But in this ignorance there is no tragedy. It is much more tragic that men pass over that which is most beautiful in man, that which renders him like unto God, over his own immortal soul and that of others. Away with that ignorance. Let everyone be conscious of his dignity as man! Let him be conscious of his royal vocation as a child of God, above all today when we celebrate the Feast of Christ the King, the King of centuries, the King of peoples, but especially the King of the immortal souls of men, to whom be glory and honor throughout the centuries. Amen.

DOCUMENT XVI

Sermon at the Closing of the Procession of Penance at Zagreb, October 31, 1943

DEAR FAITHFUL, DEAR BROTHERS:

We have just finished the great procession of penance in our city of Zagreb which is, at the same time, the close of our devotions in honor of the Blessed Virgin during the month of October. What shall I say to you at the close of this procession? A certain writer tells the story of a peasant who every day brought five pounds of butter to the baker of his town, which he needed to bake his bread, and who also, every day, used to carry away with him from the baker's a five pound loaf of bread. It happened that one day the baker set about weighing the butter, and to his surprise he discovered that the peasant had brought him only four and a half pounds of butter. He called the peasant to account for cheating. But the peasant answered him quietly, "My friend, I am not guilty, for although naturally I have a scale, I have no weights. Because of that I always put your bread on one side of the scale, and on the other side my butter. I put exactly as much butter on the scale as the weight of your loaf." The baker did not believe this. But when he used a more accurate scale he saw that the peasant was right, and since that time the baker has given his customers an exact measure of bread.

You will ask me, perhaps, what has this to do with the procession of penance. I shall apply this parable to our lives today. Whether people believe or whether they do not believe, God is our Creator, and we are the wretched of the earth who owe to our Creator veneration and obedience, in other words, we are debtors of God. And yet it is already more than two hundred years since Europe, as well as the entire world, has tried to appear more intelligent than God and refused to God the veneration due Him.

How can we describe the outrages to God in the newspapers and books of the past twenty years? How can we describe the criminal abortions over the years in the name of so-called science and of social advancement? How can we describe the corruption in the lives of numerous husbands and wives? How can we describe the evil that the pagan fashions of the women of our day have brought? How can we describe the debauchery and immorality to be seen on the beaches and at bathing places? It is enough to recall only our own river, the Sava. But what good does it do to prolong this? The prophet summed up all the vices of humanity in one word when he said, "For my iniquities are gone over my head; and as a heavy burden are become heavy upon me" (Ps. 37:5). It is thus that we have measured for God, our Creator. It is completely understandable that God has measured for us, then, just as did the peasant. For Christ has said, "with what measure you mete, it shall be measured to you again" (Mt. 7:2). And God has meted to humanity a just measure. He reduces to dust and ashes the cities which have forgotten their duty of honoring their God. He reduces to dust and ashes the villages that take His Most Sacred Name in vain and violate the Lord's Day instead of blessing Him for the bread He gives them and for the air they breathe. He reduces to dust men's works of art so that they might know that the most beautiful work is a pure human soul, the temple of the living God and which so many people have turned by their sins into a robbers' den. It is today that the words of the Apostle, St. Paul, are realized, "It is a fearful thing to fall into the hands of the living God" (Hebr. 10:31). Since we have fallen, on account of our sins, into the hands of the living God who destroys not only individual cities and villages but also entire nations, our good sense tells us that we must humble ourselves before God like the debauched Ninevites and that we must repent with a sincere penance for our sins which cry to heaven for vengeance if we wish to save ourselves from total ruin. And these are the reasons for which we have prayed this whole month and for which we had our procession of penance.

This provides the opportunity to reply in public to innumerable officious advisers, of both the Right and the Left, who suggest to the representatives of the Catholic Church how they should proceed so that the guilt for numerous crimes which have been committed and are being committed, does not fall on the Church.

Some accuse us of not raising our voice in time against crimes which have occurred in certain sections of our country. We reply to them first of all, that we are not and that we do not wish to be a political trumpet of any sort, blowing according to the desires and momentary needs of certain parties or individuals. We have always asserted the value in public life of the principles of the eternal law of God *without regard to whether it applied to Croats, Serbs, Jews, Bohemians, Catholics, Mohammedans, or Orthodox.*

But we cannot physically force anyone to fulfill the eternal laws of God, because every man has free will and each will answer for his actions according to the words of the Apostle, "For everyone shall bear his own burden" (Gal. 6:5). *For this reason we are unable to answer longer for those hotheads and extremists among the clergy.* The future will show that the Catholic Church has not failed in its duty; it will be demonstrated when things can be discussed in a calmer fashion, and the facts are all in. But today we wish to propose a question to certain groups and national organizations: Was it the Catholic Church that provoked the war which has had such terrible consequences, or was it someone else? Was it the Catholic Church which, year after year, created in the souls of men the discontent and brutality which has had such tragic results? How many times has the Catholic Church, during these past twenty years, reminded all the representatives of the intellectual and political communities that they should cease trampling on human and national rights, that they should cease destroying the generous humanity and the morality of the people through the press and the cinema. All in vain! The wind blew despite our efforts and warnings and became the terrible storm which all true Catholics regret profoundly but which all our most loyal efforts could not prevent. And for that we reply to the first group of those who reproach us: It is in you that is realized the story of the peasant and the baker. And if anyone thinks that the Catholic Church trembles before the future on account of its conduct, he is in error. The Church stands serene with a clear conscience, ready to face any situation which may arise.

We reply to those who accuse us of pro-communism, and of alleged inaction, that the Catholic Church is not an institution which lasts from today until tomorrow, but it is an organization which has survived and will yet survive innumerable states, nations, and transformations. It is not an institution which would make an agreement with communism today and tomorrow deny that agreement and fight a war of extermination. The Catholic Church has, moreover, made clear an indefinite number of times what it thinks, and where it stands. The Catholic Church can never recognize a system that seeks to take from the peasant his land; from the craftsman his shop; from a private person the fortune acquired through honest work; from the worker the fruits of his toil and, in general, from man his soul. If social reforms are indispensable, as they are, if a more just division is needed, and that is what we preach, then no one has proposed a better solution than Pope Leo XIII and Pope Pius XI in their immortal encyclicals, *Rerum Novarum* and *Quadragesimo Anno.* That is our social program. It is put to work to perfection in our religious communities where such a way of life is uniquely possible because its basis is God and the bond between subordinates is Christian charity, sanctified on the Cross of Christ. And when we say we cannot recognize the system that aspires to take from the peasant his land and render him the slave of the state, we rely on more than merely right reason; we rely on the experience which says that our peasant would prefer to die rather than let himself become a slave on his own land. We cannot tolerate a system that denies the family, which the Church sees as a divine institution and the fundamental unit of every nation. To wish to make a man and woman husband and wife only for the time that sexual relations exist, to wish to take from the family its sacred sacramental character, to prevent it from being the source of life and the place of the education of children, to wish to take the child from his parents and declare him the property of the state — all that means the undermining of the very principles of the natural law of life and the destruction not only of the family but also of the nation and the national community. We cannot recognize a system that would deny God Himself, the Creator of the universe, and reduce the profession of a belief in God to the interior of four walls, where no one could hear or see us. We cannot recognize a system which refuses to little children the knowledge of God which is given to them by religious instructions in the schools taught by priests. If the entire visible universe is the creation of God, and it is not the result of fortuitous chance, for chance is the god of fools, then the entire universe must revere God, it must revere Him in all phases of public life. *This is our point of view, from which we will not retreat even at the cost of our lives, and the future will show as always that the Catholic Church has been right and that it cannot be otherwise. We do not profess these principles from today to tomorrow; we do not profess them through fear or out of personal interests, but only because of interior necessity, conscious that this conforms to the will of God the Creator.* That is our reply to the charge that the Catholic

Church is disposed to pro-communism or is perhaps partial to it. But those persons who reproach us in such a manner would, perhaps, do better if they would knock on the door of their own consciences and ask this question: are there not a great number of people who took refuge in the forests, not because of a conviction of the truth of communism, but very often out of despair, on account of the brutal methods of a few thoughtless individuals who thought that they could do whatever they liked and that there was for them no law, human or divine? Is it not here again that the story of the baker and the peasant is illustrated? Was the Church able to prevent this terrible destruction, although it condemned it, when its teachings were so cynically spurned?

Finally, we will answer also those who accuse us of favoring racism because as you know in the minds of some people the Catholic Church is capable of anything. We have defined our position concerning racism ever since it existed and not merely now. That position is brief and precise. The Catholic Church knows nothing of races born to rule and races doomed to slavery. *The Catholic Church knows races and nations only as creatures of God, and, if it esteems one more than others, it is because it possesses a more generous heart, not because one has the strongest arm. For it the Negro of Central Africa is as much a man as the European. For it the king in a royal palace is, as a man, exactly the same as the lowest pauper or gypsy in his tent.* It sees no difference between them. Both possess an immortal soul, both have the same royal origin, finding their source in God the Creator. That is the racial doctrine of the Catholic Church, and all others are mere vulgar speculation and innuendo.

The Catholic Church cannot admit that one race or one nation, because it is more numerous or better armed, may do violence to a smaller nation with fewer people. We cannot admit that innocent people may be killed because someone, say a frontier guard, has, perhaps, killed a soldier, even if he is of a more noble race. The system of shooting hundreds of hostages for a crime, when the person guilty of the crime cannot be found, is a pagan system which only results in evil. It is absolutely certain that if order is sought with such measures, many people who up to now have obeyed the voice of the Church, although exposed to the terror, will, finally, attempt to seek safety in the forests. Is it not again, then, the realization of the story of the baker and the peasant?

Finally, I realize the question in the minds of the thousands listening to me: what order does the Catholic Church propose at a time when the entire world is fighting for a new order?

We condemn all injustice; all murder of innocent people; all burning of peaceful villages; all killings, all exploitation of the poor. We sorrow for the miseries and the sadness of all who today suffer unjustly, and reply: the Catholic Church upholds that order which is as old as the Ten Commandments of God. We are not for that order which is written on perishable paper but for that which is written by the hand of the living God in the consciences of men.

The basis of this order is God, our Lord, who does not lose Himself in rhetoric as do earthly lawgivers, but who has summed up the whole of order in the words of the Ten Commandments. We must give glory and honor to God since He is our Maker; to our parents, superiors, and to our country, love, obedience, and sacrifices if they are necessary. Our neighbor, no matter what his name, is not a cog in the machine of state, whether he be colored red, black, gray, or green; but is a free child of God, our brother in Christ. That is why we must recognize in our neighbor the right to life, to fortune, and to honor, because it is written: thou shalt not kill, thou shalt not steal, thou shalt not bear false witness against thy neighbor! We must respect his family, because it is written by the hand of God: thou shalt not covet thy neighbor's wife! We must respect ourselves, because it is written: thou shalt not commit adultery! It would be a very great mistake to think that in this order there is no Last Judgment for those who violate it. All this frightful chaos that the world endures is only punishment for the violation of the Ten Commandments of God and for contempt of the Gospel of Christ. And if humanity does not wish to recognize again the divine authority which is above it, it is certain that the hand of God will strike again more rigorously.

My dear brothers, our procession of penance comes to its end. When Jesus, our Saviour, passed by the town of Jericho, two blind men cried out to Him, "Son of David, have mercy on us."

"What would you have Me to do to you?" Jesus asked them.

"Lord, that we might see," replied the blind men. And we end our procession with an ardent prayer to the Lord, our God, "Lord, let all who are blind see and let them realize that there is neither peace nor happiness for any man, for any family, for any nation, or for any state without You, God the Creator. Because it is written for today and forever: If the Lord does not build a house, in vain do they strive who would build it; and if the Lord does not watch over a city, in vain do they watch who would guard it! Let all men learn to know You are our Father, and that we all, regardless of color, language, or shape, are Your children, and among ourselves, brothers. If we have erred up to now in taking roads that lead to ruin, let us return to the way of Your Commandments, to the path of the Gospels of Christ, which to the blind may seem hard and bitter, but which alone can make happy all men and all nations! Amen."

DOCUMENT XVII

Article published in Nova Hrvatska, *November 7, 1943, by Dr. Julije Makanec, Minister of Public Instruction with reference to the Archbishop's sermons*

THE COMPETENT AND THE INCOMPETENT

ZAGREB, November 6, 1943

Europe is the continent where the human spirit has attained its highest level. What would the world be today without all that the European spirit has created? If man is the image of God, then European man is so to a special degree; he is, without doubt, more so than a Negro of central Africa. A Gothic cathedral surely reflects eternity in a more intense and more sublime manner than a Negro's filthy hut or a gypsy's tent; and the Ninth Symphony is certainly nearer to God than the howling of a cannibal tribe of Australia.

Nationalism is the child of the European spirit, it is only the European mind that knows large groups of people united, not for any material profit but by a belief in a higher common vocation, the feeling of a need for its own common expression. Only in Europe are there nations formed as moral and political units, whose life is directed to a higher spiritual goal. If national movements have appeared elsewhere outside of Europe, they are direct or indirect consequences of European influences.

This sublime thought, that every wholly valid nation is a special idea of God, that it incarnates in itself, in a singular and peculiar manner, the idea of humanity and is for that reason indispensable to humanity; this thought was born in Europe.

Every civilized nation takes for one of its highest duties the preservation and development of its individuality. The final goal of each national struggle is the personal preservation of the national individuality, the national immortal soul, which God alone has instilled in the nation. And on account of this, each thinking member of society considers it his sacred duty to collaborate in this struggle; and rightly so, because it is directed toward the preservation of those things which the nation regards as its highest values and which alone gain for it the character of a sacred thing: and every struggle that one wages for a sacred thing is holy.

To preserve its own individuality, received from God, is one of the highest ethical, even religious duties of a nation, because in this struggle for personal spiritual preservation the nation fulfills the will of God. The national individuality cannot develop itself and be formed harmoniously if the nation has not succeeded in establishing and preserving its own national state. The value of this ideal is also appreciated from the blood that a nation is ready to spill for it. The enormous value of a national state can be measured only by the immense and formidable sacrifices that are made for it. He cannot be national who does not understand the value of a national state with regard to national freedom and independence, or, at least, who esteems it too little and speaks of it as something ephemeral and of small importance.

If its own national state, to which a nation has the right according to the will of God, is the most important and sacred thing for every living nation, then its greatest enemy is he who wishes to rob it of that national state; anyone is an unworthy son of his own nation who respects too little or disdains this national struggle for a national state, who holds himself aloof from this sacred struggle and who even appropriates for himself the right, being on the side lines out of danger, to cast words of reproach against those who suffer for their nation pain and bloody wounds; but who completely forgets to blame those who destroy his nation, his home; tear down his house, his state; and force it into a life without honor, unworthy of a servant or a slave.

The reality in which we live is hard and cruel. And the Croatian people are placed in this reality. This reality does not conform to our thoughts or to our desires, it is what it is. We must preserve ourselves in it if we wish to fulfill our duty to ourselves. Combat, blood, suffering, and misery are not novelties for the Croatian people, who bled thirteen centuries ago in the geopolitically dangerous territory on which they live. Whence come these sufferings, this blood, these pains? Are the Croatian people so wicked, so vicious that they must regard in these secular trials the punishment for the violation of the Ten Commandments of God?

Are the Croatian people in their depression and penitent discouragement now going to grovel upon the earth like worms, begging mercy from their enemies, because they are so wicked and corrupt? Is it not in this way that they would reap only the disdain and repugnance of all their neighbors and of all the strong nations that exist and that have steeled themselves in struggles and suffering?

The Croatian people are too convinced of their own value and of the justice of their struggle to accept the philosophy of a worm, crushed underfoot. The Croatian people believe in the ethics of suffering. They know that the Almighty often strikes hardest exactly those whom He loves the best, exactly those whom He has chosen for the greatest things; He strikes them with harsh trials and miseries to see if they will persevere courageously in these trials and show themselves sufficiently worthy of the vocation He has reserved for them in His great wisdom.

It is with such a feeling and such a conviction, with such a philosophy of a heroic and righteous man that the Croatian suffers the Calvary of today, and not with the philosophy of a being which has neither pride, nor backbone, nor faith in his own value and in the justice of his deeds, the philosophy of a worm.

Who appears on the scene today as an enemy of the Croatian people and their state? Who has brought to Croatia these terrible blows which bleed it today? Is it not those who wish to take "from the peasant his land, from the craftsman his shop . . . and from man in general his soul"? Is it not those who wish to take "from the family its holy and sacramental character and to prevent it from being the source of life and the place of the education of children"? Is it not those who desire "to shake the very principles of the natural law of life and destroy even the people and the community of the state"? Is it not those who would wish to "forbid little children the knowledge of God" and generally stamp out the image of God in the human soul?

The episcopate of Spain may serve as an example and model to all others respecting the just appreciation of the danger that comes from this adversary of the national liberty and the civilized life of every nation in Europe as well as of the very principles of Christian civilization. In the fight against this adversary it has not stood to one side and has not adopted a lukewarm and vague attitude.

In the bloody and inexorable fight against these satanic adversaries, Croatian lives are snuffed out every day and the best sons of Croatia are dying. All of their sacrifices, do they not merit a single word of eulogy and recognition? Do not men who find themselves in danger of death every day in the fight against the serpentine and heartless enemy; men for whose lives their dearest ones, their wives, mothers, sisters, and defenseless children tremble every day; do these heroes and unhappy men, these soldiers and martyrs who defend with their blood the sacred and just rights of their people, merit nothing else than that this man, who lives outside of all danger, thanks to their pain and suffering, should address to them words of reproach, and instead of praise and recognition speak of them just as he does of those who ravage and coldly and purposefully devastate our Croatian countryside in order to prepare for the final catastrophe of Croatian national freedom?

Croatians are, for the most part, a Catholic people. They were always good sons of the Church and want to remain so in the future. They see in a Catholic priest the servant of God who has his sphere of sublime obligations, obligations which are not of this world. For the obligations of this world Croatians had their secular leaders and they have them still today. It would not be at all opportune that men who neither know nor have a feeling for secular problems, who cannot accustom themselves to the harshness of this world, who are devoid of every political instinct and of every talent for penetrating to the essence of this fatal struggle of our day; it would not be opportune that such men, however unknowingly, spread political confusion and defection among the soldiers who defend with their lives not only the foundations of the Croatian state but also the Catholic Church against an enemy who would, without mercy, cut the throat of the organization of the Catholic Church as soon as there were no more of these soldiers, or as soon as they succumbed in battle. It is not necessary to particularly emphasize that all other sects recognized and defended by the law would meet the same fate.

Among all political faults the worst is to cut off the branch on which one is sitting. God has destined for each class its sphere of obligations; that is why it is best that everyone remain in the field to which he has been called and in which he is competent. This is entirely valid as well for that high ecclesiastical dignitary who has recently, in his sermons, passed beyond the limits of his vocation and begun to meddle in affairs in which he is not competent. He who does not understand the meaning of the political struggle, who has no comprehension of political values, and who does not know how to weigh and evaluate them, will always do best to keep himself aloof from the political sphere, leaving these things to those more competent, to those whom God has destined in this struggle to be at the head of their people as the political and military leaders who carry on their backs the responsibility of the national fate. It is in this way that he would be most useful to the Catholic Church and the Croatian people, who will not allow themselves to stray from the road of honor and pride because of any trickery, and who will not do so especially after such an example as our neighbor to the west has given us. It is easy, being on the brink of a precipice, to fall into the abyss of dishonor and infamy, but it is very difficult to climb out of it again. He alone who knows very well the land to which the road leads, because he has traveled it frequently and lived there, can successfully lead the people; but never he who is a stranger to this land. He cannot be a guide there, but rather he needs a guide for himself.

Dr. Jules Makanec
Minister of Public Instruction

Zagreb, November 7, 1943
"Nova Hrvatska" Year III, No. 261

DOCUMENT XVIII

Translations of the British Broadcasting Corporation Comments, in the Serbo-Croat Language Programs Regarding the Anti-totalitarian Character of Archbishop Stepinac's Sermons

Radio News Broadcast II   Zagreb, July 7, 1943
London — at 1:15 P.M. in the Serbo-Croat Language

Yesterday the Vatican radio station broadcast a number of excerpts from two sermons given not long ago by the Archbishop of Zagreb, Dr. Stepinac. In his sermons the Archbishop severely and bitterly condemned the persecutions of Jews and other nationalities, in conformity with measures of Nazi terrorism inspired by the Nuremburg laws. The Vatican radio station stated that the Archbishop of Zagreb said in his sermon, "Every people and every race on earth have the right to live and to be treated in a manner worthy of men. If God has given this right to men, no power in the world may take it from them; also, has not the Catholic Church always condemned all injustice and violence committed in the name of social, racist, and nationalistic principles. No one has the right to kill arbitrarily on his own authority or in any way to harm any members of a race." When the so-called Independent State of Croatia ordered that all Jews should be treated according to the Nuremburg laws, on that occasion — according to the Vatican radio station — Stepinac declared that a criminal, whose crime has been made known to him, must be judged by a state court. Also that no one has the right to destroy the sanctity of marriage as recognized by our Holy Mother Church. The married state has its rights which no secular power may take away or limit.

*   *   *

London — at 10:15 P.M. in the Serbo-Croat Language

In the moral sphere, the Axis has been dealt a heavy blow by the highest moral and spiritual power of the Catholic Church through the medium of the Vatican radio. This blow was directed against Nazism and against its satellites, of whom Pavelić is one, who must do as they are told.

Last Wednesday the Vatican station transmitted certain portions of a sermon by the Archbishop of Zagreb, Dr. Aloysius Stepinac, in protest against the persecution of the Jews. The Archbishop delivered this sermon on March 4 after the Ustashi government had ordered that the German Nuremberg laws be applied to all Jews in the Independent State of Croatia. Previously the Archbishop had declared himself against the exaggerations of the racist theory, following which the Ustashi government ordered the confiscation of property and the wearing of special insignia. The Vatican station described the Archbishop as a resolute champion of moral rights and of freedom. The Archbishop said in his sermon:

"Last Sunday I had the occasion to see the tears and listen to the groans of stalwart men and of women abandoned before the danger of seeing their homes destroyed for the sole reason that these were not in accord with the theory of Nazism." And Archbishop Stepinac added, "The Church cannot remain tranquil before events of this kind, because the fundamental rights of man are violated by these measures." Following this, he said, "Every man, to whatever race he belongs, bears the stamp of God, whether he has studied in a European university or whether he hunts in the jungles of Africa. Every man has the right to physical and spiritual life, to marriage, to a religious education, and to the use of material goods. The laws of society may not prevent this because all destruction of the rights of men can have only grievous consequences."

Previously the Archbishop had said, "God has given to man certain rights, and there is no power here below which can take them away. That is why the Church rises against all acts of violence committed against these human rights."

The most important prelate of Croatia has spoken out against the Ustashi authorities who imitate Nazi crimes. This expression needs no commentary.

❖ ❖ ❖

New York — at 11:30 P.M. in the Serbo-Croat Language

At the end of a sermon on March 14, the Archbishop of Zagreb, Dr. Aloysius Stepinac, said:

"No one has the right to destroy the intellectual class in order to aid the working class. Thus, neither Jews nor Gypsies may be persecuted for the sole reason that they are considered inferior races. If the so-called racist theories are imprudently applied, all security will disappear from the earth.

"Yes, we ask the Ustashi if they have any reply that would refute the Vatican and that would destroy the truth, preached by Christ, of the brotherhood of men and peoples."

❖ ❖ ❖

New York — at 10:30 P.M. in the Serbo-Croat Language

We are reproducing the statement of Archbishop Dr. Aloysius Stepinac against the persecution of the Jews.

This statement was recorded in the edition of the "Voice of America" transmitted from London.

DOCUMENT XIX

*Communication of Dr. Nicholas Mandić to the Head of the Croat
Government Regarding the Reaction Abroad to the
Archbishop's Sermons*

Independent State of Croatia   ZAGREB, November 29, 1943
Ministry of Public Instruction
Department of Propaganda, Zagreb
No. VT 251/43

Subject: Impression caused by a sermon of Archbishop Stepinac

To the President of the Government
To be presented personally to the President,
Dr. Nicholas Mandić

The undersigned has the honor of communicating that the radio
stations of the enemy are exploiting the notorious sermon of the
Archbishop, Dr. Aloysius Stepinac, in a way that suits their purposes.

On the twenty-eighth of this month, the London station transmitted
the following on a program in the Serbo-Croat language at 1:15 P.M.

"In Yugoslavia the Germans are making their persecutions harsher
in order to break the courage of the Serbs, Croats, and Slovenes who
are fighting for their liberation.

"According to reports from Zurich, the most recent victims of the
Germans are twenty-three priests whom the Germans have arrested
in Dalmatia. These priests referred in their churches to a sermon
delivered recently by the Archbishop of Zagreb. The priests said
that the sermon of the Archbishop of Zagreb was in accordance with
the spirit of the Catholic Church. The arrests of these priests provoked
great anger among the people. Their fate is not known but more
serious news is awaited.

"Reports state that the Quisling press in Yugoslavia announced
that the Archbishop had said, 'The Catholic Church recognizes all
races and nationalities as creatures of God and all of them are equal
in the eyes of the Church.' The Quislings say that the Archbishop
tried to justify the fight of the Partisans and that he described the
bombardment of Germany as Divine vengeance."

Za Dom Spremni!

Hail, Ustashi: ready in the service of the Fatherland.
Chief of the Section for Press and Cinema, MICHAEL TOLJ

DOCUMENT XX

Translation of a Copy of a Letter From His Excellency Dr. Joseph Ujćić, Archbishop of Belgrade, Addressed to His Excellency Dr. Aloysius Stepinac

BELGRADE, December 29, 1941

EXCELLENCY:

At the present time I have in my home the Orthodox Bishop Vladimir, from the Lower Carpathians, sent across the frontier by the Hungarians on the following mission:

The Orthodox Bishop of Gornji Karlović, Sava Trlajić, is in prison in Croatia, according to hearsay, at Lepoglava or some other concentration camp.

His mother in Belgrade, an old woman of 87, is near the end and wants to see her son before she dies.

I have also written to His Excellency the Papal Delegate Marcone, asking him to intervene with the Zagreb government so that Bishop Sava may be permitted to go and see his mother. I think that this would be a great consolation for both mother and son, a real Christmas present.

Impelled by the humanitarian reasons of a Christian conscience, and also by reason of the public interest, I take the liberty of asking Your Excellency to intervene in this case in any way that you can.

I commend myself to your prayers and wishing Your Excellency a happy and blessed New Year, I remain in fraternal charity,

Your devoted,
Ujćić

❂   ❂   ❂

Reply of His Excellency Dr. Aloysius Stepinac to
His Excellency Dr. Ujćić:

I personally intervened with the Poglavnik together with the Delegate from the Holy See, Marcone. We received the reply that this person was not at Lepoglava. What could we do?

STEPINAC

Zagreb, December 31, 1941

DOCUMENT XXI

Second Letter From Archbishop Ujćić to Archbishop Stepinac With a Request for Aid for Serbian Prisoners

BELGRADE, December 29, 1941

EXCELLENCY:

Mr. Bogdan Rasković, secretary to the Ministry of Communications and delegate of the German and Italian Red Cross, made a trip to Zagreb to intervene in Zagreb through the Red Cross on behalf of Serbian prisoners who were in various concentration camps. He has asked that, in so far as possible, they be returned to their families or at least that their families be allowed to send them packages as they may do in Serbia for their prisoners who are held in Germany.

I think that this would truly answer *"humanitati et benignitati"* which at Christmas time manifests itself from heaven, if the competent authorities could alleviate the lot of the prisoners for the Orthdox Christmas, especially of those who are held only for political offenses, otherwise being honest persons.

If you can do anything in this case, I would be most grateful.

Please accept, Excellency, my most sincere wishes for a happy and blessed new year, et memento!

Addictissimus
DR. JOSEPH UJĆIĆ

NOTE BY ARCHBISHOP STEPINAC

This Serbian from Belgrade was at my home accompanied by a German soldier so that no harm should befall him. He thanked me for what I had done for the Serbs and asked me to intervene. I told him that I was against the mass conversions to the Catholic Church, to which he replied, "Excellency, let all be converted so that they may save their lives." I promised him to intervene and went immediately to see the Minister of the Interior. What result came of it I don't know, but we did what we could.

STEPINAC

December 29, 1941

COLLABORATION: AID TO JEWS, SLOVENES, AND OTHERS IN DISTRESS

DOCUMENT XXII

Letter Addressed to Archbishop Stepinac by a Serbian Family in Gratitude for Aid Received

To His Excellency, The Croatian Metropolitan,
Dr. Aloysius Stepinac,
Zagreb.

We are very happy that you have saved our mother for us. We are infinitely grateful to you, and pray God to repay your good work through His divine blessing.

Words fail us in the expression of our gratitude to you. Now we are all happy and content with our mother at home and we pray to God.

In our most difficult moments, you, as our supreme pastor, saved us from misery and want and brought comfort into our little house and for that, Excellency, accept our thanks.

> Praise be to Jesus and Mary!
> Mother Marie, and children Joseph, Milivoj,
> Bosiljko, Smiljica, and Branko.

NOTE: His Excellency the Archbishop went in person to the Poglavnik and asked that the mother of these poor children be released.

The secretary of His Excellency the Archbishop was twice in their house while their mother was in prison. He helped them with 1,000 kronen; the mother, after she was released, received 500 kronen.

S. LACKOVIĆ

DOCUMENT XXIII

Letter From the Archbishop to Chief of Police Vragović Regarding Orthodox Who Had Been Arrested

Dr. Joseph Vragović
Chief of Police, Zagreb

THE CHIEF OF POLICE:

I have the honor of addressing you on the following matter: On

January 22, 1944, a truckload of Croatian exiles arrived from Italy among whom were some seven (7) Orthodox, whose names are listed:

1. Janković, Svetozar
2. Mutavdžić, Lazo
3. Vucetić, Borivoje
4. Vekić, Peter

5. Kukurić, Risto
6. Dokić, Philip
7. Marković, Mirko

They were all arrested as soon as they had crossed the German frontier and set foot on Croatian territory. Before their departure from Italy, guarantees had been given to all of them by our delegation which is at present in that country that no harm would be done them. They were arrested, however, that very evening and are now in the Police Headquarters in Zagreb.

According to the information I have received, my dear Chief of Police, these people who have been arrested are innocent, no charge exists against them and they were arrested for the sole reason of their Orthodox religion.

This arrest will produce a most regrettable impression on those who are still in Italy, and if they learn of what happened in this case, they will certainly hesitate to leave and return to Croatia.

Therefore, I ask that the above-named persons be released or, in case that cannot be done, that they be assigned for work at the establishment of the Carnelutti Brothers, a construction company, at 7 Vukotinovićeva Street, who will subsequently provide them with work at Ptuj.

Accept, my dear Chief of Police, my highest respect.

THE ARCHBISHOP

Zagreb, January 25, 1944
Sent on January 27, 1944 — Šalić

DOCUMENT XXIV

Letter From the Archbishop to Mons. Montini
Regarding Two Serbian Refugees

ZAGREB, July 2, 1942

MOST REVEREND EXCELLENCY:

May I be permitted to address Your Most Reverend Excellency with regard to two cases:

1. Dr. Rajko Gjermanović is in the Regina Coeli judiciary prison

of Rome. He has been assured of his liberation, but is still imprisoned. I am told that the intervention of the authorities and of charitable agencies is needed. May I recommend most earnestly this case to Your Excellency.

2. Dr. Vittorio Ružić, ex-Yugoslav minister and vice-prefect of Croatia, has been imprisoned by the Italian authorities in the city of Susak. The reason for his incarceration, I am told, was a prolonged and noisy festivity in the family on the occasion of his son's school promotion. He is in prison with his son. As minister he was always very friendly toward the Church and was decorated by the Holy See. His Excellency Monsignor Felici knows him well.

Thanking Your Most Reverend Excellency for whatever you may do in these two cases, I am happy to take the opportunity to express myself to Your Most Reverend Excellency, in our Lord,

ARCHBISHOP OF ZAGREB

Most Rev. Msgr. G. A. Montini
State Secretariat
Vatican City

NOTE:
1. Dr. Ruzić released through the intervention of His Excellency Archbishop Stepinac with the Italian Minister in Zagabria.
2. The secretary of the Archbishop in Rome acted in the case of Dr. Gjermanović at the judiciary prison.

DOCUMENT XXV

Letter From the Archbishop to Dr. Andrija Artuković
Regarding the Anti-Semitic Legislation

ZAGREB, April 23, 1941

No. 103

MR. MINISTER:

On the occasion of the announced promulgation of the anti-Semitic law, I have the honor to draw your attention to the following fact:

There are good Catholics of the Jewish race who have been converted by conviction from the Jewish religion. There are among them those who have been converted for dozens of years; there are among them also those who have excelled as good Croatian patriots. I think it necessary to take account of such converts in the promulgation of the laws.

Please accept, Mr. Minister, the expression of my sincere respect.

THE ARCHBISHOP
President of the Episcopal Conference

Dr. Andrija Artuković
Minister of the Interior
Zagreb

DOCUMENT XXVI

Letters From the Archbishop to Dr. Artuković Regarding the Application and Interpretation of the Anti-Semitic Legislation

ZAGREB, May 22, 1941

No. 117

MR. MINISTER:

I had the honor on April 23 of this year to address you a memorandum, No. 103/BK (Episcopal Conference), in which I asked that in the promulgation of the anti-Semitic laws you respect those members of the Jewish race who had been converted to Christianity. The laws promulgated on April 30, however, took no notice at all of religious affiliation. We were told then that the laws had to be promulgated in that form for reasons independent of us, but that their practical application would not be so harsh. In spite of all that, we note daily the appearance of more and more severe provisions which hit equally the guilty and the innocent. Today's newspapers carried the order that all Jews, without regard of age or sex or religious affiliation, must wear the Jewish insignia. Already there are so many measures that those who know the situation well say that not even in Germany were the racial laws applied with such rigor and speed.

It is self-evident that everyone will find it just that in a national state the sons of that nation rule, and that all harmful influences which infect the national organism be checked. Everyone will surely find just the attempt to keep the economy in the hands of the people and the ban on the accumulation of capital by foreign and anti-national individuals, and everyone will find it just that these foreign elements may not determine the fate of the nation and the state. But to take away all possibility of existence from members of other nations or races and to mark them with the stamp of infamy is a question of humanity and of morals. And moral laws have application not only for the lives of private individuals but also for those who govern states. The social organization of our day, and the general moral conceptions which are dominant, do not brand as infamous or criminal those who have been released from prison to which they had been sentenced as murderers, because it is desirable that even these persons become again useful members of the human community. Neither notorious adulterers nor even prostitutes are marked with visible signs. And, since it is not the practice of human society to hold in aversion those persons who have deserved such treatment because of their personal crimes, why treat in this way those who are members of another race through no fault of their own? Moreover, it is necessary to take into account the fact that, as a result of this, the instinct of revenge and the so-called "Minderwertigkeitskomplex" (inferiority complex) will become well developed, especially among the youth who are now growing up and who will be affected by these measures, and that this will exert an overwhelming influence on their spiritual development. Have we the right to commit such an outrage on the human personality?

In regard to what I have said, I ask you, Mr. Minister, to give appropriate orders so that the Jewish laws and others similar to them (the measures against the Serbs, etc.) be executed in such a way that the human dignity and personality of every man is respected. The provision that the Jewish insignia must be worn ought to be generally suppressed. To reimburse the state for the expenses it has incurred in procuring these insignia it could be ordered that those in question buy them, but that they may cease wearing them. Let the guilty and the exploiters be submitted to the punishment they deserve. No intelligent person is opposed to that. But let not the irresponsible mob be judge and executioner of their punishment.

I especially ask you, Mr. Minister, that you respect the baptized members of the Jewish race. Some of them were baptized a long time before the persecution of the Jews, hence at a time when baptism meant a hardship for them, especially in a material way. Many of them are already completely assimilated and no one knows that they are Jews. There are also those who have stood out in the national revolution and in that of the Ustashi. I personally know several of these who are good and enthusiastic Catholics. How will these persons now perform their religious duties? Are they to go to Holy Mass and Holy Communion with a yellow ribbon around their arms? In such a case I would be forced to tell the Jewish Catholics not to wear these insignia in order to avoid trouble and difficulties in church.

I again draw your attention to the fact that the Holy See does not look with favor on these measures. Is it opportune to create an atmosphere of distrust and discord at a time when the Holy Father has just received so graciously our Poglavnik and our delegation and when steps have been taken by the Holy See to recognize our state?

I hope, Mr. Minister, that you will not take in bad part my frank words as Archbishop.

Accept, Mr. Minister, at this time, the expression of my sincere respect.

THE ARCHBISHOP
President of the Episcopal Conference

Dr. Andrija Artuković
Minister of the Interior
Zagreb

ZAGREB, May 30, 1941

MR. MINISTER:

The ordinance concerning the wearing of special insignia by the Jews having appeared, I wrote to you, Mr. Minister, on May 22 of this year, asking that you do something to protect the Jews converted to Catholicism from the Jewish religion. Moreover, several other important interests of Catholicism and the Catholic Church will be threatened by this legislation concerning races at the time of its execution. Also I take the liberty, Mr. Minister, of reminding you of several things that you should take into consideration when you put these ordinances into effect:

1. That marriages existing between Aryans and non-Aryans, and in general all marriages of those who are now Catholics, not be jeopardized.

2. That the education of the children of non-Aryans belonging to the Catholic Church in state or religious schools be made possible.

3. That Christian non-Aryans, especially Catholics, be separated from the other non-Aryans of the Jewish religion.

4. That subordinate officials be ordered that in laying down administrative measures, especially police measures, they do not put Catholic non-Aryans in the same class with the other non-Aryans.

5. That the Catholic non-Aryans who by their unselfish work have not worked against the interests of the Croatian people, especially those who hold public or private office, be treated in a moderate and respectful manner, always conforming to their conduct and their work.

REASONS

The ordinance concerning races, which has the force of law, and the ordinance of the same kind concerning the protection of Aryan blood and the honor of the Croatian people affect in a detrimental way certain Catholics who, embracing Catholicism, have shown that they wish to become completely assimilated by the people with whom they live, in the spirit in which they were reared, and who at all times are even ready to make sacrifices for these people. In any case they have not done this out of self-interest, for certainly it would have been more opportune to have been converted to the Eastern Orthodox religion, the religion of the people who, up to April 10, 1941, were dominant in this country.

The Catholic Church, which reserves the right to judge who are its faithful and who are not, and which demands for all its faithful the possibility of satisfying their religious duties and of living according to the Catholic religious doctrine and Christian morals, is obliged to persist in this demand on the behalf of its non-Aryan faithful. In this undoubtedly, from the worldly point of view as also from the point of view of the interests of the state and the people, the fact enters again into consideration that it is precisely Catholicism which has been the cohesive and assimilating agent which has tied the different parts of our Croatian people into a whole, and which has nationalized numerous foreign elements. Consequently this conversion has created even among the Jews a strong tie with the people among whom they live and work.

It is not a question only of the moral impossibility for Christian non-Aryans to remain in the future in Jewish organizations, in schools and communal work groups for the reason that their conversion to Christianity has made them an object of the scorn and mockery of their former *milieu*, as Christianity has always from the first centuries until today found itself in an analogous position, but it is especially important that their lives be Christian and that they continue to fulfill completely their religious duties without being interfered with. It is the duty of their ecclesiastical superiors to take care of them and to be responsible for them before God, but the state would also sin against its duty to the Church and religion by hindering Christian non-Aryans in these things.

Finally, when the holy sacrament of matrimony has been validly contracted between an Aryan and a non-Aryan an indissoluble conjugal bond has been created which cannot be dissolved by any state law without violating the Catholic conscience. If in consequence of direct or indirect coercive measures, an Aryan spouse should leave his non-Aryan partner, the result would be a great number of occasions of sin by which all these souls could be exposed to spiritual ruin, a thing which could never be the goal of any ordinance in a Christian society.

The legislature itself has admitted that a person not Aryan by birth, if one regards only blood, may prove by his actions in a given direction that he has Aryan qualities. In this interpretation there are mentioned, it is true, only heroic qualities, such as the active fight for ideals, a life of sacrifice and the renunciation of material goods, whereas the Church as a Christian institution is free to show that positive Aryan qualities are still shown in many other aspects of human activities. If these qualities have found expression among non-Aryan Christians, not having the chance or not feeling themselves capable of collaborating in the most exposed part of the fight with material weapons, one cannot say that they do not have Aryan qualities which they have been able to show in other aspects of their civil activities.

For that reason I ask you, Mr. Minister, to distinguish in the non-Aryan concept of this executive ordinance between Catholic non-Aryans and non-Aryans because otherwise the former will fall into the tragic situation of being exposed to the mockery and scorn of the community which they deliberately left because of their love for Christianity and the Croatian people and which situation the Croatian people wish to avoid by these laws. At the same time by mixing non-Christian non-Aryans with Catholic non-Aryans the authority of the Catholic Church would be seriously shaken to the profit of those ideologies, communism for example, which the state combats.

In case one doubts whether such a person remains a secret adherent of an ideology, of a non-Christian religion for example, as well as of the customs that result from it, the authorities can always, through the competent ecclesiastical authorities or in collaboration with them, make an inquiry which, actually, is not difficult among people who all, more or less are publicly active.

Finally I ask you, Mr. Minister, to put in the same class as far as possible non-Aryan Catholics with Aryan qualities and Aryans, so that these men, having shown their absolute attachment to the Croatian people may not remain miserable from a psychological and social point of view and as regards Catholic non-Aryans who, despite their conversions to the Catholic Church, have not, according to the conception of the legislature, sufficiently shown their Aryan qualities, either through their activities and conduct or their social positions, I ask you to separate these from non-Christian non-Aryans in relation to their social positions and in the manner of treating them.

Accept, Mr. Minister, at this time, the expression of my best good wishes.

Dr. Aloysius Stepinac
Archbishop

Dr. Andre Artuković
Minister of the Interior
Zagreb

DOCUMENT XXVII
RESOLUTION ON CATHOLIC JEWS

The Croatian Catholic hierarchy at the plenary session of the Conference of November 18 of this year drew up the following resolutions:

As the hierarchy knows of numerous cases in which certain Jews who, either on their own initiative or through their parents', have been converted for a long time from Judaism to the Catholic religion, and who, because of the kind of life they have led, have been completely assimilated by the Croatian people, but who are treated as are the Jews who have not been converted from their religion, and are equally deprived of their personal freedom, and have had their property confiscated, the Croatian Catholic Episcopate has decided to address the following petition to the Poglavnik of the Independent State of Croatia.

Let the personal and civil liberty of Jews, or the descendants of Jews, who after their conversion to the Catholic Church no longer consider themselves Jews but who take part in all Croatian activities, religious and patriotic, be protected; and let their property and possessions be restored to them.

State authorities ought not to place obstacles in the way of Catholic priests who wish, because of their duties as spiritual fathers and in view of spiritual needs, to visit former Jews, now Catholics, who are interned in concentration camps.

STEPINAC
President of the Episcopal Conference

DOCUMENT XXVIII

*Letter From the Archbishop to Dr. Artuković
Regarding the Arrest of Jews*

ZAGREB, March 7, 1942

MR. MINISTER:

Recently there has again been talk of the arrests of Jews and of their being taken to concentration camps. In so far as there is really something to this, I take the liberty, Mr. Minister, of asking you to prevent, through your power, all unjust proceedings against citizens who individually can be accused of no wrong.

I do not think that it can bring us any glory if it is said of us that we have solved the Jewish problem in the most radical way, that is to say, the cruelest. The solution of this question must provide only for the punishment of Jews who have committed crimes, but not for persecution of innocent people.

Hoping, Mr. Minister, that you will prevent the violation not only of the Christian law of love for one's neighbor but of the most basic natural law of humanity on the part of irresponsible elements, I express my highest respect.

ARCHBISHOP OF ZAGREB

Dr. Andrija Artuković
Minister of Internal Affairs of the NDH
Zagreb

DOCUMENT XXIX

Correspondence Concerning the Wives of Jews

HIS EXCELLENCY DR. ALOYSIUS STEPINAC
Croatian Metropolitan and Archbishop of Zagreb

The undersigned women of the Roman Catholic religion, whose

husbands are of the Jewish race but Roman Catholics, send to Your Excellency a copy of the petition which we have addressed to His Excellency the Poglavnik of the Independent State of Croatia and to the Presidency of the Croatian Parliament at Zagreb praying that Your Excellency have the kindness to commend this petition to the highest authorities so that we women may be treated with respect.

Knowing Your Excellency to be an ecclesiastical dignitary who always interests himself in just cases, we hope that in this instance you will help us unhappy women through an understanding of our terrible plight.

We remain forever grateful.

Osijek, May 14, 1942

Milka Rausnitz, *nee* Veselinović
Vuka Hecko, *nee* Kovjanić
Ana Kohn, *nee* Mum
Slava Ungar, *nee* Galvić
Mica Svarc, *nee* Mic
Olga Misner, *nee* Sremcević
Slavica Salamon, *nee* Glas
Maria Glesinger, *nee* Kapaunig
Eva Zeldiner, *nee* Sorekop
Poljak Mira, *nee* Schmidt
Stefica Eisenstadter, *nee* Maracki
Josipa Gorog, *nee* Pernar
Theresa Kohn, *nee* Lukacević
Maria Kon, *nee* Valter
Emily Zimmermann, *nee* Sitar
Anna Ungar, *nee* Schweizer
Victoria Gluk, *nee* Zappe
Leopoldina Schreiber, *nee* Hartl
Antonia Schlesinger, *nee* Miklenić
Anica Sprngarn, *nee* Nefedova
Juliana Bauer, *nee* Dotlić
Maria Schiffer, *nee* De Gregori
Thilde Land, *nee* Hugo
Maria Friedmann, *nee* Ackam

Maria Edrenfreund, *nee* Baver
Spitzer Erna, *nee* Hentz
Jelisaveta Licktenthal, *nee* Fath
Maria Lichtenthal, *nee* Ift
Julka Reichnitzer, *nee* Venos
Maria Lederer, *nee* Sager
Stefica Lowy, *nee* Paradeiser
Katarina Klein, *nee* Goll
Stefica Sabo, *nee* Halter
Ela Bautel, *nee* Treml
Herma Herman, *nee* Endlicker
Maria Ullman, *nee* Salk
Ljubica Perles, *nee* Decker
Anita Goldstein, *nee* Stivi
Zozislava Reich, *nee* Magjer
Anica Weiss, *nee* Perović
Fransisca Leitner, *nee* Petelin
Mira Bosković, *nee* Sandukcić
Slezinger, *nee* Henc Katica
Anica Grinberger, *nee* Petelin
Herman Staza, *nee* Strelac
Ana Dirnback, *nee* Flecterski
Zora Kraus, *nee* Miketar
Theresa Pollak, *nee* Dijaković

I testify to the authenticity of the above and recommend the petition.

Office of the Roman Catholic Parish
SEPER, *pastor*

Osijek II, May 18, 1942

Ordinariate of the Bishop of Djakovo
No. 41/1942 — copy
HIS EXCELLENCY DR. ALOYSIUS STEPINAC
Croatian Metropolitan and Archbishop of Zagreb

We most warmly recommend to Your Excellency the enclosed petition of the pastors of Osijek, with a prayer for your intervention in the matter.

DR. ANTUN AKSAMOVIĆ
Bishop

To the Archiepiscopal Church Court of Zagreb:

The office of the deacon at Osijek has just received the message of the Archiepiscopal Church Court of Zagreb, No. 149/1942 — secret, on the following subject:

Office of the deacon.

The secretariate of the Archbishop has the honor of informing you of the following:

Yesterday, on August 20 of this year, His Excellency the Archbishop received the letter of Mrs. Theresa Pollak, *nee* Dijaković, in which the Aryan wives asked for protection against separation from their non-Aryan husbands.

His Excellency the Archbishop had already done all that he could to save mixed marriages, and he had been faithfully promised that they would be saved. After having received the above-mentioned letter, His Excellency the Archbishop immediately took steps so that the mixed marriages of Osijek would be saved as had been promised. The reply was that these cases would be examined without delay and that those persons who had acted against the law would be called to account.

You are requested to communicate the above to the parish office of Osijek and to notify all the interested parties.

The Archbishop's Secretary,
LACKOVIĆ

Zagreb, August 21, 1942

On this occasion, the undersigned representatives of the three offices of the Roman Catholic parish, express their fervent gratitude to the Almighty who crowned with His blessing the kind efforts of His Excellency the Archbishop and has given peace to these people whose marriages were endangered.

The numerous signs of this gratitude, coming from those who were directly or indirectly stricken by the events of these past several days, are touching.

They were faced with terrible alternatives: either to submit to the demands which had been imposed on them and leave their non-Aryan Catholic husbands and thereby destroy one of the basic pillars of holy religion, the Holy Sacrament of marriage, the oath taken before God and man of fidelity to one's spouse; or to partake themselves of the same fate which had overtaken their husbands.

It is clear to a good Catholic, Croatian, and man of honor that in such a case he must choose the straight and thorny road that leads him toward misery, penury, and, perhaps, even death. For such a man does not wish to lose his soul and violate his oath for his own personal convenience, nor can he abandon his best and nearest friend, powerless in misery.

As of today we do not know of a single case where any Aryan spouse has chosen, or been disposed to choose, the contrary solution.

The Aryan-Catholic wives presented a petition to His Excellency the Archbishop so that their husbands may not be affected by the civil laws.

And now Croatian, Catholic husbands, in virtue of the recent events, have addressed a petition to the deacon's office for the protection of their Catholic marriages, saying their non-Aryan wives, to whom they were married in the Catholic Church, have received not only equality of rights but also the right of residence and the nationality of their husbands according to accepted law and the civil code.

As this occurred just as the wives of Aryan-Catholics and Croatians were in danger, and on that account such marriages as well, especially in cases where there were no children, or where the children were already twelve years old, they asked that through the intervention of His Excellency the Archbishop a *definitive decision from the civil authorities be procured which would assure for their wives equality before the civil law and the inviolability of marriages.*

The parish offices at Osijek have accepted this voluntary initiative and, in turn, present the petitions addressed to them to His Excellency the Archbishop with their recommendation, praying the divine Master to bless his efforts along these lines by abundant fruits and to crown them with success.

In the hope that with such a definitive decision today's problem will be solved forever, we commend those involved and ourselves to the prayers of His Excellency the Archbishop.

Most humbly,

ROBERTO BEZETSKY

Pastor and Dean of Osijek

Copy of the letter sent to the Minister of the Interior.

S. L. (S. LACKOVIĆ)

DOCUMENT XXX

Letter of the Archbishop to Pavelić Protesting Against the Injustices Inflicted on the Innocent by the Croat Government

POGLAVNIK:

Allow me to address you in the following matter:

At Zagreb, as well as in the provinces, panic exists because of the measures against non-Aryans which has been announced, and we await the consequences with great fear. Many people are afraid that their legitimate spouses will be separated from them despite the fact that they were validly married in the Catholic Church.

Poglavnik, if it is a question of marriages which have been validly contracted in the Catholic Church, I raise my voice as a representative of the Catholic Church and I energetically reject the interference of the state in the question of such marriages, which are indissoluble regardless of the race of those involved. More than that, no state has the right to invalidate these marriages, or effect divorces by force, and if it uses physical power, then the state commits nothing other than an ordinary crime, from which no good can come.

Meanwhile, I know that there are similar marriages among the chief ministers of the national government, but these marriages are protected. It is against logic and it is against justice that these are protected and that others are abandoned to the favor or disfavor of a different law which has no basis in common sense and which, moreover, does not accord with the true interests of the people or the state. If even dumb animals protect their young and will not let themselves be separated by force, who among the judicious will believe that thousands of people in mixed marriages will be able to watch passively while their families are destroyed by force and their children abandoned to an uncertain fate? Is it not exactly in this way that the Partisans, so much decried, were created? Is it not by exactly such measures, full of injustices, that the people are driven by force into the ranks of the Partisans, as is the case with many Croatians who can no longer tolerate the injustices of the occupation forces?

In the same way I ask you again, as representative of the Catholic Church, to protect the most elementary right, the right to life, of those among the subjects of the Independent State of Croatia who have become members of the Catholic Church during the time of the state's existence, whether they were "rebaptized" or whether they came into the Catholic Church from the Orthodox; and against whom no one can prove any personal crime against the interests of the Croatian people or state.

Next I ask, in the name of the humanity that our people have always respected, not to permit any longer, Poglavnik, that the people of our state suffer unjustly. There are many in the concentration camps who are innocent or who have not deserved so severe a punishment.

Poglavnik, I am sure that such unjust measures do not come from you, but rather from irresponsible persons who have been guided by passion and personal greed.

But if there is here the interference of a foreign power in our internal and political life, I am not afraid if my voice and my protest carry even to the leaders of that power; because the Catholic Church knows no fear of any earthly power, whatever it may be, when it is a question of defending the most basic rights of men.

There is no one in our country who desires more the happiness and prosperity of our people and our new state than the Catholic Church. But this happiness and prosperity depend on our respect for the natural and positive law of God, on the respect for this law by the government of the state as well as by the people; and it is the Catholic Church which must exert vigilance. Since it does not possess physical force, but only moral, it will in the future intrepidly use this moral power, the power of protecting the rights of man and, by means of this, of contributing to the happiness and prosperity of our people.

Poglavnik, in Italy there are some tens of thousands of innocent people, for the most part women and children, from Gorski Kotar, Primorje, and Dalmatia, exiled in concentration camps. Hunger, sickness, and suffering of all kinds have caused a very high death rate among these wretched people. It is seriously to be feared that by some means the extermination of the population of those parts of our country is sought. When my delegate recently attended, in company with delegates from Croatian state and humanitarian institutions, a meeting at the Italian Ministry of Foreign Affairs in Rome for the purpose of freeing and helping these poor people, the Italians said, "Why do you interfere in our treatment of these people, after the way you act in Croatia!"

Poglavnik! Do not let these irresponsible and unwelcome elements violate the true welfare of our people. The violation of the law of nature in the name of the people and the state will bring vengeance to the people and even to the state. The bitterness that will spread the spirit of vengeance is being born within the country, while from outside the enemy attacks our moral values.

Please accept, Poglavnik, the sincere expression of my deep respect for you.

EP. A. S.

Zagreb, March 6, 1943

DOCUMENT XXXI

*Letter to Dr. Artuković With Petition of the Jewish Community
and Recommendation of Acceptance by the Archbishop*

ZAGREB, May 8, 1943

MR. MINISTER:

I am enclosing the petition of the Jewish religious community of Zagreb asking authorization to work for the welfare of those (Jews) who still remain free. Every consideration recommends the petition as just.

I ask you, Mr. Minister, to grant this request and to give to these persons, who alone of the community are left and experienced, permission to work in the area designated for the community's activity, and, in so far as several of these people are in prison, to order their release.

Thanking you, Mr. Minister, for all that you have done and for all that you will do to preserve the moral and Christian character of our people, I also express at this time my profound respect for you.

THE ARCHBISHOP OF ZAGREB

Dr. Andrija Artuković
Minister of Internal Affairs
Zagreb

DOCUMENT XXXII

Memorandum Prepared by the Archbishop's Secretary Dr. Šalić
Regarding Aid to the Jews

On March 27, 1943, at four o'clock in the afternoon, Mr. Davidović, sent by the Jewish Grand Rabbi, Dr. Freiberger, brought the following report: "We have been warned that there is a train at Novska carrying 1800 Jews on their way to Germany, most of whom come from Greece. The train is German, and all surveillance over these people is in the hands of the Germans. No one is allowed to give anything to these people, to eat, drink, or to wash with; it is not even permitted to give them a glass of water."

By the order of His Excellency the Archbishop, his secretaries Rev. John Šalić and Rev. Stephen Lacković, did everything they could to help these people. They called on the Red Cross and its president, Dr. Hukn, who made enquiries (at least he said so) among the German authorities who replied that no permissions would be granted and that consequently the Red Cross could do nothing. The priest, Dr. G. Keilback, was also called upon to intervene with Mr. von Kocijan, the German officer, who, although a good Catholic, said that he had no competence in this matter and that there was nothing to be done. The train was due to arrive at 9 or 10 o'clock that night. The members (women) of the Red Cross were ready to help but they did not dare since they did not have German permission. All hope seemed lost when Mrs. X. Y. called on the German officer on duty at the railroad station and skillfully explained the matter to him, since he alone could help these poor people. The secretary, Dr. Lacković, went directly to the German officer on duty, who got in touch with the women of the Red Cross. The démarche was successful and warm food was served to the Jews.

Today the president of the Red Cross, Dr. Hukn, talks about how these unhappy people were given food and rest and makes this statement as if it were he who had been in charge. However, if the chancery office on the orders of His Excellency the Archbishop had not done all in its power, nothing would have been done. Let God be thanked!

> On the order of the Archbishop this was recorded
> by John Šalić, *Secretary of the Archbishop*

Zagreb, March 29, 1943

On April 24, at the time of the second movement of the Jews from Greece (2000), the secretary Dr. Lacković had several conferences with the German authorities and with the H. C. K. Hrvatsk Crveni Križ (Croatian Red Cross). Assistance was permitted.

S. L.

DOCUMENT XXXIII
Various Documents Regarding Aid to the Slovenes

CIRCULAR TO THE HIERARCHY OF CROATIA

By virtue of the resolution of the meeting of the Episcopal Conference of November 19 of this year, at which the wretched state of the Slovenian immigrants was discussed, I address myself to Your Excellency on the following matter:

At the present moment there are numerous Slovenian immigrants within the boundaries of nearly every Croatian diocese. All of them have lost their belongings, as a result of which they find themselves in a state of great misery and moral depression. I beg you to give your priests orders and instructions so that, within the territory of their parishes, they may treat their Slovenian parishioners in the same fatherly manner as they treat their own. Let them interest themselves in their fate that they may ease the terrible misfortunes which have left them desolate. Let them make an effort to procure for them food, clothing, and employment; let them give information on their needs to the local welfare offices with an eye to helping them so that they may be considered by them as an *"alter Christus"* who *"pertransiit benefaciendo"* and who said, *"Misereor super turbam."*

It would also be appropriate to send, from time to time, some

Slovenian priest to those areas in the territory of your diocese where there are immigrants, in order that he may examine their condition so that, with Your Excellency's knowledge, he may send information to the Committee for Slovenian Immigrants, No. 21 Jurisiceva Street, Zagreb, which will take further measures to aid and to relieve the needy.

In the name of the Bishop's Conference,
Aloysius Stepinac, *Archbishop*

Zagreb, November 19, 1941

Monsignor Archbishop:

You have had the generosity to receive the delegate of our Regional Committee, Mr. Louis Colnar, who informed you of the situation of our compatriots who have been driven from their homes, and of the activity of our organization in seeking to relieve their misery. Also you have had the generosity to subsidize this work.

The undersigned Regional Committee, Monsignor Archbishop, expresses its most sincere thanks for your very compassionate and charitable understanding of this vital problem to our compatriots, and for the material aid we received from you. At the same time the Regional Committee begs you humbly to continue the same concern in the future for our compatriots.

Accept, Monsignor Archbishop, the expression and homage of our highest respect.

Ljubljana, June 25, 1941

SECRETARY
(*Illegible signature.*)

PRESIDENT
(*Illegible signature.*)

Monsignor Metropolitan:

A great misfortune has struck the Ljubljana Province of the Teutonic Order with half of it destroyed. Our brothers are refugees in your archdiocese and have found in your person a compassionate and benevolent father so that, informed of the fate of my brothers, I hasten to express to Your Excellency my most sincere thanks for all this that only God can repay.

The members of our province of the Teutonic Order who are refugees under your protection are the following: (1) Gregory Cesar, pastor of Velika Nedelja; (2) Dr. Vincent Bevk, Vicar of Velika Nedelja; (3) Cyril Lekšan, provincial bursar at Velika Nedelja;

(4) Remi Jereb, pastor of Ormož; (5) Leon Božić, pastor Središće; (6) Angelm Polak, pastor of Sv. Miklavz.

All the priests mentioned here have received good theological training and all, without exception, lead an exemplary priestly life.

I also venture to recommend these priests to Your Excellency so that you may care for them during the time that they devote all their energies to the service of the Kingdom of God and of your archdiocese according to the wishes of Your Excellency.

As soon as I find the first opportunity to come to Zagreb, I will ask for an audience with Your Excellency to express again my heartfelt gratitude.

My brothers here and I will remember Your Excellency in our fervent prayers. I beg Your Excellency to accept the homage of my highest esteem.

VALERIAN UĆAK
Provincial Prior and Commander of Ljubljana

BANJA LUKA, September 26, 1943

Crnomelj, May 4, 1941
Camp of Slovenian Immigrants,
Banja Luka
Subject: Request for aid.

To His Excellency Archbishop Aloysius Stepinac,
Zagreb

We ask your forgiveness for troubling you once again. We live in the most straitened circumstances and in our need we remember with deep gratitude our great benefactor, Your Excellency the Archbishop. We have received money subsidies this winter from you and from the organization *"Caritas"* through the medium of Father Camille who told us, "Every time you find yourselves in a critical and difficult situation, you must call on us."

In our Slovenian immigrant camp there are, for the most part, only old men and women, mothers and children whose sons and fathers have been enrolled in the Croatian army. They are weak and sickly and beseech help to improve their diet a little, and to make easier, at least temporarily, their miserable and suffering lives. It is an unpleasant thing to beg but misery learns to beg. These poor people are without means, clothing, blankets, and only enough linen for their most elementary needs and that at exhorbitantly high prices. Our people place their only hope for receiving aid in the priests. We Slovenians will never forget that the priests were the first to come into our camps with words of consolation to bring us aid, entering into our dwellings like the Spirit of God at a time when the whole world shunned us. Only priests know true mercy, strive to relieve misery, lend assistance, to console the despairing and give us new hope. We are convinced that this request of ours will not be useless; and whatever the kind of help, all will be accepted with the greatest gratitude.

With firm confidence in your noble heart, we send you in advance, our thanks.

Very respectfully,
THE DIRECTOR
(*Illegible signature.*)

BANJA LUKA, October 21, 1943

Office for Slovenian Immigrants
No. 435

To His Excellency Archbishop Dr. Aloysius Stepinac,
Zagreb

Monsignor, words do not exist with which we Slovenians will ever be able adequately to thank Your Excellency for your boundless generosity.

With the greatest joy and deepest gratitude we received the sum of 50,000 kronen sent by you. This help came to us just when we were most uneasy concerning our food supply. God Himself inspired you. We burst into tears, our hearts could not support the happiness of seeing you, in spirit, coming toward us as a messenger from heaven with salvation. Peace be with you. We see you, drying our bitter tears, blessing us with love, bringing us the bread we ask of God every day. Yes, you cut the bread for us poor, and the good Jesus Himself will cut for Your Excellency the largest and most bountiful portion, the eternal portion, which shall increase from generation to generation. We repeat again, the priests, and always the priests, are our constant support and mainstay. A great many among us who in other times were very hostile to the Church are today of a totally different opinion — for there are examples and proofs in abundance — they are convinced, their eyes have been opened, they have been awakened.

To what use will we put the money? We have spent 20,000 kronen for food and have ordered supplies costing another 20,000 kronen. We will distribute 10,000 kronen to the neediest in our camp, who cannot work and who do not receive aid from any other source. They aroused our compassion, these quiet and good people, and our happiness would not be complete if we could not make the trials of these unfortunates more bearable by giving them a few gifts. They suffer their misery willingly and with resignation and all their hardships. Not a Sunday goes by that they do not attend church services. Our life is monotonous, sustained by hope that we shall soon have peace.

As soon as the money is spent, we shall send you an itemized account of it, and, if you wish, all our records with the list of those who aid us and their signatures. In the meantime the entire camp expresses once again its most heartfelt gratitude for such a large subsidy and lifts its voice unanimously to say, may God reward you a hundredfold.

> Very respectfully,
> The ever grateful inhabitants of the camp.
> Director of the Office for Slovenian Immigrants
> Substitute — Dr. Čuš

Members of the Committee:
John Zadnik
Leopold Kogoj
John Gašperin

DOCUMENT XXXIV

Statement of Drago Oberzan Regarding Aid Extended to Slovene Refugees

DECLARATION

During the occupation of Slovenia, numerous citizens and even entire families were driven out of the country by the Germans, fleeing before the terror that reigned there. Their stuation was so difficult that I gave thought at time of ways to help them.

Knowing Mr. Milostislav Ciko, retired deputy minister, as a very honorable and honest man, a patriot and firm adversary of the

Germans and the Ustashi regime, I proposed to him as secretary of the Central Committee of *"Caritas"* that he take charge of assisting the Slovenian fugitives, which proposition Mr. Ciko quickly accepted. We started a secret fund immediately. Except for the two of us, the existence of this fund was known only to the Archbishop of Zagreb, Dr. Aloysius Stepinac. From this source the sum of 5,700,000 kronen was distributed in the form of subsidies to the Slovenian fugitives.

For the truth of this declaration I have made I assume all responsibility before the law.

Death to Fascism, freedom to the people!

DRAGO OBERZAN

Maribor, No. 61 Jerovškova Street

Zagreb — Maribor, September 20, 1945

DOCUMENT XXXV

Correspondence Regarding Detention of Father Francis Rihar and Letter to Pavelić Regarding Priests in Concentration Camps

ZAGREB, June 1, 1942

MR. MINISTER:

It is almost two months since two priests of the Diocese of Zagreb, Francis Rihar, pastor of Gornja Stubica, and Sigismund Majchrzak, pastor of Zokanje, have been in prison; and Francis Rihar, according to rumors, is now in the concentration camp of Jasenovac. I have received no official notice of their arrest nor of any criminal charges lodged against them. Formerly priests were brought before the court and charges made against them — nearly always because of their pro-Croatian sentiments and activities — but each time the ecclesiastical authorities were notified. After the restoration of the Independent Croatian State we have been notified only of the death sentence of Canon Dr. Lončar, although three priests have already been sent to a concentration camp.

Both priests mentioned here have lived and conducted themselves in an exemplary way, and the people have regarded them highly everywhere they have carried out their duties and have been devoted to them. Some, possibly, have regarded them as foreigners and not priests; the first is a Slovenian, the second a Pole, but both became priests in the Diocese of Zagreb and have been active there now for several years. They are not, therefore, recent refugees, but have wished to work among the Croatians for a long time. The people are downcast at their absence, and I find it nearly impossible to replace them because of the shortage of priests.

I am personally convinced that they have not deserved so severe a punishment and that such measures harm the reputation of the State. The ecclesiastical authorities should have been notified and asked to admonish them and, if necessary to chastise them with an ecclesiastical punishment before taking them to a civil prison or concentration camp like ordinary criminals.

When one undermines the authority of the clergy, that of the state necessarily suffers. For this reason Canon Law demands that the misdeeds of priests be considered before an Ecclesiastical Court.

If Father Rihar has been sent to a concentration camp, as they say, I am convinced that he will never return, because he ought to be in a sanatorium on account of his delicate health. The state will gain neither profit nor the blessing of God for the death of such a priest.

I have waited patiently and kept silent for a year, but this manner of treating priests causes me profound anguish.

I ask you respectfully, Mr. Minister, to give orders that I be sent precise information stating the reasons why they have been accused, the duration of their sentence, and where they are imprisoned.

Please accept at this time, Mr. Minister, my good wishes.

THE ARCHBISHOP

To Dr. Andrija Artuković
Minister of the Interior
Zagreb
No. 154 — Copy
Subject: Whether Francis Rihar, priest interned at Jasenovac, is still alive.

MR. MINISTER:

In the month of April of this year Francis Rihar, pastor of Gornja Stubica, was imprisoned at Jasenovac. We are convinced that the condemned is innocent but in any case the ecclesiastical authority has the right to know whether this priest mentioned is alive or not, so that if not, provision may be made for the care of his parish, his property and the priests may perform the appropriate rites in the case of deceased clergy.

I have the honor of asking, Mr. Minister, that for these reasons and in your capacity as head of your department, you secure information concerning the above-mentioned priest through sources at your disposal and that you present it to the ecclesiastical authority.

Please accept, Mr. Minister, on this occasion, my sincere respect.

THE ARCHBISHOP OF ZAGREB

Zagreb, November 2, 1942
To Dr. Andrija Artuković
Minister of Justice and Religion

ZAGREB, November 17, 1942

Zagreb
Independent State of Croatia
Ministry of Justice and Religion
Office of the Minister
No. V.T. 930-1942
Subject: Francis Rihar, priest of Gornja Stubica, Internee.

To the Archiepiscopal Church Court, Zagreb

In connection with your esteemed request of November 2, 1942, No. 159 on the above-mentioned subject, notice is hereby given that Rihar, Francis, of the Roman Catholic religion, born April 8, 1909, priest in residence at Gor. Stubica where he was pastor, was sent: (1) by the decree of this office of April 20, 1942, No. 26417/1942, and (2) at the proposal of the police guard for the city of Zagreb and Velika Zupa Prigorje of May 19, 1942, No. 7002/1942, to forced detention in the concentration camp at Jasenovac for a period of three years, that is to say, from April 18, 1942 to April 18, 1945, because as pastor at Gornja Stubica he did not celebrate a solemn high mass on the anniversary of the founding of the Independent State of Croatia, although the people came in procession with flags and demanded it of him, nor did he consent to sing the psalm, *Te Deum Laudamus,* saying that it was nowhere prescribed in ecclesiastical usage.

This is for your information.

Ready in the service of the fatherland,
DR. ARTUKOVIĆ
Minister of Justice and Religion

POGLAVNIK:

I address you, as the representative of the Independent State of Croatia, with great anguish in my soul.

Month after month I have tried to learn the fate of my seven priests who were sent to Jasenovac. All has been in vain. An official request, however, has come from the Croatian Consul in Ljubljana, forwarded by the Ministry of Foreign Affairs, concerning the pastor of Gornja Stubica, Francis Rihar, asking whether he is still alive, because his sister is searching for him.

I must conclude that they were all executed on the assumption that they were antinational. Why were they not brought before the court? If the regular court was not competent, why were they not made to appear before the court martial.

This is a disgraceful incident and a crime that cries out for vengeance from heaven. Jasenovac camp itself is a shameful stain on the honor of the Independent State of Croatia.

Poglavnik! To him who regards me as priest and bishop, I say with Christ on the Cross, "Father, forgive them, for they know not what they do."

But the public at large, and especially the relatives of those who have been killed, demand satisfaction, indemnities, and the bringing of the murderers to trial. This is a disgrace to Croatia.

Believe, Poglavnik, that I have not let myself be guided in the least by hatred, but rather by the love of truth and the welfare of the Croatian people.

THE ARCHBISHOP OF ZAGREB

Zagreb, February 24, 1943

DOCUMENT XXXVI

Correspondence Regarding the Archbishop's Intervention on Behalf of Communists

Dr. Mladen Lorković   ZAGREB, August 15, 1944
Minister of the Interior
Zagreb

To His Excellency Aloysius Stepinac
Archbishop of Zagreb, Zagreb

In regard to your letter of July 18 of this year, I notify you that unfortunately I can do nothing in the case of Professor G. Gamulin.

He cannot be liberated because he has been a member of the K.P. (Communist Party).

Please accept on this occasion, Excellency, the expression of my homage.

Ready in the service of the Poglavnik and the fatherland!

LORKOVIĆ

POGLAVNIK:

I take the liberty of addressing a petition to you to demand mercy for five condemned men — Jovanović, Bonačić, Krunić, Ilić, and Bukovac — sentenced to death by the court martial in March 29 of this year.

I ask you, Poglavnik, to use your power to modify the death sentence for one less severe. I am convinced that your act of amnesty, coming at the time of the anniversary of the foundation of our state, would have excellent results.

May I, Poglavnik, draw your attention to the circumstances in the case of Velimir Jovanović, who is considered the most guilty of the group condemned to death. As a former Yugoslav officer and an Orthodox, he married a Catholic girl in the Catholic Church and had his child baptized in the Catholic religion, and was persecuted by the former government as a result.

I ask you also to pardon Luka Mustapić, police commandant at Djakovo, sentenced to death by the court martial at Osijek. In the days of the former government he always protected Croatians in Serbia, and in our own state has collaborated with our authorities and those of the Germans. According to my information, you have already been sent his petition for amnesty.

Please accept, Poglavnik, the expression of my deepest respect.

THE ARCHBISHOP

Zagreb, April 2, 1945

ZAGREB, March 13, 1945

GENERAL:

Permit me to address myself to you in the case of five military persons who were yesterday, the twenty-ninth of the current month, sentenced to death by the court martial: Jovanović, Bonačić, Ilić, Krunić, and Bukovac.

My dear General, without examining the gravity of the crime of each of the condemned, I consider, however, that extenuating circumstances of each case, as well as general conditions justify a reduction of the death sentence.

I ask you, General, today, on Good Friday, when Christ prayed, "Father, forgive them for they know not what they do," and on the Eve of Easter, day of life, to undertake all in your power to let these five condemned men live.

I attach the petitions of the wives of the condemned which are addressed to either you or the Poglavnik and which cite the circumstances in favor of amnesty for the condemned.

In hope of a favorable decision, I send you my thanks in advance and express to you at this time, my dear General, my profound respect.

THE ARCHBISHOP OF ZAGREB

General Adolf Sabljak
Commandant of the City of Zagreb

ZAGREB, June 24, 1944

180/copy 1944

DIRECTOR-IN-CHIEF:

I send you the enclosed petition of Mr. Ivan Pandžić, addressed to His Excellency the Archbishop of Zagreb for the purpose of recommending the engineer, Zvonko Kavurić, who was arrested some time ago because of communist activities.

I ask you, Director-in-Chief, to give this case your immediate special examination, because it is possible that a man for whom such good testimony was given is not guilty as charged. There are several of our public workers who recommend him and who will be responsible for him.

With the assurance of my respect,
THE BISHOP, *Vicar-General*

To Dr. Milutin Jurčić
Director-in-Chief, Zagreb

Independent State of Croatia
Military Bureau of the Poglavnik
No. 412/45 — Secret
Zagreb, April 14, 1945
Subject: Bukovac and others, amnesty.

To His Excellency Dr. Aloysius Stepinac,
Croatian Metropolitan and Archbishop of Zagreb, Zagreb

This office has the honor to reply to your letter of April 2, 1945, addressed to the Poglavnik on the subject of amnesty for Jovanović, Bonačić, Krunić, Ilić, and Bukovac, that the Poglavnik has granted a commutation of sentence to all the above-mentioned, the death sentences changed to life imprisonment.

As to amnesty for Luka Mustapić, we have asked for an immediate investigation with instructions that the death sentence not be carried out before the results have been made available to this office for the Poglavnik's decision.

Ready in the service of the Poglavnik and the fatherland!

Chief,
Lieutenant General PERČEVIĆ

His Excellency the Archbishop intervened with the Minister of Justice and Religion in the case of Dr. Branko Gušić, on March 11, 1943, who had been court martialed. The case was suspended.

L. S.

Dr. Gušić, released, is now in Germany.

DOCUMENT XXXVII

Letters of the Archbishop Containing Evidence of His Efforts on Behalf of Numerous Condemned Persons

POGLAVNIK:

I have just learned that the intervention of the Apostolic Delegate and myself on behalf of the eleven condemned to death has not been successful. I conclude this from the desperation of the wives and mothers who, at the Archiepiscopal Palace, fell on the ground weeping with despair, and cried convulsively, "Jesus, is there no more justice in the world?"

Poglavnik, let me be very clear on one point. I do not insist on what the reaction of the people will be to these executions, but I ask once more, one last time, for a pardon for these unhappy men who, according to their confessor, have received Holy Communion nearly every day, and have protested most energetically against every communist crime which has been imputed to them. I am of the opinion that repentance as revealed by these eleven men, who will die leaving behind poor orphans, will render them useful to Croatia.

Poglavnik, I assure you that a pardon will be better for Croatia than the execution of these unfortunate men.

Accept again, Poglavnik, the expression of my very respectful esteem.   THE ARCHBISHOP OF ZAGREB

Zagreb, August 21, 1944

POGLAVNIK:

Allow me to address you, Poglavnik, to obtain pardon for the fifty-four Croatian officers, noncommissioned officers, and soldiers who will be prosecuted soon before a court martial, according to Article No. 98, Nos. 1 and 2 of the Criminal Code, the sentence for which is death.

Poglavnik, even if, objectively, the accused committed these crimes, their subjective intentions extenuate their guilt in a great many respects. According to the information I have received, they were guided by a real love for their people.

Poglavnik, I ask you in the name of the Croatian public and of Christian mercy, save for Croatia fifty-four lives that can, by your pardon and the future supervision of the proper authorities, be directed along the right path and made useful to our terribly tried people.

Poglavnik, I am convinced that the true interests of our people and of our state do not demand the death of the accused, and that it is those who demand from you as Chief of State, the sentence of death for so many persons, who are working against its interests. Croatia must not die, it must live. This natural law is ennobled by the Croatian spirit. "I do not wish the death of the sinner, but that he may be converted and that he may live," says the Lord.

When one reads a letter sent from prison by those sentenced to death and already executed, one regrets with all his heart that such men cannot serve Croatia. Those who still live, Poglavnik, can be made useful to Croatia by your pardon. If you change the sentence of death to a less severe punishment, it will have, without any doubt, a good influence on the accused as well as on their families who by their death would be left without support. That pardon would enable them to devote their lives to the true service of the people and the state.

Poglavnik, please accept once again the expression of my sincere and very respectful esteem.

DR. ALOYSIUS STEPINAC
Archbishop[1]

Zagreb, August 8, 1944

ZAGREB, October 28, 1944

MY DEAR GENERAL:

Yesterday I learned that eight soldiers belonging to the Croatian armed forces were condemned to death by a court martial because of their alleged relations with deserters. It is not possible for me, General, to enter into the details of judicial procedure or into the question of the actual guilt of the condemned men, but I ask that you try to take into consideration all the extenuating circumstances and the conditions in which we are all living and that you modify the death sentence to that of life imprisonment.

I do not say that these men are not guilty but I am convinced that a more moderate punishment will have a salutary influence, not only on the families of the condemned, but also on the people at large. The condemned are repentant for their crimes and we can hope that after the imposition of a reduced sentence, they will be grateful and loyal citizens of the Croatian state.

---

[1] On August 11, 1944, judgment was pronounced: 14 were sentenced to death.
   1. The Archbishop of Zagreb, Dr. Aloysius Stepinac, and the Papal Delegate, Abbot Ramiro J. Marcone, asked for an audience with the Poglavnik on August 12 which was not granted them.
   2. On August 14, 1944, at 12:30 P.M. the Archbishop of Zagreb and the Papal Delegate were received by the Poglavnik to whom they delivered their respective petitions and demanded the pardon of all the condemned.
   3. On August 16, 1944, at 12:45 P.M. the Archbishop of Zagreb and the Papal Delegate went to the Poglavnik and again asked him to pardon all the condemned.
   4. After the request for pardon had been refused, His Excellency the Archbishop of Zagreb wrote on August 21, 1944, to the Poglavnik and to the German commandant.
   5. The morning of August 22, 1944, ten accused and condemned were taken to Maksimir to be executed.

I hope that on your part, General, you will do all in your power so that the death sentence of the above-mentioned condemned may be changed to a less harsh punishment.

Accept on this occasion, General, the expression of my highest respect.

THE ARCHBISHOP OF ZAGREB

General Mirko Gregorić
Commandant of the City of Zagreb

To the Director-in-Chief of Public Order and Safety
Erik Lisak, Zagreb

DIRECTOR-IN-CHIEF:

On the afternoon of December 22, 1944, at my residence in Zagreb, No. 21 Trg Kralja Tomislava, the military police arrested my only son, engineer Andrija Mohorovičić, assistant and honorary professor at the Technical College of Zagreb.

I have no idea why he was arrested, but as I have heard that the military police make arrests for crimes of a political nature, I believe that my son was arrested on suspicion of such a crime.

As his father I have followed his development from birth to the present, in constant contact with him since he is unmarried and lives with me and his mother in the same apartment, I take the liberty, Director-in-Chief, to explain the impossibility of my son having anything whatever to do with, of his being sympathetic toward, or an adherent of any antinational organization, or that he has consciously done anything either by act or negligence which is or could be against the interests of the Croatian people or state.

My son is a convinced Catholic, reared in a practicing Catholic family, and an ardently Croatian milieu. His uncle, Dr. Avelin Ćepulić, the well-known leader of the Catholic crusaders and workers, stood for him at baptism and until his death was his spiritual director. My wife, sister of Avelin Ćepulić and mother of my son, was brought up in a Catholic school, the Sacred Heart, in Graz, as well as her cousins, while another cousin studied with the Jesuits. Therefore, his nearest relatives and the milieu in which my son constantly lived and from which he drew his moral education were profoundly Catholic, and the influence of Dr. Avelin Ćepulić as an active Catholic spiritual worker is well known.

I know positively that my son is a convinced Catholic and as a result a violent adversary of communism and communist ideology and therefore of the Partisan movement. I know from conversations with him, from his statements, from the life he led and the manner in which he led it, that he was guided by Croatian and Catholic ideals.

The members of the clergy who know our family and particularly my son can confirm this with their testimony.

Besides all this, my son suffered so severe an inflammation of both lungs last summer that he is still in poor health. He is of calm and retiring character, not fond of society, never having married, and shows no particular interest in political problems, being patriotically Croatian and devoted to the Croatian cause. I attribute all these characteristics to his extreme myopia because of which he is not capable of any activity outside his profession.

I believe, Director-in-Chief, that a fatal error, a fraud, or unfortunate circumstances have put my son in a position that he finds himself at present imprisoned in the jail on Savska Cesta Street, and I ask, through this letter, that you quickly take steps and give orders so that my son be questioned as soon as possible and released. My wife and I will be responsible for his conduct in the future, and guarantee it with our lives.

Ready in the service of the Poglavnik and the fatherland!

> ANDRO MOHOROVIČIĆ, *Retired Judge*
> Zagreb, No. 21/11 Trg Tomislava

His Excellency the Archbishop recommended this petition in writing. Delivered into the hands of the Director-in-Chief, Colonel Lisak, by His Excellency, Bishop Dr. Lack.

Zagreb, January 23, 1945   S. L.

DOCUMENT XXXVIII

Correspondence Regarding the Archbishop's Interventions on Behalf of Twenty-Eight Condemned Men

Minister of Internal Affairs   ZAGREB, May 16, 1944
Office of the Minister
Zagreb
No. U.M.T. 295/44

To His Excellency Dr. Aloysius Stepinac
Archbishop of Zagreb, Zagreb

With reference to your letter of April 18 of this year on the subject of the petition of the Archiepiscopal Ecclesiastical Court for our intervention in the case of Dr. Richard Hauptfeld, we inform you that the Minister for Internal Affairs gave orders to the Department of Public Order and Safety to report as soon as possible on the above-mentioned case. This was done and it was found that Dr. Hauptfeld was under arrest at Savska Cesta Street as *a prisoner of the military police* and that, consequently, neither the Department of Public Order and Safety nor the Minister of Internal Affairs has jurisdiction to decide the case, which falls within the competence of the Ministry of the Armed Forces.

Ready in the service of the fatherland,

> By order of the Minister
> *Bureau Chief*
> *Counselor* Dr. S. Nazzura

Stamp: Ministry of Internal Affairs

Protonotary:

I address you, Protonotary, in the following matter:

Dr. Karlo Radoničić, son of the physician and professor at the university, Dr. Radoničić, and nephew of the university professor Dr. Antun Dabinović, will be sentenced soon, probably to death. The whole case is in the hands of Mr. Rukavina. As you know Dr. Karlo Radoničić, I beg you to take an interest in this case.

With deepest respect,

> The Archbishop

Zagreb, June 5, 1944
To Dr. Andrija Artuković
Minister and Protonotary of State
Zagreb

> Zagreb, November 7, 1944

Mr. Protonotary:

Dr. Milivoj Gavrančić, attorney from Zagreb, has recently been arrested by the military police. He held the post of a reserve judge officer in the militia. During the year that he has been out of the army, he has occupied himself solely with his legal business. The reason for his arrest is unknown. He was not involved in politics, nor has he participated in any undertaking which could be harmful to the interests of the state. It seems that the only reason he was arrested is the fact that he bears the name, Gavrančić, and is the son of Dr. Oton Gavrančić. I have heard it said that he may even be sent to a concentration camp. Colonel Joso Rukavina has nothing against him. Dr. Draženović, against whom many people complain because of his excessive severity, seems to be the one responsible for this.

I ask you, Protonotary, to initiate immediate steps to examine the whole case as soon as possible and that Dr. Gavrančić be freed if he is not guilty.

Accept, Protonotary, my profound respect.

THE ARCHBISHOP

Dr. Andrija Artuković
Protonotary of State, Zagreb

Military Bureau of the Poglavnik
R. Br. 1718/44–taj
Zagreb
Subject: Ubl trial.

To His Excellency Dr. Aloysius Stepinac
Archbishop of Zagreb, Zagreb

In regard to your letter of December 28, 1944, concerning the above-mentioned subject, this bureau immediately made an exact and conscientious examination of the whole case of the arrest of the Reserve Ensign, Dr. Vladimir Ubl.

It has been proved with absolute certainty that this person had, as a student, belonged to the worst anti-Croatian group in Zagreb University; but he was not arrested nor brought to trial on this account, but for the reason that he committed a crime carrying a severer sentence than any other crime an officer can commit, namely, treason.

He collaborated with those who had deserted and gave false information on the disposition of the Croatian armed forces, especially in the artillery barracks at Černomerec.

The trial of the above-named is being carried out completely within the spirit of the law and he will be punished or released by the sentence of the court or by resolution of the administrative authorities — solely on the basis of the law.

At this time this bureau takes the liberty of informing Your Excellency that the highest representatives of the German Army itself have intervened on behalf of Ubl, but it not infrequently happens that people of the highest rank take up the cause of the most degenerate of communist criminals. When our own poor Croatians commit some small, insignificant misdeed, no one can be found who will say a good word for them.

Ready in the service of the Poglavnik and the fatherland!

> *Chief*,
> *General Officer* Perčević
>
> March 2, 1945

Subject: Dr. Aloysius Tovćar, university professor,
Petition of his wife for his release.

To the Department of Public Order and Safety
Zagreb

On February 28, 1945, my husband, Dr. Aloysius Tovćar, professor on the Agriculture Faculty of the Croatian University of Zagreb, was arrested according to the order of this Department for activities directed against the state.

The founders of the Agriculture Faculty of Zagreb asked my husband in 1922 to take the Chair of Plant Culture and Genetics and he has occupied that post continuously for 23 years. Besides teaching these two subjects and conducting examinations in them, he worked summers on a large experimental farm of the school and during the winter in its laboratories. My husband has contributed to many scientific journals in our own country and abroad, in which more than fifty scientific works have been published to date. During this time several manuals for students and innumerable articles for practical farmers and peasants have also been published. He spent his year's leave in America to perfect himself in his profession and there, as well as on the occasions of numerous international congresses to which he was invited, he always represented the Croatian University of Zagreb with dignity.

Thus, occupied from morning till night with his varied activities, he had no interest in anything outside of them, especially politics. He has never been a member of any political party nor of any political movement and all political activity was completely alien to him.

I am absolutely certain that his arrest a few days ago was an error or the result of slander. I ask only one thing: question him as soon as possible and bring this affair to a decision so that he may be freed as soon as possible and may continue his work at the experimental farm during the present season the continuity of which is of enormous importance for our agriculture.

I mention only one of these works which is especially pressing and which was entrusted to him by the Economic Ministry on behalf of the peasants; the preparation of the summer wheat since the state's crop of next year depends on the success of this work. This activity has been interrupted by his arrest and cannot be finished without him since he is the only competent man in this field in the country.

For this reason I take the liberty of asking again that you undertake immediately everything necessary for the questioning of my husband, so that he may not remain under arrest unjustly on account of an error or slander, but may be sent back to his work, to which he has generously sacrificed his whole life.

DRAGICA TAVĆAROVA

I warmly recommend the above petition since it is a question of a competent man and since it is not known, as I have learned, that he has committed any crime.

THE BISHOP AND VICAR-GENERAL

Zagreb, March 5, 1945

Colonel Rukavina, Joco, replied:

"Tavćar collaborated with Dr. Klinčić, who organized aid for Slovenians at Zagreb which was intended for the Partisans.

"As his crime was not of a very serious nature and since he is the only man competent to prepare wheat for the spring planting, he will soon be released."

S. L.

Zagreb, March 5, 1945

Archiepiscopal Ecclesiastic Court,
Zagreb

MR. MINISTER:

I have learned, Mr. Minister, that a few days ago a number of men were condemned to be shot by a court martial and that the following are also sentenced to capital punishment:

1. Paul Pavlin, soldier in the medical company of the IVth Mountain Regiment at Daruvar, and with him 18 others of the same mountain regiment.

2. Ivan Pindulić — deputy officer, for having contributed to the "Red aid."

3. Dr. Kadrnka — because he gave money four times to the "Red aid."

Mr. Minister, it is not possible for me to investigate their alleged crimes nor their seriousness, but I ask only that you take the necessary steps with the authorities so that the capital punishment to which they were sentenced may be changed to a less harsh punishment or that they be granted amnesty. I am sure that they will appreciate this gesture on the part of the highest Croatian authorities and this will give them the incentive to become loyal citizens of the Croatian fatherland and state.

I hope, Mr. Minister, that you will do all in your power in behalf of amnesty.

Accept, Mr. Minister, at this time, my deepest respect.

Dr. ALOYSIUS STEPINAC
Archbishop of Zagreb

Zagreb, June 28, 1944
To Colonel of the Ustashi Ante Vokić
Minister of the Armed Forces
Zagreb

MR. MINISTER:

The wife of the engineer, Mr. Košutić, who is at Lepoglava, has asked me to plead for her husband whose health is in a very dangerous condition. She is also seriously ill.

I take the liberty of asking you to do all you can so that the engineer, Mr. Košutić, may at least be placed in a Zagreb hospital, because it will react terribly on the masses of the people if they should learn of his condition.

Please, Mr. Minister, accept my deepest respect.

THE ARCHBISHOP OF ZAGREB

Zagreb, November 9, 1942
Dr. Andrija Artuković
Minister of Justice and Religion
Zagreb

ZAGREB, April 18, 1944

MR. MINISTER:

I have the honor of enclosing, Mr. Minister, the letter of the Provincial, Dr. Sibe Budrović, Superior of the Dominican Monastery of

Zagreb and Director of the Dominican Classical High School in Zagreb, in which the Archiepiscopal Ecclesiastic Court is asked to intervene urgently on behalf of Dr. Richard Hauptfeld, lecturer on the Medical Faculty of Zagreb, who was arrested on March 30 of this year.

The enclosed letter mentions the alleged reasons for which he was arrested and also the personal guarantee, on the responsibility of Provincial Dr. Sibe Budrović, by which he testifies that Dr. Hauptfeld is a worthy and honest man.

I ask you, Mr. Minister, to take immediate measures in the sense requested by the enclosed letter so that the above-named may be released and allowed to continue his work in his profession.

Accept at this time, Mr. Minister, my greatest respect.

THE ARCHBISHOP

Dr. Mladen Lorković
Minister of Internal Affairs
Zagreb

DOCUMENT XXXIX

Partial List of Persecuted and Condemned Persons on Whose Behalf the Archbishop Intervened Regardless of Nationality or Religion

Name	Profession	Sentence	Date	Results of Intervention When Known
Gabron, Stevo	Weaver	Prison	1943	Freed
Trifunović, Branko	Officer	Concentration Camp	1943	Died in camp
Galec, Vladimir	Colonel	Prison	1943	
Bakota, Patar	Second Lieutenant	Prison	1943	Refused
Kukić, Ladistaš	Miller	Prison	1943	
Basić, Jure	Law student	Prison	1943	
Dryak, Vlasta	Actress	Prison	1943	
Badel, Slavko	Manufacturer	Prison	1943	Freed
Tudjen, Juraj	Locksmith	Prison	1943	
Keresević, Vojislav and wife Stojanka		Prison Prison	1943 1943	Freed Freed
Lovrić, Milan	Student	Concentration Camp	1943	

Name	Profession	Sentence	Date	Results of Intervention When Known
Pavić, Ivan		Prison	1943	Freed
Fabijanić, Stjepan	Peasant			
Solaja, Josip	Railroad employee	Prison	1943	Shot
Premenić, Ivan	Theologian	Prison	1944	Freed
Kulisak, Vladislav	Theologian		1944	Disappeared
Niksa, Ivan	Schoolmaster at Kravar	Prison	1944	
Janković, Svetozar	(Orthodox)	Prison	1944	
Mutavdzić, Lazo		Prison	1944	
Vucetić, Borivoje		Prison	1944	
Vekić, Petar		Prison	1944	
Dokić, Felip		Prison	1944	
Marković		Prison	1944	
Potocnjak, Dragutin	Retired tax collector	Prison	1944	
Fajdetić, Grgo	Schoolmaster	Concentration Camp	1944	
Stenzer, Ana and Hansi		Prison	1944	Allowed to depart for Italy
Hajdin, Zarko	Engineer	Concentration Camp	1944	
Majseć, Stjepan	Schoolmaster	Prison	1944	
Holjac, Viktor	Student	Concentration Camp	1944	
Drevensek, Franjo	Slovenian priest	Concentration Camp	1944	
Minichreizer, Artur	Engineer	Concentration Camp	1944	
Zagorae, Ksenija (age 16, Orthodox)		Prison	1944	
Harvat, Franjo	Laborer	Concentration Camp	1944	
Otrokar, Hinko	Student	Prison	1944	
Znidarsić, Henrik	Engineer	Prison	1944	
Rusan, Matija	Notary at Sestine	Prison	1944	
Niemeić, Franjo	Priest	Prison	1944	
Pavan, Joznalda	Nun at Podr. Slatina	Prison	1944	Freed
Anić, Marija	Housewife	Death	1944	
Nemet, Branka (Communist)	Employee	Concentration Camp	1944	
Kueko, Stjepan	Innkeeper	Prison	1944	Freed
Juraj, Dr. H.	Physician	Prison	1944	Freed
Pavlin, Pavao	Officer	Death	1944	
Pindulić, Ivan	Officer	Death	1944	
Dr. Kadrnka	Officer	Death	1944	
Klemenić, Dr. Davila		Prison	1944	

Name	Profession	Sentence	Date	Results of Intervention When Known
Prakir, Ivan	Priest	Prison	1944	Taken away by Germans
Vladimir Brumen		Prison	1944	
Professor Ivo Srepe	Museum Custodian	Prison	1944	
Zvonko, Kaurić	Engineer	Prison	1944	
Radan, Adolf	Businessman	Prison	1944	
Biro, Vladislav (baptized Jew)		Prison	1944	
Livić, Zlata		Prison	1944	
Davidović, Oskar		Prison	1944	
Milcević, Stjepan	Apothecary	Prison	1944	
Samasalović, Fraujko (Communist)		Prison	1944	
Janekovic, Mirko	Lieutenant Colonel	Prison	1944	
Marine, Dr. Maks	Physician	Prison	1944	
Butković, Dragutin	Municipal employee	Prison	1944	
Belak, Stefica (Communist)	Student	Prison	1944	
Vidoni, Rudolf (Communist)	Student	Prison	1944	
Dr. Milković Vladko	Mayor	Prison	1944	Killed by Partisans
Bezi, Ivan	Theologian	Prison	1944	⎱ Taken prisoners
Segaric, Tomo	Priest	Prison	1944	⎰ by the Germans
Kezele, Vjekoslav	Schoolmaster	Prison	1944	
Cebalo, Zvonko	Lawyer	Prison	1944	
Tumbas, Adalbert	Catechist	Prison	1944	
Sever, Dragutin	Pilot	Prison	1944	
Sporen, Dr. Viktor	Veterinarian	Death	1944	Shot at Daruvar
Stanisić, Franjo	Private employee	Prison	1944	
Jesih, Dragutin	Priest	Prison	1944	
Jelusić, Ferdo (Communist)		Concentration Camp	1944	
Kereta, Patar (Communist)	Professor	Death	1944	
Wolf, Hinko (Communist)		Prison	1944	
Oresnik, Franz	Slovenian priest	Prison	1944	
Jesik, Pavao	Priest	Prison	1944	
Papec, Josip (Communist)	Peasant	Prison	1944	
Corkalo, Matija	Peasant	Prison	1944	
Lustig, Oscar	Businessman	Prison	1944	Freed
Naljković, Savo (age 71)	Businessman	Prison	1944	

Name	Profession	Sentence	Date	Results of Intervention When Known
Vresnik, Franz	Slovenian priest	Prison	1944	
Kovacević, Katarina	Wife of the Engineer Kovacević	Death	1944	
Zdelar, Gjuro	Peasant	Prison	1944	
Lepain, Nikola	Engineer, Inspector of the first section of railroads		1944	
Furlan, Ivan	Employee	Prison	1944	
Zadnik, Mirko	Student	Prison	1944	
Cepelić, Iso, and family		Prison	1944	
Kapetan, Ljubica (age 11)		Prison	1944	
Ricko, Ivan	Veterinarian	Prison	1944	
Lapter, Branko	Peasant	Prison	1944	
Novosel, Josip	Tailor	Prison	1944	
Molnar, Franjo	Employee	Prison	1944	
Vinek, Dr. Vlado	Employee of the Ministry of the Interior	Prison	1944	
Lulić, Ivan	Colonel	Prison	1944	
Rogutic, Franjo	Employee	Prison	1944	
Pintarić, Marija (aged 70)		Prison	1944	
Grbić, Maksim	Lt. Colonel	Prison	1945	
Bozinović, Petar		Prison	1945	Freed
Gudac, Ivan		Prison	1945	Freed
Sparozić, Albert		Prison	1945	Freed
Cimerman, Lovro		Prison	1945	Freed
Burić, Franjo		Prison	1945	Freed
Pavlicek, Mira	Engineer	Prison	1945	Freed
Marz, Gjuro	Counselor of the Court of Appeals	Prison	1945	
Vanjek, Franjo, his wife and 2 children	Apothecary	Prison	1945	Freed
Cvilinder, Ankica	Peasant	Prison	1945	
Hocevar, Vladimir	Police officer	Prison	1945	
Hmelj, Milan	Engineer	Prison	1945	
Vojnić, Adela	Religious	Prison	1945	Freed
Ivković, Dr. Gjuro	Deputy Chief of Police	Prison	1945	
Korenika, Vid Korenika, Mirko } Peasants from Hrasce		Concentration Camp	1945	
Bara, Ljubica, and child		Concentration Camp	1945	
Mrksa, Mira	Schoolmaster	Prison	1945	
Kuzmić, Stjepan	Schoolmaster	Prison	1945	
Zrelec, Petar	Treasury employee	Prison	1945	

Name	Profession	Sentence	Date	Results of Intervention When Known
Senoa, Zdenko	Assistant Minister of Labor	Prison	1945	
Boncelj, Dr. Josip	Lawyer	Prison	1945	Freed
Stipetić, Patar	Employee of the Sava Insurance Co.	Prison	1945	
Verk, Alojz	Storekeeper	Prison	1945	
Pandzić, Ivan	Manufacturer	Prison	1945	
Juracić, Velimir (Communist)	Municipal engineer	Death	1945	Sentence commuted
Rendulić-Cvetić, Dr. Vlasta	Physician	Prison	1945	
Mruz, Ivan	Peasant	Concentration Camp	1945	
Panić, Loso	Peasant	Concentration Camp	1945	
Sudarević, Pero	Peasant	Concentration Camp	1945	
Popko, J.	Peasant	Concentration Camp	1945	
Fister, Stjepan	Policeman	Prison	1945	
Lavcar, Dr. Alojz	University professor	Prison	1945	Freed
Sarić, Dr. Ante	Physician	Prison	1945	
Kosmac, Franjo	Engineer	Prison	1945	
Pesek, Ante	Lithographer	Prison	1945	
Kuseković, Nikola	Forester	Prison	1945	Freed
Jelovecki, Dragutin	High school pupil	Prison	1945	
Lavoslav, Bergles	Salesman	Prison	1945	
Husinec, Stjepan and Milan	Peasants	Concentration Camp	1945	
Horvat, Franjo	Laborer	Concentration Camp	1945	
Budak, Dr. Jozo	Professor of university	Concentration Camp	1945	

Zagreb, October 4, 1944

YOUR EXCELLENCY:

Released from prison and given freedom we thank you most cordially for your effective intervention in seeking amnesty for our fellow accused: Gojaković, Melorad; Sador, Stevo; and Krstić, Miomir.

TAMARA BEGOVIĆ
FEHIN KLEBIĆ
DZEMILA AJANOVIĆ

NOTE: The amnesty was the result of the petition of His Excellency the Archbishop. The Mohammedans expressed their particular thanks. By a renewed intervention of His Excellency on April 10, 1942, the released were given a complete pardon.

October 21, 1942

ZAGREB, March 22, 1944

No. 27/Int.

DIRECTOR-IN-CHIEF:

I have the honor, Director-in-Chief, to address you in the following matter:

Several days ago 18 people of the Jewish race were taken from Otocac to Zagreb where they are now in the jail of the Zagreb police. Their names are the following:

Srenger, Hinko	Room No. 17/II	Finzi, Rena	Room No. 35/III
Srenger, Miroslav	Room No. 17/II	Srenger, Berurija	Room No. 35/III
Kabiljo, Salomon	Room No. 24/II	Srenger, Elza	Room No. 35/III
Kabiljo, Avram	Room No. 24/II	Kraus, Emilija	Room No. 35/III
Kraus, Julijo	Room No. 24/II	Finzi, Flora	Room No. 35/III
Sarkić, Venecija	Room No. 33/III	Srenger, Zlata	Room No. 35/III
Sarkić, Laura	Room No. 33/III	Kraus, Edita	Room No. 35/III
Sarkić, Mija	Room No. 33/III	Kornfein, Emilija	Room No. 35/III
Kabiljo, Rahela	Room No. 35/III	Demajo, Mirjam	Room No. 35/III

As this concerns, in general, only women and children, I ask you, Director-in-Chief, to release them as soon as possible. The Jewish religious community will be responsible for them. As for the children, *"Caritas"* of the Diocese of Zagreb is ready to take care of them. If it is impossible to release the adults, I beg you to at least release the children and entrust them to *"Caritas."*

I trust, Director-in-Chief, that you will do what you can to grant this petition as soon as possible.

Accept the expression of my deepest respects.

Secretary of the Archbishop
ŠALIĆ

Dr. Milutin Juričić
Director-in-Chief for Public Order and Safety,
1 Opaticka St., Zagreb

DOCUMENT XL

Memorandum Regarding the Work of the "Committee to Aid Refugees" Organized by the Archbishop

It was in the year 1937 that Nazism began in Germany and Austria to persecute the Jews, the Catholic Church, and the Protestants.

Little by little people fled to any place where there was some hope of finding a safe refuge. At that time many of the persecuted came to Yugoslavia, that is to say to Croatia, feeling themselves safer there than in Slovenia. Their center was Zagreb. The Jews were very numerous but there were also other persons who, unwilling to adhere to the Hitlerite doctrines and the Nazi dictatorship, had been forced to take flight. Many of them had recommendations from the ecclesiastical authorities.

In view of the great number and misery of these people, and wanting to help the neediest, the "Committee to Aid Refugees" was founded under the protection of the Archbishop of Zagreb, Dr. Aloysius Stepinac, who served as intermediary with the Yugoslav authorities. The refugees received:

Financial and moral aid.

Medical care and medicine.

Information in various languages.

Visit permits, approved as a result of the special intervention of the Archbishop.

The cost of traveling to different countries.

A visa for the country of their destination, given on the recommendation of the "Committee."

Most of these people left for France, to go from there to America, England, or even to China or Japan.

Among the thousands of these refugees were:

Dr. Gere, now Minister of Justice in Austria, and the chief of the secret service in the cabinet of Beneš, who fled with numerous documents of the Czech government. After his arrival in Paris, the Czechoslovakian Minister in France sent the "Committee" a letter filled with expressions of gratitude since, according to this same chief, the Germans had put a high price on his head.

Czech and especially Polish engineers came en masse to our country. The "Committee" gave them aid at the railroad station and gave considerable sums to the "Society of the Friends of Poland."

There are today in Zagreb doctors who were helped by the "Committee" to complete their studies. Assistance was given by all the means at the disposal of the "Committee" to all these refugees, without regard to race, religion, or nationality.

A colony of refugees from Austria remains in Zagreb that was formerly under the protection of the Archbishop.

We have received letters from abroad asking that we describe the constitution of the "Committee" and how we raised the funds for our work. Similar institutions were later set up in London, Paris, New York, and Utrecht, but with the difference that Catholics were distinguished from Jews.

The Zagreb "Committee" as the nearest to the Austrian frontier, was the principal one that worked with other "Committees to Aid Refugees" throughout the world.

The "Committee" worked without interruption until the arrival of the Germans in Zagreb when it was forced to burn all its records so that all evidence of these people would be unavailable to the Nazis.

The importance attached by the German government to the "Committee" is shown in the arrest of Miss Theresa Skringer, secretary, who was sought out by the Gestapo the very day of the German arrival. She was arrested April 15, 1941, and imprisoned in Graz and Vienna where she was condemned to death, but was freed September 1, 1941, thanks to intervention from abroad.

The Gestapo intended to kill the Archbishop, according to the statement of a high Gestapo official. They wanted to arrest the other members of the "Committee" but most of them fled.

Among those competent to testify as to the truth of this declaration are:

Monsignor Milan Belukan, canon at Zagreb, member of the "Committee."

Dr. Francis Seper, rector of the Seminary of Zagreb, member.

Dr. Richard Lang, collaborator with the "Committee."

Dr. Desanka Stampar-Ristović, collaborator.

Monsignor Dr. Svetozar Rittig, member.

Because of the "Committee" the Archbishop was frequently an object of ridicule and was attacked in the press, but he continued this great work of mercy as long as possible.

THERESA SKRINGER
Former Secretary of the "Committee to Aid Refugees"

DOCUMENT XLI

*Report of Rev. Stephan Lacković to the International Red Cross
Regarding Relief in Croatia*

No. 4/P.O. — 43

Delegation of the International Red Cross in Croatia

The Undersigned has the honor of presenting to the above-named delegation a report on the aid which, through His Excellency Monsignor Dr. Aloysius Stepinac, the "International Union for Aid to Children" of Geneva sent to Polish émigrés (both mothers and children) lodged in the "Polish Home" in Crikvenica.

1. 2,000 Swiss francs (20,000 kronen): This sum was remitted by the "Committee for Aid to the Poles" of Fribourg to the Apostolic Nunciature in Berne, in agreement with which the Holy See asked the Archbishop of Zagreb to have paid from it its value in Croatian exchange to the Children's House in Crikvenica. This sum was paid on July 26, 1941, to Dr. Kujawska.

2. 60,000 kronen: This sum was sent by the tannin factory and the steam saw mill of Našice by letter on December 23, 1941. No. Eb/VC, as value in exchange for the sum to its representatives, Edward Vidoudez and Paul de Thomasson, by the International Union.

The sum sent to the Children's House in Crikvenica was received on January 2, 1942, by Mrs. Zlata Benković from the hands of His Excellency the Archbishop of Zagreb.

3. 60,000 kronen: This sum was also sent by the factory at Našice by letter on March 20, 1942, No. Eb/ — as value in exchange . . . as above under No. 2. The sum sent to the Children's House in Crikvenica was received on March 26, 1942, by Mrs. Zlata Benković.

4. 10,000 kronen: This sum was sent by the factory at Našice by letter as above under No. 3 as value in exchange for a bill of its representative, Francis Jacquemond, and was received by Mrs. Zlata Benković from the hands of His Excellency the Archbishop on March 10, 1942.

5. 10,810 Swiss francs: Christmas present from the Holy Father for the Poles in Croatia. 6,540 francs for the Children's House in Crikvenica, the rest for other Poles in Croatia.

6. 203,064.47 kronen: This sum was sent by the factory at Našice through the Prva Hrvatska Stedionica (the largest savings bank in Croatia) as value in exchange for a bill of its legal representative,

Dr. S. Charmant, on March 31, 1942, for the Children's House in Crikvenica. The sum was received from the Archbishop by Mrs. Zlata Benković on April 3, 1942.

7. 150,000 kronen: For this sum there is a certification from Dr. Kujawska of June 12, 1942, stating that she received it for the Children's House in Crikvenica. It is not known who sent or brought this money to His Excellency the Archbishop.

8. 100,000 kronen: For this sum we have a certification from Dr. Kujawska of June 9, 1942. The rest as above under No. 7.

9. 160,000 kronen: Sum received by Mrs. Staresina on September 16, 1942, sent by the Union for the Children's House at Crikvenica.

10. 20,000 kronen: Sum directed through the Prva Hrvatska Stedionica on January 5, 1943, No. 1775; sent on January 4, 1943, by His Excellency the Archbishop to Mrs. Sl. Bosnijak-Furst so that she might send it through the Prva Hrvatska Stedionica to Dr. Kujawska at Crikvenica for the Children's House. Receipt was acknowledged on January 30, 1943.

11. 250,000 kronen: Sum remitted by His Excellency Monsignor the Archbishop to Mrs. Sl. Bosnijak for the Children's House. Sent and directed through the Prva Hrvatska Stedionica to Dr. Kujawska on January 3, 1943, No. 1798. Receipt was acknowledged on January 30, 1943.

12. 498,200 kronen: Sum remitted by His Excellency Monsignor the Archbishop to Mrs. Sl. Bosnijak on February 10, 1943. This was sent through the Prva Hrvatska Stedionica to Dr. Kujawska on February 10, 1943, No. 2094. Receipt was acknowledged on February 20, 1943.

13. 300,000 kronen: Sum received from His Excellency the Archbishop on April 14, 1943, by Mrs. Sl. Bosnijak for the Children's House.

14. 400,000 kronen: Sum sent through the Poljodelska bank on August 25, 1943, to the Bishop of Senj for the Children's House in Malinska on the island of Krk where it has been transferred from Crikvenica. The sum was remitted to His Excellency the Archbishop by Mr. J. Schmidlin, delegate of the International Red Cross for Croatia.

The above amounts cannot be given more exactly because of the lack of sufficient details, especially in the question of the first expediters of a sum.

We tried to send at once, by the safest means, all sums received for the Children's House.

Very respectfully,
Dr. Stephan Lacković,
Secretary to the Archbishop

Zagreb, September 25, 1943

In December, 1942, 2,000 kilograms of potatoes were given free to the Polish children at Crikvenica; their value was 100,000 kronen at the black market rate in that place.

Stepinac

DOCUMENT XLII

Correspondence With Pavelić Regarding the Interest of the Archbishop in Providing Relief for Persons in Concentration Camps. Further Evidence of Efforts of the Archbishop to Succor the Persecuted

Poglavnik:

The blessed and holy days of the Christmas season are drawing near. Generous men, and above all the Church and fervent Catholics, should try, in this season, to help the poor and those who live in misery so that they may feel, at least during this time, relief and consolation through the Incarnate Son of God.

At this time the faithful who are in the concentration camps at Jasenovac and Labor are closest to my heart and I want some warm ray of Christian consolation to penetrate to them.

Poglavnik, I warmly request that you permit my central welfare office of *"Caritas"* in Zagreb to go to those people because many of them are in a situation worse than that of the Jews who have not been baptized.

I ask you most fervently that my special delegate, a priest: (1) may ascertain there their greatest needs; (2) that he give them, through *"Caritas"* some Christmas presents; and (3) that he notify their relatives that they are still alive.

I ask you, Poglavnik, to inform me as soon as possible of the result of this request, since Christmas is near and I must have sufficient time to organize this aid in some way or other.

Please accept my sincere respect.

DR. ALOYSIUS STEPINAC
Archbishop of Zagreb

Zagreb, December 6, 1941

Subject: Visit of a priest in the camps when they, dying, have asked for his services.

MR. MINISTER:

I have twice asked the Poglavnik, personally, to make it possible for a priest to enter the camps to bring some last comfort to the dying. Although the Poglavnik intended this, we are as yet unaware at present if access to these camps, Jasenovac, Gradiska, and Labor, has been granted any priest, although we know for certain that the dying have asked for the priests so that they might prepare for death and that this wish has not been granted them. Many people ask themselves if there is any difference between Soviet concentration camps and ours? Can the Ustashi movement count on divine blessing when it refuses to the dying what all civilized states have always granted them?

I address you, Mr. Minister, to ask you respectfully that you take all necessary steps with the proper authorities in the Ministry under your direction so that when the sick or dying in the camps ask for him, a priest will be allowed to go there and perform his ministrations without interference.

Please accept, Mr. Minister, the expression of my most sincere respect.

THE ARCHBISHOP OF ZAGREB

Zagreb, November 2, 1942
To Dr. Andre Artuković,
Ministry of Justice and Religion

To the Very Rev. Chancery of the Archiepiscopal
Ordinariate of Zagreb

At dawn on December 23, 1944, about 200–250 soldiers entered the village of Hruševec in my parish and burned down about 40–45 houses, 20–25 smaller buildings; took away 200–300 cattle, a good number of horses, calves, geese, turkeys, suckling pigs, and fattened hogs; shot 13 persons, 3 persons were burned; in addition, several other horrible crimes were committed; about 60–70 people of my parish were taken away — some old, others young — first to Savski Marof, near Zagreb, and elsewhere.

The three persons who were burned are the following:

1. Nicholas Stanišak
2. Joseph Sklebec
3. Imbro Gjurinski

The following persons, over 70 and under 15 years of age, were taken away:

Dragutin Janković	Philip Filković
Mijo Gjurinski	George Jankovich
Nicholas Kuhada	Imbro and John Kuhada
Nicholas Gjurinski	Anthony Crnoga
Dragutin Pirički	Nicholas Filković
Stephen Pirički	Dragutin Stanišak
John and George Šklebec	Joseph Stanišak
Imbro Juretić	George Stanišak
Rudolph Cvetko, father of four children	Paul Stanišak
	George Stanišak
Anthony Orgulan	Dragutin Stanišak
Stephen Orgulan	Stephen Stanišak, Sr.
Joseph Orgulan	Stephen Stanišak, Jr.
Imbro Filković	Anthony Stanišak
Joseph Filković	John Stanišak, brother of Nicholas
George Vlašić	

Besides the persons enumerated here, whose names I remember, there were at least twenty more names I do not recall who were imprisoned.

On behalf of all the people of Hruševec, my parishioners, whether mentioned above or not, I make the humble request that one of the Bishops intervene with the competent authorities so that they may come to see the burnt village in order that my people may have some help while there is still time.

For the present, I am not able to come to Zagreb, since I do not have a permit, nevertheless, I shall come soon to give still more news which cannot now be given. *Sufficit diei miseria sua.*

Firmly hoping that my wish, and that of my parishioners, will be granted, I pray you, my superiors, to accept the homage of my respectful esteem.

FRANCIS EUGENE PETREKOVIĆ, *pastor.*

Pušca, January 14, 1945
  Seal:

Parochial Office of St. George, Pušca.
The inhabitants of the village of Hruševec.

After several interventions the case was finally settled, on January 26, 1945, in the following manner by the district police, Zagreb, No. 2 Gjorgjiceva Street:

1. Most of the men able to serve will be enrolled into the army at once.

2. About 20 persons will be immediately set free if they have not already been released.

3. Seven persons still remain with the police until a decision is made on whether to set them free or enroll them in the army.

Zagreb, January 26, 1945

Archiepiscopal Ordinariate of Zagreb

ZAGREB, March 20, 1945

POGLAVNIK:

I feel obliged to address you once again as Chief of State on behalf of political prisoners who are interned at Lepoglava and other camps.

Every day the relatives of these prisoners come to me, asking me to take steps to mitigate their lot. There is no doubt that in these complaints there is some exaggeration, but the anxiety of these relatives can be understood, since they have no news from the prisoners and can send them nothing to camp, all the while knowing that typhoid fever is taking its toll at Lepoglava.

I experience considerable uneasiness in intervening in this matter after having spoken so many times to the representatives of the state. Nevertheless, Poglavnik, permit me to make a proposal for the solution of this problem. Let a commission, composed of members of the Croatian Parliament, be sent to make an inquiry on the state of these prisoners, to which the prisoners of all religions will be able to express freely their wants and their complaints. I am of the opinion that in this way the unfavorable rumors among the people will for the most part be silenced, while such a policy will greatly profit our international reputation.

Drawing your attention to this possibility, I take the liberty, Poglavnik, of asking you to let me know whether or not the relatives of these prisoners are right in entertaining fears on behalf of their dear ones.

Please accept, Poglavnik, the expression of my sincere respect.

ARCHBISHOP OF ZAGREB

DOCUMENT XLIII

The Christmas Message Addressed to the Croatian Workers in Germany

MY DEAR CROATIAN BROTHERS AND SISTERS:

I consider it my sacred duty to say a few words to you, who will celebrate this Christmas Day far from those whom you love and cherish. To you who will not, perhaps, have the chance to sing our beautiful Christmas hymns in church, to you who are forced by circumstances to think, even at Christmas time, how you can keep yourselves and yours, how to get for them their daily bread.

But, if you are far from your loved and dear ones and your Croatian fatherland, God is not far from you. His paternal eye watches over you even there, His paternal love surrounds you, and His arms protect you. Show yourselves abroad, as true children of God and as true children of your Croatian fatherland.

The first demands that you do not forget your soul nor soil it through sin, since it is created in the image of God. Since sin has existed in the world it has made no man happy but has caused the ruin of many. "Does man gain anything else from vice," says St. Gregory, "than that he makes of his own heart a prison, where he is tortured by remorse even though no one else accuses him?" Did the sin of Adam, the first man, bring anything but remorse and an immense sadness for his lost happiness? Did the murder of his brother Abel bring to Cain anything other than the infamous imprint of a fratricide which would not leave him in peace day or night? The adultery of David, did it not bring to the king remorse which pushed him into even greater sin, to the murder of him who kept him from being able to sin without self-reproach?

Drunkenness, adultery, and other vices, do they not bring to man only sadness and unhappiness for which, very often, there is no remedy?

So that this does not happen to you as well, do not forget your duties as Christians to our heavenly Father. First, do not forget to pray. When a small child wakens in his crib he first looks all around, searching for the eyes of his mother. As soon as he finds them he is glad, but if he does not find them he begins to cry. We are all children of our heavenly Father, for Christ has taught us, "Our Father who art in Heaven." Look, therefore, every day in your holy prayers to Him, our heavenly Father, who is better to you than any earthly mother, closer than any friend, and who is able to help you when no one else can. God has shown us His great mercy since He hears the humble prayers of His children everywhere. This is, above all, a great consolation for you who do not have, perhaps, the chance to go to church when you wish. God hears you from any place. St. Paul prayed in prison and obtained the help and the conversion of his gaoler. The sick King Ezechias prayed in his bed and obtained as a result a fifteen-year prolongation of his life. The thief prayed on the cross and obtained grace for his conversion, the salvation of his soul, and was the first to enter with Jesus into Paradise. The prophet Daniel prayed in the lions' den, among the lions, and remained unharmed so that not a single hair of his head was touched. The prophet Jonah prayed in the belly of the whale and obtained deliverance. Job patiently prayed to God, seated on a dunghill, separated from the world, and regained anew his health and all the wealth that had been taken from him.

Pray then, all of you, if you wish the blessing of heaven to accompany you in your work and to pass happily through the tempests of life. God does not wait for an elaborate prayer from us. The more simple it is, the dearer it is to Him. For the leper of the Gospel did not pray otherwise when he cried out, "Lord, if You will, You can have pity on me." And his prayer was granted. If then you pray as a child to your heavenly Father, He too will do his duty as a father to you, since He Himself promised, "In truth I say to you," says Christ, "all that you seek from the Father in my name, believe, and it shall be given you."

Show yourselves abroad, as I have said, true children of the Croatian fatherland. That will not be hard for you if you succeed in the first, that is to say your duty to God. Let them say what they will, for me it is certain that there is no greater patriotism, no greater love of country than the leading everywhere, in all places, of a life without sin, honest and sober. It is not drunkards, nor murderers, nor thieves, usurpers, fornicators, nor card players who form the firm foundation of the fatherland, but hard-working men, sober, honest, and conscientious. No one has ever heard of a grape grown on a thorn hedge.

I believe, moreover, that none among you have succumbed to the deadly theory of international communism, which denies all obligation to one's own people and country. The nation is one large family created by the will of the Creator in which each individual has his duty to the community, just as the community has a duty to him.

Appreciate, therefore, even from abroad, your Croatian fatherland but do not despise other nations. And you can honor it in the best way by leading an honest life and doing honest work. For you know our national proverb, "A good man is worth more than riches." And one of the most beautiful possessions of your Croatian fatherland is the Catholic religion upon which rests all of our beautiful and honorable heritage. Confess that religion in public, abroad as well as at home. I am convinced that no honest man will scorn you because of that, because it is only thieves and traitors who merit scorn, never heroes.

I hope that these few words of mine will find an echo in your hearts, since they come from the heart, warmly greeting you all, and I wish for you all the abundant blessings of God and the peace of Christ who descended to earth on the holy night of Christmas accompanied by the angels singing, "Glory to God in the highest and on earth peace to men of good will."

Your Archbishop
DR. ALOYSIUS STEPINAC

Zagreb, November 27, 1941

DOCUMENT XLIV

Communication of the Archbishop Regarding Suspension of Rev. Guberina

No. 101/Pr.

REV. JOHN GUBERINA:

Your conduct and your actions during the two and a half years that you have been living within the territory of the Archdiocese of Zagreb and elsewhere are in contradiction with your priestly vocation and have scandalized the faithful.

You are forbidden as of today, under pain of suspension, *ipso facto incurrendae*, to exercise any priestly function whatever within the boundaries of the Archdiocese of Zagreb, including the saying of holy Mass.

This decision will be reversed in the future only when you have in truth mended your ways and have given guarantees that these scandals will not be repeated.

THE ARCHBISHOP

Zagreb, June 25, 1943

DOCUMENT XLV

*Memorandum Concerning Alleged Intolerable Conduct
of Zvonko Brekalo*

No. 9/BK

Bozo Lastro, religion teacher in the technical high school for boys
at Banja Luka, has presented a report on the shocking conduct of
the Ustashi priest, Zvonko Brekalo, who had, blaspheming God and
assaulting certain persons, committed acts arising from the most
deplorable passions.

His Excellency the Archbishop is sending a letter to the assistant
of the Military Vicar, Monsignor Cecelja, asking him to examine the
case and, if what is said in the report is true, to take away from him,
ipso facto, his jurisdiction throughout the whole territory of the
Croatian Army and the Archdiocese of Zagreb *sub poena suspensionis*.
Zagreb, January 22, 1943
9/BK 1943
Received January 22, 1943
Sent January 23, 1943
Šalić

DOCUMENT XLVI

*Probative Material Presented in Defense of Archbishop
Stepinac by Dr. Politeo*

Witnesses Cited by Defense Counsel on Specific Facts
Involving the Conduct of the Archbishop

NOTE: Of the witnesses here enumerated and proposed to the
court, the court admitted and heard the following: Dr. Hren, Dr.
Cvetan, Dr. Lončar, Pecojak, Dr. Klarek, Dr. Penić, and Dr. Slamić;
the others were not admitted to the court, on the basis that their
testimony was of no importance to the case. Neither were the witnesses for *"Caritas"* admitted because this matter was not considered
decisive to the trial. Dr. Nezić was refused as a witness because he
had been present throughout the trial, and Dr. Marić because he
was one of the co-defendants.

I propose that there be called and heard as witnesses at the trial:

Dr. Dragutin Hren, canon, Kaptol 22, Zagreb, on these facts: that
upon leaving St. Mark's Church after having heard the sermon given
by Archbishop Stepinac before the opening of the Croatian Parlia-

ment, then convened for the first time, Pavelić said to the late Dosen that, "this greenhorn would not teach him politics," and that in an interview with Cecelja, the same Pavelić said that because of this sermon relations with the Church had become still worse;

that Archbishop Stepinac did not take jurisdiction away from the priests, Victor Merz and Auguste Stanzer, who had gone to join the *Partisans:*

that he had explicitly given his permission and jurisdiction to Jean Kokot, pastor of St. Klara, who asked to leave to join the *Partisans:*

that to a witness remarking that the NDH was neither an independent nor a Croatian state he replied that it was *a German colony;*

that Archbishop Stepinac constantly explained to his clergy that he would not link his name to *party politics* but only to the Croatian people;

that Archbishop Stepinac refused the invitation of the so-called NDH government to participate on April 14, 1941, in the welcome given to Pavelić at the railroad station, which is why the said NDH government resolved that the Mass of thanksgiving would not be said in the Cathedral;

that Archbishop Stepinac had warned his clergy that his first visits paid to Slavko Kvaternik on April 12, 1941, and to Pavelić on April 16, 1941, did not mean that he was in favor of Ustashism nor that he had thereby recognized the government of the Ustasha Pavelić but that, in order to protect religion and the people, relations between the *de facto* state and Church were necessary;

that Archbishop Stepinac refused to present the clergy and the chapter of Zagreb to Pavelić when the former were invited to visit Pavelić, and that Pavelić stated on many occasions that he would remove the Archbishop from his post;

that Archbishop Stepinac protested against the Ustashi oath to be taken by priests employed by the state;

that Archbishop Stepinac had ordered three priests, who alone had been appointed Ustashi officials, to resign from their posts which, in fact, they held;

that of the group of priests mentioned on page five of the indictment as having been notorious for their collaborationist activity, only three, namely Vilim Cecelja, Martin Gecina, and Anthony Djurić, were from the Archdiocese of Zagreb, while all the others belonged to other dioceses;

that Pavelić had not gone to the Cathedral until the day that the Italians had a Requiem sung there for the Duke of Aosta and that the Archbishop refused to receive Pavelić at the Cathedral entrance, and that Pavelić had been received by a simple sacristan who showed him his seat. The Archbishop, on this occasion, did not greet Pavelić.

that Pavelić openly showed his resentment toward Archbishop Stepinac for his hostility to Fascism and intervention on behalf of persecuted Jews and that various other Ustashi kept up their resentment, threatening that, as soon as Germany won the war, they would show what they were capable of doing to priests and — as they said — "to your Stepinac";

that certain Ustashi stated — according to Vilim Cecelja — that Archbishop Stepinac was guilty, in forbidding political activity to the clergy, of producing a state of affairs wherein out of a total number of about 500 priests only about 15 were of the Ustashi persuasion and that only some 30 had any sympathy for the Ustashi;

that Vilim Cecelja was, in fact, a Ustasha, but that, noting the bloody procedure of the regime, he took advantage of his position to do all he could to save Serbians and Jews.

The same witness, Dr. Hren, with the witness, *Dr. Francis Cvetan,* assistant at the University, Kaptol 31, on this fact:

that on April 10, 1941, on the occasion of the entrance of German troops into Zagreb, seeing the enthusiasm of certain young men, Archbishop Stepinac said to his entourage that this mood did not please him, that these young men did not understand what it means to live under the *Prussian boot.*

The same witness, Dr. Hren, with the witnesses, *Dr. Anthony Slamić,* canon, Kaptol 19, and *Dr. Nicolas Kolarek,* Kaptol:

that Archbishop Stepinac refused Pavelić's request that priests who received appointments from the state must resign their duties as officials of the Ordinariate, especially Dr. Slamić, Dr. Hren, and Dr. Kolarek, as well as those who were put in charge of the seminary. It was only at the time when Dr. Lončar had been condemned to death by a Ustashi court, and when the above-named persons had been notified that the pardon to be given to Dr. Lončar was doubtful, unless they handed in their resignations. At that the above-named canons resigned out of friendship for Dr. Lončar and requested the Archbishop to accept their resignations.

Dr. Hren is also a witness to certain circumstances for the proof of which we propose as witnesses, Dr. Paul Lončar and Kresimir

Pecnjak (on the subject of recommendations made to the clergy not to meddle in politics), together with John Kokot, Kaptol 11 (on the subject of the jurisdiction left to Partisan priests, see above); also these three persons are proposed as witnesses who will point out certain facts where it will be a question of their own proofs.

Next I propose as witnesses:

Dr. Paul Lončar, canon, Kaptol 14, Zagreb, on these facts:

that, contrary to the radio announcement that in the Parliamentary elections of 1938 Archbishop Stepinac would vote for Dr. Stojadinović, he really voted for Dr. Maček, and that he replied to the latter when he thanked him that he had not voted for a party but for the Croatian people;

that toward the end of July, 1941, Archbishop Stepinac had sent the witness, Dr. Lončar, to Dr. Mirko Puk, then Minister of Justice and Religion, to notify him that no priest could be a member of the Ustashi organization and still less a Ustashi official, since that would be contrary to the provisions of canon law. It was this that led Dr. Puk to order a criminal trial according to summary justice at which the witness, Dr. Lončar, was condemned to death;

that at the Theology Faculty, Canon Lončar had very often spoken against National Socialism, racism, and Ustashism, and that as a delegate of the Archbishop he had given similar lectures to priests and, having reported to the Archbishop on his activity, received from him advice to persevere in their work and to propagate successfully this Catholic ideology;

that Pavelić had on three occasions demanded from the Papal Delegate that Archbishop Stepinac be removed from his Archiepiscopal See.

Dr. Hren and Dr. Stephen Baksić, canon, Kaptol 8:

that the sermons of Archbishop Stepinac had been given precisely as they were later published in the "Katolički List" and that they were identical to the text that was submitted to this court, that most of his sermons were reproduced in thousands of copies and as illegal pamphlets, were circulated in nonliberated territory and, as far as possible, in territory liberated from the NDH — that before, during, and after the occupation the Archbishop advised his clergy to apply themselves, not to political affairs, but only to Church affairs and that he gave similar instructions to the administration of the seminary on the subject of the instruction given to the seminarians.

Dr. Stephen Baksić, canon, Kaptol 8, and *Vlado Sironić*, press secretary to the President of the Croatian Republican Government, on this fact:

that under the name of *Hrvatska straža* there existed two publications, a daily and a weekly, each separately and independently edited and under different ownership, and that approval was given, not to the daily, but *to the weekly* which, meant for the people of our villages, never took a stand for the principle of racism nor praised Hitler. (Subsidiary proof with an examination of the weekly, *Hrvatska straža*.)

Dr. Anthony Slamić, canon, Kaptol 19 (not only with *Dr. Hren* as was proposed above, but also on this circumstance):

that the censorship of books, especially of prayer books, was carried out by a special censor, who proposed them for approval at the meetings of the Ordinariate, and that it was according to his proposal that the prayer books were approved or rejected. Consequently, the Ordinariate came to a decision on the basis of the censor's report, without reading the respective manuscripts. As to most of the books published, the Archbishop had no knowledge of the censorship or what had been censored. Only books, not pamphlets, magazines, etc., were submitted to the censorship.

Kresimir Pecnjak, canon, Kaptol 25, with *Dr. Hren* and *Dr. Lončar* on this fact:

that before, during, and after the occupation, Archbishop Stepinac constantly advised his clergy to apply themselves only to Church affairs and not to political matters.

With *Dr. Lončar*, *Dr. Francis Seper*, and *Dr. Dragutin Nezić* on this fact:

that he always instructed the administration of the seminary to train the seminarians exclusively for the service of the Church and especially not to concern themselves with non-Church matters.

Dr. Francis Seper, Rector of the Seminary, Kaptol 29, and *Dr. Dragutin Nezić*, spiritual director of the Seminary,

on the circumstance that has just been mentioned, together with *Kresimir Pecnjak* (besides Dr. Nezić).

Dr. Joseph Marić, canon, Kaptol 11, on this fact:

that in 1943 Archbishop Stepinac successfully undertook the difficult work of collecting sufficient money and food *for all Croats interned in Italian concentration camps* and that the Holy See assisted him in this work; and that the Italian government along with Pavelić had taken in bad part this work of Archbishop Stepinac as well as his interventions on behalf of persecuted Serbs and Jews.

Dr. George Marić:

Conforming to a governmental request, it was necessary to establish a small seminary at Pazin where this priest, the witness, was to be a professor. But since the town of Pazin was still under the jurisdiction of the Bishop of Trieste, it was the duty of the Archbishop of Zagreb, according to canon law, to give to Dr. Marić an attestation of his character as a priest, which the Archbishop actually did.

Dr. Nicolas Kolarek, canon, Kaptol 23, Zagreb:

that Archbishop Stepinac never took an oath either to Pavelić or to the NDH, although many other bishops did so under similar circumstances.

Dr. John Penić, Kaptol 294:

that the *Katolički List* had been especially censored and persecuted by the Ustashi authorities, that its editors were directed under threats what they were to write, that the censorship was very rigorous in striking out certain words and in inserting others to change the meaning, and that this weekly was twice suspended.

Dr. Francis Seper, Rector of the Seminary, Kaptol 29 (already called regarding another point); *Dr. Desanka Stampar — Ristović,* woman physician, Gvozd 7; *N. Beluhan,* pastor of St. Mary's, Kaptol; *Theresa Skringer,* Vinogradska cesta; on this fact:

that already in 1937, under the protection of Archbishop Stepinac, a special Refugee Committee had been established which by means of money subsidies and other methods aided Jewish, and non-Jewish, anti-Fascist refugees, who had fled from Poland, Austria, and Czechoslovakia, on account of the Nazi persecutions. (Among those who were aided and given shelter there was, for example, Dr. Gere, present Minister of Justice in Austria.)

Ferdinand Feller, Mg. Ph., Jurjevska 31:

that on the occasion of the arrest of Canon Lončar, the secretary of the Pavelić cabinet, Ivanković, told him that the chapter and Archbishop Stepinac had hindered government policy, and that later, on a certain day in 1942, he told him again there was opposition and hindrance coming from the Archbishop.

Zora Feller, Jurjevska 31, on this fact:

that at her request the Archbishop intervened on behalf of her brothers, Ferdinand and Kazimir Feller, when they were imprisoned as well as in behalf of the communist, Zlata Jukić, and that he helped the Jewess, Lustbaum, to hide herself in a priest's house and later escape to Makarska.

Antoinette Termon, a nun with the Red Cross, Ninogradska 28: that at her request Archbishop Stepinac in March, 1943, intervened with the intention of saving some former Jews who had contracted mixed marriages. (All the witnesses named can testify to that as well as to interventions made on behalf of persecuted Jews, Serbs, and communists, and, in general, on behalf of all the persecuted without discrimination.)

Dr. Dragutin Nezić, spiritual director of the Seminary, Kaptol 29, as a witness on the subject of the activity of *"Caritas,"* especially on the contribution given by the Archbishop to this institution, on its expenses, on the care it gave to the children of Partisans, especially to those who came from Kozara, on the lack of foundation to the statements given by the late director, Dumić, in his declaration which has been read during the trial, on the state of health of the late Dumić at the time when, ill and confined to his bed, on December 20, 1945, he was questioned by the Commission for the Establishment of War Crimes on his quarrel with the nuns and on their moral or immoral conduct, on this same subject let there also be heard *Dr. Vilim Nuk,* Palmoticeva 3, and particularly *Dr. Marijan Dumić,* lawyer, Ilica 35, Zagreb, on the mental and physical state of her father; and on the same subject also *Joseph Panić,* pastor of Saint Barbara of Rebro, Zagreb, who will testify that the late Stephen Dumić denied the truth of his charges against Archbishop Stepinac and the institution *"Caritas,"* on which charges the article in *Vjesnik* was based, and that he denied them after this article had been read to him.

Dr. Dragutin Nezić, who directed the whole inquiry on *"Caritas"* in Zagreb, will bring the necessary documents at the time of the interrogation, and at this moment these documents are submitted with the proposal to read them at the trial: the accounts of *"Caritas"* in Zagreb, printed and put at the disposal of the public, principally drawn up by the late Stephen Dumić himself, for the years 1942, 1943, 1944.

The written statement of the lawyer, Dr. Marijan Dumić, on the state of her father's health at the time he was questioned. (*The original of the statement.*)

DOCUMENT XLVII

*Letter From General Kvaternik to the Archbishop
Regarding Chaplains*

Independent State of Croatia
Ministry of the Croatian Armed Forces
No. 3067/Taj-confidential
Zagreb, October 16, 1941

To His Excellency the Archbishop and
Croatian Metropolitan, Dr. Aloysius Stepinac:

At my suggestion, the Poglavnik appointed as Military Vicar of the armed forces the Very Reverend Monsignor Canon Stephen Vučetić and as his substitute the young and deserving priest, Monsignor Vilim Cecelja, pastor of Kustošija.

I sent word of the nomination of the Very Reverend Monsignor Canon Vučetić to His Excellency Dr. Victor Burić, Bishop of Senj and Modrus, asking him to do all that was necessary according to the regulations of the Church so that he might be named a bishop, since that is called for by the present conditions in the Croatian armed forces.

I ask Your Excellency to approve the appointment of Monsignor Cecelja on behalf of the Church and to release him from his duties as pastor.

If it is possible that Monsignor Cecelja be named canon, I would be very grateful to Your Excellency, since this action would demonstrate our solidarity to the whole world.

In this affair all material considerations will be taken care of by the Croatian armed forces.

Adjutant and Marshal
KVATERNIK

DOCUMENT XLVIII

*Record of Conversation Between Soviet Writer, Ilya Ehrenburg,
and Father Martinčić, O.F.M.*

Office of the Franciscan Provincial
No. 9 Kaptol, Zagreb
No. 1119/1945
Subject: Conversation with the journalist, Mr. Ilya Ehrenburg.

To the Presidency of the Episcopal Conference:

At the request of the Presidency of the Conference of Bishops of November 20, 1945, No. 142/BK, asking the undersigned, Provincial Modesto Martinčić, to present in writing an exact report on the outcome of his conversation with the Russian journalist, Mr. Ilya Ehrenburg, I submit the following report:

On October 25 at a little before four o'clock in the afternoon Brother Porter told me that at four o'clock Mr. Ilya Ehrenburg was coming to pay me a visit. Dr. Pallua, Secretary of the Commission for Religious Affairs of the Presidency of the Federal Croatian Government, had just a few minutes before notified the brother of that by telephone.

When, a little after 4:15 P.M., I returned from the waiting room of the Provincial Headquarters where I had been talking to a visitor, I found Mr. Ilya Ehrenburg there with his companion, Comrade Tkalec, in conversation with the priest, Dr. Leander Dedus, whom I had asked to meet Mr. Ehrenburg and to talk to him until I had finished my conversation with the above-mentioned visitor.

1. Ecclesiastical literature.

After having met and introduced ourselves Mr. E. began the conversation by saying that he had come to see me in a completely private capacity out of a desire to get some information on the state of religious literature among the Catholics of Yugoslavia. This was of interest to him inasmuch as he was a man of letters and especially so since during his stay in Italy, studying Italian literature and art, he had learned that the Franciscan Order had inspired over the centuries the incentive and content of many works in letters and art. He had found the Franciscan Order especially sympathetic because of the tendency to simplicity and poverty and their work among the poor.

After exchanging several thoughts on the "Flowers of St. Francis," he contented himself with my statement of a general nature that we Catholics have at our disposal a religious literature in the Croatian language broad enough to satisfy our needs in all the fields of priestly activity although today our priests must have recourse, especially in the scientific field, to certain religious works in different languages, mostly Latin and German. I also mentioned that in the Theology Faculty in Zagreb there was a special Chair for Oriental Theology and that much had been written in our various theological reviews on problems in this field.

2. The strained relations between Church and State.

To the question of Mr. E. as to whether I could tell him anything concerning the causes of the strained relations between Church and State, I replied approximately as follows:

"In questions concerning the relations between Church and State I am not competent to give any statement, for that is the exclusive province of the bishops, in particular of His Excellency the Archbishop, Dr. A. Stepinac, in his capacity as President of the Episcopal Conference. Even if I were competent to speak publicly on these relations I could not do so since I have not been informed of what has been done by either side for the purpose of resolving the so-called *modus vivendi* in Yugoslavia through an agreement so that these relations may be regulated in a friendly fashion."

Thereupon Mr. E. made a remark by which I could see his astonishment at my ignorance of these relations and my incompetence to give my opinion and judgment of them.

I then explained to him the role of a religious in the Catholic Church, comparing it to the role of a simple soldier in the army who knows many things but, not participating in the direction of the army, does not and need not know all that the high command does.

I concluded the conversation on this topic by suggesting that my interpreter ask for an audience for him with His Excellency the Archbishop since he alone could give the most precise information on these relations.

3. The pastoral letter.

There followed a conversation on the pastoral letter published after the Episcopal Conference which was held in Zagreb in September, 1945. He asked me the following question: "Have you read the pastoral letter?"

I replied to him, "No, because the week the pastoral letter was sent to the clergy I was ill and away from Zagreb, but I later learned its content from my brothers and other priests. I have wanted to read it carefully, but on account of my many tasks I have not yet been able to do so."

To the question: "Was the letter read to the faithful in your church and, if so, who read it?" I replied, "Yes, the letter was read to the faithful by the Father Superior, P. F. Majstorović."

To the question: "Was the letter read to an assembly of the brothers of this community?" I answered, "No, because all the brothers were present in the church at the time it was read to the faithful."

Mr. E. then asked this question: "Why did the bishops publish this pastoral letter?" I replied that only His Excellency the Archbishop was competent to give an answer to that question. When he began to dwell on what I had told him before concerning the opinion of priests with whom I had spoken, I told him that it was said that the reason for the letter was that the bishops, on the basis of the facts set forth in the letter, were convinced that the state authorities did not show a sincere desire for an agreement and friendly collaboration between the Church and State and that, any proposal for a *modus vivendi* for the Catholic Church in Yugoslavia was senseless.

Not satisfied with my answer, Mr. E. repeated the question regarding the political significance of the pastoral letter. I answered that my opinion was that His Excellency the Archbishop had not called the Episcopal Conference for the purpose of determining the bishops' own attitude or that of the faithful on the subject of the next elections, but rather in order to find, in accordance with the wishes of Marshal Tito, some way of establishing a *modus vivendi* between Church and State. I said that I did not think that the bishops wanted to make any appeal for good relations between Church and State.

At that point Mr. E. inquired why the bishops were not able to foresee the political significance of their pastoral letter.

While I was thinking of an answer to that question, he asked, "Why, during the period of the NDH, did the bishops not publish a similar letter and why did they not publicly condemn the Ustashi's crimes which were in direct contradiction to the principles of the Catholic Church?" I replied that under the NDH it was impossible to publish a common pastoral letter because the bishops were unable to get together for a conference. The occupation forces had tightly sealed off the sections of the old Yugoslavia from each other and would not permit Church dignitaries to travel from one region to another even in the conduct of business that was entirely religious.

I emphasized that our people knew very well how the Archbishop of Zagreb in his sermons, not only as Archbishop of Zagreb but also as the representative of the Catholic Church in the NDH and as the representative of the whole episcopate of the old Yugoslavia, had clearly and publicly condemned on many occasions the errors and crimes of the Germans as well as those of the Ustashi, and how in this way, as well as by his frequent oral and written messages addressed to the Poglavnik and other Ustashi officials, he had drawn upon himself the hatred and fury of the Ustashi. Then I got up, and as I walked toward the cabinet in which the archives of the Province are kept, I continued, "The Archbishop's attitude during the NDH is shown in the memorandum presented by the representatives of the clergy to Marshal Tito in defense of the Archbishop at the time when the Marshal called the clergy to a conference during his second visit to Zagreb. As I possess a copy of this memorandum, let me give it to you. "The copy of the memorandum which I handed to Mr. R. was taken by Comrade Tkalec, who put it in his pocket."

Since it had been possible in present-day Yugoslavia to publish and read such a pastoral letter specifically directed against the conduct of those in power, while under the NDH such a thing was impossible, Mr. E. was indignant at the statement of the bishops that the present regime was dictatorial and that there was no longer freedom of religion. In regard to this affirmation, he asked the question, "Why have the bishops published in present-day Yugoslavia this pastoral letter when under the NDH they would not have been able to do any such thing no matter how much they wanted to?"

I replied by exclaiming, "Very well, then, why have the present authorities not prevented it?"

"Precisely for the reason," said Mr. E., "that the present regime is not dictatorial as the bishops claim."

On this note the conversation on the pastoral letter was ended.

4. Ustashi priests and religious.

To the question: "Were there any Ustashi priests and religious?" I replied that there were, principally among the young priests.

To the question: "What was the attitude of the Church in this respect?" I answered "Negative." Instructions from Rome said that priests should keep away from them, that they should not join the Ustashi organizations, and that they must keep the rules of the Church according to which priests were forbidden, especially the ordinary clergy, to be members or officials of revolutionary movements.

To the question: "Were the priests and religious who were known to be Ustashi punished?" I answered, "Priests could not be punished merely for being Ustashi, for that was, during the time of the NDH, impossible, and because priests were not forbidden under pain of punishment to belong to the Ustashi movement. The Ustashi program emphasized its attachment to the Church and a desire to observe its principles in public life and for that reason the Church could not condemn the Ustashi movement as such nor forbid priests to enter its ranks. Rome kept aloof and hoped that priests would have nothing to do with it. For Rome foresaw that the Ustashi movement, because of its connections with Hitlerite Germany, would commit acts which would not be in accord with Catholic principles. The Ustashi priests took no notice of this advice from Rome and their Bishops because of a fatal error, a belief that the Ustashi movement would bring to Croatians independence and prosperity and to the Catholic Church freedom of action.

"Only those Ustashi priests could be punished who, as Ustashi, committed acts which could not be reconciled with their priestly vocation."

To the question: "Were there such priests or religious?" I replied, "Alas, there were such."

To the question: "Were at least such priests shown their responsibility and punished?" I replied in the affirmative. I cited in confirmation the cases of the ex-Franciscans: Tomislav Filipović-Majstorović, Justin Medić, and Hinko Prljić. I said, "In the daily press much has been written and is being written still on the crimes of Filipović-Majstorović. In May, 1942, he was expelled from the order for having, in February of the same year as Chaplain of a Ustashi unit at Banja-Luka, taken part in a punitive expedition against the Orthodox inhabitants of Drakulici, Motike, and Sargovac, three villages in the Franciscan parish of Petricevac and, according to the accusation, pointed out to the Ustashi which houses belonged to Orthodox persons and which to Catholics. Even before that, as vicar of the Petriceva parish, he had had violent quarrels with the Ustashi officials at Banja-Luka. When warnings bore no fruit he was transferred from Petriceva to Rama with the intention of making it impossible for him to engage in politics. However, he avoided this transfer by having himself named, through his Ustashi connections and against the wishes of his superiors, a Ustashi military chaplain and thus thwarted, with the aid of the military authorities, the plans of his religious superiors.

"Lately the crimes of Filipović are often written up in the newspapers and spoken of in meetings. These crimes, which he committed as a layman and as a soldier, as an apostate from the Franciscan Order and the Church, are presented in an intentionally misleading manner, as if he had committed them as a Franciscan to whom the ecclesiastical authorities had given permission to act as he pleased.

"The order, however, punished Filipović for his participation in the punitive expedition, not admitting his defense that he had done so because of a desire to protect the innocent Catholic inhabitants who had not taken part in the demolition of the coal mines, which demolition was the reason why the punitive expedition was ordered. The Franciscan Order punished him with the severest punishment at its command: expulsion.

"If Filipović, even after his punishment, did not make amends, nor attempt a reconciliation with the Church, but rather for revenge and out of hatred for his accusers completely left the Church and gave up his vocation as a priest and became a Ustashi combatant, and if as commandant of the concentration camp at Jasenovac he became a veritable murderer — one cannot hold the Church and the order responsible as has, unhappily, been done in a purposely misleading fashion in the press and at public meetings, particularly in the illustrated newspapers in which priests and nuns are represented as murderers and brigands. Such lies and such provocation will not contribute to the bettering of relations between the Church and the State. Such a reply to the pastoral letter is unjust and dishonest. If the state authorities believe the pastoral letter to be deliberately false and a lie, then, in my opinion, there is only one way to correct it. Show the responsibility of the signers of the pastoral letter and do not deride and unjustly accuse all priests and religious for misdeeds committed by those who have scorned the counsels and warnings of their ecclesiastic superiors."

Mr. E. noted down the explanation I had just made and asked me if there were any other similar cases in which priests had been shown their guilt for their nonpriestly Ustashi activities. I cited again the cases of the ex-Franciscan Medić, vicar to the Poglavnik, and the ex-Franciscan Prejić. These two priests were members of the Franciscan province of Hercegovina. After the disbanding of the Yugoslav army, in which they had performed their regular military service, they went over, on their own decisions, to the Ustashi militia. Not wishing to submit to the order of their superiors to return immediately to their province, they were suspended, with the threat that they would be expelled from the order if they did not submit. In order to escape punishment the first found a way, through his connections, of being kept on by the military vicar as a military chaplain and the second returned. Both, to avoid new quarrels with their superiors, left the order of their own free will.

With sadness in his voice and in the expression on his face, Mr. E.

then said that "Catholic priests, especially the young ones, are Germanophiles and bitter enemies of Russia. Several of them have publicly shown this in their sermons in which they have praised the Germans and the Ustashi. It is certain that the bishops knew of such expressions on the part of several priests and it is shocking, consequently, that they have not called them to account."

I answered him in approximately the following way. "The Catholic Church respects the political convictions of each one of its faithful and, therefore, also allows its priests to determine their own political views as they believe best in view of the justifiable desires and interests of their people. The Church may, in this question, give advice and it did in fact, under the NDH, advise priests as to their conduct, but the priests were not obliged to follow this advice and experience has shown that the Ustashi priests did not do so. It is not a question of Church dogma or discipline if priests are Russophile, Anglophile, or Germanophile. The principal role in this question belongs to other factors, in the first place to the education they received in school and to their daily experience. In the days of the old Yugoslavia the Serbs dominated the Croatians; at the behest of the Belgrade regime, the national individuality of the Croatian people was denied and outraged. That was felt especially by students, among whom we include the students at the Theology Faculty. And while some of them saw a solution of this situation in Communism and pro-Russianism, others looked for the solution in ultranationalism and pro-Germanism. A good part of the young Catholic clergy joined the latter out of the desire to help the Croatian people achieve its independence, prosperity, and happiness. Consequently the Church could not condemn this tendency, for it was not contrary to any dogmatic truth; it could only advise against it since it was convinced that it was a fatal error to believe that these tendencies could be realized through an alliance with Nazi Germany. For this reason the bishops could not charge with any crime the priests who made patriotic speeches pleading for the independence of the NDH since there was no question here of a religious error but only of a political one. Rome wished that we Croatians would be a bridge between the West and the East and recommended to us, especially to priests, to work with charity and patience for the reconciliation and harmony between Serbs and Croatians.

"I admit that there were some priests whom it was necessary to punish on account of their sermons and statements. So far as

I know their ecclesiastical superiors did this in the only ways that they could: with advice, reprimands, transfers, and suspensions. These means of moderating them were not, regularly, known to the public unless the priests involved spoke of them themselves to their own circles of friends to calm themselves or to console themselves by attacking their 'Anglophile' or 'Russophile' superiors."

I emphasized that if he wanted to form an exact judgment on this question it was necessary to take into account that nearly all the priests known as proponents of the Ustashi movement were in the army and as such were outside the jurisdiction of their regular ecclesiastical superiors.

To the question as what I thought of those priests who had been imprisoned or executed, I replied that among them were a great number who, in my opinion, had been judged unjustly or too severely. The ecclesiastical community could not condemn them inasmuch as it had not learned not only of what they were accused but also what they had actually done. I think that after the collapse of Germany and the NDH the people's authorities should have proceeded less harshly not only against priests but against all political opponents. Here the conversation was interrupted by Comrade Tkalec who said, "There has been too much softness in these proceedings."

5. On the Franciscans.

Mr. E. then continued the conversation, showing special interest in us Franciscans. Following the questions I gave him information on the number of Franciscans in Yugoslavia, on the administrative divisions in the various provinces, particulars on several monasteries and on the number of brothers in the province, on the activities of Franciscans, on our high schools. When I told him that the people's authorities had closed our high school at Varazdin, he asked me if I had asked permission to continue the work of that school. I said no, because at the moment it was impossible for us to run the school, on the one hand because the army did not seem disposed to evacuate the necessary buildings, and, on the other, we did not have the necessary means to repair the buildings and furnish them.

He asked me if there was any one from my province who was in prison or among the executed. I replied that up to that time the following fathers had been shot: Rikard Ribić, Beato Bukinec, and Sebastijan Santalab; and that the following were in prison: Fredo Gasman, David Pohl, Tito Thiel, Kamilo Kolb, and Casimir Herman.

In addition to these the following fathers had been taken prisoner and disappeared as military chaplains: Sabin Stefan, Hadrijan Hran, Petronije Pajtler, and Benko Ciga, who, it seems, have died as prisoners.

To the question asking if Fathers Rikard, Beato, and Sebastijan had been guilty, I replied that we were convinced that they were not guilty of the crimes for which they were accused, at least not to the extent maintained in the accusations, and that the military court had tried their case much too quickly.

He next became interested in how agrarian reforms were going in my province. I told him that they did not give me too much trouble.

Toward the end he asked me, "What is your opinion concerning the brothers at Siroki Brijeg?"

I answered: "Different from what is printed in the newspapers. I received of the brothers at Siroki Brijeg and of their tragic death the following information. . . ."

Here Mr. Tkalec got up, interrupted me, and said to Mr. E., "We must go, it is getting late. We have already stayed too long."

At these words Mr. E. got up and thanked me for a gracious welcome. We separated about 5:30 P.M. On leaving, Mr. Tkalec put down in his notebook only my religious name, Modesto. During the conversation no one took any notes.

On the basis of this report it can be seen that the words quoted as mine by Mr. Ilya Ehrenburg, in *Vjesnik*, November 16, 1945, are not accurate nor do they reflect my meaning.

Provincial of Franciscans
P. MODESTO MARTINČIĆ

Zagreb, November 30, 1945

DOCUMENT XLIX

*Letter From the Archbishop to the Military Vicar
Regarding the Ustasha Oath*

ZAGREB, October 15, 1943

Presidency of the Episcopal Conference
No. 148/BK — 43
Subject: Manner of taking oaths.

To the Very Reverend Military Vicar:

Since complaints have increased, during the past few days, that oaths are being taken in front of the Crucifix with a dagger and a revolver alongside it, thus profaning the sanctity and holiness of the Crucifix, the President of the Episcopal Conference informs you that it is forbidden to administer oaths in front of a dagger and revolver.

This statement must be communicated to all priests serving as military chaplains with the warning that in the future it is forbidden *sub poena suspensionis* to administer an oath if at the side of the Crucifix there is a dagger and a revolver.

We request that you take action as soon as possible and send us a reply on what has been done on this matter.

PRESIDENT OF THE EPISCOPAL CONFERENCE

Received by Vilim Cecelja in
person October 15, 1943
    Stepinac

III. THE "FORCED CONVERSIONS"

DOCUMENT L

Circular Letters Regarding Conversions to the Catholic Faith

No. 4104/1941

Recently a great many persons have come to the various parish offices seeking to enter the Catholic Church and also to validate their marriages which they had contracted either before the civil authorities or in another religion, and thus, according to canonical regulations, invalidly.

In connection with these facts the following is made known to the reverend clergy:

1. Reception into the Catholic Church may be permitted only to persons of whom it is sure that they desire to take this step sincerely out of a conviction in the truth of our holy faith and its necessity for the salvation of their souls. Religion is an interior matter of a free conscience and the decision in favor of a religion excludes all dishonest motives.

2. Persons who wish to be received in the Catholic Church must be instructed in the truths of the Catholic religion and ought, during the time of their instruction, to observe the commandments of God and the Church concerning prayer, attendance at divine services, hearing the word of God, abstinence, etc.; in this way these persons are introduced to the practical religious life of the Catholic Church.

3. Only persons may enter the Catholic Church who can live according to Catholic principles. Consequently, persons may be received into the Church only on condition that they promise that all children who may be born will be baptized and brought up in the Catholic Church, and that all children already born and still under their authority as parents will enter the Catholic Church.

4. To avoid excessive correspondence with the clergy regarding the conversion of persons asking to be received into the Catholic

Church or to have their marriages validated in the Church, it is necessary that the petitions presented be completely detailed, that is to say, that all essential facts be included so that these petitions may immediately be taken into consideration.

In particular it is necessary to state the petitioner's age, his profession, his marital state, single or married, and the reason for which he wants to be received into the Church. If a person has renounced the Church on account of his marriage, that is to say so that he could marry in another church and did, in fact, do so, he must indicate where and when he was married, if he still lives with his spouse or is separated, if he has children and how many, in what religion the children were baptized, to what religion they belong according to law, and finally if the impediments have disappeared which prevented the marriage from being contracted in the Catholic Church, and if the marriage may now be validated in the Catholic Church.

5. The clergy in charge of conversions is informed that in these delicate questions of the human soul they must proceed strictly according to the principles of the Catholic Church, careful of its dignity and good name, refusing to admit those who would like to be received into the Catholic Church without the correct motives, looking only to the protection of their material interests and their own selfish ends.

On the other hand, they must have above all a great deal of understanding for those who, during the past twenty years and under the direct or indirect pressure of the authorities — who at every step favored the non-Catholics, especially the Orthodox — in moments of weakness did violence to their best religious convictions and renounced Catholicism out of a desire for honors, a career, or other personal interests. Such persons merit still further special attention if it is proved that one of them, during the time of his apostasy, had relations with the Church and that, in so far as he was able, even brought up his children in the Catholic spirit. There are, alas, several thousand apostate souls of this sort with their families, and it is necessary to show them a special love and to do all that is possible to bring them back into the Church and thus to save them and their children.

Archiepiscopal Chancery

Katolički List, 1941
No. 7726

1. All those who are preparing to embrace Catholicism and who are residing within the territory of a parish must make a declaration of intent to the parish office of the same parish in which they are living; the latter must take into consideration during the time of their instruction both their instruction in general and their presence at Church services so that they may become accustomed to the practical performance of Catholic religious duties.

2. As to the work concerning conversion, that is to say instruction and parish work, the Archiepiscopal Church Court will appoint to each parish office as many catechists as they need. The catechists so appointed will put themselves at the disposal of the respective parish offices in this work as to time, place, and other circumstances.

3. In view of this, each parish office must organize a special administration and courses for small groups of ten or twenty aspirants so that the catechist may resolve the difficulties of each individual.

4. At the end of each course, those who wish to embrace Catholicism must pass, in the presence of their respective pastors or their assistants, an examination which must ascertain the good intentions, the adequate understanding, and the frequent attendance at church services of the aspirants during the time of their instruction.

5. Private instruction is also permitted, but the person preparing himself for conversion must notify in advance the parish office of the parish in which he lives; also he must pass a definitive examination before the pastor or his assistant.

6. All teachers who are in charge of these instructions must let themselves be guided in their work only by the desire to work for the glory of God, for the love of their neighbor, and the salvation of immortal souls; the dignity of our holy religion and the Church demand that we eliminate from this work any material profit under any guise whatever.

7. The teacher must, above all, know thoroughly all the rules which relate to reception into the Catholic Church. These rules are found in the "Katolički List" of this year, No. 23, under the title "Rules for reception into the Catholic Church."

8. The attention of the clergy is again called to the fact that any intervention on the subject of conversions with the Church Court is most rigorously forbidden, and that goes not only for the laity but for priests as well.

9. Instructions must not be begun before the aspirant has been certified by the authorities as having announced his conversion.

Circular Letter on Reception Into the Catholic Church

No. 2865/42

I feel obliged to warn all the clergy charged with the duties of spiritual fathers that, at the time of receiving those of other faiths into the Church, as well as in cases where petitions for conversion are presented, they must, above all, pay strict attention to the reasons for which these people wish to embrace the Catholic faith and the motives which lead to their pastors to recommend the petitions of those who intend to be converted.

These people must embrace the Catholic religion with a pure intention, without dishonest motives, with faith in the truth of Catholicism. That must be the first and essential motive for their conversion. If those who are preparing themselves to embrace Catholicism have any secondary motives they will not be an obstacle to conversion provided that they are not of a sinful character. But, if the spiritual father, despite all his instructions and good will, cannot in a sufficient measure create this first and most necessary preliminary condition for reception into the Church, then he must not present the petition for conversion, although he may still work with his aspirant if he finds it suitable and desirable.

The following are permissible motives for leading spiritual guides to recommend petitions for conversion:

In contemplating the conduct of those who are preparing themselves to embrace the Catholic religion, at the time of their instruction and in conversation with them, in watching how they put Christianity into practice according to the principles of the Catholic religion, the spiritual fathers must make sure that their conversion is sincere and that there exists a moral guarantee that those who aspire to conversion will remain practicing Catholics. It is essential, moreover, that the aspirants show in everything at least good will. If that does not exist, and despite all his efforts he cannot obtain it, the spiritual father may not recommend the petition, and consequently he will not send it in, although he may continue to work with the aspirant if he finds it suitable and necessary.

There is no doubt that the spiritual father may make mistakes despite all his attention. Then the fault will not be his but the aspirant's who has abused the charity of the priest and has scorned the Divine Grace which was offered him.

ALOYSIUS
Archbishop

Zagreb, March 2, 1942

DOCUMENT LI

Rules for Reception Into the Catholic Church
Supplement to Katolički List, *No. 23*

ZAGREB, June 11, 1941

At the time of the conversion of persons who wish to enter into the Church, whether to return to it after they have renounced it or whether to enter it for the first time, the pastors must take into account the different laws, rules, and regulations which must be applied. Such laws and regulations also exist relative to the validation of marriages in the Catholic Church. So that these regulations may be presented to the pastors as well in their relationship with persons interested in conversion as in the presentation of their petitions to the Ordinariate, we give here the most important of them.

1. Who May Be Received Into the Catholic Church?

   a) He who is instructed in all the principal truths of the Catholic faith.
   b) He who has a right intention for entering into the Catholic Church.
   c) He who can live according to the principles of the Catholic Church.
   d) He who has received the permission of his Ordinary to enter.

Concerning conditions under (*a*) and (*b*), there are questions in the Manual of the Roman Ritual, p. 16 ff.

Relative to the affirmation under (*c*), it must be pointed out that he may not be received into the Catholic Church who is living in a marriage not capable of being validated by the Church. That is why such persons, if they do not wish to leave their spouses, may not be received into the Church. There exists in relation to this positive regulation of the Holy See, which answered negatively to the question: *"num ob bonum prolis minister catholicus hujusmodi apostatam a fide* (that is to say, an apostate whose apostasy was caused by a woman) *quia a comparte separari reunit, recipere possit, saltem pro foro civili declarando nude et pure ad normam legis se ipsum recipere"* (Congregation of the Holy Office, January 5, 1927, Prot. No. 1067/1925). Only in particular special cases may the Holy See permit this. Consequently the requests for entrance into the Church *pro foro civili* need not even be sent to the ecclesiastical authorities, for they cannot receive a favorable reply. This decision applies only to those who have renounced the Church on account of their marriage, not to all apostates. For exactly this reason a request has been sent to the Holy See in this matter so that the reception *pro foro civili* may be granted to the Ordinary. The eventual favorable decision will be communicated to the clergy.

As to the point under (*d*), relative to the taxation of requests for conversion, the explanation of the President of the Episcopal Conference, No. 115/BK, is always in force. Here is its import:

"At the time of a change in religion, one pays for the customary application according to protocol, in view of reception into the Church, 20 dinars, the ecclesiastical tax in accordance with Regulation No. 44, and that as many times as one has changed religions and as many times as there are persons wishing to be converted."

Statement 182/BK — 1939, No. 11, by which it was explained that at the time of the conversion of an entire family only one tax had to be paid in accordance with Regulation No. 44, is no longer in force.

Naturally, in a case where it is a question of persons of known poverty, one can forgive them the tax in conformity with the explanation in No. 69/BK — 1939, No. 1, first part, (*c*) and (*d*). Cf. "The Official Messenger of the Archdiocese of Zagreb," Year 26, No. 1, February 10, 1939, p. 7.

2. The Validity of Marriages Contracted Outside the Church. Persons who wish to enter into the Catholic Church and who are living in illicit relations must have their marriages validated if it is possible. In this respect the question must be answered: "What is the validity of marriages concluded outside the Church?"

a) A marriage contracted by Catholics outside the Church is invalid. According to canons 1094 and 1099, a person baptized in the Catholic Church or having at any time belonged to the Catholic Church may contract a valid marriage only in the Catholic Church and before a Catholic priest. If, then, a Catholic, not being an apostate and being a free agent, concludes with his fiancée a marriage outside the Church, that marriage is invalid.

This regulation has been in force since the new Ecclesiastical

Code of May 19, 1918, for up until then, on the territories of Croatia and Slovenia, mixed marriages which were concluded outside the Catholic Church were considered invalid. (Mixed marriages contracted after that date in Croatia and Slovenia in a non-Catholic church are invalid, but, according to the decision of the Holy Office of July 13, 1921, all marriages concluded up to the time of the proclamation of this decision, that is to say marriages up to the time of August 18, 1921, inclusive in the Diocese of Zagreb, up to August 31 in the Diocese of Senj, were valid from the beginning. Cf. The Synod, 286.) Today, consequently, all marriages that a Catholic does not contract before a competent Catholic priest are invalid except in cases of danger of death or of a very great difficulty in obtaining the pastor of the place where the marriage is to take place. (Cf. The Synod, 202.)

b) A marriage concluded between non-Christians is valid if there is no impediment of the natural law to oppose it.

If persons who have not been Christian contract a marriage, the natural law is the only means by which such a marriage may be judged valid, for the Church does not bind non-Christians by its regulations. If, then, non-Christians contract a marriage it is not to be judged according to the regulations of their own religion but rather according to the natural law. That is absolutely evident for the following reasons: Marriage is a contract between persons, elevated by Christ to the dignity of a sacrament. The prescription of certain conditions for the contract of marriage may be made only by the authority to which Christ gave the right and duty of administering and regulating the sacraments. This institution is the Church of Christ which is only, as is evident from dogma, the Catholic Church. That is why only the Catholic Church may impose conditions on the marriage contract, for it alone is the Church of Christ and partakes of the plenitude of power which Christ has given to His Church. Since religious communities outside the Church have no divine right they may not impose any conditions on the validity of a marriage contract between persons who consider themselves members of that community.

Non-Catholic Christians are bound, it is true, by the canonical regulations on marriage, but they are explicitly exempt from the obligation of the canonical form of marriage, that is to say from being married in the Catholic Church.

These practical conclusions follow from that:

a) A marriage concluded between two free Orthodox persons either in the Orthodox church or outside the Orthodox church, even a civil marriage, is valid. The same thing is true for all other non-Catholic Christians.

b) A marriage concluded between two free non-Christian persons either in their temples and according to the laws of their religion or outside their temples in a civil marriage is valid.

c) A marriage concluded between a free non-Catholic person and a non-Christian person is valid whether it be concluded in a non-Catholic Church, in a temple, or in a civil manner.

The Church considers all the marriages enumerated above to be valid if they have been concluded without any impediment of the natural law being present. (Such an impediment is, for example, impotency or a matrimonial tie already existing with another person.) This also for Christian marriages if they have also been concluded without any impediment of canon law, for example, the impediment of consanguinity, of public morality, etc.

If, then, nonbaptized persons who have never been Catholic are converted to the Catholic Church, having formerly contracted a marriage to which there was no impediment in the natural law, their marriage need not be validated in the Catholic Church, for it is already valid. This marriage undergoes only one change, it becomes a sacrament at the moment the converts are baptized.

In speaking of the validity of these marriages contracted by non-Catholics, we naturally mean to speak only of this, that these marriages are valid before God and before the Church, but not at all that they are always valid as well before any civil authority, for the state may impose on the marriage contract its own conditions and recognize on its territory only marriages fulfilling these conditions. Thus, for example, in the juridical district of Croatia and Slovenia, in the time of the old Yugoslavia, it was impossible to contract a civil marriage valid in those districts, while civil marriage was possible in, for example, Medjumurje and Vojovdine.

3. Marriages Which Can and Which Must Be Validated in the Catholic Church.

From what has been said, it is evident which marriages must and which marriages can be validated in the Catholic Church if their contractors enter into the Catholic Church.

a) Only an invalid marriage contracted between two free persons, that is to say between persons who at the time of contracting the marriage were not bound by a valid marriage, may be validated in the Catholic Church. For that reason one can, for example, validate a marriage contracted in the Orthodox church between a free Catholic and a free Orthodox. Similarly one can validate a marriage contracted in the Orthodox church by a free Catholic and a divorced Orthodox person who had concluded his or her first marriage in the Orthodox church with a Catholic. This latter person is free because the Catholic could conclude a valid marriage only in the Catholic Church. One cannot validate a marriage contracted by a free Catholic in the Orthodox church with an Orthodox divorcee whose first husband or wife was Orthodox and who is still alive. The reason for that is in the theory that if two free Orthodox persons contract marriage their marriage is valid and hence indissoluble. The fact that the Orthodox church has perhaps annulled the marriage or granted a divorce changes nothing. For the Orthodox church (just as other Christian sects) has no right to impose its own conditions on the marriage contract and, since a marriage consummated between Christians is absolutely indissoluble, consequently the Orthodox church, even if it has some rights and some authority over its marriages, does not have the right or the power to dissolve such a marriage. Even if an Orthodox person, having contracted in so far as he was free a marriage with another free Orthodox person, obtains a divorce in his own church, he cannot be considered free and he cannot, during the life of his wife, contract any other marriage valid before God.

What we have just said concerning the contracting of a marriage between a free Catholic and an Orthodox is, naturally, valid for all other marriages contracted by Catholics with non-Catholics in general.

b) It is necessary to validate in the Catholic Church a marriage between two persons who were already Catholic and who contracted their marriage in a non-Catholic Church. Such a marriage is not valid for, as we have already said, a Catholic can contract a valid marriage only in a Catholic Church. And such a marriage must be validated, for the couple cannot be received into the Catholic Church if their matrimonial relations are not governed in such a fashion that they may live according to the principles of the Church.

If, then, certain persons wish to enter into the Catholic Church who have already contracted a marriage outside the Church, it is necessary to examine the marriage carefully to see if it is valid and then to see if it can be validated in the Catholic Church. In an application for admission into the Catholic Church all these circumstances must be cited, for on them depends the applicant's reception into the Church or his refusal.

c) As to the taxation of applications for validations, the following regulations are in force:

1) If it is a question of the validation of a marriage (either a simple validation or a validation *in radice*) there must be attached to the application a certificate on the amount of the direct annual tax of the applicant (the direct tax is also the tax paid by state officials and other employees on their incomes). According to the amount of that tax (No. 11 of Section 10 of the Tax Code) the application must be immediately stamped with the required stamps. If an application is not properly stamped it will be returned for proper stamping.

2) If at the same time a dispensation from the banns is requested, the application must be stamped with 60 dinars (No. 45 of the Tax Code) and with the tax of the Chancery, that is to say 20 dinars for each bann.

4. Condition for the Reception of Couples Living in an Invalid Marriage.

a) If one or both parties who cannot validate their marriage wish to enter into the Catholic Church, then, as has already been said, they can be received into the Church only if they are willing to separate. According to regulations, in such a case the person who enters into the Church is obliged to request the annulment of his marriage (a statement of annulment).

b) If the couple may validate their marriage, then the party having, perhaps, been formerly Catholic must be converted to the Church, while the party non-Catholic from birth may remain so, that is to say non-Catholic. But in such a case it is necessary that all children born up to that time, and who according to law are able, be inscribed by the Church (converted). As for other children, they must promise that in so far as possible they themselves will endeavor to enter into the Catholic Church. It is also necessary that the parties sign a contract on the Catholic education of their children and give the other prescribed guarantees.

5. Procedure at the Time of Reception Into the Catholic Church.

I. Civil regulations.

When the party has been well instructed and when he shows a true desire to enter into the Catholic Church, he must satisfy the regulations of the civil law on conversions. These regulations demand no more than that the person wishing to be converted announce his departure from his former religion to a competent minister of that religion, but it suffices that he declare his intention in writing to the authorities of first instance (in towns to the communal authorities). The authorities will then deliver an attestation of that document. For minors a declaration of their parents before the above authorities suffices and permission from the tutorial authorities is no longer necessary.

II. Reception of non-Christians on the part of the Church.

Receptions into the Church of non-Christian persons is performed through the conferring of holy baptism. The form for the baptism of adults is found in the Roman Ritual, p. 23 ff. (Zagreb, 1929).

The sacrament of baptism washes away all sins and remits all punishments. It is the sacrament of a birth into a new supernatural life. That is why at the time of baptism no absolution is given. In the case of certain ecclesiastical authorities, with a conditional baptism. In such a case it is also necessary to give conditional absolution.

All baptisms of such converts should be noted down in the record of converts and in the records of baptisms, but without a number.

III. Reception by the Church of Heretics and Schismatics.

The rite for reception is found in the Manual of the Roman Ritual, p. 161 ff. (Zagreb).

After his profession of faith, which is made in front of two witnesses and is accompanied by a renunciation of his former religion by oath, the convert is absolved from excommunication (p. 174).

Relative to the punishment of excommunication the following remarks must be made:

1) All apostates, heretics, and schismatics incur the punishment of excommunication (can. 2314, No. 1), men after fourteen years, women after twelve years (can. 2230 in connection with can. 88, No. 2). If, then, such persons re-enter the Church before the twelfth or fourteenth year, it is not necessary to absolve them from excommunication. That censure is reserved in a special manner to the Holy See. But if this crime is public, the Ordinary has the power to give absolution for it and to delegate another person for such an absolution, as is done ordinarily.

2) If a returning heretic has been a Catholic, and if he has contracted a marriage in a non-Catholic church, he has also incurred

the excommunication reserved to the Ordinary (can. 2319, No. 1). He who remains a Catholic but who has married in a non-Catholic church also, naturally, incurs this excommunication. But it must be noted here that according to Catholic doctrine this excommunication is not incurred by him who contracts a civil marriage.

3) If an apostate Catholic has not only contracted a schismatic marriage but if he has also, explicitly or tacitly, made a contract that he would have his children educated in a non-Catholic religion, he also incurs the excommunication reserved to the Ordinary (can. 2319, No. 2).

4) This excommunication is also incurred by him who has his children baptized in a non-Catholic church (can. 2319, No. 3).

5) Those who educate their children or have them educated in a non-Catholic religion, similarly incur this excommunication (can. 2319, No. 1, No. 4).

In the written application for the reception of an apostate in the validation of his marriage all these censures must be mentioned if, by chance, the applicant has incurred them.

IV. How are these censures absolved?

The priest who received from the Ordinary the power to give absolution to converts must proceed as follows:

1) If the convert has incurred only the censure for apostasy, heresy, or schism, the authorized priest will absolve him before confession *pro foro externo,* according to the formula in the Manual, p. 174. After that no priest whatsoever can absolve him from the sin of apostasy or heresy.

2) If the convert has incurred censures not only for apostasy but also for contracting a marriage in a non-Catholic church and for having had his children baptized and brought up in a non-Catholic religion, the authorized priest will absolve all these censures together according to the formula cited above.

3) Also in a case where the convert has not renounced the Faith, but only incurred censure for having married in a non-Catholic church, then having had his children baptized and brought up in a non-Catholic religion, the authorized priest will absolve him from these censures before confession *in foro externo.* If this sin and transgression was not known in the locality where the conversion takes place, it will suffice to give absolution *in foro interno* by the formula ordinarily used for the absolution of sins in the sacrament of penance.

4) At the time of the absolution of excommunication *in foro externo*

the priest must impose on the convert a serious work of penance (cf. the Manual, p. 177). Such penance must naturally be prescribed as well for those who are under censure from which they are absolved *in foro interno*.

V. Reception into the Catholic Church must be noted in the record of conversions and notice of it given to the civil authorities.

The return of apostates and the conversion of other non-Catholics must be inscribed in the record of conversions.

As to notifying of this conversion the pastor of the Christian or non-Christian church to which the convert formerly belonged, some persons are of the opinion that by the most recent ruling of the Ministry for Religion and Public Instruction of the NDH, regulation No. 17 of the Inter-confessional Law of 1906, has been abolished. According to that paragraph it was necessary for the administrative authorities to inform the pastor of the convert so that he could make a note of this new circumstance in the baptismal record as well as the records of births. However, it can be seen clearly from the text of the new law that the law modifies only the regulations on the manner of conversions and not the regulations on the registration of an accomplished conversion. For that reason, in order to avoid possible abuses and so that converted persons may not make use of double documents, the Ordinariate of the Archdiocese prescribes for the clergy in charge of administering these conversions that they shall, in the future, notify, through the administrative authorities, the proper parish offices of the conversions. It must be again emphasized that the Ordinary will demand from the above-mentioned priest a pragmatic ruling in this matter.

If at the time of conversion the validation of a marriage is necessary, this will be done in the ordinary form, that is to say by the renewal of the matrimonial vows before the authorized priest and before two witnesses. A marriage validated in this manner must be registered in the record of marriages, without number, but in the margin the date of the marriage contracted by the couple in a non-Catholic church must be noted. In special cases it may also be a question of a validation *in radice*, namely in a case in which one cannot obtain the necessary guarantees or if one of the couple is opposed to a simple validation of the marriage.

6. Notifying the Ordinariate of Reception Into the Catholic Church.

In giving general instructions on the reception of converts into the Church under No. 4104/1941 on May 8 of this year, the Chancery of the Ordinariate also gave the following important information:

Priests in charge of these delicate matters of the human soul (that is to say of conversions) are notified that they must hold themselves strictly to the regulations of the Catholic Church, defending its dignity and reputation, and that they must refuse to admit those who wish to enter into the Church without right motives, seeking only in the Church the protection of their material interests and egoistic intentions.

On the other hand, it is necessary to have a great deal of understanding, especially for those who have been for the past twenty years under the direct or indirect pressure of the authorities — who always favored those of other religions, above all the Orthodox — and who in a moment of weakness did violence to their best religious convictions and renounced Catholicism on account of their reputations, careers, or other personal interests. These persons are the more worthy of attention if it can be proved that even during the time of their apostasy they maintained their ties with the Catholic Church and perhaps as well, in so far as possible, raised their children in a Catholic spirit. There are, unhappily, several thousand of such apostate souls along with their families, and for them one must have a special charity and do all that is possible to bring them back into the Catholic Church and thus save their souls and those of their children.

7. Application for Conversions Addressed to the Ecclesiastical Authorities.

We draw attention, finally, to the very important warning of the Archiepiscopal Ordinariate of Zagreb on the composition of applications by which the pastors request the reception of a certain person into the bosom of the Church, and the validation of his marriage as well. In No. 6 of the notice of May 8, already cited, one reads the following:

"So that there may not be needless correspondence with the pastors who request the reception of a certain person into the bosom of the Catholic Church and the validation of his marriage it is necessary that the applications presented be complete, that is to say that all essential circumstances be mentioned in them so that they may be immediately examined.

"It is especially important to point out the age of the person, his profession, if he is free or tied by a marriage bond, and why he wishes to be received into the Catholic Church. If a person has renounced the Catholic Church because of his marriage, that is to say in order to be married in another church, and if in fact he was married there, it is necessary to state when and where he contracted the marriage, if he is still married or if he has been divorced, if he has any children and if so how many, in what church the children were baptized, to what religion the children now belong according to law, and, finally, if the impediment because of which the marriage in question could not be contracted in the Catholic Church has disappeared, and if the marriage may be validated in the Catholic Church."

In relation to the administration, this notification is very important, and binding on the clergy if not complied with, the applications must be returned. With such methods the clergy would charge itself and the administration of the diocese with needless work and the person desiring to be converted cannot have a prompt and favorable decision on his application.

Dr. Stj. Bakšić

DOCUMENT LII

Letter to Pavelić Regarding the Decisions of the Bishops' Conference on Conversions

Poglavnik:

The Croatian Catholic Episcopate, assembled in annual plenary conference on November 17 and 18, 1941, approved the following decisions concerning the conversions of Orthodox persons to the Catholic religion:

1. The Conference considers it a *dogmatic principle* that the solution of all questions pertaining to the conversion of Orthodox persons to the Catholic religion is *exclusively* within the province of the hierarchy of the Catholic Church, which alone, according to Divine Law and canonical regulations, has the right to lay down rules and regulations; and, as a result, all outside action on this matter is excluded.

2. For this reason no one, with the exception of the hierarchy of the Catholic Church, has the right to appoint "missionaries" to take charge of the conversions of Orthodox persons to the Catholic Church. Any missionary of this kind must receive his mission and the jurisdiction for his spiritual work from the Ordinary of the place where

he is active. It is, consequently, *contrary to dogma and to canonical regulations* that "missionaries" receive their mission, unknown to the Ordinary of the place where they work, from the commissioners of communes, representatives of the civil authority, Ustashi officials of the Religious Section of the Department of Reconstruction, or from any civil authority whatsoever.

3. Every "missionary" of this sort must in this work be dependent only to the Ordinary of the place where he works, either directly or else indirectly through the pastor of the parish in which he is active.

4. The Catholic Church can recognize as valid only those conversions which have been or will be carried out according to these *dogmatic principles.*

5. The civil authority may not "annul" conversions once they have been realized not only according to the laws of the Church, but also according to those of the State.

6. The Croatian Catholic Episcopate, elected for this purpose from among the members of a committee of three persons who are: the President of the Episcopal Conference; Bishop of Senj, Monsignor Dr. Victor Burić; and the Apostolic Administrator of the Diocese of Krijevci, Dr. Janko Šimrak. This committee will discuss and decide all questions arising in relation to the conversion of Orthodox persons to the Catholic religion. *This committee will function in agreement with the Minister of Justice and Religion in those matters which have to do with the civil regulations concerning conversions.*

7. The Croatian Catholic Episcopate has chosen the following as the executive committee in matters concerning the conversions of the Orthodox to the Catholic religion, Dr. Augustin Juretić, consultant of the Episcopal Conference; Dr. Janko Kalaj, professor of religion in the secondary schools and professor in the Theology Faculty; Nikola Bura, Director of the Chancery of the Archdiocese; and Dr. Krunoslav Draganović, professor on the Faculty of Catholic Theology. This committee will provide guidance in all matters relating to the question of conversions from the Orthodox to the Catholic religion, under the supervision of the Bishops' Committee on Conversions.

8. Only those may be received into the Catholic Church who are converted *without any constraint, completely free, led by an interior conviction of the truth of the Catholic faith,* and who have entirely fulfilled the ecclesiastical regulations.

9. As to the rite to be followed in conversions, the Croatian Cath-

olic Episcopate takes for its own the regulations of the Sacred Congregation for the Oriental Church of July 17, 1941, Prot. No. 216/36, addressed to the President of the Episcopal Conference and which reads as follows in the Croatian translation:

"The Sacred Congregation for the Oriental Church draws the attention of Your Excellency to the fact that the Roman Catholic pastors of Croatia ought to be requested by the Most Reverend Bishop, in cases of the conversions of non-Catholics, when it is a question of persons who were formerly adherents of the Oriental rite of the Catholic Church but who left the Catholic Church because of the threats and pressures of the Orthodox Church, that they *do not obstruct the natural return of these persons to the Oriental rite.* If Your Excellency will present this necessary rule to his venerable brothers, the Bishops of Croatia, they will merit recognition through this valuable contribution to a progressive expansion of Catholicism in a region where so many hopes are nourished for the conversion of non-Catholics. I renew to Your Excellency the assurance of my greatest respect.

> Your devoted brother,
> Eugene Tisserant
> *Ant. Arata, Archbishop of Sardis,*
> *assessor*"

The Croatian Catholic Episcopate accepts the regulation of the Holy Apostolic See of October 18, 1941, in the following terms: *"In all places where there are already parishes of the Greek-Catholic rite, let the non-Catholics who wish to be converted be directed to those parishes.* It is recognized that if the non-Catholics do not wish or are not able to keep their Oriental rite, they may choose the Latin rite."

The Croatian Catholic hierarchy accepts these two regulations inasmuch as they are, in their broad outlines, in accord with the directives of the circular letter of the Government of the NDH of July 30, 1941, No. 46468/1941, namely:

a) That it is necessary to consider as a Greek-Catholic parish not only the region of the parish seat but also the whole of the territory already marked off by canon and civil regulations, consequently, not only the parish seats but also the subsidiary churches.

b) That it is not permitted to ignore conversions made in Greek-Catholic parishes since that is in opposition to canonical regulations and, moreover, these conversions have been made in complete accordance with the regulations of the civil authorities.

c) That all misunderstandings in these matters be presented to the Bishops' Committee for Conversions which will settle them.

d) That local authorities are forbidden to interfere in these questions. In the spiritual work of the Church no lay organization nor the Ustashi may interfere, for that could only harm the cause of morality.

10. The Bishops' Committee for Conversions will organize courses for priests who take charge of conversions to Catholicism. They will receive in these courses practical and theoretical instructions for their work.

11. It is necessary to create among the Orthodox inhabitants a psychological basis for conversion. Toward this end they shall not only be promised but actually be guaranteed all civil rights, especially personal freedom and the right to hold property. All proceedings contrary to law in regard to Orthodox persons shall be strictly forbidden and they shall be penalized as other citizens through due process of law. And, most important, all private actions in destroying the churches and chapels of the Orthodox or the stealing of their property should be severely punished.

POGLAVNIK:

These decisions have been determined by a great love and concern for the Croatian nation, for the NDH, and for the Catholic religion which is the religion of the great majority of the Croatian nation.

Only those *mistakes* are emphasized which obstruct the legitimate conversion of Orthodox persons and which will contribute to a successful policy.

We do not accuse the Government of the Independent State of Croatia of these mistakes. We do not intend to present these faults as if they were systematic, but rather as the acts of irresponsible officials who are not conscious of their great responsibilities and the consequences of their conduct.

We realize that these acts were a political reaction to the past twenty years and to the crimes of the Chetniks and communists who have committed so many outrages against our peaceful Croatian people.

We thank almighty God for the fact that through your efforts, Poglavnik, the situation is becoming more stable and the Croatian Catholic Hierarchy urges, not in a spirit of recrimination but as a guarantee in the future, that the activities of these irresponsible elements be eliminated, so that the effectiveness of legitimate conversions may be assured, and the efforts made be reasonable and realistic.

Let me cite, Poglavnik, the opinions of several distinguished members of the Croatian Catholic Hierarchy, opinions that were given to me in writing at the time of the last meeting of the Conference. His Excellency Monsignor Jazo Garić, Bishop of Banja Luka, on November 4, 1941, wrote as follows, "I do not know what I can say on the subject of the principal question to be discussed at this conference. Generally speaking, I am not an optimist. In many cases, not only of individuals but of entire villages, I think that there will be defections at the first opportunity. From now on the Chetniks and the communists will take revenge on those who have become converted to the Catholic religion. They will burn their houses, steal their cattle and other properties. And on the part of the Mohammedans, crimes of indescribable savagery have been committed on the poor Orthodox population. Called to account for this, they said in their defense that they did what they had been ordered to do. *Many of those who had already been converted to our religion* have died in the districts of Bihać and Cazin. *They were forced to be converted to Islam.* The only consoling thing among all this tragedy is that the priests conducted themselves very nobly in taking care of these poor people. They took no notice of threats. . . . Banja Luka has suffered, but Banja Luka has known moderation in comparison with the bestial cruelties committed in other places. The movement for conversion diminishes in places under the domination of the Chetniks and the communists, and these latter are attacking especially vigorously the territories of my diocese, except that of Livno. The pastors of many parishes have fled to a safer place. . . ."

The Bishop of Mostar, His Excellency Monsignor Aloysius Mišić, wrote on August 18, 1941, No. 968/41, among other things, "The circumstances in which we are living are lamentable in every way. It is necessary to admit and recognize this. There are difficulties for the state authorities, but there are also difficulties for the Church in connection with its divine mission and its work for immortal souls. A large part of the Orthodox faithful in the diocese of Mostar is favorably disposed toward conversion to the holy Catholic religion. The high state officials in Zagreb have on several occasions given to subordinate officials instructions on conversions from another religion. *As a matter of fact, according to general indications, these instructions are not of a sort to serve the general welfare of the*

Church or even that of the State. By the grace of God we have been given a chance today as never before to help the Croatian cause, to save the souls of innumerable men of good will, that is of the peaceful peasants living in the midst of Catholics! They know the Catholics and the Catholics know them. Conversion is acceptable and easy. *Unhappily the authorities by their extreme views are, without perhaps intending to, placing obstacles in the way of the Croatian and Catholic cause. The leaders are not guilty. But all kinds of people are interfering in this matter, youths without learning or experience; in place of intelligence and reason, there is force and violence. It is not surprising that evil consequences for the Croatian and Catholic causes have resulted.* . . . In many parishes of the Diocese of Mostar, for example, Duvno Polj, Stolac, Klepeci, Goranci, Gradac, etc., a number of honest peasants announced their intention of being converted to Catholicism. They went to holy Mass, they learned the Catholic catechism, had their children baptized, but then *the intruders gave their order.* While the neo-converts were at Church attending holy Mass, they seized them, the young and the old, men and women, and drove them before them like cattle . . . and soon sent them to eternity, *en masse.* That can serve neither the holy Catholic cause nor the Croatian cause. Everyone condemns such unreasonable acts and we have lost an excellent opportunity which could have furthered the best interests of the Croatian Catholic cause. We might have emerged into a majority in Bosnia and Hercegovina and instead of coveting favors from others be able to dispense them ourselves. I consider this a holy and worthy cause. In the interests of Croatia and the Church, I say to His Excellency that we must do all in our power to prevent these disastrous consequences, to show the way, and prepare for happier times for the Croatian and Catholic cause."

The same bishop wrote on November 7, 1941, No. 1253/41, as follows, "At one time it seemed that a large number of schismatics would be converted to the Catholic Church. However, those who have been *stožernik,* designated *logornik* (Ustashi officials) have abused their positions, exploited the worst instincts of the masses and the weakest side of human nature, with the result that a reign of terror has come to pass. And there is nowhere a remedy for it. Men are captured like animals. They are slaughtered, murdered; living men are thrown off cliffs. The under-prefect in Mostar, Mr. Bajić, a Mohammedan, has stated with the authoritative voice of his position — he should keep silent and not utter such statements —

that at Ljubinje, in a single day, 700 schismatics were thrown into their graves. From Mostar and from Capljina a train took six car-loads of mothers, young girls, and children ten years of age to the station at Šurmmaci. There they were made to get off the train, were led up to the mountains, and the mothers together with their children were thrown alive off steep precipices. In the parish of Klepci 700 schismatics from the surrounding villages were murdered. Must I continue this enumeration? In the town of Mostar itself they have been bound by the hundreds, taken in wagons outside the town, and there shot down like animals. We come finally to the deportation of the Serbs into Serbia. In tears, lamentations, and misery, they gradually disappeared. A delegation went to wait on Mussolini in Rome and we can readily imagine what they asked for. The result was a renewed Italian occupation of Hercegovina under military and civil authority in their hands. The schismatic churches came to life all of a sudden and the pastors of the Greek churches, coming out of hiding, showed themselves freely because the Italians were amiable and favorable to the Serbs. The Catholic Church does not countenance the commission of acts of violence. It condemns vio-lence and it condemned it as well on these occasions. But the transition from one extreme to another is significant. The new occupation au-thorities have suddenly become friendly toward the Serbs, severe toward the Catholics, and there have been imprisonments, even executions. The poor have paid the bill for this tyranny. It is not astonishing that in light of these events the conversion of Orthodox to Catholicism has been a complete failure. The ferocity and the savagery of certain individuals, the lack of understanding of the highest authorities have seriously damaged the welfare not only of religion but also that of the State. If the Lord had given to the authorities more understanding to handle the conversions to Catholi-cism with skill and intelligence with fewer clashes, and at a more appropriate time, the number of Catholics would have grown by at least 500,000 to 600,000.

The Archbishop of Vrhbosna, His Excellency Monsignor Dr. Ivan Šarić, wrote on November 15, 1941, No. 4107/41, "There is a tendency on the part of the civil authorities to seek the conversion of more Orthodox but, unhappily, they do not do what must be done. From many places we have received complaints that in sections where the highest positions are occupied by Moslems these officials are no carrying out the requests of the Orthodox who wish to be converted to the Catholic religion. In other places overly high taxes are imposed on religious conversions, taxes which these poor people cannot afford to pay. Thus, at Sarajevo, the district authorities demanded by way of a tax, 500 kunas, with the result that we have been obliged to petition the government in Zagreb and ask that this order be revoked. It is understandable that such acts on the part of the local authorities make great difficulties for the conversions." His Excellency the Archbishop speaks further on — of the propaganda of the Evangelical religion (the Protestants). Its representatives have said that the Orthodox ought not to be converted to Catholicism, that their own priests would return, and that, if they do change their religion, they should rather be converted to Protestantism.

His Excellency Pavao Butorac, Bishop of Kotor and Apostolic Administrator of the Diocese of Dubrovnik, wrote on November 4, 1941, No. 10/1941, "I realize only too well the importance of the subject on which we shall have to speak. From a recent order from the Ministry of the Interior it may be noted that in the highest circles a more precise understanding of the subject of conversions to the Catholic religion is beginning to prevail. Any use of force can have the most catastrophic effect on the reputation of the Catholic Church. It is necessary to consider all eventualities, even the possibility that the Serbs, through caprice, might decide to be converted *en masse* to Islam. Precisely for this reason I think it is necessary to choose with special care the missionaries who are to be sent among the Serbs and not to entrust this charge to priests or religious who are not prudent and in whose hands a revolver might better be placed than a crucifix."

Poglavnik!

From the statements of these four Croatian Bishops, as well as from comments made orally by other bishops at the conference itself, it may be clearly seen that *grave mistakes have been made* in connection with the conversions.

The source of these mistakes lies in the fact that work concerning these conversions has not been entrusted to *the authority to which alone, according to Divine Law and canonical regulations, it ought to have been entrusted; that is to say to the Croatian Catholic bishops who alone are called to give to this work for souls an apostolic character of holiness and charity, to direct this effort toward the well-*

being of the Holy Roman Catholic Church and the Croatian nation.
These conversions have been managed by men who frequently acted
as if the ecclesiastical authorities did not exist. Because of that,
mistake followed mistake.

In the first place they did not keep in mind the fact that the
question *of rites* in Croatia is *not a dead issue* or even a mere formality which one can easily forget while continuing to live in another
fashion. There are customs which do not date from yesterday but
from the first centuries of Christianity. They have lived in the souls
of men for more than 1600 years, they give form to piety and to
the whole of spiritual life and guide the emotions. In simple people
they have become a part of their spiritual life, often more so than
the truths of the faith themselves. For this reason the Sacred Congregation for the Oriental Church in its decision of July 17, 1941,
Prot. 216/36, "draws attention to the fact that it is necessary for
Roman Catholic pastors in Croatia to be advised by their bishops
*not to prevent the Orthodox from their natural return to the Oriental
rite in case of their conversion. . . ."*

This means that the psychological aspect of this problem is vital.
It is necessary above all to know the man whom we approach with
Catholic truth. It is necessary to know his past, his traditions, and
his feelings. It is particularly necessary to know the Orthodox religion,
its structure in the past across the centuries and at present. It does
not suffice to know only the dogmatic differences and to explain
them at the time of conversion, but it is also necessary to recognize
what effects these differences have had on the souls of the Orthodox.
It is indispensable to understand the Orthodox religion in its social,
political, and cultural aspects. Its errors have exerted a profound
influence, and communism has found nourishment and encouragement in the Orthodox religion. This schism was inspired by opposition
and this opposition through the centuries has produced bitterness
and hate; a hatred which has gnawed at souls and minds and whose
fruit has been negation, revolution, nihilism, and destruction. This is
demonstrated in Russian Bolshevism, and in the religious struggle
in Russia between the old traditions and the new trends.

We must not deceive ourselves with illusions. The Orthodox religion
has forged a type of man who cannot change his way of thinking
overnight, mechanically, as if he were a machine. It is precisely this
mechanical way of proceeding that has had disastrous consequences.
That was remarked at the time of the conversions in Poland. All

that was erected artificially, without a profound spiritual basis, fell in ruins at the first opportunity like a paper house. We have witnessed the experience in Spain, where disconcerting examples of conversions without conviction threatened Catholicism and the Spanish nation. This experience characterized the Latin Empire at Constantinople. This mechanical process carried with it a hate which concealed itself for a time, but at the propitious moment, burst into a flame of passion. This unfortunate method of building is fragile; on sand and not on rock, and when the storms and the winds come, nothing remains but ruins.

A second fundamental mistake in relation to the conversions is that local authorities and Ustashi officials frequently forbid in their own name, despite the NDH circular letter of July 30 of this year, any reception of Orthodox converts into the Greek-Catholic rite. What is even worse is that they forbid such conversions in regions where those who are Orthodox today were for several centuries united with the Catholic Church and were turned away from union and from the Croatian nation for a time by Serbian propaganda and force. It seems that these conversions have been forbidden because of certain apprehensions of a political nature which, however, have no foundation, for the Greek-Catholic clergy have shown their pro-Croatian sentiments over a period of three hundred years in the face of the most difficult circumstances. The work of this clergy has been crowned with success, as is attested in the vigor of Greek-Catholic intellectual life and the strength of the faith among the masses of peasants in the Žumberak and elsewhere. Cannot this Greek-Catholic clergy from the Diocese of Križevci accomplish the same thing with the same results in other regions in view of its experience and its three-century-old tradition? Instead of giving freedom of action to the Diocese of Križevci in conversions in the spirit of the circular letter of July 30, the Greek-Catholic priests were overwhelmed by threats as, for example, Alexander Vlasov of Disnik in the Garesnica district who was bringing about conversions in the territory of his parish, in complete accord under the regulations of the circular letter. He was told that he would be driven out of the country as an "undesirable" in spite of the fact that he was a citizen of the NDH. In other regions, as in Veliki Zdenci in the same district, conversions from the Orthodox to the Catholic religion according to the Greek-Catholic rite were simply "annulled" although they had been realized not only in conformity with ecclesiastical regulations but also with the regulations of the civil authority then in force, and, with the special permission of the Ministry of Justice and Religion. In still other places the president of the commune and the notary, as, for example, Dr. Jurija in Sokolovac near Koprivnica, published pamphlets for their subordinates against the "uniate religion" and the "uniate church." Indirectly they threatened anyone who dared to seek reception into the Catholic religion according to the Greek-Catholic rite. In still other regions, as for example at Križevci, during Holy Offices, the persons who had been converted according to the regulations of the civil and ecclesiastical authorities were taken from the church by force before the eyes of the faithful and sent off to a construction camp. Following the state directive for the restoration of the regions, the Greek-Catholic priests were sent notices — naturally without the knowledge of the Ordinariates of the respective places — in which they were threatened with punishment and in which the Greek-Catholics and the non-united Greeks were put on the same footing. In other cases, as that of the notary at Barensnica, it was stated that only those who had distinguished themselves in the fight against the Croatian nation entered the Greek-Catholic Church, when the contrary was true, for these were the converts who signed the message sent to the Poglavnik in which they expressed their sincere loyalty to the NDH and the Chief of State and their gratitude for admission to the community of the Croat nation to which they had always belonged but from which they had been torn for a time by a policy of violence. In the regions of Prnjavoo and Bosnia, the Chetniks and the communists have driven, with one exception, all the Greek-Catholic priests out of their parishes and have robbed their houses. Consequently the Chetniks, who on the one hand ought to be the converts of the Greek-Catholic rite, are its worst enemies! It is necessary to state that the above-mentioned Dr. Ante Jurina, president of the commune and notary at Sokolovac, has within the past few days published a decree in which he again speaks of a "uniate religion" which does not exist in the NDH. This is the name which has served the Yugoslavs and Serbs who mocked Catholics of the Greek-Catholic rite and sought to separate them from Catholicism and Croatia. In order that you may better judge the acts of Dr. A. Jurina, a copy of this decree is enclosed along with a copy of his order to the village leaders against the "uniate church and religion."

Poglavnik!

No one can deny that these terrible acts of violence and cruelty have been taking place, for you yourself, Poglavnik, have publicly condemned those which the Ustashi have committed and you have ordered executions because of their crimes. Your effort to insure the reign of justice and order in the country merits applause.

The Croat nation has been proud of its thousand year old culture and its Christian tradition. That is why we wait for it to show in practice, now that it has achieved its freedom, a greater nobility and humanity than that displayed by its former rulers.

The Church condemns all crimes and outbursts of passion on the part of irresponsible elements and inexperienced youths and demands full respect for the human personality without regard to sex, religion, nationality, or race, for all men are the children of God and Christ died for all, *qui vult omnes homines salvos fieri.*

We are sure, Poglavnik, that you hold the same position and that you will do all in your power to restrain the violence of certain individuals and to allow only the rule of responsible authority in the country. If the contrary were true all work for the conversion of schismatics would be illusory.

Please accept, Poglavnik, the assurance of my sincere respect.

THE ARCHBISHOP, *President of the*
Episcopal Conference

Zagreb, November 20, 1941

DOCUMENT LIII

Correspondence Regarding Conversions of the Orthodox
in the Požega District

District Authority of Požega
No. Official Copy, 1942
Subject: Conversion of the Orthodox People
to the Roman Catholic Religion.
(in the prefect's handwriting)

NOVA GRADIŠKA

With reference to his oral statement of the 12th of the current month, I inform the Archbishop of the following:

By reason of absolutely accurate information, and personal observation, it appears that several of the priests here do not show sufficient interest in the movement for the conversion of the people from the Orthodox to the Roman Catholic religion. Without doubt, all the pastors here, as well as their assistants, are very busy with their regular duties as priests, but that ought not to be a hindrance — in the opinion of the undersigned — to sacrificing a little time in the interests of the converts or to instructing them. It is my opinion that each priest, as soon as he has received the decision of the authorities that they will permit the conversion of certain persons or of whole villages, ought immediately, on his own initiative, to establish contact with the people, without waiting for special petitions or delegations, in order to associate himself personally, as soon as possible, with those who are preparing themselves for conversion; and that he ought to encourage them and strengthen them in their decision and at the same time refute the propaganda of the opponents of conversion who in such cases ordinarily become most powerful and dangerous, because at that moment — as we have been shown by our experience up to the present — intimidation and threats reach their peak.

Too long a time passes from the moment a decision is made to allow conversions to the initiating of religious instructions, and the opponents of conversion are the only ones to profit by it while our spiritual leaders have remained waiting, arms folded, "for the Orthodox to agree with them and send their carriages for them." This conduct can no longer be excused because of overwork. It shows that they are not taking this obligation seriously, which is scandalous, because the conversions are a patriotic duty for every priest. What is even more serious is when a priest, at his first meeting with the "converts," declares frankly that the Church is not at all happy about their conversion.

For this reason it would be useful to advise the clergy, by some adequate means, to undertake this work with devotion and tact so that progress may be made in this district as soon as possible and with greater success.

I emphasize especially that the priests in this district, on account of their national Hungarian feelings, as the pastor at Rusevo and the chaplain at Kutjevo, are not suitable persons for work of this kind, because they are lacking a spirit of nationalism. The apathy with which they work leaves a very disagreeable impression on

Catholics as well as on those who are preparing for conversion. For this reason it is indispensable that others come to replace them and that they be sent somewhere where they will not be required to fulfill this sort of mission.

As all the members of the former (Orthodox) parish of Gradiška have already been converted, it will be necessary to establish a (Roman Catholic) parish at Gradiška and to send them a priest as soon as possible, which they want and ask for themselves because the pastor of Kutjevo, whose parish is very large, is not able to perform successfully the duties of spiritual guide at Gradiška and its neighborhood. There is the question of the Church there, which must be repaired or torn down and a new one built; but all that can be done only after the arrival of a pastor so that the work for converts in a Catholic and Croatian spirit may proceed.

For the fatherland!
CHIEF DISTRICT OFFICER
Signature

L. S.

NOVA GRADIŠKA, January 28, 1942

Independent State of Croatia
No. secret 253 — 1942
Subject: Conversion of Orthodox persons
        to the Roman Catholic religion — remarks.

To the Archiepiscopal Ordinariate of Zagreb:

I have the honor of enclosing the proposal of the chief officer of the Požega district with a request that it be examined and that an adequate system to administer it be set up in the proper department.

No difficulties have been raised on the part of the state authorities in any justifiable case of religious conversions, but it is requested that instructions and warnings be given anew so that the conduct of the priests may in the circumstances be beyond criticism.

I have the honor to add that the presence of the pastor of Rusevo and the chaplain at Kutjevo at their posts is undesirable for national reasons.

For the fatherland!
PREFECT
(*Illegible signature.*)

L. S.

NOVA GRADIŠKA

The Archiepiscopal Church Court of Zagreb
No. 1911/42

The Archiepiscopal Church Court has the honor of replying to your letter of January 28, 1942, No. 253, as follows:

The Church authorities, on the subject of conversions from the Orthodox and other religions, act according to the laws and rules of the Church. The Church forces no one to embrace the Catholic religion, but when someone comes to the representatives of the Church, they instruct him with the greatest zeal, and if he shows that he is embracing the Catholic religion with good intentions, they welcome him. According to the report of the chief officer of the Pozega district it is understood that the Orthodox people of the Rusevo parish have asked for permission to be admitted into the Catholic religion, but it is not shown that they have also declared such an intention before the parish office which it is also necessary to do. The pastor may not go into the villages to instruct these people before the "converts" have done this because then it would seem as if the representatives of the Catholic Church were forcing these people to be converted which the Catholic Church must not do. It is not shown in the letter from the district officer that the converts have declared their intentions to the representatives of the Church or that the latter do not wish to do their duty. If this were so, this Archiepiscopal Church Court would take most energetic measures against those priests. However, this matter will be investigated and if it is proved that there is some guilt on the part of the priests mentioned, they will be ordered recalled and transferred.

This Archiepiscopal Church Court up to now has never heard any criticism of the pastor of Rusevo, who is of Hungarian birth, or of the chaplain at Kutjevo, both zealous priests. Rusevo is a poor parish, and the two priests barely manage to perform their regular duties, despite the best will, and they cannot be as active regarding the conversions as the civil authorities apparently wish. The pastor of Rusevo, as soon as he learned that there was a large number of persons preparing to embrace the Catholic religion, asked that he be sent two priests as assistants, or in so far as possible, even more. This was done and on Saturday, February 7, two priests were sent for the instruction of these converts. It is hoped that all the work

regarding the conversions from the Orthodox to the Catholic religion
in the parish, may be carried out effectively.

Dr. F. Salis
Vicar-General

Zagreb, February 8, 1942

DOCUMENT LIV

Petition of Priests for Cessation of Deportations of Orthodox

Monsignor Archbishop:

We, the undersigned priests, assembled at Zazina on the day of
St. Elie's fair, sent a petition to the Poglavnik in which we asked that
the deportation of the Orthodox inhabitants, converted to Catholicism,
be stopped. These poor people hopefully call on us Catholic priests,
and through us on Your Excellency, to support our request.

These people have already suffered many reverses of fortune and
punishment; and now they are to be driven into Serbia, to which they
are strangers, in which they have never been, and which will receive
them as aliens.

These people are peaceful and are sincerely and honestly attached
to our Holy Church, and we can hope that they will be good
Catholics.

We humbly ask Your Excellency to add your valuable recommendation to our enclosed petition addressed to the Poglavnik.

It will create a favorable and widespread impression when it is
learned that these deportations have been stopped at the request of
the clergy and its Archbishop.

As the affair is most urgent — *Periculum in mora* — we ask Your
Excellency to expedite this matter without delay — so that the people
may not be deported before action is taken.

Very humbly devoted to Your Excellency in Our Lord, Zazina,
July 20, 1941.

Thomas Stare, *pastor of the parish of Mala Gorica*
Charles Joseph Iskra, *pastor of Pešćenica*
P. Charles Jelusić, *from Sela near Sisak*
P. Denis Drnić,
Joseph Mikelić, *spiritual counselor at Pešćenica*

This memorandum in question was sent with the recommendation of the Archbishop to the Poglavnik, July 24, 1941. Seper.

The Archbishop took charge of the case as far as he was able so that the request might be favorably received.

DOCUMENT LV

Report of Pastor Augustin Kralj to Pavelić Regarding Forced Conversions

To the Poglavnik of the Independent   October 25, 1942
State of Croatia, Zagreb

The undersigned, following his conscience, feels obliged to present to you a report of all that he experienced on the occasion of the deportation of Orthodox persons converted to Catholicism from the parish of Crkveni Bok on October 13 and 14 of this year. The parishioners were taken to the concentration camp at Jasenovac by several detachments of Ustashi. I thought it necessary that you yourself, as Chief of State, learn from a Catholic priest the bitter truth concerning the methods employed there.

On October 13 at seven o'clock in the morning the first rifle and machine gun shots were heard in the neighborhood of the Crkveni Bok parish. I learned later that Ustashi detachments had earlier blockaded the whole district. At half past seven I decided to go to the church and say Mass. Suddenly, out of breath and pale as death, my housekeeper, a convert herself, came into my room and asked me to save her because the Ustashi were arresting people and killing them.

At first I didn't believe this. So I went out to see for myself what was going on. I turned in the direction from which I heard people crying and I had proof that the evacuation of Crkveni Bok had indeed begun. Ustashi were leading the people away, machine guns in hand. I went up to one of them and asked him what all this meant. No reply. "Everything in our village has been in order. Neither the police nor myself," I continued, "has been notified of any disturbance. I ask you, in the name of human feeling, what is the reason for measures of this kind?" I received the reply that such orders had been given and that the Ustashi had to carry them out.

When, after that, I was walking in front of the group toward the police station, I perceived that the people did not know what was going on, and that some of them were quietly waiting for order while others tried to flee, the Ustashi running after them and shooting at them. From that time on shots were heard in all directions which showed that people were fleeing from their homes to save their lives.

I arrived at the police station where Lieutenant Ljubo from Jasenovac had already come. Sergeant Abramović and the notary, Gavrić, were also there. We tried to save certain people, but did not succeed. We succeeded only in drawing up a list of all the Catholics by birth who were taken along with the others so that they might be separated from them. Later this was done.

Then Lieutenant Ljubo left us. As he went he told Sergeant Abramović to make sure that there be no pillaging in any place whatsoever, only one sentence being ordered for pillagers, that of death.

Leaving the police station, I went home. Only Ustashi were about in the village. I met many of them and nearly every one of them was going about with either a small or large bottle of brandy. Some were already drunk. I met several of them who were looking for things to steal. I reprimanded them severely, telling them to stop if they wanted to escape being sentenced to death. They replied that they had been given permission to take food and drink from the houses. Returning to my house, I found two Ustashi searching it, although they must have known from the prie-dieu and the crucifix hanging above it, from the radio set, and from your portrait that it was the room of a priest. After having taken my things back, I threw them out.

The inhabitants of Crkveni Bok were already gathered on the other bank of the Sava, at Lonja. But at Crkveni Bok the shooting did not stop. It continued all day. I didn't know what to do. From Crkveni Bok there was nowhere else to go and I didn't know what I could do there. Late in the afternoon the first wagons, sent from neighboring villages by the Ustashi authorities, began to arrive to collect the villagers' possessions. During the whole of the next day 500 wagons, which came from the neighboring villages of Bobovac, Suvaj, Lonja, and Puska carried these goods away to Jasenovac. I saw on these wagons not only bed clothes, pillows, and clothing but such furniture as sewing machines, iron pots, and side boards.

I crossed the village several times in all directions, being myself obliged to go and get a place to stay in Sunja. I perceived that in every house there were people who were gathering and hiding something for themselves. They took all objects of any value that they could find. These were people from Bobovac, Puska, and from Lonja. All of a sudden half of them were wearing two overcoats. People came to Crkveni Bok with horses only, then they took wagons from the village in which they carried loot away, without returning the wagons. Others brought their horses to Crkveni Bok where they exchanged them for better ones which they found there. Some Ustashi were watching to see that no objects were stolen, but I saw one who surprised someone who had some linen sheets under his coat and who did nothing about it. The school mistress of Crkveni Bok, Anne Pintar, told me that the Ustashi had found 100,000 kronen in the house where she boarded. They offered this money to her but she did not wish to take it, so they kept it themselves. She was not able to tell me whether or not they have returned it.

One thing especially struck me, the swearing by the Ustashi of the most gross oaths, and not only by one of them but by most of them, even the officers. Then also the thefts committed by Catholics in charge of collecting the villager's possessions for the state. Only the smallest group of them came from Jasenovac. My position as priest does not permit me to denounce these persons for the reason that there were too many of them and that they would all lose their lives for these crimes, which in other circumstances would not warrant so severe a sentence. On October 14 it was a sad thing to see the appearance of the buildings. All were empty, damaged, and turned upside down.

Poglavnik, the impression received by the undersigned when he was gazing at all these things was more than terrible. I am not called upon to judge whether there were reasons for such measures, but I must say that neither myself nor the police in this district had any knowledge that Partisans had established contact with the inhabitants of Crkveni Bok. Several persons from the district office who came to Crkveni Bok and learned of the fate of these converts couldn't get over it. The Subprefect Bošnjak came on October 14 in the afternoon and, having seen all this, said that it would not go unpunished. The Ustashi captain, Majer de Kostajnica, who apparently was used to visiting Crkveni Bok and knew people there, condemned most severely the methods of the Ustashi from Jasenovac.

Crkveni Bok is a rich place because its soil is fertile and its people very hard working. They fulfilled all their duties to the state. Colonel Stephen Faber, requisitioning hay for the army, recommended that all Catholic villages model themselves on Crkveni Bok in the matter of gathering supplies. Last year fats were requisitioned for the army at Crkveni Bok and the people gave about 250 kilograms of fat free. When appeals were made to these people to enter military service, the largest percentage of them answered the appeal. It is true that about fifteen persons disappeared from the district, from which one can conclude that they joined the Partisans, but they were instantly scorned by the villagers as lazy. The Partisan propaganda has not been successful in Crkveni Bok.

That is why the methods used by the Ustashi authorities against these people are astonishing. The more so since the people of Crkveni Bok this summer gave 250 wagons to Jasenovac and took them wood for their fires. It was the younger element among the Ustashi who did these things which, it seems, they did reluctantly. Even in itself the attempt to deport people from one place to another is horrible, for men are tied to all sorts of things that remind them of home, but the methods used for such a deportation as that which occurred in Crkveni Bok are, as I have seen, even more terrible. What I have seen there I shall never forget. A boy of 15 was leading an old woman who had remained behind. He saw a horse at the edge of the road which he mounted and began to spur. Riding the horse quite fast, he yelled without stopping, "Get along there, hurry up," to the old woman upon whom I cannot say whether the years or her bundles weighed heavier. Another woman was arrested along the route who had a baby at home in its crib, but she was not allowed to return to her home to get it.

Many people came to ask me how these events came about at Crkveni Bok. I came to Crkveni Bok because I wished to, so that I might work there for the good of God, of the Church, and of the Croatian people. In my work I met many obstacles which were not, for the most part, deliberately placed before me. But I felt myself upheld by the hope that one day the success of this work would be seen. The older people were not receptive, clinging to what they had learned in their youth. But the children listened willingly to my instructions and accepted my counsels. Evident progress could be seen on that point. But in repayment I have received such a blow as to leave me without my flock. How much better never to have come here, never to have experienced these things of which at present I am trying to draw a partial and very inadequate picture.

Poglavnik, let these people return to their homes. For the most part they have been robbed by their Catholic neighbors. And let no one, anywhere, adopt further measures of this sort, since in that way our good Catholic people may become corrupt who otherwise would not commit such acts.

The inhabitants of Crkveni Bok were this past summer hard-working farmers and they have reaped a very good harvest. Now, if another should eat the fruits of their labor and become the owner of their goods as a thief, it will bring no good to anyone. Rich people have suddenly become paupers, without home, clothing, or bread. At the time of the evacuation the village of Crkveni Bok contained about 2500 persons. I have learned that all are not at the Jasenovac concentration camp. That is a sign that all have not been captured. Those who were not taken will not return to their homes. No one is willing to give them food because even without them there is a shortage of food. There remains only force, the armed hand; they will rob and take revenge against our people. I am afraid that the same thing may be done even by the 300 persons who are working for the state in labor battalions when then learn how their mothers and fathers, children and wives have been treated and of their fate while they were sacrificing themselves for the state.

Poglavnik, through your mercy allow these people to return to their homes. Even if they find empty houses, they will still be grateful to you. And on my part you would have my most sincere gratitude, from me who has been pastor to them for a year, if, Poglavnik, you order that they be sent back to their homes.

Za dom spremni!

Hail, Ustashi: ready in the service of the fatherland!

AUGUSTIN KRALJ
Pastor of the Parish
Crkveni Bok-Sunja, October 16, 1942

Augustin Kralj in person brought the letter and asked for an audience with the Poglavnik.

The original was sent to the Poglavnik by His Excellency Bishop Lach.

DOCUMENT LVI

Testimony of Father Žužek of Glina Regarding the Efforts of the Archbishop to Save Lives

TESTIMONY

On August 29, 1941, Second Lieutenant Rolf with about fifty young

Ustashi came to Glina. He immediately arrested all Serbians, for the most part widows of those who had been massacred on May 12, 1941. He showed mercy to only a few who had had contacts with the bank of the then Minister, Dr. Puk, in monetary matters.

As I was returning from the Bureau of Taxes I met in the street a group of those who had been arrested; they said to me, crying, "You told us, when receiving us into the Catholic Church, that we would have nothing to fear." I replied at once, "I will take your case to the Archbishop."

I left for the district government and I requested the officer in charge of the district, at that time Imper, to take care that these people were not killed and he replied, "What can I do now when Second Lieutenant Rolf has taken over command of the district? And beyond that you know that I can do nothing against Puk and Jerec" (who was Prefect at Petrinja, and, moreover, a drunkard, runner after women, and a cheat).

I then went to see the Second Lieutenant of the Ustashi, Rolf (a man about 50, completely gray), and I said to him, "The women and young girls you arrested today have been converted to Catholicism. The Minister of the Interior has decided that such persons have the same rights as other citizens, and His Excellency the Archbishop of Zagreb has personally obtained from the Minister an attestation of that decision. The Church would be betrayed if any harm should come to those who were arrested." I noticed from Rolf's expression that these remarks were displeasing to him, and he said to me, "I have only the Mandate to arrest them and to bring them to justice." I saw that he wanted to get rid of me as soon as possible.

At the court where I next introduced myself I was told that nothing at all was known of the case and that Rolf was using the jail as his headquarters.

After all that the Ustashi had done here under the aegis of the infamous Puk and Jerec, I clearly foresaw that the following night all the arrested persons would be taken off somewhere and killed, so I went again to the officer in charge of the district, Imper, and asked his permission to use his telephone to call the Archbishop. He allowed me to do this, remarking that I should be careful of what I said because a Ustashi was seated next to the telephone switchboard in the post office.

I called the Archiepiscopal Court. The porter answered the telephone and I asked him to call the Archbishop's secretary; in a few minutes someone came to the phone, Dr. Stephan Lacković I think, to whom I explained for the most part in Latin, on account of the Ustashi seated next to the switchboard at the post office, what the problem was. The secretary replied that His Excellency the Archbishop was not at home but that since it was a question of a delicate case, he would go look for him and that I should wait at the telephone. That was at noon and I had at my house J. Crnković, then administrator of the parish of Crkvena and today assistant at the parish of St. Mary; my father, Joseph Zuzek, now catechist at Kranj; and my assistant, Francis Bratušek, of the Levantine diocese. That is why I left for my house after having asked the employee who was on duty that day, Stephen Klobucar, to advise me when the Archbishop's secretary called — the rectory is only a few minutes away from the phone.

We had just sat down to lunch when there was a knock on the door. Second Lieutenant of the Ustashi Rolf entered alone and said to me, giving me a piercing glance, "I have just received orders from the Poglavnik that all persons who have been converted to Catholicism are to be set free. You, pastor, will come at two o'clock, with the district officer Imper, to the jail and read the names of the converts. You will give them a talk and tell them to be very careful, because as soon as anyone opens her mouth (*ipsissima verba*) she will be arrested and then no intervention will help her. (He was thinking, naturally, of His Excellency the Archbishop.)

At three o'clock I went with Imper to the jail where I told those who were gathered whom they had to thank for their deliverance, and, while Imper went to look for some cigarettes, I opened the large outside door and released nearly all the arrested women, crying with emotion.

That evening, Krnić, the jailor's son, my pupil in the high school at Glina, brought the others whom we had not been able to release at once, since they were Orthodox, to my house. My sister and I hid some of them in the cellar, others in the attic, and about eleven o'clock that night sent them off in a direction where there were no Ustashi soldiers. And thus the arrested were restored to their homes. And since many Orthodox had been arrested, there were, together with those from Glina, about 150 of them.

The next day an envoy from Puk and Jerec came to my house, the infamous Vidaković, brother of the murderer who had killed the administrator of the Bucica parish, Vedrina, and said to me brusquely, "Yesterday you emptied the jail, you will be responsible for that, especially since you have no rights in the Independent State of Croatia because you are Slovenian." I replied to him, "Know well that I was driven from Istra in 1923 because of my pro-Croatian sentiments! Shall I be repaid by Croatia in such a way? In any case I am nothing, let the Archbishop of Zagreb answer you!"

And that is how there are today in Glina, and the surrounding villages, women who are still alive, who were saved by the intervention of the Archbishop, Dr. Aloysius Stepinac, and who will always remember with gratitude him to whom they owe their lives.

All the above (*ut supra*) can be attested to by J. Crnković, parish assistant at St. Mary's.

FR. ZUZEK, *pastor*

Glina, November 10, 1945

DOCUMENT LVII
Statement of the Archbishop Regarding Interventions with Pavelić on Behalf of Converts

Through my intervention with the Poglavnik made on behalf of the converts, formerly Orthodox, taken from Pakrac to Stara Gradiška, I got the Poglavnik to order the Department of Public Order and Safety in Zagreb to put itself immediately in touch with the professor of religion in Pakrac, who averred that the persons taken away had had no relations with Partisans or traitors, but that they were honest and worthy citizens, and that according to the outcome of this inquiry they were to be freed at once.

So that this affair might be favorably settled as soon as possible and the Poglavnik's orders carried out, and the persons taken away be able to return to their homes, I sent Father Thomas Sruk, religion professor at Pakrac, to Zagreb so that he might be at the disposal of the Department of Public Order and Safety. Having received the statement given by the religion professor from Pakrac, the Department took the necessary steps to have this matter finally examined and terminated.

Through this letter I ask the authorities of the concentration camp at Stara Gradiška to put themselves in touch with the Department of Public Order and Safety in Zagreb so that the Poglavnik's order concerning the freeing of the citizens from Pakrac may be carried out as soon as possible and then to allow the religion professor, Thomas Sruk, to visit his faithful from Pakrac and to calm and console them.

ARCHBISHOP OF ZAGREB

Zagreb, September 17, 1942

DOCUMENT LVIII

Correspondence Regarding Destruction of Orthodox Property .

Independent State of Croatia   ZAGREB, February 13, 1942
Ministry of the Interior
Secretariate of the Minister
V.T. No. 81/1942
Subject: Demolition of Greek Orthodox churches.

To His Excellency Dr. Aloysius Stepinac,
Archbishop, President of the Episcopal Conference.

In reply to your letter of February 10, 1942, on the subject of the demolition of Greek Orthodox churches in the country and of the Orthodox parish church of the Assumption in Senj, I inform you of the following. This Ministry did not give any order whatsover in this connection and was unaware of this matter until receipt of your letter.

As soon as the Ministry received your letter it sent an order to the Prefect of Senj to forbid and prevent any future attempt of this sort.

> Za dom spremni!
> Hail, Ustashi, ready in the service of
> the fatherland!
> By the authorization of the Minister of
> the Interior.
> The Prefect of the Minister of the Interior
>
> DR. A. NIKOLIĆ

S. L.
No. 223/1942
Parish Office of Kanjiska Iva.

In reply to your letter of April 27, 1942, No. 67, we communicate the following: According to the decision of the Holy See on the subject of the appropriation of former Greek Orthodox churches, such Churches cannot, at present, be transformed into Roman Catholic churches. Only in the case of certain localities where there is no Catholic Church and in which all the Greek Orthodox, or at least a considerable majority of them, have been converted to the Catholic religion may these churches be used for Catholic services with the permission of the Archiepiscopal Ordinariate. Prior to use they must be blessed *simplici benedictione*. It is in the latter sense that this right was accorded to Father Pasicek. As a result, these churches have not become Roman Catholic and their properties may not be transferred to the Roman Catholic Church at the land office. Until further notice, nothing in these churches may be transferred, one may only set up a provisional altar.

THE VICAR-GENERAL

Zagreb, May 1, 1942

DOCUMENT LIX

Statement of Several Zagreb Priests in Regard to Efforts of the Archbishop to Prevent Injustices and to Avoid Persecution

The undersigned members of the Consistory from 1940 to 1946 make the following statement:

1. In 1941, under political pressure from Ustashi authorities, several Orthodox Serbians wished to enter the Catholic Church, thinking that as a result they would be protecting their lives. They sent petitions to the Archiepiscopal Ordinariate in Zagreb asking to be received into the Catholic Church. The Archbishop, Dr. Aloysius Stepinac, in reply adopted a policy regarding reception into the Church in strict accordance with practices of the Church. He said that only those should be received who declared that they came freely and were well instructed in Catholic truth.

2. In this same spirit the Archbishop, Dr. Aloysius Stepinac, published several official circular letters informing the clergy that in such receptions they must consider the dignity of human freedom and the principles of the Church. At the same time he gave instructions on the subject of reception into the Church to his Chancery and to teachers that in answer to requests for permission to become Catholic they adhere exactly to the regulations of the Church.

3. When certain pastors presented petitions requesting permission to receive the Orthodox in groups, they were refused by the Arch-

bishop, Dr. Aloysius Stepinac, who demanded that reception always be individual and based on the prescribed instructions.

4. When several pastors asked for the advice of the Consistory as to whether they were free to accept for Church use certain objects taken from plundered or demolished Orthodox Churches and offered to them by Ustashi officials, Dr. Aloysius Stepinac took a strong stand against the acceptance of such objects.

DR. F. SALIS, DR. C. DOCKAL, DR. E. BAKSIĆ,
DR. F. ROZIĆ, DR. J. MARIĆ, DR. K. PECNJAK,
DR. P. LONČAR, DR. D. HREN.

Zagreb, October 6, 1946

*Statement of Joseph Crnković, Assistant Pastor at St. Mary's,
Zagreb, in Defense of His Excellency Monsignor
Archbishop Dr. Aloysius Stepinac*

1. From 1941 until 1945 I was employed in the Archiepiscopal Chancery. It is true that in my work I had nothing to do with the reception of Orthodox and other persons into the Church, but I know the procedure that was followed. Priests had received precise directives on the subject of how to receive converts: instructions had to precede conversions, and it was necessary that they enter the Church through a conviction in the truth of Catholic doctrine. For the most part, answer to requests for the chance to be converted were given by His Excellency, Bishop Salis. While a search was made for all that was required for conversions and lest their requests be refused, *the people wishing to be converted* themselves begged us, crying, to grant them their requests *more quickly,* hoping to find, by becoming Catholics, help in avoiding persecution. They believed this and we received them as we wished to help them. *If we had not done this for them, today we should be reproached for not wanting to aid the Serbians and others when we were able.* If later these converts have been badly treated, can the clergy, and least of all the Archbishop, be held responsible for it?

2. I am a native of Glina and in July, 1941, I spent my vacation at my parents' home. One day the Ustashi dragged all the Orthodox women and young girls to the court of the Glina district. The pastor, Francis Zuzek, at their request immediately went and telephoned Archbishop Dr. Aloysius Stepinac. Returning to the rectory, he told me that he had spoken to the Archbishop's secretary who had promised

to tell the Archbishop about what had occurred at Glina. It is to be added that these poor women were afraid of meeting with the same fate as their husbands, killed one night in May by the Ustashi. After dinner, the Ustashi officer Rolf came to the rectory and said that he had received orders from Zagreb, from the government, *to release all the Orthodox women who had been arrested.* It is certain that the Archbishop had intervened with the Ustashi authorities on behalf of these women and that is why a counterorder providing for the release of these Orthodox women followed. Thus, then, *thanks* to pastor Francis Zuzek and to *Archbishop Dr. Aloysius Stepinac the lives of many Orthodox women were saved.* Full of gratitude they recognized that and recognize it still today. Released, they came to the rectory and thanked the pastor with tears in their eyes, kissing his hand.

JOSEPH CRNKOVIĆ
Assistant Pastor of St. Mary's

Zagreb, September 24, 1946

IV. THE MILITARY VICARIATE

DOCUMENT LX

Letter Regarding Designation of Archbishop Stepinac
as Military Vicar

The Presidency of the Episcopal Conference
Zagreb
No. 351/BK

The Holy Father, in order to satisfy the desire of the Episcopate on the subject of military chaplains, has entrusted me, in case of mobilization, to exercise *functiones-quamquam sine titulo — Vicarii Castrensis* with all the powers *cum potestate subdelegandi* which are found in the *Index Facultatum, quae a Ss.mo. D.no nostro Pio Papa XII Vicariis Castrensibus pro casu belli aut convocationiis ad arma conceduntur,* Congregatio Concilii, December 8, 1939.

I have the honor, according to the decision of the Episcopal Conference, to send you copies of the above-mentioned *Index Facultatum* so that you may send them to priests who would be called into military service as chaplains in case of mobilization. In such a case I will send the necessary jurisdiction to all by telegram.

In Ss.mo Corde
ALOYSIUS, *Archbishop, President of the*
Episcopal Conference

Zagreb, November 20, 1940

DOCUMENT LXI

Letter of Colonel Vujanić Regarding Recruitment of Chaplains

Ministry of Croatian Armed Forces
1st Section
No. 2042
Zagreb, September 18, 1941

To the Presidency of the Episcopal Conference
The chief of the Religion Section, to whom the petitions of priests desirous of becoming chaplains in the Croatian Army have been sent,

412

has found that only a very small number of them are capable of exercising this function in the Croatian Army.

He has proposed that the Ministry of Croatian Armed Forces announce a meeting where the conditions will be explained and a better choice can be made.

At the same time he has asked that a message be sent to the Presidency of the Episcopal Conference in Zagreb.

Included is an announcement of the meeting as well as the proposed allocation of Roman Catholic chaplains in the Croatian Armed Forces.

Chief of the 1st Section
Colonel of the General Staff
VUJANIĆ

Two enclosures
Stamp of the Ministry of
Croatian Armed Forces
1st Section

V. CONSPIRACY AGAINST THE NEW AUTHORITY AND RELATIONS WITH IT

DOCUMENT LXII

Pro Memoria Regarding the Foreign Ministry Archives
Entrusted to the Archbishop

The Archiepiscopal Ecclesiastical Court of Zagreb
No. 58 — copy

The Ministry of Foreign Affairs of the Independent State of Croatia, fearing that as a consequence of the eventual bombardment of Zagreb several documents already published by the Ministry would be damaged, deposited several of the above-mentioned documents in the palace of the Archbishop since they believed the palace to be very solidly built.

The documents are in the underground rooms of the palace.

For the same reason, several state officials left at the Archiepiscopal palace a few of their private belongings which they declared had been their private property prior to 1941. His Excellency the Archbishop learned of this and declared that he could not give absolute guarantees for the above-mentioned articles.

His Excellency the Archbishop notified the President of the Government of the Croatian Federation, Dr. Vladimir Bakarić, of this on June 4, 1945, at the time of his official visit.

This "pro memoria" is published in view of providing authentication and evidence.

At the order of the Archbishop
The Secretary of the Archbishop,
Ivo SALIĆ

Zagreb, June 6, 1945
58 — copy, 1945

The original was sent to Dr. Paulua, secretary of the Office of Monsignor Rittig, June 6, 1945.

National Croatian Government
The President of the Government's
Commission for Religious Affairs
No. 44/1945
Received June 13, 1945

THE REVEREND SECRETARY OF THE ARCHBISHOP OF ZAGREB:

In regard to the "pro-memoria" of the 6th of this month (No. 58, copy), this Commission has the honor to inform you in regard to the documents left in the cellar of the Archiepiscopal palace by the Ministry of Foreign Affairs of the former NDH that they are to be delivered to the commission in charge of the collection and conservation of cultural and artistic monuments, antiquities, and works of art, which was transferred from the former NDH and now works under the Ministry of Public Instruction of the Croatian Federation, 1 Jesuitski St.

You are asked, concerning other objects left at the Archiepiscopal palace by third parties, to directly notify the above-mentioned commission in so far as it is a question of art works, antiquities, libraries, or archives, and if it is a question of other personal property to notify the National Administration of Public Property of the Croatian Federation of Zagreb.

Death to Fascism, freedom for the people.

For the Commission
DR. S. RITTIG

L. S.

60 — copy

Archives of the Ministry of Foreign Affairs

June 6, 1945

DOCUMENT LXIII

Letter of the Bishops of the Republic of Croatia to the Faithful,
Issued on March 24, 1945

DEARLY BELOVED:

In the past we Bishops of Croatia have made known to you our thoughts on matters of supreme moment for our spiritual welfare. In this tragic time of war we lack adequate means of contact with our flock and it has not been given to us in all places and in every parish to alleviate the very grievous ills which have afflicted the faithful of every diocese of Croatia. Because your sorrows, and those of the entire Croatian nation, have been multiplied by your anxiety for the fate of your country upon which a deluge of falsities and calumnies has descended, we, empowered to act in the name of all the Bishops of Croatia gathered in council, consider it our bounden duty to speak to you, most dearly beloved, to rectify certain calumnies and vicious lies which affect the most sacred rights and existence itself of the Catholic Church and the Croatian nation.

Profoundly mindful of present-day events, and the dangers of the future, we call upon the faithful to unite themselves more closely with us in professing the true faith in God, the author, the lawgiver, and the ultimate end of life, so that in all things we have before our eyes the immortality of the soul, and the inestimable value of the moral dignity of man, today so gravely challenged. United with the successor of St. Peter we protest to the Holy Apostolic See, as did our predecessors in the times of Pope St. Agatho and John VIII, our unshakable loyalty regardless of the false accusations of the enemies of the Church and despite persecution.

Considering furthermore how much suffering the Croatian nation has undergone in this 20th Century, we beseech all who are afflicted in whatever way not to despair, not to allow themselves to be drawn away from the Catholic Church and the charity of God and men, even if it means the shedding of your blood.

False witnesses have come forth accusing us Catholic Bishops, priests, and eminent laymen of bloodshed in Croatia. God, the all-seeing witness, knows what we Catholic Bishops have done over the past twenty years to preserve peace in the Croatian nation and to further Christian works of mercy. The whole world is aware of this. The love of peace is the essence of the Croatian spirit, and this love of peace, despite the greatest obstacles, particularly after 1918, was avidly cultivated by the spiritual and civil leaders of the Croatian people.

The blame for the futility of our labor rests with those who dealt death to the Croatian leaders, who perpetrated acts of rapine upon the helpless populace, and in consequence turned our people away from the path of peace, rendering them discontented with their lot.

Innocent Croatian blood has been poured out in the course of two world conflagrations in the cities and villages of Croatia, even in the Belgrade Parliament. In Belgrade a concordat, i.e., a most solemn pact between the Holy Apostolic See and the former kingdom of Yugoslavia, was concluded, but it happened that the rights of the Croatian Catholics depended on the whims of the government. In silence we pass over the shameful breaking of promises made to our Croatian leaders. This is not unknown to those who have followed recent events.

When war engulfed our land, the Croatians remained unmoved because they lacked civil liberties and arms while an iniquitous enemy instituted a reign of terror whose one and only purpose was the extinction of the Croatians as a nation. Consequent upon this, and sad to say, some Croatians were found who returned killing for killing. The Bishops of Croatia decried and condemned such retaliatory measures.

The Bishops collectively, as in their meeting of 1941, raised their voice in protest against those who transgressed the limits of just defense and against men of violence of whatever party, race, or creed. To the innocent we extended aid. Always, when means were open and available to us, we interceded with those in power to lighten the misery which through no fault of ours has fallen upon our country. We condemned vehemently all opinions and doctrines, whether of rightists or leftists, as well as everyone who violated divine precepts and deprived others of their human rights.

Today we demand equality of law for all, exhorting each and every man, party, and people not to render evil for evil or abuse for abuse (1 Pet. 3:9). We addressed this admonition to individuals and political parties who under the cloak of justice instigated men to murder as war criminals especially the clergy and intelligentsia and to deprive them not only of life but even of their reputations.

All criminals, of whatever political leaning, must be brought to justice and punished for their crimes. It is evident to all true lovers of justice that guilt cannot be fully and truly judged by those moved by hatred. If any priest, a rare occurrence, has injured others in their rights, we shall not hesitate to impose ecclesiastical sanction against him even to deprive him of his sacerdotal or religious status.

But from the depth of our soul we protest before God and mankind against the systematic murder and persecution of innocent priests and Catholic faithful, many of whose lives excel in sanctity, upon whom the maddened enemies of the Church have brought death.

The enemies of the Catholic Church, especially the followers of materialistic communism which the entire Croatian nation rejects (he who would dare to assert the contrary, would be lying to the whole world), have in Croatia exterminated with fire and sword priests and the more outstanding of the faithful.

It is apparent why they accuse all Bishops, priests, and religious as war criminals; why they attempt to foist totally false accusations upon them. In the civilized world, however, not a single person will be found to approve such flimsy and arbitrary charges, or believe that Bishops, priests, and well-known religious communities are war criminals, worthy of capital punishment; as perpetrators of massacres. Perpetually shall the blood of these heroic martyrs cry out in accusation against those who use murder as a means to power.

The Catholic Bishops of Croatia are prepared and ready to have each individual case investigated by representatives of other nations and by an international commission. In this way the charge of war criminality will be proved a lie, and simply a means of exterminating those who oppose and want no part of communism.

Wherefore the Croatian Bishops recommend that a committee be set up to examine all cases, and to gather facts for presentation to an international commission. Thus the truth will become apparent, how lies have been made the instrument of an ideology, whose followers seek in every possible way to enslave the entire world, despite their numerical inferiority. In Croatia their number is literally microscopic.

In spiritual matters we acknowledge the supreme jurisdiction of the Church; in civil affairs the state; just as we must render an account concerning ecclesiastical administration, so too must we to the civil authority within its jurisdiction. The Church has imbued the priests and people of Croatia with a will to render to God what is God's, and to its own country, its due. History testifies that the Croatian people for nearly a thousand years have never renounced their right to nationhood. In like manner, they wish freedom for all other peoples on earth. During World War II, the Croatian people realized their desire and right by establishing their own independent state; cognizant of the will of their people, the Bishops of Croatia assented, as was right. No one therefore has the right to accuse any citizen of the Croatian Republic or its Bishops because they acknowledged the will of the Croatian people in what is their right according to both divine and human law.

The Croatian Bishops, inasmuch as lies in their power or concern, agree that in the Republic of Croatia law must be respected, mindful that justice is the basis of government; and justice should be to all without discrimination of race, kind, religion, and circumstance.

Most Dearly Beloved:

We are now on the eve of Holy Week which commemorates the Passion of our Lord Jesus Christ. Mankind is passing through its week of passion. Christ the divine Messias, the eternal Truth and Love, teaches us what our feelings during this sacred time should be. To those whose charges affixed Him to the Cross He replied: "Father, forgive them, for they know not what they do" (Lk. 23:34). We are fully aware that suffering oppresses thousands and thousands of our countrymen. Hence, to you, grievously wounded souls, we say: If anyone wishes to be a follower of Christ, it is necessary to be ruled by His spirit, which leads men's souls to echo the words of the crucified Christ: "Father, forgive them. . . ."

In conclusion, we, your pastors, admonish you to observe the divine law most faithfully, to confide in the mercy and providence of God, the Creator of the world, to preserve your faith in the Holy Church till God ends this horrible catastrophe, till God extends to all mankind and our nation, which has undergone such terrible evil, His holy peace.

May the omnipotent God the Father, the Son, and the Holy Spirit bless you.

Dr. Aloysius Stepinac,
*Archbishop of Zagreb, Metropolitan
and the President of the
Bishop's Council*

Dr. John E. Šarić,
*Archbishop of Sarajevo
and Metropolitan*

Joseph Garić, O.F.M.,
Bishop of Banja Luka

Dr. Anthony Akšamović,
*Bishop and Apostolic Adminis-
trator of Gjakovo*

Dr. Janko Šimrak,
*Bishop of the Croatian
Greek-Catholics*

Given at Zagreb, the 24th of March in the year of our Lord, 1945.

DOCUMENT LXIV

*Note on the Meeting of the Higher Clergy with the Marshal of
Yugoslavia, Joseph Broz Tito, President of the
Federal Republic, on June 2, 1945*

When Marshal Tito came to Zagreb, the state authorities expressed
a desire that, in the name of the Catholic Church, the higher clergy
pay him a visit. The Croatian government itself put automobiles at
the clergy's disposal. The Archbishop of Zagreb, Dr. Aloysius Stepinac,
had at that time already been in prison for about two weeks.

The Vicar-General, Bishop Dr. Francis Salis, said in his speech of
welcome, "I myself am not competent to give in the name of the
Church a statement of any validity at all, it is only the Ordinary, Dr.
Aloysius Stepinac, who can do that, but he has been deprived of
his freedom. All the same, we hope with confidence: (*a*) that the
Catholic Church in the new state, will have complete freedom in
carrying out its mission, (*b*) that it will be able to teach freely
religion in all classes, (*c*) that the Church will continue to have its
Catholic high schools and boarding schools, (*d*) that Catholic Action
and its other religious associations will function freely, and (*e*) that
it will continue to publish its newspaper and journals without interference. On this basis a cordial understanding between the Church
and the State can develop.

I

Marshal Tito's Speech

emphasized these two points: (1) we desire the greatest possible
freedom for the Catholic Church of Yugoslavia in regard to Rome,
and (2) we want the Slav idea to be propagated. We are not content with the attitude shown to date by the Church and clergy. We

admit that religion is, in the life of the people, a thing of such a nature that it cannot be settled by decrees but rather by mutual agreement.

THE CLERGY'S REPLY TO MARSHAL TITO

Marshal, you should recognize what the Vatican means to us Croatians and how discreet and judicious its attitude has always been toward the Croatian question. Here are proofs of it:

1. Thanks to the Vatican and to the Holy Father, Pius XII, now reigning, the Medjmurje has been retained by us. For the Hungarian army having occupied the Medjmurje, Hungarian diplomats demanded from Rome that in ecclesiastical jurisdiction the Medjmurje be subordinated to the Hungarian Episcopate.

Rome stated in reply that Medjmurje is a purely Croatian region from the ethnic point of view. For hundreds of years it has been under the jurisdiction of the Archbishop of Zagreb. We do not know how this war will end. We must make no prejudgment in this question.

2. Occupied Dalmatia was treated in the same way by the Vatican when Italian diplomacy asked that it be subordinated in ecclesiastical jurisdiction to the Italian bishops.

3. Up to now the Vatican never recognized the NDH.

4. When Pavelić visited the Holy Father, he was received not as the Chief of State of the NDH but as a simple Catholic.

5. When the Ustashi youth visited the Holy Father, they were received not as Ustashi youth but as young men and women of Croatia.

6. His delegate, His Excellency Dr. Marcone, was not accredited by the Holy See to the NDH government but to the Croatian Episcopate.

7. As for us priests and Catholic faithful, we are bound to the Holy See in matters of religious dogma and discipline, while in our national and social activities we are completely free.

We Croatians should be grateful to the Holy See for its wise attitude toward us and its thoughtful regard for our feelings. *That is why we Catholics neither demand nor will demand from it any greater freedom than we already have.*

8. As for the Slav idea, in that the Holy See places no obstacle. That is seen from the fact that, in a special way, he has proclaimed Sts. Cyril and Methodius, the Slav apostles, as our patrons; that in their honor he has given us a ritual for a special Mass and feast day;

that he has published Missals in the language. We Catholics live in the greatest tolerance toward the Orthodox.

II

Marshal Tito, on the Subject of Archbishop Stepinac

Marshal Tito: "You would like to know something about Archbishop Stepinac, but I can say nothing about him since he is where he is at present." (That is to say in prison.)

Reply of the Clergy

Marshal, in brief this is what we have to say on the subject of Archbishop Stepinac. He is the greatest Croatian alive today and a devoted worker for the nation and society for the following reasons:

1. There are members of your government whose lives were saved by his intervention.

2. During the war he fed 7000 Partisan children without asking whether they were Croatian or Serb, Catholic or Orthodox.

3. By his interventions and sermons he defended the Serbs, the Jews, and Gypsies, and saved the lives of a great number of them.

4. He preached sermons and made protests against the racist laws, against hypernationalistic acts of violence, against the custom of taking hostages and of hanging innocent persons.

5. He intervened with Pavelić and his police, while knowing that they were making an effort to remove him from his episcopal see and did not appreciate his interventions.

6. He intervened on behalf of the poorest people who call on him in their misery.

7. He went to see Dr. Lončar, imprisoned at Lepoglava, sentenced there by the Ustashi for having protested to priests and seminarians that they ought not to engage in Ustashi politics and that they ought not to become Ustashi officials.

These are the acts of this great man, a worker for the nation and society, who is today in prison. We hope with confidence that you, Marshal, will set him free so that together with us he may continue his labors. (The next day the Archbishop Dr. Stepinac was set free.)

III

Marshal Tito Objects

that so many priests had been Ustashi and Ustashi officials and that with the Ustashi they fled the country; some were captured and are now in various concentration camps.

REPLY

Marshal, permit us to reply to you as follows:

1. You should know that for several centuries the Croatians have hoped that their desire for freedom and for an independent Croatian state would one day be realized. It seemed that this desire was fulfilled by Pavelić and the action of the Ustashi. Is it, then, surprising that many persons were taken with this idea from the first and that they associated themselves with the Ustashi movement? The acts of violence, the murders, and spilling of blood brought about by the Ustashi movement turned many away from them.

2. Many of them fled the country along with Pavelić and the Ustashi because: (a) they were military chaplains of the Ustashi, (b) others among them were taken away by force, (c) others went because they had heard that the Partisans would kill and exterminate all those who had sympathized with the Ustashi, and, finally, (d) the *domobrans* (that is to say, the Croatian soldiers) had been incorporated by force into Ustashi formations and had to leave the country with the Ustashi, but they did not leave voluntarily.

Marshal, in view of this, we take the liberty of warning you that the numerous concentration camps full of innocent people will engender great unrest and discontent which would not be at all profitable to this young state.

Permit us to bring especially to your attention an incident that occurred at the Lepoglava prison on the day that Dr. Lončar arrived there condemned to death by the Ustashi and later pardoned, his condemnation to death being changed to a prison sentence of twenty years. The prison guards, seeing a priest dressed in prison clothes, made this remark, "Now we see that the state is going to the devil for it persecutes the Church and the clergy." We stress the fact that this was said by simple people, prison guards, "the state that persecutes the Church and the clergy is going to the devil."

MARSHAL TITO'S REPLY

(1) I do not ask that everyone hold the same opinion on politics as I do, but I do demand that no one interfere with us in the work of consolidating the state. (2) Religion is a very important factor in the life of the people, so that nothing in this domain should be done

by decrees but only by agreements. (3) I am going to have a speedy investigation made of all those who are interned in the camps and free all those whose hands have not been bloodied.

THE CLERGY MADE THE FOLLOWING REMARKS

Permit us, Marshal, to draw your attention to what the Partisans are doing. We are convinced that you neither know nor approve of this. They are going around in Zagreb, armed with revolvers, (1) preventing the nuns from praying with the children to God, (2) in the nuns' quarters they are transforming the chapels into dormitories, and (3) in these places they are removing the crucifixes, etc.

MARSHAL TITO'S REPLY

"You are quite right that I did not know of this nor approve of it, and the situation will be remedied." After that Tito said to the President of the Croatian government, Dr. Bakarić, "Bakarić, write all that down."

DR. RITTIG TOOK THE FLOOR AND SAID,

"Do you know, Comrade Tito, that the clergy is guilty and must do penance?"

THE CLERGY PROTESTS

"Monsignor, that is not true, one cannot say that. One can say, some priests or a few of them have made mistakes, but not the clergy. That is not true."

MARSHAL TITO

"That is right, to know that some or a few priests have made mistakes, but they are considered as a moral whole."

With that the meeting ended, the clergy left.

DOCUMENT LXV

The Meeting of Marshal Tito (Josip Broz) and the Archbishop of Zagreb, Monsignor Stepinac, on June 4, 1945

The purpose of this meeting was to find a common basis for a clarification of the situation and to prevent, as far as possible, conflicts between the Church and State. Present at this conversation was also the President of the Federal Government of Croatia, Dr. Vladimir Bakarić.

The Archbishop stressed the following thoughts:

1. The creation of a new state is incontestably a great and difficult task. But more important still is the pacification and organization of the state; according to the French proverb, "When there are dissensions in a country, things go badly."

2. A state is secure when its citizens are secure. That is why wise statesmen respect the religious feelings of the citizens and their freedom of conscience.

3. Always, for the state as well as for the Church, it is best that this freedom of conscience be determined by juridical norms. The old State, for example, ruled over the status of the Orthodox people in a juridical fashion, but not over that of the Catholics, and that was a serious error.

4. For Catholics it is the Holy See that is competent to make decisions in these questions. Interviews with individual bishops may be very useful, but not a single Catholic may, be it even at the price of his life, ignore his supreme authority, the Holy See, for otherwise he ceases to be a Catholic. The best form for the regulation of such relations is in any case a concordat. But one can find a solution as well in another way. There is the example of the old Czechoslovakia which ruled on questions of Czech Catholics by a *modus vivendi* which in practice proved to be good and satisfied both parties. There are still other means. They should be left to the diplomats.

5. The re-establishment of regular diplomatic relations with the Holy See and the regulation of these relations by a treaty would have a very great significance for the new state that has just been created. For it must not be forgotten that the Catholic Church is an organization of 400 million men who, it is true, are not all practicing Catholics, but who in every country where they live exercise a direct or indirect influence on the public life and it is, consequently, understandable that the Catholics of the whole world are interested in the status of Catholics in the new Yugoslavia.

Marshal Tito understood the importance of this matter and was, in principle, ready to settle it. He expressed his fear over the lack of benevolence on the part of the Holy See in regard to Slavic peoples and, particularly, in the concrete case, the Yugoslav people.

The Archbishop replied thus: "So far as I can see, this fear has no foundation. During this war the Holy See has, in a concrete manner, shown itself very benevolent. For example in the question of Medjmurje, a very delicate subject for the Croatians, the Holy See did not for a moment give in to the offensive of Hungarian diplomacy with the result that the Archbishop, finding himself completely alone in facing the Hungarians, was the sole holder of ecclesiastical jurisdiction in Medjmurje during four whole years of the war, although Hungarian troops had occupied Medjmurje and had even annexed it. Cardinal Maglione, Secretary of State of the Vatican, gave his word of honor to the Archbishop of Zagreb that there would be no change of the status quo in the province of Medjmurje so long as the war lasted, and he kept his word despite the difficulties for the Holy See made by the Hungarian authorities. There was a similar question in Dalmatia, occupied then by the Italians. The Holy See did not think for a single instant of taking Croatian dioceses from Croatian bishops and annexing them to Italy. Also, in a general way, the Holy See showed great respect and friendly feelings toward the Slav nations. It is only necessary to recall Leo XIII when Strossmayer had entered into conflict with the imperial Austrian court on account of Russia. It is necessary to remember Pius XI who founded a special institute in Rome under the name of 'Russicum.' The Sacred Congregation for the Oriental Church has as its head today a great friend of the Slavs, Cardinal Tisserant, a Frenchman."

Marshal Tito expressed the desire that the Church give its support to the state authorities in Istria since Istria was one of our provinces. The Archbishop replied that if Istria was Croatian, hence Slav, it was so only because of the Catholic Church. All the intellectuals had fled or else become denationalized with the exception of the Catholic clergy who, at the price of great hardships, stuck it out during an occupation of 25 years and kept their native language. On account of these the Holy See had endless difficulties with the Italian government which is shown by the case — to cite only one — of the Archbishop of Trieste, Monsignor Fogar, who was very impartial and friendly toward the Slavs and who finally, under government pressure, was obliged to resign.

Finally, the benevolence of the Holy See toward Southern Slavs is also seen in the fact that it had, informally, been favorable to a concordat (which was made a fiasco because of the stupidity of the leading negotiators from Belgrade), in the fact that it conceded the use of the paleoslavic language for all of Yugoslavia, and consequently conferred a privilege which is not shared by even the largest nations in the world, such as Germany, France, England, etc.

The Archbishop added at the end of this, "Until now I have spoken to you as a bishop. I would like now, if I may, to add something as a man, as a man who considers circumstances in an objective manner. If it is desired to consolidate the situation as soon as possible, it is necessary in my opinion, to meet frankly and courageously with the representatives of the Croatian Peasant Party and with the *honest* adherents of the Ustashi movement. You can talk with all of them, you do not have to accept any decision. Let all who wish to collaborate honestly and sincerely in the reconstruction of the country be welcomed. If they refuse to collaborate, the fault will be theirs. Why not try such a meeting? A wise statesman omits nothing that can contribute to the happiness and contentment of his country."

Finally the Archbishop added that human lives everywhere be spared if it was possible, for we are a great people and up to the present our losses have been so numerous that another catastrophe would be equivalent to an extermination of the Slavic peoples in Southern Europe.

The Marshal replied that he would keep that in mind and do all he could. "It is not very easy," he said, "for justice must be satisfied for the gravest violations of humanitarian sentiments."

In all, the Archbishop was of the opinion that with good will on all sides the greatest difficulties could be surmounted, for the Church recognizes the principle, "Render therefore unto Caesar the things which are Caesar's, and to God the things which are God's."

It is possible that the plenary conference of the Episcopate, which will take place soon, will make its contribution in these matters.

DOCUMENT LXVI

Letter from Archbishop Stepinac to Dr. Vladimir Bakarić,
President of the People's Republic of Croatia, Regarding
the Persecution of the Church in the New Yugoslavia

Presidency of the Episcopal Conference   ZAGREB, July 21, 1945
No. 64/BK

MR. PRESIDENT:

I have had occasion several times so far to write to you regarding certain questions which are important to the proper regulation of the relations between Church and State. Although I have received no answers to those letters, I consider it most urgent that I write you again concerning these matters. There is first the question of the death sentence given to my priests who are momentarily awaiting execution. In connection with this circumstance I consider it necessary to explain to you, who are the responsible holder of the governmental authority in Croatia, a number of things which are obstacles to the pacification of our present situation and to that contentment which the people have awaited as following the war's end. I feel it to be my duty toward you to explain these things to you frankly so that you may avert in time the causes of the discontent that I see every day in my association with great numbers of my faithful who, literally, besiege my palace asking for aid. In doing this I hope to find on your part a sincere and complete understanding, for all that I am explaining is in the interest of the people in general and of the national community.

I

1. At the time of the meeting of the higher clergy of Zagreb with the Marshal and the President of the Federal Government on June 2 of this year, the Marshal solemnly declared to complaints that certain agents of the government were acting arbitrarily and arresting priests, that all priests who were in the concentration camps and prisons would be questioned without delay and that those who were found to have no blood on their hands would be quickly pardoned and set free. This statement was made under solemn circumstances and it should be the foundation of cordial relations between the Church and civil authorities.

It is true that a certain number of seminarians and some priests have been released from the camps and prisons during the past two months. But the seminarians from Zagreb were immediately called to the colors. And it is also true that a number of my priests were taken before a military court and sentenced to death. These are: Professor Kerubin Segvić and Professor Stjepan Kramar who were condemned to death by the court martial of the town commandant of Zagreb on June 29. Besides these two, the court also condemned to death the nuns Blanda Stipetić and Fanika Splajt; Sister Beata Nemec was sentenced to three years at forced labor. The military court at Karlovac condemned to death by firing squad Dr. Matija Kranjcić, pastor at Ozalj; Father Rikard Ribić, guardian of the Franciscans; and Father Dr. Beato Bukinac, professor in the high school at Karlovac. I have learned, although the news has not yet been completely confirmed, that the court martial at Krizevici has condemned to death Stjepan Pavunić, pastor at Koprivnica; Michael Kanoti, pastor at Varaždin; Josip Kalajdzić, pastor at Biskupec; and Petar Kovacić, pastor in Zagreb. These four are waiting for their sentences to be confirmed by the court martial of the Second Army Command at Zagreb. Besides these, Dr. I. Guberina, a priest from the diocese of Sibenik, has already been sentenced to death.

Mr. President! I cannot refrain from making some observations on the subject of the procedure of these courts martial.

Every man with a sane mind and an honest heart knows that an accused person has the inalienable right of defending himself and of demanding in his defense the questioning of witnesses before any court that merits its name and which intends to exercise its functions in the name of justice. Without the questioning of witnesses, who personally participate in the most important part of the proceedings, namely the trial, there cannot be a just sentence. I affirm that the military courts do not admit witnesses in their trials. If eventually it is permitted the defendants — *who learn the nature of the accusation against themselves for the first time at the trial* — to bring to their aid from among their associates some witnesses on their behalf, that does not satisfy the fundamental demand of human justice to be able to defend oneself with witnesses, for these statements are not taken into consideration at the time the sentence is handed down, as harsh experience has shown. Such statements, in any event, cannot replace the oral questioning of witnesses for the simple reason that neither the defendant nor his associates know the nature of the accusation. Consequently such testimony cannot be *ad rem*. For that reason as well it has no effect on the sentence.

The courts martial function to the complete exclusion of the public. And the names of the military judges are not known, at least publicly. That is possible and understandable in a regime which does not call itself popular and democratic but which is openly known to be authoritarian. But it is impossible to understand that such a trial system exists in a regime which emphasizes its democratic character and the fact that the people rule. I think, Mr. President, that you, as all honest men everywhere, will agree on this point, that one cannot call the rule of the people the practice whereby the newspapers print articles on the eve of a trial aimed at a given defendant and on the next day the news of his condemnation. Still less can one call the rule of the people the contents of the communiqués published after the decisions of the military and civil courts. Such communiqués are usually cynical comments concerning the condemned and hence are as a blow struck at the face of justice rather than a justification of a severe penalty.

2. The example of the death sentence given to Professor Kerubin Segvić may be advanced as proof of what has just been said. Although the Marshal clearly stated that priests who had not bloodied their hands, but had only been indiscreet, would be pardoned, an old man of 79, K. Segvić, was condemned to death, although no proof of criminal conduct was adduced. He was accused of supporting the Gothic theory of the origin of the Croatian people. That is a somewhat preposterous scientific theory which can hardly be proved and he might more properly have been accused of insanity. The holding of this scientific theory does not justify according to right reason sentence to death. It was not proved that Professor Segvić incited men to murder on account of his theory. Such an explanation for the capital sentence given to old Professor Segvić has caused dismay in legal circles because of its lack of juridical sense, and has provoked among the people, sympathy for the cruel fate of a powerless old man. These, Mr. President, are most natural human sentiments and no theory or propaganda can accuse them of being "false humanitarianism."

The insufficiency of the explanation given for the death sentence of Professor K. Segvić is also shown by the article entitled "The People's Judgment Is Inexorable," in the *Omladinski borac* (*The Young Fighter*) of July 5 of this year. This article states on the subject of Segvić that he was "an old priest resembling a monkey," "the formulator of what is called the Gothic hypothesis of the origin of the Croatians." In this article it is explicitly admitted that the "Herrenvolk" (that is to say the race of leaders, the Germans) never wanted to recognize that the Croatians were, from a racial point of view, the same as themselves and that hence this monstrosity was never officially approved. In this "explanation" there are several other evident contradictions. Segvić protested against the excesses of the Ustashi who had used his theory to justify their crimes against the Serbs. It was, moreover, universally known that Segvić did not approve of the massacre of the Serbs but that he had condemned such a procedure on several occasions in my presence. For all the other deeds with which he was charged, Segvić should rather have been taken before a court of national honor than before the courts martial which condemned him to death for a reason which no judge in his right mind could accept.

Moreover, can the natural good sense of the Croatian people accept the explanation of the death sentence given to Sister Blanda Stipetić? For the first time in the history of the Croatian people a nun has been sentenced to the supreme penalty by which the most hardened of criminals are punished. And how has Sister Blanda bloodied her hands? By hiding a Ustashi, the murderer Stjepan Hripka, under the name of Barić. She was assisted in this by Anka Zbornik and by Sister Beata Nemec. Let us assume that Stjepan Hripka was a proved "murderer." The question was open whether Sister Blanda Stipetić knew that he was. This fact was not brought out in passing sentence. On the contrary, Sister Blanda Stipetić asserted (cf. *Omladinski borac,* July 5) that she did not know what he was nor whether he was a Ustasha. Hence, so long as subjective guilt for an objective act was not proved, no sentence could be pronounced according to any human law or to any reason; and least of all could the accused be sentenced to death. This Hripka lived far away from Sister Blanda Stipetić and Anka Zbornik. It has not been proved that either of the two had any knowledge of his former activity. This man had helped both Sister Blanda Stipetić and Anka Zbornik to bring food to Zagreb for the hospital and the welfare kitchen for the poor. If they hid him without knowing what he had been, is that an act meriting the death sentence? By this sentence Sister Blanda Stipetić and Anka Zbornik are punished in the same way as the acknowledged murderers, Juco Rukavina and Majstorović-Filipović. Does there exist any real basis for judging her guilt? These acts were performed by a nun who frequently saw how Partisans and their families were hidden in the sister's hospital and who, without having done anything whatever to make their situation more difficult, kept silent. Could not that have been taken into consideration at the time her guilt was being judged?

But there is something even more important. Hripka was arrested. Up to today he has not been taken before any court, his crimes have not yet been legally proved. So far as I know, he was still, ten days ago, living in the concentration camp at Maksimir. By what law, by what logic can two death sentences be pronounced because of aid given to a man who himself has not yet been tried and whose guilt has not yet been legally proved? Mr. President, that is indeed an example of "justice" and law unique in the annals of our courts.

Now to cite another case. The pastor of the Holy Family parish in the Kanal District of Zagreb, Petar Kovacić, was punished for having accepted a decoration from the Ustashi regime, a distinction which was given him against his will. He was also charged with having warned parents from his pulpit to see that their children do not remain on the streets until the early morning hours in mixed company. For such a "transgression" on the part of a Catholic priest exercising his functions, a sentence of 18 months at forced labor was imposed. In this connection we note the unique character of our judicial procedure. On the proposal of the public prosecutor, the judge himself accused the defendant of having forced one of his Orthodox relatives to be converted to Catholicism several years ago; he was on that count sentenced to six years of forced labor. "The judge accuses, the judge condemns," was said by the people of the Turkish courts three centuries ago. Here in the progressive people's court in Zagreb in 1945 is a practice of the sixteenth or seventeenth century. The misfortunes of Pastor Kovacić did not end there. He was taken to the court martial of the city commandant of Zagreb and condemned to death. The mind nor the heart are no longer capable of understanding justice in this sense.

I have not been able to verify the recent news concerning the pastor of Koprivnica, Stjepan Pavunić, who has been condemned to death at Krizević. I know Pavunić as an exceptionally conscientious man who would not harm a fly and was incapable of inciting anyone to do wrong. He had expressed himself in favor of the Independent Croatian State, at a time when the NDH still possessed real coercive power. If he was a member of the Sabor, it was not voluntary, but, as everyone knows, by the order of the authorities then in power. It is well known that those who did not come into the Sabor upon invitation, were put in prison. Does a man with the moral qualities of a Stjepan Pavunić deserve the death sentence?

Moreover, why was the pastor of Varaždin, a peaceable and sober man, well thought of in his town, for several years the teacher of Varaždin's youth, shot as a malefactor? Should the words of the Marshal not be applied here, when he said those who had not bloodied their hands would be released after all the troubles and pain they have endured up to the present? The same thing applies to the pastor of Biskupec, M. Kalajdzić, and the pastor of Kamensko, Bucmanić, who were, as we have learned, also condemned to death by the court martial at Karlovac.

I am citing examples at length, Mr. President, to show upon what foundations the procedure in the courts martial is based. I think that it is as clear as day that such a procedure can inspire no confidence whatever in the courts' objectivity. It is equally clear that these courts do not serve justice, but vengeance and hatred. If they are handing down death sentences *en masse*, they have become the creature of a mass terror. It is not surprising that the president of the court martial of the commandant of Zagreb has been called by the people another Vignijević, the ill-famed president of the Zagreb court martial at the time of the Ustashi regime.

There is a universal demand to stop all this as soon as possible, or to speak more accurately to stop at once the activities of these military courts in Croatia and to restore civil courts for civil cases. If these courts are to be called popular, the qualified judges should be elected by the people. Not one member of the regional court nor of the district court, and still less of the military court of Zagreb was elected by the people; all were appointed by the higher authorities.

3. Besides the above-named priests from the Archdiocese of Zagreb, a whole group of priests are still in the prisons and the concentration camps. I am enclosing a list of the imprisoned priests from the Archdiocese of Zagreb. As to other dioceses I have not yet been able to obtain exact information. But so far as I have been able to learn, their number must exceed the number of imprisoned priests from Zagreb.

4. I receive more information every day on the subject of arrested priests. And at the same time as the news of their arrests, the news of the forceable requisitioning of their property. The parochial offices are closed and the care of souls is often impossible. The lesser state officials proceed without any legal authorization to divide ecclesiastical property and to solve, on their own authority, the agrarian problem with Church property. There are incessant attacks in the newspapers against certain priests. Priests are dubbed "reactionaries." My person is attacked and lies and caricatures fil the newspapers as if I had given my protection to those who acclaimed Pavelić. The clear sense of my circular letters is distorted in the daily press — and without the slightest chance for those attacked to defend themselves publicly or in the same newspaper All this makes it perfectly clear that in this country the Catholi clergy has been placed outside the law. Anyone can attack them with

impunity, defame them, and they can only remain silent, fill the
prisons, and enrich with their names the cruel list of those condemned
to death. All this occurs at the very time that speakers, and even
the public prosecutors, are explaining to the people of Zagreb the
government statement on freedom of conscience and of religion.

5. I state too that the voice of the Catholic press has, in reality,
been silenced. The publication of a pamphlet by some priests from
Zagreb has not been permitted. The reason given was that there
was a shortage of paper. A little later some soldiers took from the
basement of the *Narodna tiskara* (the Catholic printing press of
Zagreb) and from my place wagon loads of paper for the communist
Naprijed ("Advance"), as if the printing presses of the party were
a state enterprise. This constitutes a unique example of the juridical
situation in which we are living. The Catholic weekly, *Novi život*,
has been allowed only monthly publication, and in a reduced number
of copies so that it is curtailed before it makes its appearance.
The *Narodna tiskara*, in which most of the capital involved belongs
to the Church, has been accused of collaboration with the occupation
forces and with enemies of the people and all of its activities have
been suspended. Prior to any court decision, soldiers, and consequently state employees, took away its paper reserves for the profit
of another press, that of the party. Thus all freedom of the press
is in fact rendered impossible although this guarantee figures among
those in the declaration of the Federal Government. We have reached
a point where every day we are attacked but are not permitted
to publish any Catholic paper. All this occurs in a period of liberation
and under a promise of freedom.

6. This year's procession of the citizens of Zagreb from Marija
Bistrica has become a subject of newspaper attack and other methods
of reprisal against the Catholic clergy. I must on that account refer
to this procession.

But first an observation. Nothing that occurred at the time of
that procession had been organized in advance. I challenge most
vigorously the assertion that reactionary circles had organized the
shouting of political slogans. The hymn known as "We want God"
has been sung in Zagreb for a long time. It is, to characterize it
properly, a French hymn about 25 years old and has already been
sung here for many years. The shouts and cries as a form of mass
demonstration are something new and in the style of our own day,
certainly not an invention of the Church. The interruption of my

sermon was definitely not a part of the ceremony. I have always demanded and emphasized that the Church must be separated from politics.

I state next that in the procession and during the religious ceremonies no political sentiments were uttered, although I know very well that the USACH (the Popular Front Youth Organization) had sent several of its members to scream political slogans which might have provoked a reaction from the people present. Neither the Church nor the clergy are guilty if a crowd of the faithful made a pilgrimage from Marija Bistrica this year. Responsibility for this falls upon those who have filled the concentration camps and prisons with the relatives of the participants in the pilgrimage. The Church and the clergy are not guilty if thousands have acclaimed these victims. Publicity has been given to them by those who have put the clergy in prison and condemned them to death. In relation to the procession from Marija Bistrica, a rumor is being spread in certain circles of high government officials that Bishop Cekada recited on several occasions, along with the gathering of the faithful, five Pater Nosters for the émigrés. I repudiate this lie which thousands of pilgrims can at any moment show to be a calumny.

7. The question of religious instruction in the schools has not been posed by the Church but by those who have, without the agreement or consent of any authorized representative of the Church and without asking the opinion of the great numbers who today send their children to the schools, have made their decision. Despite the affirmations that religious instruction would not be abolished, the following facts have been proved: (*a*) that religious instruction has been entirely abolished in the higher classes of the secondary schools. This is not in accord with the principles of freedom of religion and freedom of conscience. If these principles determine the optional character of religious instruction in the lower classes of the secondary schools, why is that not also valid for the higher classes? It is plain that in the decision to abolish religious instruction from the higher classes, another reason was decisive. It is certain that this was not a motive of friendship toward the Church and religion. And the masses of the people realized this clearly.

b) In the lower classes religious instruction has been reduced to an optional matter and to one hour a week.

c) In the elementary schools it is optional and has been reduced to one hour a week.

These are proved facts. If those who made this decision regarding religious education in Croatia had foreseen the reaction of the masses of the people, they would certainly have hesitated to make such a decision, for it is not in accord with the opinion of the people. I again add that the students in the higher classes have, in great numbers, spontaneously demanded the catechism. Why has this freedom been taken away from them in the name of "liberty"? These facts show the need for a revision of the regulations concerning religious instruction in the elementary and secondary schools so that it may be given for two hours a week in the former, and introduced into the higher classes.

8. A final word on the charge of the communist newspaper, *Naprijed* of July 14, 1945, that a priest, a catechism teacher, had his pupils learn to chant, "We want religious instruction in the schools." I will proceed to make an inquiry on this matter. But I cannot understand how the *Narodni list* of July 14 could have carried a cartoon of the procession from Bistrica as if the children had shouted this slogan. Does this not mean making the procession an object of mockery? Does that not fall under the law of incitement to religious hate? Can such buffoonery be called "a scientific criticism of religion" or is it "a criticism of an incorrect activity of representatives of religion," a criticism which is not itself considered as an incitement to religious hatred? Be sure of this, that tens and tens of thousands of men and women who took part in the procession from Marija Bistrica were profoundly indignant at this mockery in the *Narodni list*. It is even less understandable how the Minister of Public Instruction, Mr. Vekljan, could have said before the people of Donja Stubica that, "the reaction tried to exploit this [that is to say the return of the procession from Marija Bistrica] . . . and it had engaged several children to cry that there was no religious instruction in the schools." [See *Vjesnik* of July 19, 1945, p. 3.] I regret that the Minister was so badly informed on the procession from Marija Bistrica, as to make, in so uncritical a fashion, the statement that I energetically repudiate.

It is true that the day after the procession from Marija Bistrica all the priests teaching catechism in the elementary schools of Zagreb were stricken from the lists of appointees and were told, as I have been informed, that they would be paid henceforth by those who wanted religious instruction in the schools. Mr. President, I ask you, how can such actions be interpreted? Do they conform to the principles of the freedom of conscience and of democracy as affirmed by the Minister of Public Instruction in his speech at Donja Stubica? Must those who conform in practice to their consciences, according to the principles of democracy, pay a special tax for the maintenance of priests to teach catechism in the elementary schools? And are not these the overwhelming majority of parents? I ask you, Mr. President, to make an inquiry into this case, so that the priests teaching catechism in the elementary schools may not be the victims of anyone's hatred and that they may not be punished for something for which they cannot be declared collectively guilty. That can be done only if hundreds of thousands of parents are not penalized by a tax for the support of priests to teach catechism in the schools, if these parents are to avail themselves of the right to freedom of conscience. The decision by which the priests teaching catechism in the elementary schools were struck from the lists of appointees is another striking case of the way in which certain persons understand democracy and justice. That is why I hope, Mr. President, that you may try successfully to have this decision revoked.

9. Mr. President! When all that I have stated concerning the actions of the military courts against the priests is taken into consideration; when the list of the priests condemned to death is reread; when the great number of priests in prison are taken into account; when day after day the attacks against the clergy are repeated, and they are denounced as "reactionaries," which in the vocabulary of the times means defaming them and thus placing them outside the law; when the position of the church in today's schools is realistically appreciated; when it is recalled that nearly all ecclesiastical buildings, such as schools and seminaries, are used for secular purposes; when it is, moreover, shown that a Catholic press in Croatia has been practically destroyed; when in Catholic institutions, teachers are named who, in their classes attack directly the Catholic principles of education; is it not then legitimate to conclude that the Church in Croatia is being persecuted? I have purposely not mentioned the kind of treatment to which Catholic priests are exposed in the concentration camps and in the prisons, for that is too tragic a story. But the facts speak for themselves in a very loud voice. Their words are clear. The Catholic Church in Croatia is in a state of confusion. It is not persecuted openly, for today that is not yet opportune, but under the pretext of the regulation of its activities in the political sphere and, in reality,

by the evident tendency toward the destruction of all that forms
the basis of the life of the Church, namely the freedom of the clergy
and their activity in administering to the souls of the faithful. For,
as statistics show, the clergy is rapidly disappearing from the surface
of free life, either in the prisons or under the bullets of the
firing squads.

II

Mr. President! I remarked in the beginning that great numbers
of my flock come to see me every day, presenting various requests
that I might aid them in their need. As their pastor I cannot turn
a deaf ear to all these appeals, and for this reason I must discuss them
so that you may take them into consideration.

1. In the first place I attach great importance to the fact that
those who are condemned to death by the military courts ought
to be able to receive a priest in the last moments of their lives and
obtain religious consolation. Everyone condemned to death has the
right to receive the sacraments, even those who are condemned to
the loss of their rights. The priests who have been executed, without
such spiritual consolation, should especially have this right. During
the Ustashi regime I tried very hard to assure that all the condemned
have a priest in their last moments and I finally succeeded in
assuring this. I do not think that the present regime wishes to be
inferior in this respect and that as soon as possible the question
of a priest's presence with the condemned will be solved. Let the
military authorities designate the priests in whom they have confidence and I will give them the necessary authorization so that this
question may be finally settled. I have already received on several
occasions oral promises on this subject, but the matter has so far
made no progress whatever. Meanwhile the military courts have
pronounced death sentences *en masse,* as is confirmed by the events
that occurred on the 20th of this month before the Zrinjevac court-
house in Zagreb when several dozens of women learned that their
husbands or their brothers had been shot.

2. In connection with this question there is an important circumstance, namely that there is no court which, in the case of a death
sentence, is competent to pardon the condemned. Such an institution
exists in every juridical system of the twentieth century. True
progress in the cultivation of the soul and the heart demands that
in the administration of a state the principle of the pardon be

respected alongside that of justice. This principle is deeply rooted in the Christian soul of the Croatian people. For that reason the absence of a supreme authority which, in the case of death sentences, can exercise the right to pardon is doubly felt. I cannot and I must not pass over in silence the fact that such an authority during the Ustashi regime saved the lives of several persons who are today in high office. Why go backward in this respect, when at the same time it is emphasized that we are a progressive people?

This is all the more necessary for, in so far as I know, the military courts proceed in a singularly rapid manner. They say that as many as eighty sentences a day are pronounced. In a few minutes they reach a decision on the fate of a life or of long years of nonfreedom. Can it be supposed that such a procedure in the courts can be careful and just? The real necessity for this authority cannot be considered as satisfied by the fact that the sentences of a lower military court must be confirmed by the high military court of the army. For that is not an agency for granting pardons but, in fact, a court of appeals. And a court remains always a court, that is to say, it remains always within the sphere of the application of law, and hence of justice. Account is taken of the fact that the overwhelming majority of the accused do not and cannot know the regulations of the military courts which today judge their acts retroactively — which also is not regular — it is clear that the existence of an authority able to pardon those condemned to death would be highly desirable.

3. The relatives of the executed do not have the right of knowing where the tombs of their dear ones, their brothers and husbands, are located. It is known that the Roman law permitted the burial of the executed. After the execution "justice is satisfied," and there is no reason why the body of a Christian should not be decently buried. In place of this, executions today are carried out in unknown places. The corpses are thrown into a common ditch and no one of their relatives can learn where the graves of their loved ones are to be found. The men in power today trembled with horror and cried out against the actions of the Ustashi when the latter buried the condemned in unknown places or at the site of the execution. I myself fought hard so that the bodies of the executed might be given Christian burial. What was abhorrent formerly must not be repeated today. For that reason it is necessary to permit relatives to take the bodies to the family graves, in Christian cemeteries as

pious Christians have done with their dead from time immemorial. It is also necessary to introduce the practice whereby the courts which pronounce death sentences and have them carried out, inform the Bureau of Vital Statistics so that the death of any individual can be officially proved. That is necessary because of the great consequences in relation to their property and their families.

4. Our prisons and our concentration camps are still full, too full. I leave aside the question whether all who are imprisoned are in fact guilty and whether they ought to be there. For in not a few cases persons remain for six or eight weeks in prison without being questioned. After their first interrogation they are released. Should these latter have been put in prison? In the press it is admitted that the authorities have been led into errors by false accusations and that they have put innocent people in jail. . . . Such cases could easily be avoided if those who were the objects of accusations were not immediately jailed. On the basis of an accusation, the accused ought to be called in for questioning. Then only should it be decided whether it is necessary to imprison him or to release him so that he may defend himself, if such should be the case, while free. Mass arrests must necessarily produce the effect that many innocent persons are put in jail for the sole reason that someone has committed an act of personal revenge against them. Such acts of revenge and such indictments of innocent persons can and must be checked by the punishment of those who turn in false accusations. But that must be said clearly in the invitations issued to the people by the authorities. Unhappily not one single invitation from the authorities asking the people to denounce the guilty has contained this singularly important sentence, namely that those who turn in a false accusation shall be punished. To uphold the morale of the people that is an absolute necessity. In contrary circumstances a system of secret accusations and revenge is favored and on such a foundation the prosperity of the people and the state cannot be built. How much easier the task would be made for the authorities if arrests were carried out more prudently and if easier cases were resolved by an interrogation without arrest! How much discontent, how many tears, and how many troubles spared! These things must also be considered.

5. In the manner of treating the prisoners there are many things against which the masses of the people are complaining. First of all, the prisons are too full and cannot hold the number of persons as-

signed to them. Measures at the time of arrests such as I described above would greatly alleviate this evil.

I have already requested that several priests be designated to visit the prisoners and give them the sacraments in case of illness. As of today this request has not been satisfied adequately.

Besides the prisoners, there are relatives who suffer greatly in bringing them food and spare clothing. The policy in this weather is incomprehensible. Certain prisoners are never allowed to receive food and spare clothing from their families. They have been in prison for weeks. Their wives bring food and the guards tell them that they are not there, although the wives saw them — let us suppose such a case — a moment before. Why not allow all prisoners to receive food on certain fixed days? If there have been abuses in regard to this, they can be avoided by reasonable precautions and control.

The relatives of the prisoners must wait hours for their turn. Once the food is received by the guards, they must again wait for long hours for the baskets to be returned. There have been cases where relatives had to wait for four to six hours in the sun to finish this task. Why torment those who are not guilty? Cannot the procedure for the reception of food and clothing be accelerated? I know of many cases where women fell ill on account of such a procedure and were so weakened that they became unfit to work.

But these persons are still comparatively happy for at least they know where to take their food. But what can I say about those who for whole weeks must go looking from prison to prison before they finally find their husband or their son? Why such a procedure? Does it not mean unnecessarily tormenting and embittering so many families? They already suffer from the knowledge that someone from their family is in prison. Should the measure of their suffering be unnecessarily increased? I find no reason for such procedure. The excuse which holds those who were in the forests suffered and that now those who were in the towns must suffer is not human. Of what would the liberation consist, at bottom, if only the roles of the suffering should be changed? That is why I hope, Mr. President, that in agreement with the military authorities you will obtain the establishment of a bureau which will give to the relatives of the prisoners exact information on where the members of their families are located. Then that all prisoners will be permitted to receive food and spare clothing, especially the latter. And, finally, that the method of delivering this food and clothing will be speeded up. In that way many justified complaints will be avoided and with them much discontent.

6. I have received in the past few days several hundred questions and requests in regard to the fate of the officers and soldiers who were taken to other places. Thus there have been many complaints on the subject of the group of air corps officers who made their way from Zagreb to Bjelovar, then across the whole of Slovenia to Petrovaradin and Vršac. The relatives who visited them at Vršac reported that these men, together with other prisoners, would be sent to work in Russia. This news does not seem to me to be truthful but, naturally, it troubled the relatives of these unfortunate men. It would, on that account, be useful if this report were officially denied, since I have learned that several of these officers have returned to Zagreb.

Hundreds of thousands of Croatian soldiers who were marched away from Zagreb were enrolled, as I have learned, in the Yugoslav army and stationed far from their homes in Macedonia and Serbia. The fate of these men, the flower of the Croatian people, is hard. They did their duty in good faith. Now they must wander from one misfortune to another, exposed to the outpouring of chauvinistic hatred, as prisoners of war in their own country. Months pass without being able to send their families news. Others are still in concentration camps and suffer from hunger in their own fatherland. When all this is seen, the question is asked, has the Croatian people ever in its history suffered so many calamities as in the last four years of the war and the few months since the end of the war?

If to this is added all the sufferings of Croatian intellectuals and civil servants, intellectuals returned from the service or who are still in concentration camps or prisons for having exercised the functions by which they lived under the old regime, then the question is asked, where is this leading us? Thousands of civil servants and professional men have no bread. What new work can be undertaken by men with a university education at forty or fifty years of age? That has today become an acute social question. These intellectuals are told to go and build roads, by illiterate leaders; a cynical and cruel mockery of Croatian culture. One cannot but think that it is a question of the extermination of Croatian intellectuals. But in any case it is a miserable attempt. In the place of trained Croatians are put persons without any experience or background, whom even the responsible state authorities publicly acknowledge to be sometimes incapable of signing their own names.

7. Finally the question is asked, where does there exist a moral justification for the persecution of thousands of Croatian officers and hundreds of thousands of Croatian soldiers who, in the greatest good faith and with many sacrifices in order to serve the Croatian people, fulfilled their duty as soldiers? In conformity with the moral principles of war not one of them should be punished except those who violated the international rules of war or unjustly attacked the peaceful civil population who took no part in military operations. It will not be too much to point out also in defense of these Croatian officers and soldiers the fact that they considered their fight to be a defensive fight against all the injustices that were committed, which injustices were even admitted by the NOP (the chauvinist regime of prewar Yugoslavia). Moreover, these officers and men are ready today to collaborate in the reconstruction and rebuilding of a Yugoslavia that would be a true guarantee of the legal and real equality of all the peoples of the nation.

I conclude. All that I have explained is with the intention of assuring a sincere collaboration between Church and State. This was always my wish and the guiding idea in my work. This work is of an ecclesiastical character, and so assumes no responsibility for political actions. It has been accomplished within the limits of ecclesiastical law, for the benefit of the Croatian people, and consequently of all of the Federal Yugoslav Democracy.

Please accept, Mr. President, the expression of my sincere respect.

ARCHBISHOP OF ZAGREB, *President of the Episcopal Conference*

Reply From Dr. Vladimir Bakarić

ARCHBISHOP:

Through Monsignor Rittig I received your letter containing complaints against our authorities' methods of procedure.

I am grateful to you for having sent me your sincere opinion.

I find that on certain subjects you are badly informed, on other subjects that I do not share your point of view, on still others I am of the opinion that you are absolutely correct.

I hope in a few days, as soon as my health permits, to discuss these matters with you and find a solution which will satisfy both parties.

Please accept the expression of my respect.

Dr. V. BAKARIĆ

Zagreb, July 26, 1945

Letter From Archbishop Stepinac to Dr. V. Bakarić
No. 67/BK

ZAGREB, August 2, 1945

MR. PRESIDENT:

I have the honor of acknowledging receipt of your letter and thank you most cordially. You have been kind to give me a summary reply to my letter of July 22 of this year and to announce an interview on the questions I raised with you. However, I see in the newspapers that in your address to the Sabor, you touched upon several of the questions in my letter. I think it necessary to make some observations on several points of your speech to the Sabor:

1. First of all, I note with satisfaction that you have clearly expressed the government's intention not to meddle with religious principles and the internal affairs of the Catholic Church. You have, by clarification of Marshal Tito's speech, set aside all doubt on the subject of alienating the clergy and the faithful from Rome, that is to say from the supreme head of the Church, the Holy Father. It is hardly necessary to emphasize that such a policy would be a flagrant contradiction of religious freedom. It would likewise be sterile and condemned to failure, for it does not take into account the dangerous upheaval that would be provoked in the life of the state. I must at the same time express my profound regret that a member of the Sabor attacked the Holy Father in a speech, an attack which even the President of the Sabor regretted. Such an unqualified attack shows that it was basically motivated by religious hatred. It is an affront to millions of Catholics, and I am only doing my duty in raising my voice to protest against this act. I hope that such an outburst will not occur again for it is in open contradiction to the rules of good conduct and to the respect for the religious head of millions of Catholics in this country, especially in Croatia. I do not think that the appeal to democracy can justify so uncivil an action.

2. You mentioned the procession from Marija Bistrica in your speech and said that you "possess authentic statements from the highest ranking ecclesiastics that most of the pilgrims were members of Ustashi families many of whom had fled, were in hiding, or in concentration camps." If these words refer to my letter, I reiterate that I made no such statement and that this conclusion does not follow from what I did write. My words were as follows: "Responsibility for this falls upon those who have filled the concentration camps and prisons with the relatives of the Marija Bistrica pilgrims." It does not at all follow that the relatives of the Marija Bistrica pilgrims were "Ustashi." There were a great many who were not Ustashi, but who have relatives in the concentration camps and prisons. That is universally known. In my letter I also drew attention to the great numbers of former Croatian soldiers who were arrested, put in concentration camps and prisons, and, after a time, set free by the authorities as innocent men. You stated elsewhere in your speech that you did not wish to prevent the procession because of "the attitude of certain men without a conscience."

I emphasize again that the ecclesiastical authorities had no political motives in organizing this procession. I assert that during the procession no political slogans were uttered. I cannot accept your statement that at the time of the procession "a fundamentally Ustashi campaign was organized." The reason is that I am convinced that the great majority of pilgrims had nothing in common with the Ustashi movement and consequently were not pro-Ustashi. If anything could be conceded, it is "that there were certain men without a conscience," whose attitude was not that of a religious procession. These were completely lost in the mass of the faithful. In a word, I take vigorous exception to the charge that the Church is political and, especially, that the organization of the procession from Marija Bistrica was pro-Ustashi in character.

3. In two places in your speech you refer to a list of imprisoned men to be given to the "English." At one point you speak of an office that draws up these lists and at another you say that, "among the priests are those who are making these lists — for the 'English' — of men in concentration camps, those whose whereabouts are unknown, whether they have fled into the forests or abroad. The families of these men are asked to gather together information required for the 'English.' In fact a political party is in the process of formation. All this is the work of enemies."

Mr. President! As I pointed out in my letter, I receive every day a great many petitions asking for aid and information. I stated this sincerely and openly. Hence, I must energetically reject the accusation that anyone in my secretariate is making up lists for the English. I do this because the whole city knows that hundreds of persons have come to my office with the addresses of their relatives from whom they have had no news up to the present. This was not the result of my own initiative or that of my priests. If you have been otherwise informed I assure you that the information is inaccurate.

The reality was as follows. About twenty days ago a group of women, wives of officers who are at Vršac, came to ask me to sign their petition to Marshal Tito that he might have them brought back onto Croatian territory. I recommended this petition and it was given to Monsignor Rittig to pass on to the Marshal. Since these women had not yet collected all the signatures of interested parties, they left the petition with the porter of the Archiepiscopal palace so that others might sign it. At the same time I received inquiries regarding other prisoners, with requests to aid them.

I could neither reject these requests nor turn these persons away. For four years I did not turn away people from among your ranks who came to me to intervene for them. None of my priests told anyone that this was being done for the "English," for none of my priests are capable of conceiving such a thing. I energetically reject the statement that in this organization (that is the Catholic Church and the clergy) any new orientation has been introduced or that it has deviated, even a little, from its traditional path; I reject such a statement as to the activities of my secretariate in the matter of petitions requesting information about the missing members of many families. Mr. President, all this was done publicly in my office. Is it possible to conceive that such action as the government esteems hostile to the state was carried out publicly through my secretariate?

4. In concluding this reference to the gathering of information, you stated further in your speech: "We affirm that we know whence comes the inspiration for these actions and we are following the development of these matters attentively." In regard to these words I say sincerely that I am unaware whence comes the inspiration in gathering information on the subject of missing persons.

I have thought it necessary to submit the preceding observations on your speech to the Sabor.

Please accept, Mr. President, my expression of the greatest respect.

Dr. A. Stepinac
*Archbishop of Zagreb, President of the
Episcopal Conference*

DOCUMENT LXVII

*Communication From the Archbishop Regarding Education and
Other Matters of Vital Interest to the Church*

Presidency of the Episcopal Conference   Zagreb, August 11, 1945
No. 71/BK

To: (1) Dr. Vladimir Bakarić, President of the Croatian Government
    (2) Religion Commission of the Presidency of the Croatian
        Government
    (3) Federal Ministry of Public Instruction of the Yugoslav
        Democratic Federation, Belgrade.

Within the past few days the right to teach in the primary and
secondary schools has been officially taken away from us. Prior to the
beginning of the new school year, the representatives of the Ministry
of Public Instruction are preparing proposals for the projected reform
in instruction in the state schools. In regard to this I feel obliged to
explain the position and the point of view of the Catholic Church
relative to education, especially the religious education of the young.
Toward this end I have the honor of submitting this letter, in the
hope that it will be used in solving the school problem under
present-day conditions, especially as now there has been no agreement in this matter between the Catholic Church and the state
authorities.

1. I wish to draw your attention first to the position of the Catholic
Church between April, 1941, and May, 1945. This is necessary so
that difference between the situation of the Church today in the
sphere of education and that prevailing before the outbreak of
the war.

In prewar Yugoslavia the Church had the right of collaborating
in the education of the young in all state and private schools,
religious instruction being obligatory for two hours each week, except
for the schools under the jurisdiction of the Ministry of Commerce.
Even in that case religious instruction was approved in principle,

although it was not actually taught during the school year of 1941–42. Along with religious instructions, the performance of religious duties was prescribed: attendance at divine services, reception of the sacraments three times a year, participation in spiritual exercises for three days, and once a year, on the eve of Easter.

The Church had the right, guaranteed by the unratified concordat, of establishing private schools. Among them were the Archiepiscopal and Episcopal high schools in Zagreb, Travnik, Split, and Sent Vid; a number of the boarding schools of the various religious orders, such as the Franciscan high schools in Visoko, Široki Brijeg, Badija, Sinj, and Varaždin and the Dominican high school in Bol on Brać Island; the high school and normal school of the Sisters of Charity in Zagreb, of the Daughters of Divine Charity at Sarajevo, and a great number of elementary schools throughout the nation. All these schools had the right to teach publicly since they functioned in perfect accord with the state schools and were under the supervision of the Ministry of Public Instruction in Belgrade.

At the same time as the Church supported these small seminaries and the Archiepiscopal and Episcopal high schools in Zagreb, Travnik, and Sent Vid, and the various orders had, besides these high schools, boarding schools such as those as Visoko, Široki Brijeg, Badija, and Bol, the schools of the Sisters of Charity, the Salesians, and the Ursulines in Zagreb, and the school of the Archdiocese of Zagreb at Požega, the state also aided the small seminaries in the form of a regular subsidy guaranteed by the state budget.

On the territory subject to the old NDH, the above-described position of the Church remained the same, only the number of the private schools directed by the religious orders was increased.

This position in prewar Yugoslavia had been achieved after a long struggle and did not correspond completely to the educational principles that the Church has held through the centuries as the wisest and best. It was, nevertheless, acceptable, and the regular religious education of Catholic youth was rendered reasonably effective. It is necessary to point out especially that the day and boarding schools run by the Church enjoyed the complete confidence of parents because of the sound education they provided. The government, through official inspectors, recognized their great success. It is well known that the Catholic schools occupied first place among schools throughout the country. More than 95 per cent of the students from Catholic private schools regularly passed their state examinations. In some schools an average of from 98 per cent to 100 per cent was constantly maintained. I emphasize that these Catholic private schools were not sectarian in a narrow sense. They were attended by students of the Orthodox, Moslem, and Jewish religions as well as by Catholics; and even in cities such as Zagreb where they had the chance of attending public or other schools, nevertheless, their parents paid a special school fee so that they might send their children to Catholic private schools. Their existence was amply justified by their brilliant success.

2. The end of the war in May of this year brought an essential change in the position of the Catholic Church in Yugoslavia in the field of education; when in the states of the Federation having a preponderantly Catholic population, such as Croatia and Slovenia, as well as in Bosnia and Hercegovina, obligatory religious instruction was abolished in all primary and secondary schools. This is an undeniable fact. In the higher classes of the secondary schools no religious instruction, even on an optional basis, is permitted. In the lower classes of the high schools religious instruction has been reduced from an obligatory to an optional status and at the same time the number of hours has been reduced from two a week to one. In the primary schools religious instruction has ceased to be obligatory and has been made optional and the hours reduced likewise from two to one a week. Moreover, religious instruction which, for centuries, was given first place in the course of studies, is today grudgingly reduced to last place, behind all the practical disciplines. It is clear that among us that which ought to be first in the scale of values and human life has been reduced to the lowest rank.

I feel bound to express my dissatisfaction over this action on the part of the school authorities in Croatia. This action violates the right of parents to rear their children in a religious atmosphere as well as the inviolable right of the children themselves to have a religious education. This policy is clearly contrary to the wishes of a considerable majority of Catholic parents, in whose name I speak. These were the parents who, when questioned by the school authorities themselves as to whether they desired religious education for their children, voted "yes" in a plebiscite religious instruction in the schools. Are the actions of the school authorities in Croatia, based — as is said — on the will of the President of ZAVNOH (*Zemaljsko Antifašističko Vijeće Narodne Omladine Hrvatska —*

Regional Anti-Fascist Council of Democratic Croatian Youth), in accord with the clearly expressed wishes of the people to respect its religion as the most sacred of all things? Is this policy a faithful interpretation of popular preference, or an arbitrary and even sectarian imposition on the people? This action was taken without any understanding with the Church authorities and the great masses of the Catholic faithful, as if in Croatia the Catholic Church with its faithful did not exist and could be forgotten and ignored.

Moreover, the school authorities do not devote to religious instruction the minimum attention they give to other nonobligatory studies as to attendance and observation of discipline. They are, moreover, indifferent on the subject of the performance of religious duties on the part of the students. They rarely give permission to announce in class a Mass for the students.

It is true that in the towns of Croatia, Bosnia, and Hercegovina the school authorities questioned the parents of children in various ways whether they desired religious education for their children in the primary schools and in the lower classes of the secondary schools. Nearly one hundred per cent of the parents requested a religious education and religious instruction in the primary schools. The percentage of parents who desired religious instruction in the lower classes of the secondary schools varied from 93 to 96 per cent. Moreover, in several secondary schools the students in the higher classes themselves requested by a considerable majority that religious instruction be introduced into their course of studies.

In Zagreb and in the country there are many cases in which the crucifixes have been removed from the classrooms. Nearly everywhere the students themselves, from the lower as well as the higher classes, have replaced them in the classrooms.

There has been a change in the matter of saying a prayer before and after classes. This practice, as old as the schools themselves, is merely tolerated today in certain schools, while in others the school authorities have abolished it on the oral order of the Ministry of Public Instruction. There occur innumerable instances of the students themselves, from the higher and lower classes of the secondary schools, saying these prayers spontaneously without paying any attention to the contrary orders of their superiors.

Private schools run by Catholic religious or by the Church itself, must discontinue their regular school work at the end of this school year. As to the next school year, 1945–46, an announcement appeared in the *Vjesnik* of Zagreb which carries exact statistical details on the schools, students, and professors. In this announcement it is said, "These private high schools will end their work this year, so that next year the students may transfer to public schools since all private schools will be abolished." (*Vjesnik,* Zagreb, August 4, 1945, No. 90, p. 5.)

The Archiepiscopal and Episcopal high schools of Croatia and Slovenia have not received any subsidy from the government for two months and are going to be closed according to *Vjesnik.* The buildings of the minor seminaries are nearly all occupied by the army. Thus the work of training seminarians for the Church has been made impossible or considerably limited. The same thing is true in regard to the buildings of the Catholic private high schools of the various orders.

As can be seen from all this the position of the Catholic Church in the field of education has deteriorated. This position is so precarious that one can reasonably say that the Church has been deprived of nearly all possibility of educating its children and young people. And what has been left to it in the public schools has the character of a favor which is given for a certain time and then arbitrarily taken away.

3. It is clear that the Catholic Church cannot accept the existing situation, and still less consider it a normal thing. That it cannot do for several reasons.

First of all, this kind of state monopoly in the education of children infringes on the right of parents in the education of their own children. Parents — good sense tells us — have the sacred right and duty of preparing their children for their mission in life as independent beings. Children need the care and protection of older persons so that they may harmoniously develop their spiritual and physical capacities. This aid — education — is due them first of all from those who have given them life, of whom they are a prolongation and an alter-ego; that is, from their parents. That is why parents have the inalienable right to fulfill their duty of rearing their children. This right of parents is primordial and of first importance no matter what rights the state may claim in the education of children. Children are the property neither of the state nor of the people, but are independent subjects over whom their parents exercise the fundamental right of education. By their very nature parents are the most capable teachers of children, having more than others all the qualities of a good teacher; knowledge and understanding; the love and confidence. The parents' right of education extends not only over religious and moral education but social and physical as well. To parents belongs the right to establish schools by themselves and, if the state establishes educational institutions, to choose the school which their children attend. In cases where the state establishes and supports schools, parents have the right to demand that instruction conform to their principles of education.

It follows that the state monopoly as it has been introduced among us makes this impossible through denial of the basic right of parents to educate their children.

Besides parents, the Catholic Church also has the right and power to educate its people in faith and morals. This right was given it by its founder, Jesus Christ, and through the centuries it has been recognized by all secular states who respected the freedom of religion and the freedom of conscience. The state which, in principle or in practice, does not respect this right of the Church denies arbitrarily the most sacred rights of men. No modern state that aspires to civilized rank can deny the Church this fundamental right of giving a religious education to Catholic youth. Initial religious education is given to Christian children by the family, representing God and the Church, while in the schools it is the Church itself which provides it through its representatives. These latter must have the authorization of the Church for the fulfillment of their mission.

Like parents, the Church has the natural right to establish schools, especially if religious education in state schools is endangered or made impossible or if the whole tenor of education is contrary to the doctrine of the Church. Naturally in cases such as these the Church conforms to the practical regulations of the state relative to courses of studies and the qualifications of teaching personnel.

In particular, the Church has the right to set up seminaries for the education of future priests (can. 1352 of Canon Law). In their internal administration, the Church is completely free and independent and cannot sacrifice its right to set up seminaries, even in concordats.

The right to establish schools also belongs to the state. It does not, however, perform a primary duty, but a supplementary one, in as much as it provides what parents alone cannot supply through private or church schools. Moreover, in the interests of the common good, the state has the right to set up the courses of studies and to see to it that all teachers fulfill their duties and that they have the necessary qualifications.

These are principles which the Catholic Church professes everywhere in the sphere of the education of children and youth.

In the light of these principles it is clear that the present state of education, as has been explained, not only does not satisfy the Church but must be rejected.

4. Present practices cannot be justified from the point of view of the principles of freedom of religion and conscience as upheld by the Federal Government and the Croatian Government.

It is inconsistent and contrary to the principles of freedom of religion and of conscience that the teaching of religion in the lower classes is permitted, while in the higher classes of the secondary schools in Croatia it is forbidden. In Belgrade, at least up to now, these principles have been correctly understood, so that the teaching of religion has been permitted even in the higher classes of the secondary schools. If the authorities base their policy on the principle of the freedom of conscience and consider it a sacred thing and therefore *do not permit the imposition* of any religious instruction on those who do not want it, by what right can these same authorities *forbid* it to those who, according to their consciences, *do want* religious instruction in the higher classes of the secondary schools? The decision of the President of ZAVNOH (see above), which forbids religious education in the higher classes of secondary schools in Croatia, is an evident violation of the principle of freedom of conscience and can be explained in no other way than as a hostile act against religion in general, and the reflection of an exclusivist and materialist attitude. Whatever the opinions of those who made the decision to forbid religious instruction in the higher classes of the secondary schools, according to the freedom of conscience that they claim for themselves, they are not justified according to the dictates of common sense in refusing this freedom to others. The fact that all the decisions of the Presidency of ZAVNOH are called democratic and that all who understand their illogical nature are quite simply called reactionary and pro-fascist, and that the justified criticisms of these decisions is called an attack on the peoples' government does not change the situation. That is all very simple and easy. But it is, at the same time, very far from that democracy that respects the national traditions, the will of parents regarding their children's education, and the will of the young people themselves who want to have religious instruction in the higher classes. If in Belgrade religious instruction can be permitted in the higher classes of the secondary schools in harmony with the principle of freedom of conscience, why not in Zagreb? Does another logic hold for Zagreb, or another kind of freedom of conscience? Where is democracy practiced, in Belgrade or in Zagreb?

I may mention too that religious instruction has always been considered an outstanding medium of education. To look upon it as an educational subject no different from any other is entirely false. Those who hold this opinion are obviously unaware of the end and the nature of religious instruction in the schools. We have created a program of studies in our schools to the end of meeting the demands of modern pedagogy. From this point of view we cannot be content at all that only one hour a week is devoted to religious instruction as an elective. That does not satisfy the real need of religious knowledge and an adequate moral education for students, particularly urgent in difficult times such as the present. The reduction of religious instruction to one hour a week is a positive step backward. This is equally true, in perhaps still greater measure, in the primary schools.

The practice, introduced in Croatia by the Ministry of Public Instruction, of forbidding any prayers in the schools and not tolerating a crucifix in the schools is also incompatible with freedom of conscience and religion. Croatians are a Christian, Catholic people and they have the right to have a crucifix in their public schools, in line with their venerable traditions. This demand is included in the declaration of parents in the plebiscite in which they voted to have their children attend catechism classes. Authorities who call themselves "popular" are obliged to respect this wish of the parents and to allow a crucifix in the schools established in wholly or preponderantly Christian regions.

Freedom of conscience and religion means that students desiring and attending religious instruction may freely fulfill their religious duties and that the schools not hinder them in this. This could be done if they were given free time, not taken up by classes, to attend divine services on Sundays and to frequent the sacraments, as was done in prewar Yugoslavia. If the students can, for many less important reasons, receive permission to be absent from classes, then it is logical that they be given free time for the practice of their religion.

The principle of the freedom of religion and conscience demands that the state permit the Church to support its seminaries and the private high schools of the religious orders. The Church cannot consider adequate the religious and moral education that is given in the state schools. It is on this account that the Church, in canon law, provides for the establishment of seminaries where it gives to candidates for the priesthood the education that is necessary and suitable for them. It is incompatible with the freedom of religion if seminaries are closed by the occupation or confiscation of their buildings or the loss to the Church, through agrarian reforms, of means for the support of these students, who are mostly the sons of peasants.

It is incompatible with freedom of conscience if private Church schools are abolished. True democracy and truly popular government does not force parents to send their children exclusively to state schools if religion is disregarded by the whole trend of instruction and where it is excluded in the most important years of their psychological development, the age of puberty. This tendency in education may have been given much thought but that does not mean that it is in accord with the spirit of the people and with their time-honored traditions. On the contrary, we openly state that irreligious education such as the decision of the Presidency of ZAVNOH means to favor in the higher classes of the secondary schools is contrary to the national Croatian and Slovenian spirits which were formed essentially by Catholicism. I am convinced that in time most parents and the young people themselves will demand a Christian education in all schools. From the point of view of the freedom of conscience, in a true democracy it goes without saying that the private schools of the Catholic orders and the Church are allowed. Even in secularized France where they are not, in 1906 school legislation hostile to the Church led to a violent separation of Church and State and to the open persecution of the former. But the France of 1939 and of 1945 is no longer the France of 1906. And if anyone wished to introduce among us the conditions of 1906, it would be clearly an open declaration of a Kulturkampf against the Church. But that is not the temper of our times.

Freedom for private schools is desirable for economic reasons. Today when the whole country is in ruins, when insufficient means exist for the enormous work of national reconstruction, economic considerations demand in an almost imperious manner that the state preserve the private schools. In this way, as in prewar Yugoslavia, a popular and national education is assured through a unique program of studies under the supervision of the school authorities.

5. To sum up briefly, the Catholic Church presents to the school authorities the following demands:

1) That in all state schools, primary and secondary, in the higher and lower classes, religious instruction be given two hours a week.

2) That students who freely enroll in religious instruction classes be obliged to attend these classes regularly.

3) That in the annual certificates last place not be given to religious instruction but rather the honored place it has always occupied.

4) That students attending religious instructions be allowed to perform their religious duties and that they be given free time so that they may receive the sacraments (three times a year) and attend the Easter retreat once a year.

5) That private Episcopal, Archiepiscopal, and religious orders' high schools be allowed and that they be given the right to teach publicly at least those who have attended them up to the present.

6) That ecclesiastical seminaries be permitted to function and that their buildings be evacuated so that they may fulfill the end for which they were founded. The same thing is meant for the buildings of other ecclesiastical institutions and schools.

I note in conclusion that in all this we are faced with problems whose solution depends on the success of the negotiations for an agreement between our state and the Holy See. It would not be proper to create in advance through unilateral decisions an unfavorable situation for the Catholic Church and then engage in negotiations with the Holy See. It is understood that such procedure would give no proof of our good intentions to preserve regular relations between our state and the Holy See which form the only possible basis for the proper regulation of the situation of millions of Catholics in the spirit of true democracy and for the welfare and to the profit of both Church and State.

THE ARCHBISHOP, *President of the Episcopal Conference*

DOCUMENT LXVIII

Correspondence Regarding the Proposed Agrarian Reform

Memorandum presented to: (1) Marshal Tito, Belgrade.

(2) Dr. Vladimir Bakarić, President of the Government of the People's Republic of Croatia.

(3) The Presidency of the Council, the Commission for Religious Affairs.

No. 72/BK

A month ago, toward the end of July, with the first indication that the agrarian reform then under study would be actually applied, I had the honor of sending you a letter in which I set forth briefly the position of the Catholic Church on this question. I expressed my hope, based on the promise of the President of the Federal Government, Marshal of Yugoslavia Josip Broz, made to the representatives of the Zagreb clergy and to me personally, that all questions touching on the relations between Church and State would be worked out by agreement and that, in the question of agrarian reform, the Church would be given a chance to examine the proposed law. Had this been done, it would have been possible to come to an agreement with the Church and draft a statute more just and complete than that now presented to the Provisional Popular Assembly.

Unhappily my proposal was not taken into consideration. Today, when the proposed agrarian measure in detailed form has been received by the Legislative Committee of the Provisional Popular Assembly, it is only through sketchy newspaper articles that I have discovered the principal provisions of the law. On the basis of this information it is my duty, in defense of the rights of the Catholic Church, to draw attention to the following points before this law is finally approved by the Assembly.

1. According to the article of the Federal Minister of Agriculture, Dr. Čubrilović (*Zagrebački Vjesnik*, No. 98, August 13, 1945, p. 2), the fundamental principle of agrarian reform is this: land should belong to him who cultivates it. Since the Church, that is, its priests and religious, do not themselves cultivate their own land, for they are not farmers by vocation, its landed properties are looked upon as held in mortmain and, in principle, are to be expropriated without indemnity with the one exception, up to five

hectares of land can be left to churches, convents, and other religious institutions for their support or to be used for humanitarian purposes; in the case of certain institutions of a more significant historical character, up to twenty hectares of arable land may be left to them. (Cf. *Borba*, August 14, 1945, p. 1.)

Without examining the question of the validity of the principle or its justification, I draw attention to one vital feature, namely, that by this solution of the agrarian problem the Church in Yugoslavia is dealt a severe blow in the fulfillment of its normal activity and is gravely jeopardized.

I have already stated, in my letter of last July, that the ecclesiastical properties which the Church possesses in Yugoslavia represent, as a result of the first agrarian reform (following the War of 1914–18), the remnants of the great Church holdings of former times. The Minister Dr. Čubrilović recognizes in his article that, "it is difficult to tell the number of such properties." If this principle should actually be put into effect and all ecclesiastical properties confiscated, it would deprive the Church of most of its means of subsistence. The Catholic Church supports its clergy and religious by means of its landed properties: archbishops, bishops, members of the chapters of archdioceses and dioceses, the central offices of the dioceses, pastors and vicars, major and minor diocesan seminaries, high schools and boarding schools, hospitals, orphanages, and numerous parish churches. The loss of all these properties by the above-mentioned ecclesiastical institutions means rendering the normal activity of the Church impossible. It means the loss of the resources for the education of so many thousands of peasants' sons in its schools and seminaries. The loss means that it will be impossible to educate its future priests and in reality cripple all forms of activity in the future. It is plain that the new agrarian reform represents a piece of legislation hostile to the Church. This is evidenced eloquently when the confiscation of its properties is put on the same basis as that of enterprises for profit and feudal institutions which have no particular reason for survival in the new order. This law reveals as do other measures, that in this nation the Catholic Church has become an entity without rights, exposed to the constant blows of a premeditated, systematic persecution, under the guise of freedom of religion and conscience and respect for private property.

It must not be forgotten that by means of its landed properties — which it received because of its religious mission — the Church has performed a noteworthy cultural function in the past and continues to do so today. The Church is proud of the activity of that patron of learning, Bishop Strossmayer, without which neither the University of Zagreb nor the Academy of Science would be in existence. It is equally proud of the magnificent works of Archbishop Bauer who, at the time of the most serious housing shortage in Zagreb, aided in its solution by the erection of a large block of apartment houses and who was responsible for the most modern type of residence halls for the education of future priests at Salata (Zagreb). The same observation holds for the school building of the Sisters of Charity and their hospital in Zagreb. These cultural and social works, performed for the benefit of the community and all the people, were made possible only because the Catholic Church possessed the necessary material means from its landed property. Today it is proposed, in the name of social justice, to take the remainder of these properties away from the Church as from a mortmain or an ordinary capitalistic enterprise.

As a result of the new agrarian reform the priests and religious of the Church will no longer have means to support themselves. They will necessarily become the charges of their faithful who have shown on many occasions that they do not desire to receive lands belonging to the Church. They appreciate that the seizure of the few properties of more than twenty hectares still left in some areas will not constitute a solution of the agrarian problem. These small bits of property will not satisfy the need of the peasants for more land and only a few among them would receive anything at all. The majority of the faithful consider the property of the Church a parish matter and they do not welcome outside meddling, not even from the State. If these parish lands were taken away from the Church and divided, those who need the Church and its priests would be forced to support them. For this reason the majority of the people consider that any such interference harms the entire community and imposes new responsibilities on it. If the agrarian reform becomes law in the form in which it has been proposed to the Provisional Popular Assembly, it will provoke, instead of the pacification of the masses of the Catholic people, a new unrest among them. For these masses have a very highly developed sentiment of respect for the property of others, especially that of the Church.

The large properties of the Church are very few although they usually merit the attention of the uninformed. I suggest that these holdings, in so far as they still exist today, have a considerably different importance from other large properties. These few large estates support not only the bishops but entire Ordinariates, that is to say the chancelleries that direct religious affairs with their priests and other employees who, up to the present, have received state subsidies. Moreover, every bishop still has obligations toward a certain number of parishes of which he is the patron and where he must, consequently, support the pastor and the parish church. There are also the chapters with ordinarily a large number of members. It would not be just to treat the large holdings of the chapters as a single legal entity as in the case, for example, of the properties of the Metropolitan Chapter of Zagreb. This embraces twenty-eight separate entities, to all of whose members it provides their entire material support. The members of the chapters function as councilors in the administration of the dioceses and the chapters have in turn obligations toward the parishes of which they are the patrons. There are several religious communities with large holdings, as the Sisters of Charity who, from their large possessions at Luznica — which they cultivate themselves — support several convents of their community.

I call attention to the fact that the agrarian reform passed in Poland and Hungary, occupied at the time by Soviet troops, left to the Catholic Church far more land for the support of its priests and religious and ecclesiastical institutions than is proposed here at home. Is it not proper to conclude that in Yugoslavia the new agrarian reform seeks to strike a blow against the Church and make it impossible for it to carry on its normal activity?

All these reasons clearly show that the proposed agrarian reform ought to consider the social and cultural circumstances in deciding who is to be adversely affected by its provisions and who is not. For otherwise the result is *"summum jus summa injuria."*

2. The fundamental principle of the new agrarian reform, that the land should belong to him who cultivates it, is of such a nature that it is impossible to realize it fully. Strictly speaking it would make impossible any ownership of landed property that a peasant did not cultivate himself or with the aid of his family. I wonder how much of such property the average peasant holds; this average peasant who was told by the President of the Legislative Committee, Mr. M. Pyjada, that he would be vigorously protected by this law (*Vjesnik,* August 14, 1945, p. 2), since it is customary for many peasants to cultivate his lands with the aid of others in his village

and often that of a day laborer. These persons will keep their land while the Church will lose it. What an inconsistency shows itself here between principle and practice! That is clear to any man who knows a little about the conditions of village life. These inconsistencies are inevitable because it is impossible completely to realize in actuality the principle that the land should belong to him who cultivates it.

The Minister of Agriculture, Dr. Čubrilović, recognized in his article that this fundamental principle has been abandoned in the case of intellectuals to whom five hectares have been left although the cultivation of the soil is not their principal occupation. It is seen, then, from this article that the State itself is going to establish a fund of landed properties for the benefit of the Federal Government, the various ministries, and other state institutions. It is clear that in these cases the principle that the land should belong to him who cultivates it is not considered. Is not the Catholic Church itself also a public law institution with which our state desires to negotiate for the solution of their mutual relations? How can these negotiations with the Holy See be effected if, before they begin, the Church is despoiled of all the landed properties necessary to it for the performance of its duties and its normal existence? Is not such action calculated to nullify in advance any basis for a sincere agreement with the Holy See, without which it is impossible to imagine the peace and contentment of millions of citizens, as the experience of prewar Yugoslavia shows? For these reasons I cannot in the name of the Church accept the new agrarian reform, for it is obviously unjust to the Church by reason of its insistence on an unrealistic principle that the land should belong only to the one who cultivates it.

3. The explanation by which the Minister of Agriculture justifies the confiscation of Church properties, describing them as "a contribution from the benefactors of the people" is, moreover, not legitimate. This would mean that these properties had been given by the community to these institutions and that, consequently, it would have the right to take them back without paying any indemnity (*Vjesnik*, August 14, 1945, p. 2).

That explanation cannot be the foundation for a true order in a lawful society. The Catholic Church has in its possession the written documents by which the persons who gave it these properties stipulated that they were to be used for certain specific purposes:

the support of priests and religious as well as its charitable and social institutions. These persons transferred their properties to the Church in accordance with their own desires in conformity with the civil regulations in force at the time of the transfer, and the Church in receiving these properties assumed the obligations imposed at the same time by the donors. These transactions had the character of a bilateral contract in which the state may not interfere, for by unilaterally annulling these contracts and confiscating and expropriating the lands, the state overthrows the legal foundation of every contract concluded by the members of society. The state that seeks to annul such contracts necessarily loses the confidence of its citizens. It fails to respect rights which it is obliged to uphold for these rights existed before the state itself. Such a reversal can least of all be committed by a state which, in solemn proclamation to the whole world, declared its respect for private property. Hence the explanation by which the Minister of Agriculture attempts to justify the complete expropriation of Church lands is not admissible.

It cannot be said that there is not sufficient unoccupied land in our country today. Without examining the reasons why over 750,000 acres of land are at present abandoned, I would suggest that these lands can be allotted to those to whom land has been promised and to those others who do not have enough. The properties of the Catholic Church that can be considered large are so few that they can be counted on the fingers of one hand. They came into existence as a result of the cultural and social activities of the Church and for that reason they have merited in the course of history the confidence not only of their founders but also of the masses of the Catholic people. Why destroy them now when so many social and cultural reasons fully justify their existence? These lands have not been neglected as the official press has attempted, inaccurately, to make us believe. They have suffered the ravages of war just as have most of the properties of the state. Their past is witness to the enormous benefits they have brought to the whole community. The lands of the Catholic Church have made possible the material existence of the Church which is the basis for its spiritual activity. They are the source of the support of the priests and religious and, consequently, relieve the faithful in large measure of that responsibility. These Church lands are indispensable for the maintenance of ecclesiastical establishments, and of social and charitable institutions. I strongly urge that they be exempted from the effects of the new agrarian reform, for once before they were subject to the same policy and knew the unjust intervention of the state.

I urge this the more strongly because I myself and the representatives of the Zagreb clergy received the promise of the President of the Federal Government and Marshal of Yugoslavia, Josip Broz Tito, that questions concerning the relations between Church and State would be worked out by an agreement. Unilateral agrarian reform conceived in a spirit hostile to the Church, such as is now before the Provisional Popular Assembly, would, in the event of approval, be a new proof that in this nation the Catholic Church, despite all the assurances of religious freedom and respect for private property, has been deprived of all its rights. I hope that this second letter on the subject of agrarian reform will be considered for the welfare of both Church and State.

> Dr. A. Stepinac
> *Archbishop, President of the*
> *Episcopal Conference*

Zagreb, August 17, 1945

Presidency of the Episcopal Conference,
Zagreb
No. 74/1945/BK

Marshal,

Permit me, Marshal, to address you personally on a question of principle and of the gravest importance.

At the time of your visit to Zagreb at the beginning of June of this year, a delegation of the Zagreb clergy visited you at your request, accepting your initiative in discussing with the representatives of the Catholic Church matters concerning the Church and State. In your address you explicitly emphasized the desire to work out everything through mutual agreement. You suggested the idea of forming a committee of experts by the Church to enter into negotiations with the representatives of the State on questions of common interest. In the conversations that followed your talk you pointed out your desire to come to an understanding with the Church before the definite promulgation of laws concerning both Church and State. You expressed this desire and this promise to me personally at the time of the conversation I had with you on June 4 of this year that the state authorities would promulgate laws concerning the Church in agreement with the Church.

It is clear that the Church considered and still considers this attitude on your part not only as a condition for sincere collaboration with the state authorities but still more as an obligation of the state to promulgate laws concerning the Church on the basis of a frank exposition of its opinion after an exchange of ideas with the representatives of the Church.

Unhappily I must call attention to the fact that from that time to the present a series of laws and ordinances regulating the relations between the Church and State have been promulgated without such an exchange of ideas. I undertook to set forth the point of view of the Church but met with no understanding from the other side.

I informed, through a special memorandum that I had the honor of sending to you toward the end of July, all the competent lawmakers of the viewpoint of the Church on the question of agrarian reform. Now that bill is before the Provisional Popular Assembly, I would like to point out most emphatically — along with the letter of justification I am sending you — that the Catholic Church cannot accept such a solution to the agrarian problem. The provisions of the law which unilaterally expropriate, without any full or equitable indemnity, the properties of the Church are unjust. They put the Church in a position which makes impossible the maintenance of the institutions indispensable to its normal activity, such as the seminaries, the Ordinariates, and educational establishments. Moreover, the maximum amount of land left to the churches and convents is too small to assure the support of their priests and religious, who are bound to certain fixed obligations according to the letters of foundation, without their becoming the charges of the Catholic faithful. I add that this law leaves to the Church as the maximum amount of land that it can keep far less than in the neighboring countries where agrarian reforms have also been instituted. For that reason it is obvious that this law reflects a spirit hostile to the Church.

Therefore, in the name of the Church, I protest against this agrarian law which in addition to all the injustices it contains, is being approved hastily on the eve of the elections and without the existence of a sufficiently trained personnel to put it into practice justly.

I draw your attention, Marshal, to the fact that passage of this law on agrarian reform as it stands will only make worse the relations between the Church and State, relations which, alas, through no fault of the Church are already bad enough. I am convinced that it will not contribute to internal pacification or the projected negotiations with the Holy See. I think that in this matter the words you spoke to the Zagreb clergy are altogether valid, that Church-State relations can only be solved by mutual agreement.

Please, Marshal, accept the expression of my greatest respect.

Dr. Aloysius Stepinac, *Archbishop,*
President of the Episcopal Conference

Zagreb, August 20, 1945

Zagreb, August 20, 1945

Presidency of the Episcopal Conference
Zagreb.
No. 75/1945/BK

To the Presidency of the Provisional Popular Assembly, Belgrade.

I have the honor of addressing the Presidency of the Provisional Popular Assembly on the subject of the agrarian reform law.

I have already had the opportunity of explaining the point of view of the Catholic Church on this subject in a letter. I did that because the President of the Government and Marshal of Yugoslavia, Josip Broz Tito, had personally declared to me, as well as to the representatives of the Zagreb clergy, at the beginning of June this year, that in general all questions concerning the relations between Church and State would be settled by mutual agreement.

The Assembly has placed on its agenda the law concerning agrarian reform and resettlement. This law has been drafted without advice of the representatives of the Church. The provisions of this law reflect a unilateral point of view. They expropriate all the lands of the Church without a just indemnity; lands which it has legally acquired. This law removes the necessary material conditions for the exercise of its normal functions, and which are guaranteed by the principles of religious freedom and the respect for private property. A maximum amount of land is left to the seminaries, the Ordinariates, and educational institutions which is not large enough to support the hundreds of children in their care, most of them the children of peasants. So little land is left to the priests and religious of the Church who are bound by certain obligations to the donors of this land that they will be unable to subsist without becoming a special charge on the faithful.

For that reason, in the name of the Catholic faithful, I strongly protest against this solution of the agrarian question, in an atmosphere of haste without any prior consultation with the Church. This law will not improve the relations between Church and State but will furnish a fragile basis for the projected negotiations with the Holy See.

> Dr. Aloysius Stepinac
> *Archbishop, President of the*
> *Episcopal Conference*

Telegram   August 21, 1945
No. 77/BK

To Marshal Josip Broz Tito, President of the Federal Government of Yugoslavia.

In regard to your conversations with the clergy of the Archdiocese of Zagreb and with the undersigned on the manner of solving ecclesiastico-religious questions by the Federal Government as well as by the provincial governments, I sent you a letter in which I explained the point of view of the Church on all these matters and also on the agrarian reform which, I see by the papers, is now on the agenda of the Provisional Popular Assembly. Stop. I protest vigorously as President of the Conference of the Yugoslavian Catholic Hierarchy, against the method of carrying out the agrarian reform as provided for in the bill before the Legislative Committee.

> Dr. Aloysius Stepinac, *Archbishop*
> *President of the Episcopal Conference*

To the Presidency of the Provisional Popular Assembly, Belgrade

(The same text as above was sent with the following addition at the end. "I have sent a similar telegram to Marshal Josip Broz Tito.")

To Archbishop Dr. Aloysius Stepinac,
President of the Episcopal Conference.

SIR:

I have received your letter of August 20, 1945. I have also been informed of the content of your letters and your telegrams addressed to the Presidency of the Provisional Popular Assembly.

On the subject of the question of agrarian reform, especially as it concerns the Church, many discussions as well as meetings took place before this session of the Provisional Popular Assembly, but there was always unanimity on one point; that agrarian reform must include the Church lands. This unanimous point of view is, of course, the result of the state of mind of the peasant masses, not the will of the deputies themselves. All that could be done in this matter was to leave to the possessors of these lands ten hectares instead of five, as was originally planned. Moreover, by the agrarian reform a much more considerable amount of land is left to monasteries or institutions which have a certain historical character. The definitive solution in this latter question is left to the various provincial governments which will determine to what institutions this right will be extended.

I cannot agree with your reproach that I promised something which has not been done. I have awaited the outcome of your Episcopal Conference which, unhappily, either did not take place or, as far as I know, the government has received from you no written information or resolutions.

I reiterate the possibility of reaching an agreement on questions pending between the Church and State, for I think that that is in the interests of an easier domestic readjustment.

> *President of the Government,*
> *Marshal of Yugoslavia,* J. B. TITO

Belgrade, September 1, 1945

DOCUMENT LXIX

*Letter to Marshal Tito Regarding Discussions of the
Hierarchy, September 17 to 22, 1945, and Setting
Forth the Demands of the Church*

Presidency of the Episcopal Conference,
Zagreb

ZAGREB, September 22, 1945

No. 107/BK

MARSHAL,

The Catholic Hierarchy, meeting in plenary session in Zagreb from September 17 to 22, 1945, considers it its duty in these critical times to address you, as the highest authority in Yugoslavia, in the interest of both Church and State and for the general welfare of all the people.

The Catholic Hierarchy had on its agenda a discussion of the general situation of the Catholic Church in Yugoslavia. In the course of its meetings the Catholic Hierarchy was compelled to take cognizance of certain distressing facts, which compel us to present to you, Marshal, our attitude regarding the future relations between Church and State.

Out of one hundred Catholic magazines and newspapers not one exists today; almost all our publishing plants have been confiscated, as well as our paper supplies. This means that the existence of a Catholic press has become impossible.

The seminaries have been, with few exceptions, liquidated as have been to a greater or lesser degree all Catholic educational and welfare institutions.

By the abolition of compulsory catechism in the schools, the education of youth has been placed, to our greatest regret, in gravest danger, and through action contrary to the freedom of religion which is guaranteed to all citizens by law and by government declaration.

The abolition of all Catholic private schools has been announced in contradiction to the elementary rights of parents and the Church, these two essential elements in education.

By the constant organization of all sorts of celebrations which last late into the night, the youth of our cities and villages are exposed to great moral danger.

The performance of religious duties on Sundays has been made difficult because different classes of persons, such as youths and office workers, are called upon on that day to perform compulsory work or engage in sports contests.

In the delicate question of marriage the Church has had the following *faits accompli* placed before it: the introduction of civil marriage and the practices of certain local officials of making marriage decisions which are not lawful and which are even opposed to the provisions of the civil code in effect up to the present.

As a result of the agrarian reform and the suspension of the salaries of the clergy and other officials of the ecclesiastical institutions, the reduction of the Church to a state of pauperism has been brought about.

The graves of soldiers in Catholic cemeteries have not been spared although contrary to international law, the cultural traditions of Europe, and the practices of Christianity.

Marshal, the Catholic Hierarchy has reached the conclusion that the present situation of the Church in Yugoslavia is tantamount to open persecution, however much the government may deny it.

Marshal! We consider it necessary and our duty to communicate these facts to you as the President of the Federal Government.

The Church wants no conflict with any government, especially with that of Yugoslavia, our fatherland. For that reason we address you directly, Marshal, hoping by personal contact to avoid possible misunderstanding between Church and State.

We demand most urgently the reparation of the injustices listed above. We await from you the unconditional release of Bishop Šimrak so that the Holy See will not be called upon for a decision in that case. We await from you the release of all our priests who are innocent of crimes.

We demand complete freedom for the Catholic press, for Catholic private schools, other educational and welfare institutions, seminaries, and the restitution of all confiscated property.

We demand absolute respect for Christian marriage, a complete course of religious instruction in all primary and secondary schools, the possibility for the performance of Sunday religious duties, a revision of the agrarian reform in agreement with the Church, and respect for Catholic cemeteries.

We await, through your intervention, the solution of the question of the admission of priests to military and civilian hospitals, as well as to prisons. In our opinion this constitutes one of the most essential features of religious freedom.

These are our demands and our requests. We set them forcefully before you as our faith and our conscience as pastors dictate.

Marshal! We are profoundly convinced that a peaceful solution to these misunderstandings can be found, for the benefit of both parties, Church and State. We hope for peace and harmony with the state. If on the state's part there is equal good will, we can arrive at a peaceful solution by means of an agreement with the

Holy See, such as the President of the Bishop's Conference proposed in his first conversation with you. If, on the contrary, this good will does not exist, the state will suffer as much as the Church. You may be certain, Marshal, that the Church cannot, at the price of all its sacrifices, recede from its fundamental principles, for that would be a denial of itself.

Marshal! We confidently express our hopes to you who, a son of our country, knows the soul of its people, its religious sentiments and needs. On the basis of your statements to the Zagreb clergy, we are convinced that you will understand us; for we ask this in the name of the religious freedom that is guaranteed by all modern states.

In spite of the difficulties we have just set forth, we declare ourselves to be loyal citizens of the state in which we live, that we will respect its authorities, and are ready to collaborate for its reconstruction.

One more request, Marshal! We call on you, in your generosity, to proclaim anew a more complete amnesty on behalf of prisoners, both lay and clerical, which would be a motive for rejoicing among all the people and would confirm them in their loyalty to the state.

Finally, we are persuaded that the wisdom of our statesmen will bring us victory and that through your efforts you will succeed in bringing lasting peace in Yugoslavia.

Please accept, Marshal, the assurance of our greatest respect.

Signatures of the Bishops:

Dr. Aloysius Stepinac, Archbishop of Zagreb and President of the Episcopal Conference.
Dr. Nikola Dobrečić, Archbishop of Bar and Primate of Serbia.
Dr. Josip Ujcić, Archbishop of Belgrade and Apostolic Administrator for the Banat.
Dr. Jerome Mileta, Bishop of Šibenik.
Dr. Kvirin Klement Bonefačić, Bishop of Split, formerly of Solin and Makarska.
Dr. Josip Srebrnić, Bishop of Krk.
Monsignor Miko Pušić, Bishop of Hvar.
Dr. Ivan Josip Tomažić, Bishop of Maribor.
Dr. Viktor Burić, Bishop of Senj and of Modruč.
Dr. Smiljan Čekada, Bishop of Skoplje.
Dr. Petar Čule, Bishop of Mostar.
Dr. Antun Akšamović, Bishop, Apostolic Administrator of Djakovo.
Monsignor Lajco Budanović, Bishop, Vicar General of Subotica by a special authorization signed by Dr. Viktor Burić.
Dr. Antun Buljan, Vicar General of Sarajevo.
Monsignor Božo Ivaniš, Vicar General of Banja Luka.
Anton Vovk, Vicar General of Ljubljana.

Ivan Jerić, Vicar General of Prekomurje by a special authorization signed by Dr. Ivan Tomažić.

Dr. Ivan Djuro Visošević, Pro-vicar of Krizevici.

DOCUMENT LXX

The Pastoral Letter of the Yugoslav Hierarchy
Issued September 21, 1945

DEARLY BELOVED FAITHFUL IN CHRIST:

We Catholic Bishops, assembled in plenary session at Zagreb, consider it our pastoral duty that on the occasion of this conference we also make known our thoughts to you, our beloved flock.

After long years the war has finally ended, a war which bled mankind as never before within human memory. Its gore-stained whip did not spare our land. The attendant horror of war has oftentimes visited our homeland, and in its wake has left devastation and desolation. Entire sections of our country are razed; and untold numbers of families have been broken up to the anguish of distraught parents and to the whimpering cries of orphaned children. All over Croatia each person grieves for some beloved departed one. Every one of us has known privation, hunger, and disease which inevitably accompany war. In very truth the war has lashed us doubly. To our great abiding sorrow civil war ensued with its consequent sanguinary horror and hate. Enemy occupation and internal dissension wrought such suffering as is rarely experienced in any land. The war's cessation leads us to offer unceasing thanks to God for His mercy in sparing us from further calamities of war and fratricide.

The war's finale inaugurated for us all great changes in every phase of life. Before our eyes has vanished what once was considered the basis of everyday life. The state bears a new name, Democratic Federated Yugoslavia, radically reorganized with no regard for the past and with a new governmental structure and program breathing a new and revolutionary spirit.

It does not pertain to the Catholic Church to prescribe for its members in what manner they shall solve their political, national, and economic problems; providing that such solutions are in accord with universally binding moral principles. In purely political questions the Church adheres to the dictum of its Founder: "Render, therefore, to Caesar, the things that are Caesar's and to God the things that are God's" (Mt. 22:21). Thus guided, the Church embraces all peoples of all lands with equal indiscriminate love, for in every man and all men the Church sees a brother of Christ redeemed by His Blood. Her primary concern above all else is the spiritual good of her children; thus, irrespective of the form of government and economic system individual nations may freely choose, the Church exerts all possible care for the safeguard of their spiritual welfare.

This concern for your eternally priceless souls, beloved flock, inspires us at this moment when we address our first pastoral letter to you in Democratic Yugoslavia. Deeply conscious of the tremendous responsibility we bear before God for your souls' welfare, we long to see the speedy solution of post-war problems which beset our own and all nations. In this spirit we address this pastoral letter to you, dearly beloved.

Prior to the cessation of hostilities the government in Belgrade pledged its solemn word to honor and respect freedom of worship, conscience, and private property. This was accepted by the Federated Government of Croatia conditionally on the grounds of the alleged unsatisfactory attitude of the Catholic Church. In the first days of this new government, when we were able to establish contact with its officials, we acquainted them with the various problems, needs, and attitude of the Catholic Church but because of the new spirit reigning a hostile reception was accorded to the Church's position and rights, a reception, therefore, necessarily of consequent spiritual detriment to you. Dearly beloved, we pointed out and admonished those in power that questions affecting both Church and State should be solved in an atmosphere of mutual understanding, and from the highest government sources we received assurance that such would be the case. The final word in all questions which mutually concern both Church and State, so far as the Church is concerned, belongs to the Holy See which is the final judge in matters of faith and the religious life of its followers. From time to time we took it upon ourselves to inform the government of the mind of the Church in every individual case of concern to us, always bearing in mind the common good of all.

In the meantime, however, circumstances and developments arose which nullified our good will and endeavors. Aware of the jeopardy in which the Catholic Church and the priceless spiritual good of its millions of faithful have been placed, we consider it our duty to bring out into the open all the calamities and vicissitudes which confront and plague the Catholic Church. All of us make up one spiritual society, the Mystical Body of Christ. "So we, the many, are one body in Christ, but severally members one of another" (Rom. 12:5). And to us in these days is directed the fiery call of the Apostle of nations, St. Paul: "But doing the truth in charity, we may in all things grow up in him who is the head, even Christ: From whom the whole body, being compacted and fitly joined together, by what every joint supplieth, according to the operation in the measure of every part, maketh increase of the body, unto the edifying of itself in charity" (Eph. 4:15–16).

Above all, most dearly beloved, the cruel fate of many priests, the pastors of your souls, has saddened us. Many priestly lives have been extinguished, not only because of the war, but because of the present civil and military rule. The number of priestly victims according to our knowledge is as follows: 243 dead, 169 in prisons and concentration camps, 89 missing; total 501. To that number must be added also the death of 19 clerical students, 3 lay brothers, and 4 nuns. Balkan history for many a century has not witnessed such a slaughter of God's chosen ones. But what has most grievously offended us is that they, like hundreds and thousands of other Catholic faithful, are denied the Sacraments in their last moments — which all civilized nations allow even to the most depraved criminal. Capital punishment is decreed by the courts quickly and summarily. The accused often have no inkling of the crime under which they are charged until the opening of the trial, where often they are deprived of the right of defense by counsel and witnesses, a practice common in all courts of justice.

Sincere and unbiased judicial minds will decry this lack of the basic elements of justice in the death sentences pronounced upon God's anointed ones. Who can show or prove that so many priests condemned to death were in truth criminals or deserving of capital punishment? Were all these priests murderers? For example, in the Franciscan monastery at Široki Brijeg 28 religious were put to death without the semblance of a trial. They did not take up arms against the army of national liberation as was so calumniously charged; and furthermore, practically all these massacred Franciscans were well known for their opposition to Fascism. There were instances when thousands of the faithful, loudly protesting the innocence of their priests, sought their release. Yet priests were still condemned to death. It is obvious that such condemnations were not carried out in the name of the people and of Christian justice; it is indisputably evident that it is inconsistent with the sentiments of the people and their ideals of Christian justice, that death be dealt to those differing in political thought and who were never guilty of any criminal offense. The laws of justice are above political views and bind equally all times and peoples. In the name of that eternal justice we raise our voice before all mankind, most dearly beloved, in defense of unjustly condemned priests, and for the thousands and thousands of your sons and brothers who shared the same unjust fate.

That we come to the defense of innocent priests does not mean that we seek to shield the guilty. We grant there were priests who by their extreme nationalism sinned against Christian justice and charity, and therefore deserve to answer before the court of earthly justice. Their number is, however, insignificant. The serious charges hurled against the greater part of the Catholic clergy in Yugoslavia by the press and in public utterances are a planned campaign of lies to besmirch the name of the Catholic Church in the minds and hearts of the people.

A great number of priests languish in concentration camps, doomed to long years of forced labor. To this day the Greek-Catholic Bishop, Dr. Janko Šimrak, is deprived of his freedom, and the fate of Bishop Carevich is unknown to us. In the humanly uninhabitable concentration camps many priests are made to perform duties degrading to their sacerdotal dignity. Often they are not allowed to hear Mass on Sunday — much less to say Mass — thus depriving the priests and other internees of great spiritual comfort and benefit. Their crime — political views at variance with those of their accusers. Many of these interned priests, who were seized by government agents, have disappeared and we have no knowledge of their whereabouts. All our appeals, all our searchings are in vain. All traces have been erased.

Such a loss of priests has had serious spiritual repercussions. Numerous parishes are without pastors. The religious life of the people has been weakened and the faithful have been placed in spiritual jeopardy. The press openly attacks the clergy which cannot defend itself in any way, since the laws allow such attacks and the papers tolerate no reply.

The situation of the Catholic press is another source of anxiety for the Church. Of some hundred publications in existence before the war, not one today is published. When permission was sought to resume publishing, every possible subterfuge was employed for refusing permission. The excuse was made of the lack of paper, yet wagonloads of paper were confiscated even from the residence of the Archbishop of Zagreb. The Catholic press for the greatest part has either been shut down or rendered powerless.

All imaginable means were used to do away with the Zagreb diocesan press. When that failed, they arrested the director, and seized the press. Our protest finally proved effective — and that only a few days ago. The well-known Catholic Press Society of Ljubljana has been taken out of Catholic hands. The same fate has overtaken the Catholic press in Mostar, Šibenik, Maribor, and Sarajevo. There is a systematic plan of confiscation, and the freedom of the press is a question for the Catholic Church in which the welfare of many souls hangs in the balance. How can the Catholic press function under such crippling and nullifying circumstances?

Nor are our seminaries in any happier condition. The Church by great material sacrifice built and maintained these institutions through whose portals have passed hundreds of priests and outstanding laymen. But today, to all practical purposes, these seminaries have been suppressed, for they have been militarily occupied or confiscated, as for example, those at Zagreb, Salati, Split, Travnik, Sent Vidu, Ljubljana, Maribor, Sinj, and elsewhere.

In the field of education the Church has sustained blow after blow. Classes in religion were placed on a non-obligatory basis, dependent on a declaration of intention. It has been a cause of joy, in the midst of so much sorrow, that Catholic parents, where voting on the question has been permitted, declared for religious instructions in the schools. In the annual educational report for Croatia, religion has been listed as the least important of all subjects; furthermore, in all elementary and secondary schools religious instruction has been shortened from two hours weekly to one — and that when these calamitous times shriek for religious training. Such crippling blows mean nothing else than the curtailment of religious freedom and education. In the higher grades of the secondary schools of Croatia, religion classes were absolutely forbidden on the pretext of freedom of conscience! Such action on the part of the government officials in Croatia is incomprehensible, for if in the lower grades of the secondary schools freedom to attend religious instruction is allowed, then why not in the higher grades where the youths of eighteen have the right to vote? Does this right to vote, then, mean the exclusion of freedom of conscience?

While on this question we wish to state that in the voluntary attendance at religious instructions in the case of young children the decision rests with the parents, for it would be ridiculous and the height of folly to leave such a decision to the young who have scarcely begun to think. The same was explicitly affirmed by the National Liberation Committee of Yugoslavia Ministry of Education in Belgrade, February, 1945; hence, the contrary action of some teachers and educators who insist that the children must decide for themselves is in open defiance of the Belgrade directive.

The Catholic Church maintained a great number of state-recognized private secondary schools. Their excellence and high scholastic standing were recognized in pre-war Yugoslavia by the state and the parents of the Catholic and non-Catholic students alike. But today, newspapers under government inspiration announce that these schools will not be able to function again. We fail to understand why these educational institutions must be closed when parents, upon whom the burden of educating their children rests, have the greatest confidence in them and clamor for their reopening. The spirit of true democracy demands compliance with the parents' demands in regard to the schooling of their children; furthermore, the Church has the right by natural law to maintain private schools, and all civilized governments rejoice that the Church bears with them the burden of maintaining educational institutions.

The Catholic Church also possessed an extensive institutional system for the care of small children and education of the youth of all classes; and here, too, they are either shut down or under government control; anonymous persons attack the work of the Church by false accusations and indecent caricatures in the daily newspapers which proclaim religious training as medieval and sinister; the Church is unable to defend itself from such charges because she is without means of defense, and the hostile press affords no possibility of refutation. Moreover, state-appointed supervisors in our confiscated institutions openly and covertly strive to nullify Catholic efforts. Freedom of conscience and religion is as a consequence an empty phrase and serves as a cloak for anti-religious activity.

The youth, both in urban and rural areas, is exposed to new moral dangers through the continuous organization of dances which last far into the night and even to dawn. Thus it happens at times that the young of both sexes remain together without parental supervision throughout the entire night under the influence of alcohol. Let no one dare say that in this there is no great moral peril for the youth. Irrefutable experience testifies that many a boy and girl as a result of such a morally dangerous environment live to regret for many a year the consequences of such occasions. But our greatest concern and anxiety is that parents and guardians are powerless to object against such misconduct on the part of their children and their wards.

The youth in many instances cannot fulfill their Sunday duties in attending Holy Mass because of the many meetings and programs which take place at the very time Mass is being said. In some places they are forced to participate in so-called "progressive enterprises." Thus Catholic youth is alienated and barred from compliance with their religious duties. In many army units and youth organizations the theory of man's origin from the apes is propagated. It is obvious in what direction they are endeavoring to guide our Catholic youth and the picture becomes clearer when we note that in the secondary schools man's origin as explained by religion is ridiculed as merely legend and the statement is made that the question must be "scientifically explained."

The sanctity of Catholic marriage has been besmirched by the introduction of civil marriages. Steeped in Catholicism, our nation has always held that the matrimonial bond is holy and sacramental, and must be made in the presence of God. Today that is discarded. The character of marriage is firm and indissoluble; but civil authorities dissolve Catholic marriages without the Church's consent and in open violation to God's laws. In the past few months such divorces have rapidly increased even here in the diocese of Zagreb. What consequences this will have upon family life, which is the cornerstone of all progress and happiness for nations and states, is obvious. How many children, through no fault of their own, will be deprived of the necessary and beneficial influence of family life in childhood and youthful years we dare not contemplate.

Even in purely charitable endeavors the Catholic Church suffers constant restrictions. The work of the Catholic *Caritas* of the Archdiocese of Zagreb is well known to all. It has saved some 7000 children, regardless of creed. To our suffering brethren in many districts we sent tens of wagonloads of food and saved many hundreds from starvation and death. We were deeply concerned about feeding our compatriots in the concentration camps in Italy as well as after their return home. But today there is strict government supervision for the state has no faith in its activity; although the public is aware that Catholic *Caritas* issued regular reports of its income and expenditures, and enjoyed universal confidence.

The agrarian reform adopted by the temporary People's Assembly has worked great injustice on the Catholic Church. Whatever land possessions the Church has, were obtained lawfully and honestly, and never served as a means for further enrichment; but rather to support officials of the Church, its seminaries, and central agencies. The income from these lands, therefore, was in truth for many and for the greater part for the sons of peasants and those of poor circumstances. Furthermore, the Church was bound to fulfill the conditions as laid down by its benefactors.

Besides all this, many priests have made generous donations for national and cultural purposes as for example, the University of Zagreb among whose greatest benefactors were Bishop Strossmayer, Archbishop Bauer, and the Rev. George Zerjavić.

The confiscation of Church land through the agrarian reform was carried out without compensation — as if the Church had obtained these holdings nefariously. The little that was left to the Church will by no stretch of the imagination be sufficient to support the seminaries, cathedral parishes, episcopal offices, and parishes; consequently, these agrarian reforms render impossible even the fulfillment of ordinary ecclesiastical functions, and this means that the burden of support is thrown not on those few who have benefited but on those who did not receive any portion of the land at all.

To justify the confiscation of Church properties the press attempted to show that they were poorly run or even in an abandoned condition. When proof to the contrary was offered to the papers, they refused to print the truth because those who were responsible for the sorry conditions were known to all.

We wish to declare that the Church does not stand in opposition to any needed and justifiable social reform, even if it affects her material interests. The Church seeks, however, that in all questions pertaining to its life, the State not employ unilateral and dictatorial methods, but come to an understanding with the Church as an independent and equal party.

Catholic Sisterhoods together with their educational and charitable institutions almost daily experience constant harassment from the new spirit now prevailing. How bitter is the frustration of the Sisters not only in government-owned hospitals but in their very own! The treatment accorded these Sisters by the state supervisors in their own hospitals is undisputed evidence that they wish to render powerless the Sisters' work of mercy toward the sick, and to appropriate these institutions founded and supported by the Sisters through their own efforts, and incalculable sacrifices.

Finally, we must acquaint you, dearly beloved faithful, with a most sorrowful and unusual fact. The graves of the dead are not spared or left unmolested. In the cemeteries of Zagreb, Varaždin, and elsewhere the government has ordered that the crosses be stripped from the graves of the Ustashi and Germans. These graves have been so vandalized that there is no way of telling who is buried there. Such procedure must be condemned and censured. Before death all men must bow. In death all men cease to be enemies. The unwritten law of human decency, springing from Christian love, gives to all men the right of decent burial. It is well known that after the first World War the graves of the one-time enemy were honored and guarded. Today, our own sons are denied this in their own land.

Most dearly beloved, our worries concern not only the immediate needs of the Church, its institutions, and its priests. Knowing full well the sufferings and hardships of so many of our flock, we did all that was possible to alleviate and aid in the days of trial and grief. On many an occasion we interceded with the authorities in person and by letter to pardon and spare those condemned to death. With obstinacy we sought for their last moments the consolations of religion. We sought that the relatives of the dead know of their last resting place. All this was done at the behest of the relatives of the unfortunate victims of fatricidal butchery.

For those in concentration camps we sought to lighten their burdens, that they might regularly receive food, that their relatives might know where they were sent. We took it upon ourselves to hasten their day of liberation, if it were shown that they were not guilty. We came to the aid of many of the intelligentsia who as a result of unemployment were unable to provide for self and family. To all who asked for aid, we gave to the best of our ability, having always in mind Christian charity and justice to all, never questioning political thought, creed, or nationality. No propaganda accusing us of political intentions in such action hindered us from carrying on for we were convinced we were acting in the spirit of Christ's love for neighbor. If we did not succeed at all times, it is not our fault. We are convinced that we did our duty fully. We grieve that we were unable to extend aid where help was necessary and where many a tear could have been wiped away.

There is something else that especially pains us. It is the materialistic and godless spirit which today is being openly and secretly, officially and unofficially, propagated throughout our country.

We Catholic Bishops of Yugoslavia, as teachers of the truth and representatives of our faith, condemn unreservedly this materialistic spirit from which mankind can hope for no good. Likewise, we condemn all ideologies and social systems based not on the eternal principles of Christian Revelation, but on shallow material foundations, that is to say, on philosophical atheism.

All that we have stated has been carefully sifted. It is abundantly evident that the Catholic Church in Democratic Federated Yugoslavia is in a more difficult position than ever. The present situation regarding the Catholic Church in Yugoslavia, as we see it, is only separated from open persecution by a tenuous fiction.

Most dearly beloved flock, we wish to bring these facts to your attention, so that you may understand clearly the present situation in which the Church finds itself. Come what may, we look with confidence to the future. We take courage from the awakening religious spirit in the great masses of our faithful in all parts of our country. Especially, are we consoled and made joyful by the lively and overflowing devotion to the Mother of God, who is so near and dear to our Catholic people. This is proven by the overwhelming number of pilgrimages, such as never before visited our national shrines of Mary. Cherish and nourish in your hearts and that of your families that deep abiding devotion to the Mother of God. Pray her Rosary together in common, imitate her virtues, and it is certain that the Mother of God will be our special protectoress. Under her powerful protection our flock in all circumstances and vicissitudes shall remain faithful to their forefathers' religion. The Mother of God will not abandon us, but will through her intercession provide God's guidance in all our needs. May the blessings of God be ever more abundant for all of you and in all of your necessities.

All that we have laid before you, dearly beloved, has been said with no intention of provoking a conflict with the new authorities. We do not seek it nor have we ever sought it. Our thoughts are directed toward peaceful, orderly civil and public life. That peace today is necessary to all, but if there is to be peace and if the wounds of war are to be healed, it can only be done by respecting our Christian religion and its moral laws.

We anticipate that there will be unjust attacks and accusations that we are aiding the reactionaries and enemies of the people, and we are not concerned or fearful. We are one with our people, we guard its most precious heritage, its faith, its honor, its desires to be free in its own in unity and love with all citizens of this state, regardless of creed and nationality.

Therefore, we seek — and under no circumstances shall we desist — full and complete freedom for the Catholic press; full and complete freedom for Catholic schools; full and complete freedom for religious instructions in all grades of elementary and secondary schools; full and complete freedom for Catholic societies and organizations; full and complete freedom for Catholic charitable works; full and complete freedom for man's dignity and personality and inalienable rights; full and complete respect for Christian marriage, return of all confiscated properties and institutions. Only under these conditions can the situation in our country be solved and lasting internal peace be realized.

May the Almighty bless all men of good will who work to realize these aims. May He, who is the one source of peace, which the world cannot give, grant to each and everyone of you to see the day of true and lasting peace. As a pledge of those desires may the blessings of God the Father, Son, and Holy Spirit now descend upon all of you!

Given at Zagreb, the 20th of September, 1945 — on the occasion of the Bishops' plenary conference.

Dr. Aloysius Stepinac, Archbishop of Zagreb and President of the Bishops' Conference
Dr. Nicholas Dobrečić, Archbishop of Bar and Primate of Serbia
Dr. Joseph Ujčić, Archbishop of Belgrade and Apostolic Administrator of Banat
Dr. Fra Jerome Mileta, Bishop of Sibenik
Dr. Kvirin Bonefačić, Bishop of Split, formerly Solin and Makarska
Dr. Joseph Srebrnić, Bishop of Krk
Msgr. Miko Pušić, Bishop of Hvar
Dr. Ivan Josip Tomašić, Bishop of Maribor
Dr. Victor Burić, Bishop of Senj and Modruć
Dr. Smiljan Čekada, Bishop of Skoplje
Dr. Peter Čule, Bishop of Mostar-Duvno
Dr. Antun Akšamović, Apostolic Administrator of Djakovo
Msgr. Lajco Budanović, General Vicar of Subotica
Dr. Antun Buljan, Vicar-General of Sarajevo
Msgr. Božo Ivaniš, Vicar-General of Banja Luka
Anton Vovk, Vicar-General of Ljubljana
Dr. Anton George Višošević, Provicar of Krizevac

DOCUMENT LXXI
Letter of Archbishop Stepinac to Dr. Vladimir Bakarić

Presidency of the Episcopal Conference   ZAGREB, November 10, 1945
Zagreb.
No. 138/BK

MR. PRESIDENT:

The events to which we have lately been witness compel me to send you this letter.

The campaign directed against the pastoral letter of the Catholic Episcopate, waged in the newspapers, in political meetings, by posters plastered on walls, by the jeering words painted upon the houses of priests and religious, reached its culmination on the fourth of this month in the physical attack made on me and my attendants at Zaprešić. On All Saints Day the state officials, more exactly the OZNA, warned me that the people would rise against me in church if I were to attack, in their opinion, the popular government. Against the Bishop of Dubrovnik, while he was interpreting the pastoral letter, voices were publicly raised in the church crying, "Down with Christ!"

These facts demand that I call your attention, as the responsible state official, to certain facts which are of essential importance in our present situation as well as in its further development.

1. First I must mention the communiqué of the 6th of this month, issued by the Ministry of the Interior of the People's Government of Croatia on the subject of the events at Zaprešić. It contains gross errors that, out of a regard for the truth, I must correct.

The whole of the attack on my car came exclusively from the right side of the automobile and not from the left. The damage done to my car is witness to that. At my arrival in front of the church at Zaprešić, the peaceful peasant population of the place was on the left side of my automobile. On the right side there were about twenty persons, armed and in uniform, and a group of women wearing Partisan caps, also a few peasants. It is a fact that the great majority of the parishioners hailed with joy the establishment of a new parish in Zaprešić. Most of the parishioners of the new parish could not, however, even come to the front of the church, their way having been barred. Even the communiqué of the Ministry of the Interior showed that the attack had been organized, saying that, "the assembled group began to make a demonstration, to hail the agrarian reform, and to throw eggs, mud, and small stones at the Archbishop's automobile." It is obvious that these eggs and stones did not suddenly fall from heaven into the hands of the demonstrators but that it was all planned in advance. I have proof from certain witnesses to the fact that on the same day the SKOJ [*Savez Komunističke Omladine Jugoslavije* — Communist Youth Union of Yugoslavia] had held a meeting where it was decided to attack me. These witnesses testify that an hour before the incident occurred it was publicly said in Zaprešić that I would be assailed. Immediately before my arrival in Zaprešić, two motorcycles came toward my automobile and took a good look at where I was sitting then hastily turned toward the church after their riders had exchanged a few words. I watched them attentively. They were obviously a reconnaissance patrol.

These, Mr. President, are the facts that the communiqué of the Ministry of the Interior passed over in silence. These facts throw light on the background of the physical attack made on me. They constitute irrefutable proof that the attack was organized by the persons who were standing at the right side of my automobile. The communiqué of the Ministry of the Interior, on the contrary, reports the incident in a way calculated to show that by my arrival to conduct a purely ecclesiastical affair I provoked the attack against my person. I most energetically deny such an allegation. In what a superficial way — to speak of it with the greatest moderation — in what a deliberately misleading manner was this communiqué composed! The fact remains that two stones were found in my car, one weighing about 70 decagrams (1⅜ lbs.) and another 20 decagrams (⅜ lb.) while the communiqué speaks of "small stones." I am keeping these stones as an historical document and I can show them to you, Mr. President, so that you may be convinced of the character of the Ministry of the Interior's communiqué and of its conception of what constitutes a "small stone." To be struck on the head by such a stone would, in the opinion of physicians, cause either a serious wound or death.

2. Another very serious violation of the truth in the Interior Ministry's communiqué is the statement that Pastor Pasicek drew a revolver and lightly wounded V. Simunić. That is completely untrue. Far from drawing a revolver, Pastor Pasicek did not even have one. He stood with folded arms when the demonstrators began to strike at him with stones, knives, and fists. It is ridiculous to suppose that he could have drawn a revolver under the rain of knife thrusts and

against fifteen to twenty heavily armed persons. All the witnesses declare that the shooting began at the time my automobile arrived in front of the church and that it stopped before the pastor, after my arrival, came out of the church among the demonstrators. After my departure not a shot was fired and during the shooting Pastor Pasicek was in the church. It is a fact that after Pastor Pasicek was assaulted, he was searched and a number of his assailants said, "He has no revolver." This testimony is borne out by Pastor Pasicek himself and by persons who were standing close to him and heard the previous statement. It is a transparent and exceeding clumsy lie to assert that a priest would carry a gun in front of the altar on the occasion of the establishment of a new parish. No man in his right mind would believe it. While he was there, however, powerless, a revolver was thrown at him to make it appear as if it were his own so that the assault against him could be justified and so that the shots fired at the moment I arrived in my car in front of the church could be made to appear less unprovoked. Let the Ministry of the Interior inquire a little more carefully into the question of who fired the first shot from the demonstrators. Let the Ministry of the Interior also inquire into the question of who the persons were who, after I left in my automobile, went with arms to Lužnica demanding, "Where is the bandit Stepinac?" These persons searched the house and grounds there looking for me. Their intentions were surely not peaceful.

The question is then, how could this attack on me at Zaprešić have taken place?

3. Mr. President, this question must be posed, for the nine hundred years history of the Archdiocese of Zagreb contains no incident comparable to that which occurred at Zaprešić. Who were the moral instigators of this incident? The immediate guilty must be sought among the people of Zaprešić. But all the instigators are not to be found there. The intellectual authors of this assault are to be found farther away. I draw your attention to the fact that on Saturday, the third of this month, an unknown man came from Zagreb and that he met at the railway station a boy from the Children's House. He went to the commune office and speaking there with him of the opening of the new parish, to take place the next day, said that I would not have time to open the parish. As one can see, the trail of the intellectual instigators of the attack leads to Zagreb. The instigators of the attack must be sought among the editors of the Zagreb

newspapers who unceasingly publish attacks on me and insult me as if there were no juridical protection in the state. All this is done in such a way that a request for retraction according to the press laws is useless. And what is to be said of those speakers in public meetings who openly threaten me and the clergy? Does not the speaker belong among the intellectual instigators who, on October 7, in Zagreb, speaking to an audience in the Workers' Hall on the pastoral letter, said, "If someone needs to be shown our power, we will know how to choose the time to show him, since he has asked for it. We force no one to be our enemy, make no one provoke us into showing him our fangs, but if anyone has not sufficient wit to see for himself what is going on around him, then it is our duty to show him what is happening." (*Vjesnik*, October 8, 1945.) As you see, Mr. President, the time was chosen and the fangs were shown at a moment when I was on my way to perform an ecclesiastical function and to say Holy Mass.

Do not those persons, unknown to me, belong among the intellectual instigators who organize the propaganda campaign of caricatures by which they directly provoke attacks on the clergy? Who is it that draws in the streets of the city the caricatures of priests shooting on the people from the cathedral? Priests are shown as if, in giving Communion, they are keeping people away from the elections. And when a certain priest was attacked and he strongly protested against it, the Zagreb radio station announced that something similar had been said in confession and therefore in circumstances such that the priest, because of the seal of the confessional, could not defend himself. In spite of everything the caricatures of the Communion remain on the walls. The houses of the priests in the Kaptol (a street near the cathedral) have been painted with offensive inscriptions, directly across from the church, thus provoking the indignation of the people. "For the cassock-wearers the Church, for the people power." "Down with the black robes." "Down with the clerical fascists." "Death to the remains of Fascism." "Death to the conspirators." "Death to the signers of the pastoral letter." Are not these inscriptions an open appeal to attack the priests and their houses? The hammer and sickle, emblem of the Communist Party, appear on every priest's house in the Kaptol. Is that the freedom the Church enjoys in this state? And what is the significance of the fact that at the meetings of the AFZ [*Anti-Fašističkie Žene* – Antifascist Women] in Palmotićeva and Josavski Streets, a woman speaker, Vuković, openly incited the people to insult priests in the streets and even to kill them and to spit at the faithful attending church? Would you please, Mr. President, inquire into these facts by all the means which are at your disposal?

The incident on All Saints Day when government officials warned me in advance in my palace of the reaction of the "faithful" in the cathedral shows that the authorities foresaw very clearly the excesses and attacks. The government delegates could not have proven that better than by their reply given to my question, "What are these people who want to attack me?" "That is our business," they replied. That is precisely it. And it is for exactly that reason that I have set these facts before you, Mr. President, to draw your attention to them in time. I must hold you personally responsible for all future excesses, now that you are in possession of the above facts. I hold you all the more responsible for you are also the highest official of the Communist Party in Croatia, which — as everyone knows — controls all public political activity. In this double capacity you carry before the court of history full responsibility for events which follow from the above enumerated facts.

Please accept, Mr. President, the expression of my respect.

Zagreb, November 10, 1945
To Dr. Vladimir Bakarić
President of the Croatian People's Government, Zagreb

DOCUMENT LXXII

Circular Letter to the Zagreb Clergy Regarding a Number of the Accusations Made Against the Conduct of the Archbishop

No. 897/45

REVEREND BROTHER PRIESTS:

In the daily press of Zagreb there appeared on December 16 of this year the statement of the President of the National Croatian Government, Dr. Bakarić, "On Ustashi Activity in Ecclesiastical Institutions."

Out of respect for truth and justice, I propose to examine the charges made in that statement. I want to inform you, as my collaborators, who support "pondus et aestus diei" in the vineyards of the Lord, of the events of which President Dr. Bakarić speaks in his statement.

1. To all the complaints directly or indirectly lodged against us we can reply that we have nothing with which to reproach ourselves. Our conscience is clear and tranquil before God, who is the most faithful Witness and the Just Judge of all our actions. Our conscience is clear and tranquil as well before the Catholics of this country who judge events calmly and soberly.

Our conscience is clear and tranquil before the Croatian people to whom we belong, according to the Will of God, by ties of blood and whom we serve wholeheartedly in our position, without regard to their different points of view or political parties.

2. My reverend brother priests, you know our point of view as to the activity of priests in politics. In my circular letters, from 1935 to 1938, I forbade, in the spirit of the Ecclesiastical Code, all active priests to become candidates for the elections on any ticket whatever. I insisted on the same point of view in 1943 and I have emphasized it in my sermons. I am of the same opinion today and can see no reason for changing it. I wished to avoid all responsibility on the part of the Church for the public political activity of priests. Each priest is alone and personally responsible for what he does in the political sphere. Consequently, if a priest does something contrary to the regulations of the law now in force, he must personally answer the consequences of his action.

3. Numerous persons have sought entrance to the Archiepiscopal palace at all times. Innumerable persons visited the palace during the later years of the war. Their opinions, religions, nationalities, and political affiliations were the most diverse. We welcomed all these people paternally as is befitting our ecclesiastical position. If someone came to the palace under an assumed name, we are not omniscient, and cannot penetrate all manner of disguises, nor are we responsible for those who abuse our Christian charity.

4. We declare that all those who stayed in our palace under the flag of the "Križari" were unknown to us. It is not known to us if Erik Lisak once spent the night in the Archiepiscopal palace. If so it was without our knowledge or approval. We reject most vigorously the assertion that Erik Lisak had the least connection with the pastoral letter, which under ordinary circumstances would be absurd, or that he came to the palace at the time when the Episcopal Conference was being held. We also made clear that the Chancellor, Canon N. Borić, had no idea that the high school student Krema had shot Captain Glonbcnik, and that in ignorance he received him under his

roof once, out of pure Christian compassion, after he had found him, unconscious, in the cathedral.

Canon N. Borić has explained this incident in a special letter to President Bakarić to demonstrate his innocence.

The archives of the Ministry of Foreign Affairs of the former NDH were brought to the Archiepiscopal palace on account of the dangers of the war, but they have long since been transferred by the present authorities. You are aware that the former minister, Aljbegović, did not leave any "box containing the complete record of the speeches of Pavelić" in the Archiepiscopal palace.

We were quite unaware that there existed in the Archiepiscopal palace a kind of depot for the collection of supplies destined for the so-called "Križari" in the forests. It is impossible to speak of some sort of headquarters, depot, or channel through which Ustashi were brought into the country from abroad as existing among our closest advisers; if anything of this kind existed, it was certainly without our knowledge or approval. I have at hand the declaration of the priests of the Diocese of Zagreb and other dioceses who resolutely deny the so-called charges against the pastoral letter as printed in the daily press.

The assertion that we maintain any political communication whatever with anyone is a lie.

We have defended, defend, and will defend until the last breath of our life the right of the Catholic Church to complete freedom in fulfilling its mission.

We do not intend to employ any other defense of our activity, because it would be completely useless.

5. The daily press carried some photographs of a reception on the occasion of New Year's Day in 1945. Civic courtesy demands that one perform certain conventional acts on such occasions, but they do not in any way signify the approval of a particular political attitude, therefore this photograph does not disturb us. The same applies to the flood of caricatures by which we have been ridiculed in the different newspapers, magazines, and posters. You, brother priests, are able to judge clearly on the basis of published documents what my relations were with the former authorities. It is characteristic that we were then, as today, attacked and humiliated when we defended the principles of justice and Christian charity.

6. The above-mentioned statement is welcome to certain people as providing, because of the actions of several individual priests, an

argument to weaken the Church and its institutions, and an opportunity to reduce its right to accomplish its mission freely.

However, neither material measures, mockeries, threats, nor physical attacks, such as that at Zaprešić, will shake us in defense of the Church and its right to fulfill its mission.

We have presented our demands to the proper authorities which the Church did not renounce in its effort to seek a rapprochement with the state, but as of today we have received no concrete reply to them. The Church demands that it fulfill its mission and regulate its relations with the authority of the state as the free representative of a free Church in a free state.

Whatever may happen in the future, we have nothing to add to our defense. Our defense is in God, our conscience clear, and our witness, besides all of you, reverend brother priests, the mass of our faithful people and the representatives of the Holy See in Zagreb. The Holy See has the last word in any conflict between Church and state as far as the Church is concerned.

And you, my Reverend brother priests, remain completely untroubled, following the directions of the Church, of its Code, and your Archbishop, and carry out your spiritual and religious mission in such a way as to give rise to no attacks on the Church.

ALOYSIUS
Archbishop

Zagreb, December 17, 1945

DOCUMENT LXXIII

Letter of the Yugoslav Bishops to Marshal Tito, September, 1952

MR. MARSHAL:

We, the undersigned Bishops and the Apostolic Administrators of the Catholic Church in the territory of the F.N.R.J.,[1] have examined during our joint conference in Zagreb, held from September 23rd to September 26th, 1952, among other pastoral questions, also the conditions under which the Catholic Church exists in Yugoslavia, and consider it our duty to address to you, as the Supreme Chief of State, the following memorandum concerning some of the more important problems of the religious life of our faithful.

---

[1] F.N.R.J. — Federal National Republic of Jugoslavia: the official name of Yugoslav State.

The Catholic Bishops of the F.N.R.J. first of all state that in Yugoslavia there is no complete religious freedom. The freedom of conscience and religion to which the Constitution of the F.N.R.J. (Art. 26) refers is in practice reduced to partial freedom of worship (*cultus*) or, as our law says, the freedom of religious rites. We say *partial*, because the freedom of worship is in some respects limited to such an extent as *de facto* means the negation of genuine religious freedom.

The churches are, it is true, *still open,* although some of them, sometimes with high artistic value, as for example the Church of the Trappist Fathers at Delibašino Selo, near Banja Luka, have for a certain period been used as store-houses for wheat or agricultural machinery. The monumental Church of St. Joseph at Ljubljana has been transformed into a film studio, while the ancient Church of the Crusaders, also at Ljubljana, a real gem of ecclesiastical art, was taken from the Catholics and simply, without consultation, given to the Old-Catholic sect — which, incidentally, at Ljubljana, lacks almost any adherents.

Very many roadside crosses and paintings have been destroyed, but the perpetrators of these violations can never be discovered. The same thing has happened to some of the smaller chapels in Slovenia and in other parts of the country.

The large and beautiful Church of the Holy Redeemer at Rijeka[2] was mined over night and destroyed at the beginning of November, 1949, although it stood in the very center of the town. The Church of the Carmelite Sisters at Selo, Ljubljana, was destroyed and without any reason the beautiful chapel Salita al Calvario, on the island of Krk, was demolished. As far as we know in the same way many Catholic churches in Banat have been destroyed, while, in different parts of the country, many public oratories, in the former institutions of the nuns, have been closed down by force.

The Church of Our Lady at Ptujska Gora, the biggest place of pilgrimage in Maribor diocese, was, without consent, and against the will of the ecclesiastical authorities, transformed into a museum.

The State authorities give no permission at all for the building of new churches (Osijek, Bitoljic, near Sinj, Novo Selo, near Djakovica, etc.), and it is difficult to obtain permission for the repairing of old ones.

---

[2] Fiume.

The Registers of Births, Deaths, and Marriages were taken away from the Church authorities even in 1946. Nevertheless, the State authorities arrogate to themselves the right to make evidence at their will also in the new record-books, which the Church has been making since May 9th, 1946, solely for her internal use. The old record-books have not as yet been given back to the Church though the time for it (the end of 1951) has already passed.

The UDBA authorities require *organists, both men and women,* and masters of ecclesiastical chant, to leave their duties.

Processions are, in the most parts of the country, forbidden, and the bigger religious celebrations, where the faithful from several parishes assemble, are frequently obstructed in various ways. In particular *the celebration* of so-called *first Masses* is obstructed. The hostility of the authorities goes so far as to take away from the young priest also the gifts *in natura,* which he used to be given by the faithful on this occasion, according to the ancient custom.

The freedom of preaching is also endangered. Priests are sometimes cited for responsibility because in quotations of Holy Scripture or in positive explanations of religious truths are seen actions against the State and the existing social order. The State has even gone so far as to forbid priests to oppose atheistic propaganda amongst children. "Priests," so it is written in an instruction of the internal section of the S.N.O.[3] in Bosnia and Hercegovina, "are not allowed to influence the parents, lest their children should not become atheists." From another priest it was required that in his sermons he should persuade the faithful not to go to church.

Priests *are not allowed to give religious instruction* in schools, presbyteries, and other ecclesiastical premises; there are many cases where priests were prohibited from giving instruction to the youth in the churches themselves, even such as the preparation for first Holy Communion or Confirmation. The priests, because of the breach of such prohibitions, are cited and punished by fine or arrest.

The Church and her institutions are overcharged by *disproportionally high taxes,* and when the priests are not able to pay them they are distrained and deprived of their belongings, or the goods of the presbyteries are seized (Trsat, Volar, Desinić, Draganić, Novalja). There are even cases where from a Diocesan Curia and from some Sanctuaries of Our Lady (Brezje, Ptujska Gora) all money of Mass stipends,

---

[3] S.N.O. — *Sreski Narodni Odbor,* or National District Committee.

which was temporarily deposited in their treasuries, was distrained.

Many churches *are not allowed in any way to collect ecclesiastical alms.* The cathedral at Ljubljana had to pay 10,000 dinars fine, because its sacristan removed 10 dinars from the altar: an offering which had been left there by one of the faithful.

In Slovenia, and in other parts, it is made impossible for ecclesiastical institutions even to receive gifts from abroad. At the beginning of May this year there arrived at Rijeka some large parcels of used clothing and a certain quantity of powdered milk and eggs, a gift from American Catholics to the priests, religious, and seminarians of the dioceses Rijeka, Senj, Krk, and Zadar.[4] This gift had to be returned to America, because the authorities required in taxes and customs duties more than six million dinars — more than these poor dioceses could afford. In July this year there arrived at Rijeka from the same American Catholics gift parcels of flour and oil for the dioceses of Senj, Krk, Rijeka, and the seminary of Rijeka. These parcels had to be returned to America, because the duties on them were so high that the flour which had been sent as a gift, would be much dearer than the flour from the home market.

The arrest of the priests goes on, and the punishments received by them exceed in severity the already rigorous standards which are generally applied to our legal practice. For example, Karlo Gnidovec, the seventy-five-year-old and much respected parish priest and dean of Žumberak, was, a few days ago, sentenced to death by shooting for acts supposedly committed during the war.

There are still in Yugoslav State prisons more than two hundred priests, and one can say with a clear conscience that during the past eight years a *considerable* part of the Catholic clergy have experienced, for longer or shorter periods, the disgrace and hardships of the prisons. Among the imprisoned clergy there is also the Bishop of Mostar, Dr. Peter Čule; while the Archbishop, Dr. Aloysius Stepinac, does not yet enjoy full freedom. It is indeed astonishing how the clergy, which in all the civilized countries of the world has the least to do with penal code, in our own country has become incorrigibly criminal!

Physical attacks on priests are not rare. During the past seven years about eighty priests have been killed by ambush, secretly, and in the majority of these cases the perpetrators have not been discov-

---

[4] Zadar is Zara in Italian.

ered and punished. This ferocity reached its climax in the attack on the person of Msgr. Anton Vovk, Bishop of Ljubljana, while he was officially traveling. On January 20th, 1952, he was physically attacked at the railway station at Novo Mesto; petrol was poured on him and ignited. But for his presence of mind he would have been burned alive. Here is the strangest thing: the attacker was only sentenced to nine days' conditional jail for his crime!

This same Bishop is not granted permission to visit places in the border zone, even in cases where he is obliged to make canonical visitation and administer Confirmation. His canonical visitation to Jesenice was regarded as a provocation, and a terrorist group, on his arrival at Jesenice itself, forced him to return to Ljubljana, while thousands of people inside and outside the church were expecting their Bishop.

Nor is permission granted to the Bishop of Maribor, Dr. Maximilian Držečnik, to visit his parishes in the border zone. We also possess certain information about the obstacles placed in the way of the other Bishops performing canonical visitations in the territory of their diocese.

The State authorities, wherever they can, *ignore the Church* and her institutions. The Catholic Hierarchy, in its references, from 1945 up till the present, has addressed to the Government of the F.N.R.J. at least six documentary memoranda, and has never received any answer, except that the Religious Commission at the presidency of the Government of the F.N.R.J., on May 19th, 1950, laconically informed the President of the Episcopal Conferences, the Archbishop of Belgrade, that the memoranda of the Hierarchy from April 26th, 1950, "are compiled in such an impossible spirit that they cannot be taken as a basis for negotiations to regulate the relations between the Government of the F.N.R.J. and the acting President of the Episcopal Conferences, and the other signatories of the mentioned memoranda." And that was all.

And how many memoranda, applications and complaints the individual Ordinaries have addressed to different departments of the Federal Government, to the Republican Governments, and to other authorities of the State administration, without receiving any answer! The ecclesaistical offices are not organs with which the State authorities would condescend to correspond. The Church must be humiliated at any price!

There is, finally, the very painful question *of the official atheistic course in the schools and in the whole public life of the F.N.R.J.* Atheism is the religion of the régime. Atheism is taught in the schools, preached in the conferences, propagated in the press, enforced on State employees and on the Army. Teachers in the elementary and middle (grammar and similar) schools are formally forbidden to frequent the churches. Teachers who do not obey this command are dismissed from their posts. In a State employee religiousness is considered to be the worst possible characteristic. Officers of the Yugoslav Army dare not even think of getting their children baptized.

The schoolchildren, too, are summoned, if they go to church on Sunday or express their religious feelings in any other way. There are cases where students are excluded from teachers' training colleges for the sole reason that they have declared themselves to believe in or to be fulfilling their religious duties. Although physical punishment is strictly prohibited in the schools, yet it happens that teachers in villages severely beat schoolchildren because the children dared to attend Mass or to take part in religious instruction in the church.

Recently, on the feast of the Nativity of Our Lady (September 8th) a scene developed in a village church, for which a trustworthy witness guarantees. He stood at the back of the church, and suddenly noticed how the children present in the church hid like frightened birds under the skirts of their parents, or ran amongst the groups of women, who were in great number in the church, so that the children could remain amongst them unnoticed. A father covered his son with a cloak so that it seemed as if the child would be suffocated. A man who observed this, astonished, asked the father: "What are you doing? Do you not see that your son will be suffocated?" And the peasant answered: "The teachers have come into the church. If they see my little one, they will beat him!" And, indeed, three local teachers came into the church, apparently not to pray to God but to find out which schoolchildren were in church, so that they would be able to punish them later.

To these proofs of lack of religious freedom in the F.N.R.J. must be added the old ones, already stated in the memoranda of the Hierarchy from former years.

Among them is to be mentioned *the liquidation of the whole of the Catholic schools in the territory of the F.N.R.J.* The whole series of classic and real gymnasia, teachers' training colleges, civil schools, technical and elementary schools and kindergartens have been abolished with the stroke of a pen, and their buildings confiscated from their legal owners.[5]

The Church's right is only recognised in the so-called religious schools — i.e., the schools for the education of the clergy. But these schools are exposed to so many vexations and limitations that it is clear that their existence is only tolerated as a necessity and temporarily. To mention but one thing: these schools are deprived of public recognition, although their teaching staff is qualified, and their students are denied all the privileges which the students of the public schools enjoy (reduction on railway tickets, a shorter term of Army service, etc.).

All printing presses belonging to the Catholic Church and her institutions in the country *have been seized,* without compensation having been made. Twenty big printing enterprises and literary publishing societies passed overnight into the hands of the State: this is a loss which cannot be overestimated.

Thus, one can say, *the Catholic press is completely destroyed.* A couple of small insignificant religious periodicals, which are still published, are so limited in volume and circulation that the religious press in the F.N.R.J. can no longer be said to exist. And even these miserable remnants of the once powerful Catholic press, which possessed before the war 152 Catholic publications, can hardly exist. High taxes and frequent confiscations because of — as it is alleged — the tendentious publication of articles — and yet these are often simply reprints of articles already published in the State press, or quotations from the speeches of the State leaders — all these things obstruct the correct functioning of the Catholic Press. Finally, there is hardly any use to us from these insignificant periodicals, which must be kept silent, while the monopolised State press daily attacks the Catholic Church, her Bishops and priests, sneers at the Faith, falsifies the historical facts, thus damaging the Church, and makes a mockery of ecclesiastical persons, religious rites, etc. But what causes us the deepest grief, Mr. Marshal, are *the coarse and bitter attacks on the person of the Holy Father the Pope,* whom we honour as the Supreme Pastor of the Church and the Vicar of Christ on earth.

---

[5] The Bishops are referring to the types of school which have been abolished, and these were similar to the old Austrian schools (for instance, the civil school corresponded to the old *Bürgerschule*). The present State authorities made a complete change in the school system.

We mention further *the suppression of the convents* and the liquidation of the Congregations of Sisters in whole provinces (Slovenia, Bosnia, and Hercegovina), the prohibition of almost all religious societies, and the lack of any organized form of Catholic public life. We mention finally, although unwillingly — because we ascribe to this problem only secondary importance — that, in the nationalization of the ecclesiastical possessions, in some cases not even the laws issued by the actual authorities have been observed.

All this undoubtedly proves that in the F.N.R.J., freedom of conscience and religion does not exist, and that the Catholic Church is refused the most elementary liberties and her vital rights are endangered. In this short review we could not, of course, enter into all the details possible. We are, however, ready at any moment to provide exhaustive documentation for all the statements made above, on the sole condition that we are granted liberty to collect and publish the evidence.

After all we have stated, it is not difficult to answer this question. If it required from the Church that she, for the sake of the agreement, or, as our authorities say, for the sake of friendly collaboration with the State authorities, is to give up her essential vital rights, then such an agreement is impossible. The Church has never in her history agreed to unconditional surrender, and she will not do this now. To require from the Church that she recognizes the actual situation in the F.N.R.J. as lawful and definitive would mean the same as to ask her to deny herself or to sign her death sentence.

The Church in the F.N.R.J. is always ready for negotiations and for reasonable concessions, but on condition that her moral and juridical status is completely recognized, and that all her rights, which she has as regards her nature and end, are guaranteed. That means that if the State honestly wants correct relations with the Church, before anything else all the injustices crying out to heaven are to be removed, injustices to which ecclesiastical institutions and persons are exposed daily, and the course of persecution, which has been in force from the beginning of the F.N.R.J. up to today, must be stopped.

If this is not done the Hierarchy will be confirmed in the conviction that the F.N.R.J. aims at the complete destruction of religion. This destruction has to be performed in stages. Some such stages are already behind us, and at present, according to our opinion, we are at the last but one. The aggressive atheism has already reached the church doors, and now, as we have seen, it makes preparations to penetrate into the last asylum of religious freedom.

The State authorities in the F.N.R.J. enforce, as particularly suitable means to regulate the relations between Church and State, the establishment of priests' professional associations. Such associations exist already, mostly without the permission of the competent Bishops, in the whole territory of the N.R. Slovenia, in Istria, and in Bosnia and Hercegovina. We are convinced that such associations have not the required conditions to achieve such a great task. First of all, because their setting up is always urged by the State authorities, who for this purpose go around visiting the priests. Then, among other things, the way of their activity and the suggestions which the members of the association receive from the State authorities entitles us to the conclusion that the priests' associations, according to the intentions of their patrons, must serve the purpose of breaking the ecclesiastical discipline and of progressively weakening religious life, and not of regulating the relations between Church and State.

If it is required from the Hierarchy to permit such associations, then it is necessary to bring their rules into harmony with canonical prescriptions, and to secure for the ecclesiastical authority full control of their activities. Only on these conditions is the Hierarchy willing to take into consideration the possibility of recognising such professional priests' associations.

The Catholic Hierarchy has always maintained a position of loyalty towards the existing State authority; and the Hierarchy holds it today. We do not wish to develop revolutionary activity. On the contrary, we sincerely love our fatherland, and we will ask the priests and faithful to assume a friendly attitude toward everything that is positive in the actual social-political system. It is obvious that we, together with our faithful, uphold the integrity of our State borders, and that we are prepared for every sacrifice for the benefit and prosperity of our State community. One thing cannot be yet expected from us: active participation in the political life of the country. Politics and the responsibility for it we leave to those who have a vocation for it. We will care for the moral and spiritual foundations of our social and political life. This is our domain, and our part on this field cannot be compensated with anything.

In return we do not claim any privileges. We shall be satisfied if what belongs to us according to divine and human right is recognised and given to us. We understand by this term not only freedom of worship but the whole complex of liberties which are included in the idea of freedom of religion and conscience. They are: freedom of confessional schools, freedom of the Catholic press, and freedom of religious organizations, and, together with this, the right to dispose freely of the material means which we need. We do not expect to receive these means as a present from the State: the people, who believe in their Church and love her, will provide them for us.

If the present State authority accepts these principles, we Catholic Bishops consider that the tension between the Catholic Church and State of the F.N.R.J. will soon decrease, and even that these relations will be settled for mutual benefit. And this is an aim which is worth some sacrifice.

This memorandum, Mr. Marshal, we Catholic Bishops of the F.N.R.J., from our Plenary Conference in Zagreb, address to you as the supreme head and chief of our State community, having the hope in full confidence that our memorandum will receive the reception and understanding which is appropriate to its importance.

Please, Mr. Marshal, receive the expressions of our loyal regards. *Zagreb, on September 26th, 1952.*

BIBLIOGRAPHY

The following bibliography does not pretend to be exhaustive. Neither are all the works listed favorable either to Archbishop Stepinac or to the Catholic Church. Its purpose is to list a number of more important studies of Yugoslav backgrounds, contemporary history, the Tito regime, and the specific case of the trial and conviction of Cardinal Stepinac.

Adamic, Louis, *My Native Land* (New York and London: Harper and Brothers, 1943).

Ancel, J., *Peuples et nations des Balkans* (Paris: Librairie Armand Colin, 1930).

Benkovic, Theodore, O.F.M., *The Tragedy of a Nation,* Chicago, 1947.

Cavalli, Fiorello, S. I., *Il processo dell'arcivescovo di Zagabria* (Rome: Edizioni "La Civiltá Cattolica," 1947).

Comincia il processo Stepinac (Pamphlet), Centro Informazione pro Deo, Rome, 1946.

Constitution de la République fédérative populaire de Yougoslavie (Belgrade, 1947).

Committee on foreign affairs House of Representatives. Report of the special study mission to Germany and certain other countries. Supplementary report on Austria, *Yugoslavia,* Italy, Spain (Washington: Government Printing Office, 1952).

Curran, Rev. Edward Lodge, *Stepinac or Tito?* (Pamphlet) (Brooklyn, N. Y.: International Catholic Truth Society, n.d.).

Derrick, Michael, *Tito and the Catholic Church* (Pamphlet) (London: The Sword of the Spirit, 1953).

Evelpidi, C., *Les Etats Balcaniques* (Paris: Rousseau et Cie, éditeurs, 1930).

Fotić, Konstantin, *The War We Lost* (New York: Viking Press, 1948).

Guberina, Ivo, *La formazione cattolica della Croazia* (Pamphlet) (Rome, 1943).

Korbel, Josef, *Tito's Communism* (Denver, Colo.: The University of Denver Press, 1951).

Latu, Roger, *L'Eglise derrière le Rideau de Fer* (Paris: La Bonne Presse, n.d.).

MacÉoin, Gary, *The Communist War on Religion* (New York: The Devin-Adair Company, 1951).

Markham, R. H., *Tito's Imperial Communism* (Chapel Hill, N. C.: University of North Carolina Press, 1947).

Martin, David, *Ally Betrayed. The Uncensored Story of Tito and Mihailovich* (New York: Prentice-Hall, Inc., 1946).

Martirium Croatiae, Rome, 1946.

Migliorati, V. S. J., *La chiesa nella Repubblica Federativa Popolare Jugoslava* (Pamphlet) (Rome, 1946).

Mousset, Albert, *Le royaume serbe, croate, slovène. Son organisation, sa vie politique et ses institutions* (Paris: Editions Bossard, 1926).

Mousset, Jean, *La Serbie et son église 1830–1904* (Paris, 1938).

Programme et statuts du parti communiste de Yougoslavie (Belgrade, 1948).

Religion in Yugoslavia. A report on conferences with Roman Catholic, Orthodox, Moslem, Jewish, and Protestant leaders, and investigations through the medium of religious institutions and documents. By seven American Protestant clergymen and editors of religious journals who visited Yugoslavia in the summer of 1947.

Roucek, Joseph S., *Balkan Politics* (Stanford University Press, 1948).

Spinka, Matthew, *A History of Christianity in the Balkans* (Chicago, 1933).

Sudjenje Lisaku, Stepincu, Šaliću i Družini, Ustaško-Križarskim Zločincima i njihovim Pomagačima (Zagreb, 1946).
The printed text of the officially transcribed examination of Cardinal Stepinac and several of his codefendants.

Ulam, Adam B., *Titoism and the Cominform* (Cambridge: Harvard University Press, 1952).

Watson, Hugh Seton, *The European Revolution* (London: Methuen, 1950).

West, Rebecca, *Black Lamb and Grey Falcon* (New York: The Viking Press, 1948).

White, Leigh, *Balkan Caesar. Tito vs. Stalin* (New York: Charles Scribner's Sons, 1951).

Yanochevitch, Milorad, *La Yougoslavie dans les Balkans* (Paris: Les Editions Internationales, 1936).

Yugoslavia, Edited by Robert J. Kerner (Berkeley and Los Angeles: The University of California Press, 1949).